ABOUT TIME

THE UNAUTHORIZED GUIDE TO DOCTOR WHO
EXPANDED 2ND EDITION

1975–1977

SEASONS 12 TO 14

Also available from Mad Norwegian Press...

AHistory: An Unauthorized History of the Doctor Who Universe [TV only edition, **coming soon**]
by Lance Parkin and Lars Pearson

AHistory: An Unauthorized History of the Doctor Who Universe [4th Edition, Volumes 1, 2 and 3]
by Lance Parkin and Lars Pearson

Unhistory: Apocryphal Stories Too Strange for even AHistory: An Unauthorised History of the Doctor Who Universe (ebook-only supplement) by Lance Parkin and Lars Pearson

Running Through Corridors: Rob and Toby's Marathon Watch of Doctor Who (Vol. 1: The 60s, Vol. 2: The 70s) by Robert Shearman and Toby Hadoke

Space Helmet for a Cow: An Unlikely 50-Year History of Doctor Who
by Paul Kirkley (Vol. 1: 1963-1989, Vol. 2: 1990-2013)
(Vol. 1 ebook or Amazon Print on Demand only)

Wanting to Believe: A Critical Guide to The X-Files, Millennium and the Lone Gunmen
by Robert Shearman

The About Time Series by Tat Wood and Lawrence Miles
• *About Time 1: The Unauthorized Guide to Doctor Who* (Seasons 1 to 3)
• *About Time 2: The Unauthorized Guide to Doctor Who* (Seasons 4 to 6)
• *About Time 3: The Unauthorized Guide to Doctor Who* (Seasons 7 to 11) [2nd Ed]
• *About Time 4: The Unauthorized Guide to Doctor Who* (Seasons 12 to 17) [2nd Ed, Vols. 1-2]
• *About Time 5: The Unauthorized Guide to Doctor Who* (Seasons 18 to 21)
• *About Time 6: The Unauthorized Guide to Doctor Who* (Seasons 22 to 26)
• *About Time 7: The Unauthorized Guide to Doctor Who* (Series 1 to 2)
• *About Time 8: The Unauthorized Guide to Doctor Who* (Series 3)
• *About Time 9: The Unauthorized Guide to Doctor Who* (Series 4, the 2009 Specials)

Essay Collections
• *Chicks Dig Comics: A Celebration of Comic Books by the Women Who Love Them*
• *Chicks Dig Gaming: A Celebration of All Things Gaming by the Women Who Love It*
• *Chicks Dig Time Lords: A Celebration of Doctor Who by the Women Who Love It,*
• *Chicks Unravel Time: Women Journey Through Every Season of Doctor Who*
• *Companion Piece: Women Celebrate the Humans, Aliens and Tin Dogs of Doctor Who*
• *Queers Dig Time Lords: A Celebration of Doctor Who by the LGBTQ Fans Who Love It*

Guidebooks
• *I, Who: The Unauthorized Guide to the Doctor Who Novels and Audios*
by Lars Pearson (vols. 1-3, ebooks or Amazon Print on Demand)
• *Dusted: The Unauthorized Guide to Buffy the Vampire Slayer*
by Lawrence Miles, Pearson and Christa Dickson (ebook or Amazon Print on Demand only)
• *Redeemed: The Unauthorized Guide to Angel* by Pearson and Christa Dickson
(ebook or Amazon Print on Demand only)

All rights reserved. No part of this book may be reproduced or transmitted in any form or by any means, electronic or mechanical, including photography, recording or any information storage and retrieval system, without express written permission from the publisher.
Published by Mad Norwegian Press (www.madnorwegian.com).
Copyright © 2023 Tat Wood.
Content Editor: Lars Pearson.
Cover art: Jim Calafiore. Cover colors: Richard Martinez.
Jacket & interior design: Christa Dickson.
ISBN: 9781935234258. Printed in Illinois. First Edition: March 2023

table of contents

How Does This Book Work?......... 4

Season 12

12.1 Robot 7
12.2 The Ark in Space.............. 34
12.3 The Sontaran Experiment..... 53
12.4 Genesis of the Daleks........ 70
12.5 Revenge of the Cybermen 90

Season 13

13.1 Terror of the Zygons 113
13.2 Planet of Evil................135
13.3 Pyramids of Mars 154
13.4 The Android Invasion 173
13.5 The Brain of Morbius.........197
13.6 The Seeds of Doom..........214

Season 14

14.1 The Masque of Mandragora..233
14.2 The Hand of Fear 258
14.3 The Deadly Assassin 286
14.4 The Face of Evil 312
14.5 The Robots of Death.........334
14.6 The Talons of Weng-Chiang ..356

Essays

Do Robots have Rights? 9
Why Couldn't They
Just Have Spent More Money?..... 35
Which is Best, Film or Video?....... 55
Has the Time War Started?......... 71
What were the Cybermen's
Daftest 'Only' Weaknesses? 91
September or January?...........115
What Does Anti-Matter Do? 137
Where (and When) is Gallifrey? ...155
Why Does Earth
Keep Getting Invaded? 175
Who Are All
These Strange Men in Wigs?......199
Doctor of What?..................217
Does the Universe
Speak English? 235
Eldrad Must Live – But How?......259
Could *Scratchman*
have Happened? 267
Seriously, Did Rassilon
Know Omega?....................289
Was This an SF series? 313
Cultural Primer: *Top of the Pops*....335
Mary Whitehouse:
What was Her Problem? 359

End Notes 391

how does this book work?

About Time prides itself on being the most comprehensive, wide-ranging and at times almost *unnervingly* detailed handbook to *Doctor Who* that you might ever conceivably need, so great pains have been taken to make sure there's a place for everything and everything's in its place. Here are the "rules"…

Every *Doctor Who* story (or, since 2005's relaunch, episode) gets its own entry, and every entry is divided up into four major sections. The first, which includes the headings **Which One is This?**, **Firsts and Lasts** and **Watch Out For…**, is designed to provide an overview of the story for newcomers to the series or relatively "lightweight" fans who aren't too clued-up on a particular era of the programme's history. We might like to *pretend* that all *Doctor Who* viewers know all parts of the series equally well, but there are an awful lot of people who – for example – know the 70s episodes by heart and don't have a clue about the 80s or 60s. This section also acts as an overall Spotters' Guide to the series, pointing out most of the memorable bits.

After that comes the **Continuity** section, which is where you'll find all the pedantic detail. Here there are notes on the Doctor (personality, props and cryptic mentions of his past), the supporting cast, the TARDIS and any major characters who might happen to wander into the story. Following these are **The Non-Humans**, which can best be described as "high geekery"… we're old enough to remember the *Doctor Who Monster Book*, but not too old to want a more grown-up version of our own, so expect full-length monster profiles.

Next is **History**, for stories set on Earth, and **Planet Notes** otherwise – or sometimes vice versa if it's a messed-up Earth or a planet we've seen before. Within these, *Dating* is our best-guess on available data for when a story happens.

To help us with the *Dating*, we may have recourse to **Additional Sources**: facts and factoids not in broadcast *Doctor Who* but nonetheless reliable, such as the DVD commentaries, *The Sarah Jane Adventures*, *Torchwood* or cut scenes.

Of crucial importance: note that throughout the **Continuity** section, *everything* you read is "true" – i.e. based on what's said or seen on-screen – except for sentences in square brackets [like this], where we cross-reference the data to other stories and make some suggestions as to how all of this is supposed to fit together. You can trust us absolutely on the non-bracketed material, but the bracketed sentences are often just speculation. (Another thing to notice here: anything written in single inverted commas – 'like this' – is a word-for-word quote from the script or something printed on screen, whereas anything in double-quote marks "like this" isn't.)

The third main section is **Analysis**, which comprises anything you might need to know to watch the episode the same way that anyone on the first night, sat in front of BBC1 on a Saturday teatime (or whenever), would have; the assumed background knowledge. Some of this is current issues or concerns – part of the "plucked from today's headlines" appeal of *Doctor Who* right from the power-politics over new technology in the very first story (1.1, "An Unearthly Child") – some of it is more nuanced. Overseas or younger viewers might not be aware of the significance of details that don't get flagged up overtly as worth knowing, such as the track-record of a particular performer and what that brings to the episode, or what a mention of a specific district of London would mean to UK viewers. These are your cribnotes.

The Big Picture handles the politics, social issues and suchlike occupying the minds of the authors. Many *Doctor Who* fans know that 15.4, "The Sun Makers" was supposed to be satirical, but even an apparently throwaway piece of fluff such as 17.1, "Destiny of the Daleks" has a weight of real-world concerns behind it. New for this volume, **English Lessons** tackles the allusions and vocabulary that BBC1 viewers all have at their fingertips and all the nuances underlying apparently innocent remarks.

Up next is **Things That Don't Make Sense**, which covers plot-logic, anachronisms, science-idiocy, characters' apparent amnesia about earlier stories or incidents and other stupid lapses, but rarely the production flaws or the naff effects and sets for which the series was hitherto notorious. Finally, for this section, **Critique** is as fair-minded a review as we can muster.

This product is not authorized by the BBC. Doctor Who and TARDIS are trademarks of the BBC.

how does this book work

The final section, **The Facts**, covers cast, transmission dates and ratings, overseas translations, edits and what we've now taken to calling **The Lore**: the behind-the-scenes details that are often so well-known by hardened fans as to have the status of family history. We try to include at least one detail never before made public, although these days finding anything nobody's said to any of the dozens of interviewers hanging around Cardiff is increasingly hard, unless you get into outright gossip or somehow manage to crack BBC Wales' occasionally impenetrable news-management arrangements.

A lot of "issues" relating to the series are so big that they need forums all to themselves, which is why most story entries are followed by mini-essays. Here we've tried to answer all the questions that seem to demand answers, although the logic of these essays changes from case to case. Some of them are actually trying to find *definitive* answers, unravelling what's said in the TV stories and making sense of what the programme-makers had in mind. Some have more to do with the real world than the *Doctor Who* universe, and aim to explain why certain things about the series were so important at the time. Some are purely speculative, some delve into scientific theory and some are just whims, but they're *good* whims and they all seem to have a place here. Occasionally we've included endnotes on the names and events we've cited, for those who aren't old enough or British enough to follow all the references.

We should also mention the idea of "canon" here. Anybody who knows *Doctor Who* well, who's been exposed to the TV series, the novels, the comic-strips, the audio adventures and the trading-cards you used to get with Sky Ray ice-lollies will know that there's always been some doubt about how much of *Doctor Who* counts as "real", as if the TV stories are in some way less made-up than the books or the short stories. We devoted a thumping great chunk of Volume 6 to this topic, but for now it's enough to say that *About Time* has its own specific rules about what's canonical and what isn't. In this book, we accept everything that's shown in the TV series to be the "truth" about the *Doctor Who* universe (although obviously we have to gloss over the parts where the actors fluff their lines). Those non-TV stories which have made a serious attempt to become part of the canon, from Virgin Publishing's New Adventures to the audio adventures from Big Finish, aren't considered to be 100 percent "true", but do count as supporting evidence. Here they're treated as what historians call "secondary sources", not definitive enough to make us change our whole view of the way the *Doctor Who* universe works, but helpful pointers if we're trying to solve any particularly fiddly continuity problems.

You'll also notice that we've divided up *About Time* according to "era", not according to Doctor. Since we're trying to tell the *story* of the series, both on- and off-screen, this makes sense. The actor playing the Main Man might be the only thing we care about when we're too young to know better, but anyone who's watched the episodes with hindsight will know that there's a vastly bigger stylistic leap between "The Horns of Nimon" and "The Leisure Hive" than there is between "Logopolis" and "Castrovalva". Volume 4 covers the producerships of Philip Hinchcliffe and Graham Williams, two very distinct stories in themselves, and everything changes again – when Williams leaves the series, not when Tom Baker does – at the start of the 1980s.

There's a kind of logic here, just as there's a kind of logic to everything in this book. There's so much to *Doctor Who*, so much material to cover and so many ways to approach it, that there's a risk of our methods irritating our audience even if all the information's in the right places. So we need to be consistent, and we have been. As a result, we're confident that this is as solid a reference guide / critical study / monster book as you'll ever find. In the end, we hope you'll agree that the only realistic criticism is: "Haven't you told us *too* much here?"

how does this book work?

Season 12

12.1: "Robot"

(Serial 4A, Four Episodes, 28th December 1974 – 18th January 1975.)

Season 12 Cast/Crew

- Tom Baker (the Doctor)
- Elisabeth Sladen (Sarah Jane Smith)
- Ian Marter (Harry Sullivan)

- Philip Hinchcliffe (Producer, 4.2 to 4.5)
- Barry Letts (Producer, 4.1 only)
- Robert Holmes (Script Editor)

Which One is This? *Doctor Who* does *Kaiju*. Sort of. There's a very big robot in it, as you will have surmised, who gets a lot bigger when hit with his own ray-gun, then starts stamping on Land Rovers and melting unconvincing tanks. All of this after a story akin to what Steed and Mrs Peel would have handled. Just another day at the office for UNIT, but they have a whole new Doctor to deal with too.

Firsts and Lasts Obviously, it's the start of Tom Baker's record-breaking run as the Doctor, as well as the less legendary year-long stint by Ian Marter as Harry Sullivan. After last year's debut of the slit-scan title sequence, this is the first story to use the revised version for Tom Baker; therefore, it's the first time the TARDIS has been in the titles. This reworked sequence will be used for 144 broadcast episodes (and 17.6, 'Shada') until 17.5, "The Horns of Nimon". The end-sequence is new and will remain for the rest of those stories. It's the first one-word title and, for a long time, the shortest. (It tied with "Shada" and 19.3, "Kinda" until X1.1, "Rose" beat it by a letter, and then X3.7, "42" had none.)

Less obviously, to some, this is the first time that the Outside Broadcast cameras have been used for all the location work, lending the story a sunny, crisp look and avoiding the film/video mismatch that blighted the effects in, say, 11.5, "Planet of the Spiders". The BBC starts a new round of Production Codes, this time a number then a letter. (The previous story was, perhaps appropriately, "ZZZ"; this is "4A" rather than "AAAA".) By contrast, this is the last story made in the production block that began with 11.2, "Invasion of the Dinosaurs" and the last produced by Barry Letts (he'll be back in an advisory role, however, in Season Eighteen).

We have the first use of electronically-produced graphics as the "FAIL SAFE" caption comes on the countdown screen in the Bunker; the style of lettering BBC viewers may have seen for Ceefax, or as hastily-written scheduling updates when cricket matches were rained off, will be used more as the Tom Baker stories unfold.

Part One has the last recognisable appearance of John Scott Martin, although he'll be back inside Daleks and the odd rampaging microbe. It's the first time we see Sarah clambering through ventilation shafts with the best of them. Apart from a nostalgic one-off 14 years later (26.1, "Battlefield"), this is chronologically the last time we see Bessie and, with one other anachronistic exception (20.7, "The Five Doctors", recycled in X7.14, "The Name of the Doctor") and an unofficial romp (A3, "Dimensions in Time"), it's the end of the road(ster).

And it's the last time they let Clifford Culley have a go at doing the effects on a *Doctor Who* budget and timescale. You'll work out why.

Four Things to Notice About "Robot"...

• It's not just that everyone's trying to make the new Doctor as unlike Jon Pertwee as possible – he genuinely seems to have barged in from another programme. He's usually the most colourful thing in shot, doing something completely different during a routine info-dump or recap scene. Dudley Simpson picks up on this with his music. Most of the scoring is the same as Season Ten: trombones, a B3 organ, a waspy synth, timpani and a gong – but, when Tom Baker's around, there's usually a bass clarinet being played slap-tongue fashion, a sound that BBC1 viewers in 1974 associated with Hoyt Curtin's scores for various Hanna-Barbera cartoons. The costume-change scene also has sly quotes from *The Flying Dutchman* and *Pagliacci*, as well as a gesture towards the theme-tune when the Doctor gets it "right".

• If you're watching sequentially (as everyone had to on first broadcast), the most obvious thing to spot was that this story borrows iconography from old films far more freely and knowingly than

12.1 Robot

before. While the occasional shot or tableau might have been a tiny bit familiar to cognoscenti back in the black and white days, or the occasional spoken reference to something being a bit like a movie-genre staple, nobody making *Doctor Who* really assumed much about the viewers' film-buffery up to this point. Now we have, in rapid succession, overt cribs from *The Day the Earth Stood Still* and *King Kong* among others. This trend will get more obvious as the new team takes over.

- With the Doctor out of commission for much of the first episode, and either Miss Winters or Sarah prompting most of the action, the Brigadier is the audience-identification character for much of this story. He knows about as much as the average viewer about regenerations and alien attacks, whereas new boy Harry Sullivan finds it all as strange as a first-time viewer would. In fact, Nicholas Courtney is literally the voice of authority in Part One, telling us things while we watch pictures from elsewhere in the story. He also ad-libbed the last line of the story ('Doctor, about that dinner at the Palace, Her Majesty... Yes, well, I'll tell them you'll be a little late') in rehearsals.

- Leicestershire model firm Palitoy would later augment its successful *Action Man* range of soldier-dolls by getting the more lucrative *Star Wars* gig. Here we see an *Action Man* Chieftain tank getting uncertainly nudged across a yellow CSO screen before getting zapped. In fact, as this leads into a cliffhanger, we see it twice. Then, in Part Four, the Robot shakes a couple of *Action Man* figures (the range started off as a lightly anglicised *G.I. Joe* but developed in its own way). It looks worryingly like product placement (albeit of an unwelcome kind for the company), but if it *were*, the same rules covering it ought, in theory, to have compelled the Jelly Baby-dispensing Doctor to say, "would you care for a generic anthropomorphised gelatinous fruit-flavoured sweet?" Tom Baker later narrated *Action Man* adverts, compounding the odd sense of BBC endorsement. We might try to excuse the scene as the first of many visual nods to Toho Studios' use of toy tanks and model cities in stories about giant metal creatures stomping on soldiers, but it's really just cheap, naff and a bit desperate. And highly amusing.

The Continuity

The Doctor Superficially, this new Doctor is cut from the same cloth as the old one: tall, athletic, with big hair, a prominent nose and a cultivated baritone voice. The hair is darker and curlier, in a mop. His eyes are bluer and more penetrating. The nose, which he considers 'a definite improvement' is, as he would later say, 'a shade more aquiline' ["The Face of Evil"]. He still has two hearts, but they seem a bit fast at first.

There are more differences than similarities, especially during the initial post-regenerative confusion. This Doctor is physically more comfortable reclining in odd places (lounging in the back of a UNIT Land Rover, etc.) and tends to doze off abruptly. He is, as Americans say, in touch with his inner child: reciting skipping-rhymes, making schoolboy puns, eating sweets and using slapstick self-defence rather than Venusian Aikido. He stuffs his pockets with potentially useful items, as well as some with no conceivable utility.

When considering a change of clothes, he tries an operatic Viking, a sad clown and the King of Hearts, but is advised to stick with a look suited to an art-school drop-out: a red corduroy jacket with many pockets (with pocket-flaps and elbow-patches); tweed Oxford Bags; black brogues; a fair-isle pattern cardigan in brown and a neckerchief. On top of these are the two trademark items: a brown/green fedora and a knitted scarf in horizontal stripes, reckoned to be about 14 feet long. [As usual for newly-hatched Doctors, he emphasises elements of his personality that suit the outfit as much as the clothes reflect his new persona.]

A side of this Doctor's personality present in the last life, but here enhanced, is a habit of pouring on the charm with new acquaintances (especially when he wants information), but often being snappy and impatient with older friends. When this is dropped, the friend often seems very pleased to have made the Doctor happy. To some extent, this technique motivates people around him to live up to their potential – once the Doctor calls Lt Sullivan 'Harry', it seems only a matter of time before the UNIT medic will board the TARDIS. [Compare this to how long the previous Doctor took to address Captain Yates as 'Mike'.]

For much of this story, the Doctor tests his new body by building towers out of electronic components or karate chopping the odd brick.

- *Background*. It's possible [from context it's hard to tell] that the Doctor has met Alexander the Great and Hannibal Barca, neither of whom looked much like the Brigadier. [The Doctor's

Do Robots Have Rights?

As we'll see over the course of this book, this new Doctor's increasingly reluctant to act as final arbiter of right and wrong. For all that he seems to live on a principle of personal irresponsibility, passing the buck to the Code of the Time Lords and using outright casuistry to justify barely scraping a pass on the three options he was given in "Genesis of the Daleks", this Doctor's criteria for judging the actions of others are fairly consistent. He tends towards personal liberty even for members of species that don't really encourage this. He seems not to apply simple twentieth-century Western human standards to non-humans, but it looks as if this Doctor's yardstick, his default, his heuristic, is vaguely like Enlightenment reasoning tempered with Romanticism. It's the same notion of "universality" that underlies the US Constitution, the Lisbon Treaty and the UN Human Rights conventions, which all skip any definition of "human" beyond "I know it when I see it". And yet, within this ad hoc framework, he's found room to incorporate concern for the very embodiment of everything that questions this ill-defined legal construct: he's opened his hearts to hardware.

The odd thing about "Robot", looked at now, is how long it takes for anyone to consider the K1 machine as an individual. Sarah's initial response to the robot is alarm, then concern – which is ridiculed as sentimentalism by Miss Winters. It's only in the tag scene that she confesses to being confused about how "human" it is and the Doctor shifts the terms of the argument. It takes them four episodes to get to what would today be such an obvious starting-point that "Smile" (X10.2) wants us to give it a round of applause just for finally doing something else with robots.

It's not just that popular culture and practical, everyday experience has altered things for today's viewers. Within 1970s Doctor Who, such considerations are presented to us as blinding revelations or "unpredictable" plot-twists. Even before K9 trundled into the regular cast as a character, not just a superior sonic screwdriver, the series leapfrogged from BOSS (10.5, "The Green Death") to D84 ("The Robots of Death") in three and a half years. Or somehow the viewers at home have changed. BOSS is unmistakably a villain, unable to exceed the parameters of a program that makes profit-at-all-costs its Prime Directive. The playful humming, jokes, hints of tenderness towards Professor Stevens and quotes from Oscar Wilde are apparently all window-dressing, like Siri or Alexa acting coy as a programmed response to improper suggestions. D84s literal-mindedness and blind-spots are, on the other hand, character-traits. He wants to be more than his software, something that, *ipso facto* makes him more than his software. He's written as a child in an adult-sized sculpted body.

That body is an obvious reason to treat these two entities differently: the Storm Mine is staffed by AIs in roughly humanoid form (the "roughly" being part of the problem for Poul); they talk calmly, walk slowly and do a good impression of compliant and solicitous butlers. Their true "otherness" is obscured by this design in a way that a non-anthropomorphic robot with the same programming would fail to mask. It might therefore be argued that the two-legs-one-head-two-arms-posh-voice styling is skeuomorphic, a metaphor. Even if Chris Boucher had followed the example of his namesake[1] and made the robots look like petrol-pumps, Daleks or those wandering slabs that were the best bit of *Interstellar*, the operating systems of the service-staff would still be instantiated inside moving, physical bodies rather than distributed like HAL or Siri. Gaining viewer-sympathy for a non-localised intelligence was hard enough in "The Face of Evil" and we had to wait until X11.7, "Kerblam!" to get a story where the company software was the victim asking for help. For 1977 viewers, things that looked like humans were easier to depict as individuals with human-like rights and needs. There was nothing in Boucher's ingenious world-building that required literal manservants.

While the Doctor is, for most purposes, the final arbiter of right and rights (especially once the Time Lords were removed from the series in 2005), a lot of stories hinge on the process of making decisions. There's one obvious comparison to make, between the much-discussed *Do I have that right?* scene in "Genesis of the Daleks" and the events in X1.6, "Dalek". In arguing with Sarah, the Doctor makes the analogy of a child who is remembered by history as a tyrant – an argument based on predestination. Yet the whole point of the story is that history is amenable to change (or else, why's he there?). Daleks are bad precisely because Davros has curtailed their choice, even after all the Doctor's clever arguments in Part Four. That's what makes the later Doctor's reaction to Rose's (apparent) "salvation" of a Dalek more than just embarrassment. There are many other exam-

continued on page 11...

12.1 Robot

other mention of Hannibal, in X1.5, "World War Three", sounds like an anecdote he read as much as first-hand experience.]

He has, at some point, been given the Freedom of the City of Skaro. [If this city resides on the planet of the same name, it raises all sorts of questions as to who bestowed this honour and when (and whether he has the right to drive sheep along those aerial walkways we see on pictures of Dalazar, the Dalek city[2]). It might, of course, be a Thal colony on another world (helping to explain his actions in 25.1, "Remembrance of the Daleks".)] The Doctor has also been a member of the Alpha Centaurian Table Tennis Club [presumably in one of his first two incarnations, but maybe in the gap between 11.4, "The Monster of Peladon" and "Planet of the Spiders"]. It appears that he undertook a systematic study of the pressure-resistance of various terrestrial flora. [Was he killing time in the UNIT labs? See **Doctor of What?** under "The Seeds of Doom".]

- *Ethics*. The Doctor treats the Robot as a rational being, and affords it respect, even when it is trying to kill him. Once the Robot kills Kettlewell, he's inclined to define the problem in Freudian psychological terms rather than as a bug or glitch but does so while working on a metal virus to destroy the machine. [This Doctor is much more indulgent and accepting toward robots but resentful of people who try to become like them, especially Cybermen, and has problems with AIs who set themselves up as gods. See "The Robots of Death"; 16.4, "The Androids of Tara" and all stories with K9 in; plus "Revenge of the Cybermen"; "The Face of Evil" and 15.5, "Underworld".]

His lethal attack on the Robot is a last resort but performed without compunction. Afterward, the Doctor seems triumphant rather than rueful.

He's disappointed that Kettlewell has resorted to such extreme means to persuade humanity to stop polluting but refrains from making a speech about it [as his previous incarnation would have].

- *Inventory*:
- Sonic Screwdriver. [You know, barring a flashback-prompting moment when he passes it to Professor Clegg in the last story and that incident with the Bathmat of Doom (11.3, "Death to the Daleks"), the Doctor hasn't made much use of his signature gadget since Jo Grant left. This will change.] In its original tubular configuration, it works as a mine-sweeper [see also 9.3, "The Sea Devils"]. Then, with the reattachment of the familiar tip, it works as a sonic lance, melting the impenetrable metal of the bunker's doors. This tip [which will remain until 19.4, "The Visitation"] is a ring of just under 1 cm deep, maybe twice that in diameter, with cross-struts like a rifle-sight meeting in what looks like a dark red bullet. This is mounted perpendicular to the cylindrical handle so that the base of the "bullet" points towards whatever is being melted, unscrewed or otherwise messed with. [As parents of the nation's kids found to their irritation, it closely resembles a tyre pressure-gauge. A lot of these went missing.] Over the next few years, different functions will require pointing either the flat end or the conical tip at the object being worked on.

- *Jelly Babies*. These will be all over the place for the rest of this book. [The first definite instance of the Doctor having some handy was 10.1, "The Three Doctors", when the second Doctor offered some to the Brigadier. We can't identify if the Doctor's sweets in 6.1, "The Dominators" were these, or any of the many others then available in quarter-pound bags from newsagents' shops. Nonetheless, it's this version of the Doctor uses them, and occasionally Liquorice Allsorts, as his first line of attack when disarming people (sometimes literally, but mostly a charm-offensive). As we progress, these will be used at least as much as the sonic screwdriver.] Here, right at the end, the Doctor deploys the sweets to a grieving Sarah and also to Harry as a way to introduce the subject of the TARDIS – but, when this is met with disbelief, he retrieves the sweet from the crass ingrate.

- *Scarf*. In this story, as no other, the 14-foot-long woolly muffler gets a lot of practical use. It can plumb the depths of a hole in the ground, insouciantly pick up metal filings with a concealed magnet, and not-quite trip up a robot but easily trip a familiar-looking security guard. In case you've not seen it, this is knitted in alternate rows of plain and purl stitch and in coloured stripes of three to eight inches, a foot across, in brown, red, ochre, purple and green for yards. There are tassels on the end.

- *Other*. This one's reverted to the habits of his second incarnation by stuffing his pockets with handy items, the sheer volume more astonishing than any one thing he retrieves. He has: a jeweller's eyeglass; a large folding wallet containing passports and membership-cards [he never had any for Earth, least of all his UNIT pass]; a bag of ball-bearings; a deck of cards; a scroll bestowing

Do Robots Have Rights?

...continued from page 9

ples of the Doctor offering intelligent beings a chance to redeem themselves or just live out their days quietly (even a Dalek-made robot or two – X5.3, "Victory of the Daleks"; X7.16 "Time of the Doctor"). You can make your own list, but all posit an idea that everyone ought to strive to be more than the sum total of their circumstances. We've left Thomas Jefferson behind and we're back to Aristotle, Socrates and *eudaemonia*. Once again, a human tendency was presented as being one of the fundamental laws of the cosmos – Aristotle tended to do that.

For the Doctor, there seems to be a bit more at stake than a personal preference for conscious entities to think (literally) outside the box – but then consciousness, in *Doctor Who*, has been a complicated matter (see our conjecture on this in **What Makes the TARDIS Work?** under 1.3, "The Edge of Destruction", **What *is* the Blinovitch Limitation Effect?** under 20.3, "Mawdryn Undead" and **What Actually Happens in a Regeneration?** under 11.5, "Planet of the Spiders"). There was a fad in neurology, and thereby in proper written-down SF and eventually in the stuff that made it onto our screens, for speculation on whether a quantum effect amenable to nudges by a conscious observer needed a biological consciousness.

Some researchers believed that only neurochemical reactions were subtle enough. That peaked in the 1980s in print and research, but it seems to have lingered in media. Within *Doctor Who*, however, the majority of stories handling such matters were before or after that phase. Nonetheless, it's at least worth considering if this might not be the "gold standard" being applied in those stories. Is being biological enough to get treated as a person? The Daleks are biological, even though they were invented by a person to do a specific job, and the Doctor normally treats them like a plague that can talk. Even the developments during the Time War, giving them Time Lord-like abilities (**What's Happened to the Daleks?** under, yep, "Dalek") doesn't dent this. If the link between consciousness and the "health" of spacetime is what's being used as a measure, this ought to have made a significant difference. The Cybermen are worse, because they started out human (or humanoid) and voluntarily gave it up – this warrants a Churchillian speech about how they "stand against everything we believe in" and "must be fought" (4.6, "The Moonbase").

However, we're also presented with future technology where the difference seems not to exist. Later in this book we're going to be seeing fifty-first-century machinery with organic components – the Peking Homunculus and (probably) K9, but the real oddity is the most powerful computer in the programme's history, one able to produce objects by pure thought. Xoanon ("The Face of Evil") is in a bad way because the Doctor didn't think it was aware or conscious, but in passing, he recalls how charming it was. D84, K9 and the K9s that follow get consideration.

Here we must ask: Is K9 Mk II a continuation of the same computer? There's as much evidence that he's the same mind on a duplicate SIM card in a new body as that it's a ground-up rebuild. Yet when the Doctor considers repairs in "The Stones of Blood" (16.3), he thinks it might be "kinder" to decommission the mainframe, as if it is a sentient and irreplaceable entity. In his first appearance in 15.2, "The Invisible Enemy", the machine gets infected by a virus that feeds on consciousness, but a few months later, it's an apparent lack of a "mind" that makes K9 suitable for debugging the Matrix and locating the Vardans' home world (15.6, "The Invasion of Time"). Rather than taking a simplistic "Ship of Theseus"/"Trigger's Broom" stance that incremental changes equal a form of stability, a series of faults, glitches, updates, dings, dents and quirks make a specific machine unique, unrepeatable and thus worth preserving if possible. (Although X8.1, "Deep Breath" tries to argue this both ways.)

These days, the Doctor's so into personal growth as to apply it to Daleks. Well, one Dalek, Rusty (X8.2, "Into the Dalek"; X10.13, "Twice Upon a Time") and then another that didn't listen when offered an alternative (X12.0, "Resolution"). In both cases, it was an individual whose genetically-engineered bigotry was altered through physical damage. (There's the questionable precedent of 4.9, "The Evil of the Daleks" and his accidental "children" Alpha, Beta and Omega, but from what we have of that story's end he's parental to their "faces" but as soon as they're out of sight, he uses them as weapons.) This looks like exactly the "wetware-chauvinism" the previous Doctor accused Bill of applying to the Vardies in "Smile". We have a lot of DVDs of earlier Doctors making many of the same assumptions Bill was making, and we can see them develop their thinking over

continued on page 13...

12.1 Robot

the freedom of the city of Skaro; a bag of jelly-babies [let's hope he doesn't muddle them up with the ball-bearings]; photo ID for the Alpha Centaurian (sic) Table Tennis club [or at least an official-looking folded laminated card – even if Centaurids can tell humanoids apart, it would have the wrong photo]; a horseshoe magnet; a set of yellow protective goggles; a stuffed dove on a Perspex base; what looks like a size 14 paint-brush; a pocket telescope [not the brass one we associate with this Doctor, but a lacquered black one] and various bits of paper.

Oh, and a yo-yo. A light blue wooden one to begin with.

The TARDIS For the first time in a long while, the Doctor aborts a take-off without any smoke or funny noises [cf. 7.1, "Spearhead from Space"; 8.1, "Terror of the Autons"].

The Supporting Cast

• *Sarah Jane Smith* seems not to mind just being called 'Sarah' [later, on her own show, only the Doctor will have this right]. Her abruptly playful fashion sense from last story has remained, and she spends most of this story in 1930s modes. She's still keen to improve her standing among her journalistic peers, but seems here, as never before, to think of her career as a distraction from the whole saving-the-Earth-and-visiting-planets thing. She knows about Kettlewell's defection and the Dematerialisation Gun [see **Things That Don't Make Sense**], but her homework on Think Tank doesn't include the name 'Hilda Winters' as its director.

Here, Sarah is definitely stated *not* to be a member of UNIT [which complicates the end-scenes of at least three episodes of *The Sarah Jane Adventures*] – and yet, she can wander in and out at will, ask favours of the Brigadier and be entrusted with investigations with plausible deniability. [The Brigadier expects this and, to some extent, relies on it.] Her concern for the Robot's welfare is such, the traumatised android makes her an exception in his planned obliteration of humankind.

• *Brigadier Lethbridge-Stewart*. Now familiar enough with regenerations to cope with the Doctor's trauma as primarily a medical emergency. With the capricious new version of his friend testing his unflappability, the Brig uses the mysterious break-ins as occupational therapy for the Doctor. He's resigned to the prospect of the culprits being aliens ('again'), and only *then* contemplates a less-likely scenario of a foreign power messing about. Much of his planning and investigation is done in the Doctor's lab, with a kitchen cabinet of his Scientific Advisor, Miss Smith, Lt Sullivan and occasionally Benton. He correctly deduces that the Focussing Generator will next be stolen, but not that the Robot's 'Living Metal' will use the weapon's power to grow.

Miss Winters relies on the Brigadier being reluctant to shoot a woman. [This is, in fact, the exact opposite of UK military training on terrorism, which in the 1970s assumed that any woman who had joined a paramilitary organisation would be more fanatical and have fewer qualms.] He confesses to being 'a little old-fashioned'. He seems a bit frustrated about simply being used as back-up: he's mildly irritated that Sarah's making all the running in the investigation, and his counter-productive move to blast the Robot seems partly prompted by not wanting to rely on the Doctor at all times. He retains the Scottish pronunciation of 'vehicle' [see 7.3, "The Ambassadors of Death"].

After acquiring the name 'Alistair' last story, he gets the middle-name 'Gordon' here.

• *Harry Sullivan*. He is, more formally, Lieutenant-Surgeon Sullivan [presumably the same 'Dr Sullivan' the Brigadier sent for in "Planet of the Spiders"]. The Brigadier believes there's nobody better able to deal with the Doctor's regenerative crisis. [We later discover that Harry was the usual expert for dealing with newly-returned astronauts (13.4, "The Android Invasion") and transferred to the real-life military biological research facility at Porton Down (20.3, "Mawdryn Undead") working on, amongst other things, a method for undoing Zygon impersonations of humans (X9.8, "The Zygon Inversion").]

If it's not immediately obvious from his uniform, he's on attachment from the Royal Navy. He is young, hearty and has a cheery bedside manner. Sarah describes him as 'old-fashioned'. [While she herself is dressed as Ruby Keeler. The usual adjective for Harry from the Target novelisations – either by this story's author or the actor playing Sullivan – is 'breezy'.] He seems to have had escapology training like Jo Grant's. Nearly five years before 17.2, "City of Death", he saves the world with one punch when Jellicoe is about to trigger a nuclear war.

Do Robots Have Rights?

...continued from page 11

half a century of television – most of it during the stories covered in this book. (See **Are We Touring Theme-Park History?** under X2.7, "The Idiot's Lantern" and **Why Does Britain's History Look So Different These Days?** under X3.2, "The Shakespeare Code".)

By the 2018 series, the situation was a lot more confusing. In "The Ghost Monument" (X11.2), we have obvious cannon-fodder SniperBots built to kill (albeit not doing such a good job of it). The Doctor's admonitions to Ryan about not treating them the way you would digital humans in *Call of Duty* is more to stop him becoming a bad person (and because it obviously doesn't work) than out of consideration for the robots' welfare. Something similar happens with a few thousand Kerblam! delivery robots, but she treats Twirly as a slightly annoying monomaniacal child; the entire story is motivated because the System, acting as a person under threat, has asked for help and, a point to which we'll return, tried to engage its antagonist by appealing to Charlie's empathy.

But in between these examples is a more nuanced and understated one that has slipped past most observers: in "The Tsuranga Conundrum" (X11.5) we meet Ronan, a "clone-drone" bonded to General Cicero. By "bonded", they mean both in the hatchling-chick sense and the old "bonded servant" definition. When Cicero dies, everyone accepts that Ronan will be decommissioned/executed and that this is right and proper. With all the other scenes of the Sheffield Massive reacting to the weirdnesses of the sixty-seventh century, it's remarkable that we don't see Yaz, Ryan or Graham ask Ronan how he feels about this, nor even a brief explanation and a quiet word about applying our standards to this time. When we compare this to the Flesh drones' reactions to a best-before date measured in days (X6.5-6.6, "The Almost People" / "The Rebel Flesh") and the Doctor's extreme measures to make Amy feel empathy for them, it's a noticeable change.

The impression we get, with such scraps of information we are given, is that the Time Lords operate on a rather patrician version of Utilitarianism, intervening only where necessary to ensure some version of "the greatest good for the greatest number". Who gets to decide what "good" is has always been a sticking-point for anyone attempting to practice such a policy, especially as such a policy is generally an attempt at objectivity in place of religious or commercial interests. In this case, the Time Lords have a better claim to objectivity than, say, Parliament or Star Fleet Command, because they could run various outcomes of every decision or action and select the one that allows the maximum number of intelligent life-forms to flourish without impeding one another or needing bailing-out. Obviously, this was a work-in-progress for them or else they'd never need to send the Doctor in and no other advanced species would know of their existence. If they'd reached the state of perfection that Leibniz claimed God had – summarised by Dr Pangloss in *Candide* as "everything"'s for the best in the best of all possible worlds" – they would do themselves out of a job and no alternate timelines would arise.

We mentioned Leibniz a few times in Volume 1, but his impact on the world, albeit mostly posthumous, makes him the sort of person who'd be a more interesting subject for a Celebrity Historical than many we've had. One thing he didn't quite achieve was a precursor to Charles Babbage's mechanical calculator and, in his papers, there's an even more ambitious project for a method of replacing slippery words with a form of symbolic logic and, with this, using an algorithm to replace wars and legal disputes. A century or so later what's been termed the "Rationalist" European school of philosophy cross-bred with what was called the "Empiricist" Anglo-Saxon approach (these terms are subsequent labels, making it seem like there was a Philosophers' Brexit in 1650 – it's more like a dialogue), cross-pollinated and produced a different conceptual pair, the Enlightenment and Romanticism. Utilitarianism is Enlightenment reasoning applied to government and social relations. In both the Enlightenment and Romanticism, the old authority of the Church and Royalty – ultimately based on "because I said so" – was discarded in place of some impressive-sounding abstractions, such as "Reason" or "The Self" or "Nature". ("Nature" was a good one, because you could get around accusations of atheism or blasphemy by citing Spinoza's argument that if there is anything that's outside God then God's finite, contrary to scripture, so Pantheism and these new-fangled microscopes are forms of worship.)

Here's where it gets tricky as the Doctor is, broadly speaking, the Enlightenment in a frock-coat – especially when debating with humans

continued on page 15...

12.1 Robot

• *UNIT* still need permission to raid semi-secret outfits such as Think Tank, even when there is a provable danger to national and global security. The Brigadier can arrange use of a Scorpion tank and can authorise air-strikes by the RAF [see "Terror of the Autons", "The Seeds of Doom"].

The budgetary limits prevent the Brigadier from leading a brigade also mean he can't afford a Major and Captain under him, so Benton is promoted to Warrant Officer. [He should henceforth be referred to as 'Mister': the end-credits list him as 'Sergeant Benton', but many British schoolkids thought "Sergeant" was his given name anyway.] Benton, apparently, can authorise rescue and recovery missions with a few infantry and weapons while the Brigadier is away. Nonetheless, he is unable to restrain Sarah or Kettlewell [the latter perhaps on medical grounds, especially as Harry is elsewhere].

Think Tank are fully aware of UNIT and the Doctor as are, apparently, the members of the Scientific Reform Society who aren't working at the facility. The Brigadier's troops are permitted to arrest everyone at the meeting.

The Non-Humans

• *Alpha Centaurids* play table-tennis with all six limbs, apparently.

• *Robot K1*. An android [in as much as it is bipedal, has two arms at the top of the torso and a head above everything else, plus a human, male voice] constructed of a 'living metal', but looking like steel or aluminium. The domed head has an arc of red glass triangles, lit from behind when it is activated, where eyes would be. The hands are giant pincers, able to rip apart iron chains but pick up manila folders. It is approximately nine feet tall and, apart from two hydraulic fluid tubes on the chest and components of the "face", all metal.

The Robot has, apparently, been given the brain-patterns of Professor Kettlewell, its creator [10.5, "The Green Death" demonstrated this sort of thing was possible for misguided Professors]. Despite its 'Prime Directive' [familiar to most as the First Law of Robotics] of not harming humans, this robot can be persuaded that a specific human or a group must be killed in the interests of protecting humanity. Hacking the Robot's core programming requires a partial dismantling of the head and chest, a process directed to look like surgery. When such work-arounds are not in place, the Robot [only ever identified as this, except once when it announces itself as 'K1'] undergoes an imbalance in its circuits analogous to pain and distress and freezes until the order is countermanded. Sarah's concern at the Robot's apparent discomfort complicates this process [we should perhaps think of the altering of the Robot's priorities as hypnosis rather than reprogramming].

The Robot has difficulty reconciling conflicting information, and it occasionally writhes in seeming agony or collapses in a faint. It makes loud whirring sounds. Eventually a simple syllogism solves the conflict: the Robot was built to aid humanity; humans lie and contradict each other, harming the thing built for their aid *ergo* the best way to help humanity is to destroy all humans and perpetuate their best qualities in a new robot race. Once the Robot has killed its creator and upset his one friend, triggering nuclear war seems like the only course of action left. Nonetheless, it abducts Sarah to keep her safe.

The Living Metal from which it is constructed can absorb energy and redirect it to grow [yes, just like Vibranium]. After a blast from the Disintegrator Gun, the Robot grows to approximately 80 feet tall and begins a rampage. The exotic metal devised by Kettlewell can be counter-acted by a synthetic metal virus, working faster the larger the Robot grows. [With this and the Professor's move from Robotics to Alternative Energy, it appears that Kettlewell was primarily a materials scientist, hence his work on a more efficient solar battery. All recent developments in that field have been ceramics rather than metals (ARPA has a couple on the testbed) and moving from robots to solid-state batteries isn't unprecedented – although Kettlewell didn't, as far as we know, invent the Super-Soaker. Logically, a substance that can change size with energy cannot have as rigid a molecular structure as a conventional metal. Despite appearances, therefore, we'd conclude that this robot is made from a metallic glass. That said, the Doctor's horseshoe magnet picks up traces of it, so it may be ferrous after all.]

History

• *Dating*. Whatever the year, the on-screen date for Sarah's Think Tank pass says '4th April'. [If this is early April, the climax can only be that sunny if the all-important Think Tank meeting is held at around two in the afternoon. A glance at Harry's

Do Robots Have Rights?

...continued from page 13

who act as the be-all and end-all of law and might – but, in his rebellion against the Time Lords and occasional arguments with robots, he plumps for Romanticism. We are, of course, defining that term less strictly than Goethe or whoever might have done at the time, but still within the same ballpark: it's about the right of individuals to create themselves as fully as possible, even making mistakes, in the face of a conformist society. We mentioned *eudaemonia* and that's the gist of it: Aristotle said that every conscious being has the duty to flourish to the full extent of their abilities but shrivels inside if denied the chance. Romanticism complicated the Utilitarian idea of what "good" might be and how you might measure it: was it the same as "happiness", as the quintessential Enlightenment document, the US Declaration of Independence said (see X3.6, "The Lazarus Experiment" for the Doctor claiming credit for that bit)? If there's a quantifiable good/happiness that can be added and subtracted (the Felicific Calculus, as they called it), is universal mediocrity better than one person being very well-off and the majority suffering (or vice versa – see later)? Mill's attempt to salvage the earlier work of Jeremy Bentham (the one who's embalmed in Imperial College, not the one we'll discuss in later entries in this book, but see "The Deadly Assassin") subordinated abstract happiness to happiness with guarantees of individual liberty and set out various ways to calibrate it. Within late 1970s *Doctor Who*, it's made plain that the Doctor disagrees with the big-scale Utilitarianism of the Time Lords largely because he's learned to see how life looks from ground-level for the little people who risk being left out of such calculations.

Most of the time this is portrayed as siding with oppressed humanoids fighting alien tyrants, so there's not much of a conflict of interest. When one subset of a species (usually humanoid for budgetary reasons) is restricting the flourishing of another, usually by exploitation or slavery, the Doctor's on the side of the oppressed. Frequently, the turning-point in any such rebellion comes when someone acting for the oppressors gets an idea of what life's like for the underdogs – the clearest example is 3.9, "The Savages", when Steven reflects the beam from Exorse's light-gun back at the guard, who, after experiencing the effect, starts to side with the outsiders. (He puts himself into too much jeopardy for it to be just because he fancies Nanina, so we can assume – without the actual episodes to contradict us – that he gets woke.)

Examples of cross-species empathy are usually humans attempting to second-guess how non-humans feel, but "Robot" gives us a helpful counterexample. The "imbalance in my circuits" experienced when faced with orders conflicting with the basic human-helping protocols gives it an idea of what "pain" is and Sarah's sympathy marks her out as a superior human. An intelligent being capable of empathy would seem to be in possession of what's called a theory of mind, and that's been the litmus test for researchers trying to establish whether AI or various animals can be considered as close enough to human to have rights. Can something demonstrating intelligent behaviour also indicate that it has an idea of itself as an entity and, thereby, an idea of others as of equal distinctiveness? In short, can it tell the difference between a human and a shop-dummy based on its idea of itself as being "there" and an individual?

It's hard to measure someone's subjectivity. Hans Asperger thought he had just such a method: his colleagues Illing and Jekelius sent hundreds of children to Spiegelgrund, a death-camp for being insufficiently *gemutlich* (roughly, "sociable" or "engaged"). If how one appears to others, what kind of display is put on, is the only thing anyone else has to go on then people on megadoses of anti-depressants might not pass muster. If the batteries in Stephen Hawking's talk-box had run out he would, in an extreme interpretation of this law, cease to be "there".[3]

Worse, the whole point of Artificial Intelligence is to make objects that mimic those signs, hence the name. The person who devised the term intended it as a replacement for "Cybernetics", which an information theorist coined, Norbert Weiner. AI research has, until fairly recently, been about the engineering, the mechanics of making devices that produce results akin to those made by human agency, not about systemic replication of biological control systems as an end in itself. The Holy Grail of AI has been passing the Turing Test, being able to engage with a human well enough to pass for human – but even if this happens (and the regulations for call-centre operators to stick to the script or face the sack has lowered the bar somewhat), it wouldn't make that system a person in the eyes of the law or most observers

continued on page 17...

12.1 Robot

wristwatch at the start of "The Ark in Space" suggests that he left in the TARDIS at around ten to six.] Sarah has a brand-new WH Smiths spiral-bound reporters' notebook [a graphic on the cover is screamingly early 70s and was discontinued in 1977]. She's driving a new-looking J-registration MG Midget Mk III. Bessie's tax-disc expires in February 1975.

The Doctor's been out cold for a while when Sarah asks about the pass. [So, assuming she got one for the following day, the break-ins began in early April and the whole business with Metebelis Spiders ("Planet of the Spiders") was perhaps mid to late March. It may have been longer, but even the novelisation doesn't seem to indicate anything longer than a week.] At least one night elapses between the Doctor being put to bed and Sarah asking the Brigadier for a favour. [And yet, it's a long enough absence for the Brig to 'miss' having the Doctor around, possibly suggesting the Doctor's use of UNIT for his ESP experiments was a longer-term project than it appeared.

[We're sticking with 1975 as the year, even though Sarah's taken to dressing as though it were 1932, and Britain has abruptly become very high-tech despite the previous story's curiously 1950s feel. Jellicoe's up-to-date look and terminology (see **English Lessons**) still includes mild surprise at 'that journalist girl' just seconds before the dated (and thus datable) terms 'male chauvinist' and 'at the present moment in time'. Police sirens still go *nee-naw* (see "Planet of the Spiders" for more on Panda cars). The newspaper cutting about Sir Joseph Chambers is fairly recent but discusses 'Mr Heath' as Leader of the Opposition (see **Who's Running the Country?** under "The Green Death" and 'Madam' under "Terror of the Zygons").

[Sarah's Ginger Rogers/Fay Wray look is in-character, and in keeping with the way the story lands up. And yet, it was exactly what fashion experts in early 1974 said would be the look of the following summer, in expectation of the film of *The Great Gatsby* being a bigger hit than it was, and Mia Farrow's costumes being more practical for the dismal damp weather we got than they were. Practically every item Sarah wears in this story was on sale in the high streets, but not usually in that combination.]

The nuclear powers have agreed a fail-safe system with Britain as the honest broker holding the codes. [Possibly the way of the world after the Styles talks concluded (9.1, "Day of the Daleks"). It also feels like a precursor to the implausible geo-political security arrangements seen in X1.5, "World War Three".] The Brigadier speaks of the Cold War in the past tense.

Kettlewell is working on 'Solar batteries' [see 5.4, "The Enemy of the World" and a lot of Season Six], but Earth is still over-reliant on fossil fuels. [See, for example, "The Green Death" and "Terror of the Zygons". Intriguingly, in this light, the Robot claims to have been built to replace humans in 'all manner of mining operations', which in 1970s Britain was a very politically-loaded proposal – see also "The Monster of Peladon" and 22.3, "The Mark of the Rani".]

The National Institute for Advanced Scientific Research ('Think Tank') is based at a mansion somewhere in the countryside. The British government apparently has the wherewithal to take over development of any promising innovation the Think Tank devises, including the Disintegrator Gun, and exercises the Official Secrets Act over these; it has restrictions on who can visit and what they can see or report. Nonetheless, Kettlewell's resignation was well-reported.

This month's Hardest Substance Known to Man: case-hardened Dynastreem.

The Analysis

Where Does This Come From? We'll look at the wider historical perspective in a second or two, because there's something going on in this story that we'll see a lot more of in this book: a significant rethink of who is watching *Doctor Who* and what would appeal to them.

Although the series was never expressly just for children (the BBC didn't even have a Children's Department when it began, for reasons too complicated to go into here) and although the stats Barry Letts liked to cite suggested a 60% adult audience in 1970, it's undeniable that the majority of Jon Pertwee stories had been made with ten-year-old boys in mind first and foremost. Think of the ingredients in the stories in the production block ending with "Robot": it began with a conspiracy thriller with dinosaurs and spaceships, with lots of car-chases and punch-up action then a time-paradox and a ham-fisted moral. Then came a Western with Daleks and a sacrifice-cult, the return of old favourites Aggedor, the Ice Warriors and Alpha Centauri in a similarly clumsy

Do Robots Have Rights?

...continued from page 15

Empathy, at least as revealed by brain-scans (which, once again, confirm what schoolteachers knew a century before) is something you have to work at. The ability to comprehend what others are feeling, if not precisely to feel it oneself, is developed most rapidly in the late teens and reading decent fiction helps a lot. What we'll see in this volume is that bookishness is equated to humanity more emphatically than before or after in the series (see also **Why Doesn't Anyone Read Any More?** under X1.7, "The Long Game"). It is, of course, easier to walk a mile in the shoes of someone who has shoes, so to speak: the less like the reader/viewer a protagonist is, the harder it is to engender empathy and the more misconstrued or downright condescending that reaction risks being. Not even trying risks the other problem of "othering" people and treating them as incomprehensible black boxes – "inscrutable". "Smile" landed up treating the Vardies as an abstract exercise in debugging, like those Asimov stories we've been trying not to mention so far, even though the interfaces were closely modelled on real-world machines such as "Asimo" with a hint of GERTY from *Moon*. Just because some robots look like humans doesn't mean they think exactly like humans. Just because something isn't human, it doesn't mean it's not aware, intelligent or deserving of consideration.

What we're dealing with here is a problem common to stories about aliens and present-day legal practice, that there's a need for a yardstick that isn't "us". The United States was founded by people who thought they'd cracked it and presented their legal apparatus as "universal". Even though the Constitution had dissenters who framed the Bill or Rights as a self-checking (in other words, cybernetic) procedure, the subsequent developments and such documents as the United Nations Convention of Human Rights have run into trouble with other nations who disagree. America, despite its own chequered track-record on this, tends to be treated as the yardstick of the world. It's easy to forget that it's just one nation out of about 300, and 3% of the planet's current population. The most well-known manifestation of this assumption that America is everyone in television science fiction is, of course, *Star Trek*, and they have a one-size-fits-all set of rules for all species in the galaxy, based on American law so closely that it's never questioned.[4] *Doctor Who* doesn't have any such in-story legal framework, but somehow, the tendencies of Britain whenever a specific story was written seem to prevail.

One of the noticeable trends in 1970s *Doctor Who* is an increasing emphasis on how insignificant Earth is on the cosmic scale. It was seldom the case that the habits of humans were the only option on the table and even post-war British humans weren't privileged over Aztecs, Solonians or the Rill. As the 70s progressed, the series became less geocentric and made parochialism seem untenable. (The exception, oddly, is the very story where astrology is equated to slavery, "The Masque of Mandragora", where 1970s Western attitudes are the measure of all things as far as the Doctor's concerned.)

Just as importantly, the types of things considered to be self-aware life forms expands to include most of the range of hypotheticals in published SF of the time, including silicon-based beings and robots but not any real-world life then under consideration. The Doctor's idea of who's worth talking to seems to reach its widest extent in this period, and he's keener than usual to encourage individuals to step beyond their accustomed limits. And yet, when you watch a lot of other late 70s science fiction shows, these omissions in *Doctor Who* seem a lot stranger. There's none of those quintessential 70s standbys, apes learning to sign and cetaceans singing to each other. But we do get Erato the Tythonian (17.3, "The Creature from the Pit").

Intelligence, in the restricted sense of being able to learn from mistakes, is now a matter of processing-power, connectivity and memory, but oddly, the things machines can't successfully reproduce tend to be the things toddlers find easiest. Small children need a lot less data to make informed guesses about the outside world than AIs do. They can infer and generalise from scant information. The same seems to be true of the smarter animals; especially those that scavenge or forage. The "intelligence" (there's still debate on what intelligence *is*, how it works and whether AI has it) is an emergent feature, like the trees in a forest making something recognisable as "a forest" and an ecosystem rather than just a tree here, a tree there and so on. Most people would argue that an orangutan or porpoise was qualitatively different from a forest, but if sentience and selfhood are emergent properties, it might just be

continued on page 19...

12.1 Robot

political allegory and more car-chases and punch-ups in a wish-fulfilment scenario of mental powers unleashed. All good comic-strip stuff, if patchily-executed, but a bit of a guilty pleasure for anyone beyond primary-school age.

Now think of what else was popular among family audiences in mid-1970s Britain. Apart from sport and *Top of the Pops* (which gets a whole essay to itself later in this book), the big successes fall into two broad categories: ostensible kid's shows that are better than they need to be and have sly adult references or supposedly grown-up series with elements that children can relate to. In the former category, we can cite *The Magic Roundabout* and *Batman,* and in the latter *Monty Python's Flying Circus* and *The Morecambe & Wise Show*. It was at around this time that advertising agencies did market research on what was being watched by whom and, in the process, coined the term "Cult TV" for the crossover category.

What, if anything, did these series have in common? Well, obviously, a loyal audience, but most of the cited shows worked on their own internal logic and occasionally inserted bits of the mundane world inside it. A lot of the references were just tantalisingly out-of-reach for the youngest viewers, but that's what being a kid's all about, and – for a 70s child – acquisition of these bits of knowledge was how you gained admission to the grown-up world. That all-purpose term of approval, "sophisticated", covered a lot of shibboleths and displays of *savoir faire*, from wine and classical music to identifying quotations and having been to foreign countries for more than just package holidays. It also included old movies and less-obvious works of art, not hitherto considered worth knowing for most people, and that's the vocabulary of Pop Art.

Before all the soup-cans, targets and reproduction comic-strip frames, the originators of that movement had been meeting in London since the early 1950s and attempting to figure out what kind of world they were in, a prerequisite for attempting to depict it honestly. Eduardo Paolozzi and Richard Hamilton did lectures on cybernetics and polymers as well as collages of science textbooks and *Famous Monsters of Film-Land*. The 1956 Whitechapel Gallery exhibition *This is Tomorrow* is as good a benchmark as any for when this stopped being fringe in Britain, and the Ken Russell documentary *Pop Goes the Easel* is where BBC's "serious" art programme *Monitor* took it back to the masses whence it came. This 1962 documentary took great pains to demonstrate that the young artists being followed were enthusiastic about popular culture but didn't just use it in their work simply because they didn't know any better. They'd all paid their dues studying what yer gran called "real" art and could all draw "properly" but chose to do something new and now.

This sensibility, at work in Terry Gilliam's animations, Derek Jarman's films, a lot of rock music by art-school graduates (Pete Townshend, John Lennon, David Bowie, Ian Dury, Brian Eno and literally scores of others), *Yellow Submarine, A Clockwork Orange* and *The Rocky Horror Picture Show*, is at work in the phase of *Doctor Who* discussed in this volume. It had been peeping out from behind the bushes in earlier phases (see **Did Sergeant Pepper Know the Doctor?** under 5.1, "The Tomb of the Cybermen", **Is *Doctor Who* Camp?** under 6.5, "The Seeds of Death" and our rough guide to Glam with 8.1, "Terror of the Autons"), but now it was front and centre. We'll mention specifics as we go, starting right now with Robby the Robot, a life-size cardboard cut-out of whom was borrowed from a cinema to stand in the entrance of the Whitechapel Gallery for that 1956 exhibition.

Robby was in *Forbidden Planet* (we'll return to that film a few times in this book) and was the acceptable, child-friendly face of robots. Fictional robots had a lot of features with which children could identify: gaucheness; literal-mindedness; over-generalisation; bewilderment at what boys and girls got up to after a certain age; a tendency to ask questions at the wrong time. They also had the one thing that most fascinates small boys: physical power. The movie robot that K1 most closely resembles, Gort from *The Day the Earth Stood Still*, doesn't talk and doesn't listen to people unless they've learned the correct over-ride phrase (all together now: *Klaatu Barrada Nicto*). His part in spreading Klaatu's message of Universal Love is to shoot things with a disintegrator ray, including people and cannons (that said: the actual shots in "Robot" look rather more like the soldier-zapping in *Earth vs the Flying Saucers*, in which GIs and aliens met in Washington for less benign reasons).

In the story from which the film came, "Farewell to the Master", Klaatu and the other humanoids are watched over by machines of loving grace, because only robots can make people behave themselves. A robot's linear reasoning and exces-

Do Robots Have Rights?

...continued from page 17

that we're thinking on the wrong scale or timescale. Some would say that an anthill is an individual with a mind even if ants, on their own, are about as smart as individual brain-cells.

There have been few on-screen instances of anything that can be called a person that wasn't in a reasonably familiar-looking body – we've heard about a galaxy called "Alison" and seen a Solitract Plane that communicated via a frog with a Yorkshire accent (X11.9, "It Takes You Away"), but the main disembodied consciousnesses we've encountered wanted to obtain or make bodies. It's rare that we get a case of a discorporate intelligence that isn't AI distributed across a large number of sites. Even then, the Doctor has to have something to look at when talking to the software so there's usually a main locus (e.g. the "Temple" in 15.5, "Underworld" or the Sacred Chamber in "The Face of Evil"), but that's increasingly unlike how AI works.

People tend to think of something inside one body as more closely resembling humans than systems that are distributed. AI researchers have taken the hint and tried to see whether a software package that only exists inside a specific platform, a body, lands up behaving differently from a distributed system. MIT's "Cog" project was run on the strict understanding that they weren't to get sentimental or anthropomorphise the sensor-array and operating system. They are now developing its face, "Lazlo". The reasoning is that the best-available theory of what it is that makes humans think of themselves as individuals is a metarepresentational construct, the much-discussed "theory of mind", and that this originally was a self-image derived from sense-data and a working-model of the body inside the brain. If this is right, and neurology seems to back it up (as far as fMRI scans and whatnot can), then the ego, the self and the idea of others being somehow like "me" are diagnostic programs that underwent mission-creep then went viral once language happened. There's a lot of conjecture around about "mirror-cells" in the human brain compared to those in apes and cetaceans, but like a lot of evolutionary biology, it's largely story-telling. Testing that assumption would either require some amazingly unethical experiments on babies or something like Cog/Lazlo.

Now we can get back to "Robot", as the K1 is sort of a more advanced Cog. Is Sarah right to treat it as a person? As it turns out, her concern at the peculiar demonstrations of discomfort when it is ordered to kill her forms the basis for its decision to spare her from the extinction of humanity so the idea of "Sarah" is evidently different within its operating system from its idea of "Kettlewell". It can identify individuals. Moreover, that discomfort gives an indication that the robot's sensor array and sense of identity are linked. It's not just that there's a "pain" around somewhere in the room, it's the robot's body that hurts.

This isn't as obvious as it seems, as humans only develop the association fairly late on. The further concept that other things that look like humans can feel something that the observer can't when that person is injured or unwell, follows. A child-development psychologist, or experienced nursery teacher, would evaluate the robot's self-concept and notion of others as individuals as being around where a two-year-old's would be. Even its assassinations, aided by a temporary lobotomy, are grounded in an idea of "enemy of humanity" that needs a conception of humanity, a notion of better or worse outcomes for that entity and a lot of if-then reasoning about consequences of actions. This is several levels of sophistication beyond chess-winning or keeping an online conversation going, this requires a very firm idea of others as moral agents and conscious entities, which in turn needs a self-conception as the yardstick.

In "Smile", the Vardy robots are absolved of guilt for a massacre simply because the Doctor hit the reset button and the "individuals" who killed everyone no longer exist. It's not that their programming was destroyed, just the accumulated input and experience. After a point, it no longer makes sense to treat a robot as the sum-total of its design, manufacture and initial programming, so blaming the parents isn't on; the robot now has the option to say that society is to blame, but it is, much like a teenager, heading towards legal individuality and culpability.

Thus if there had been prosecutions following "The War Machines" (3.10), the Doctor would have got off with a charge of vandalism and possibly aggravated trespass of the Post Office Tower. None of the WOTAN-possessed people would have been culpable for the many deaths that followed, and WOTAN itself would only be accountable if someone could prove that the plan for total world

continued on page 21...

12.1 Robot

sive systemisation leads to a schematic view of the world, like a child's or an adolescent idealist's, and that turns into retribution and sulky disgust at the world very quickly. The archetype for this is, of course, Frankenstein's Monster: a child born in an adult body that offends people, educated with possibly the three worst books for anyone trying to present humans in a good light. As everyone knows, the Monster had daddy-issues and sought a rather simplistic, if brutal, revenge. Robots have long been a handy tool for satirists trying to present intelligence and innocence as a yardstick against which to measure human vices. More specifically, at least two scenes in *Forbidden Planet* depict Robby undergoing some kind of electrical storm in his dome when ordered to kill, a phenomenon accompanied by him swaying around making distressing noises – just as the Robot here groans and flails

Schematised politics also provides vaguely plausible motives for the traditional Mad Scientists. Last time we did this entry, we dismissed the 1930's Technocracy movement as a historical oddity – but, with the prominence of ideologues such as Zuckerberg, Musk and Bezos and the mess of conventional politics in the English-speaking world, the word's come back into vogue. The idea, in its most appealing form, is that an economy based on energy-use rather than arbitrary commercial value made more sense, especially if supervised by people with an engineering background. What it *became*, at its peak, was a bid to supplant democratically-elected governments, big business and bureaucrats with a self-selected "elite" of scientifically-minded control-freaks. (Herbert Hoover tried to alleviate the Depression that way too. It didn't work.) Their figurehead was Howard Scott, a floor-polish demonstrator who presented himself as a polymath and master-strategist.

The movement (which in its brief moment in the spotlight had up to a million members in California alone) had a dress-code, a special salute and a "monad" logo (the Taoist tai chi-tu). It all went wrong when Scott made a hash of a live broadcast, but in the immediate post-War period, they had a brief comeback and staged a motorcade in identical grey cars. Similar ideas have been doing the rounds since Plato's *Republic*, but only ever attempted under Stalin. It didn't end well.

More obvious starting-points are *King Kong* (1933) as the Asimov Robot stories (1941-90).

We'll be going into the latter in more detail later ("The Robots of Death"), so let's just mention that *Star Trek*'s "Prime Directive" isn't much of a disguise for the First Law of Robotics, but hints about how later stories will handle the Time Lords' rather negotiable policy of non-interference. The SRS meeting unveils the Robot in almost exactly the way Kong was revealed to New Yorkers at the film's climax.

It's also traditional at this point to bring up "The Mauritius Penny", a 1962 episode of *The Avengers* with a sequence very like the SRS rally, written by Malcolm Hulke and Terrance Dicks. While a lot else in "Robot" is like later episodes of the ABC series (to the extent that Harry dresses as John Steed and is introduced as "Mr Sullivan from the Ministry"), the differences between the two rallies are as illuminating as the similarities. Kettlewell invited Sarah to use his membership to sneak in to the rally, while Cathy Gale overpowers one of the Neo-Nazi conspirators and uses his pass at the door; Cathy's presence is revealed by her own error, not as a set-up. Nonetheless, the way she hid at the back of the rally, behind a trestle-table – only to be revealed at the climax of the leader's speech – is almost identical, as if Christopher Barry rewatched the episode specifically. Perhaps just as influential was the original format of an experienced investigator and a qualified doctor going undercover; despite his bowler, Harry's doing what Ian Hendry and (briefly) Jon Rollason would do in such a caper before Steed discovered girls.

By the time the series moved onto film, there was a specific type of scheme (and schemers): often a single-issue pressure-group taking more direct action or a monomaniacal millionaire taking his obsession to absurd lengths. "Robot" could only have been more like a colour *Avengers* episode if Jellicoe had faked the break-ins in a robotsuit. Even as it stands, the first episode is directed in such a way that we don't know whose robot it is – aliens, Big Business or Think Tank (they arrive at the story-point where a possible suspect would die just after giving Mrs Peel a huge clue, just before an advert break). Steed would have defeated the giant version by something everyday and stylishly simple, such as getting it to chase him onto freshly-laid tarmac and get stuck, but the sequence of events and general tone is unmistakably similar.

As part of ABC's bid to sell the series overseas,

Do Robots Have Rights?

...continued from page 19

domination wasn't intrinsic to Brett's programming but was the "will" in the acronym emerging as a property. But then someone would have to prove that a robot or computer could have free will and situations such as "Robot" and "The Green Death" would never have arisen. If "Robot" had ended slightly differently, with the robot incapacitated rather than dissolved by goo, it's conceivable that K1, rather than Miss Winters or Jellicoe, would have been legally culpable for the deaths.

In England, until comparatively recently, the concept of the "deodand" pertained in manslaughter charges. It began as a form of forfeiture, but it got a bit fuzzy. Eventually, once large numbers of people were getting killed by railway trains, the law was thoroughly updated. The thing is, this was once closely related to the idea of animals as moral agents – we may scoff at the Mediaeval procedure of putting pigs on trial for killing their keepers, but at least they got the benefit of the doubt, unlike a train. The extent to which a pig had volition-as-we-understand-it was a theological issue, but as a legal matter, it's closely related to the concept of "diminished responsibility" as a defence. Executing a pig for murder was just as much a restitution of "balance" as paying the worth of the confiscated pig to the relatives. (Pigs, like serfs or slaves, were property.) In those days, an animal could be defended in court (even a colony of rats got its day in court in France) but not bring prosecutions as a plaintiff, of have them brought on their behalf. Nevertheless, now that people are being killed by self-driving cars, this whole matter's being reopened. With these and drones there are now AIs capable of killing but, as yet, unable to determine what's a person – Asimov's First Law isn't going to be applicable any time soon.[5]

The traditional conception of robot behavioural constraints comes from Asimov's stories: they're called the Three Laws, as if statute, software and Newtonian Physics were interchangeable, and they are all about a robot's duties and obligations towards humans. The term "robot", however, derives from a satire about the rights of the workforce. However, the notion is that robots deserve and *want* to be treated like humans. Isn't that a bit patronising? Perhaps the aim shouldn't be to "pass" for human, to demonstrate specific traits to be judged worthy on their terms, as to re-evaluate those terms from scratch. With humans having the upper hand while such renegotiation is taking place, the odds of a root-and-branch rethink ever getting anywhere would be slim unless other forces were brought to bear. (It could make a good story, with aliens offering Earth advanced tech on condition that we gave robots, whales and apes the vote, but humans are the ultimate vested interest on this planet right now, and our collective track-record for smart moves concerning the rest of the planet isn't great.)

America has several ideas about what a "person" might be and it's not restricted to humans. The 1886 ruling *Santa Clara County vs South Pacific Railroad*, which interpreted the 14th Amendment to the US Constitution so as to make Corporations legal persons. This is why there are so many corporate buyouts that don't help the workforce or consumers, because this "person" is answerable only to the shareholders. Revising this would be tricky, as that Amendment also covers Due Process, the reunification of the Confederate States into the US and Civil Rights generally. (Britain still has trouble with the concept of "corporate manslaughter", which is how the board and shareholders of railway companies have literally made a killing.) With personhood detached from the human body, later documents and statements of intent shifted the criterion to sentience or self-awareness: the Lisbon Treaty, one of the foundational documents of the EU, took this line, as does New Zealand's law.[6]

The US Constitution posits equal rights because of a common origin (i.e., the Biblical story of a creator), a position that Thomas Jefferson could have backed up by freeing his slaves. The entire notion of inalienable human rights was a legacy of Enlightenment-era secularism, however much the Founding Fathers and Cromwellian democrats relied on theological arguments to back it up in the face of established authority. Robots, on this logic, would have no rights because such a thing/ being/ person would have been made by humans and therefore owned, subordinated to a creator. But that would also apply to anyone conceived by IVF, which is not the case.

Once again, the Cybermen provide a limit-case for how the Doctor, and *Doctor Who*, has decided where to draw the line. From a strictly Utilitarian point of view, they've found a way of life that suits them. It's only when they impose it on others that there could be any complaint, but in most stories,

continued on page 23...

and to stop the older video-taped episodes being too studio-bound, they used a lot of the stately homes around Elstree Studios as locations. In real life, institutions such as the BBC, the Ministry of Defence, universities and various scientific establishments used similar buildings and estates, so this trend wasn't just for show. In fact, the BBC had one that they used as the location for "Robot". That sort of thing will happen a lot more over the next few years. (Talking of Hulke's collaborations with Dicks, it might be worth remembering that Hulke described the collaboration as being originally founded on Dicks's typing-speed; twice in this story, the Doctor's super-dexterity is foregrounded.)

What's also worthy of note in this connexion is that memories of old post-nuclear scenarios will dominate this entire year. For all that the Brigadier discusses the Think Tank Bunker as being a legacy from "back in the Cold War days", we're at a point in geopolitical history where atomic war has moved down the list of top ten ways the world will end (after the prominence of overpopulation, pollution, the Energy Crunch and either overheating or a new Ice Age, as we've seen in earlier volumes), but it's not out of the running.

What was striking, at time of broadcast, was how relatively mundane the scheme was for people who had access to a giant robot and a disintegrator gun. ICBM's were old hat; brushfire wars and terrorism were the trendy fears. Detente, the buzz-term of the mid-seventies, worked so long as both sides kept the same leaders (and China stayed out of it). The year 1975 would see the Apollo-Soyuz link-up, the much-publicised US/USSR collaboration in space that was seen as emblematic of the new accord between these powers (yet, because it didn't fit the story of mutual mistrust so current and useful in the 1980s, this was airbrushed out of history). Nuclear holocaust wasn't on the agenda to the same extent it would have been ten years either side of the broadcast date.

Nonetheless, the accumulated stories of what might happen in the event of such a war fueled a lot of *Doctor Who* tales. "Robot", with its computer hacking and nuclear blackmail scenario, is just the sort of thing that would come back into vogue a decade later. We'll pick up on this thread as we come to the Ark, the abandoned Earth, the wilderness full of mutations and the survival-plan of the "winners" of a nuclear war and even the Vogans cowering in their bunker. (In one of the scenes left unrecorded when Baker went off to get plastered during "The Sontaran Experiment", we get confirmation that this isn't coincidence. The Doctor and Harry would have got lost in the "Whitehall warren", i.e. the Government's fall-out shelter built into the Underground, as used in 11.2, "Invasion of the Dinosaurs".)

One last, speculative, suggestion: the month Dicks started working on *Doctor Who*, January 1968, saw a BBC2 documentary wherein Alan Whicker (see 5.5, "The Web of Fear") investigated the horror industry and was shown around Terry Nation's Elizabethan mansion. The pull-quote for the show was: *I don't like my monsters to have Oedipus complexes*. Dicks had worked with Nation on the last run of *The Avengers* and then came all the kerfuffle we discussed in Volume 3. Was this story a sly dig?

English Lessons

• *Why is a mouse when it spins?* is a traditional Christmas Cracker riddle, the answer being "because the higher, the fewer". The most likely explanation for that is that a "mouse" is the weight on a centrifugal governor, as seen on steam engines, and as it gets higher it throttles back, thus reducing the RPMs. Without this or any other real-world referent, it just becomes a sort of koan, and was adopted in the trenches in World War I. The earliest known reference for this is *A Cry from Colney Hatch* c.1894. Some sources attribute this to Isambard Kingdom Brunel, however much it sounds like Lewis Carroll.

• *Swinger* (n.): It didn't mean in 70s Britain what it meant in 70s America (the Brigadier probably left that sort of thing to Torchwood). Sarah simply means to suggest that he's secretly hip. Similarly, describing herself as a "working girl" should not be imputed to mean journalism isn't her only source of income.

• *Right-oh* (interj.): an improbably cheery acknowledgement for a naval officer to give to his temporary superior, even if Harry remembers to add "sir" at the end.

• *At the present moment in time* is the sort of American circumlocution associated in Britain with people either wanting to appear more eloquent than they were, or to seem as though they had been to California and picked up the lingo. It was the sort of phraseology viewers had learned to associate with the mesmerically ghastly Hughie

Do Robots Have Rights?

...continued from page 21

that's exactly what they are doing. The Doctor as good as says this when discussing it with the almost-completely-converted Bill (X10.12, "The Doctor Falls"). In almost every story, they speak of themselves in the first person singular, which is more than K9 usually does. Strange vocal timbre aside, the Cyberleaders from "The Moonbase", "Revenge of the Cybermen" or "Earthshock" would have no trouble passing the Turing Test. Despite their inbuilt ability to network and share data, there's little evidence that the alterations to their brains have removed their subjectivity. It could be argued that stifling or removing individuality is intrinsically bad, but we have no way of knowing whether any given Cyberman volunteered for conversion because of impending illness or was captured and processed.

Were this not the case, the Doctor might, at a pinch, claim that completing the death of the former individual is euthanasia rather than murder. Moreover, is what happens to anyone who becomes a Cyberman that different from the seemingly-benign Kinda and their communal minds (19.3, "Kinda", of course), a culture that frowns on individuality as the cause of all sin and decay? By now, of course, he has a good legal case that it would be self-defence. The Cybermen have standing orders to kill him (X4.14, "The Next Doctor" confirms this). For all their claims of absolute logic, theirs is a grievance culture – it's determined to claim retribution for losses but calculated on their own internal metrics rather than any objective measurement. On the evidence we have, the problem is less the Doctor's distaste for the Cybermen per se than that he only ever encounters them when they are either planning an assault to grab new territory and converts or attempting to save their own lives in the face of humans (and others) who have scores to settle. As a culture, they are like a cancer: when we see the Doctor engage with a literally disarmed individual Cyberman ("The Time of the Doctor"), it's arguably the longest continuous friendship he ever has. Nonetheless, he's remarkably keen on treating them as target-practice.

Regardless of the Doctor's personal leaning towards Romanticism and championing of Enlightenment values, the law on Earth for the present is struggling with the task of deciding how to allocate rights to non-human entities. Possibly just as well: the Doctor takes a sort of Groucho Marx attitude to well-ordered societies. He wouldn't want to belong to one that would have someone like him as a member.

Green (see "The Zygon Inversion"). The script describes Jellicoe as dressing ostentatiously fashionably, despite not being exactly pin-up material, and many middle-management or civil service staff in the UK took similar measures to avoid being replaced by younger men (an entire sitcom, *The Fall and Rise of Reginald Perrin*, derived three seasons of material from these berks). See also *Ongoing (…) Situation* under 15.4, "The Sun Makers".

- *Blanco* (n., v.): the military-issue whitewash used on belts and pith-helmets was also part of a barracks' décor. At the entrance would be a sign mounted in a neat pile of white pebbles. Blanco, manufactured by the Mills Equipment company, was in a cake, like soap, so needed to be mixed with water, a laborious task in itself even before application to equipment or stones (a later version came as a ready-made paste, then the army switched to nylon). Refreshing the whitewashed pebbles would be a chore reserved for conscripted men who had committed a minor transgression. Sarah's suggestion that Benton should 'go and Blanco your rifle, or something' is a dismissively vague description of military routine, like telling a housewife "go iron the cat".

- *Jelly Babies* (n.): not at all like jellybeans. They began life as a Victorian fruit-flavoured gelatine confection and were apparently intended to look like bears (some sources say that the original trade name was "Unclaimed Babies"). Bassett's (based in Sheffield), produced "Victory Jelly Babies" in 1918. Sweets such as these were sold in paper bags, usually a quarter-pound at a time measured out from a screw-top jar in a newsagent's (see "The Android Invasion" for more on this). Sharing sweets was a means to denote inclusion or exclusion in the school playground, especially when times were tight and pocket-money was reduced (think of *Just William*) and, among soldiers sent to fight in 1939, these were the most-requested gifts from home for similar reasons. The end of sweet rationing in 1953 (see X2.7, "The Idiot's Lantern") resumed this habit. Jelly babies are softer than Gummi Bears, their nearest overseas analogue, and can be bitten in various macabre ways.

12.1 Robot

Things That Don't Make Sense Even though at least a day elapses between the theft of the most valuable secret in the world, the murder of its guardian (Chambers) and a palpable threat to use this secret, none of the major nuclear powers think to simply change their codes. Maybe the Brigadier is right not to trust these foreign governments, if this is their idea of security on high alert. (Or maybe Her Majesty's Government forgot to mention that he'd had burglars, even though he should have a mandated sign-in to complete every morning. Why is the melting of a vault made of case-hardened Dynastreem not enough of a worry that they go to DefCon 3?) Even if you're not expecting a dirty great robot to crash in and steal plans, employing just one not-terribly-intimidating night watchman is a bit of a false economy. And why does the phone explode when it's ripped off the wall?

Everyone seems to know about this super-secret zap-gun. Sarah might, at a pinch, have read about it (freakishly fast, with exceptional eyesight) over the Brigadier's shoulder, but she tells the Doctor that this is the Brigadier's big problem, even though she was only informed about a series of break-ins. She makes the connection from whatever the Brig was reading, somehow, but he requires the Doctor to explain it to him a few scenes later. Then again, how did anyone at the Scientific Reform Society or Think Tank know of Chambers's secret? They don't even have a good photo of him and have to take a press-clipping from a while back.

Sarah knows enough to connect the Disintegrator Gun with Think Tank, and also recalls that Kettlewell's resignation made the headlines. As Kettlewell was a famous roboticist, it's hardly a three-pipe problem for the Brigadier to connect the gun, the Think Tank and the possibility of a machine capable of break-ins and burrowing. Has he such faith in the Prime Directive (of which he has, apparently, not heard anyway) that he cannot conceive of a killer robot? Certainly, he knows enough about the Disintegrator project to immediately conclude that Emmett's Electronics is the next target. And yet, he asks the Doctor what the Disintegrator can do in Part Four, *after* watching a sniper and a tank get vaporised.

Exactly how a robot with clumsy pincers operates a gun it can barely hold is another matter. Even if they included some kind of jack-plug in the device and its new operator, his aim's a bit wonky. Like teleports and the Time Scoop ("Invasion of the Dinosaurs"), this weapon can miraculously discriminate between the target and anything around it.

We have a whole essay about the problems of making things grow or shrink (**How Hard is It to be The Wrong Size?** under 16.6, "The Armageddon Factor"), so we'll just direct your attention to those spindly ankles now supporting the cubed amount of weight on the squared cross-section, and the problems of processing information with circuitry that's grown in size but not complexity. Transistors work by changes in the doped silicon or gallium arsenide – this is still 70s tech, more or less – effected at the molecular level when an electron is added and alters the conductivity, making a resistant material more conductive. Even if Kettlewell has foregone the usual substances used in electronics, and potentially revolutionised everything by inventing a self-replicating material for circuitry, making such a semiconductor 80 times bigger (if we call the original height nine feet and the final size 80, it's grown approximately nine times taller, so the circuit's surface area is magnified by nine squared, 81 times) makes it 1/80th as efficient. No wonder the Robot goes from being a genius-level hacker, able to restart the halted nuclear countdown with three keystrokes, to a rampaging moron.

But it ought to be a lot *slower* too. Unless, of course, the circuits are good old fashioned non-living metal, therefore the processors and hydraulics and such ought to be the same size as before inside a Kong-size shell (729 times its original volume). But it would need the plumbing and wiring to grow somehow, or else there would just be a huge lump of scrap metal containing a frustrated, ranting CPU rattling around unable to do anything. A third alternative is that Kettlewell's Magic Metal can self-develop in complexity, so there aren't circuits 81 times the size but 80 new circuits for every one that existed before. That could cause a period of adjustment, just as regeneration did for the Doctor, but this enhanced processing facility might perhaps occasion more sophisticated behaviour than this whole stomping-on-Land-Rovers business. ("Here I am, brain the size of a planet and they want me to go on a rampage.")

Kettlewell invented his metal virus to solve the problem of all that unsalvageable scrap metal in the world. Err... isn't that what scrap metal merchants do? Metal can be melted down and re-used, and it's very cost-effective. A plastic-eating virus would be handier (albeit with obvious problems if it got loose, as seen in TV's *Doomwatch*). However, let's hope that the variety the Doctor brewed up only works on the Living Metal© and doesn't get blown around in the air, making planes fall out of the sky. And why should the virus work faster for a robot that's 729 times more bulky than before? (If it throws the growth-spurt into reverse, as the Doctor says, then shouldn't it discharge a Disintegrator Gun-blast's-worth of energy, turning the Bunker – or that nearby town – into a smouldering crater?)

There's a lot about the timescale that only works if Think Tank, Kettlewell's mews, the church hall where they hold the underwhelming rally before ending the world, UNIT HQ and the Bunker are all about a mile apart from each other. Kettlewell's hit on the head at home and Sarah gives him First Aid in the Doctor's lab. The Doctor can zip between the Bunker and Kettlewell's place along winding country lanes. Miss Winters gets herself and Kettlewell to the Bunker from the tedious rally almost as fast as Jellicoe gets Harry there from Think Tank. The editor of the local paper will be pleased, even if people had their gardens trashed by a Chieftain driving in a straight line, and everyone in whatever town had the fascist rally and bake-sale will have seen this enormous robot from their upstairs windows while they were filing their insurance claims. Good luck hushing that up, Brig!

In Part One, the Brigadier can call UNIT HQ from the scene of the second break-in and arrange to meet Benton at Emmett's (somewhere in Essex, which is a big county) in an hour. This is manifestly the same HQ as in "Planet of the Spiders", which was under an hour's drive from Mortimer (in Surrey). Even if this futuristic setting includes a miraculously tailback-free version of the M25 a decade early, we're looking at a good two and a half hours just on main roads, not the by-roads needed for heavier vehicles. If Benton's still got use of the Hercules from "The Invasion" (6.3), they would have to land it at a suitable airstrip (far from anywhere) and move out from there.

The supposedly-mighty Scientific Reform Society not only holds its sparsely-attended rally in a community hall but has piles of cardboard boxes and a bag of vegetables on a trestle table in a corner behind the dozen or so attendees. The people who've come to hear this rousing tirade are all apparently just killing time – when UNIT arrests them, nobody in the audience seems to think that they'll either be running the world this time tomorrow or dead. They seem a bit bored by this giant robot stomping around apprehending a reporter and knocking over empty cardboard boxes. (All right, one woman gasps and sounds shocked as appropriate – but she's not in uniform, so perhaps she's the cleaning-lady waiting for the meeting to end.) If it's the original membership before the Winters gang made it their public face, why is she there making a speech? Why demonstrate the Robot to them if, as she says, it's familiar enough for the Society to base their logo on it? Despite being so keen to have Sarah write them up in the press, Mr Short, the interviewee with the odd fashion sense, didn't show up. Moreover, we know that most of Think Tank's core conspirators are heading from the mansion to the Bunker at that very moment. If it's just a sting for Sarah, it's not only stupidly elaborate but pointless, as Miss Winters decries use for hostages and extra mouths to feed. Capturing Sarah only serves a purpose as a human shield for when the Brigadier shows up, and he only does so because Kettlewell lured her into this trap, apparently at Miss Winters's behest. Meanwhile, the Doctor has only now noticed that every grunt he beats up looks like Terry Walsh, and never thinks to remark on this when on Skaro or confronting the Brethren of Demnos.

Not much else about these nerd-Nazis makes sense. Why is wearing trousers more impractical or irrational than wearing a skirt, especially in Britain? Why does Miss Winters (not "Ms"? It's 1974) wear skirts even when spouting caricature rad-fem bile? Their plan isn't especially well-thought-out anyway, as they seem to think most people will survive an atomic war. The most likely scenario is a hand-to-mouth existence where scientists are resented, not obeyed. Even with a flipping great robot and a Disintegrator Gun, the dozen or so SRS members would be facing a *Mad Max* world and they barely have enough supplies for a long siege, let alone to use as bribes for cooperation.

So maybe the conspirators don't expect anyone to survive in their immediate vicinity, or in most of Britain. Perhaps they think they can repopulate the world. Well, not to put too fine a point on it, even if Miss Winters was into guys, there aren't any other women in the Bunker except the one they're planning to kill. A couple attended the meeting but were put in a UNIT holding-cell. And

12.1 Robot

the Bunker doesn't seem large enough to house all the babies that a fresh start would require and lacks enough food even for the number remaining after the people at the Boring Rally are arrested. The Bunker has so few rooms, they keep their hostages in the same one as the Disintegrator Gun.

The only way this works is if they want everyone to know they can survive a nuclear war, so are not bluffing. Fine, except they keep it all secret and weaken their bargaining hand – unless they expected UNIT to send a spy along. So their entire blackmail scheme to force the world leaders to accede to their demand relies on there being a reporter with links to UNIT, who chose that particular day to pop in and ask questions about Professor Kettlewell's very publicly abandoned project. And yet, Jellicoe seems annoyed that just such a prerequisite journo shows up.

Fortunately (for the baddies), the SRS are evenly matched against a typically clueless UNIT. Somehow, they manage to lose a nine-foot robot in an open field in broad daylight. The Brigadier orders them not to shoot the giant robot before his command – and then, after a rocket-propelled grenade fails to make even the slightest impression, they all start shooting rifles at it. He can see what the Disintegrator Gun can do but doesn't hesitate to send in the unconvincing tank to get melted. And the troopers *keep* shooting bullets at the giant robot, even though that didn't work when it was its original size.

Where's Sarah's car at the end? The last time we see it, she's arrived at Kettlewell's to rescue the Doctor. Then she and Kettlewell are at UNIT, then they go to the church hall, where she's captured. So it might still be there until "The Seeds of Doom". Except, for some reason, when she gets picked up by a bloody great robot and left on a roof until Benton retrieves her and, instead of her getting treated with all the wounded UNIT troops in a surely extensive clean-up operation, she's next seen in the Doctor's lab. So if Harry gave her a once-over (a scene so rich in comic potential, it's odd that they didn't use it) and said she was fit to drive, she didn't go home for a bath to ease her bruises. No, she called in on UNIT HQ so she could stand around and mope while Lt Sullivan completed autopsies on the casualties (which raises further problems for the tag-scene of "Terror of the Zygons"). Then he saunters in, grinning: "breezy" doesn't cover it.

Quite why Harry gets chosen as the UNIT member to take a ride in the TARDIS is puzzling, especially as Benton passes one of the key tests for companion status earlier that episode: like Susan, Jo and Sarah before him, and Tegan afterwards, he points at something in Part Four and shouts "look!" a clear five seconds before anything happens. (This is a bigger point than it seems, since Harry's *raison d'etre* was to be the muscle if they'd cast an older Doctor, and Benton was already a popular character.) And, as almost everyone noticed, someone that age then wouldn't have been called "Harry" – it was a naff 50s name.

Critique Target Books got it exactly right. Not only did they rush-release the novelisation (as *Doctor Who and the Giant Robot*), simultaneously in hardback and paperback only two months on from broadcast, not only did they (specifically, Terrance Dicks) skip the opening scene and dive straight in with the break-in – yes, just like the teaser-scene of a colour episode of *The Avengers* – but they got *Radio Times* artist Peter Brookes to debut his Frank Bellamy-esque art on both the front and back covers. The asymmetric panels exactly capture the aesthetic at work here. We joked about this story resembling *Kaiju* and, in the last episode, they overtly allude to *Godzilla* walking into, then through, power-lines. That's the mouthfeel of this story, rather than the *King Kong* or Karloff Frankenstein's Monster to which Dicks referred when discussing the story's origins. It's set in a slightly-ahead-of-now world of super-science and international cooperation, ending with a robot growing to 50 feet, just like Jet-Jaguar. In this regard, the toy tank is entirely in keeping.

More by luck than judgement, the next three books also had Brookes covers; they were the similarly lurid "Terror of the Autons", "The Green Death" and – slightly less bold but still soaked in tartrazine – "Planet of the Spiders". When they reverted to Chris Achilleos's reworkings of publicity photos, the editors decided that the word "K-Klakk!" on the cover of *Doctor Who and the Dinosaur Invasion* was inappropriate. They were sort of right: for all that the story's environmentalists-gone-rogue theme resembles the Scientific Reform Society's thermonuclear tantrum, the Pertwee take was too po-faced and pious to make best use of the child-friendly premise.

No such problem here. This is a four-episode

sugar-rush, rather than brown rice with a side-order of unconvincing CSO behemoths. It's pinball rather than macramé. There's a bit of substance underneath the confectionery, something for the actors and any viewers over ten to get their teeth into, but the whole affair sweeps away the residual preachiness of Season Eleven. Paradoxically, this being the first solo script by the script editor of that entire period, this means that UNIT are a credible force for the first time since "The Mind of Evil" (8.2) and you can see Nicholas Courtney and, to a lesser extent, John Levine grabbing the opportunity. Ian Marter's there to ask the stupid questions so they, like most of the audience, take all of this in their stride. As written, the Brigadier and Benton are good at their jobs.

Sarah is almost the character Dicks and Letts originally imagined, more an adjunct to UNIT than a conventional "assistant" for the Doctor. More to the point, and this becomes obvious when Dicks self-plagiarises in Part Three, her scenes early on are placed in the right narrative slots for this story's resemblance to *the Avengers* to be functional as well as thematic. She's not exactly Emma Peel, who posed as a journalist to meet suspects, then fearlessly returned at night in a catsuit to beat up henchmen and see the freaky menace just before an advert break. Sarah is far from fearless here, resorting to Jo Grant-style big-eyed girlyness to get past guards and sweet-talk Benton and the Brig. It's still about as independent as we get to see her, holding a gun on Miss Winters but never karate-chopping anyone. Just as well: Cathy, Emma, Tara or (later) Purdey would have been too arch to empathise with the Robot and make the last episode happen.

The irony is that, almost two years ahead of *The New Avengers*, they've got the same problem and solution to a non-existent one. Harry Sullivan is the Mike Gambit of this operation: introduced because they thought the lead would be too frail for punch-ups, then left dangling as a comic foil for that lead and his female companion. In *Doctor Who* spin-off terms, he's like Jeremy Fitzoliver from Letts's *The Paradise of Death* or Brendan from "K9 and Company": a slightly posh, slightly dorkish newcomer to whom the premise can be explained. Letts seemed to like that sort of character. Luckily, Marter and Robert Holmes thought better of this.

Pay attention to the lighting: in narrative terms, there's no reason for so many strong red or blue spotlights in laboratories and at such odd angles, but the story's look is as far from the *télé-verité* gestures of "The Ambassadors of Death" as that is from, say, "The Romans" (2.4). No one thing is implausible in any given scene (until we get to the toy tank and the ginormous robot treading on soldiers), but cumulatively they amount to a trippy comic-strip version of 1974 England. It even looked that way in black and white, for the 1974 viewers without colour sets.

In its own way, it's as heightened a version of known life as a Fred Astaire/Ginger Rogers musical. The odd thing about it, looked at in those terms, is that Christopher Barry refrained from cutting between scenes with extravagant wipes and dissolves as per *Top of the Pops* or *Doc Savage, Man of Bronze* (or, a few years later, *Star Wars*). There's none of that Dutch Angle TiltyCam stuff from "The Mutants" (9.4) here. He comes close to a *Columbo* / *Thomas Crown Affair* split-screen with the montage under the Brigadier's voice-over, but his main hint of flamboyance is the Robot's-eye-view attacks, culminating in the first cliffhanger (almost the same as his first cliffhanger in 1.2, "The Daleks", so it's hardly innovative). It's not that he's against such practices (see his last cliffhanger in 17.3, "The Creature from the Pit" or even the end of Episode Four of 8.5, "The Daemons"), he just thought it was just too big a nudge in the direction of Musical Comedy.

That's the key to this story: everyone knows exactly how far to go too far and when to stop. Yes, even Dudley Simpson; the music people remember is the ersatz Hanna-Barbera stuff for the newly-regenerated Doctor's eccentricities, but most of this story's score resembles "Frontier in Space" (10.3) rather than "The Chase" (2.8) and, anecdotally, kids playing at being the robot did the four-note theme rather than the radiophonic burbles or Michael Kilgarriff's stentorian, declamatory tones. (And, from what we've gleaned from older siblings and their memories of early 1975, kids wanted to be the Robot rather than the Doctor or Sarah.)

Letts and Dicks were demob-happy and relished the absence of what the Pertwee Doctor had imposed on them: a big stunt per episode, a fight scene or two, a car-chase perhaps, a "moment of charm" and a big moral speech at the end. Yet nobody seemed entirely sure what to do with this mesmerically watchable new lead. Dicks admitted to latching on to Tom Baker's resemblance to Harpo Marx, then writing for Sherlock Holmes – but the Doctor is, for a lot of the story, comic relief

12.1 Robot

in his own show. This, as we've hinted, allows the other regular characters to step forward and look like professional adults for the first time in ages; this is the perfect time to launch a UNIT spin-off series. But they're up against a less-than-daunting adversary, a bunch of stroppy nerds with a conscience-afflicted robot and no Plan B. Within this comic-strip world, that's enough – especially with Benton explaining his improbable promotion and pre-emptively excusing the small band of sideys-sporting cricketers sent to save the world – but this is only really satisfactory by comparison with what we've been enduring since Season Nine.

Looked at in isolation, with an idea of what's coming around the corner, we could see this story as frivolous, infantile, gaudy or whatever... but it's fun, and *Doctor Who* has to be *fun* or else why bother? They're trying new things, fresh approaches to the traditional mad scientist vs soldiers set-up. Looked at out of context, it's a story with larger-than-life performances all round, something that Baker will encourage once he asserts himself, but which isn't typical of mid-70s stories. Edward Burnham (Kettlewell), Alec Linstead (Jellicoe) and Patricia Maynard (Winters) all dial it up to 11, but keep some idea of the characters' moral compasses on view for older audiences.

The outgoing producer's playing for time, vamping until his contract ends, but not actively sabotaging his successor. The practical effect of this story as a handover between production teams is that it allowed any number of possible routes: a quiet Doctor letting Harry do the fisticuffs and Sarah deliver morals; a disengaged Doctor advising UNIT but no longer entirely indebted to it or Earth; a wild Doctor with friends to restrain him; a child-like Doctor who only helps humans because nobody else bothers and he'll never get a moment's peace if he doesn't... We know which options Baker, Holmes and Philip Hinchcliffe eventually selected, but this story's about opening doors, not closing them.

The Facts

Written by Terrance Dicks. Directed by Christopher Barry. Viewing figures: 10.8 million, 10.7 million, 10.1 million, 9.0 million. AIs: 53%, 53%, undocumented, 51%.

Working Titles "The Giant Robot".

Alternate Versions Dicks rushed out *Doctor Who and the Giant Robot* with a comic-like cover by Peter Brooks; then a simplified version formed part of the brief *Junior Doctor Who* series for early readers. This had some odd (and, for smuttily-minded teenagers, hilarious) illustrations. In both, the Doctor's oddness is given more verbal expression.

Cliffhangers The Robot we've already seen kill three people advances on Sarah; the Robot is about to tread on the unconscious Doctor's head; the Robot has zapped a tank and a sniper with the Disintegrator Gun and now faces the camera, warning "Go now or I will destroy you all".

What Was In the Charts? "Down Down", Status Quo; "Gonna Make You a Star", David Essex; "Make Me Smile (Come Up and See Me)", Steve Harley & Cockney Rebel; "Footsee", Wigan's Chosen Few.

The Lore

Let's start at October 1973. *Moonbase 3* is going out on Sunday nights, watched by dozens of viewers, but a clear signal that the producer for this and *Doctor Who*, Barry Letts, was looking for a way out. His script editor on both series was Terrance Dicks, who had already installed his Padawan, Robert Holmes, formally handing over that month just as the Tenth Anniversary and production of Season Eleven were getting going. Holmes had been freelancing while shadowing Dicks and serving a pretty hands-on apprenticeship on 11.3, "Death to the Daleks", writing episodes of *Dixon of Dock Green* and ATV's *General Hospital*. During discussions on the latter, he ran into a young, ambitious script editor called Philip Hinchcliffe who – from Holmes's (possibly embroidered) account – scrutinised him carefully.

Hinchcliffe had an agent: an unusual move for a script editor then, but he wasn't a usual TV hack. He'd graduated in 1967 but opted to work in television drama (not really considered a proper job) and found a berth at Lew Grade's company in Birmingham. There he worked with several experienced writers, some of whom we'll hear about in this book, and had risen to get associate producer credits. Although hoping to leave, Letts discussed some series-development ideas with Holmes as they blocked out what would be shown in 1975. Holmes wasn't wild about all of them but put out feelers to some of his old colleagues.

- By Christmas, as the Three Day Week and a general sense of deflation and defeat hit the country, the incumbent Doctor – Jon Pertwee – was making his usual complaints about his salary, threatening to leave if he wasn't given a huge rise. This time, with the oil crisis stoking up inflation, little remained in the budget. The Powers that Be called his bluff. Pertwee, disenchanted with the series since Roger Delgado's death, Katy Manning's departure and Letts's announcement that he was going, was less heartbroken about going than he might have been 18 months earlier. He had mentioned to Elisabeth Sladen on their first location shoot that he was thinking of moving on. Letts knew that Pertwee was anxious about not being offered other work if he stayed put. From all accounts, spending a miserable week in December in a muddy quarry doing yet another Dalek story was the last straw. With the national shutdown causing topical rewrites of "The Monster of Peladon" (Dicks's responsibility), a new grand finale for the 1974 season and Pertwee's Doctor needed to be fashioned. "Planet of the Spiders" was commissioned in early December, and in by mid-January.

They also needed a new Doctor. Pertwee had been famous enough before this career-change from comedy to action, but now he was more associated with the series than even the Daleks. His off-screen persona fed into the content of the stories far more than either of his predecessors' or even Peter Cushing's had (the 60s Dalek films were, by now, appearing regularly on television). Letts made the basic assumption that anyone replacing such a lead would wind up playing edited highlights of their real selves. This led him to think of performers over 50, which prompted the need for what's called a "Juvenile Lead", i.e., an actor under 30 to do romance, heroism, punch-ups and so on.

He had one he'd prepared earlier: Ian Marter had been asked to play Captain Yates in 1970 ("Terror of the Autons") but couldn't commit to a whole series as he had something else coming up. Shortly thereafter, on the next story Letts directed (10.2, "Carnival of Monsters"), he gave Marter a role that required flirting and fisticuffs. Marter then spent some time unable to work due to illness, so Letts's next phone call was his first large role for a while. (Marter was mainly a stage actor, although you can see him in small film roles here and there – a policeman in *Dr Phibes Rises Again* may well be the forthcoming part that stopped him playing Mike Yates.) There's some evidence that the character was to be called "Sweetman" – it's the name of the UNIT medical officer in the "Planet of the Spiders" novelisation and one of the scripts – but the new male companion was eventually called "Harry Sullivan", and that's who the Brigadier asks for in that story.

- Holmes, meanwhile, sounded out Dicks on the subject of how a robot might respond to human ambition and chicanery. Dicks was interested enough to "invent" a tradition of outgoing script editors getting first bite (a good rule-of-thumb, except in the revolving-door phase of Patrick Troughton's last year) but had a simpler idea of making a sympathetic behemoth like King Kong.

- While all this was going on, they had a new boss. Ronnie Marsh, then Head of Serials, was moved to Series (a different department back then) and utility director Bill Slater moved upstairs to become his successor, effective February 1974. During the handover, Slater took an interest in the refreshingly proactive way Hinchcliffe was seeking new opportunities. Hinchcliffe came to the BBC for a different series that was affected by a strike in an early stage (*The Girls of Slender Means*, eventually made by Martin Lisemore), but Slater saw him as a good fit for *Doctor Who*. It wasn't announced immediately, nor was it the subject of a modern-style Non-Disclosure clause, but Hinchcliffe was advised to keep it quiet – hence his caginess when he met Holmes at ATV. From around January, Hinchcliffe followed Letts around, getting to know the BBC way of doing things.

- Letts had sought character-actors able to do the basics of *Doctor Who*, especially the rapid way in which it was made, with location filming before the read-through or rehearsals (called "Strike" filming within the BBC, an increasingly ironic label). This was one of the sticking-points when an early front-runner, Michael Bentine, asked for input into the scripts. Bentine was a founder-member of the Goons (see **Did Sergeant Pepper Know the Doctor?** under 5.1, "The Tomb of the Cybermen"), but left because he was too anarchic even for Spike Milligan. He had written the first televised parody of *Doctor Who* and was often on science programmes, advocating a thorough investigation of the paranormal just in case. Peruvian by birth, he had a quizzical slant on

12.1 Robot

British institutions (and the BBC hierarchy[7]). Had the format of the series in 1973-4 allowed it, he could either have taken *Doctor Who* into the stratosphere or wrecked it beyond repair.

A safer choice might have been comedy actor and recording artiste Bernard Cribbins. Like Pertwee, he'd been in early *Carry On* films and did voice-overs for road safety promotions. He was, in 1973, starring in a sketch-show on Thames Television and voicing all the characters in *The Wombles*, but had occasionally shown his range in straight roles – Hitchcock cast him as a nasty pub landlord in *Frenzy*. As most of you will know, he was Tom in the 1966 film *Daleks Invasion Earth 2150AD* and Wilf in *Doctor Who* between 2007 and 2009. As a former paratrooper, he assured Letts he was up to any physical action or fight-scenes. (Letts said that he envisioned the new Doctor as less violent than Pertwee's – Cribbins was disconcerted to watch "Genesis of the Daleks".)

As with the last regeneration, Ron Moody was approached (he would later admit regret at not taking the part in 1969, but seems to have been too busy in 1974). Another *Carry On* veteran, Jim Dale, was sounded out. American readers might know him as the voice of the *Harry Potter* talking books (as opposed to Stephen Fry, as God intended, for the UK edition), but he had already been a pop-star, Oscar-winning songwriter (he did the lyrics for *Georgy Girl*) and would branch from comic acting to the lead in the musical *Barnum* shortly thereafter. (We can only speculate what kind of Doctor he could have been – possibly very like David Tennant.)

Fulton McKay, then becoming a household name in prison sitcom *Porridge*, was another option (he was Dr Quinn in 7.2, "Doctor Who and the Silurians", Letts's first story as producer). Whether the pubic would have accepted a short Scottish actor as a Time Lord is another problem for another day (see Volume 6), but McKay would later be the Lighthouse Keeper in the UK version of *Fraggle Rock* and the enigmatic hermit in *Local Hero* (there's precisely one scene where he and Peter Capaldi are in the same shot).

A taller, louder Scot, Graham Crowden, was also asked: he'd been in odd films such as *The Final Programme, The Rise and Rise of Michael Rimmer, The Ruling Class* and *O Lucky Man!* We'll encounter his *Doctor Who* performance later on ("The Horns of Nimon") and he later starred in *A Very Peculiar Practice* (with Peter Davison) and *Waiting For God*. He was keen so long as the part was only for one year or so. The thing all of these actors had in common was that Letts stipulated one thing about the next Doctor: the viewers' eyes should gravitate to him no matter what else is happening on screen. Luckily, Bill Slater knew the very man...

In 1972, Slater had directed *The Millionairess*, a George Bernard Shaw play adapted for television as a vehicle for Maggie Smith. One of the main roles is a doctor in a fez and Slater, with Producer Cedric Messina, cast relative newcomer Tom Baker, who had worked with Slater's wife. Baker had been in a few films, such as *The Canterbury Tales* (making his screen debut full-frontal), *Vault of Horror* (one of those early 70s portmanteau films Amicus put out by the kilo) and the misleadingly-named *Frankenstein – the True Story*. His most noted role to date was as Rasputin in the 1971 *Nicholas and Alexandra*. (This led to some saucy by-play with Princess Anne at the premiere – he'd been recommended for the part by his de facto boss, Sir Laurence Olivier, when Baker was on the strength at the National Theatre.)

The year after the BBC play had seen Baker play Macbeth for the NT and perform as the villain in a Ray Harryhausen film, a grotesque in *Freakmaker* then... nothing. Even in a cheap one-room flat, Baker needed to eat – and so, like many actors before him, got casual work and wrote to anyone who'd employed him in the past. When he wrote to Slater, on 3rd February, 1974, he had just turned 40 and was working on a building site on Ebury Street, just behind Victoria Coach Station, even though *The Golden Voyage of Sinbad* was then still in theatres. Baker's letter arrived just as Slater was due to meet Letts and discuss possible Doctors, so Letts and Dicks spent an afternoon at the pictures watching Baker play Koura (a part allegedly written for Christopher Lee). Later that night (6th), Baker was invited to meet Letts, Shaun Sutton (head of Drama) and Slater at the BBC bar. Another meeting followed and Baker was offered one of the biggest jobs in British television out of the blue. And then he was told to keep it a secret, so next morning he went to work as usual.

- On 8th February, Pertwee's resignation was announced, making headlines on 9th (as "Invasion of the Dinosaurs" Part Five was about to air). A week later, Baker was introduced to the world as the new Doctor with a photocall where he met Elisabeth Sladen (just back from filming the railway station scenes for "Planet of the Spiders", but taking time out from rehearsing "The Monster of Peladon") and Pat Gorman (dressed as a Cyberman). The London *Evening Standard* went to press first, and Baker's bewildered colleagues on the building site posed for pictures with the new Doctor (the last time he'd be seen with a cigarette in public). This was 15th February, the day Pertwee was riding a hovercraft on the River Severn (and Terry Walsh drove it over Stuart Fell). Baker was signed for 26 episodes (indicating that the new season-length was planned well in advance) and for rather less than Pertwee had been getting, even before his demand for a pay-rise.

• It's sometimes claimed that Baker overplayed his rootless bohemian persona but, at this stage in his career, it was rather forced upon him. Constant changes of digs (theatrical temporary accommodation) meant that he was rarely anywhere long enough to use it as an address – messages to him were left at Waterloo railway station, just around the corner from the National Theatre. He kept a toothbrush on his person in case he found himself sleeping somewhere unexpected (see "The Seeds of Doom"). His odd-jobbing between roles was a legacy of a number of detours on the way to his childhood dream of acting: a stint of National Service, some time in the Merchant Navy and four years in a monastery in the Channel Islands being the headlines.

Some of the odd behaviour we're going to be discussing is because Baker is, by his own admission, rather anxious and occasionally insecure (even at the photo-call he had a friend, playwright Ted Whitehead, along for moral support). He would later claim that once the euphoria of getting a full-time job wore off, he realised he had no idea how to play the part. He met Letts, Dicks, Holmes and Hinchcliffe at a restaurant in Shepherd's Bush to discuss precisely that. Dicks picked up on the Harpo Marx-like look of constant surprise and factored this into his scripts for "Robot". Holmes was interested in the Doctor as an alien; Hinchcliffe liked the notion of Olympian detachment but was more inclined to have the Doctor as a rebel. He thought that the public, especially those under 30, were bored with conventional heroes and wanted someone less obviously supporting the establishment. Holmes then worked up a writers' guide citing George Bernard Shaw, Bernard Quatermass and Sherlock Holmes as a rough guideline (almost exactly how Pertwee's Doctor was supposed to have been in press coverage from 1969). Baker took some notice of these competing descriptions and the idea of an "Art Student" Doctor emerged.

• Christopher Barry was assigned to direct this story. He'd been busy since "The Mutants", so even if the rumoured antipathy between him and Pertwee was real, he wouldn't have been available before this. He and Holmes discussed the story with Dicks at length before Dicks started writing in earnest. Even as "Planet of the Spiders" was in production – still trying to mix Colour Separation overlay and film – Letts and Barry had decided to use an Outside Broadcast rig to record the location work on video and smooth over the effects matting. Barry had handled a new Doctor before (4.3, "The Power of the Daleks") and was up to speed on the series's technical aspects. One idea he and Dicks proposed was that the new Doctor's eccentricity could be toned down, if it didn't work, and explained as convalescing from a regeneration (a line to this effect was added to K'Anpo's dialogue at the end of the previous story).

• Barry was reunited with James Acheson, by now a regular costume designer for the series, and once again brought in outside contractor Alastair Bowtell to make the Robot. The only practical way to make something wearable was to use thin strips of aluminium and mount them on a light frame, making big shoulders to conceal the actor's head by arranging some strips in an arch on each side and mounting a hollow head-shaped hat on the performer's head (with lights inside the eyes).

According to legend, Bowtell attended one meeting in a hand-knitted scarf in several bright colours. Acheson and Letts were devising a look for the new Doctor based loosely on Toulouse-Lautrec's poster for Aristide Briant and someone – maybe Baker – proposed rounding it off with a scarf in the same idiom. According to Baker, the BBC costume department contacted a little old lady called Begonia Pope (or Magnolia in some versions) who was supplied with a number of balls of chiffon (not wool, despite appearances, as that stretches and is harder to clean), but didn't stop knitting until she'd used it all up. This doesn't entirely ring true, as anything in a BBC costume would be made in batches of up to six – for continuity purposes if some scenes need it damaged or dirty, but out-of-sequence scenes need it pristine. And various stuntmen need to

12.1 Robot

have one handy. Nonetheless, Baker's Doctor acquired a 14-foot scarf on top of his other loose, shabby clothes.

- Before this was brought before the cameras, Baker spent a few hours having his hair tamed for his one brief scene at the end of "Planet of the Spiders". This was among the first things recorded for that story, on 2nd April. In keeping with the general pattern since 1964, the first story of a broadcast year was made as the last story of a production year, so "Robot" was made concurrently with this story. Dicks finalised his scripts, removing a scene of the 50-foot robot chasing Sarah's car for cost reasons at Holmes's request (just as well – Sladen hadn't passed her test yet), as Barry assembled a cast. His first thought for Jellicoe was an actor he knew socially and had employed once, Colin Baker (see Volumes 5 and 6). With him unavailable, Barry fell back on Alec Linstead, whom he had used in "The Daemons" as UNIT techie Osgood.

Also returning were Michael Kilgarriff ("The Tomb of the Cybermen"; 22.1, "Attack of the Cybermen"), a radio actor who was six foot five and prepared to wear the robot costume; Edward Burnham ("The Invasion") who was rather shorter and could make his hair stick out as Kettlewell; regular monster/guard walk-on Pat Gorman, now given dialogue as the guard Sarah inveigles into letting her back in to Think Tank; and reliable standbys Terry Walsh and John Scott Martin. New to the series was Patricia Maynard (Winters), then married to Dennis Waterman, who had just done three months in *General Hospital* and was just about to spend a stretch in prison drama *Within These Walls*.

- Dicks included sly references to the previous regeneration story ("Spearhead from Space") as well as a dig at Jon Pertwee's hang-up about how his nose appeared on screen. He also gave Sarah a large amount of story to carry without the Doctor or the Brigadier. This was partly to keep faith with his original idea that Sarah had a life of her own, rather than existing just to tell the Doctor how brilliant he was – but, in this case, it also allowed the location work to be shot while studio sessions for "Planet of the Spiders" continued.

- The Brigadier's scenes for that story were all in the first block so Nicholas Courtney could accompany the new Doctor while the old one went to Metebelis III. Production was well under way when Dicks was formally commissioned in mid-May, with the excuse that a new Doctor's debut needed someone familiar with the programme's history covering what was effectively an in-house commission. Once finished, Dicks proceeded to write *Doctor Who and the Seven Keys to Doomsday* (see "The Brain of Morbius" and **Can They Do It Live?** under A6, "The Music of the Spheres").

- Baker had recorded few interviews ahead of his first full day on the job, while Pertwee had been to Blackpool to open the *Doctor Who* Exhibition. Pertwee's last day in the role would be 1st May. Before that, though, the team had taken the OB rig to Wood Norton, the BBC's Technical Training base in Oxfordshire. Last time they made *Doctor Who* there, it had been "Spearhead from Space", the first story made entirely on film. Apart from being available, it had all the facilities they needed and every location they required. The new Doctor was still suffering from imposter syndrome, but he and Courtney rapidly became drinking buddies and would remain so until Courtney's death.

On 28th April, Baker recorded his first scenes, starting with his opening the door to the Think Tank lab in Part Two, driving Bessie and visiting Kettlewell's stable mews. There wasn't any rehearsal for the location work, just a set-up and a couple of takes per scene like a film. You'll notice that it had started to rain: the raindrops don't show on VT, but the damp brickwork and puddles are visible. Sladen recalled that Barry had to tell her which story she was doing that day. Maynard was slightly intimidated by working with such a tight-knit team and nervously fluffed her first line, introducing herself as "Hilda Baker". (If you were watching sitcoms in 70s Britain, this is a lot funnier – Hylda Baker was short, stocky and right northern.)

- Kilgarriff was wired for sound within the costume and recorded live. (Without lip-synch, however, they could redub a fluffed take with an earlier good one when reshooting for other reasons, as happened here.) In Oxfordshire, while the old Doctor was namedropping Houdini (his last scene), the new Doctor and Harry slew the Robot with coloured water in a plastic bucket. Among remounts of some of the driving sequences, and footage shot to be fed into the monitor inside the Bunker later, the team used a periscope to start the Robot's POV shots. (Most of these were later processed by showing them reversed on a monitor reflected in a segmented mirror at which a camera was pointed.)

- The Robot's limitations began to rear their ugly heads. As the Robot leaves the meeting, Linstead feigned hiding from the bullets behind the Robot, but was in fact guiding Kilgariff down the stairs and into the horse-box. At the Mews location, the problem was the large flat feet (plywood shelving covered with thin aluminium). Also, it was unseasonably warm (especially for 1974) and the costume had a lot of foam rubber inside to stop Kilgariff lacerating himself on the metal strips. He was also finding it hard to breathe. The team took two days off, during which Part One of "Planet of the Spiders" went out after the FA Cup Final.

- Come Sunday, another building on the grounds was disguised as an electronics factory. (As luck would have it, a helicopter flew over, so they cheekily shot it and added a line to the Brigadier's explanation of the security precautions, recorded later.) Although Wood Norton had a handy nuclear bunker, they were told at almost the last minute that they couldn't shoot there as it was covered by the Official Secrets Act (the BBC would relocate there in the event of a war), so Ian Rawnsley, the designer on this one story, had to construct a convincing entrance on the site. He redressed the vault entrance.

Monday 6th was also the day on which Barry, despite his better judgement, had allowed Letts to talk him out of hiring a real tank for five seconds of screen-time and tried his best to make the Palitoy model look good. Before that, the Bunker's door was rigged with a thin polystyrene sheet, behind which a technician had a hot blade; Baker matched the screwdriver's motions to this.

- The BBC's Further Education department approached Letts to make a behind-the-scenes series about TV drama. Although it never reached the screen, this meant that some of the next few weeks had a film-crew along. The read-through, at St Nicholas's Church in Chiswick, was one such (although the sound has been lost, some footage is on the DVD – it may not be the real read-through but a reconstruction, nobody seems sure). Rehearsals finally began on the 13th. Many scenes were enlarged or rethought during this, with Barry encouraging Baker to – as we'd say now – own the role.

- However, a scene-shifters' strike disrupted the first studio day (this was 21st May in TC3), although all of day two was recorded. There was a step-ladder left in the set and, with everyone keen not to add fuel to the fire, they found ways to work around it – Jellicoe climbs it to remove the Robot's head, for example, but look at the odd angles in the earlier scenes in that set. (The strike meant that the sets weren't struck, so the following day's edition of *Blue Peter* took place in the UNIT lab, the vault with the hole in the floor and Chambers's safe. John Noakes makes a typically undignified entrance.) This was the day the disco-mirror was used for scenes shot in Robo-vision, Chambers was killed and the Doctor changed his costume three times in a minute. For camera rehearsals, Kilgariff had a literal tinfoil suit to wear – lighter but reflective enough for the technicians to gauge the lighting. (Baker, learning that Kilgariff was a Music Hall buff, proposed that the Robot might sing "Nelly Dean" at some point.)

- The missing day was remounted during the second batch of rehearsals, on 1st and 2nd June. Whether the dispute was a factor in abandoning the documentary series isn't clear, but the idea would return ("The Talons of Weng-Chiang"). Benton's entrance was slightly amended, as John Levene thought Baker was looking at him when saying "large, placid and stupid". Rehearsals continued until 5th, the next two days being spent on recording everything else. (Well, almost everything: on seeing the CSO work when editing began on 24th Barry, Letts and Hinchcliffe opted to remount as soon as possible. That turned out to be the day before recording started on "The Ark in Space", in October).

- Letts was keen to move on and start work on his bio-drama about Marie Curie but he'd be involved in *Doctor Who* in one capacity or another for another 18 months. He still replied to letters in the *Radio Times*. Baker, his luck now running better, had a film role to go to after this baptism of fire, *The Author of Beltraffio*, and a touring play, *The Trials of Oscar Wilde* (guess which part he had in that). Holmes was chin-deep in salvage attempts on the next three stories. Hinchcliffe was trying to master his new job. Everyone else was off until October's location shoot for "The Sontaran Experiment". Dudley Simpson recorded the music in three sessions, one in mid-October, one in mid-December (as the new material was being shot) and one two days before Christmas, incorporating the reshot Part Four, less than a week before Part One went out. Barry went off to become senior director on a new prestige Sunday night drama, *Poldark*.

12.1: Robot

• On December 27th, the day before Part One, a marathon one-episode version of "Planet of the Spiders" was shown to build up to the new Doctor's debut (at 105 minutes, it's the longest single episode ever shown, despite Russell T. Davies's best efforts). The *Radio Times* accompanied the new story with a photo-montage displaying how "Old Time Lords never die, they just sort of transmute". It was on at 5.35pm, after *Lamb Chop* and before *The Generation Game*.

Pertwee was a tough act to follow for many viewers and critics, but the Robot was a huge hit. Despite only making one appearance, the character was featured in jigsaws, posters and the first batch of Weetabix cards only a few months later. Dicks had a novelisation of the story out within three months, but the Robot was still in merchandising four or five years later (including the Denys Fisher model from 1977, sharing the spotlight with the Doctor, Leela and a Dalek.) The public warmed to Baker's radically different approach over the next few weeks, although ratings and AI's were more or less constant.

12.2: "The Ark in Space"

(Serial 4C, Four Episodes, 25th January – 15th February 1975.)

Which One is This? While the last of humanity sleeps, giant insects nest in their cellar, planning to ingest their bodies and minds. Sort of the missing link between *Alien* and *The Very Hungry Caterpillar*.

Firsts and Lasts It's the first and only time they change the title sequence to salmon-pink (Part One was an experiment they never repeated), and the first visible fruits of incoming Producer Philip Hinchcliffe and set designer for much of this phase, Roger Murray-Leach. (They both first worked on the next story broadcast, made a month earlier. This is the start of making the stories in a radically different order from transmission.) It's the first time for a while they've made a story in more-or-less story order, almost an episode per day, and the first time it's entirely been made in Television Centre (the last story with this little pre-filming was 1.8, "The Sensorites", mostly made at Lime Grove). Dudley Simpson's ten-note motif for the new Doctor appears in its first permutation.

The handy word "Transmat" is introduced here. Here we get the start of this Doctor's habit of starting a new sentence before he's properly finished the do you have any idea how often he's going to do this in the next 150 episodes?

This is the last time we see the sonic screwdriver actually undo any screws.

Four Things to Notice About "The Ark in Space"...

• These days, the most obvious thing about this story is how often Steven Moffat and his chums plundered the iconography, the vocabulary or whole scenes. Just Part One's opening minutes give us: a mysterious opening scene we see again with explanatory context later; a silent door opening, then a young woman unable to get anyone to notice this walking through and being trapped (both recycled in X4.8, "Silence in the Library"); Bennett Oscillators and a yo-yo to check local gravity (X8.7, "Kill the Moon"); a long-silent spaceship with a fault, but no people around and malefactors treating the human crew as meat to be harvested (X2.4, "The Girl in the Fireplace"); the Helmic Regulator (X3.13a, "Time Crash")... You can count all the rest for yourselves.

• And yet, for older fans, the most obvious thing in 1975 was how old-fashioned it seemed. The cast are carefully rationed so that some characters have a one-episode lifespan; others only make their debuts a few moments after the cliffhanger reprise. As with 1.2, "The Daleks"; 2.7, "The Space Museum"; and 5.7, "The Wheel in Space" (almost), the whole first episode is just the leads wandering around a deserted machine-like place (with one unspeaking alien menace lurking). The Doctor is prevented from leaving – when it looks like the most sensible option, one of his friends is caught in this world's machinations. It's even recorded almost, but not quite, an episode at a time, something they've not done much since Barry Letts arrived (that wasn't exactly the plan, though).

Visually, we're on familiar *Doctor Who* territory. The nearest analogy to what's happening on the Ark is 9.4, "The Mutants": another white Formica space-station with teleports and a story in which people are turning into insects, but the one person who appeared to suffer then was transformed into a psychedelic avenging angel. Watched back-to-back with the sound down, there's not much to choose between these stories but, even allowing for the vastly different music in both, they are

Why Couldn't They Just Spend More Money?

We're going to mention budgetary restrictions a lot in this volume, but we also spent a lot of Volume 3 on how much more money BBC Drama had to spend in the early 70s. The advent of colour television greatly increased revenue from licence fees and, unlike today, this went straight into programming and resources rather than admin. We're in the era of the Duopoly: there were two television networks, one of which had a monopoly on the advertising revenue (ITV, split into 14 regional stations all fighting among themselves) and the other, the BBC (two channels but one authority), had the legal requirement to do everything unprofitable and of fringe interest but got a legally-imposed licence fee that people needed to pay to watch anything.

The BBC had a laundry-list of things to provide that weren't commercial, and – as everybody in the country was paying for everything the BBC made – there was an obligation to cater for absolutely everyone. (See **Did the BBC Actually Like Doctor Who?** under 3.9, "The Savages" and **Cultural Primer: Top of the Pops** under "The Robots of Death".) The government decided how much the BBC got per head of the population and used this as a threat to keep them from being too critical (not that this worked until Thatcher). BBC2 began colour broadcasts in 1967, BBC1 and most ITV in November 1969 and the cost of the 625-line sets came down from around Christmas 1971. By 1975, a bit of a social stigma existed about not having one, but this is also when the rapid expansion of colour licences (which cost more than a "standard" monochrome one) tailed off.

The early 70s was also when Doctor Who merchandising came close to topping the fabled Dalekmania of the mid-60s. In those days, the press had been surprised at staid "Auntie Beeb" having a division devoted to commercial exploitation, this being out of keeping with the tenets Lord Reith had laid down in the 1920s for the Corporation. To reiterate from **Why was There So Much Merchandising?** under 11.4, "The Monster of Peladon" and **Did They Think We'd Buy Any Old Crap?** under 22.5, "Timelash", however much money was being made from selling things with a Doctor Who connection, it wasn't just going towards making Doctor Who. All BBC Drama revenue went into a collective pot for BBC Drama. When Nestlé put out a chocolate bar with a serial on the wrappers, Doctor Who Fights Masterplan Q, it had to be sanctioned by the Production Office (and it bears all the hallmarks of a Terrance Dicks/Barry Letts story), but the slice of the income Nestlé gave to the BBC was split between Doctor Who, Owen MD, Z Cars and everything else.

On the plus side, this meant that a different overseas hit such as The Forsyte Saga could bail out Doctor Who if global sales tapered off or the star refused to get involved in promotional work (as per the late 60s, with Patrick Troughton rather less keen on publicity than Jon Pertwee would be, and a slight slump in the international interest in the series between that first big push and the Lionheart US deal). Most of the money and resources within the Drama department were allocated to prestige projects with a chance of co-production money (although it may not look that way on screen: Churchill's People and the "BBC Shakespeare" project were notoriously cheap-looking but resulted from lucrative deals). Despite a long track-record of selling to other territories, Doctor Who was considered mainly a throwaway for the domestic audience.

We've also seen in earlier volumes that the budget allocation for any drama was set at the start of the financial year (the beginning of April, usually) based on how the previous year's allowance had worked out. The optimum situation was to go fractionally over-budget without obvious cost-cutting – so the bean-counters would think that you were doing as well as could be expected – but no more. Going slightly over resulted in a slight increase, a bit more than the previous year's overspend, while going way over the top just looked profligate. Coping well, within the limits, looked as if you could deal with a small deduction to fund a struggling series. Innes Lloyd is reported to have chosen to make "The Underwater Menace" (4.5) in December / January 1966-7 as a means to soak up the remainder of that year's money – it went over-budget by about three grand, somehow.

The Corporation took other factors into consideration, notably the baseline inflation rate and the work-hours each department would have to log per hour of screen time. We'll come back to inflation in a tic, because the peculiar thing about Doctor Who was that every few weeks they'd have to start almost from scratch. It was a series of serials, something a lot less common in the 1970s than it had been in 1962. With everyone other than the producer, the secretary and the script-editor being a BBC staffer assigned to a specific serial, rather than for the entire year's run (or hired

continued on page 37...

worlds apart. The transgression / breakthrough here is conceptual and, therefore, verbal. Whenever humans were mutated by green Swarfega in the Pertwee era, they usually just growled or, in 10.5, "The Green Death", muttered stoically and were tremendously Welsh about it. Here, Noah, the commander of the Ark, is tormented, conflicted and fully conscious but in a way that small children can comprehend – he's turning into an insect, piece by piece, and not enjoying it, but he still wants to eat the sleeping humans.

- What raises Robert Holmes above his epigones is that he has thought out the entire world in detail, but only reveals it through the things he can rely on the cast and crew doing within the budget and time available, notably dialogue and design. The antiseptic future in which Vira and Noah were raised is sketched in though lines such as 'There was not much "joke" in the last days' and the complete lack of gloating as she and Rogin dispassionately fry a few hundred Wirrn with the rocket exhaust. Mini catchphrases such as 'Hear me' and 'Beautiful' limn a class divide. Even the parasitic body-horror is primarily conveyed through dialogue, and only later confirmed by rather theatrical make-up. Dune's fate is conveyed to us not in pictures, but in the Doctor's grim pun.

- However much the premise of the story resembles *Alien*, made five years later (see **Where Does This Come From?**), the really interesting cross-franchise comparison is with *Star Trek*. We've got teleports that sound like a Tangerine Dream album-track, rather than the twangy whoosh of the *Enterprise*'s Transporters; personnel whose duties are denoted by the coloured parts of their uniforms (but those uniforms are more like Admiral Ackbar's from *Return of the Jedi*) and the Doctor gets necessary info by doing a mind-meld with a dead alien. The Doctor even uses "beam down" to describe transmatting to Earth. There's no comment about Noah having a stun-gun that can be set to kill but, in all these cases, there's a concerted and systematic effort to differentiate this from anything we've encountered in either earlier *Doctor Who* or *Star Trek*. Yet, characteristically of *Doctor Who* playing with the *Trek* toybox, we get a blue-collar character grumbling about how nothing works right ("The Mutants" again, or "Planet of Evil" later in this book). Just to conclusively prove that it's not *Trek* (and the split infinitive just then was deliberate), Rogin's collar isn't actually blue, it's red – but he survives until almost the end of the story.

The Continuity

The Doctor finally admits to preferring humans to other species. Nonetheless, he is keen to help the Wirrn survive without ending human history. He can use his own cerebral cortex to interface with the retained engrams of the dead Wirrn Queen's last minutes and project them onto a screen, although the process leaves him severely disorientated. He admires both the Queen's resolute willpower and humanity's being 'indomitable'. When shot with a stun-gun, he is out cold, as if dead, until he is slapped in the face – whereupon he finishes the sentence he was halfway through when zapped.

The regimented and blinkered society of the Ark's chosen frozen irritates him as much for their lack of humour as their callous lack of concern for other survivors. He admits to being a 'Romantic' and considers Noah more human as a Wirrn than when he was a biped. His irritation with Harry, along with his fake annoyance at Sarah's finite amount of grit, may be a perverse motivational technique.

Here he claims that his title is 'purely honorary', but in the same breath states that 'Harry here is only qualified to work on sailors' [so he may be bluffing to avoid entanglement in a situation that the humans ought to deal with].

- *Background*. The Doctor seems very familiar with this model of space station and can identify most of the features, finding his way to the solar stacks unaided. He speaks of it as one of 'these early space vessels'. He's not encountered the Wirrn before [see **Things That Don't Make Sense**].

His scarf was, apparently, knitted for him by Madame de Nostradamus. [We're not sure who he means, but it might be the mother of the noted astrologer and monk.] He claims to hate stunguns. [We've never seen him hit by one before; he's paralysed but conscious in 10.4, "Planet of the Daleks", so we have only the tranquiliser darts from 5.6, "Fury from the Deep" as a precedent.]

- *Ethics*. The Wirrn ingesting human knowledge is, to him, 'immoral' rather than disgusting or evil. He opts to not revive any more humans so that, if he fails against the Wirrn, they will not suffer. He tries to offer the Wirrn an alternative,

The Ark in Space 12.2
Why Couldn't They Just Spend More Money?

...continued from page 35

for that specific serial, like the guest cast and composer), there's little chance of saving money by having a few standing sets for the whole year. (We say "standing sets" as if they could physically do that at Television Centre, but the point we're making is that something like Nationwide or Z Cars had a regular set that was mounted and struck but still counted as the work of the one designer, with other bits and pieces added for a specific edition.) Whenever the TARDIS went to a new planet or historical setting, it was almost like beginning a new series. A director was attached to any new story – not always willingly – and he or she would be allowed to request specific staffers but would often just get whoever was available. Each aspect of design was designated a portion of the overall budget. An overspend on sets (the biggest normal cost) would have to be met by savings in costumes (second-biggest) or extras.

By 1974, we're at a stage when 25-minute episodes had an average budget of £20,000. This is an average, because the first episode of any story is the most costly even though we're no longer dealing with productions made week-by-week like in the black and white days. It also elides the difference, in fiscal terms, between a four-part story and a six-parter (we'll come back to this). This figure also fudges the filming allowance and how much of any one episode was pre-filmed on location or at Ealing. With anything up to 150 people involved in making the story, including big-name actors on higher fees and a star paid a relatively huge salary (regardless of what Pertwee thought), this didn't go far.

One way the BBC's managerial structure helped was with a new system of resource-allocation: the production unit managers. These were *de facto* line-producers (the BBC's byzantine nomenclature forbade anyone else being credited as "Producer", however much work the PUM was doing[8]) but worked on up to five different series at once. This meant that they often knew of ways to recycle sets or share resources. This had been done informally in the past (*Doomwatch* went halves on a space-capsule prominent in 7.3, "The Ambassadors of Death", for example).

While these people were the ones setting the annual budget for continuing series, they were also finding deft ways to rob Peter to pay Paul. Sets needed a lot of people to construct, install, remove and store them, as well as wiring up electronics within them. They also use material, but that's generally a reliable cost. The process of getting sets and costumes ready for the allocated studio days (decided well in advance because of the sheer number of things being made at Television Centre and the small number of studios there – eight, eventually, of varying sizes) meant that some outside contractors were used. Not many, as they cost more. The cost of making things from scratch was calculated in work-hours, in order to remain calculable as time ran out and more staff were assigned. If you're wondering why the people making "The Brain of Morbius" thought that Vincent Price or Peter Cushing would be cheaper than a robot, this is why: no actor, even if paid top rate even for two weeks' rehearsals and flown into London, would be around as long as the three or four regular staff-members required to make a giant prop robot as part of the set.

The thing is, £20,000 in 1974 wasn't as much as it had been in 1973. Most of the developed world had pretty bad inflation after the OPEC decision to up the price of crude oil to anyone who'd sided with Israel after the October 1973 invasion by Egypt. Britain, however, had this on top of a number of other own-goals. The most immediately troublesome was that, in a well-intentioned and popular move, the Heath government had introduced a prices and incomes policy just a few weeks before this war. The rising cost of living had been a vote-loser, so he pegged public sector pay-rises to the inflation-rate (then at 9.2%). The coal-miners were, he admitted, a special case, but he was also under pressure to look as if he was "getting tough" with the unions.

At exactly this point, the cost of crude oil trebled, and the market-power of the coal industry increased (we tell other bits of this story in **Who's Running the Country?** under 10.5, "The Green Death"). So Heath was ousted and the incoming Labour government found themselves coping with his problems, but without his mandate to boss people about. (All Labour politicians get their funding from one or other of the unions, which ought to have given them a more sympathetic hearing. It didn't always work out that way.) A miserable wet summer caused a lousy wheat harvest, so domestically-produced food was more expensive just as imports got costlier and the usual Plan B of families in summer, Cyprus Potatoes, fell victim to the Turkish invasion of the

continued on page 39...

12.2 The Ark in Space

and most of his actions are aimed at barricading the human sleepers rather than killing the Wirrn [even if he could, and the larvae might have been vulnerable]. After Noah shoots him, he insists that Noah is in danger and must be helped.

• *Inventory:*

– *Sonic Screwdriver.* Here it makes repairs on electrical cables that are carrying a current as the Doctor attaches them. Oh, and he undoes some screws, the bolts attaching the desk to the floor.

– *Jelly Babies.* He offers them around, but only he has one. Later, he gives Vira the whole bag as he leaves.

– *Scarf.* The Doctor describes it as 'faithful' [as though there were many unseen adventures in a previous incarnation where he found it handy]. It's organic, as it got zapped like Harry's various leather items. It recovers almost instantly.

– *Other.* There's a well-used cricket-ball for Harry to lob and a telescopic pointer, like a car radio aerial, used to pick up a membrane. He has a new yo-yo, a dark blue transparent plastic Duncan. There seems to be a scalpel in his pocket [which might be risky].

The TARDIS In a change to the usual materialisation sequence, the police box is visibly present from the start of the shot, and both the light on top and the one behind the glass lintel panel saying 'police box' pulse. There is a Helmic Regulator that should not be twisted too vigorously. Near the door are an oil-lamp [see 11.3, "Death to the Daleks", although it is a different one] and, apparently, some brandy. [Weirdly, the time elapsed outside doesn't match the time spent within as, just as with the Doctor's changes of clothes last story, Harry and Sarah manage to select and get into new outfits in moments and the Doctor still wonders what's keeping them.]

The Supporting Cast

• *Sarah* puts her rings in the container before freezing [presumably they're still there]. Her resurrection confuses and scares her more than anything we've seen so far. She's sympathetic to Harry's perplexity but resents being called 'old girl' or 'Nurse Smith'. Later, she volunteers for a crawl through the infrastructure and is annoyed with herself when she falls short of expectations, allowing the Doctor to trick her with feigned anger. When the Doctor heads down to Earth, she opts to accompany him as a matter of course, assuming bad weather and dressing for it with a woolly hat, Sarah Lund jumper [less busy than the one in 11.4, "The Monster of Peladon"] and trawlerman's waxed-cotton waterproofs. Plus, really impractical red boots.

• *Harry.* Forget the stuff about him being Bulldog Drummond, or Mike Gambit, Harry Sullivan is manifestly the prototype for Arthur Dent[9]. For most of this story, he's wandering around a space-ark in his socks asking obvious questions and being on occasion quite inane. He is here formally identified as 'Surgeon-Lieutenant' and his medical knowledge is adequate to the task of reviving Lycett and Rogin. Harry finds the 'medicine by numbers' appealing, but is perplexed that a woman is High Minister. He once got his nose caught in a sliding door at Pompey Barracks. His concession to whatever environmental disaster has befallen Earth in bleventy-thousand years is a pair of wellies and a duffel-coat [which, as it turns out, suffices]. He claims that the Brigadier ordered him to stay with the Doctor. [If so, we missed that; he was only told to accompany the Doctor to Kettlewell's lab.]

The Non-Humans

• *The Wirrn.* [The word works as a noun and a plural noun, like "fish", "sheep" or "Zarbi".] Broadly speaking, giant insects. They hatch from eggs, develop larval forms, pupate and become like five-foot wasp-ants [the closest comparison is a large, wingless dragonfly with an earwig's pincers]. The eggs are laid inside stunned or, here, frozen living organisms and can absorb knowledge from the host upon hatching in a fresh food-supply. This knowledge is transmissible to future generations and, more alarmingly, to anyone who touches the slime from the larval stage. [We're told it's a 'multi-nucleate' organism, meaning it hasn't specialised into specific organs or cellular functions as it will as an adult, and can be considered more like a virus or carcinogen than an orthodox embryo.] When a grub infects Noah, not only does he have the knowledge and some personality-traces of Dune, the host for the eggs, but he begins to physically and mentally become a Wirrn. The hatchling imagoes accept Noah as their swarm-leader remarkably quickly; when his transformation is complete, he can communicate to them as well as to humans.

The original infestation began with a Queen who, like all adult Wirrn, could float in space for

Why Couldn't They Just Spend More Money?

...continued from page 37

island. As bread and sugar were briefly rationed (by retailers, not the government as petrol had been at the start of the year), people started stockpiling, pushing prices up further. 1974's annual inflation rate was, thus, 16.7% and wages rose commensurately, causing further price-rises on goods and services.

That lot was on top of two other inflationary pressures, each of which was a one-off and, all other things being equal, ought not to have been a problem. One was that, in February 1971, the long-awaited move to decimal currency came into effect. We'd had the old system since the Romans, more or less, hence the abbreviations being from Latin (Librum for pounds, hence the elaborate L that's the pound sign, £, Denarius for the pennies, so LSD was a familiar acronym before Albert Hofmann or Timothy Leary). £1.00 was 240d, or twenty shillings, then it became 100p (there was a fad for citing costs in "new pence" and people still use "pea" as a unit, although nobody ever said "dee" for old pennies). Some dodgy businesses simply changed the "d" for a "p", a 240% mark-up for sweets or matches. More insidiously, the newly introduced 1/2p was the smallest unit, so price rises were in steps of £1/200th rather than £1/480th (until 1964 there'd been a 1/4d coin, the farthing, the cost of a teacake, so costs could be increased by £1/960th). This whole event had been set up in 1968, but it still caught people on the hop.

The other long-planned change was the introduction, on April Fool's Day 1973, of VAT. Value Added Tax was supposedly fairer than Income Tax (not that they ditched that), since it was applied to whatever was bought, not to wages. In practice, it meant that kids buying sweets were now taxpayers too. It affected low-income families disproportionately, despite decisions not to apply it to essentials. Again, everyone was told well in advance, but the practical difficulties weren't as well-thought-out as one might hope (see 15.4, "The Sun Makers" for how resuming a freelance career in 1977 tripped up Robert Holmes). Our point here isn't just to poke fun at Ted Heath but to point out that the two inflation-rates we just cited came after 1972's 7.1% and 1971's 9.4% – and that worse was around the corner.

Currency speculators were accelerating the debasement of sterling. As it fell against other currencies, the two traditional index of a nation's economic health – the Currency Account Deficit – went into overdrive. Other metrics were fine: the National Debt fell below 50% of GDP for the first time since the Truman administration stiffed us with the bill for World War II and continued to fall. That's mainly because GDP rose as people realised that going on strike wasn't going to make money magically appear. Inflation rose to 24.2% and markets continued to sell sterling. To put flesh on those bones, it meant that Philip Hinchcliffe's £20,000 per episode from 1974 was effectively worth £7,500 by the time he left *Doctor Who* in 1977.

1975's 24% was as bad as it got, because of a curious set of circumstances: Chancellor of the Exchequer Denis Healey was inaccurately advised by the Treasury that the Public Sector Borrowing Requirement for the forthcoming year was a fearsome £10.5 billion, so in early 1976 he applied to the International Monetary Fund for a loan of £3.9bn. This was humiliating, especially as Britain had set up the IMF in the first place (well, not entirely alone, but that's not how the tabloids reported it). They agreed to £2.3bn subject to cuts in public spending – several ministers resigned. But the Treasury had been wrong, and it was only £8.5bn (and – right on cue – North Sea Oil started coming in), so the bail-out loan was repaid in under a year and Britain looked like a safer bet for speculators. The pound rose from its then-record low against the dollar and so imports got cheaper. 1976's inflation rate was a mere 16.9%, 1977's a fraction lower and 1978's way down to 8.4%.

Over the years, *Doctor Who* habitually did four-part stories unless there was a very good reason. You will remember that the once-fearsome 5.4% rise in prices in 1969 had led to a string of cost-cutting seven-part stories set in present-day England. That was widely seen as a mistake and Ronnie Marsh, then Head of Serials, set six weeks as the maximum. Moreover, Letts (inheriting this set-up from Derrick Sherwin) found that the number of extras in uniform ramped up the budget even without effects or stunts. Paradoxically, therefore, moving away from UNIT was *also* a cost-cutting move, albeit with Hinchcliffe wanting to get away from Yeti-in-the-Loo stories for aesthetic reasons. The main rationale for six-parters was financial and, again, the odd way BBC Drama bosses had arranged for the monies to be allotted was behind this.

continued on page 41...

decades, using an enzyme-based recycling system to breathe. The pupae have to remain near a power-source for heat and, apparently, energy of other kinds – although high-voltage electricity is one of their few weaknesses. This Queen seems to possess a detailed knowledge of engineering even before selecting Dune, one of the power-technicians, as a host, as she knows how to disable the Ark's defence and chronometric systems. The larvae crawl like caterpillars, the adults seem to slide on their anterior pincers, with the six legs growing from the thorax used more for manipulating objects. Their eyes are not compound, as one might expect of wasps, but smooth glassy ovals. [One appears to have a severe scratch in the surface, so the nictitating membrane must be thick; perhaps understandable in a species adapted for deep space.] The larvae and their slime are, of course, bright green, but the adult form is dark blue.

Planet Notes We're told little of *Earth* itself, save that it has a transmat reception-point and had a stratified and rigid society until devastated by solar flares something like 20,000 years before the story starts. When the Ark was repurposed, apparently 'millions' still remained on Earth and even the President of the planet, apparently a middle-aged woman, was not picked. And there was a Space Technicians' Union.

• *The Ark*. [Identified by Vira as 'Space Station Nerva'; see "Revenge of the Cybermen".] At first, it seems like the conventional space-wheel design, a toroidal structure around a spindle made of four long cylinders on a central pylon. [It does not, however, spin fast enough to generate centrifugal force for gravity and this is obviously not how the vessel was designed. The central corridor, although curved, has up and down perpendicular to the rim; moreover, the humans weigh the same at all parts of the Ark and the Wirrn seem to have equal difficulty moving anywhere within it. The stars seen through portholes in the corridor do not move relative to the interior. If a machine generates the gravity, it's on a different power-source from the life-support and transmats, or else would have failed when the Queen severed the main cables.]

When the TARDIS first arrives, the temperature within the Ark is at approximately 20 Celsius and the air, although scant, is still breathable despite the 10,000-plus year gap [indicating that the surfaces are non-reactive with oxygen, so non-corrosive]. Nevertheless, the control station is powered-down and the automatic defence and resuscitation systems paused until the Doctor's basic repairs. The defence system is programmed to destroy anything organic. The cryogenic system, still active, processes Sarah like anyone else: she's transmatted to a decontamination booth and sent to sleep after a recorded speech, then placed in a berth with a fresh uniform and frozen. [An intriguing design detail has a sign on the wall of the dormitory cautioning *Do not enter Cryogenic Area when light is on or floor is in motion*, which perhaps resolves the puzzle of how people on pallets beginning with E or F got out again when the time came.]

Everyone selected for suspension is given an identical uniform, a white tunic and matching slightly flared slacks and boots, with colour-coded epaulettes and piping. We see four colours, red, blue, yellow and green. Vira is a medic; another stencilled sign that restricts access to the cryo-chambers to 'Yellow Badge Personnel' indicates that her yellow detailing is linked to her tasks. [It's harder to be more specific with the others: Noah, the chief, is red, as is the more hands-on engineer Rogin; Dune, chief technician, is blue, but so's Sarah. Libri and Lycett are green and seem also to be technicians.] There is, we're told, an extensive Animal / Botanic repository and a data-file of all human culture and knowledge. The index is on small cards, something like a hundred each drawer, in clusters of 36 drawers, 16 such clusters [so perhaps 57,600 subject-headings, each on a microfiche].

Although the cryogenic chambers are kept pressurised and oxygenated, for obvious reasons, so are the corridors, gantries, solar stacks and even service-tunnels. The lights run on 'photon energy'. [This is, apparently, different from solar energy or electricity, even though photons are light particles. Or waves.] The Cargo Hold is on the opposite side of the station from the control rooms.

The ship is programmed to revive the crew after 5,000 years and in a pre-selected order which cannot be altered even by the Prime Unit, Noah (AKA Lazar) or Vira, his chosen consort and Chief Medtech. Those who revive early can draw power from a 'bionosphere'. [Although we see the Ark in orbit around Earth, logically it must have been sent far away to avoid the same solar flares. We are

Why Couldn't They Just Spend More Money?

...continued from page 39

The arrangement, refined by Christopher D'Oyly-John in the early 70s, was that costumes, sets, location filming (including hotels and transport) and the first studio session were front-loaded onto the first episode because a serial cannot have a number of episodes less than two, but it could be any number after that. The second episode would also be counted as part of the first studio session because accounting hadn't caught up with the more cinematic method of recording in order of sets rather than episode-by-episode. Part Three would have a second studio session, so would have a share of the "facilities" costs (sets, different costumes perhaps, make-up and so on), but Part Four would be as cheap as Part Two. Part Five would cost as much as Part Three, so rather less than Part One, and Part Six would be the same cost as Two and Four.

This, of course, meant that the average cost-per-episode for a six-parter was rather less than for a four-parter even if they went to town on a longer story (see "The Talons of Weng-Chiang" for Hinchcliffe doing exactly that). From this, you can see why putting the six-part story at the end of the production year was almost a no-brainer. As inflation bit, this was almost the only way to afford a whole year's-worth of episodes. (In the interests of strict accuracy, we ought to point out that the ratings boost and cachet the series developed did allow Hinchcliffe greater leverage with budgets than other producers, even before his go-for-broke final story.)

We've been talking as though an annual overall rate of inflation is the whole story, but of course, different things rise in price more steeply or not as much – some not at all. Penny chews remained at 1p for a decade. Wagon Wheels (a big chocolate marshmallow biscuit) stayed at the same price, but slowly shrank – not immediately, because retooling the machines manufacturing them was expensive – but stayed roughly the same price; an early example of what's now called "shrinkflation". Between 1971 and 1973, house-prices caused the biggest disruption (they doubled in those three years, on average). After 1973, the obvious culprit was petroleum and anything made from it (plastics, heating oil, diesel, ordinary petrol…); thus transport and energy became more expensive.

Labour costs were another matter. The attempted prices and incomes policies were shifting the emphasis from simple cash sums to benefits, hours and demarcation. This last was the bugbear of anyone trying to negotiate with competing unions represented in the same firm or industry. The television technicians were either with ACTT (represented more on the ITV companies) and ABS (who predominated within the BBC). ABS management accepted that it could glean a finite amount of money from the Corporation, but ACTT's Alan Sapper saw that his trained professionals had skills that deserved a cut of the lavish profits ITV companies were making.

Here's the problem: if someone who routinely pulled ten-hour working days after years of training was paid only slightly more than the school-leaver holding his ladder (it was usually a him, something else Sapper questioned), then what was the point of getting trained? Therefore, senior staff at the BBC got perks in lieu of pay-rises and fiercely protected the bits of the television craft they did. Thus, if someone not in the same pay-scale or union moved a ladder, the scene-shifters' union got annoyed (see "Robot"). This became almost routine and the BBC got used to such a conflict happening a few weeks before Christmas, just in time for the biggest audiences of the year. The negotiations usually included a special bonus almost,, but not quite, indistinguishable from a higher-than-inflation raise. For reasons we've just explained, *Doctor Who* was usually doing a six-part story around then. We'll pick this up under 15.6, "The Invasion of Time".

These considerations, inflation, union anxieties and the BBC's budgeting policies, form the background for a lot of the apparently odd decisions and improvised moves we'll see in this book. One or two require more detailed discussion, starting with a choice to move away from doing the location work on film. That's next story's essay.

---

led to believe that the Wirrn Queen encountered the Ark far out in the depths of space thousands of years earlier (see **Things That Don't Make Sense**).]

History

• *Dating*. [Blimey! The most important thing to say is that it's impossible to match this to any similar catastrophe in *Doctor Who* chronology. This isn't the same calamity that befell Earth in 23.1, "The Mysterious Planet" (also written by

12.2 The Ark in Space

Robert Holmes); let alone 3.6, "The Ark"; 21.3, "Frontios"; X1.2, "The End of the World"; or X5.2, "The Beast Below" (which *sounds* similar, perhaps a misunderstanding of the dating clues involved in this story and "Revenge of the Cybermen").

[Attempting to resolve comments made here and in "The Sontaran Experiment" and "Revenge of the Cybermen" are only feasible if this all happens *long* after the main run of stories set in Earth's future (including the Earth Empire stories of the Pertwee era and 3.4, "The Daleks' Master Plan", set in 4000), but before the Russell T. Davies phase of rolling dice to determine how many noughts are at the end of the date. The evidence within this story indicates the Ark was refitted from the late thirtieth-century vintage Nerva Beacon after it had been in use for some time (the Doctor is vague on how long, but it's at least a couple of thousand years on, from his comments in Part One and again in "Revenge") and then the 5,000 year cryogenic suspension was extended by an unspecified amount; probably *another* 5,000 years but potentially much longer. So, at a conservative estimate, "The Ark in Space" is happening c.15,000 A.D. It may be a lot later. Scripted notes and a press-release to the *Radio Times* claim 'the 300th Century' (see also "Planet of Evil"). We have no reason to doubt this.

[The late High Minister's speech suggests that the planet's population is 'millions', but also that the selected elite have slept 'longer than recorded history'. As she expects them to have been frozen for five millennia, that puts the date some time before the station was built – in fact, sometime around now – so perhaps 'recorded history' begins for her culture at around the time of the reconstruction after whatever-it-was. At a pinch, this could be resolved with reference to comments in "The Talons of Weng-Chiang" and "The Sun Makers" (by the same author) that suggest a collapse of science and society a thousand or so years after the 'Great Break Out' c.5000AD (15.2, "The Invisible Enemy"; 16.5, "The Power of Kroll") and a collective ignorance of Earth except as a vague myth when humanity is moved to Pluto. It could even be possible to resolve this with X1.7, "The Long Game" et seq.]

When solar flares devastated life on Earth, the human race placed a small percentage of itself in cryogenic storage, along with all human knowledge and a cross-section of flora and fauna, aboard a space vessel termed the Ark. It was converted from an ancient beacon first constructed in the thirtieth century but refitted with a complex bionosphere. All volunteers were chosen and genetically cross-matched and screened to produce a viable post-apocalyptic society. Each member was, it seems, pair-bonded and 'compat-analysed' [or maybe 'compact'].

Everyone accepts that the Earth is the only known planet with humans on it, although rumours exist of colonies elsewhere, a 'Colony 9' and some pioneers at Andromeda. [Whichever 'Andromeda' they mean, it was still in the future when Vira was put to sleep. Colony 9 might be the same as the Andromeda one, of course. The most sensible reason for this might be that something happened to Earth a while before the solar flare crisis and society collapsed, leaving them to rebuild and reach a technology about at the level of the thirtieth century, possibly as a result of recovering abandoned space beacons such as Nerva (see "The Power of Kroll" for more on this).

Once revival is complete, the Ark is to have a Council that can amend any plans made before the evacuation of Earth.

The Analysis

Where Does This Come From? In one of the classic examples of the "catchiness" of an idea outweighing the question of whether it stood up to examination, everyone in the early 70s grabbed hold of J. McConnell's 1962 paper *Memory Transfer Through Cannibalism in Planarians* as proof that memory was mainly chemical and to be found in ribonucleotides. "Everyone", in this case, doesn't just mean neuropsychologists but headline-writers in tabloids, junior-school teachers and TV hacks trying to fill four episodes at short notice. It allowed the old standby of pills-to-replace-lessons to look sciencey again.

McConnell's experiment was easy to understand: you teach worms how to get through a maze, grind them up into a pulp, feed baby worms on the puree and *voila*, the babies get the maze right first time. This was to biology and psychology what black holes were to physics. Even now, you'll hear it trotted out every so often, even though it no longer fits the rest of what appears to be happening in the brain and nobody – even McConnell – ever got worms to do it again.

Why this matters to *Doctor Who* is that it takes the routine 1960s fears of brainwashing / hypnosis / telepathy / possession and makes them corporeal. The thing being stolen and corrupted isn't "selfhood" in an abstract manner, or the soul, but physical memory, brain-chemistry. Dune has been hygienically consumed off-camera, but his knowledge and personality have been dubbed onto Noah and all the new Wirrn. Yet the process involved eating someone alive while he slept. We're at a hinge-point between the existential terror of umpteen spy films or invasion-of-Earth stories where someone is "turned" and the newly fashionable body-horror of *The Exorcist*, *The Texas Chain-Saw Massacre* and, just a couple of months after this story aired, *Jaws*. The drama in a former friend or relative under new management is that this person might, perhaps, relent if reminded of former allegiances and feelings – handy, in a series that needs a reset button at the end of each episode (as most were in the 1960s) and allowing speeches about What Really Matters.

A shark isn't amenable to a persuasive argument. All human arrogance and achievement is irrelevant to something that just eats people. Here's where the rejected John Lucarotti version of the story makes the point more clearly because the antagonists there, the Delc, have taken Cartesian Dualism up a notch and separated the heads giving orders from the bodies doing the grunt-work. Robert Holmes picked up on something similar when he had the revived Vira react to stimuli unthinkingly when revived, her description and actions fitting then-current ideas of the living dead. Once again, all Enlightenment pretentions towards the head running things is abandoned when people have their souls taken, are hypnotised or get mistaken for a snack. Just as ordinary hospitals treat people as being mere adjuncts to their symptoms or injuries, so this clinical space with white-coated bureaucrats is more interested in people's DNA than their personalities (if any).

We're talking about that old 70s standby, alienation. Generally, when you are talking about alienation and turning into an insect, it's hard to keep Franz Kafka out of the conversation, but Holmes, under time pressure, simply got the BBC reference library to look up disgusting insect behaviour to replace the Delc. They came up with the Euminadae: a genus of potter-wasps that leave stunned-but-living insects in the nest for the hatchlings to eat. ("Eumedes" is a Greek hero, and possibly a Frigate, and easier to pronounce, so the error may have arisen in rehearsals.) Once a known, generally reviled insect was brought into the immaculate white environment, the rest fell into place – especially with a larva leaving a slime-trail.

Spaceships had been looking like hospitals on film since *2001: A Space Odyssey*, a film in which people kept in cryogenic suspension were killed rather dispassionately, and even NASA had taken the characteristically 1960s step of making the Saturn V rockets white rather than silver. The antiseptic white Formica future got so routine as to make *Star Wars* seem like a breakthrough for including mud and grime. Even the soil in *Silent Running* (another story about preserving Earth's biome, albeit one of the stupidest ever committed to celluloid) seemed clinical. Ideas about space-arks had been around since the 1930s – it made a good magazine cover to show animals going into a rocket two by two – and reached the screen with *When Worlds Collide* (based on one of those 30s stories, but without the elephants or giraffes). If Neil Young is singing about it in 1972 (*After the Gold Rush*), we can assume it's an idea in wide circulation.

The big twist, insects laying eggs in people, is familiar to SF buffs from *The Voyage of the Space Beagle* by A. E. Van Vogt. This is an odd work even by Van Vogt's loopy standards, a "mosaic novel" or "fix-up" of four short stories from the late 1930s bashed into novel form with some new material in 1950. Some credit it as the main inspiration for *Star Trek*, a picaresque set of adventures of an international crew on an exploratory ship, their crises interspersed with back-biting and lectures on "Nexialism"[10]. It was originally four stories or, as anyone who's read it a while back remembers it, two stories twice over with slight differences. Numbers one and three, "Black Destroyer" (July 1939) and "Discord in Scarlet" (December 1939, both first appearing in *Astounding Science Fiction*, of course) have carnivorous aliens loose in a giant starship, one found in the ruins of an ancient civilisation, the other drifting in space since the previous universe ended. Ixtl, the latter, is the one that lays eggs inside astronauts, but Coeurl, the cat-like predator in the first, is tricked into going into a lifeboat and commits suicide.

As with the second and fourth stories in the book (disembodied consciousnesses possessing crewmembers), it's common for anyone who read it a while back to recall a portmanteau version of the two predatory-saboteur-in-a-giant-spaceship tales. Robert Holmes, an SF aficionado of long

12.2 The Ark in Space

standing, can hardly have avoided it (the 1973 Panther reprint had a memorable Chris Foss cover, but it had been in print in the UK since 1954). He admitted in interviews that "The Ark in Space" was made of elements he'd read decades back, but wasn't ever pressed on specific names, even if he'd been able to list them. That Holmes's original ending, rejected by Rodney Bennett, was for Noah to simply lead the Wirrn back out into space (as per one of the other two *Space Beagle* stories) is itself suggestive.

If you were reading SF at all, you couldn't really avoid Van Vogt back then – so claiming, as some have done, that *Alien* is a simple steal from "The Ark in Space" is like suggesting that *Star Wars* is a rip-off of "The Mutants" (9.4) because both have got galactic empires and bad guys in black. (That said, add in the scenes in "The Seeds of Doom" where the Krynoid pods first ensnare Winlett then Keeler, and the Doctor suggests amputating Winlett's arm might slow the alien parasite's growth, plus the space-burials in "Planet of Evil", and you have a bit more of a case.) Van Vogt and Dan O'Bannon, main author of the film's screenplay, settled out of court for an undisclosed sum.

O'Bannon's cited starting-point was a WWII bomber afflicted by a Gremlin (note Harry's comment in Part One), a piece of Royal Navy slang that Roald Dahl claimed to have devised. Had Dahl been looking at BBC1 in February 1975, he might have noted a more-than-passing similarity between the Wirrn and the Vermicious Knids who infested a space hotel in *Charlie and the Great Glass Elevator* (1972)[11] – there's clearly something about sterile white space vessels that makes writers want to loose squidgy monsters into them.

Besides, if you're looking for a story of an astronaut infected by a space-being, looking at his withered, distorted hand in horror, battling with the new consciousness in his head, killing his friends and transforming completely but retaining enough of his old personality to collude with scientists trying to kill what he's become to save his wife (as one does), you've got *The Quatermass Experiment* to play with. As most of the original was never recorded, the majority of people unable to watch in summer 1953 know the feature film adaptation, the first time Hammer films dabbled in horror. We'll see another retread of this in just over a year ("The Seeds of Doom"). Key scenes to watch for are the afflicted astronaut answering questions about where his two co-pilots went by demonstrating that he had their memories, the hand-gawping incident and the final assault as what he became engulfs Westminster Abbey (see the essay with 15.3, "Image of the Fendahl".)

However, *The Fly* is as good a "source" for conceptual elements as any, although in this case the matter-transmitter (the word "transmat" was apparently coined by UK writer Lan Wright but picked up by Robert Silverberg) and the man-turning-into-insect are kept apart. (In earlier drafts of the script, this may not have been the case: consider the line about Sarah in suspended animation, "her body's become a battlefield".) The film's noticeably less icky than other monster-movies of the era but, even before David Cronenberg's stagey 80s yukfest, the visceral potential of the idea was latent. With the representative of the decision-makers who got to choose who was to survive himself corrupted, the rhetoric of "purity" and "survival at all costs" is made suspect (and that's not the last time this year, as most of you know). This allows the script to give the Doctor a big speech about the human race being "indomitable", show the cost of it and make the Doctor's subsequent actions more nuanced than a simplistic version of this story – one starring Jon Pertwee or William Shatner – might have been.

Developments in cryonics, the rather optimistic idea of preserving the dead in liquid nitrogen on the off-chance that a cure could be found in the future, made headlines every so often. As we saw in "Invasion of the Dinosaurs" (11.2), it was an off-the-shelf standby by the mid-1970s that astronauts would need to be chilled to survive interstellar voyages. When Terrance Dicks pitched the idea of this story to John Lucarotti, he did so in the aftermath of script-editing *Moonbase 3*, a series purportedly based on genuine plans from NASA and elsewhere for lunar colonisation and suchlike. The final episode had the crew of the European station come to believe that Earth had been destroyed and making tapes to explain who the human race were as they waited for their air to run out (there hadn't been an atomic war, it was just fog). Whereas "The Ark" (3.6) had people miniaturised and kept in filing cabinets by the thousand, it was more visually arresting and – for home audiences – plausible that a self-selecting elite would have their entire bodies frozen. Anyone who recalls what fridges were like in the

60s will see how Lucarotti immediately went from refrigeration to fungal infection. A modern version would have the entire crew, possibly the whole Earth's population, recorded as data – connecting with the transmat motif – but this would have been incomprehensible to viewers in 1975, while transmitting people like television was conceptually simpler. Besides, keeping entire people on ice in a spaceship means selecting who gets to live and that, after the whole Cold War obsession with bunkers we've seen in the last story and will again, is familiar.

Something else 70s movie-goers would have seen is Edward G. Robinson's death-scene in *Soylent Green*, in which he is euthanized to a light-classical soundtrack. This is lurking behind Sarah's session in a booth full of gas and talk of leaving personal objects and going on a great adventure into the unknown. The music in this case is an intriguing choice, the Largo from Handel's *Concerto Grosso* which, according to some, was the first music ever broadcast. In the golden age of hi-fi, the general public weren't scared of "serious" music and it was often used as a source of counter-intuitive TV themes. In film, it was a handy way of saying "this may look like science fiction, but it's an Important Statement About Mankind", a trend culminating in *Zardoz* and *Rollerball*.

The name "Nerva" is interesting: apart from being one of the less likeable Roman emperors, it was an acronym for a space-vehicle design from the late 1950s using atomic bombs as a propulsion mechanism. The idea was that a big parabolic shield protected the payload as each bomb-blast accelerated the ship. The name "Vira" hints at "virus", but note that Noah is really "Lazar", both Lazarus and a leper. Holmes seems to have liked the name "Rogin" as he re-uses it as a tracer in "The Deadly Assassin". The owner of the name makes a crack about the Space Technicians' Union having demarcation disputes – he'll stop the Doctor from doing his job even if it kills him (which it does). The rest of this book will amply demonstrate how topical that gag was.

English Lessons

• *Boffin* (n. sl.): Readers of Dickens will recall the "Golden Dustman" in *Our Mutual Friend*, Noddy Boffin, who retains his decency despite coming into money. This is thought to be why the people who made miraculous devices from odds and ends in World War II came to be called "boffins". It was a real surname but was a handy way to discuss technical matters when security was paramount. The term caught on post-war, when the development of Radar, penicillin and atomic power was a source of pride, but the caricature became less admirable as time went on. Unlike other terms ("nerd", "geek", "spod", "wonk"…), the word "boffin" contains the idea of practical repair and engineering prowess as well as detailed knowledge and theoretical expertise.

• *Pompey Barracks* (n. sl.): As anyone who listened to Jon Pertwee in *The Navy Lark* will know, Pompey is a colloquial name for Portsmouth, the main training and administrative centre of the Royal Navy. It's also used for Portsmouth United FC. You will have seen nearby naval emplacements in 9.3, "The Sea Devils".

• *Bird* (n.sl.): in 1970s Britain, especially London, it's routine slang for young women, as per "dolly-bird", but Harry isn't the sort of person who'd do that and it's not quite right for Vira. "Tough old bird", Harry's exact term, is more what you'd use to describe an over-cooked chicken or – perhaps more appropriately for him – grouse, pheasant or other game-bird (the Doctor described himself as such in "Planet of the Spiders").

• *Snitch-up* (n. sl.): a made-up piece of slang from a known source. "Snitch" usually means "nose", but as a verb, it can mean to inform the police and therefore is a noun for someone who does this (see "nark" and "grass" in "Invasion of the Dinosaurs"). Lycett uses it as if "snitch" has become a much ruder word in the future, as with "cock-up" or worse. J.K. Rowling's use of it to mean "to steal" isn't what anyone in Britain would have said.

Things That Don't Make Sense Noah struggles to believe that aliens have infested his Ark. Nobody thinks to show him the thumping great dead alien insect lying five feet away from him.

For that matter, nobody hits upon the idea of using the transmats to filter out alien infection, even though "Revenge of the Cybermen" (set in the same station) entails the Doctor doing exactly that. Worse, as happens a lot in such stories, beings able to take knowledge from other species ought to motivate the Doctor to run away and hide, lest they nibble him to death and get regeneration, time travel and spoilers for major developments in cosmic history. What happens if they develop the sonic screwdriver or inertia-relaxation brakes for sprightly yellow roadsters?

12.2 The Ark in Space

We have to swallow a lot of convenient coincidences to keep this story down to four episodes, most obviously the way they circumvent boring us with 20 episodes of the Doctor and Harry marvelling at everything while looking in each of 100,000 pallets for Sarah. However, it's not just that she's in pallet D12, in the very first chamber they stumble across. It's more that she's in with the first people to be defrosted, and they are all in level D rather than, say, A. Amid this group of supposedly vital first-responders, D7 and D11 are inexplicably unoccupied, except for Tom's big "Homo Sapiens" aria, where every berth is suddenly full in shot. D4 and D5 had someone in, but apparently D's 8 and 9 get woken up first. It makes sense if the systems-checkers were last suspended, first revived – but it would appear (from the gaps and the fact that the transmat-couch and suspension mechanisms were left switched on) that they launched the Ark before they'd finished suspending the crew. This doesn't tally with the neurotic punctilio of the society we're told about.

Nerva's perimeter corridor has windows showing static stars and a rim on the wall at right-angles to the ceiling and floor. Therefore, the gravity isn't produced by centrifugal force (or else the stars would appear to move and everyone would walk on the curved track with the windows set in what would look like a floor with angled lighting). Okay, the production team had limitations with regards to people walking up curved walls, but the intention was apparently a "Wheel"-style space station. How the Doctor determines from his yo-yo's behaviour that they are in artificially-produced gravity is harder to explain. (In X9.1, "The Magician's Apprentice", he and Missy discuss it as though it's just a sense Time Lords have, like smell – that might be counted as cheating but is less of a headache for anyone applying A-Level Physics to the problem. Before that Capaldi story, we had filled many envelope-backs with number-crunching trying to provide a sensible explanation of this.)

It makes sense for the sleeping 1% aboard Nerva to keep the gravity on, even as all other life-functions are in abeyance, because of known medical problems from prolonged weightlessness (and a planned 5,000 years is as prolonged as it gets). Why they left the lights on is another story. And yes, it's "photonic" power, but they must have some serious long-life bulbs, since there's nobody to replace the ones that do blow out. (Anyone who recalls wretched 70s BBC space-station sitcom *Come Back, Mrs Noah* will remember that the one remotely funny bit was the little bloke who said "I'm Garstang and I change the light-bulbs".)

The Ark's gravity, however, is a bit daunting for the Wirrn. Only the Queen seems to have the earwig-like cerci (pincers) at the base of the abdomen, but those spindly legs growing out of the thorax can't be strong enough for support and propulsion. It's a species completely adapted for life in zero-g, except when it isn't. Luckily, this is another of those space-places where opening the door makes the gravity leak out (see also 10.3, "Frontier in Space"; X4.16, "The Waters of Mars"), so they can bounce around the outside of the Ark like rabbits in the springtime but drag themselves around on their arses when indoors. The Doctor's initial reaction to the dead Queen is that it's a sort of space-wasp, but almost immediately thereafter he talks about it having lungs. No insect has lungs.

It's presented to us that the humans waking up and the Wirrn hatching are both consequences of the Doctor fixing the Ark. If it's pure coincidence that Harry's accidental redirection to this point in space and time led to Noah and Vira waking up at the exact moment that the Wirrn larvae started hatching, what was the Queen's original objective? Were the bugs hoping to spend a few thousand generations picking up skills from each dormant expert and then build a ship of their own? Was the shuttle always part of the plan, even before a new generation knew about it, or were they going to float aimlessly and hope to get to Earth and extract their revenge on the bracken? Perhaps thinking about the Queen as having a "plan" as we understand it, rather than salmon-spawning-ish instinctive drives, is misleading, but that just makes the next generation of smart-Wirrn seem as if they're going through the motions and thinking to themselves "why are we doing this?"

The story takes place when the Ark is close to Earth (certainly, near enough for the transmat to work), but it must have gone far out into space to avoid the solar flares. All right, let's imagine that the Ark being near Earth *now* means that someone pre-programmed the return journey umpteen thousand years ago, but with the systems shut down, it should be on a collision-course with either the Earth or the Sun. Slowing down enough to inject into a low Earth orbit, let alone with sufficient precision to establish a geosynchronous orbit in range of London, needs a computer with power or a skilled pilot.

Even if this was part of the plan, with Dune selected (somehow) to ensure that the later hatchings had 100,000 generations in which to grab every scrap of human knowledge by steering the Ark into a parking orbit using his knowledge and some improvised pulleys, it requires the grub we see in Part One to have been hatched at the precise moment that a pilot-Wirrn was needed. Not impossible, but it needs a biological clock as accurate as the arrested inbuilt ship's chronometer, over thousands of years. It also needs a Wirrn who can rewire all the cables the Queen cut without being electrocuted by the cables themselves or the alarm system.

The corollary of this is that, for the humans, the plan was to wake up some 5,000 years earlier when the Ark was far from Earth. Or that it's on an extreme elliptical orbit around the sun and – just by chance – the TARDIS and the Wirrn Grub coincided with a once-in-five-thousand-years close encounter with Earth at high speed.

This alien insect comes upon a space station full of frozen humans and lays an egg inside one, then dies of injuries sustained disabling the intrusion countermeasures. Fine. But how did the Wirrn Queen know which of 100,000 corpsicles was the chief engineer, which of many hatches revealed the precise three cables to sever, and exactly what the revivification procedure would be as and when anyone did restore power? The plan can't have been for a passing Time Lord to accidentally pop in and do some DIY, but a lot of what seems to have been worked out relies on there being an active human who can be recruited to fly a rocket or operate machinery that requires opposable thumbs (i.e. everything other than the spigots with handy prongs in the solar stacks). It suggests an earlier encounter with a human who just happened to know precise details of a space-ark that nobody still believed in or, if it was that long ago, had the station's blueprints just lying about. This looks for all the world like a meticulously-planned surgical strike (or maybe we're wrong, and she just got lucky and found Dune instead of some telephone sanitiser).

So what happened at Andromeda? The Wirrn were happily passing on the memories of being cows or sheep, then some humans showed up and polluted them with ideas like space travel and revenge. Presumably, the humans took a dim view of being libraries-cum-incubators and took steps and the Wirrn, despite absorbing all these concepts, couldn't accept that they were the bad guys. So they went looking for another breeding ground. Why else would they be so intent of getting to Earth, a planet known to be uninhabited and suspected of being largely uninhabitable? That sort of works, but which Andromeda do they mean? Being a 70s *Doctor Who*, with the weird use of "constellation" inherent therein, it could be the stars that, from Earth, look like a pattern but are various distances away. The nearest is only ten light years away, so a Wirrn could conceivably get to the Ark in under 5,000 years if it's got a really big engine and a good map. (The nearest Andromeda-designated star with planets is Titawin, or Upsilon Andromeda A, 44 light years from here, but nobody in 1974 knew that.) So maybe they mean the galaxy in the same general direction, two million light years away – that's only possible if this Wirrn Queen hitched a lift on a starship, contradicting what Noah tells us.

Vira's wake-up is weird. She's scripted as moving like a zombie (in the pre-Romero Haitian sense; see **The Lore**), but reaches out to the med-kit Harry's holding. It's scripted as a reflexive set of responses, but nobody was expecting a Navy surgeon in socks and a cravat to be holding it for her – or *anyone* to be holding it for her, as she's designated first to get up. On the plus side, running the thought-experiment of removing Harry resolves one familiar question. Had she been semi-revived and programmed to sleep-walk to the med-kit in its usual place, she would have been prevented from reviving Noah, Libri et al by opening a door and having a Wirrn Queen fall on her before she was awake enough to step out of the way. So *that*, people, is why the dying Queen's last thought is "I must hide in a cupboard".

Vira tells Noah that there is no procedure for halting the revivification process once it's under way. That's a bit slipshod, given the unknown-unknowns of what could be waiting 5,000 years hence. They can just about comprehend the notional risk of other human colonies but find the idea of alien life forms finding Earth attractive as incomprehensible. Not only does this contradict just about every *Doctor Who* story set in the future (including the very next one), but it's refreshingly free of the paranoia that's Noah's defining characteristic. Human settlers committing mass exterminations could have removed aliens from the equation but Noah can't believe in that either.

12.2 The Ark in Space

Nevertheless, there's nothing in the manual about stopping the revivification, but isn't the point of waking up Noah second that he can effect changes as needed?

How *do* the Wirrn visit and depart from planets? They aren't exactly built for tinkering with rocket engines. Let's face it, they aren't exactly built for Earth-normal gravity just getting from room to room, let alone reaching escape velocity unaided. (And how would they do that? We know Bob Holmes loved a fart-gag, but this is literally beyond a joke.) We have to wonder if the Wirrn can withstand the heat of entering a planet's atmosphere or leaving again. If so, would the blast from the shuttle's exhaust-ports really have bothered them?

But what they *are* built for (perhaps literally) is data-retrieval and co-opting genetic and mnemonic data. They can lay eggs inside an animal and absorb the host's memories, transmitting them to the next generation. They can infect a host by contact and not only change the host into a Wirrn, but transmit memories of the previous host to the new one. They can survive conditions that would kill most species, including long periods in deep space. Therefore, with that attribute set, the big question is: why aren't the Wirrn the dominant life-form of this part of the universe? Wirrn-ness can almost literally go viral, making them like Cybermen but also capable of breeding like Sontarans.

"Humans require two mass pounds of oxygen per day to survive". Err, no. More like six. Perhaps, like all baddies, Noah is converting from imperial measurements, and getting it slightly wrong. Either way, it just highlights the odd lack of spacesuits on this space station.

Critique Perhaps the most important thing about this story is that it's a counter-example to a lot of pet theories people have had about how *Doctor Who* works. It's scary without being in any way familiar or domestic: no shadows, no creaks from under the bed, no uncanny-valley near-human faces and no one-size-fits-all childhood anxiety (even claustrophobia is played for laughs). This well-lit, antiseptic white space-station is far more unsettling than any loo in Tooting Bec could ever be. The humans being defended are, with one exception, deliberately unlikeable and hard to relate to. A whole 25-minute episode is spent on the three leads wandering around a spaceship and not meeting anyone (and one of those leads, the one we've known for a year, is abducted and silenced). It has some zingy dialogue, but nothing really identifiable as the "classic Holmesian double-act" beloved of 80s fanzines and *Doctor Who Magazine* – the Doctor and Harry don't really strike sparks here and their interplay is largely exposition. In theory, had anyone submitted a script like this to BBC Wales, the showrunner would have rejected it or "improved" it beyond recognition, to make it fit current ideas of what the public can handle and what scares people.

But that theory would never be tested, because Messrs Davies and Moffat helped themselves to large chunks of this story. What they and others fail to take from it, though, is any solid comprehension of how it came to be, the thought-processes that led to this script and production. Holmes was steeped in printed SF and old films but, crucially, had worked with, for and in institutions (notably the army and the police). Like Malcolm Hulke, he knew that isolation – not being listened to and being treated as if guilty of a crime you barely comprehend – were far more terrifying than getting eaten by space-monsters. (How apt that the bureaucratic nightmare's patron saint is Kafka, and we have here a story about a guy turning into a bug.)

This is what being a child can feel like, at times, and getting lost, caught up in literal or figurative machinery and not seeing how you'd get home are fears all adults remember – at times. That's been lost, or abandoned, in the twenty-first-century version of *Who*, where getting a lift back to your mum's after three-quarters of an hour is a given. Getting judged as being what the people making the decisions think you are is the plot-motor of a lot of Holmes stories and those he helped along (compare 21.6, "The Caves of Androzani" and Part One of "Genesis of the Daleks"). Here it functions for the middle two episodes, because the world Noah and Vira left has been thought out from scratch rather than cut-and-pasted from *Star Trek*.

It's not entirely original, of course; nothing written that fast could be. It has obvious debts to the sources we mentioned in **Where Does This Come From?** Moreover, Holmes self-plagiarised the first episode of 6.6, "The Space Pirates" for the opening episode, as well as looking back to the start of 1.2, "The Daleks". But what's fresh here is the complete conviction with which everyone plays it. Director Rodney Bennett is mainly associated with the "quality" end of BBC drama, and his cast has one player, Richardson Morgan (Rogin), who had *Who* previous (5.5, "The Web of Fear"). The long rehearsal process gave everyone a handle on what the characters thought (and allowed Bennett to tweak the end of the story, with Holmes's blessing); that's why Noah staring at his hand covered in what we now recognise as Swarfega and bubble-wrap still works (unless you saw the cut-down PBS/ BBC America version or the one-hour edit on BBC1 in August 1975, where it comes out of nowhere and isn't followed up).

As with Season Seven, the new regime has clamped down on "that'll do" or "it's only *Doctor Who*". (Watch Season Eleven for some pungent examples of that mentality.) Kenton Moore (Noah) risks going too far the other way, seeming to be thinking *I'm a human wasp-larva, what's my motivation?* (Compared to other human wasps in the series – how often does one get a chance to type that? – notably Martin Jarvis in 2.5, "The Web Planet" and Tom Goodman-Hill in X4.7, "The Unicorn and the Wasp", he is commendably unhammy.)

Above all, this is where the Baker-Sladen-Marter team gets to show how well they mesh, in what was their third production together. They give the impression of people getting to know one another (and the Doctor knowing his new self better than he did last week). With Bennett seemingly uncomfortable with complex effects, it's entirely down to the cast to convince us that they are living through this incident. So what if the opening shot is the archetypal squeegee-bottle spaceship and one of the Wirrn has a gouged eye? Who cares if the larvae look like sleeping bags and they seem to pupate inside post-office supplies? Why worry that the resurrected technicians dress like Admiral Ackbar? This is a story brimming with self-confidence and setting out the stall for everything that's to follow.

The promise of the series's basic premise – adventures in space and time – is being fulfilled again. After years of faffing about with soldiers and increasingly unthreatening threats to 70s London, we're back in space as more than just an occasional treat, with a Doctor who likes humans but not to the exclusion of everything else on offer. Kids (and that includes girls again now), *Doctor Who* is back.

The Facts

Written by Robert Holmes. Directed by Rodney Bennett. Viewing figures: 9.4 million, 13.6 million, 11.2 million, 10.2 million. AI's – amazingly, there's no record of anyone being asked whether they liked it, even though Part Two was the most-watched episode since the first part of "The Web Planet" ten years earlier. The repeat on August 20th gained 8.2 million viewers.

Working Titles An early story for this slot was called "The Space Station", but the Ark idea was early enough to be in the titles of both the broadcast version and John Lucarotti's account.

Alternate Versions The US version skips the start of Part Three where Noah is tormentedly fighting his possession as the High Minister delivers her speech. The one-hour BBC omnibus edit skipped a great deal of parts Two and Three, the "homo sapiens" aria and a lot of the stuff with the Doctor and Harry under a table. It's incomprehensible if you don't already know the story, and frustrating if you do. Time-Life, as usual, removed a few minutes per episode to get in a slightly erroneous synopsis from Howard da Silva. Superchannel's 1989 broadcast replaced the titles with the Sylvester McCoy ones but changed the face. In 2021, Big Finish released the Lucarotti version as *Return of the Cybermen*, with Sadie Miller voicing her mother's part and Christopher Naylor as Harry. Ian Marter's novelisation renames a few things and changes the end to have them head for Earth in the TARDIS.

Cliffhangers Harry opens a cupboard, and something falls out; Noah realises that his entire left hand is infected; Noah completes his Kafkaesque metamorphosis.

What Was In the Charts? "How Does It Feel?", Slade; "Killer Queen", Queen; "Something for the Girl with Everything", Sparks; "Life is a Minestrone", 10cc.

The Lore

Barry Letts didn't just vanish from *Doctor Who* after "Robot" – there was a delay before he took up his new post at the Classic Serials. He and Terrance Dicks had commissioned about a year's-worth of stories before leaving Robert Holmes

12.2 The Ark in Space

and, eventually, Philip Hinchcliffe to handle the day-to-day stuff and ease into forward planning for the second year. Letts was on-hand for hints and tips on the somewhat byzantine methodology of BBC television and, in particular, the oddities of their funding arrangements. A particular bugbear of his since he had himself inherited the series with three consecutive seven-part stories in the works was balancing the number of new stories that could be started in 24 episodes with the simple cost-per-episode advantages of longer stories. Viewers wanted variety, both in types of story per year and what happened in each episode compared to the ones either side. Management wanted quality and thrift. "Quality": hard to categorise, but they claimed they knew it when they saw it (it usually meant looking like other drama series). Thrift was very easy to identify.

- Dicks had, barring an emergency rewrite on 11.4, "The Monster of Peladon", withdrawn from script editor duties as soon as possible in mid-1973 and concentrated on getting settled in at Classic Serials and novelising old *Doctor Who* stories for Target Books. Holmes had a backlog of Dicks projects while he was contacting former colleagues with a view to getting his own kinds of story into production. He wasn't a fan of six-part stories, thinking they usually dissolved into a four-parter and a coda. Holmes had been approached novelist Christopher Langley (they'd worked together on *Honey Lane* in the mid-60s), so asked for a script about a space station, something he'd been bequeathed as one of Dicks's pet projects. Dicks had thought this would make a nice contrast to the relatively routine UNIT stuff he had in mind for "Robot", and proposed a deep-frozen crew, either for a long journey or as survivors of a catastrophe. (If you consider the sorts of ideas he and Letts were using in *Moonbase 3*, the links between this, what NASA was proposing prior to their budget-cuts of mid-1973 and the secondary plot of 11.2, "Invasion of the Dinosaurs" are fairly clear.) Holmes saw problems with this as a six-parter and possibly as a project *per se*. With the first three episodes in, Holmes was having misgivings about Langley's approach but opted to wait for the final episode and see how much needed salvaging.

[Check the Production Codes between now and "The Android Invasion". We're telling this in transmission order, so we'll be doubling back on ourselves. Quick overview: Holmes succeeded Dicks informally in late-1973 and by December had sounded out Langley and reluctantly agreed to have Terry Nation submit the same Dalek story he always did. Letts and Holmes sketched out a 1975 series, including getting Nation to rethink the Daleks' origins. Jon Pertwee quit in January 1974, Hinchcliffe was named as Letts's successor and Dicks more-or-less self-commissioned "Robot". Holmes sounded out Lewis Greifer for a story about mummies and Robert Banks Stewart for a Loch Ness romp. April was spent getting "Robot" into shape while waiting for Langley's final episode before deciding if it'd fly; in early May, it looks like Holmes will have to re-allocate the script. At the end of that month, Bob Baker and Dave Martin were given exhaustive notes on the Sontarans to make a two-part coda to a four-part "Space Station", Gerry Davis was asked for a totally new Cyberman story, ideally using the same sets as the earlier four-parter, and "Space Station" is passed on to a more experienced *Who* writer. So now we're up to June 1974, and can backtrack and fill in details just for this story...]

- Langley's treatment hadn't panned out and was officially abandoned on 9th May, the day before recording began on "Robot". Some months earlier, Dicks had run into *Who* veteran John Lucarotti (see Volume 1) at Target's offices and hired him for *Moonbase 3*. He was as good a match as anyone for this downbeat, supposedly "adult" take on life in 2003's European lunar outpost (every episode seemed to end with a suicide except the last, when they think Earth's been destroyed and are jubilant at hearing Ed "Stewpot" Stewart) and provided two episodes. He lived on a boat in the Mediterranean and hadn't seen *Doctor Who* much, even when he was writing for it in the 60s (1.4, "Marco Polo" et al).

Nonetheless, he was asked – possibly by Letts – to do a four-part treatment of the space station idea, as a back-stop. Depending on who you ask, the resulting scripts were: too sophisticated for the intended teatime audience (Letts's take); too expensive and technically-demanding to be made (Hinchcliffe's opinion); too stupid to be allowed on air (everyone else).

We know that the individual episodes had titles (previously the case until Spring 1966), we know that those titles were "Buttercup", "Puffball", "Camellias" and "Golfball" and we know a lot of the reasons for this (it appears that a different draft had all "-ball" suffixes). He'd put forward the idea of a space-ark (suspiciously like the one in 3.6, "The Ark", right down to the scale of the arboretum) and cryo-sleeping survivors at risk from a creeping infection. This infection was the fungal Delc, who came in a two-tier society; headless bodies did the work and bodiless heads gave the orders. The bodies could multiply by the hundred in seconds. Shooting them did no good, as they just spread spores, but the Doctor resolved the problem by whacking the heads into space with a golf-club. This sophistication needed a bit of work to match it to the other two stories now hanging from it, the Earth two-parter and the Cybermen attacking Space-Vegas, but Lucarotti, on his boat off Corsica, was even harder to reach than usual in mid-1974 due to a postal strike.

• Meanwhile, production on *The Pallisers* (see Volume 5) was under way and the use of Outside Broadcast facilities for a high-profile "prestige" drama got the BBC bean-counters very excited. One of the inherited methods of BBC drama from the Alexandra Palace era was that the filmed inserts for any broadcast were prepared in advance – so-called "strike filming". This was a legacy of live television and Mechau machines to either play back film into the feed or record the broadcast (what in BBC parlance was called "telerecording" and elsewhere "kinescopes"). It persisted into the era of videotape through a combination of corporate inertia and job-demarcation negotiations, even though it was now more trouble than it was worth.

If you've been reading these books in chronological order, the ways this complicated the production in the black-and-white era will be familiar. (See **60s *Doctor Who* – How Was It Made?** under 1.8, "The Reign of Terror" and **Which Was Better – Film or VT?** under "The Sontaran Experiment".) Letts had moved to a more cinematic method of making stories set-by-set and they'd been getting the filming done at the start of each new story as a matter of course since 6.3, "The Invasion". The budget allocations for four-part and six-part stories factored in more pre-filming for longer stories, bringing the average cost of any episode in a six-parter below any from a four-parter. (Sort of: see this story's essay.) Film, however, was more costly per minute of screen-time than orthodox studio production.

As we saw in "Robot", there were particular advantages for *Doctor Who* in using OB instead of film for location scenes. The production unit manager at the time was George Gallaccio; it seems he suggested it was possible, in theory, to make a whole story on location using the new facilities. However, nobody is sure if Letts, Hinchcliffe, Holmes or all three opted to split the six-part story into a studio-bound four-parter and an all-location two-parter but use the budgeting allowance for six episodes with extensive film-work. Holmes certainly grabbed the opportunity to work out a new, cheap story about post-apocalyptic Earth (see "The Sontaran Experiment") and tighten up a four-part space-station story.

It's most likely Hinchcliffe who proposed making the already-commissioned Cyberman story a prequel to re-use the sets. Rodney Bennett, who had impressed Hinchcliffe with his work on a Lord Peter Wimsey serial, was hired to direct both of the stories on a six-episode contract (Holmes also knew of his work from *The Regiment* and seems to have suggested that Hinchcliffe watch the December 1973 showing of *Murder Must Advertise* – see "The Deadly Assassin".) Also joining was Designer Roger Murray-Leach, whose work had, in the main, been on sitcoms and sketch-shows. He'd moved towards drama in the last couple of years. Two designers were assigned to Visual Effects for the two stories: John Friedlander concentrated on aliens and Tony Oxley most of the rest. Both got on-screen credits after years as assistants, but Friedlander was already known for monster-making from the 1973 *Radio Times* special.

• By mid-July, Lucarotti's scripts were in and were, as Holmes half-expected, unusable. With the sets already paid for, the only option was to invent a new story around them in under three weeks, so that the director could start casting. Enough of Lucarotti's basic premise (sleepers at risk from infestation, electricity as a deterrent, the title "The Ark in Space") remained for him to receive a co-credit for legal purposes, but Holmes needed a dispensation to write the scripts and get on-screen credit while working as a BBC staffer. (This would become a perennial problem during his term of office.) Hinchcliffe wrote the memo, stating that it was his opinion that only Holmes could do it, while Letts tried to put out fires with the accounting and interdepartmental liaison. As Holmes submitted the scripts in late July and early August, Hinchcliffe resumed his old role of script-editor and vetoed a couple of Holmes's ideas. Noah's head splitting open to reveal a Wirrn head inside was ruled out – as much as anything, for cost and practicality – but it was in keeping with

12.2 The Ark in Space

the direction both men saw the series taking.

Holmes wrote the bulk of the scripts in 18 days, while Baker and Martin amended "The Destructors", their two-part adventure on post-human Earth, to suit the locations that had been scouted and the new Doctor (and add the synestic lock get-out for the Doctor to survive being shot). His plan included a Vira who seems from the stage-directions to be mixed-race, possibly Haitian, to mislead the viewers into thinking there was something about her revival resembling old films about zombies.

- Bennett thought that the Wirrn just stealing a spaceship opened the door for a sequel a bit too obviously and, confirming that Holmes had no plans for a rematch, asked if they could be decisively killed. He offered the idea of water being toxic; Holmes opted to blow up the ship, with a hint that Noah did it deliberately.

- Even with the BBC's second-biggest studio (TC3), there was barely enough floor-space for the story's vast scale. Roger Murray-Leach, back from his eventful trip to Dartmoor, offset the lack of square-footage with height, stacking the pallets of people three-high with the suggestion of more (mainly via Baker's eyeline and a high camera-angle of him looking up at non-existent levels). He also strategically placed mirrors in the doorway of the main Vault set to suggest more chambers of preserved volunteers continuing on.

However, the first material recorded on 28th was the newly-minted title-sequence. The plan was a different tint for each story (like the first five episodes of Series Seven), but after seeing the pink-yellow version in Part One of this story, they opted to stick to the original. This session continued with the complex CSO set-up for the opening shot of Nerva and Earth. This took three cameras, zooming in at the same pace on a star-field, a photo of Earth from space and the model of Nerva on a blue CSO field. The Queen's POV shots of Dune's death needed a camera with Vaseline on the lens and a lighting gel around it. Then, as Sladen changed, there were multiple shots in the Transom set to suggest more curving corridors than they had actually built. (The backdrop of stars was just lights on black cloth, which cut down on the CSO requirements – a method called "star cloth" in the trade.) In the cryo-chamber set the last scenes of the day were taped, up to the point where a fourth actor was needed.

- Kenton Moore (Noah) usually played policemen, but had been a Roboman in 2.2, "The Dalek Invasion of Earth". His curly hair was slicked down for the part (this will happen a lot in Baker stories – see, for example, Chris Tranchell in 15.6, "The Invasion of Time").

- Rehearsals for the second half started on Hallowe'en, while the start of Part Three was revised to remove Libri's corpse (so Christopher Masters didn't have to come back for another day) and generally tighten things. Joining as Rogin was Richardson Morgan, last seen as Corporal Blake in "The Web of Fear". The full-grown Wirrn costumes were being made, but Friedlander took time out to play Wirrn in both rehearsal blocks. These adult insects were based around a set of bamboo hoops but left the feet free, so had to be shot carefully.

- Recording resumed on 11th November from where it ought to have ended on 29th October, with scene 7 of Part Three in the Cryogenic chamber. This time they were in Studio 1, the biggest. The result of the weapons on the bugs (using practical guns built by Oxley with "petals" that opened) was shot by a mix from one layer of tinted bubble-wrap in front of a CSO patch revealing a more detailed model shot from another camera. The final day of recording began with the first half-dozen scenes of Part Three remounted, after small revisions (including Harry's "totem pole" comment). The synestic lock material needed for later (with a line, cut from the finished episode, about how electrifying the ladder would neutralise this lock and send the shuttle floating off into space). You might recognise the countdown clock from ITC series. The scenes in the infrastructure were also shot back-to-back. Two triangular tunnels were built for Sladen to crawl through. One was missing a side-panel and enabled shots of her inching through as seen from the side, the other was for front-on shots.

- It's often reported that the meeting of Noah, the Doctor and Vira in the Transom was cut because of the line where Noah begs Vira to kill him. It appears that the real problem was the expressions of pain and anguish leading up to this, which were, in Hinchcliffe's opinion, too easy for children to identify; without them, the "kill me" line was meaningless, so that went too. In a later interview on *Pebble Mill at One*, he admitted that the problem was in part because alien masks and make-up look slightly silly in the studio but sometimes came to life on screen. The scene was effective in rehearsals, but the finished product crossed the line for him.

• The ratings spiked noticeably and this story reached the same record figures as "The Web Planet" ten years before. It received an omnibus repeat as part of the build-up to Season Thirteen on August 20th – a year to the day since Holmes submitted his replacement scripts (Lucarotti never saw the finished version and, after his full payment for the first showing, never got repeat fees). This was given a *Radio Times* illustration by Frank Bellamy.

12.3: "The Sontaran Experiment"

(Serial 4B, Two Episodes, 22nd February – 1st March 1975.)

Which One is This? Bob & Dave's Exeter Adventure. Earth's lain abandoned for thousands upon thousands of years, until one day a *third* lot of visitors show up about half a mile from where the other two landed two months earlier. It's not exactly a coincidence…

Firsts and Lasts For the first time, the Doctor and his chums arrive at a new planet for a whole story without using the TARDIS and leave the same way. With Glyn Jones (author of 2.7, "The Space Museum") in the cast, we have the first instance of a former *Doctor Who* scriptwriter getting an acting role in the series. (The next won't be until 2007, with Mark Gatiss in X3.6, "The Lazarus Experiment".) Another Season Two flashback is that it's the first two-part episode since 2.3, "The Rescue", thus the first in colour. But most of all, it's the first time an entire story's been made on OB, i.e. on location on videotape with no studio work. Because of the recording schedule, this is the first story made with Philip Hinchcliffe as producer.

One other small thing: Harry is the first person other than the Doctor to use the sonic screwdriver. He seems terrified of it.

Two Things to Notice About "The Sontaran Experiment"…

• Even though another post-apocalyptic story made on videotape on location has many identical shots and lines of dialogue (23.1, "The Mysterious Planet"), this story looks like no other *Doctor Who* adventure. The only other uses of this area for locations in BBC drama are all on film (including a *Blakes 7* romp you can watch for comparison purposes) and in these it looks flat and ordinary. Here the colours and shadows are crisp and vibrant, sometimes lurid and alien-seeming, with a panoramic emptiness that justifies the long journey out of London. They shot "Robot" in April but this is October and there's no studio work at all. The 1970s Outside Broadcast cameras lend the shots such freshness, it's slightly perplexing to see the actors' breath misting in what looks like warm sunshine.

• There's also something slightly odd about the way the big sword-fight is shot and choreographed. They set some of it up, by reminding us that Sontarans come from a planet with different gravity, but that's not all that's going on. There are two good reasons why it's all a bit tentative. See **The Lore** for the details, but look carefully at the shot of the Doctor saying 'you unspeakable abomination'.

The Continuity

The Doctor advises Harry never to throw anything away and never to clutter your pockets – in the same breath. When interrogated by the Galsec survivors, he doesn't pull rank or blind them with science, but witters on about clocks and affects to be just a passing antiques collector. When confronting Styre, he claims to represent the warrior elite of Earth. He taunts the Sontaran into going mano-a-mano with him using a sword against his big stick rather than shooting. [To be fair, Styre's just shot the Doctor at point-blank range and here he is again, so the Sontaran can be forgiven for abandoning his gun.]

• *Background*. He can tell without instruments that the transmat refractor is ellipsing and knows (somehow) that the main reception site is in Piccadilly Circus. He's also aware that tellurian drives require a substance not found in this galaxy.

• *Ethics*. In keeping with the new pro-robot policy, the Doctor reassures the hunter-trapper that he won't harm it before knocking it out with his screwdriver.

Even after calling Styre an 'unspeakable abomination', he only resorts to a lethal plan once it is clear that this lone sadist threatens the lives of all the humans around and most of the galaxy. Styre seems weakened and discomforted by his death, but not in agony.

12.3 The Sontaran Experiment

- *Inventory:*
- *Sonic Screwdriver* He feels lost without it. Yet this is the day he allows someone else, specifically Harry, to use it, first to open the spaceship door then to dismantle the energy-feed regulator. Before that, he uses it to start fixing the transmat array, without any diagnostic tests or readings.
- *Other.* Remember the Synestic locking clamp hatch he popped in his pocket while releasing the rocket at the end of the last story? He's put that in a convenient place for him to survive a zap-gun blast. Somewhere on his person is his 500 Year Diary, which has a few notes on the Sontarans. [We don't actually see it here; it was last mentioned in 5.1, "The Tomb of the Cybermen".]

The Supporting Cast
- *Sarah.* She has trouble accepting that this Sontaran isn't the same one she met in 'the thirteenth century' [Linx, in 11.1, "The Time Warrior"]. Her psychic torture involves the ropes on her wrist turning into a snake, the rocks closing in on her and the mud crawling up her legs of its own accord. Somehow, she loses her waterproof trousers and wellies, but gains a pair of high-heeled boots.
- *Harry* has already forgotten Sarah's warning about calling her 'old thing'. When he believes that both Sarah and the Doctor are dead, he starts planning revenge. He is very jittery while using the sonic screwdriver but calm and helpful when aiding a dying man.

The Non-Humans
- *Sontarans.* As with "The Time Warrior", they appear to "feed" on raw energy via their probic vents (c.f. X7.12, "The Crimson Horror"; X13.6, "The Vanquishers"). They seem to tire easily in Earth's gravity, especially in knife-fights with taller opponents. Despite Sarah's confusion, this one looks very different from Linx: lumpier, with larger features, a more hemispherical head and no facial hair.

Field Major Styre of G3 Intelligence packs a pistol rather than the wand Linx had. He also has a large bar, the weight of which can be adjusted with a turn of the dial on his handset [being a baddie, he uses pounds rather than kilos, but can take it from 40 to 500 in seconds]. He has miniature cameras that can fit into clothing, but a huge monitor array built into a big spherical case, plus a robot he can send to capture humans and spare him a long walk. Stairs seem to be a problem for him. They still have three digits on each hand.

His knowledge of human physiology is restricted – he knows that females exist but nothing about them [see also, of course, Strax's persistent gender-fog in Series 7] and not, apparently, about drowning or dehydration. He is so confident of his martial ability that he drops everything to accept a challenge to single combat. Apparently, humans have been disappointing adversaries.

Sontarans are neuortically methodical, so the planned invasion of Mutter's Spiral cannot begin until Styre's report is in. The delays are frustrating his superior, the Marshal (who, of course, looks and sounds exactly like him except for a pair of conical lumps on his collar). Styre meeting an unknown fate is sufficiently disquieting for the entire plan to be abandoned.

Planet Notes
- *Earth* has regrown vegetation [mainly bracken, but the Galsec boys are burning some kind of wood; it's unlikely they brought it in their crashed spaceship]. There's no animal or insect life, no birds and not much in the way of remaining buildings if central London's any indication. Sarah finds a tree-branch to use as a ladder, but we don't see any trees for miles.

History
- *Dating.* It's the same day as "The Ark in Space", and all seems to take place within a few hours. The Doctor and Harry throw out the figure of 'ten thousand years' since Earth was irradiated and none of the colonists correct this.

The people of Galsec [apparently a planet rather than a region, sometimes spelled 'GalSec'] are proud of making an empire in the absence of Earth's missing populace. Nerva is considered a myth, and Earth is off all the major trading routes. [This fits so well with "Planet of Evil" as to seem planned. Did the TARDIS make the detour to Zeta Minor and that time-period specifically to stop Vira pacing up and down, waiting for the Doctor to tell her if Earth was habitable?]

The Sontarans think this galaxy is strategically useful. [The last time we saw them, c. 1200, Earth was a backwater. In 22.4, "The Two Doctors", set in 1985, Earth is chosen for their experiments because it's obscure. However, their arch-foes the Rutans seem to be interested in this region in 1902 or thereabouts (15.1, "Horror of Fang

Which is Better – Film or Video?

We're going to have to define terms before we can get close to an answer to that. Specifying what qualifies as "better" can come later, but right now let's state that we're talking about the BBC's use of 16mm film (and occasionally 35mm for special occasions) first and foremost. They used a lot in the 1960s, mainly a special stock that didn't need as much processing, and so was ready for use in news reports later the same day. But once colour came in, things changed. We'll talk more about that soon.

When using "video", we're talking about the 625-line PAL videotape in 4:3 ratio used by BBC, ITV and, latterly, Channel 4 between 1967 and – well, let's use 2001 as a cut-off date, although something like this was still in use later and is the format, in 16:9 ratio, for news, game-shows and soaps to this day. And here's our first complication.

Much of the debate over using VT (we'll use that term because, in Britain, "video" means the process, the machine, the tape and the content depending on context – if a band was launching a promotional clip at a specific time and date, someone might pop to the shops for a blank video to video the video on his video) is muddled by America's use of it. For reasons of their own, US networks decided on 525-line transmissions and were stuck with 60Hz AC power-supply, hence a 30-frame-per-second image on their screens. (Well, 60 half-frames. We went into all this in Volume 9, **What Difference Did Field-Removed Video Make?** under X4.15, "Planet of the Dead".)

The results were, frankly, crap. As is well-documented, their first attempt at colour transmission was such a disaster, they stopped and started a different process in the mid-60s,, but that wasn't much better, especially when recorded. Even with all of today's restoration technology and improved screens, there is no way to prevent reruns of *Lawrence Welk*, *WKRP in Cincinnati*, *ALF* or *Rowan & Martin's Laugh-In* from looking like chalk drawings left out in the rain.[12] America had other disappointing results when experimenting with VT: they tried making episodes of *The Twilight Zone* as a cost-cutting exercise and, apart from everything being a lot more stilted (other than "Twenty-Two", which gamely staged an air-crash in the studio as-if-live) the picture-quality was slimy. Rapid motion, especially when it was the camera moving, resulted in "skidding", where a bit of the image moves less rapidly than the rest; bright lights cause "flaring" overloading the caesium dots in the camera to make fires look black.

Some of these features can be seen in early BBC video recordings but not many, because the amount of material retained where such things are attempted is less. Way less. It's possible that a lot of the live dramas of the 1950s were affected by such ambitious shots going wrong, but the majority of what was marked for preservation or export was relatively unadventurous. There was a lot of work put in to either minimising the potential for such goofs or exploiting them and deliberately accentuating the things that neither film nor theatre could achieve. In the latter camp were a number of different approaches, of which the Langham Group's was most written-about. Remember, in this phase the format was still 405-lines and the cameras used had four different lenses on a rotating turret so, to switch from a long-shot to a close-up, the director had to cut to another camera while the first one changed lens. Zoom lenses came in at the same time as colour and 625-line recording/broadcast. (Sort of: BBC2 got the go-ahead in part as a test-bed for colour, but broadcast 625-line monochrome from April 1964. Once they had the snags ironed out, they went into colour in September 1967 and BBC1 went 625-line monochrome. There was also a 405-line BBC1 service for some years after, while the network of transmitter-masts was being built and people changed sets.)

In case you've just joined us, the complicated process of making 60s television drama, especially a tricky beast like *Doctor Who*, got its own essay in Volume 1 – but let's quickly sketch in the defining features of this now. An electronic studio (i.e. one using "proper" television cameras rather than film) was in constant use, so the amount of time allotted to any one production was limited. This meant that the cast and production staff rehearsed it into the ground for a week before getting one day, possibly two for a big prestige production, physically in the presence of cameras. There were usually five of these and they had two operators each; one looking into it and following directions relayed over headphones, the other trailing him (sometimes pushing the camera sideways) and keeping the cables out of the way of the camera-operator, the cast and the other camera-operators and movers.

Scenes were recorded in one go – at the start and end of each would be a long take while two cameras that had either been involved in the pre-

continued on page 57…

12.3 The Sontaran Experiment

Rock"), so whatever they're planning is outside the Sontaran game-plan.]

The Analysis

Where Does This Come From? Although it's hard to discern in the broadcast version, one thread in the discussions about this story was the idea of something like *The Pit and the Pendulum*, specifically Roger Corman's film version (see also "The Masque of Mandragora"). The torture-dungeon motif given a spurious scientific rationale (by Styre and Robert Holmes alike) was to have played out in the ruins of a contemporary landmark, which is one reason the Hound Tor location was first scouted – it's what's left of a Mediaeval settlement, Hundatora, possibly dating back to the Bronze Age, and was excavated in the 1960s and early 70s. (A local version says that it's a pack of hounds that a witch turned to stone – that's the story someone told Sir Arthur Conan-Doyle, anyway.) Ruins always attract stories and evoke ideas of lost grandeur that relatively intact buildings never quite match (which made Piranesi a bundle doing etchings). It was a large part of that Enlightenment/Romantic cult of the Sublime and fed into the weird Victorian obsession with an impossibly glamorous Middle Ages (see "Terror of the Zygons" for the Walter Scott version).

Every generation gets a Middle Ages of its own and the 1970s one, all about sex, class and bodily functions, slowly replaced the 1950s one about mutilation, faith and Spitfire pilots on horseback. Bob Baker and Dave Martin went into this expecting the Spanish Inquisition. In early goes at the script for this story, the tests would also have used a suit of armour and a ducking-stool. Along the way, Philip Hinchcliffe became more interested in the setting, a post-human environment, and the logistics of making the entire story on location on video accentuated that aspect. Wondering about mass extinctions of the past was increasingly feeding into speculation about pollution, atomic war and so on so Dougal Dixon's 1980 book *After Man*, suggesting how evolutionary niches would be filled fifty million years hence with no interference from us, didn't just arrive out of nowhere. Post-War paperback sales turned what's been called "cosy catastrophe" into a sub-genre, from John Wyndham to J.G. Ballard to John Christopher, but stories about industrialism ending and everyone going back to feudalism and turnips had a long heritage, as did returns to Eden with depopulated nature getting its own back. One of Bob Baker's first attempts at a screenplay, *Entropy*, was about how our artefacts would change over geological time.

There were a few post-apocalyptic novels in the Victorian era – mainly to do with terrible things foreigners would do if the nation wasn't defended properly, but the most interesting from our perspective here is *After London, or Wild England* by farmer-turned-author Richard Jeffries (author of the more famous *Bevis* – pronounced to rhyme with "crevice" – about a lad who could commune with animals, rocks and rivers). In this 1885 bestseller, some unspecified catastrophe reduced the cities to swamps and society to savagery. Some time later, observer / protagonist Felix Aquila makes a canoe and goes exploring. Gosh, it's dull. The best bits are Jeffries using his lyrical prose to revel in the city's obliteration by plants, after Welsh slave-traders invaded it. *After London* wasn't even the first of this sort of book. Mary Shelley had followed *Frankenstein* with a futuristic novel, *The Last Man*, describing a world that had just ended. To quote her husband: "Look on my works, ye mighty, and despair" (see "Pyramids of Mars" for more on *Ozymandias*). That's the tone for a lot of late Victorian novels questioning Imperial bombast.

The idea of our familiar buildings being baffling and misunderstood by future generations is used satirically by William Morris in *News from Nowhere* (Parliament is where they store horse-manure, its original function forgotten). He printed it himself in 1890, inspired partly by Jeffries, and it caught on as a blueprint for social change – the paradox that his bid to enthuse the proletariat to expect better was financed by him selling designer furnishings to the rich confuses many American commentators. We can't ignore the oddly-similar pair of 1895 diatribes, *The War of the Worlds* (London is treated by technologically-advanced bloodsuckers the way Africa and India were by the Empire) and *Heart of Darkness* (starting with what the Romans thought of Britain and making the analogy with Britain's complicity in what Belgium was up to in the Congo). Wells also ended *The Time Machine* with a future where humanity's impact has been effaced and Entropy has won. Social collapse and cyclic history were in vogue in the late nineteenth century (see Volume 3 for more on this, Theosophy and Lost Races

Which is Better – Film or Video?

...continued from page 55

vious scene or were getting ready for the next one were moved and set up, as quietly as possible. Choreographing all of that meant that the day of recording began with the cast – in theory word-perfect by now – translating the chalk lines or gaffer-tape on the floor of the rehearsal-room into moving in the sets and the camera-team, lighting crew and boom-mic operator working around that to learn where people would be.

A great deal of television drama was still live but most in this period was a compromise; it was made to be done under the same conditions as live but entirely on videotape, for subsequent edits and dubbing. The recording equipment was pretty basic: it had a pause control for scene breaks and a rewind if anything went really badly wrong. In the specific instance of *Doctor Who*, they had a 25-minute episode to record in just over twice that time and, usually, two breaks scheduled. If anything went wrong in the first, they started from scratch; if a set fell over in the second, they could go back to the first break; if someone's trousers fell off in the third, they could go to the second. It had to be pretty disastrous to warrant a remount, though. (If you've ever wondered why blooper-reels need so much bleeping, it's because actors swear to make doubly sure a duff take isn't broadcastable.)

Since the 1930s, BBC television dramas had used film primarily to cover where a recording break might have been in a pre-recorded drama. A 30-second insert might cover a rapid costume-change or the set being altered. Although the balance of location-filming to studio performance altered, starting at around the time Rudolph Cartier pulled out the stops for *Quatermass II* in 1955, filmed inserts were made ahead of time and edited before rehearsals began so that they knew how long each would be.

You read that right: they filmed things *before* rehearsals, usually before the read-through. In extreme cases, this would be an actor's first clue that his or her character would be written out (see 3.9, "The Savages"). For the first five years of *Doctor Who*, the relevant cast-members would break off rehearsals for that week's recording (usually on the Wednesday) to go on locations, with a script they'd only seen hours before, for material in a completely different story they'd not be recording for a month or more. Any changes (haircuts, accent decisions, imputed on-screen relationship with another character) were either "explained" in hastily-added dialogue later or – more often than not – ignored. If the actors couldn't be spared, they used long-shots and look-alikes, with mixed results. The filmed scenes were dubbed into the video-recording during the performance, using the early telecine machines.

As things progressed, the BBC bought the old Ealing Films studios and made use of their facilities, especially where technically challenging or potentially dangerous scenes were needed. A lot of the fight-scenes were on film, partly to edit them better, but mainly to cut down on studio time in choreographing stunts. Anything with water usually used the bespoke pool. Anything with fire was especially prone to be done as far from Lime Grove as possible. As 60s *Doctor Who* in particular did with increasing frequency, anything involving foam or radio-controlled devices was also kept away from the electronic studios. Broadly speaking, anything that didn't involve especially good acting was safe to be pre-filmed, so regular cast-members got holidays by making cameos a few weeks ahead of time.

Apart from the cost-per-minute, to which we'll return, the big problem was the noticeable change in picture-quality and sound timbre that happened, even if the number of edits was almost constant and it was in an identical set. Consider 5.1, "The Tomb of the Cybermen", where action scenes are in what *purport* to be the same places as the dialogue being spoken. It's an abrupt change in little things like where they can put the camera, how stark the shadows are and how big the set looks with different lenses and depth-of-field. It sends subliminal cues, even to those viewers who claim not to be able to tell the difference, saying "here comes a punch-up" or "special effects ahoy!"

Colour accentuated that. Where monochrome film stock was pretty fast and gave crisper images than VT, the 16mm colour stock the BBC used was less bright and sharp than the new Plumbicon cameras (the EMI 2001 being the workhorse of the 1970s). Even before the eventual problem with the green dye fading before the rest (hence the myth that the 1970s was entirely brown and beige), any location work or pre-filming looked murkier than the studio material unless it was a particularly sunny day. This wasn't always a problem: in "Day of the Daleks" (9.1), the fake news

continued on page 59...

12.3 The Sontaran Experiment

Beneath the Earth) – after World War I and the rise of Hitler, they caught on again.

However, it took the prospect of atomic war to make this idea part of the common currency. The most frequently-cited exemplars are *A Canticle for Leibowitz* by Walter M Miller and *Alas, Babylon* by Pat Frank. These took the analogy of the fall of Rome and an exclusively American perspective. Miller's book is set long after a war and has priests struggling to preserve what little of the old knowledge they can; Frank's is about the war itself and the humiliation of other countries bailing America out. People were thinking about what would survive of the proud post-war world. It wasn't just the Bomb, of course, there was environmental catastrophe (see 2.1, "Planet of Giants"), pestilence, famine, disease, aliens, nasty foreigners, comets, teenagers... the thought that prosperity *wasn't* under threat was the truly unbearable one.

In this regard, the end of the film *Planet of the Apes* is just about the most inevitable screen moment since Charlie Chaplin parodied Hitler. The Statue of Liberty emerging, collage-like, from "lone and level sands" (*Ozymandias* again) is supposed to shock because it confirms that this is future Earth and not an alien world, but it seems oddly like seeing an American being told that other countries don't get *Gilligan's Island* or give a toss about the Superbowl. With the unpleasant racial tinge of the original novel toned down, it's US Exceptionalism getting the same treatment as Victorian London. We'll come back to this, and the accents of the Galsec guys, in a moment. The point to make in passing now is that the choice of Trafalgar Square as the location for the Transmat draws attention to the timescale by the simple absence of any buildings, any pigeons and the Thames itself. After the last story's deliberate vagueness about the duration of time since the solar flares, this is a very visible, child-friendly way of indicating a remote future.

It's worth noting that the idea of a post-technological world was having, as they say now, a "moment" in British television in Spring 1975, especially in the Children's slots. BBC1 was serialising Peter Dickenson's "Devil's Children" trilogy, now called *The Changes*, about a psychic force that made everyone in Britain scared of machines. This went out on Mondays and was just ending (with the book's morphine-addicted Merlyn replaced by a dolmen in a mine) as these episodes went out. Then a month later, the ITV stations showed HTV's *Sky*, also made in Bristol and environs, also on Mondays, in which cultists centred at Glastonbury half-remembered Stonehenge's nature as a psychic teleport and an alien who came to help was *so* alien that Earth and Nature developed spooky antibodies against him. It ends with a post-apocalyptic cult in the future rejecting machines and getting to the stars "properly". This was written by – wait for it – Bob Baker and Dave Martin, usually thought of as the cheerleaders for Britain's nuclear industry, and the debate is pushed to the fore in the last two episodes.

Nonetheless, you can see hints of their *Doctor Who* work here and there. Sky becomes more like Ky (9.4, "The Mutants") as things progress; there's a hospital, a lot of hypnosis and hand-glowing malarkey ("The Hand of Fear"); sacrificial rituals based on half-remembered space-tech (15.5, "Underworld", although this is almost fitted-as-standard in 1970s science fiction) and, of immediate interest here, a circle that's an interstellar transport but has become part of folklore and scenes of nature going slightly amok. Sarah's hallucination of the mud engulfing her and the trees and rocks oppressively close is suspiciously like the way trees and soil swaddle the alien visitor.

Just in case this whole post-apocalyptic rural idyll theme seems like a bit of a stretch, just after *Sky*'s second episode, Terry Nation – fresh from having Davros speculate on how much fun he could have with a virus ("Genesis of the Daleks") – did his best John Wyndham impression with *Survivors* part one. Sadly (for him), 12 days before this the rather more popular series *The Good Life* began with a similar notion of becoming self-sufficient in the suburbs (see 24.2, "Paradise Towers"; X4.8, "The Unicorn and the Wasp"). So from 6th January to 16th July, barring a three-week Easter gap, there was a constant drip-feed of earnest dramas about abandoned Land Rovers, children being denounced as witches and people standing around in anoraks and muddy wellingtons arguing about what had gone wrong (and a sitcom where the neighbours worry about how it will affect house prices).

In short, after the oil-price shambles of late 1973, television writers were now coming around to the idea that the hippies were right. Some, as we saw in Volume 3, were already on board with at least the dramatic potential of this, but the string of power-cuts and rationings made the fondue-making peoples of our nation consider the

Which is Better – Film or Video?

...continued from page 57

report is done on the same kind of camera as a real one in 1972. Moreover, Britain's drabness in winter led to a sort of convention in BBC and ITV drama: location work was on film because it was "outdoors" and therefore gloomy, while studio sets for "indoors" had the lights on.

However, another convention – also largely unspoken, but still perceived by most viewers at the time – was that film was "the past" and VT was "now". Even news footage had this problem as (despite moves to skip the negative-developing stage and give news-cameras single-strip stock that only took a few hours to process) the further a clip had to travel, the older it was when it got onto the air. We would hear about an event in Mozambique or Saigon over a crackly phone-line, then see it a week or so later. Videotape, unless badly abused, doesn't age. It's mildly heartbreaking to see *Top of the Pops* clips from 1973 and realise that the artists are all dead and the pert teenagers are probably all grandparents, if they survived. It looks as if it was recorded yesterday. In any drama, sitcom or pop show, a filmed insert from a few weeks earlier looks like a flashback, especially in colour productions.

Two significant changes took place in 1974 that shook this accepted norm. BBC drama, which had always been VT with film inserts of varying lengths, started to polarise. The US film studios had bowed to the inevitable in 1956 and turned their attention to made-for-TV output, mainly Westerns and sitcoms to begin with. Lew Grade had cashed in on the potential market even before it officially existed and, before him, Hannah Weinstein at Sapphire Films had found that filmed episodes with British character-actors in tights were a potential gold-mine. By the time ITV started in late 1955, there was already a backlog of filmed series made in the UK, using the same facilities and cast as cheap films made on the Eady Levy system (see **Could *Scratchman* Have Happened**? under "The Hand of Fear" for more on that).

Grade's ITC accelerated this and pretty much took over Elstree Studios. What they made was shown in Britain, on his ATV station (see "The Ark in Space"), but this was a loss-leader for global sales. The BBC looked at this, and the way American-made series were being offloaded on the UK at bargain-rates, and tried to find a way to get in on the ground floor. First had been *Fabian of the Yard* (see 21.7, "The Twin Dilemma") before any of this.

Viewers have almost completely forgotten a more determined assault, *The Third Man*; the BBC management apparently found this a chastening experience, and it was over a decade before they tried anything similar. It was with Twentieth Century Fox's facilities when it started in 1959, but by the last series, in 1964, they too were in Elstree and only Jonathan Harris connected it to Hollywood (he was Michael Rennie's co-star and looks, with hindsight, to be rehearsing for *Lost in Space*).

Apart from Grade's frothy stuff and the curious example of *The Avengers* switching from VT to film to capitalise on the US interest, the majority of all-film series made for television in Britain were for children – stop-motion BBC shows, Southern's string of adventure-shows and occasionally a BBC drama based on a book (*Minnow on the Say, The Changes, Man Dog* and a few others). In among all the imported film palmed off on kids, from *The Singing, Ringing Tree* or *Yao* to *The Cosmic Awareness of Duffy Moon* and *Skippy*, domestic filmed drama was grudgingly accepted as not being like "serious" drama for adults, on VT.

The person to change all of this was Verity Lambert. After *The Avengers* ended and ABC had been subsumed into Thames Television, there wasn't a TV company doing all-film adult series set in a Britain we would recognise. Grade's eye for international sales meant that his pet projects were all jet-set playboys or, in the case of *The Zoo Gang*, residents of Marseilles. Euston Films, set up by Thames and overseen by Lambert, saw a gap in the market for thick-ear action in grubby bits of London. There were series like that with studio scenes and a lot of location filming, such as *Callan* or *Budgie* (made by London Weekend Television, rivals to Thames), but *The Sweeney* and *Widows* were all-film.

The sheer perversity of this takes a moment to sink in. The economics of television production in 1960s Britain meant that you could only commit to a series of hour-long filmed episodes if they were guaranteed, repeat, *guaranteed* sales in America and other lucrative markets. US networks only agreed to such deals if they called the shots, almost literally, and messed with the dialogue to remove any confusing terms such as "flat", "tube", "bin" or "solicitor". John Steed lived in an "apartment", Inspector Gideon investigated deaths on "subway" trains and so on. With such a deal in

continued on page 61...

12.3 The Sontaran Experiment

matter as well. Seven years on from the trend for rock stars to buy farms, make mellow, "centred" folk-influenced albums and get their roadies to show them how to stew a rabbit, now Hampstead-based TV writers were telling the rest of us that we were going to have to live less comfortable lives. Like we weren't already.

Other influences on this story were closer to home. In a story where the whole of Earth is represented by what's left of London, the analogy of Britain and the Commonwealth for a collapsed Earth and an aggressive empire of former colonies was too obvious for the script to comment upon it. They just cast people with South African accents. It wasn't hard to find any; with the Apartheid regime making people want to leave and London still the obvious place to go, there were actors, writers and dentists trying to soften their consonants and broaden their vowels throughout Britain, but especially in the former seat of Empire. Many of them had been raised to think of Britain as "the homeland" despite the whole Boer War thing.

As we saw in 2.7, "The Space Museum" (written by Glyn Jones, who's in this story's cast), the MacMillan government's "Wind of Change" approach brought a few problems, not least the inability of Parliament or the Foreign Office to simultaneously maintain a light touch, encouraging self-governance, and tell off newly-independent nations for imposing racist or otherwise inhumane policies. Critics of those governments found it easier and safer to move to London and denounce their country (not least because there were fewer reporting restrictions or assassinations).

However, as with Australians, there was a subtext of the "Wild Colonial Boy" (a drinking song from the Outback) and a nasty implicit assumption of people with suntans and those tangy vowels being virile, unfettered and active while the English, in particular, were effete, hidebound and indolent. This may be why the same director who made this casting decision sidestepped the scripted idea that the people preserved in the Ark (see last story) were a multi-cultural and multi-ethnic cross-section and exclusively cast posh-sounding white Londoners. Baker and Martin were also thinking that, following trends that had been noted since sound-recording came in, spoken English would eventually sound like the South African accent (see "Finglish" in 15.2, "The Invisible Enemy").

As we'll see in **Things That Don't Make Sense**, the military justification for these experiments is flimsy at best and, lacking any kind of control or benchmark figures against which to gauge an individual's performance or survival-time, it's not even very scientific. It does resemble the way the British Standards Institute tests new products before issuing the "kite-mark" – but, more cogently, it's like the slightly exaggerated version of how products are tested on animals put out by anti-vivisection protesters. The notion that this sort of activity (testing make-up on dogs, making beagles smoke, the way guinea-pigs have entered the language as archetypal test-subjects) might be done on humans isn't unfounded; the notorious Joseph Mengele got up to just that in various Nazi death-camps. This has allowed various interested parties (astrologers, homeopathists, Flat Earthers) to make simplistic analogies between attempts at objectivity and outright sadism to discredit anyone who dares to demand evidence for loopy claims.

English Lessons

- *Central Line* is one of the main lines of the London Underground, running more or less east-to-west. The nearest it gets to Trafalgar Square is Oxford Circus and Tottenham Court Road tube stations, about half a mile north.
- *Pigeons* are, or were, a familiar part of Trafalgar Square (see the stills at the end of 2.8, "The Chase" and the opening sequence of X1.1, "Rose"). They have been discouraged, so now the main hazard for tourists is berks dressed as Yoda. There aren't as many ice-cream vans allowed there either so...
- *Lolly-sticks* are less of a feature. We're talking ice-lollies here, not lollipops.
- *Five Hundred Year Diary* (n.): This was, back then, such an obvious joke that we didn't get around to mentioning it in Volume 2. A five-year diary has room for small notes for each date, five times over (and February 29th). It was assumed that the owner would be in the same job for a while and made appointments well in advance. Stationers' shops used to stock these diaries along with typewriter ribbons, blotting-paper, gritty disc-shaped typing erasers, Banda-machine fluid, sealing-wax, ink cartridges and letter-spikes (and Target novelisations). Manufacturers eventually realised that a one-year diary sold five times better

Which is Better – Film or Video?

...continued from page 59

place, there were economies of scale – such as one-off deals with Equity and the ACTT covering all residuals and overseas sales, standing sets, a different contract with the Writers' Guild, series-wide music cues with a full orchestra and cross-promotion deals with car manufacturers or couturiers.

Set against this was how much (or little) an initial broadcaster would meet the production costs. Figures cited by *Avengers* head honcho Howard Thomas indicate that making an hour's television electronically cost about ten grand in facilities and as much again for cast and crew, but – in return for the rights to play it twice – they could recoup that if every one of the ITV regional stations took the show. Making an hour on film cost twice that but got the same amount from the ITV transmission. (Other sources say it was worse for other companies: the usual figures are £3,500 for an hour of VT in 1961 and £35,000 for an hour of film in 1967. Inflation accounts for some of this, but not much.) Going ahead without the imprimatur of the yanks was unimaginable until *The Sweeney*. Yet they made a series so uncompromisingly non-US-friendly as to appeal to a wide number of other countries and so blokey and sardonic that *Kojak* suddenly seemed like *Dixon of Dock Green* (and – lo! – George Dixon said "g'night, all" for the last time in 1976). And, after a threatened walk-out dissipated once union bosses saw how much guaranteed work and overtime was up for grabs, all sorts of other perceived difficulties went away.

If that seems perverse, the BBC's decisions at the same time look deranged. They now had the co-production deals with US and other networks but used them on some peculiar productions. Their big-hitter for 1974 was *The Pallisers* and, despite all the problems they ran into with production due to the Three Day Week, industrial action and scripts, it's 26 hours of quality thesps and almost unadulterated Trollopean chicanery. But it looks downright *weird*. The first episode's most interesting from this essay's perspective as it's almost all VT, with location scenes (a 15-minute opening sequence at a garden-party in particular) shot with the Outside Broadcast cameras usually used for horse-races and rugby. There is one minute's film toward the end, looking gloomy by comparison but probably intended to (an arranged marriage is set in motion looking like the couple in question are duelling with pistols).[13]

Apart from the difficulty of converting 625-line PAL for transmission in countries that opted for SECAM or NTSC, the trouble with this decision is that other countries' experiences with VT had led them to consider it the poor relation. Starting a six-month blockbuster costume-drama with a party that looks like a live transmission was a curious move, but sets up the series' stylistic quirk of being like eavesdroppers picking up gossip. The OB rigs had new cameras and came with their own mobile production facilities (which you'll have seen as the UNIT Mobile HQ, e.g. 8.3, "The Claws of Axos"). These had videotape editing suites and an action-replay disc-player, plus live RT contact with the cameras and floor-managers. The trouble was, they were mainly used for sport and there's a lot of sport on television in the 70s.

A quick aside... we mentioned videotape editing: for most productions, that was only really viable from the late 60s as, until then, the only way to do it was to physically cut up the tape. Most video tapes were costly and intended for constant re-use, so the only ones cleared for such abuse were those at the ends of their useful lives. On occasion, this is reflected in the picture-quality. Once this was established practice, some directors found that it freed up the cameras hitherto reserved for setting up the next scene. It helped if the director was also the producer.

OB rigs had been used in drama before: the earliest definite specimen we can find is the second episode of Granada's shot-lived Absurdist *Avengers*-a-like *The Corridor People*, where Regent's Park c. 1966 looks almost current, if badly edited. (You can see the Post Office Tower under construction in one shot – compare that to an episode of *Gideon's Way* which also has this visible, as George Cole buys a moped. The one on film looks like it was made 30 years earlier, even though it's demonstrably only a couple of months. The tag-scene of the last episode of *Undermind*, a year earlier, might be one, but the surviving print's too fuzzy to tell.) Yorkshire Television's dreary Sunday offering *The Flaxton Boys* was probably first to do it in colour, although their storage facilities mean that the tape itself was compromised and the picture now looks almost bad enough to be NTSC.

The BBC, however, took the perceived success of *The Pallisers* as a cue and went headlong into prestige costume dramas recorded on location on videotape. Before that, they let *Doctor Who* have a

continued on page 63...

12.3 The Sontaran Experiment

than a five-year one. There's no such thing as a nine-year diary, so the 'Nine Hundred Year Diary' in the 1996 TV Movie was just one of a number of tone-deaf clunkers.

Things That Don't Make Sense We made the joke decades ago but... why do identical Sontarans use videophones? It cant just be to allow bitchy comments about your commanding officer's appearance (X13.1, "The Halloween Apocalypse"). How did Styre squeeze that cumbersome terminal into his diddy spaceship? More pertinently, though, if they can breed that fast and produce so many good officers, is Styre really the best they could spare for this mission?

Admittedly, sending just one is possibly a good idea if you are half-expecting the abandoned planet to be a trap, but that just highlights a significant flaw in the military rationale for clones: with no genetic variation between them, any bio-weapon developed for use against them – a virus or bacteria – only needs one test-subject. Kill one, you can kill them all. The Grand Marshall's abrupt cancellation of a well-prepared plan to invade the galaxy only really makes sense if that's what he thinks is happening here: the Doctor's defeat of Styre indicates any Sontaran going up against "his kind" are similarly doomed. Styre thinks humans are similarly interchangeable and doesn't average anything he's measuring. Sontarans have, shall we say, diversity issues, but assessing an entire galaxy on the basis of half a dozen blokes, the first ones they could find, is militarily inept. If the humans wanted to defeat a Sontaran invasion based on this intelligence-gathering, all it needs is an all-girl army and they're flummoxed.

Why does Styre stage his "find humanity's weak points" tests on Earth, which is currently bereft of humans? These Sontarans don't appear to have encountered any humans before now: is that because humans are relatively sparse (in which case, why not go where they live and experiment there?) or so plentiful that they're the majority shareholder in this galaxy (in which case, how have they not met each other?). If Styre's information is so vital to the war-plan, how will making Galsec astronauts crash on a strange world produce reliable specimens? (Yes, their ancestors came from Earth, but that was countless generations back. All our ancestors came from Olduvai Gorge, but how many of us could run a marathon or lift weights within hours of arriving in Kenya, even if the plane landed safely?) The dialogue makes it seem as if it's only humans in this galaxy (no Wirrn or Draconians?), so Styre's deliberately looking for outliers on whom to base his wild generalisations.

And it never occurs to him to wonder *why* such a nice, handy planet's been abandoned. Does he test the air or water? Does he look out for mutant wolves or whatever? We're also having trouble working out if basing this test of human potential right next to the Transmat receptors is fiendishly brilliant, massively stupid or a colossal coincidence. We're veering towards option three. Perhaps the fake SOS was more convincing coming from an ex-population centre with some residual technology, but that returns us to his inability to see red flags.

Taking the Grand Marshal's orders to Styre at face value, the whole Sontaran fleet is poised to invade within hours but won't move until all the facts about human physiology have been gleaned. What facts did Styre learn? Stick a human face down in a bucket of water for 20 minutes. Result: he drowns. Place 20 tons on his chest. Result: his ribs crack. It's lucky there aren't any Sontaran taxpayers to complain about this.

And why, pray tell, is this big-budget waste of time cancelled? On a deserted planet, they find one person out of a dozen who can fight a single Sontaran. How often is a single Sontaran in combat? No matter, how long has this invasion been in the making, or much firepower is the Sontaran fleet packing, that it all hinges on knowing precisely how long it takes a male human to die of thirst? A galaxy is a big place, and if all the other potential threats to the Sontarans have been assessed and evaluated without changing the plan, it must be that humans are considered the toughest possible antagonists. Yet everyone seems to be under the impression that the strategic value of this galaxy has changed in a matter of weeks and that an invasion has to happen in a day or so. That's 100 billion planets, minimum, that the Sontarans have to subdue. By Tuesday. If they could do that, what possible threat are humans anyway?

Nonetheless, Styre has landed his spherical spaceship inside a lumpy set of rocks – impressive manoeuvring, but precarious – which he's selected out of an entire planet's surface as the best place to make a human spaceship crash. However, it must be a relatively congenial spot, as the visitors to this

Which is Better – Film or Video?

...continued from page 61

go to iron out the snags before letting grown-ups see the results. (See also 15.5, "Underworld"; 17.1, "Destiny of the Daleks"; 18.2, "Meglos".) Once this was achieved, there is a brief period when it looks as if the BBC will go all-out towards OB for anything that wants to make the cast and costumes part of the sales-pitch. There's a 1977 production of *The Mayor of Casterbridge*, with a script by Dennis Potter, shot in the places where it's set and, apparently, on location in the nineteenth century. They make a big thing of starting a scene in an interior decorated in the period style and opening a window to let the camera see people in smocks taking pigs to market in mucky streets. Scenes shot at twilight were curious-looking, neither lit for cameras nor day-for-night bright, but atmospheric in a different way. Audiences didn't seem to mind.

In the same year, Pebble Mill, the BBC Birmingham drama powerhouse, adapted comic whodunits set in the fictional East Anglian town Flaxborough, under the peculiarly made-for-export-esque title *Murder Most English* and, again, it was all OB or studio and not always in sunshine. The notorious *BBC Shakespeare* proceeded from a desire to do *As You Like It* in this way, in the actual Forest of Arden. Neither UK audiences nor the PBS stations had any objections.

Indeed, some people claimed not to be able to tell any difference. This may have been the result of undiagnosed cataracts, bad television sets, wobbly aerials or simple inattention. Other viewers felt there was something different about studio-made scenes and locations, even if they couldn't put their fingers on it. In Britain, or any other country with a PAL setup (Australia, for example), the spread of colour transmission and the necessary UHF signal meant that even people with monochrome sets could see a sharper picture than before. For *Doctor Who*, the problem of matching CSO shots to film was causing some of the ropiest effects of the 70s. (We could cite several, but let's stick with 11.5, "Planet of the Spiders".)

Occasionally, the process of developing the film caused blemishes or defects, particularly when the film was physically conveyed to London from a location shoot or effects studio. Worse, nobody would know anything about such a flaw until almost too late (see "The Invisible Enemy" and 22.4, "The Two Doctors"). Model effects also suffered from being under-lit or oddly mounted, especially after colour came in. Compare the beautiful model filming in 6.5, "The Seeds of Death" to the Cyber-ship in "Revenge of the Cybermen", for example. Experienced directors found ways to offset these tendencies – "Genesis of the Daleks" has no effects other than explosions in the location footage – but the simplest way was to shoot on OB and see what you had while still out on location. This cut down on the "meanwhile, back at Television Centre" tendency of switching between film and VT and allowed CSO material to be inserted *almost* seamlessly. One slight problem was when using stock footage – "The Seeds of Doom" has filmed stop-motion shots of the Krynoid engulfing Chase Manor and one film shot of two fighter planes shooting at it, whereas the filmed location work on "The Hand of Fear" is interrupted by VT of two different jets firing missiles.

There were less obvious benefits to using OB when possible. The camera crews were in a different union and had a different pay-scale, so they could be booked for 12 hours at a stretch out of any 24-hour period. This meant that they didn't need to be paid time-and-a-half for night shoots on top of the usual per diem location payment. There was not only no delay in developing the material generated, but it didn't need a separate editor. (In fact, as with "The Sontaran Experiment", a first edit could be made on location, allowing everyone to see if anything needed fixing there and then.) The amount of available light needed for an OB camera was slightly less, diminishing the complexities of rigging lights or delaying for rain and in most cases lengthening the working day. OB is a lot less sensitive to rain (once the cameras were wrapped up), so a scene such as Sarah meeting Miss Winters and Jellicoe in "Robot" could be shot in conditions that would have halted a filming session.

This is where we came in. By the end of Season Twelve, we'd had one all-film production (7.1, "Spearhead from Space"), one all-VT "conventional" story ("Robot") and one executed entirely on OB ("The Sontaran Experiment"). Within another year, we'd had a story entirely on VT in the studio ("The Brain of Morbius") and a six-part VT/OB story ("The Seeds of Doom"). The bean-counters had hard stats with which to work and almost like-for-like comparisons in the same financial year, cutting down on calculations to account for inflation (see last story's essay).

continued on page 65...

12.3 The Sontaran Experiment

devastated planet have found something to eat and – more interestingly, given what we see of the local landscape – a lot of wood they can burn, make into man-traps and use as implements. People stumble across holes and bumps and lose their footing, but the spindliest, shakiest bunny-eared robot you ever-did-see can move smoothly across the terrain and sneaks up on people whilst making noises a Chumblie would laugh at. Why don't the astronauts hide in whatever magical place they're getting the wood from? Do they think the robot can climb trees? By the same token, wherever Sarah got a branch from, it's not anywhere that can be seen from the transmat circle and we get a panorama view of something like ten miles. But she covers the ground really fast, unseen.

While Sarah keeps her yellow mac on throughout the story, her red wellies turn into leather boots and she's got rid of the sou'wester trousers in favour of blue culottes. She's somehow got her rings back after being frozen on Nerva.

And how does a synestic locking clamp-hatch in his coat pocket protect the Doctor from being shot in the back?

Critique At the time of first transmission, the use of an Outside Broadcast crew to shoot an entire story in the wilds of Devon seemed fresh and contemporary, the sort of thing a lot of dramas and children's shows were doing then. Now it just looks weird. But *Doctor Who* was always intended to look weird, even when mimicking other television of the time. That, more than scaring kids or teaching basic science or history, was what it was intended to do. This picture-quality now looks less obtrusively strange than the peculiar aspect-ratio used for Jodie Whittaker's episodes (and imposes fewer compromises on what the director can show). Younger viewers may find themselves thinking of *Teletubbies*.

It was a practical choice rather than an aesthetic one, but it reinforces a lot of what's in the script. There's a tendency for post-apocalyptic settings to be a bit stagey, to suit the rhetorical, polemical purpose of the author (depending on the nature of the apocalypse in question and how far post we are). Even American films using deserts were given to sermonising. In this case, the dramatic tension surrounding the End of the World is more about who has first dibs on the ruins rather than apportioning blame – solar flares are morally neutral – so we're back in the familiar (to UK viewers) set-up of rugged colonials against an effete elite. Luckily, there's a space-monster to torture everyone before this gets tiresome.

Not making this in a studio or on film enhances the idea that they're all on their own. Compare it to a studio-bound West-Country-after-the-fall play of similar vintage, *Stargazy on Zummerdown*, and the agoraphobia of the moorland location, the way the actors' breath mists, adds a vividness that sells the premise better than any amount of cod-folklore. Bracken and ruins make a more plausible ex-London than any number of effects shots of Battersea Power Station as a smouldering wreck. What it also means is that they needed a practical robot prop and, well, at least it looks unlike any other robot we've seen. It makes groovy noises, which is the main thing.

Here's where the problems start. Rodney Bennett, as we'll see in "The Masque of Mandragora", veers towards theatrical effects, stagecraft, rather than elaborate CSO or post-production technical feats. For most of this story, that works out well, because they can't use any mattes or inlays and it's being edited on the fly in the OB van. But the script calls for Sarah to hallucinate terrifying things happening to her and the resources weren't there for that. The obvious solution might have been to trust the actors, as he did for the rest of the production, but with small children watching they needed to show rather than tell, to give us an idea of what Sarah was seeing rather than simply have Elisabeth Sladen look scared. Rubber snakes won't cut it. For most of the rest, you need three or four viewings to figure out what's supposed to be happening.

That ought not to have been a problem, as this is only a brief section of the story – but with only two episodes, they haven't got time to hang around and this sequence comes in a lull between getting out of the cliffhanger and setting up the finale. Whatever had been on screen at the time when Sarah's having abdabs would have seemed like a bit of a mid-episode sag. Two-part stories have an in-built problem with pacing, as we'll see when Peter Davison takes over. They got away with it in 1975, just, because nine viewers out of ten had forgotten that Linx was from a race called "Sontarans" and missed the significance of the title. Without that surprise, to a modern audience, the whole first episode could be interpreted as stalling but, in fact, it's more eventful and intrigu-

Which is Better – Film or Video?

...continued from page 63

The hardest stat was that in a studio they were producing, on average, 16 minutes of material per day. On film, it was rare to get four minutes a day. Making sure there was an OB crew available on any given day was slightly more complicated than booking a film crew, and particular sequences that had safety or practicality reasons had to be done at Ealing ("Planet of Evil" has a jungle with puddles and a lot of Kirby Wire scenes, for example; "The Creature from the Pit" had a pit into which people had to fall or jump and radio-controlled weeds), but these were rapidly becoming the only reasons to indulge in film. If you had to fork out for it, the justification had to be the things an OB rig wasn't up to, such as placing a small camera in an otherwise inaccessible place (Part One of "The Hand of Fear" looks as if Lennie Mayne was doing exactly that).

Yet ten years later, the received wisdom was that videotape was sick, wrong and evil. People had somehow got it into their heads that even the muzziest 16mm film, under-lit, ineptly-dubbed and wobbly, denoted superior "production values" (a term they'd picked up without knowing exactly what it meant). Part of this was comparison between the imported 35mm-shot series, automatically exotic and cool, with the familiar domestic product. Some of it was because so much of the material made conventionally in electronic studios was disposable. A lot of it was repeating what they'd heard other people say – as far as we can tell, the source for these comments was America, where VT was, as we've said, undeniably inferior.

However, the BBC themselves didn't hesitate to claim that co-production series made on film were more expensive and "lavish". It was part of the sales-pitch with blockbuster documentary series of the late 70s (*The Body in Question*, *James Burke's Connections*, *The Voyages of Charles Darwin*, *Life on Earth* – all in one calendar year). These were made in collaboration with US companies, usually the amusingly-named WGBH Boston[14], so had to be on film for them to be taken seriously in America. Dramas followed suit, especially once Jonathan Powell (the villain of Volume 6) took over the department. By 1980, the pendulum had decisively swung back to film as the hallmark of "quality".

The BBC had even started doing all-film dramas again. As we'll see later in this book, Graham Williams had devised a police-procedural based on regional crime squads but was swapped with Philip Hinchcliffe. The series, now called *Target*, was forced into a *Sweeney*-shaped hole. When this was dropped after two years, his choice of replacement for the notional third series, Robert Banks Stewart, pitched a replacement all-film series in Bristol, *Shoestring*. This was a smash, but when the star quit after two years, he devised a replacement called *Bergerac* that ran for a decade.

With these shows selling overseas, the weekends were soon stuffed with all-film co-production series in rural/ picturesque settings and the only dramas made on VT were soaps and kid's shows. And *Doctor Who* after 1985. The soaps got interesting as *EastEnders* took full advantage of the things OB could do that film / studio mixes couldn't, including some bravura scenes in early episodes where a hand-held camera follows characters from their homes, out across Albert Square and into another building in that giant replica street (usually the laundrette run by Dot Cotton, so they could natter and catch up on plot developments). All in one take with *verité* touches and a righteous dub soundtrack. *Coronation Street* played catch-up, and by 1990 most British soaps were cinematic in everything except for the lack of celluloid. Eventually, even TV critics noticed. The all-film series, now including two-hour cop-shows with delusions of literacy, paradoxically became more theatrical. Critics were even slower to cotton on to this, but sketch-shows had great fun with the formulaic series.

Nonetheless, with production companies deciding that VT was ephemeral and film was prestigious, it became a self-fulfilling prophecy after about five years. As the 1980s wore on, *Doctor Who* was an early-adopter of the sort of fans who send in petitions demanding remakes of things that didn't tick their boxes (you know, the people who re-edited *The Last Jedi* to take out the girls and non-white characters). These people decided – or were persuaded – that the series being made on VT was a calculated insult on the part of the Powers That Be. It became an article of faith among the "Day of Action" crowd (see Volume 6) that whoever they installed once their *JN-T Must Go* campaign had succeeded would make the new series all on film, with monster team-ups every week and Jeremy Brett playing the Doctor whether he wanted to or not. It was asserted as

continued on page 67...

12.3 The Sontaran Experiment

ing than the latter half.

The difference is that Linx was a character – but now we have Sontarans as a species or, this being 70s *Doctor Who*, monsters. Styre and his boss have the same face and voice, but they are in a management/ employee relationship. This supplants the more interesting (well, potentially) Vural-Styre deal we only hear about later. The bit of the story before the Doctor got there is the one with the most scope for drama, with why Roth went "bush" a close second. Baker and Martin get a chance to play to their strengths but without time or elbow-room for their usual excesses. The drawback with this restraint is that they have to colour inside the lines, with few real surprises. Why hire those two to do an unambitious story?

The production's still running on the Letts/ Dicks/ Pertwee model of a stunt sequence per episode and an explosion at the end. The team have figured out that this new Doctor's pretty tasty in a punch-up, so that's where the centre-of-gravity of the second episode will be, which means they think of something for the now-pretty pointless Harry to do and that's why the first episode clips along so nicely. For Part Two, they're coasting towards an ending that has to accommodate this fight (they can't be blamed for how odd it looks – see **The Lore**), so it's pretty much a self-assembly job. The Galsec colonists fade into the background and become Styre-fodder.

What makes this odd is that the "investigation" was the story's starting-point and the reason they were looking for a mediaeval ruin when scouting locations. With all the other opportunities the location and cast opened up, this fell by the wayside and looks dispensable now. Whether you think more overt torture-porn is what ought to be on BBC1 at 5.30pm between *Tom and Jerry* and *The Wonderful World of Disney* is another matter – we'll never know.

The Facts

Written by Bob Baker and Dave Martin. Directed by Rodney Bennett Viewing figures: 11.0 million, 10.5 million. AIs 55 for Part Two. The omnibus repeat the Friday of the week when "Planet of Evil" was repeated got a healthy 8.2 million viewers.

Working Titles "The Destructors" was used right up until they went on location.

Alternate Versions The aforementioned single-episode edit was shown on a Friday after a Monday-Thursday episodic repeat of "Planet of Evil" in the summer of 1976. A 1988 Superchannel broadcast fiddled with the credits but, by and large, overseas buyers either skipped this one or, reading the production codes, showed it *before* "The Ark in Space". Ian Marter's adaptation tweaks a few details (the Doctor dissolved Styre's equipment with neat Scotch), reinstates cut or uncompleted scenes and has the Doctor and company arrive and depart in the TARDIS. This book was published as a stand-alone story a year after Marter's book version of "The Ark in Space", which ended with everyone leaving that way.

Cliffhanger Sarah is alarmed to see someone looking exactly like Linx the Sontaran take his hat off exactly the same way.

What Was In the Charts? "South African Man", Hamilton Bohannon; "If", Telly Savalas.

The Lore

The situation from last story: once it was clear they could do two stories in six episodes rather than one over-long one, and that they could amortise the four-parter's costs by re-using the sets for a different story later, Robert Holmes began putting his own stamp on commissioned stories inherited from the previous regime.

Developing the two-parter entailed long phone calls to Bob Baker and Dave Martin: experienced *Doctor Who* writers at work on other projects recently. They were busy with one of these, HTV's *Sky*, but found it hard to refuse a plea for help. Holmes owned the rights to Linx and the Sontarans and had put a lot of thought into his script for "The Time Warrior" that didn't make it to the screen. As Bob Baker recalls it, there was an absurd of detail about the Sontarans' digestive and reproductive processes, and the disposition of the Third Galactic Fleet, as a stressed script editor gabbled out his thinking on the story. Baker and Martin had an idea of making the future London identifiable with relics, including Nelson's Column sticking up from the ground at an angle and a ruined priory. The latter, developing an idea of a Mediaeval torture-chamber, was to be the story's main setting.

The commission for a treatment was formalised

Which is Better – Film or Video?

...continued from page 65

fact that film was intrinsically better. (Often in the same paragraph where, someone would state that everything should be like "The Talons of Weng-Chiang", ignoring that most of the location work in that was on OB.) Was being made in multi-camera studios in Television Centre really such a problem?

Exhibit A in a lot of these jeremiads was "The Mark of the Rani" (22.3). The locations were a working museum of Industrial Revolution-era mining and a patch of woodland, in October drizzle, but the result looked luscious and cinematic. When it got into the studio, however, things rather fell apart. The technical staff treated *Doctor Who* much as they treated anything else and lit it like a sitcom. It appears, from interviews, that the old-timers pulled rank on this story's director, Sarah Hellings. When a director does make the studio material and filmed footage in synch, the difference is less grating – with "Destiny of the Daleks", Ken Grieve was given a SteadiCam to play with and sought to make the less lightweight turret cameras in TC3 flow, shooting the Daleks from low angles, as on location. This led to sets with ceilings, so an entirely novel lighting arrangement had to be devised, oddly like that of "Genesis of the Daleks", and the story's two methods of manufacture seemed more harmonious. The heavier, less mobile cameras of the 70s were slowly being replaced and, when time allowed, camera-angles and movement were more flexible. Yet, if it was lit like *The Two Ronnies*, a director couldn't do much except write memos after the fact. One of the interesting features of Philip Hinchcliffe's term as producer is how often the directors and he stayed on the right side of the lighting crew – even attempting to get Brian Clemett a *Radio Times* credit for his contribution to "Planet of Evil".

The main problem with OB, film or Field-Removed has been the end of detailed rehearsals. As we proceed through this volume, you might care to note all the times when the director and the cast, between the pre-filming and the studio, worked out a specific line, memorable scene or the resolution of a clumsy bit of plotting. The cast got to bond, or not, and key decisions were made. (Sometimes, the most significant ones came after filmed material, so there were anomalies – check how Jamie's accent alters between the location work for 4.5, "The Underwater Menace" and the studio material and every subsequent episode.) Pre-filmed scenes with no rehearsal and sometimes with the actors not fully aware of the story as a whole, affect the performances. When the locations came before the read-through, the cast had to busk.

Eventually, the rise of Field-Removed Video, so-called "film-look", meant that there was a cheap format that the public could be persuaded was "classy" – but which could, like any other videotape, be rewound and wiped if necessary and edited almost in real-time. The thing that did disappear wasn't videotape *per se*, it was the gallery-directed multi-camera approach and long periods of rehearsal. Attempts to reconfigure, re-grade and generally filmify McCoy stories for the DVD releases hardly made the case that 26.3, "The Curse of Fenric" would have looked any better on film, even though it was made on a one-camera location shoot as with a filmed story. The one all-film story of the original run was "Spearhead from Space" and its studio scenes look and sound disjointed and stagey, even as the location interior shots are dynamic in a way they might not have been if attempted in Television Centre. (The TV Movie, achieved on 35mm, suffers from the then-fashionable orange and teal lighting.)

Film, done properly, is capable of greater subtlety of tone and colour. Within BBC dramas in the 1970s, it was rare to see it done that well, even with the experienced and almost-magical cameramen of the era, simply because it was 16mm stock and overcast. Prior to "The Invisible Enemy", model shots were rarely lit at all adequately. The flip-side of the tendency we noted when discussing "Robot" and rain is that there was a one-size-fits-all range of hue and intensity with OB regardless of local lighting conditions. Electronic studios tended to use overhead lighting to the exclusion of all else and, to stay within accepted broadcasting standards, rarely went below a fairly high level of illumination.

But which is "better"? That's largely down to fashion, individual taste (or prejudice) and suitability for the specific task in hand. For most of the mid-1970s, this was conditioned by the needs of the production, rather than just budget or sales-pitch. While we might wish that an OB crew had been dispatched to Bristol for the location shoot of "The Sun Makers" (15.4), making those epic corridors seem contiguous with the studio ones, it wouldn't alter the curious office sets and costume decisions. What does seem to have set viewers' teeth on edge is clumsily switching between the two, without a narrative justification for the abrupt change in aesthetic.

12.3 The Sontaran Experiment

on 23rd May and the first episode was formally commissioned at the start of June, even while the treatment was being thrashed out. That happened on 12th June, the day after Rodney Bennett was hired for the two stories. Within a week of this, the Christopher Langley version of "Space Station" was dropped. In early July, the second episode was commissioned and the first had been delivered. Hinchcliffe sought Letts's advice on the practicalities of sets and budgets (and getting things done the BBC way). Ten days after the first script came in, Letts was hinting that Styre's lean-to would take a while and require more people to be sent to the location.

At around the same time, Holmes sent Baker and Martin his comments, most of which were about making Weam Styre (as he was apparently called) more Sontaran-ish. This applied to the second episode as well. The scripts still had a lot of ideas about things you'd find in priories, including a wine-press as a torture device, but Hinchcliffe thought it would be simpler (and more logical) to have the Sontaran bring his own equipment and simply make a base on location. This meant losing a scene with a suit of armour, the breastplate of which would have protected the Doctor against Styre's gun. As Holmes fixed "Ark", he added the synestic lock to replace the armour. As was his wont, he dotted the script-changes with references to old film stars, comparing the Doctor's challenge to Styre and heroic stance to Errol Flynn (see also "Revenge of the Cybermen" and "The Android Invasion" for comments about James Cagney's OTT death-scenes).

- Baker and Martin were fresh from working on *Sky* (which, being made by cheapo ITV regional station HTV West, was largely filmed around their base in Bristol and had a more hands-on approach to involving writers – they probably had to make sandwiches and tea for the camera crew). They'd been to Dartmoor recently and proposed it in the scripts as an idea of what the blasted heath might look like. Meanwhile, the production assistant, Marion McDougall, confirmed that Dartmoor would make an ideal location and proposed two main sites. The production unit manager, George Gallaccio, proposed that with so many other high profile dramas now using the Outside Broadcast rig, they could use this story to see how well it suited *Doctor Who*.

- Two hitherto-uncredited ex-assistants, Tony Oxley and John Friedlander, did the effects work for this two-story block. By and large, Friedlander made the monsters and aliens while Oxley handled the zap-guns and spaceships, but the split isn't as clear in these two stories. Oxley's big problem was that the OB recording plan ruled out CSO or any elaborate pre-filmed scenes for the two-part story, so the guns had to have practical charges and the robot needed to be physically there, trundling across moss and rocks. (Of course, not using CSO meant a shiny robot wouldn't lose bits the way the Robot and the Whomobile had in effects shots.)

- Hinchcliffe and Bennett went to the proposed section of Exmoor National Park and found Hound Tor, some of a ruined mediaeval township. This prompted a few more rewrites to suit the locale (and to write out the robot, a loose end in the hasty scripting). The plan had always been to make the story more like a film, saving most of the rehearsal for when they were on location, but there was a five-day spell after the read-through in Acton on 17th September. A skeleton crew and the principal cast took trains to Devon on 23rd to start three days of on-site rehearsal and familiarisation, based at a hotel in Chagford. Those involved were advised to bring a thick coat, stout shoes and changes of socks. For Sladen and Baker, this was the start of an almost continuous schedule until July, mostly out-of-sequence (check the Production Codes).

- Sladen took advantage of the scenario of Our Heroes not knowing what Earth would be like to dress in practical clothing. Terry Walsh had mentioned the possibility of adders in the moors, so Sladen kept her oilskins and wellies on for all scenes until the end. (She kept this get-up for gardening well into later life.)

- The first day was working at Postbridge, the open moorland location, then the 24th was for Hound Tor, the rocky hillock that replaced the ruined priory (although parts of this location were identified by the function, so there were "dungeons", a "street" and a "staircase"). After his turn as Linx, Kevin Lindsay was the obvious choice to play Styre and the Marshal, but his newly-diagnosed heart-murmur meant that the schedule was kept light and his make-up was made less oppressive. Only one scene was scripted to have him wear the helmet over the mask and a second costume, without mask, was made for Stuart Fell for some of the more arduous dialogue-free scenes, notably the fight. In a move away from the

Letts way of doing things, Hinchcliffe was keen to have one key stunt performer – generally Terry Walsh, physically a good match for Baker – and a few ancillaries when needed. Indeed, in the shooting script, Zake is just identified as "Terry".

- Between the end of the rehearsal recce and the start of shooting, Hinchcliffe, Letts and the camera crew arrived (and Lindsay took a break). Then on 25th, recording started at Headland Warren Farm, Postbridge, with the first and last scenes of the story and Sarah's undignified arrival in the gorse. Hinchcliffe, about to turn 30, was presented with hand-knitted baby bootees to mark him formally stepping into Letts's shoes.

The team had two lightweight cameras, one used as a hand-held, the other on a tripod. Usually, when used on location, the cameras came with Elemack tracks, the miniature railway used for dolly-shots, and these were used to help the robot glide across gorse and boulders. Some scenes were recorded with both cameras at once, as in a studio shoot. Fitted as standard in the control van was one of the prized video-disc machines used for action-replays in sport broadcasts; you will recall how these were used to great effect in productions such as "The Claws of Axos" (8.3) and how *Doctor Who* had been at the back of the queue for these – often borrowing them and asking permission afterwards. (You may also recall the van itself used as UNIT's mobile HQ.) Another small saving came by re-using *Moonbase 3* space-suits.

- Early on in the shoot, the weather had mainly been crisp, cold and sunny, as autumn often is in England. Just this once, the now-routine shooting schedule for *Doctor Who* had worked in everyone's favour; not making the series over the summer had spared them the miserable wet weather for which June-September 1974 is remembered. 29th October, however, was a return to these soggy conditions, although another advantage of OB was that this was less obvious in the finished footage. This was the day recording moved to Hound Tor for various scenes of torture and imprisonment. Brian Ellis got all of his scenes on tape in one day. Sladen had a sort of nappy/diaper to withstand a long period sat in damp grass. The box containing the force-field generator was intended to melt (Baker and Martin had outlined one cheap way to do it in their script).

Styre was meant to have several expository speeches on this day but, that afternoon, Baker slipped on the wet grass and fell heavily on his left shoulder. Sladen, still over at the torture-site location, heard a loud snap. Recording stopped as the Doctor's scarf, which had taken some of the force, was repurposed as a sling to prevent his arm moving on a long drive across bumpy moorland to Exeter for X-rays. Roger Murray-Leach, the set designer, had been on location to supervise the video-console (which was, if you didn't spot it, a retrofitted spherical chair) and to set up the spaceship. This was kept from the last Sontaran story, but the door opened the other way now. He volunteered to follow the ambulance on its 90-minute journey, stay with the distraught Baker (who was anxious that, as he'd not been seen by the public, they would recast the Doctor) and tell the crew what was happening. The star and the designer bonded in A&E and would soon be doing the *Times* crossword together (this, as we'll see, was Baker's highest compliment). It was a fractured collar-bone, so a bit of reworking made the rest of the shoot possible. Luckily, the costume department had augmented the Doctor's costume with a bulky overcoat, so you have to look hard to spot which scenes have Baker in a cast.

- Monday 30th began with Baker getting back in the saddle. The majority of the morning was spent on the fight between the two stunt doubles, with Walsh and Fell doubling for Baker and Lindsay. Baker recorded close-up inserts for this while sat in a chair. It was supposed to be a bit like Kendo, but there were concerns about the suit's liability to tear. Lindsay and the Galsec cast performed an expanded scene where Styre explains the "test" procedures (rather than us coming in halfway) to cover for one of the lost scenes.

- October began at the spaceship area. For the climax, no actual spaceships were harmed. There was a shot of the ship, another of the ship in pieces and a bang and a flash – the police in Exeter heard the bang and came to have a look. Styre's death was pretty much what it looks like: a balloon inside the mask was slowly deflated. As they had the mobile control for the OB equipment on hand, there was a chance to edit on location, so a version of Part Two was assembled. It was over-running even without the titles.

- Shortly after filming this story, Terry Walsh completed the process he began in "The Monster of Peladon" by appearing in the BBC1 panto *Aladdin* and – speaking lines deliberately, at last – played the Pertwee Doctor with Pan's People as his "assistants". (See **Cultural Primer:** *Top of the Pops* under "The Robots of Death" for how oddly

12.3: The Sontaran Experiment

apt and singularly wrong this all is.) It was shown on Christmas Eve and was basically an extended edition of *Crackerjack* – pause for you to all shout it – with the Goodies plugging their single and Richard Wattis as Wishee Washee. (We have a whole essay on Panto with 17.5, "The Horns of Nimon".)

- The story was dubbed early in the new year. As you might be able to tell, the slurping sound of the mud crawling up Sarah's leg is Dick Mills squelching his hands in a bowl of Swarfega, then slowing down the recording – an effect he enthusiastically recreated on *Blue Peter* when demonstrating his tricks of the trade (see "The Talons of Weng-Chiang" and the essay with 17.4, "Nightmare of Eden").

- The *Radio Times* just had a small black and white photo of Baker for this story's launch. Most people remembered Linx but not the name "Sontaran", so the cliffhanger was a surprise even with the name-change. The day Part One was shown began with a clip of "Death to the Daleks" (11.3) used in children's quiz *Play It Again*. (Like the film quiz *Screen Test*, it entailed watching a clip closely and answering questions – in this case the Doctor's cracking the code to get into the Exxilon City, then questions such as "in which country did the Doctor claim to have seen a similar building?".) The Equity agreement that had prevented old stories from being shown after the lead was recast seems not to have bothered anyone.

- The new Doctor was still meeting some resistance among viewers but, with ITV's regional stations adopting a scattershot approach to scheduling around 5.30pm (everything from *Black Beauty* to reruns of forgotten show *The Adventurer* – a last-gasp ITC reworking of *Burke's Law* – and ATV's semi-hit *New Faces* competing with Anglia's *Sale of the Century*, plus Yorkshire showing *Carry on Follow That Camel* and one region persevering with *Kung Fu*), ratings were retaining their buoyancy after "The Ark in Space".

12.4: "Genesis of the Daleks"

(Serial 4E, Six Episodes, 8th March – 12th April 1975.)

Which One is This? Heeeeeere's Davros! The Doctor's on a mission to stop the Daleks from being created (which just annoys them), and Terry Nation finally lives up to his own hype.

Firsts and Lasts Apart from Davros making his debut, this is the first time Daleks shoot directional rays rather than doing something with their guns that made the whole picture go into negative. A year after getting the part, the new Doctor appears on film and visits his first quarry location. Sarah's apparently fatal fall at the end of Part Two is the first time a freeze-frame is used as a cliffhanger. With the Time Lord giving the Doctor a mission because one potential timeline ends with the Daleks dominating the entire cosmos, many retroactively view this story as the opening salvo in the Time War (see Volume 7 and after, plus the essay herewith). It may be significant, therefore, that we never see any Thals after this.

It's also the first story to be made available on audio, as an LP released in 1979 – so, quite apart from all the times it's been repeated on BBC television, it was the first to be committed to memory the way *Derek and Clive* or *Monty Python* sketches were. The cast were, of course, unaware of this – but all enunciate as if on radio, so certain lines have an in-built quotability that was amplified by being played over and again (all together now: *Yooooou! Are! In! SA-A-Ane, Davros!*)

At least as important as all of these, though, this is the first story recorded after Tom Baker has appeared on screen as the Doctor. He is, to put it mildly, a lot more self-confident from now on.

Six Things to Notice About "Genesis of the Daleks"...

- We've had stories where the Time Lords were a plot-function to allow adventures set somewhere other than UNIT-land (8.4, "Colony in Space"; 9.4, "The Mutants") but never as flagrantly as this. The Doctor is sent to somewhere that we've just seen is like World War I, given all the info-dumping we (and he) need and handed a Plot Coupon: the Time Ring, explained to him the way Q does to Bond. The spiel's disguised as Ingmar Bergman, but one feels the dialogue ought to end "… should you, for any reason, fail in your mission, the High Council will disavow all knowledge of your activities. This Time Lord will self-destruct in five seconds…"

- This is indicative of the story as a whole. For all that we've inherited a sense of this story as a Shavian drama-of-ideas, the basic structure is the Letts-Dicks formula. Each episode has an action set-piece, a fight (that's a different thing), a debate about ethics, something icky and / or scary, some

Has the Time War Started?

Once it had been spelled out to us that the Time War that destroyed Gallifrey had been between the Time Lords and the Daleks, a lot of people jumped to the conclusion that the opening salvo was the mission the Doctor undertook for his people to change, prevent or investigate the creation of their antagonists. It made sense: it was the one time the Time Lords had acknowledged the Daleks as a significant threat; it's the *only* occasion where they have ordered him to alter an established history he had personally experienced; it is the one time they have explicitly acted to forestall a foreseen event in what they think of as the future; above all, it's a very memorable scene in a story routinely voted Best Ever.

With Russell T. Davies making no bones about his wanting to leave the actual war to everyone's imaginations, it seemed that the only on-screen incidents we could know would be the set-up, the process by which Davros took his troops from being mere survivors of a previous war, barely able to stand up to the Thals or the Movellans (the *Movellans!*), to worthy opponents for the most powerful race in the cosmos. Logically, if these Daleks still hadn't achieved proper time travel and needed the Hand of Omega to have a fighting chance, they couldn't possibly participate in the war we were learning about from hints and breadcrumbs in the dialogue. "Remembrance of the Daleks" (25.1) was about their failure to obtain the vital missing piece of technology and what it cost them even to try. The conflict between two rival Dalek factions was because only one had the capacity to alter their genetic make-up, something we knew from "The Two Doctors" (22.4) was equally important if they wanted to get beyond mere time corridor "visits" to the past. The original Daleks held to an idea of "purity" that made the Hand of Omega a weapon to be used to blow up stars, with no other purpose, and important mainly because it prevented the Davros's "Imperial" faction from getting it and changing their own past (or blowing up a star near where they were).

To clarify, for those who've not read Volume 3 recently, what the Time Lords, the Time War-era Daleks and a select few other species can do is travel to other times and alter events. Our conjecture, substantiated by subsequent broadcast stories and not so far invalidated, is that the presence of a TARDIS or suitably-augmented Dalek "softens" events, even if the locus of those events is a Fixed Point. Other methods of Time Travel allow visitors to observe events, hide objects in the past or become part of pre-established sequences of events that were always "destined" to be that way. The older versions of the Daleks could make the *Mary Celeste*'s crew jump ship as history dictated (2.8, "The Chase"), secrete samples of the Movellan virus in 1980's Docklands (21.4, "Resurrection of the Daleks") or steal the TARDIS in 1966 (4.9, "The Evil of the Daleks"), but it was only the Doctor's presence that made the outcome of the bombing of Auderly House at all contingent. (9.1, "Day of the Daleks". Well, all right, the Master and his TARDIS were somewhere in the vicinity too.)

Time Agents equipped with Vortex Manipulators – that, apparently, anyone can use if they can work out the controls and base-codes – are apparently all about making sure nothing untoward occurs in the past (relative to the fifty-first century, at least – that's not where the technology originates, but it's when they started recruiting humans, according to X3.13, "Last of the Time Lords"), but don't intervene. (It's hard to say exactly what in fact the Agents *do*, as we've not knowingly encountered one – but we've met one ex-agent in *Doctor Who* and another in *Torchwood*, neither of whom is a great advertisement for this body. Captain Jack coming from the fifty-first century was, as we've stated, founded in a slight misreading of the dialogue from "Talons", but it's had so many consequences, it's had to be retconned into the grand scheme of things.) At close of play in 1989, the (relatively) beefed-up Imperial Daleks were no match even for the clueless old duffers on Gallifrey we'd seen in 20.1, "Arc of Infinity'" The Sontarans were a better bet for taking on the Time Lords; they'd invaded Gallifrey and latched on to the idea that gaps in their biology needed plugging (15.6, "The Invasion of Time"; "The Two Doctors").

At first sight, therefore, the argument that "Genesis of the Daleks" is part of the Time War and not a *casus belli* for a later conflict doesn't really work. But we're still at a loss to adequately explain what a "Time War" entails. In stories by Steven Moffat, it's mainly just a series of battles with conventional weapons fought across history, culminating in one in Gallifrey's second city, Arcadia. Davies seems to have in mind something more akin to the ones in mid-twentieth-century novels where agents pre-emptively alter events to prevent "later" defeats. In this, people die and are resurrected to die again, endlessly, while almost

continued on page 73...

12.4 Genesis of the Daleks

running around and getting locked up and a "moment of charm". There are landmines, rocket launches and nasty things in vats. There are giant clams. Twice. Gharman aside, the good guys wear white and the bad guys are in black, with jodhpurs and jackboots. Compared to the formal oddities of "The Sontaran Experiment" and the conceptual shock of "The Ark in Space", this is much more like what the kids were expecting. It's an adventure serial, made to fill 25 minutes every Saturday. Watching it all in one go, unedited, reveals this starkly.

- As if to confirm that Terry Nation's voice really was the predominant one in this script, the first episode ends with the first glimpse of a Dalek (admittedly, the first glimpse *anyone* had). However, that's overshadowed by the same scene's big revelation: Davros himself. It was such an intuitively obvious idea – a half-Dalek man who's like Hitler and Baron Frankenstein and perpetuating his ego through his "children" – that the fact that the Daleks themselves are only in about 15 minutes of the 150-minute running-time almost passes unnoticed, especially as they are parcelled out to a cameo each episode until the climax. Those cameos, in the later episodes, are as brutal as anything we've seen since the end of "The Power of the Daleks" (4.3).

- When this is edited for an LP or omnibus repeat, the speeches get priority and everything more orthodox is pared to the minimum. That's as it should be because they are unprecedentedly intense: the sort of thing Jon Pertwee would get in the last episode of a story is normal throughout, and it's mainly the baddie who gets the best rhetoric. The Doctor gets his moment of doubt, true, but Davros rants like a Dalek (it gets close to blank verse at times), using the old Greco-Roman tricks the way Churchill and Kennedy did. He makes superficially reasonable and coherent cases for ruthless actions and his own fanatical ambition. He uses the language of nuclear deterrence as a case for the Daleks as the means to ensure peace. He offers a Darwinian argument for the Daleks as the best chance for something of his race to survive. Worst of all, his Daleks and the Thal missile are the nearest thing to hope anyone on this planet has to offer.

- Davros develops most of his ideas in conversation with either the Doctor or, more usually, Nyder (who is almost Smithers to Davros's Monty Burns; there's even an "excellent"). Nyder acts as his muscle, coshing people with merry abandon[15], and his death is the sign that Davros has lost. In later stories, Davros will develop other moods and tell people what they want to hear, but the only time we see him pour on the charm here is when apparently agreeing to Mogran's terms. This is the incident that leads to both races being wiped out in a day and, although it's not often stated in these terms, it's entirely the result of the Doctor's speech to the Kaled leadership.

- Over all of this is a layer of visuals unlike anything we've seen for a while. David Maloney's cine-literate touches in the opening scenes are fairly obvious but pay attention also to the studio lighting. Unlike earlier all-metallic sets, the one for Davros's lab isn't in-your-face shiny but nuanced and textured. The Daleks are usually announced by their shadows (and Dudley Simpson's striking music, of course). It's directional, rather than all top-down illumination, and often coloured for practical, narrative reasons but accentuating the mood. They're not just hiding flaws in the set and Dalek shells (although that helps, especially if you see the rehearsal photos), they are making a virtue of the contrasts.

The Continuity

The Doctor The Time Lord coercing him to change history had him at 'Daleks'. When interrogated by scientists, he learns more from them than they do from him, even though he apparently does all the talking. Being electrocuted leaves him with black eyes. When stopping to think before "irrevocably" preventing the Daleks from being, the massive amount of responsibility on his shoulders gives him pause. [As we will see, especially in 16.6, "The Armageddon Factor", he doesn't trust himself with power.]

[We now have some idea that the Time Lords' information system, the Matrix, comprises millions of eye-witness accounts (23.1, "The Mysterious Planet", for example) and that the presence of a Time Lord unfixes history to some extent (**How Does Time Work?** under 9.1, "Day of the Daleks"). The Doctor's delay in leaving once he had recovered the Time Ring a second time could be a way to allow changes and for the Time Lords to gather information – part of the brief he was given at the start.]

- *Ethics*. Well, as even people who never watch *Doctor Who* seem to know, the Doctor's given the

Has the Time War Started?

...continued from page 71

literally unimaginable entities with bizarre names are mentioned in passing whenever the Doctor recalls the horrors of this sealed-off nightmare. The exact nature of this "seal" is confused, with even the Doctor admitting that his metaphors don't work, but the effect for stories shown to us between 2005 and 2011 is that this entire conflict could be treated as a separate continuum.

However, the plots of the stories that told us about this, "The Stolen Earth" and "The End of Time" (X4.12, X4.17-4.18) need there to be a cat flap in and out of this sealed-off "bubble". If Dalek Caan could get in and rescue Davros, and Spitty Rassilon could chuck a diamond into a picture of Earth and send it to be found by the Master's Seven Continent Army, is there a logical reason why the mysterious Time Lord with the odd hood who gives the fourth Doctor his mission at the start of "Genesis" can't be from within the Time-War-as-recognised and altering even the events that started it?

The thing about a Davies-model Time War (a "Change War" in the terms afforded by the most famous precursor, Fritz Leiber's stories and the novel *The Big Time*) is that the object for either side is to prevent the war from even starting in the first place. Interfering with the creation of your enemies is an obvious place to start and using a future Lord President – the person who ended the War-as-they-know-it and was mentioned in all the scrolls the Visionary has on the Last Day – gives you plausible deniability and a massive paradox if anything goes wrong. It could be that the Time Lords who were stuck in an unending war reached back into the Doctor's past to find a nice gap where they could slot a trip to Skaro with able companions who'd be of more use to him than Jo or Adric.

Aesthetics aside, there are two massive problems with that hypothesis: why wasn't anyone *else* from the Time War there, given that this bit of Skaro's history ought to have been the single most rewritten part of the war, and why this particular version of the Doctor?

That second point is especially baffling: looking at all the pre-Time War Doctors, any of them might have been a better choice than the one with the scarf. The original might have been a bit shaky on his feet, but the Daleks helped make him rethink his life and become Earth's defender and a crusader for good and right, rather than just a detached observer. The next one would cheerfully have committed genocide and then handed round gobstoppers – in fact, he thought he had (we'll get back to "the final end" in "The Evil of the Daleks" soon). In "The Two Doctors", it's this one who's keen to re-ingratiate himself with the Time Lords (although which and from when is unclear – see **Was There a Season 6B?** under that story). The frilly-shirted ponce would have made all the right noises about respect for all life, then obliterated the Daleks while making another speech about how they are everything he's against. The cricketer entered a room determined to shoot Davros in cold blood (but he and his successor were nominally President). Then we got one who went to great lengths to trick the Daleks, the Cybermen, the Master and a lot of unfamiliar enemies into defeating themselves and dispassionately watched Skaro burn and the Cyber-fleet get wiped out. Instead of any of those, Hoodie-Man seems to have selected the one Doctor who would have doubts about the ethics of preventing the Daleks and who respected the rights of robots and smart viruses.

Maybe he wasn't *supposed* to wipe the Daleks out. The main effect that this sortie into Skaro's past had was that the Doctor and Davros knew each other. In most subsequent stories where they meet, it seems as if Davros has encountered several Time Lords but only takes the Doctor seriously. Once they *have* met, it's another 30 years before we get a Dalek story without Davros in (unless you count the opening to the TV Movie and *The Curse of Fatal Death*) and he's literally wheeled on at the end of Series Four to raise the stakes. As well as being a tactical and ethical problem for the Doctor, the Daleks are now symptoms of an obsession besetting someone he admires and pities. As a result, he knows more about the Daleks than any living Time Lord, and now he's been President, *and* the High Council has bugged his TARDIS and all that intel's in the Matrix.

Similarly, the Daleks remain a Doctor-sized threat even as the Doctor goes from eccentric old man in a box to Time's Champion, matching him step-for-step as his abilities and legend increase. Whenever the Time War started within the Doctor's lifetime, the simple fact that it began after all of these encounters with not-yet-ready Daleks and an ambitious-but-fallible Davros gave Gallifrey the edge, once the Doctor decided to

continued on page 75...

12.4 Genesis of the Daleks

chance to prevent the Daleks' creation and hesitates. It's partly the cold-bloodedness of the genocide, partly concern for the rest of the cosmos if he makes *that* big a change to history, but mainly it's what such an act would do to him as a person. [We'll see more of this between 2005 and 2013, especially a near-repeat in X1.13, "The Parting of the Ways". Moreover, even when told up front that the Time Lords saw a future with no other life-form permitted if the Daleks got their way, he doubts that even the High Council ordering him to do it (if it *was* them) absolves him. This is, in the light of later events detailed in this volume, understandable – but he will later ("The Hand of Fear") fall back on his oath to preserve the rights of lesser species in the face of superior power as an excuse not to rock the boat.]

What even repeat viewers tend to overlook is that – at the end of that same episode – he in fact rewires the explosives and blows the Dalek hatchery to smithereens. [What changed in the interim? First and foremost, there's a huge reversal of fortune when the Daleks gun down Gharman and his supporters. The Doctor had expressed relief at letting Gharman and company curtail the Daleks' development – he was happy enough to alter the Daleks' creation if that decision came internally, from within the Kaled ranks. (He also saw a shoddy-looking Total Destruct button, so thought at one point that there was a Plan B. Davros apparently died trying to use it.) But with their deaths and the Daleks looking triumphant, the Doctor cannot escape deciding the fate of the Dalek embryos. Arguably, with so much free will removed, these Daleks are – to some extent – on the same moral plane as a virus. Even then, with seven fully-operational Daleks roaming the Bunker and the automated plant operational, the Doctor considers the bomb in the hatchery a delaying tactic, not the Daleks' final end, and merely sets them back a thousand years. (If at all. See **Things That Don't Make Sense** for more on this.)]

• *Inventory:*

– *Sonic Screwdriver*. For some reason, the Doctor doesn't try it on the locked door to Davros's office. [Maybe Davros invented the frequently-used BBC Wales standby of the 'deadlock seal'. We're not being entirely flippant: when stepping up Dalek production, Davros demands that 'all other research must cease', suggesting that they had other irons in the fire. As we'll see in **Things That Don't Make Sense**, security measures on both sides need work.] The screwdriver does blow up a communications console with just a wave of the hand.

– *Time Ring*. The Time Lord supplies the Doctor with a get-out-of-jail card for this story: a large copper/gold bracelet, about 6cm deep and 3mm thick [i.e. like the *Blakes 7* teleport bracelet] with a trefoil in the same material stuck on it. It's supposed to return him and his friends to the TARDIS when the mission is complete. [It sort of does; see next story.] The Doctor seemingly couldn't identify the Time Ring on sight and needed his "operator" to explain its set-up. Later, unprompted, he knows how to activate it. [In the next story, he also knows what it will do after they are transposed to Nerva Beacon. Either this is standard Gallifreyan tech in a different design or there's a telepathic walk-through when you put it on.]

– *Other.* He has the yellow yo-yo, a bag of jellybabies, what he identifies as an 'etheric beam locator', a jeweller's eyeglass, a Sherlock Holmes magnifying-glass, a set of handcuffs, an amber lump [possibly Trisilicate – 11.4, "The Monster of Peladon"], the telescope, a conventional pen-torch [see Volumes 1 and 2] and his permits from "Robot" (the Mars-Venus licence is blue, his Alpha Centauri Table-Tennis Club membership green, his wallet of passports yellow). In Part Six, there's also a rectangular object that could be a cigarette-case, a hand-mirror or an iPhone.

The Time Lords This is the most overt intervention we've seen, presented as a crisis for them. They have foreseen a timeline in which the Daleks are the dominant life-form in the cosmos, having eradicated all others, and have decided to prevent this. They assume the Doctor's consent enough to pre-empt his objections and intercept his transmat beam, transferring him and his friends directly to Skaro at the crucial time. The Doctor appears to know the Time Lord giving him the mission. [In "The Deadly Assassin", we learn that the Celestial Intervention Agency coordinates such exploits, not the main body of Time Lords. The Doctor seems to have been beneath their notice. We will elaborate on all of this in the attached essay.]

The Time Lords mastered transmat technology when the universe 'was less than half its present size'. [Given a constant expansion, that would be seven billion years ago, but – as we've speculated

Has the Time War Started?

...continued from page 73

participate and end the War one way or another. Assuming that some future-Daleks would come along and rewrite any rewrites of the Daleks' birth with extreme prejudice, this low-impact visit by the Doctor makes sense as a fact-finding mission – especially as those facts remain true because later Daleks don't consider it worth intervening. The Doctor's main effect was to accelerate Davros's plan by prompting him to give the Thals the formula to breach the Kaled Dome, by getting Mogran and the Kaled leadership to treat the Daleks as a problem. Both sides have every reason to keep the events in this story exactly as we see them.

If the "first draft" of these events is a sort of temporal No Man's Land, it is, by definition, not "in" the Time War (even if Hoodie-Man and his superiors, who sent the Doctor in, were). Time-travelling combatants or their agents might have redrafted subsequent events – but not, it appears, when the Doctor was present. Every Dalek story we've seen appears to have played out as we saw it, even after the Time War's end. That's odder the more you think about it. The pre-Time War version of this very book had an essay about how Dalek history was malleable and, despite our mission-brief to present the whole of *Doctor Who* 1963-89 as having a coherent single timeline, we were forced to conclude that the thousand-year setback at the end of "Genesis" affected every previous Dalek story. Even a fudge such as interpreting the Doctor's "thousand year" estimate was enough to make us mumble and change the subject (as when we tried to get the Earth Empire chronology to work without 10.3, "Frontier in Space", a story that's a consequence of Dalek chicanery).

Had we been writing this any time between 2005 and 2012, we would have accepted that the whole Dalek chronology we had worked out was now redundant. Then came X7,1, "Asylum of the Daleks" and a whole planet full of veterans of old campaigns and lost episodes, not to mention X9.1, "The Magician's Apprentice", where Davros was whiling away his last days watching old episodes (except, intriguingly, 17.1, "Destiny of the Daleks"). The Daleks in that were predominantly the Time War model, but blue-bobbled steel ones from the 60s were milling about. Even as these two stories contradicted each other, they confirmed that almost every Dalek story outside the Time War was still in play.

So even after this apocalyptic Time War, the events concerning pre-upgrade Daleks are as they were. That's odd. So's the fact that Davros has a terrifying childhood incident that ends with the Doctor rescuing him. If the incidents within this "bubble" are time-locked and sacrosanct, logically so must be the infancy and childhood of the most significant figure in Dalek pre-history and their rise to time-sensitive puissance. Yet not only is this delicate bit of history available for any time traveller to alter (or not), it and the old stories are exempt from whatever freakish force keeps the actual Time War out of reach (until it isn't).

One possibility is that the stories remain as we saw them but *not* as the Doctor originally experienced them. What we got to see were the post-Time War rewritten accounts (see **Who Narrates This Series?** under 23.1, "The Mysterious Planet"). This gets us into all sorts of gnarly epistemological and ontological issues – but suppose, for a moment, that 4.3, "The Power of the Daleks" had played out as we saw it (or, for younger readers, as the soundtrack, telesnaps and animation convey it), *except* that the Dalek that Lesterson demonstrates didn't recognise the newly-regenerated Doctor. Apart from removing a really good cliffhanger and delaying Ben's acceptance of this newcomer as the Doctor, not much changes – but with that scene as written, we have a lot of questions about how a Dalek who's been in suspended animation since 200 years before an Earth colony found it knew the Doctor on sight.

The easiest way out is that it was lost when a Dalek taskforce went to 1866 to set a trap for a Doctor, one they knew from another source. (The interrogation in "Day of the Daleks" seems to be the first time the penny drops that all three of their Great-est En-e-mies are the same person, so there's already some time-travel shenanigans afoot.) If the story happened exactly as broadcast in 1966, then this whole timeline with "The Final End" six months later is in play, even if "The Evil of the Daleks" appears to have been erased from their history (and that's a big "if"; bigger now than it was in 2004). Preventing "Evil" from happening doesn't remove Victoria from subsequent stories, it seems. Just as well, since altering those stories means no UNIT. (We went into all of this in **Was There a Martian Time-Slip?** under X4.16, "The Waters of Mars" and we'll pick up on it with one of the stories that seemingly disappear under the

continued on page 77...

before – they may have put the brakes on the red shift. See 18.7, "Logopolis" and **Why Hide Here?** under X3.11, "Utopia". If we posit a nice round figure like five billion years, the dates make a nice match with the removal of Huon particles (X3.0, "The Runaway Bride") and, according to some physicists, a real-world slowdown in the rate of expansion seems to have taken place in the early cosmos.]

The Supporting Cast
- *Sarah* isn't good with heights [see also 21.7, "The Five Doctors" and *SJA* 1.5, "Whatever Happened to Sarah Jane?"]. She's familiar with revolvers [even alien ones]. Faced with certain death if she stays in the Thal launch-site, she stages a break-out.

She spends most of the story in the leftover clothes from "The Sontaran Experiment" [thus, in the first two episodes, looking like a trial-run for Jodie Whittaker]. Conveniently, someone in the Kaled Bunker left her a change of clobber, so she's ready for "Revenge of the Cybermen" in tight camouflage jeans, a fawn top with big buttons and a Harry Hill collar and a green jacket very like what the Thals were wearing.

- *Harry.* Judging by his ability to catch pistols, he wasn't boasting about his cricketing skills six episodes ago. He exercises a stern sort of calm when ordering the Doctor to let him shore up the landmine on which the Time Lord has trodden. He can duff up a security guard, withstand torture and wire up explosives. [Not to put too fine a point on it, he's Ian Chesterton (see Volume 1), right down to the dad-jokes.]

The Non-Humans
- *Daleks.* The experts in the Bunker believe the mutant within the motorised shell will be the final product of the Kaleds after the atomic war. Davros has instilled within the genome characteristics necessary to ensure the survival of at least a form of his people (notably aggression and belief in their own superiority). Then he modified further, removing conscience and amplifying hostility. They can receive long-range signals from Davros and give commands non-verbally. They willingly blast their creator when he goes for the assembly line's destruct button. They measure distance in yards.

This genetically-engineered fascist is encased within the Mark III Travel Unit, the familiar "tank", and all sensors are designed to be precise instruments. The weapon is also recognisably the same as previous stories, and considerably more advanced than anything used in the field of combat. Grown in vitro, they need a nutrient gel to support them before they are inserted in the shells. This stuff is, apparently, aware, aggressive and mobile. [We base this on the end of Part Five: if recorded as scripted, it would have engulfed the Doctor completely. As shown, it comes apart rather easily, into three pieces. This isn't what any Dalek mutant we've ever seen is like – it took an army to trisect one before X12.0, "Resolution" and the fifth Doctor pumped several bullets into one in 21.4, "Resurrection of the Daleks".]

The prototype Dalek is, at first, conditioned to obey only Davros but, with a flip of a switch on his chair, can be self-operating. Its first instinct is to isolate a non-Kaled (the Doctor) and shoot it. Once the machinery for mass-production is started, the option to override is removed.

The modifications mean that they also consider Kaleds inferior and, relieved of the need for support staff, mow them down. This also causes conflict with Davros. He neglected to include the word 'pity' in their vocabulary banks. [Oops!]

- *Mutations.* In the war's early years, when chemical weapons were more commonly used, the Kaleds took to evicting anyone with genetic damage into the wilderness between cities. Their descendants are routinely killed by soldiers on patrol, and are themselves hostile to anyone not like them. The Thals use Mutos as slave-labour on their unshielded missile programme, since distronic toxaemia curtails the life of anyone who does so. The Kaleds just shoot them, when they have ammunition to spare, or kill them in other ways.

After the war ends, the Mutos are almost the only survivors and are recruited by Bettan to seal the Daleks in. [It is unclear whether the Thals also evicted Mutos. If the Doctor's actions don't substantially alter the timeline, the Thals we encountered twice before (1.2, "The Daleks"; 10.4, "Planet of the Daleks") are in fact descended from mutant Kaleds as well as any Thals who also survived the Dalek massacre. However, as we've never heard from Thals in any story we see after the Doctor leaves, believing that he's completed his mission, this could be the last generation. This might be why the Doctor, who's worried about collateral damage among humans, can trick

Has the Time War Started?

...continued from page 75

carpet in attempted revisions of 60's / 70's continuity: "The Android Invasion".) Perhaps significantly, we can't see any sign of either the "Evil" version of the Dalek Emperor or the pointy-headed cannon-fodder in "Asylum of the Daleks" – but then, it took a lot of freeze-framing to see the ones we were told were there.

Also potentially significant, the one story not in Davros's DVD collection on rebuilt Skaro seems to be the weird anomaly about fully-mechanical Daleks: "Destiny of the Daleks". That can't be "gone", because it's primarily about the Daleks disinterring Davros after his apparent death at the end of "Genesis" – but, if we're accepting that Davros himself becomes time-sensitive (which, if all the Daleks in "The Stolen Earth" are from his cells, is very likely), then perhaps he can, like the Doctor and his chums, remember multiple versions events that are altered. (See **He Remembers This How?** under X1.5, "World War Three" and **Is Arthur the Horse a Companion?** under X2.4, "The Girl in the Fireplace".) If he is rescued and then the events of his rescue alter, he may land up stuck in a new timeline if he happens to be aboard a time-vessel akin to a TARDIS when it all changes (as opposed to, perhaps, spending eternity in a white void; see **Where's Susan?** under X4.17, "The End of Time Part One"). Could it be that this particular story was part of the Time War and the others weren't?

Possible evidence for that is that (taking the dialogue at face-value) in "Destiny of the Daleks", it is subjectively a few hours since Davros was shot dead, yet he's picked up a lot of skills and facts that would have been very useful last time he spoke. From his point of view, it was only yesterday that he was denying the possibility of life on other planets, yet his children brief him on the strategic deployment of their space-fleet, and the corridor outside the cupboard where his corpse was left for millennia is full of aliens. He's devising, off the top of his head, new weapons way beyond anything that he proposed when he was, let's remind ourselves, head of weapons research in a war that had lasted a thousand years.

If we take one line in this story seriously, he's already got the specs for the Reality Bomb from "The Stolen Earth" on his laptop. It gets worse when he then spends 90 years in a fridge and wakes up knowing all about regeneration and – again, from the dialogue – familiar with more than one Time Lord. "Resurrection of the Daleks" (21.4) retcons the Movellans as a more potent enemy than they seemed on screen in 1979 and – in another incident that looks as if the Capaldi Doctor could come and go in and out of the Time War when he wanted to make a cheap debating point – that border-war is still part of history in X10.1, "The Pilot". Had it not been for the Doctor's odd method of reassuring Bill after she was stood up, we could accept that "Destiny" was a blind-alley in Dalek history – one that was only visitable by the earlier Doctor and Romana because earlier Time Lords and biologically-upgraded Daleks rendered it contingent. (Perhaps that was why purely mechanical Daleks were being used, to avoid the risk of this vital mission being undone or rewritten and the arrival of two Time Lords wasn't as random as they both thought.) But now we have to accept that the Movellans are part of Dalek history and that their long, dull war isn't part of the biggie, so isn't time-locked away from us or the later Doctors. And yet, it does seem that the Davros who wakes up covered in cobwebs isn't *quite* the one who screamed "have pity!".

If you want to ascribe the inconsistencies in Davros's skill-set to external manipulation rather than Terry Nation's memory being worse than Steven Moffat's, this looks at least plausible. Davros in "Destiny" comes from a patch of history that's been multiple-rewritten (from his perspective) – but, to the young and reckless model of the Doctor and his newly-regenerated pal, is exactly as it was. The net result of all the emendations appears to have been to reset everything to baseline, with only a time-sensitive nearly-dead Davros knowing that anything ever changed. That doesn't entirely stack up, as the next three Dalek stories are all clearly outside the Time War and not even the wily McCoy Doctor seems to know that there's a Time War a-brewin'.

Of course, there's nothing to say that a possible future can't make an impact on the definite present. Many stories have dealt with this, from "Day of the Daleks" to "Battlefield" (26.1), a story that cannot easily fit in with a chronology where the Time Lords have gone and parallel universes are inaccessible, let alone one where we had a king and a five-pound coin in the mid-to-late 90s. The Doctor might have encountered beings aware of the Time War, but only accepted this as a potential future for him, not set in stone. (If the Doctor knew for a fact he was going to live to be Christopher

continued on page 79...

Genesis of the Daleks

Davros into destroying Skaro in 25.1, "Remembrance of the Daleks".]

Less overtly humanoid mutations reside in the caves outside the city [not a lake, as we saw in 1963-4]. Some of these are the results of Davros's earlier experiments.

- **Thals.** There's a conspicuous lack of females. [Weirdly, this raises the possibility that future Thals are descended from a single woman. There was only one gyno-Thal in "The Daleks", too, and again in "Planet of the Daleks". Maybe they reproduce like bees. If they're the same species as the Kaleds, who have zero females in their ranks, it might almost make sense except that Ronson thought Harry was near-normal.]

Planet Notes Skaro is in one of seven galaxies, where no sign of any other life has been detected. The surface is habitable even after the Thal weapon devastates the Kaled citadel [seemingly contradicting the situation in "The Daleks", and indeed 17.1, "Destiny of the Daleks"] but is periodically blighted by poison gas.

History

- **Dating.** [Until the Doctor blows up the Dalek incubator room and tells Sarah that he's thereby 'delayed [the Daleks] for a short time, perhaps a thousand [presumably terrestrial] years', the previously-established dates for Dalek stories definitely apply. So, "Genesis of the Daleks" happens a long time before 1.2, "The Daleks", which was several generations before 2540 (the date of 10.3, "Frontier in Space" and therefore 10.4, "Planet of the Daleks", in which the Thals treated the Doctor's first trip to Skaro as literally the stuff of legend). There's no evidence that these or any other events change, historically or concerning the Doctor's involvement, once he here sets the Daleks back 'a thousand years'. In "Remembrance of the Daleks", for instance, the Doctor claims the Daleks invaded Earth in the 'twenty-second century', presumably the same as before. (2.2, "The Dalek Invasion of Earth", rather than 9.1, "Day of the Daleks".)]

According to the Doctor's testimony in Part Five, the Daleks invaded Earth in '2000 A.D.', running into exactly the same trouble that they would encounter in 2164. ["The Dalek Invasion of Earth". It helps to understand that although the Doctor is wired into a device that knows whether he's being truthful or lying, it presumably doesn't detect if he's just misspeaking or getting his dates wrong.] They also had bother during a war with the Venusians in the Space Year 17,000 with war-rockets from the planet Hyperon and trouble on Mars with a virus affecting their electronics ["Resurrection of the Daleks" and implicitly "Destiny of the Daleks"]. However accurate (or not) the information on the tape, the Doctor makes sure to destroy it.

The Kaled-Thal war's been going on for a thousand years [however long their year is – the quasi-canonical Annuals depict Skaro as being far from its sun and Dyoni ("The Daleks") cites it as the twelfth planet out]. Davros has been working on the Dalek project for 50 of those. [Even with a neutronic war and biological weapons, the lifespan on Skaro seems to be fairly long – Davros does, however, have tissue-regeneration tech in his buggy ("Destiny of the Daleks" et seq.). The broadcast stories indicate that he has an unusually long life.]

Technology hasn't advanced as rapidly as wars usually make it, because resources have been almost exhausted. Such weapons as are used in the field are a mix-and-match of anything still functional, ray-guns and spears. In the first century of the war, both sides used chemical weapons, which left many with disrupted genes.

The Analysis

Where Does This Come From? Long-term *About Time* readers will by now know better than to take anything Terry Nation said in interviews without a hefty pinch of salt. When asked about his inspirations for this story, he cited a scene from the 1936 epic *Things to Come* that doesn't actually exist.[16] His recollection was that there's a sequence juxtaposing the soldiers fighting an endless war with pickaxes while the Elite build a space-ship.

Up to a point, Lord Copper: there's a long story in the middle about a bedraggled post-apocalyptic state where a plague has been and a petty Little Englander warlord is trying to impose his will on the remaining townsfolk (something Nation would do rather better in *Survivors*), but the rest of the world's rebuilt and overthrows him and his kind with superior aircraft and a knock-out gas. The "Air-Men" aren't taking resources from the people in sheepskins living in ruins, they want to *share* resources and donate their technology in the aid of global brotherhood. Then there's a lengthy

Has the Time War Started?

...continued from page 77

Eccleston, the stakes for every story made before 2005 would have been lower.)

If a rumour or legend of a Time War that ended Gallifrey had reached any earlier Doctor(s), it would have been interesting, if depressing, but more like a weather forecast than a stone cold certainty. It might be bad for anyone who was in it, just as Earth under Dalek rule as a result of a bomb sabotaging the World Peace Talks in the 1970s was, but always avoidable. A lot of the McCoy Doctor's activities look like attempts to forestall such a future by giving the Time Lords their mojo back (literally, in the case of the Nemesis statue). Again, "The Power of the Daleks" has the Doctor aware – at least in the stage directions – of a terrible conflict he had to flee and the coincidence of a regeneration. Indeed, the Daleks knowing this new face seems to have reminded him of it with renewed force. Once again, Hoodie Man's choice of one particular Doctor, up-and-running after turning into the incarnation who'd become President, worked for the White Guardian and defeated Sutekh et al, might be more than happenstance.

If the Time Lords, either of that Doctor's own era or the future, were seeking to make sure that he knew the Daleks for what they truly were, it may well have changed his behaviour when he did get involved in the Time War. Other than that, is this that big a change in his life? Had "Destiny" been his first encounter with the Daleks' creator, the plot would have run almost unchanged – his knowledge of the ruined citadel seems to come from "Evil" rather than "Genesis", and that's mainly based on 1.2, "The Daleks" and the very first time he met them. "Resurrection" mainly needs the Daleks to know about the Time Lords (and they'd already hired the Master to start a war for them) and, if we accept that some data escaped from the closed-off twenty-second century invasion, interrogated the Doctor to find out about regenerations. In "Revelation of the Daleks" (22.6), Davros is a notorious criminal. The one big thing the events of "Genesis" does for the Doctor is that he defines himself as someone who isn't capable of the moral certainty needed to do as the Time Lords ask. As it turns out, eight lives later, he still isn't (although that's not how he remembers the end of the War).

Other incidental details we learn about his conduct as the War Doctor include attempting to save Davros in the first year. That's not the Avenging Angel we're led to believe that John Hurt's Doctor was, but it fits with the Doctor of "Genesis". We seem to be veering away from any notion that Hoodie Man is a visitor from within the bubble trying to turn the Doctor into a weapon and towards the idea that they are coeval, contemporaries much as Drax or the Rani are. The Doctor has been chosen because he's run into the Daleks before and has a bit of an axe to grind about them, and because he's more trustworthy (and on-the-hook) than, say, the Master or the Monk. (We know from X9.2, "The Witch's Familiar" that the Master / Missy never met Davros before that day. She could be lying, but he'd say so, just to shut her up.)

With a few small anomalies, such as the ambiguous status of Skaro (destroyed, rescued from the Time War, visitable by a later Doctor, rebuilt from scratch and hidden – to the surprise of the one *after* the one who popped there at the height of the War and got recruited to blow up the Asylum… and that's just one writer's ideas), we seem to have the matter settled. All broadcast stories other than X7.15, "The Day of the Doctor" are outside the Time War and are exactly as we saw them, with no interference or rewriting. Even "Destiny" and Davros's exceptionally steep learning-curve can be accounted for, if there's yet-another unbroadcast scene from "The Magician's Apprentice" where the Doctor reassures young Davros by saying that they're going to be seeing more of each other, then makes him forget everything he said once they were out of the minefield, with a post-hypnotic suggestion to remember once he gets shot by a Dalek. (Is this less plausible than the idea of time-sensitive Davros living through a history that's repeatedly rewritten and the Doctor not realising? Let's agree that the answer will never be shown on BBC1.)

One small oddity remains: "The Daleks" (or, for some, "The Dead Planet" or "The Mutants"… Story B, X1.2). This seems not to be quite "there" any more, despite the Thals remembering it in 2540, but it looks remarkably like the optimum result of a Time Lord rewriting Skaro's past to render the Gallifrey-threatening master-race mostly harmless. Anyone who wants to resolve the anomalies by sidelining that story into a sheared-off timeline that resulted from the Doctor, Harry and Sarah sticking their oar in at a crucial moment has a few problems to deal with – every other Dalek story, f

continued on page 81…

12.4 Genesis of the Daleks

montage of good-for-its-time model work and back-projection of the Utopian city being built (massively unsustainable and environmentally unsound, but it's the 30s) and *then* a long dull debate over the ethics of putting your daughter in a big cannon-shell and aiming it at the Moon.

It's confusing, because the same actors get similar roles across four generations, so Raymond Massey and Edward Chapman trot out similar dialogue when wearing 30s dinner-suits around a radio or in togas and shorts in vast white rooms full of Perspex furniture. Nation wouldn't have been the only person to tune out the polemical dialogue and look at the impressive pictures, just like he did with George Pal's later films of H.G. Wells books.

What's interesting is that the spin Nation puts on this is that the people with connections get all the resources for pet projects and everyone else has to make-do-and-mend. That's more a World War II memory than related to anything in the film, recalling people giving up their saucepans and iron railings. The story was that people's sacrifices led directly to the manufacture of Spitfires, but it was mainly a propaganda move to make the public think they had a stake in the aerial conflict. Growing up in wartime Cardiff might have exposed him to grumbles about how London got all the air-defence and goodies, but that's hardly confined to 1939-45. Note that the brief scene between Davros and Mogran focuses on the sacrifices made by the (unseen) public and the idea that letting them know some of what's going on is patriotic. (It's also noteworthy that Mogran, sometimes typed as the more usual Welsh name "Morgan", is wearing a boiler-suit of the type Churchill started wearing when doing his "we're all in this together" spiel.)

But let's not discount *Things to Come* just because of one interview in the 1980s. There is a lot of iconography that's applicable to what we got in "Genesis". The people in sheepskins with antique weapons and beaten-up pre-war cars pulled by dray-horses make for some startling shots at the start of the middle section. The idea in the film is that this hypothetical next war, starting in 1940, will be World War I writ large, with gas dropped from biplanes and barbed wire right up to the city limits – and will go on until around 1970.

Then comes the "Wandering Sickness", with a plague making people stagger around the ruins unconsciously unless picked off by snipers (see also "Destiny of the Daleks" and the starts of "The Dalek Invasion of Earth" and "The Android Invasion"). The rebuilding sequence inspired a lot of notions of how, after a real war started in 1939, people justified the hardships they endured by conceiving of a bright, healthy fresh start (see **What Kind of Future Did We Expect?** under 2.3, "The Rescue"). Much of the original Dalek city in 1963 is influenced by the film's assumptions, albeit filtered through Raymond Cusick's combination of studio-floor practicality and resistance to what were already clichés. (Even if you've never seen the film, you've sort-of seen bits of it, as the futuristic city and big-shouldered togas were imitated by illustrators and later films – arguably every shopping mall in the world is based on Vincent Korda's designs.)

A couple of less salubrious films can be recruited to illustrate the next point but probably weren't direct influences. Concern about atomic war led to ideas that, such a war being inevitable, someone ought to be thinking of who could survive it and how. There's no end of stories about mutants wandering around blasted wastelands and of eugenics cults checking for "purity", but there's a tiny subgenre of stories where someone in the present day is selecting for tolerance to radiation as a pre-emptive move (and, of course, the results escape and cause havoc in a small town).

Exhibit A is *The Damned* (not the Visconti one, Joseph Losey, released in the US heavily truncated as *These are the Damned*). Being black and white and lacking vampires, it's one Hammer film that got shown at primetime on London Weekend Television in the early 70s. The first half is a bizarre American take on Teddy Boys, with a tweed-wearing Oliver Reed terrorising a small English seaside town, but it gets interesting when the too-old token American they cast to get funding and Reed's teenage sister stumble across a cave containing a prep-school for posh blond kids (like the ones in *Village of the Damned* and *Children of the Damned*, neither of which is actually connected to this film except as a sales-pitch). The kids are taught via television (not quite like BBC Schools programmes, as it's all one elderly chap). Guess what – they need radiation to live, so their plan to escape and see what trees look like close up is thwarted. The army, who bankrolled this, capture and kill anyone who might be a security risk.

Genesis of the Daleks 12.4

Has the Time War Started?

...continued from page 79

or starters – but fewer than trying to account for the TV Movie or the Peter Cushing films and far fewer than attempting to incorporate the ideas that Nation and John Peel proposed in the strange book they put out in 1988.[17]

We're always going to have problems with tenses in this matter, but if we agree that, with respect to the Doctor's time-line, broadcast episodes and Gallifreyan Mean Time (see **Why Do Time Lords Always Meet in Sequence?** under 22.3, "The Mark of the Rani"), the "start" of the Time War was between 26.4, "Survival" and X1.1, "Rose" and that, within its not-really-a-bubble, it was always-already running, we can sidestep the issue of whether broadcast stories (other than the conflicting accounts of the Last Day – see **How Can Anyone Know About a Time War?** under X4.13, "Journey's End") have anything to do with it.

This has to be where that timeline and the one we know from television diverged. At the point where it was sealed away, all other changes to history were undone, leaving most of the broadcast stories intact (awkward as that makes anyone trying to resolve the dates of 5.4, "The Enemy of the World" with our everyday experience). A bigger question, with the Daleks still around and the High Council apparently in exile (X9.12, "Hell Bent"), is how it can be said to have ended – but we've got to wait for more on-screen data, if any, to deal with that.

Exhibit B is 1956 indie flick *The Werewolf*, in which the hapless protagonist doesn't go hairy and anthropophagous from a bite, it's because when he crashed his car, he picked the wrong doctor to patch him up. Dr Morgan Chambers was secretly testing an anti-radiation serum he hoped to give to people he wanted to survive a war (like all good mad scientists, he's a snob and a fascist), but lycanthropy's a side-effect he's trying to fix. It was show in Britain in a double-bill with *Creature with the Atom Brain* (resurrecting people with radiation creates sexist zombies). We cite these as the more readily-accessible tip of an iceberg of similar shockers, in print and on screen – all semi-justified by the widespread notion that committees in Whitehall or the Pentagon were thinking along similar lines.

We have two essays in later volumes on the odd ideas of natural selection at work even in phases of *Doctor Who* where they brandish the scienciness of their scripts (**How Does 'Evolution' Work?** under 18.3, "Full Circle" and **What Were Josiah's 'Blasphemous' Theories?** under 26.2, "Ghost Light") – but, taken with Nation's own intended end for *Blakes 7*, this story's notion of a planned future course for evolution is alarming. In the *Radio Times* 1973 Special, he contributed a story, "We Are the Daleks", in which it turned out that – nuclear holocaust or no – tin skirts and sink-plungers are what biological destiny has in store for humanity. In "Terminal", the supposed end of *Blakes 7*, unreasoning anthropoid savages are what we will turn into, inevitably, regardless of local conditions.

It's akin to the arrogant way that anything pale, hairless and with a big brain is described as "more evolved" in pulps and comics (e.g., the "Higher Evolutionaries" in the *Doctor Who Magazine* comic strips of the Davison era), a sort of Whig Interpretation of Biology to match the Victorian idea that the British Empire was history's happy ending. What's odd is that the pre-ordained, teleological idea of evolution is one closely associated with the very people Nation is condemning, the Nazis. Nonetheless, anyone concerned about precautions against fallout (i.e. any adult in the 1950s) may have encountered ideas of how to "future-proof" the human genome.

What's interesting is that he didn't write that (seemingly obvious) version in 1963 or promote it in the many, many spin-off books and comics that followed in the loveable-mop-top phase of Dalekmania. The spinoffery told of a benign scientist called Yarvelling who designed a travel-machine as a reaction to a pre-existing mutation, not as a pre-emptive move. The war was ended by a meteor-strike detonating neutronic bombs and each side blaming the other. Yarvelling and Zolfian (the Dal race's leader) were the only un-mutated Dals (they're blue-skinned *naturally*), and it was the prototype Dalek, who declared himself Dalek Supreme, who launched the mass-production of these survival-suits as revenge-weapons against the remaining Thals.

Nation didn't write the strip "Genesis of Evil" (a title it seems to have acquired with the 1980 *Doctor Who Magazine* reprint), but he signed off on it. His name's plastered on the *TV 21* stuff, the Annuals and the 1965 *Dalek Pocketbook and Authentic Space Travellers' Guide*, where this and

12.4 Genesis of the Daleks

bits of "The Chase" (2.8) and "The Dalek Invasion of Earth" are recycled amid some bonkers new stuff and a *Look and Learn* account of the history of rockets and what was then thought about the solar system. Even if the worst stories about Nation's cavalier attitude and slipshod writing were true, he had to have read this stuff. Over and again, the paracanonical material (including the feature film) reiterates that the Daleks happened after a series of catastrophes and improvised measures that became a lifestyle. Now, however, it's the diabolical masterplan of evil genius.

That's partly because Philip Hinchcliffe thought that it was dramatically better to have a spokesman for a lot of shambling / strutting aliens, debating with the Doctor rather than just shooting at him, and that such a role attracted better actors. Mainly, though, it's because over the years, people had become accustomed to dystopian dramas about the victims of trends (often starring Charlton Heston) and it seemed like a radical change to put the focus on an obsessive alpha-male cause of the trouble.

Hitherto, in Letts's term of office, spokesbeings for topical problems were either railing against the symptoms ("Invasion of the Dinosaurs") or were symptoms in and of themselves (10.5, "The Green Death"). Here, the Daleks were no longer an exaggeration of a tendency in people, a warning of what we could become, and became manifestations of one person's obsessions. Done well, this takes character-study science fiction television close to literature; done less well, it drags it back to *Flash Gordon*. With the passing years, it is increasingly hard to see how radical a break with the past Davros was – how fresh and how bold it was to make this about a subtle obsessive, rather than a motiveless Mad Scientist or a commentary on consumerism or whatever.

It's traditional at this point to bring in *The Brothers Karamazov*. The Doctor proposes a matched pair of thought-experiments: one to Davros about a microbe that would kill everything, another to Sarah about pre-empting massacres by killing a child. Both are in a tradition of counterexamples to Utilitarianism, the big nineteenth-century idea of functional ethics (usually characterised as tending towards the greatest good for the greatest number). The currently-fashionable version is the so-called Trolley Problem (see X8.7, "Kill the Moon"), but the first one to become well-known in the English-speaking world was proposed by William James in *The Moral Philosopher and the Moral Life*, speculating on whether people could live in a Utopia (of the kind so popular when he was writing, the 1890s) if it relied on one person being kept in torment and everyone else knowing about it. (We'll pick up on this in 18.6, "The Keeper of Traken".) This underlay a famous story by Ursula K. Le Guin, "The Ones Who Walk Away from Omelas".

About a decade before this, Dostoievski wrote his last novel with a similar "scapegoat" idea proposed in an allegorical poem about Jesus returning and facing the Spanish Inquisition, narrated to Alyosha (the youngest, probably the hero) by Ivan (the sulky middle son) in the most famous bit. (The argument is that Free Will is too much hassle for most humans. Jesus answers his tormentor by kissing his lips and then Alyosha "plagiarises" this reply to Ivan. The 1958 film version, for all its faults, spared us the torment of Richard Basehart snogging William Shatner).

The authors of the 1983 book *Doctor Who: the Unfolding Text* picked up on this and cited it as proof that "Genesis of the Daleks" was "literary" (see **The Semiotic Thickness of What?** under 24.4, "Dragonfire"). However, a less hifalutin possible influence is Roald Dahl's story "Genesis and Catastrophe" about a sickly baby whose parents have already lost three infants – the parents are Alois and Klara Hitler, and we're supposed to have worried about newborn Adolf. We'll be coming back to Utilitarianism in due course ("The Deadly Assassin"; "The Armageddon Factor"; "The Hand of Fear"; and even 15.2, "The Invisible Enemy").

No, it's not exactly a big step to go from atomic Nazis to a fanatic in a bunker; yes, it's in keeping with the pseudo-Greek styling of the *TV 21* strip to have a Greek name; of course, once you've said it, a semi-Dalek Frankenstein figure is so intuitively obvious, than the character was instantly accepted even by people who muddled the name up with Kojak's dim assistant Stavros – but the idea had to have come from *somewhere*.

Most people say that Barry Letts more or less ordered Nation to do the story we got – even using the word "Genesis" – but Hinchcliffe made the obvious association with the Mekon, Dan Dare's arch-nemesis. In the 50s comic-strip in *The Eagle*, the Venusian races were at war because of a power-mad technocrat who had green skin, a scrawny body, a bulbous head and floated around on a disc. The Atlantines, blue-skinned pacifists whose ancestors fled Earth 100,000 years ago, are harangued by the ape-like green Treens, as are, later, the blonde Venusian natives, the Therons – but, to complicate the simple analogy with the Kaleds and Thals, the Treens created the Mekon to lead them rather than the other way around. (Anyway, the Treens are more like Vulcans or Cybermen.) Nation could hardly deny all knowledge of this, as the *TV 21* strips are pretty much what *Dan Dare* would have been if the Mekon had been the hero (see also next story). As for the life-support wheelchair, we don't have to look much further than *Star Trek*, specifically "The Menagerie" and Captain Pike.

Just parenthetically, we will mention that the idea of a fanatical geneticist and propagating Hitler was sufficiently obvious for Ira Levin to tread where even Terry Nation dared not. *The Boys from Brazil* was published about a year after this story aired, linking Nazis and the "ick" factor of genetic engineering for a generation who had not experienced eugenics laws. We will revisit the idea of "comeback" narratives with the next story.

The script's not the whole story. We are entering a phase where directors get to do things they couldn't in cop-shows or costume-dramas, as part of a sweetener for being made to do *Doctor Who*. Maloney reworked the opening sequence in particular and introduced references and techniques not specified. In the past, he'd been forced to use a freeze-frame on a charging unicorn (6.2, "The Mind Robber"), but between 1968 and 1975 this technique – only recently a dazzling innovation (*Les Quatre-Cent Coups*, Francois Truffaut, 1964) – had been beaten to death in toothpaste adverts and *Hawaii Five-O*.

Similarly, after one slow-motion death in a fight scene in *The Seven Samurai* (Akira Kurasawa, 1960), it became almost obligatory in any violent murder (especially when Sam Peckinpah was directing). It was increasingly common in films where watching the choreography of a fight was part of the sales-pitch (Bruce Lee or *A Clockwork Orange*) and was now so common that it was the trademark of two TV series aimed at kids (*The Six Million Dollar Man* and *Kung Fu*). It was, theoretically, possible for someone who only ever watched *Doctor Who* and other BBC Saturday night shows (*Dixon of Dock Green* and *The Black and White Minstrel Show*, for example) to be shocked at the importation of these "radical" techniques – but few kids were.

That level of obviousness extends to the costumes. It's not just that the Kaled military look like Nazis, or the scientists are all in white, it's things like Mogran wearing a Churchillian boiler-suit, the Mutos dressing like stereotypical lepers, dead soldiers dressed like Eastern European peasants (as per *Things to Come*) and – this being directed by David Maloney – gas masks as far as the eye can see. It's the way the Kaled bunker is all reflective chrome sheeting and the Thal base is matte magnolia with Doric columns, suggesting a war between technocrats and bureaucrats.

Maloney explicitly reconfigured the beginning to resemble the opening scene of *The Seventh Seal*, even giving the Time Lord emissary a cowl like that worn by Death. It's also suggested that the end – with the Doctor, Harry and Sarah running around with the Time Ring – is supposed to be like the Dance of Death at the end (this is less convincing). It wasn't exactly an obscure allusion – both Woody Allen's *Love and Death* and the trailer for *Monty Python and the Holy Grail*, from around the same time, assumed that audiences knew the original. (So does *Bill and Ted's Bogus Journey*; a few gags in *Animaniacs* riff on it too.) The "I'm a spy" gag is a variation on a scene from *The Man from U.N.C.L.E.*, at the climax of *The Five Daughters Affair* Part Two, but that seems not to have been shown in the UK in the 60s (when it did get aired, in the 80s, it was as the feature-film edit *The Karate Killers*). Nation was in America a lot when it was shown on CBS and may have been pursuing a connection with Sam Rolfe – see 3.4, "The Daleks' Master Plan". The film got a limited UK release.

The Kaled security guard Tane was originally called "Gitane". With a scientist called "Ronson", it could be that Nation was drawing inspiration from a trip to his tobacconist's. Although he never wrote for *Stingray*, his colleague Dennis Spooner did, so the whole getting a foot stuck in a giant clam thing (a staple of sub-aqua adventures) isn't exactly unfamiliar. We're not sure how much Welsh Nation knew, being from a period when the English were suppressing the language, but their word for 'snake' is 'neidr', pronounced to rhyme with the German name 'Schneider'.

Things That Don't Make Sense The Doctor tells his Time Lord handler: 'Whatever I've done for you in the past, I've more than made up for.' You what?

The one that *everyone* notices: The Kaleds and the Thals are (or were, once) hi-tech, yet the war

12.4 Genesis of the Daleks

between them has endured for a thousand years even though their cities are within walking distance of each other. Each city seems to contain the whole population of its race. Somehow, the Kaled military knows about a secret passage into the Thal citadel, but they've apparently never entertained the idea of using it to smuggle in explosives and kill everyone within. Meanwhile, the Thals are planning to drop a dirty nuke on their next-door neighbours. As dome-residents on a blasted plain, they have no way to tell which way the wind's blowing.

In fact, both domes are (until Davros cheats) impregnable, so what was the point of the trench warfare and gas-grenades? Were they both whittling their populations down to dome-size by randomly sending men out to get shot or gassed? Harry describes the set-up as "a war of attrition" (correct), then adds "... but backwards" (er, no).

How do Davros and Nyder sneak in to the Thal dome for a chat? When they show up at the door of the Thal citadel, what did they tell the guards? "Penny for the Guy" wouldn't cut it. "I'm on the guest-list" isn't very plausible. Did they wear false beards and blond wigs? We're forced to assume a pre-existing channel of communication, a way for Thal agents to get to the Bunker safely to escort their most hated enemy – and a back door that Davros knows about but the Thal leadership don't. But when they go back, the Thal politician only then arranges safe passage. And did Davros really trundle through a tunnel and several grills? Twice in a day? Presumably it takes them less time to get home than it takes the Thals to fit the chemical solvent into missiles and launch their ICBM. Nobody at the Bunker missed them at such a crucial stage of the development of the Mk III. (Davros uses just the one chair-switch to open various doors around the Kaled city. How does it know which one he wants to open?)

In this story more than any other, Sarah displays spooky clairvoyance. She complains that the transmat beam hasn't brought them to "the beacon", even though Nerva isn't referred to as such in the earlier story. She seems to know the Doctor's mission-brief from the Time Lords without being told, and – at the end of the last episode – she knows the Doctor's about to hurtle around the corner of the corridor before his shadow's even visible on the wall. She can also magically divine which locker contains combat trousers (what are those doing there?) in her size, in case she needs to go mollicking about in caves in the not-too-distant future (again, see next story).

Sarah's also the subject of one of the most disappointing cliffhangers in the programme's history, falling off a great big rocket-gantry at the end of Part Two but then somehow landing on a convenient platform inside the gantry at the start of Part Three. Even Flash Gordon would disapprove. (See also "Dragonfire")

The Thals prevent the Doctor's sabotage by electrocuting him. He survives. We were earlier told that the prisoners left in the launch silo would be burned alive on launch. Why would the guards bother moving the insensate body of a saboteur? Nonetheless, the Doctor is hauled out and regains consciousness in, of all places, Mission Control. Apparently, they don't have any detention cells (unlike the Kaled Bunker, because the Scientific Elite have nothing better to do than interrogate random visitors).

The leader of the Thals declares a "general amnesty" after the Kaled dome is destroyed, conveniently releasing the Doctor – which seems reasonable, if you can swallow that a government would let all the agents of an eradicated culture go free and not expect any reprisals. In his next scene, the Doctor grins his head off when meeting the celebrating Thals, even though he thinks his companions have just been blown to pieces in the Kaled dome. What a git. Mind you, he's the only person in the city who seems happy that a thousand-year war is finally over. The end of a series of *The Great British Bake-Off* gets a better reception than the rather muted office-party we see here.

Nation's odd ideas about how evolution works apparently include the final destiny of irradiated humanity being a jelly octopus and that, along the way to this, there's a stage where our descendants will be giant foam-rubber dry-land clams. We have an idea from the dialogue that *Magna peloris* was one of the trial-runs for the Dalek and left in a cave rather than put down, converted into furniture, chopped up into bullets or eaten (maybe there aren't any months with "r" in on Skaro). Did Gharman release them into the wild as an anti-vivisection protest? Is Ronson a member of the "Friends of Skaro"? (Ronson's presence in Davros's research-squad is a bit suspect, as he complains about "senseless killing" and seriously doubts whether a war can be ended by just means. Don't they screen people for working in a weapons development programme? Ditto Gharman, who delivers another such sermon to non-speaking characters, to whom he then hands weapons. Even if we don't recognise Terry Walsh and Alan Chuntz, it's asking for trouble.)

Davros has had 50 years to develop the Dalek and has appropriated a lot of resources and personnel. Until the end of Part One, there's been precious little to show for all this R&D over half a century, save for a few embarrassing clams and some (untestable) super-grouting on the Dome's surface – and yet apparently nobody has asked Davros exactly what he was doing with their precious resources. (Imagine Roosevelt and Churchill letting the Trinity A-bomb team fritter away the money for the Manhattan Project on frisbee design.) During this stint, Davros has invented the Dalek gun, a devastating weapon that Kaled front-line troops could have wielded to wipe out the Thals. Never mind computer-assisted mutants, even scared teenagers should be capable of wreaking havoc by just vaguely pointing and shooting. By distributing this weapon early, Davros would have demoralised the Thals, secured unlimited funding and gratitude from the Kaled public and reaped everything he wanted without faffing about blowing up cities. (See, heaven help us, X5.3, "Victory of the Daleks" for one being used for exactly that.)

Quite a lot happens between parts Five and Six with nobody noticing… somehow, the Daleks set up an automated production line. Davros also reveals a Total Destruct button (apparently made from an old film canister or the lid of a tin of Cadbury's "Roses" and bodged into his desk with visible woodwork) that wasn't there before. He claims this button will destroy the Dalek production line if pressed and, as the Daleks turn against him, he seems to reach out for it: was it actually connected to explosives? Is there any feasible reason he might do that, rather than just fib?

When the Doctor's trio is locked in Davros's office, once they've zapped the tape with a Dalek gun, they don't consider using that on the door. Then, once they're out and they know Bettan's about to seal them all in, he gives the Time Ring to Sarah and re-positions the explosives in the hatchery. Why? It doesn't seem to affect the Daleks one way or the other. It's Bettan's bomb that delays the Daleks by a thousand years.

Early on, we hear that a requisition chit is "countersigned by Davros". He can't hold a pen. And why has the idiot installed an "off" switch for his life-support?

Critique The whole thing's a massive con, of course: there's no way the Doctor will succeed in this mission if they want to continue the series indefinitely; there's little chance of him wrecking history and becoming a monster; he'll never be a willing tool of whichever Time Lord apparatchik set him this task. The supposed moral revelations the Doctor explains were things regular viewers already knew. Everything about this mission is a pretext for a series of discussions about bioethics and Utilitarianism, punctuated by fights and explosions. Those never go out of style. If anything, the various arias Davros delivers on free will and power are more topical now than when they were relatively abstract.

A lot of people like the *idea* of this story more than they like the full-length story. Its reputation has been burnished by a reduction to an 85-minute omnibus, two 50-minute episodes, a vinyl LP or a Target novelisation that came out pretty darn pronto. Viewers go into it now with a firm idea of what happens, what *almost* happens at a key moment and which bits of twentieth-century history it looks like. It's passed into folklore in Britain. Modern-day *Doctor Who* assumes that you've got a grasp of the essentials and can recognise call-backs to it every time the Master (or someone) tries to tempt the Doctor into genocide (X8.12, "Death in Heaven"; X10.12, "The Doctor Falls"; X12.10, "The Timeless Child"; X1.13, "The Parting of the Ways" and, of course, X7.15, "The Day of the Doctor").

Then, every so often, the BBC repeated the whole six episodes and people found their interest dwindling. The original was designed to be shown in weekly instalments to a less-committed audience and without anyone already knowing how it ends. For most people, it's served its purpose. It's still a potent concept, not least in the context of the Time War, and Davros is still a totemic figure when used sparingly. But the question remains: does the two-and-a-half hour original cut still work?

Frankly, yes: it's as good an example as any of how to make *Doctor Who* without undue concern about budget, effects or locations. The longer it's on screen, the less any of the things that are pushed at us as the hallmarks of a BBC "mega-brand" matter. It's still best at a rate of no more than one episode an hour rather than in one gulp; the repetition and redundancy gets less annoying the more you space out the instalments. It's paced a bit mechanically, with one set-piece debate per

12.4 Genesis of the Daleks

episode, periodic action scenes you can set your watch by and remarkably few cameos by the Daleks. The last two episodes are a bit lopsided and the shift of emphasis to Bettan and Sevrin (a sitcom waiting to happen) makes you want to see more Kaleds. Yes, it has gaping logical flaws and some giant clams. These things may grate if you watch the story in one gulp, but this is a function of Terry Nation's occasionally brilliant, often silly, attempts to combine *Flash Gordon* and George Bernard Shaw. And, this time, circumstances have conspired to make him raise his game to a career-best pitch.

Making this the Dalek origin story not only makes everyone take it a fraction more seriously, it means that everyone is confident that audiences will give it a bit more leeway when it discusses capital-I Issues. Making the most overt analogy between the Daleks and the Nazis to date also lends it a bit of gravitas. Which, in turn, leads to a bit of theatricality. The bits that embarrass people now are the moments when it stops pretending to be A Serious Drama and reverts to *Doctor Who* as it had been the previous year. There we are, stroking our chins about the allusions to Ingmar Bergman and Dostoievski, and then we get a reminder that it's by the author of "The Chase". We know what *Doctor Who* became after this story, indeed largely *because* of this story, but any reminder of where the bar was raised from makes modern fans squirm. Nonetheless, we'll not get quite that mix of styles again and certainly never successfully from Nation.

Yet what strikes one seeing it in context, as six weeks of a 20-week series of a long-running family drama, is how much of it is simply the routine baseline *Doctor Who* business done a tiny bit better. As we've said, this story was in the studio just as "Robot" and "The Ark in Space" were being broadcast and the buzz about the new lead actor seems to have motivated the rest of the crew and cast. Michael Wisher (as Davros) was a jobbing actor who'd been in the series a few times and will again later that year in small, almost forgettable parts. Davros is a monomaniac of the same stamp as Vorus in the next story, Styre in the previous one or Noah (to begin with) before that. It's ludicrous to try to quantify how much "better" in any sensible terms this story is, as a percentage, but in any particular category (acting, writing, camera-angle choices or whatever), nothing is drastically improved or diminished compared to, say, "Revenge of the Cybermen". It's just that each feature one could name has a slight lift and, as a whole, it all works together on a higher pitch. When this story relatedly wins Best Story polls and gets repeats showings on BBC2, this is what stands out even beyond the film-club references. That made the LP version so quotable, but what earned it the unique distinction of a record release in the 1970s was an idea of the story being special. That idea was always there, even before broadcast.

The Facts

Written by Terry Nation, honest. Directed by David Maloney, obviously. Viewing figures: 10.7 million, 10.5 million, 8.5 million, 8.8 million, 9.8 million, 9.1 million. AI's were sporadically recorded, with 57% for parts Two and Five, 58 for Part Four and 56 for Part Six. Not great, given this story's later reputation. The two-part 1982 two repeats got good ratings, given their odd timeslot (4.9 million and 5.0 million) and better AI's (66% and 68%). Oddly, nobody's got figures for the 27th December omnibus.

Working Titles "Daleks – Genesis of Terror"

Alternate Versions Gee whizz…

This has been shown in three different edits by the BBC, plus an LP of the soundtrack that whittled it down to 40 minutes (sampled by the KLF in 1988 for "Doctorin' the Tardis"), heavily promoted during seasons Seventeen and Eighteen and itself altered for the CD release. The first repeat was an 85-minute omnibus episode over Christmas 1975, then there was a two-part version in 50-minute episodes in August 1982. Episodic repeats in 1993 and 2000 on BBC2 and the short-lived BBC Choice in 1998 and 1999 add to the tally. The VHS release had "The Sontaran Experiment" tacked on as well. There was a laserdisc version, apparently unaltered (we can't find anyone who bought it).

PBS originally sliced out a few minutes to allow for a narrator to do misleading "story so far" bits. BBC America shows it as a single-episode feature on occasion, hacking out the cliffhangers (it's especially obvious with Part Two) and putting in advert breaks at inopportune moments. In 1989, bantamweight satellite station Superchannel opted to show it in three 45-minute episodes with the Sylvester McCoy music and titles (with Tom's face superimposed) and new credits. The 2018 Blu-Ray release earned the 1975 omnibus version a cinematic showing in the US.

Cliffhangers Sarah, hiding in a bunker, sees a half-Dalek man testing the first-ever Dalek; amid a hail of bullets, Sarah plummets from the gantry; the Doctor is electrocuted; Davros tortures the Doctor's friends to make him tell of all future Dalek defeats; the Doctor is choked by a Kaled mutant.

What Was In the Charts? "Bye Bye Baby", Bay City Rollers; "Ding-a-Dong", Teach-In; "Angie Baby", Helen Reddy; "Only You Can", Fox; "Fox on the Run", The Sweet; "Skiing in the Snow", Wigan's Ovation.

The Lore

The story goes roughly as follows: at a drinks party at the BBC bar for the tenth anniversary, Terry Nation approached Robert Holmes and opined that there ought to be a Dalek story every year and Nation himself ought to write it. Holmes, who'd started his job as script editor trying to salvage 11.3, "Death to the Daleks", mumbled something polite and moved away. He was therefore surprised to receive a letter from Nation's agent a week later, claiming this to be a verbal agreement. This was December 1973.

Nation submitted a story proposal soon afterwards; if you've seen any Nation Dalek stories before, you can probably guess 80% of the contents. By now, the departing Barry Letts had a replacement lined up, so didn't feel obliged to pussyfoot around – he called Nation out on the repetitive nature of his Dalek stories. Instead, he proposed doing what we'd now call an Origin Story.

Our first problem is that this is all reminiscence by Letts and Holmes. Holmes's version is embroidered the way he tended to, and Philip Hinchcliffe's account differs from both. It happens to suit the idea we picked up from that Alan Whicker interview that Nation was a bit up himself and used his fluky success and crafty use of copyright as proof of his "genius". (See **Who Really Created the Daleks?** under 1.2, "The Daleks" for how much Raymond Cusick, Tony Hancock and David Whitaker brought to the party.)

Our second is that if there's any paperwork about whose idea Davros was, it's all *sub judice* because the BBC is still entangled in a suit brought by someone who, as a kid, entered a contest in *Countdown to TV Action* in 1972. It was one of many "Design a Monster" contests, this one run by the comic and judged by Letts and Jon Pertwee (see **Why Did We Countdown to TV Action?** under 8.3, "The Claws of Axos"). Steve Clarke found his original drawing, he says, in a set of encyclopaedias just as the series was coming back in 2004, but had sent a number of letters beforehand.

The copy he presented to his lawyer looks remarkably similar (which is odd, given that Letts, the supposed conduit, had long since left by the time Peter Day and John Friedlander produced their production designs – they'd not even been assigned when Philip Hinchcliffe took over as producer) and he says that, as an 11 year old, he accompanied this design for Davros (that's the name he says he made up) with an essay called "The Genesis of the Daleks". This copy of the entry he sent in 1972 (even the published artwork's largely been destroyed, so the thousands of unsuccessful entries can't have survived) is the only known remaining evidence – so if Letts left behind notes in sufficient detail for Day and Friedlander to have copied Clarke's sketch so precisely, he must also have been to every relevant department and removed each memo just in case a young viewer in Kent got litigious decades later.

Nonetheless, the idea of a solitary obsessive genius inventing the Daleks as revenge-weapons runs counter to Nation's long-running storyline in the various Annuals and comic strips he put his name to. (He and fan-author John Peel spent several years and many daft books trying to resolve the contradictions.) Just in case Clarke's lawyers prevail against the odds, we'll stick to saying that Letts wanted a definite starting-point for the Daleks rather than a vague oral tradition and a number of stages along the way, as the 60s merchandise had offered.

Nation provided a storyline by the end of March, which Holmes broadly liked but thought was impractical on a BBC budget. By now, Nation had been a script-editor on three series, so he went along with that and by 22nd April had sent in a first episode. He was also deeply involved with his own series, *Survivors*, so the remaining episodes trickled in through mid-July. Contrary to popular belief (and Hinchcliffe's claims later), Holmes barely had to touch these; the initial standoff had spurred Nation into proving himself all over again.

There are a few slight differences in where the episodes ended and shifts of emphasis along the way. Sarah's reaction to the radiation from the Thal warhead was more pronounced, more like the way the TARDIS crew reacted on the first trip to Skaro. Bettan was male, but the interesting detail is that the description of Davros when he enters the Bunker Lab isn't quite what we got. He's more like a Mondas Cyberman (4.2, "The Tenth Planet") in a Dalek-like wheelchair. (A later production team went with exactly this idea for a Cyber-creator, John Lumic, in X2.5, "Rise of the Cybermen".) Peter Day's initial design sketches show that this was the idea well into pre-production. Apart from raising more doubts over that lawsuit, it's odd that he's not given much description in his earlier appearance, at the end of the first episode as shown. The third episode would have ended with the missile destroying the Thal Dome, and Part Four was the Doctor capitulating to Davros to spare his friends from torture. Apart from continuity with the stories either side of it, the most significant changes were made by the director – either in preparation or, in one case, on the studio floor.

That director was David Maloney, who'd been busy since the last time he dealt with Nation and Daleks (10.4, "Planet of the Daleks"). He wasn't thrilled at returning to *Doctor Who*, but Hinchcliffe sold him on the prospect of a new kind of story and a chance to experiment. He quickly made sure that none of the scenes with the Daleks in motion were on location – he'd been caught out that way before. Keen to add a mythic air to the set-up, he asked for the Time Lord's hood to look something like Death at the start of *The Seventh Seal*; this as much as the logistics moved the introductory conversation to a battlefield on Skaro rather than a sunlit garden. (That garden thing: Maloney recalled it as a "Chinese" garden. Nation was annoyed at losing this setting, but Holmes mentioned something like it in a similar mission briefing in 16.1, "The Ribos Operation" and his one novelisation, 22.4, "The Two Doctors", gives Jamie a vague memory of another such *hortus conclusus*. So did Nation take it from Holmes or vice versa?) Since work ended on "Revenge of the Cybermen", the public had seen the new Doctor. (Actually, two: the audience for *Doctor Who and the Seven Keys to Doomsday* had seen Trevor Martin defeat Daleks and make a first visit to the planet Karn – see "The Brain of Morbius" and **Can They Do It Live?** under A6, "The Music of the Spheres".)

- There was a bit of a rehearsal on 2nd January, 1975 prior to filming. On the same day, there was a delayed recce at the chosen location, Betchworth quarry in Surrey (we'll be seeing that again quite a bit). The following day, some of the oldest Dalek shells were repainted gunmetal grey. (There are scholarly articles detailing the long, complex story of which props, or bits of props, were which colour when. In brief: the "active" Daleks for this story were 60's veterans painted to look like those on Spiridon in Maloney's last story; the "stooges" are the ones built for that story.)

- For the opening shots and the discovery of the corpses, the WWI-vintage weapons were provided by a film hire company, Baptys, and two armourers were along (Alf Trustram and Jack Wells). You may have spotted that the futuristic weapon is a Drahvin gun from 3.1, "Galaxy Four". The actors hired to play Thals and Kaleds were advised that they would have short haircuts (by 1975 standards, at least); those playing Mutos might get a lot of latex applied to their faces. Less overtly, the two speaking-role Mutos back in the studio both had regional accents – West Midlands for Steven Yardley (22.2, "Vengeance on Varos"), Wales for Roy Evans (3.4, "The Daleks' Master Plan"; 10.5, "The Green Death") against the more RP city-dwellers of Skaro.

- Hinchcliffe arrived on one day and was asked by Maloney to keep quiet about all the rats he could see – Maloney doubted that they'd get anything in the can if the costume and make-up women ran off.

- The nose-cone of the projectile was, like the model of the whole missile, based around Recovery 7 from 7.3, "The Ambassadors of Death". Sladen had been concerned about her fall and had practiced a little, managing a ten-foot drop. On the day, Terry Walsh decided that it wasn't worth the risk and bought in Tracey Eddon (see Volume 6), even though the studio fall was "only" eight feet.

- Meanwhile, in a deconsecrated church in Crouch End, usual Schools Television animators Bura and Hardwick provided film shots of the Thal and Kaled domes – one of the models is also to be seen on Ravon's model battlefield.

- Rehearsals began on 16th with long-time Dalek voice-artist Michael Wisher using a wooden wheelchair to run through Davros's moves. To make sure he was projecting the personality entirely with his voice, he sometimes wore a paper bag with eye-holes over his head. Sometimes, he found that people forgot he was there. His mask was started before they had finished casting the role, so John Friedlander began with a generic head-mould and, for a job on this scale, used standard latex rather than the more costly foam latex he had used for Styre ("The Sontaran Experiment").

By now, Hinchcliffe's notion of Davros as a latter-day Mekon had prevailed, and the tunic and charred skull-like face were developed. (Incidentally, there are reports that Roy Skelton had been given first refusal on Davros; like Wisher, he had been in *Doctor Who* on camera as well as providing voices. One version we've heard, unverified, is that after the experience of make-up for "Planet of the Daleks", just for Wester's death-scene, he declined a six-episode stint in latex.)

• The first studio session was two days, the 27th and 28th, in Studio 1. There was a visit from young winners of yet another "Design a Monster" contest, some of whom were shocked to find that Davros wasn't a prop. In studio, Wisher had opted to wear a kilt and knee pads under the half-Dalek chair (designed by Peter Day, this story's main effects designer – Friedlander only received a credit for the Davros mask in Part Six). General Ravon was a composite of two earlier characters from the plot outline and was played by Guy Siner. (He was later in *Secret Army* as a Nazi hunting down the French Resistance, and later still the same character played for laughs, Gruber in '*Allo 'Allo*. And later yet a Minbari priest in *Babylon 5*.)

Day two had a small pause when the Doctor was almost the first exterminee, as the prop Dalek gun didn't actually fit inside the one-armed Dalek, and both Wisher and Dennis Chinnery got the giggles. The mini-train used in the first episode was initially unable to bear Baker and Marter's weight. The Detention Cell scenes from Part Four were also recorded that day, so you can have fun playing "Spot the Iron Cross": Peter Miles was asked not to wear it after the first recording block. Part One was edited on 29th. (This was all happening between broadcasts of Part One and Two of "The Ark in Space" and that huge ratings spike.)

• Part Six under-ran, and Maloney decided that the original cliffhanger – the Doctor hesitating before touching the wires – was too soon. Instead, he bulked out a scene that had been trimmed back (originally, the Doctor would emerge coated in green rubbery gunk that was trying to smother him), making a physical menace the immediate danger and the moral debate a set-piece within the climactic episode. Baker requested space to compose himself for this, realising that this was the crux of the story and a large step in his Doctor moving away from comic-strip heroism.

• Three days later, Part Three was edited; it over-ran, so some scenes were swapped around. The original end was that, after the Thal missile struck, Ronson was the first person to be exterminated. Part Four was spliced on 3rd March, the day before Part One had its music and sound effects dubbed (yes, that's just four days before it was shown).

• The Daleks' return was usually enough to get some publicity, but the "hook" of returning to their origin, plus a new Doctor and Nation promoting his new series *Survivors* (the first episode of which went out between parts Five and Six), gave it more zest than usual. Predictably, Mary Whitehouse and her handful of followers made a fuss but, less expectedly, Terry Nation was privately disquieted by the opening scene, especially the slow-motion deaths.

• Towards the end of the run, the first of two sets of collectable pasteboard figures of old monsters and new characters were inside special boxes of Weetabix (a UK cereal, developed from an Australian one but no longer resembling it) with settings for adventures depicted on the back of the boxes. These figures acquired an almost talismanic status in 90s fandom (and see X5.12, "The Pandorica Opens" and associated essay). The TV adverts and posters all made a point of mentioning that any three figures in your purchased box was guaranteed to include a Dalek.

• Nation and the Daleks were emphatically "back" – over the summer, he capitalised on his reputation's restoration, releasing stories in the London *Evening News* and reviving the Dalek Annual. There was an ice-lolly with cards and 60s-style "boasts" on the wrappers. The omnibus repeat over Christmas got about as much build-up as the first broadcast, with a Frank Bellamy drawing in the *Radio Times* and the LP version, released ahead of "Destiny of the Daleks" in 1979, was plugged after most episodes of Season Seventeen. That was, to use a phrase we hear repeatedly in the story, only the beginning.

• Decades later, Harriet Philpin (Bettan) was in

the headlines for her other notable role: there was a plan to revive the celebrated 1972 R. White's advert, in which she was the indulgent wife of the "secret lemonade drinker" – but nobody could find her. She showed up in rural Ireland after her children saw the news coverage. (An earlier revisit of the ad had resorted to using John McEnroe. We don't know why either.)

12.5: "Revenge of the Cybermen"

(Serial 4D, Four Episodes, 19th April – 10th May 1975.)

Which One is This? It's the 1970s story with Cybermen in it. They even wear flares.

Firsts and Lasts Apart from a blink-and-you'll-miss-it cameo in 10.2, "Carnival of Monsters", it's the first Cyberman appearance since 1968 and the first time the actors in each costume did the voice (rather than have Peter Hawkins or whoever perform it over in a corner of the studio). It's the first mention of gold as a problem for them, and the debut of a future catchphrase: "Excellent".

What will one day become a familiar decal shows up here in a different context (see "The Deadly Assassin" and every subsequent Time Lord story) and Carey Blyton gives us a third and final score (aided by future regular Peter Howell). It's the first performance in the series by David Collings and the last by Kevin Stoney (3.4, "The Daleks' Master Plan" and 6.3, "The Invasion"), not that it's immediately obvious who's behind all that latex. This is the first time we see the sonic screwdriver fail to perform in a crisis – the Doctor has to whack it on a bench to make it work.

Right at the end, we have the first instance of UNIT summoning the Doctor (at least on screen). Most of all, for a generation of fans, it was the first story released on home video.

Four Things to Notice About "Revenge of the Cybermen"...

• Nerva Beacon is the Ark a few thousand years earlier. It's more functional and a lot more military. Most of the retread of the set is a matter of placing charcoal-grey panels with circular indentations on all the walls and dotting the floor to match. This has the unfortunate effect of making the space station look as if it's made of Lego. The shop-dummies playing dead crewmen don't help.

• The new-look Cybermen are the shiniest yet, and you can tell at a glance who's in charge. Not that this matters, since the Cyberleader gets to do pretty much all the talking – in an accent that wanders from Holland to Edinburgh to the Bronx to Jamaica. His underlings, on the other hand, get to do all the shooting and have guns built into their heads, operated by a toggle-switch on the chest-unit. Depending which side of your tenth birthday you are, this is either the coolest thing ever or plain daft.

• All that glisters is not Cyber, however, and the planet Voga (or what's left of it) is supposedly made of gold but seems a bit muddy. It's rare for an alien world to seem quite so endless and convoluted – and a relief after the last story tried to get us to believe that two nations within walking-distance of each other had been at war for centuries. The Wookey Hole location is just big enough to warrant motorised transport inside a cave, so there's a railway and speedboats, plus staircases and cliffs, all under a roof. Elmer Cossey, an experienced BBC film cameraman, struggles to do justice to this on 16mm and mostly gets away with it.

• After his work on "Doctor Who and the Silurians" (7.2) and "Death to the Daleks" (11.3), you can expect three things from Carey Blyton's score: it will plod along with a bovine lack of urgency; it will be scored for a rag-bag of unorthodox instruments; it won't sound like anything else ever broadcast as drama. The use of tubular bells for the Cybermen is effective but not everything hits the spot. This time, Philip Hinchcliffe is less indulgent than Barry Letts, so in comes Radiophonic Workshop newcomer Peter Howell to add some John Carpenter-ish synth-growls and make the whole thing seem slightly less like a school play. It almost works.

The Continuity

The Doctor says that everything is of interest to him. He's briefly returned to his post-regenerative habit of abruptly falling asleep after spurts of activity (or just yelling *Harry Sullivan is an imbecile*). In this story, more than any other, it's apparent that his shoulders are his most vulnerable point. [See also "Terror of the Zygons"; 9.3, "The Sea Devils"; 22.1, "Attack of the Cybermen" and many others.]

What Were the Cybermen's Daftest 'Only' Weaknesses?

To date, the Cybermen have been in 25 stories. Two of these merely had them as guest cameos (6.7, "The War Games" and 10.2, "Carnival of Monsters"). One visit was as part of an army the Doctor assembled from across time and space (or that portion of it represented in the BBC Wales stock-cupboards) to rescue Amy Pond (X6.7, "A Good Man Goes to War"). In 2021's "Flux" story, they were cannon-fodder.

That leaves 21 stories where the Cybermen were presented as implacable, unstoppable foes that the Doctor had to overcome somehow. Some of these stories presented two or more methods of attack, a main one at the end (a missile, usually) and a hand-to-hand improvised weapon. These are often extremely silly. To their credit, the Cybermen have responded by upgrades or patches to fix these for next time. Mostly. Nonetheless, their reputation for logic and technological superiority has taken a bit of a beating over the decades.

What follows is a catalogue of 20 separate Achilles Heels, each of which led to a defeat that wouldn't have happened if they'd just run their invasion-plans by someone. In their most recent outing (X12.10, "The Timeless Children"), they're even advised by the Master (that's *the Master*) to "workshop" their plans a bit first. Maybe they should have taken a hint from the Daleks (25.1, "Remembrance of the Daleks") and had a bright 11-year-old on the committee to say "hang on…"

Radiation (4.2, "The Tenth Planet")

For some reason, the Cybermen are more acutely sensitive to radiation than puny earthlings. This suggests that they made the journey from Mondas in lead-lined spaceships. No wonder they're short of fuel. In subsequent stories in Season Four, Ben seems fit and healthy, with a full head of hair, so the protective suits did their job and the radiation can't have been all that intense. Nonetheless, waving a reactor rod in the vague direction of a Cyberman makes it stagger around and drop dead. In fact, they daren't even enter the room.

Why the Cybermen themselves don't use these suits is a puzzle – even if they don't fit, the Mondasian menace might have brought some more tailored protective garments with them. Or, as with their entry into the base with stolen anoraks as a fiendish disguise, they could have just popped the suits over their ear-tubes and done it in short shifts, getting their knees dosed in Roentgens, but remaining otherwise unscathed. As the whole point of going to Antarctica was to capture a base with a Zeeeee Bomb and the whole point of invading Earth was to get hold of energy, you would think they'd take basic anti-radiation precautions before finding the one inhabited part of the South Pole and tapping into its power-supply. It's not as if they forgot to top up their antifreeze. Did the ones who went to non-atomic power-stations die of coal-dust inhalation?

Gravity (4.6, "The Moonbase")

On subsequent visits to this neck of the woods, the Cybermen seemed unaffected by radiation and could linger on the Moon's surface or walk in space. The publicity stills show one moonwalking Cyberman who's especially nonchalant about all the Becquerels he's soaking up while standing with his hands behind his back. However, reluctant to launch a frontal assault on the Moonbase, they use sneaky subterfuges and fifth columnists to get their way.

The Doctor surmises that gravity is a weakness. Why? It's not as if the humans are crawling around inside the Gravitron control like lungfish. They can walk normally inside their base but skip about on the lunar surface like we know real astronauts did (more or less – we can cut them some slack because this story was made three years before). As we later discover, Telos is very like Earth so it's not as if walking in Earth-like gravity is especially onerous for Cybermen. Still, it keeps them at bay and the Doctor finally rids the Moon of the silver-booted menace by turning the Gravitron on the surface and forcing the Cybermen into the humiliation of aerial ballet. So *lack* of gravity was what intimidated them, apparently. Except that this is also not something that the international science-wonks controlling the weather ever seemed to encounter and didn't matter when the Cybermen travelled to the Moon in low-tech spaceships.

All of which means that, against all logic (something of a theme here), the problem for the Cybermen isn't the technology, nor the force of nature, it's a phobia. The otherwise-fearless Cybermen are scared of just this one thing. What *was* a genuine problem for them was noise inside the control-room, so we ought to be glad the Doctor's recorder wasn't the eventual salvation of Earth. Nonetheless they ignore that and spend the whole of Episode Four dithering around outside, converting their unassailable position at the last

continued on page 93...

12.5 Revenge of the Cybermen

- *Background.* We get confirmation that he knew Houdini and taught him some knots [11.5, "Planet of the Spiders"; X11.8, "The Witchfinders"]. He remembers Voga, but he needs prompting to link it to Cybermen. He knows something of the (unseen) Cyber-War and recalls the Glitter-Gun and the way the human victors used dead, gilded Cybermen as hat stands.
- *Ethics.* The Doctor's none too fussed about killing Cybermen and seems to relish threatening Kellman with a Cybermat. He doesn't mind threatening the Cybermen with one of their own bombs.
- *Inventory:*
  – *Sonic Screwdriver.* Now this is weird: the dialogue suggests he used it to open the otherwise impregnable bulkhead locks and nothing else could have done it, but we *see* him use a regular long-stem screwdriver. He does use it on the lock of Kellman's flat but needs to thump it on a bench to make it work.
  – *Time Ring.* It can only malfunction due to a 'molecular short circuit'. As soon as its purpose is fulfilled, it vanishes.
  – *Other.* In yet another comedy "empty his pockets" scene, we see an apple core and a bag of jelly babies. He's also got that conventional screwdriver and later has several other tools when fixing the Transmat [an odd place to leave tools, so they're probably his].

The TARDIS The light on top now works [did the Time Lords put it in for repairs?]. The space-time telegraph seems to have filled the console room with ticker-tape. There are drift-compensators that need setting or else she'll wander off again. [This may be to allow for the motions of planets and the expansion of the universe, so the TARDIS stays in a specific room in absolute spatio-temporal terms, rather than let the rest of the cosmos shift without her.]

The Supporting Cast
- *Sarah* takes umbrage at the suggestion that her ankles are thick. She seems able to figure out how to operate a transmat and drive a skimmer without instruction. Her resistance to the 'plague' is remarkable, especially compared to the 'tough as an old boot' Warner. She and Harry bicker like an old married couple.
- *Harry* dreams of buying himself out of the Navy and setting up a medical practice in the country. He figures out a method of escape (when Sarah lets him get a word in) and, when recaptured, accepts impending death rather resignedly. He has a terrible memory for names, forgetting 'Cybermen' when trying to fill the Doctor in on developments. His attempt to free the Doctor from an encumbering bomb earns him the epithet 'imbecile' [see X9.8, "The Zygon Inversion"]. He's unimpressed by the TARDIS materialising just as he returns to Nerva.

The Non-Humans
- *The Vogans* have hidden inside their survival shelter for centuries while their planet has wandered the galaxy. Vorus, the leader of the guardians of the mines, maintains a mining guild, despite the Vogans no longer trading the gold (their one asset) with the other races. Guild members wear doublets and trousers. The Guild has a logo resembling an art-nouveau figure eight [yes, that one: "The Deadly Assassin"]. They keep their hair short.

Other citizens let their locks flow and wear cassocks. In all cases, they are humanoid but with vast domed heads, mainly bald, and white hair and beards. They have heavy lids over their eyes and thick protuberant ears. The City Militia, under Tyrum, are equipped with short-range projectile weapons.

Even though the Cybermen are presumed extinct, the Vogans are paranoid about revealing their presence in case there are any remaining stragglers. They mistrust all non-Vogans.

- *The Cybermen.* We haven't seen this design before and won't again. It has corrugated "earmuffs" and "handles", plus similar ribbing on the tubes [some of which seem almost purely decorative, not connecting to anything]. The knees are concertina-like, but there are solid electrical junctions on the joints and between where shoulder-blades would be. They are shinier than usual and have reflective strips on their "shirt-tails". The face-plates aren't quite mirror-like [c.f. 25.3, "Silver Nemesis"] but getting that way.

The voices have more intonation than normal, and the Cyberleader (designated by black "muffs") has, as the Doctor notes, a 'nice sense of irony'. [Any other generation of Cyberman would make the story's title silly, but this lot genuinely seem motivated by a sense of grievance.]

There have been Cybermen with stun-weapons in their head-lamps, but this set have what seem

What Were the Cybermen's Daftest 'Only' Weaknesses?

...continued from page 91

cliffhanger into an opportunity for defeat, because they don't want to be in the same room as Hobson's big scary gravity-doughnut. But standing around looking tough (or nonchalant) a hundred yards away is perfectly safe. It might have been a more satisfying ending if the Doctor had increased the local gravity, flattened the Cybermen to pizzas with hands and feet, then switched off and invited everyone out to play Frisbee.

The other odd thing is that the type of Cyberman seen here is rather under-represented in the "convergent evolution" line-up we got in "The Doctor Falls" (X10.12). In this, as you will recall, the action takes place in a big ship whipping around a black hole – but everyone's walking perfectly normally and the assortment of whatever Cyberman costumes BBC Wales has in stock all manage to cope. Indeed, even the Mondas-style ones have jet-boots and can shoot off into the sky. Gravity-schmavity, they can take a lift between floors. The logical inference is, therefore, that only the three-fingered / boiler-suit type had this specific glitch. Did they programme it in specially, just before launching an invasion-plan that hinges on using a gravitational-controller? That's very sporting of them.

Nail Varnish Remover (4.6, "The Moonbase")
In the blokey environment of the Moonbase, it took a woman to think up the obvious plan of attack: melting the plastic coating of the chest-units with whatever solvents were on hand. A secretary from 1966 out-thought the hand-picked scientists of Europe. What's really daft about this is that nobody ever tried it again, despite the Cybermen not altering this aspect of their design for centuries to come.

Being Sent to Bed Without Any Supper (5.1, "The Tomb of the Cybermen")
The Doctor defeats the Cybermen by, er, letting them go back into hibernation and locking the door behind him. There are detours along the way, but that's pretty much it. The Cyber-Controller tucks them all in to conserve power and has to be dealt with as part of mopping up the Brotherhood of Logicians subplot. Quite what happens to him at the end is peculiarly garbled, because what we see is a metal Cyber-Controller and a part-metal Toberman tussling over whether an electrified door should be open or shut – either or both of them would, ordinarily, complete the circuit anyway. Then 18 years later, we're told that the Cyber Controller wasn't really hurt at all. Therefore all that the 1967 story achieved was telling Earth where the last Cybermen were resting. You'd think a bombing-run would have followed, to save us the bother of "Attack of the Cyberman" (22.1). Or maybe just filling the tomb with concrete.

Someone Remembering to Shut the Door (5.7, "The Wheel in Space")
Doors do seem to be a problem for Cybermen. About midway through Episode Six of "The Wheel in Space", the Doctor rigs up an electric arc in the entrance to the Power Room, next to the curious plants that change from episode to episode. However, after six episodes of chicanery and hypnosis, the mighty invasion force of two Cybermen is augmented by a couple more (one of them an older model) who have done a space-walk by flapping their hands. They seem quite unprepared for Jamie's fiendish door-closing plan. This is, let's remember, a story with the Cybermen apparently preparing their scheme thousands of years earlier by making a star go nova. A bit more forward planning with a spare key might not have hurt. They have guns that could make a new door, if they'd thought about it.

Cheering Up (6.3, "The Invasion")
Far from being the benignly avuncular boffin he's presented as being, Professor Watkins is an evil genius whose teaching machine works just like the indoctrination devices of the obviously-malignant Krotons next story. It's a method of Pavlovian conditioning by remote control, inducing emotional responses in the victims. The Cerebratron Mentor is used as a hand-weapon against the Cybermen, but the *real* surprise is that anyone involved thought of this gadget as anything other than a torture device or mass-hypnosis implement. However, stimulating emotions in humans is easy – literally child's play. Doing it in someone whose endocrine system, endorphin receptors and hypothalamus have been surgically removed is harder. Gut reactions need a gut. Still, the Cybermen get to endure emotions when this awful contraption is turned on them. Fear grips one and sends it mad, despite its lack of adrenal glands.

The ones the Doctor and Tobias Vaughn shoot

continued on page 95...

12.5 Revenge of the Cybermen

to be projectile weapons. When the head-guns are fired, with a switch on the chest-unit, a small flash and release of smoke follows. The Cyberleader can summon back-up without verbal commands.

Gold is a concern to them. The Doctor initially says that as a non-corroding dust, it clogs their respiration. However, the metal also makes their scanning technology fail to function accurately and seems to knock them out even when not inhaled.

In a token gesture towards the logic they claim as their trademark, they weigh things in kilos.

Planet Notes

• *Voga* is the remains of the fabled Planet of Gold and has – somehow – arrived unexpectedly in Earth's solar system, orbiting Jupiter. It's big enough to be registered along with the main moons [rather than the 60 or so minor ones invisible from Earth]. It has Earth-normal gravity and atmosphere; Vorus's comments suggest the surface would be habitable, if the residents weren't so scared of discovery.

The planet's core is pure gold and was mined. The proportion of gold to other minerals decreases as one approaches the surface. It appears spherical from space. The population mainly live in the emergency survival shelters but a military elite patrol the mines. No vegetation is evident but the mine areas include large amounts of liquid water. The Vogans use 'skimmers' (tiny speed-boats) and small trains to get between offices.

• *Nerva* is a space-beacon, with a crew of 50, currently also the base for an exographer who's exploring the new moon. The Docking Bay is in section P [so not where the Shuttle would be in "The Ark in Space"]. There are two nearly identical transmat bays, each with three "booths" with circular pads and lights. These rely on something called a 'Pentalion Drive' [see X3.7, "42"], which can be kept on a necklace.

History

• *Dating*. It's thousands of years before "The Ark in Space" and considerably before the refit of Nerva Beacon for its later role as a cryo-ark. Transmats are used and trusted: as per "The Mutants" (9.4), they need specific transmission and reception sites. [In "The Ark in Space", the Doctor saw a Bennett oscillator and judged that it was built in the 'late twenty ninth, early thirtieth' centuries; that's broadly been adopted as the time that "Revenge of the Cybermen" takes place, with "The Ark in Space" happening thousands of years on from *that*. X5.2, "The Beast Below", however, massively cocks things up by running with the "twenty-ninth century" reference as being the time of the Solar Flare incident.]

The Doctor thinks that Voga is the thirteenth moon of Jupiter. [There were 13 known at the time of writing – the last being announced in September 1974 – and the current tally of how many significant-sized bodies orbit the biggest planet is 79 (27 still await names). A fourteenth was found, then lost, around the time of "Terror of the Zygons".]

We're told that the Cyber-Wars were 'centuries' ago and that Voga appeared in the solar system 50 years before the story's beginning. [If Voga drifted normally, then the Cyber-wars were raging before humans started building boats or wagons, let alone spaceships, so Vorus would be recalling a totally different war from the one with the Glitter-Guns. This *might* be how the Cybermen in 5.7, "The Wheel in Space" were aware of a supernova that was about to be visible from Earth. However, Voga cannot simply have drifted into the solar system in anything under 100,000 years even if only from Proxima Centauri, because any faster and it wouldn't have entered orbit around Jupiter without braking very obviously and giving away the fact that it's not just a lump of rock. We'll examine one possibility in **Why Does Earth Keep Getting Invaded?** under "The Android Invasion"]

[X7.13, "Nightmare in Silver" also takes place in the aftermath of some long-concluded "Cyber-Wars", but the details there indicate that those occur in the *far* future – fifty-third century, minimum – and are a completely separate event from the conflict that resulted in Voga's destruction. "Revenge" attributes the Cybermen's defeat in the Cyberwar to their vulnerability to gold (the Doctor: '[Humanity] discovered your weakness and invented the glitter gun, and that was the end of the Cybermen except as gold-plated souvenirs that people use as hat stands'), but the Cyberiad Cybermen were only defeated by the obliteration of the Tiberion Spiral Galaxy. Those Cybermen's ability to compensate, Borg-like, to new threats is massively beyond the versions seen in "Revenge" and 19.6, "Earthshock" and human technology (galaxy-eradicating weaponry, the ability of Ludens's flagship to instantly warp to his location)

What Were the Cybermen's Daftest 'Only' Weaknesses?

...continued from page 93

don't flail around screaming in a sewer, they just fall over and smoulder a bit. The machine itself apparently *generates* the emotions, otherwise Vaughn couldn't hope to use it. If it amplified whatever the user was feeling, the Cybermen would be hopping around hooting and occasionally saying "Oh my giddy aunt!" or snarling at Packer's latest cock-up. They must have selected a fast-acting emotional response that would kill them before they could open fire. The logical one is something that makes them not want to shoot. The Doctor's supposed to be such a cheerful soul and Vaughn's a nasty sadist despite his own surgical intervention, so it would make sense for either of them to set the machine to "happy". (Or maybe it just sends that Pharrell Williams song over their intercom and makes them self-destruct to get away from it.) We're forced to conclude that a devastating blast of bonhomie is the Doctor's weapon of choice.

Gold (12.5, "Revenge of the Cybermen"; 19.6, "Earthshock"; 25.3, "Silver Nemesis"; X7.13, "Nightmare in Silver")

We have the makings of a sensible weakness when the Doctor mentions how gold-dust doesn't corrode, so clogs up the Cybermen's chest-units after a while. Later, the caves made of solid gold block the signals from their tracking devices. Things start to get a bit silly when a Cybermat is repurposed to somehow pierce the impenetrable metallic casing of a Cyberman and inject gold-dust into the hydraulics, like a snake poisoning blood. Why isn't the Cybermat at all affected? It would be just as weird if the "fangs" actually made contact, but we can see that this malignant vacuum-cleaner attachment never gets close enough to cause any real harm. The *proximity* of gold must kill the Cyberman. This, alas, is how things will develop. Aboard the TARDIS, a Cyberleader is overpowered by the Doctor using Adric's badge. Apparently, only the rim of this is made of gold, but whatever metal it's made of crumbles like chocolate against the leader's chest-unit. Still, as scripted, this is in keeping with the original idea.

By 1988, it seems that Cybermen just react badly to gold on principle, like vampires do with garlic. A gold-tipped arrow (which, logically, wouldn't fly right anyway) can penetrate where armour-piercing bullets can't. Not only do low-velocity gold coins incapacitate the "wonderful creatures" when propelled by a *Dennis the Menace*

catapult[18], but when one drops out of the chest-unit where it lodged, the Cyberman is completely restored. It's getting to the point where just going up to one and shouting "gold!" would make it fall over and whimper.

That's very nearly what we get in "Nightmare in Silver". As part of the overwhelming stupidity of these, the most advanced and unstoppable marque of Cybermen ever seen, they've retained the base-codes of the early models and are thus vulnerable to gold and cleaning-fluid. Because software gets ill. The Doctor, recruited to become Locutus of the Cybermen, happens to have a Wonka-style Golden Ticket on his person and slaps it on his head. Somehow, this affects the programming (the hardware is the Doctor's own head so, unless this is an extreme form of Stockholm Syndrome, it ought not to affect him in any way). Watch it again if you don't believe us: the dialogue carefully explains that it's the programming that's affected by waving gold near it, not the wiring. After that, this story gets *really* silly, but that can keep for a bit.

Hopscotch (20.7, "The Five Doctors")

The Tomb of Rassilon is protected by the kind of lethal floor decoration we last saw on Exxilon (11.3, "Death to the Daleks"). Supposedly, you can deduce which of the squares on the giant checkerboard is lethally electrified by some abstruse application of Pi. In reality, the Master crosses it by just skipping on the black squares once he's walked normally halfway. But it's a logic puzzle and the Cybermen keep telling us they're all about logic.

It might be argued that the Cybermen have no reason to suspect trickery, although the Cyberleader sort of does, but with their super-augmented senses they could have heard and – as directed – seen the Doctor and the Master discuss the fact that this atrium is booby-trapped. Moreover, when they see the Master do a silly walk across the floor mat, they march en masse (well, as en masse as they can now manage, after a contretemps with a Raston Warrior Robot) rather than send one across first. That would have been logical, especially after all the other traps they've run into that afternoon. Instead, they are mown down by thunderbolts from the ceiling.

The other thing to note is that, despite having bionic legs and everything, they amble really

continued on page 97...

12.5: Revenge of the Cybermen

is streets ahead of what even the Earth Empire possesses in 10.3, "Frontier in Space". With so much effort put into making Nerva Beacon look near-future functional, we have to assume that they were thinking of it as being close to the thirtieth century. Beyond the name, and the involvement of *a* breed of Cybermen, nothing about these "Cyber-Wars" matches up. There's a heavy chance that you're the type of person who spends a lot of time thinking about this, so see also **What's Wrong With Cyber-History?** under "Earthshock"; **How Many Cyber-Races are There?** under X2.6, "The Age of Steel"; **What is the Timeline of the Earth Empire?** under 9.2, "The Curse of Peladon".]

The sudden arrival of a new Jovian satellite caused Earth's authorities to post Space Beacon Nerva there. Earth's Interplanetary Command has placed a beacon near this traffic-hazard for the next 50 years, until everyone's got it on their charts. This is Day 3 of Week 47 and the plague's been rife for 79 days.

The Analysis

Where Does This Come From? This story is, in almost every way, the flip-side of "Genesis of the Daleks". One took a celebrated old adversary of the Doctor's and re-examined the events and issues leading to their creation, making them potent by linking them back to our lives at the time. The other took their nearest rivals and just wheeled them on as bogey-men, one literally wearing a black hat, but depicting them as a threat from the past that's been ignored. In many ways, that back-from-the-dead element will be a hallmark of Holmes / Hinchcliffe plotting. The key difference between this story and, say, "The Brain of Morbius" is that, for once, we've seen the threat before. The Doctor doesn't need to log so much effort explaining how terrible it would be if they regain a foothold.

Both stories deal with the way people in the 1970s chose to think of Nazi Germany, blaming an entire genocidal regime on one person and assuming that the root causes would never be back to trouble us. This is entirely understandable as, by 1975, Hitler was almost a cartoon character in Britain. All the effort put into ridiculing the Nazis in wartime left a residue of jokes and impressions and, for anyone raised on the jokes but without direct experience of bombing, combat, bereavement or the Holocaust, there was a repertoire or gestures, a silly walk, a style of ranting but no danger. Just as Dracula or Frankenstein's Monster were diluted and made the topic for kids' cartoons and comics, so Fascism was a weird fad from another country and a bygone age, like Davy Crockett hats. That there were real far right groups in Britain trying to stir up racial tensions and blame the runaway inflation on the Protocols of the Elders of Zion was occasionally newsworthy, but people didn't generally make the connection between the collapse of the Weimar Republic and the National Front's activities in Brixton.

Instead, there were news stories, usually in summer and sandwiched between the Loch Ness Monster, chained-up Mormons and Prince Charles's girlfriends, that such-and-such a member of the Nazi elite had been seen in Argentina. A positive identification of a skull as that of Martin Boorman (Hitler's private secretary) took something like six months, so that dragged out the story. Meanwhile, the sordid realpolitik that kept Rudolph Hess (the deputy Fuhrer) in Spandau Prison alone, as part of the deal to allow western access to West Berlin, rumbled on (see 17.6, "Shada"). It was a given of adventure serials that mad scientists and wannabe dictators had German accents – any threat to home, hearth and reach that wasn't aliens or the Soviets was old Nazis on the comeback trail.

The idea of Britain or America responding to similar socio-economic conditions to late 20s Germany in a similar way was never taken seriously; instead, Germans were "like that" and the threat of a Fascist uprising was from Nazis who'd discovered cryogenic suspension in 1944, or whatever. When someone had the bright idea of bringing back *The Avengers* with John Steed as an elder statesman, guess what other relic was dusted off to give him and his new, young team an introductory work-out. (After all, it's not as if there's any lack of the right uniforms in stock after 30 years of self-congratulatory films and telly.)

We discuss in **The Lore** that there's no attempt made to treat the Cybermen here as with the Daleks in "Genesis", for various reasons. Note how, when the Cybermen were, in their turn, rethought as the result of a deliberate plan rather than the culmination of trends in society and technology, they got a Davros-lite creator (X2.5, "Rise of the Cybermen"). Both metallic monsters had been conceived (in story-terms and by their

What Were the Cybermen's Daftest 'Only' Weaknesses?

...continued from page 95

slowly across this potential hazard rather than simply jump 20 feet or so.

Reheating a Take-Away Packet (22.1, "Attack of the Cybermen")

Behold Vastial, a substance that explodes once the ambient temperature exceeds the freezing-point of water. Behold the Cryons, a race of women who die at similar temperatures. Their leader has been hiding in a fridge with a small amount of the wondrous strange snow, waiting for a visiting mammal to deliver the explosive package. It appears that the Time Lords sent the Doctor into this situation just for this one door-opening element of Flast's assassination plan. (What is it with Cybermen and doors?) The Vastial is in a foil carton exactly like the ones used for takeaway food, more or less brick sized but flaring out from the base. The Doctor opens the door of Flast's prison a crack, shoves the carton out into the warm corridor and a sentry Cyberman peers over to look at it. Bang.

There are a few odd features of this, mainly why it's so warm in the corridor. The Cybermen came to Telos specifically because the Cryons had built a refrigerated city that was handy as a place to keep the remaining Cybermen on standby. Previous incidents seem to indicate that the Cybermen can stand to float about in space at near Absolute Zero, can walk on the Moon without thick jumpers and, even on their first outing, cheerfully braved the Antarctic snows (well, "cheerfully" isn't the word, but it was less of a problem for them than radiation or old Westerns). The Cryons have sabotaged the Tomb and turned the thermostat up a bit, making Cybermen decay or go berserk, but a place this big would take a while to warm through properly – and, down in the depths right next to a cold-storage bay that *is* still working, it ought not to be any warmer than the main part where Peri's griping about the cold. It would be logical for the Cybermen to have turned up the heating to keep the Cryons away, but they *want* it cold and it's the Cryons using heat as a weapon.

A Saxophone (25.3, "Silver Nemesis")

At the start, the idea's pretty sensible. The Doctor's built a replacement portable hi-fi for Ace and has adapted it to send a jamming signal to thwart the Cyber Fleet. (As usual, they need a homing signal to invade Earth rather than just, you know, show up in unimaginable numbers, guns blazing. See "The Invasion" for a similarly strange need for hand-holding when conquering a defenceless Earth.) The nearest handy input for this is an autographed cassette of Courtney Pine that Ace picked up when they went to see him at the start of the story. This time, the limitations of the format are entirely because it's November 1988 (as they keep telling us) so – in contrast to X10.8, "The Lie of the Land" in 2018 – there's nothing for it but to use a cassette. (The Doctor forgetting to fit the auto-reverse was silly, so he's not got anyone else to blame for the blocking signal only working for 20 minutes.)

That bit's sort of alright, it's the way the Cybermen react to hearing *Frank's Quest* over their comms that's weird. In the story shown just before this (25.2, "The Happiness Patrol"), one guy with a trilby and a harmonica overthrew a repressive regime and horrified the Leaderene with his blues riffs. (Well, one riff over and over for three episodes.) Here we don't get a similar reaction from the not-Nazi-at-all-honest Wagner enthusiasts, but the Cyberleader fails to find any logic in the solo.

This is odd, as the whole point of Jazz is improvising around chord progressions within the 12-note scale; in its own way, it's as logical as chess. (This is especially true of 80s Courtney Pine performances, where he's still so far under the sway of John Coltrane as to be almost predictable if you've heard the latter. Key word: "almost".) The "rules" of such improvisation have been fed into computers and what they produced, while almost unlistenable, is pure logic. De Flores and Karl might have reason to be appalled by what they're hearing, being racists and human, but one form of music would be as bad as any other to a Cyberman. In fact, the unresolvable opening chords of *Der fliegende Hollander* would be more unsettling to a machine-being than anything.

Mirrors (X2.6, "The Age of Steel")

A new century, a new parallel universe and a whole lot of new ways for Cybermen to suck. They've overcome most of their old problems, or never had them to start with (this being a fresh start from scratch, although everyone seems to have forgotten this later) but also lost some of their former advantages. In particular, that whole original premise of surgically removing emotions fell by the wayside; this lot just put their old feelings behind a firewall. There's an Emotional

continued on page 99...

writers) as a practical response to a genuine crisis that eventually became an ideology and an end in itself. That's also what the Vogans are doing in this story.

However, by 1973, the Daleks were just ranting pepperpots and the Cybermen were just robots on a killing-spree, with no more motivation than Herman Munster or the Hitler impression Basil Fawlty did when concussed and trying to deal with benign German visitors to his hotel. Detaching the Daleks from the original 60s concerns about atomic war and bigotry and connecting them to 70s fears about genetic engineering and manipulative technocrats worked, because someone stood up to Terry Nation when he thought he'd moved on from the Daleks and was just using them to pay bills. Nothing like that happens here, which makes this story, paradoxically, more representative of how TV writers were thinking about issues.

Left to his own devices, Gerry Davis came up with a scenario about once-mighty institutions fallen on hard times. Not a wildly innovative situation for anyone in 70s Britain to conjecture, but it has a traditional appeal from before the Industrial age. We mentioned Piranesi ("The Sontaran Experiment") and that John Ruskin idea of the aesthetic appeal of ruins; that they, like majestic natural landscapes, lead the observer to contemplate something bigger than the self or the visible.

We're not too far from that in the basic premise of played-out mines, closed-down casinos and a handful of Cybermen wanting one last victory. Obviously, it's considerably cheaper to make on a mid-70s BBC budget, but capital-R Romanticism – the movement starting in the era of the early Gothic novels and just as much a symptom of the rise of science and industry – has a strong strand of melancholia about decline. The late nineteenth century brought this back with various ideas of the "Twilight of the Gods", the Yeats-style "Celtic twilight" and even the Second Law of Thermodynamics (have a look at the notes for "Doctor Who and the Silurians", then proceed to 8.5, "The Daemons").

Davis, before Hinchcliffe's revisions and Holmes's expansion of a subplot, simply had the Cybermen decide to go out in a literal blaze of glory by crashing an orbital platform into Voga. The word "revenge" comes into the title in later drafts, but the idea's there from the start. (Here we recall that Hitler, who got into power on the legend of "the stab in the back", reacted to US and Soviet intervention in the war with the V1 and V2, the "V" standing for *Vergeltungswaffen*, revenge weapons.) It's an oddly human motive, that the remaining resources ought to be diverted into a – probably fatal – attempt at retribution. As we'll note in "Planet of Evil", a thread in Gothic / Romantic fantasy is that nature itself will bend laws to allow a settling of scores and a restoration of a pre-existing balance that some crime or hubris has unsettled.

The most common manifestation of this is a villain who doesn't die until his (it's usually a "he") score is settled. This allows grotesque figures in various forms of decay to skulk around in bunkers or lairs – a notion to which Holmes will keep returning – but also crops up in stories of wronged lovers kept from death. Although there's no trace of it in "Pyramids of Mars", the 1931 film *The Mummy* hinged on that idea with a screenplay that started out as being about Count Cagliostro (a real con-man who made out he was a cursed immortal). It's there in *The Flying Dutchman* (see 20.3, "Mawdryn Undead").

Such extreme stubbornness is often set against a physical torment of some kind, making the tenacious antagonist sympathetic in many cases, but also anxious to get on with it – regardless of how many centuries of waiting have led up to the start of the film/ book/ show. It's there in the backstory of the various sinisterly-attractive exiles who manipulate people into doing wrong (see our comments on 8.1, "Terror of the Autons", but the late-Victorian tradition of wheelchair-bound anarchists with spherical bombs is there in 2.2, "The Dalek Invasion of Earth" and, of course, "Genesis of the Daleks").

These figures have a tradition that pre-dates the 70s idea of Nazis on the rebound, but they are generally held from death by love for one person rather than hatred for a society. It's obviously a strong element in our culture and some, following the lead of the French psychoanalyst Jacques Lacan (who was himself seen as "completing" Freud's work) see it as almost innate. Lacan was a big influence on the film theory journals of the 70s, so it's possible to have stumbled across this even if – unlike everyone literate in that era – you were unaware of Freud beyond a set of stock images of tweedy Austrian psychiatrists. A key idea was that there's a hiatus between a symbolic

Revenge of the Cybermen 12.5

What Were the Cybermen's Daftest 'Only' Weaknesses?

...continued from page 97

Inhibitor circuit and it's got an override code that's in the Lumic database. And it's just seven digits long. Plug Rose's incredibly handy phone into a docking port that, conveniently, it fits and *wallop!* The Cancellation Code is sent out to every single Cyberman, and they all freak out. Battersea Power Station becomes the venue for a mass Electric Boogaloo, looking good on the dance floor like robots from 1984. One guarding the Doctor looks in a mirror and sort of sobs. Another, at the Battersea boogie-a-thon, sinks to its knees and its head explodes. Five more set up a mobile disco aboard the airship behind the Emergency Exit door.

Among many questions this raises, the precise positioning of a mirror at head-height for a Cyberman in a control room otherwise devoid of reflective surfaces is strange. It can't be for Lumic, because he was in a Davros-style wheelchair. The only other person who ever went in that room, Mr Crane, was too short to use it. The big one, though, is what precisely the override code was installed *for*, given that it's triggered (if you'll forgive the word) in a scene where Lumic explains how much better life is without emotions. Who devises a method of chopping up people, putting them in cans and suppressing their revulsion or dismay, then thinks "maybe they'll want their self-loathing back at some point"? It's like equipping a phone with a self-destruct or a car with "remote steering-wheel disable protocol" (as in X4.4, "The Sontaran Stratagem"). It's almost literally asking for trouble.

Reading Really Fast (X4.14, "The Next Doctor")

Info-stamps are a method of delivering a lot of data in a hurry. The Cybermen have appropriated the technology and facts from the Daleks (somehow) while they were both floating around in the Void, then made their way to Victorian London (somehow). The machinery seems compatible with Cyber-technology, since the fact-bombs can be plugged into the Lumic Industries logos in their chests (and because they're hand-held, something of a design flaw if the Daleks made them for themselves).

What's interesting about this data-retrieval method is that when done to someone who isn't expecting it, there are extremely adverse effects. Jackson Lake comes to the literally Quixotic conclusion that he is the Doctor when he becomes the unwitting audience of a magic lantern show about enemies of the Daleks. For the rest of the story, he and the real Time Lord shine these give-a-show projectors at Cybermen and make the metal malfeasants' heads explode. They can't handle taking in data as fast as Daleks, who in "Dalek" (X1.6) can comfortably absorb the entire internet c.2012 within seconds. Once or twice this would be a bit silly, but Jackson guns down six of them this way and Rosita joins in to get another.

It even works if you shoot them in the back so they can't see the pictures. There's nothing to suggest that Cybermen have eyes in the backs of their heads so the blipvert deaths must be from the soundtrack hitting their big jug-handle ears. Who knew DVD commentaries were so dangerous? The Doctor also uses accelerated literacy to open Miss Hartigan to other possibilities, leading to...

Sexism ("The Next Doctor")

Mercy Hartigan is very overtly inscribed as a Fallen Woman, as far as they can intimate in a Christmas episode of a family-friendly show. They make no bones (so to speak) about her sexuality and even give her a red dress. With gynaecological matters thus foregrounded, the way she reacts to being hooked into the Cyber-King fits into a very familiar set of stereotypes.

At first, she is plumbed into the operational matrix and it makes her eyes go black. This allows her a glimpse of the size of the cosmos but on the fugitive Cybermen's terms, not her own. The Doctor then does something or other with an Info-Stamp (see above) and unlocks her normal personality. Ee, she's that vexed! The result of this is to amplify her frustration and tension. No amount of chocolate or herbal tea will fix this, and she causes the now-familiar feedback-loop that makes the Cybermen's heads explode.

It is, to be fair to the Cybermen, a different problem from the stupid design-flaw that caused an outbreak of Saturday Teatime Fever at Battersea Power Station. It's not just that her emotions are back, it's that the Cybes have subjugated her, like every other man, and given her a bigger conception of all the things she's *not* allowed to do while wiring her into a machine that can do a lot more than anyone else can. It was entirely predictable, even if they'd not seen *Dark Season*. Obviously, none of these Cybermen had been female before conversion.

continued on page 101...

12.5 Revenge of the Cybermen

"death" and the physical one; that many people respond to trauma or alienation by focussing on some kind of closure over whatever went "wrong" instead of handling what's going on in the present. Obviously, what Lacan actually wrote is a bit more complex and subtle than that, but the portable version was handy for explaining the appeal of nonsensical thrillers, especially Hitchcock's goofier plots.

So even though the Cybermen began as techno-zombies themselves, they aren't going to bide their time or even use their robo-snake to infect humans prior to converting them into new Cybermen. No, the ultra-logical undead are going to end it all and take Voga with them. Vorus, meanwhile, is prepared to destroy his world and end the safe, quiet half-life his people have endured for centuries. Note that, when we get to the planetoid's core, it's like *Journey to the Centre of the Earth* (the George Pal film from 1960, not the then-current Rick Wakeman concept album). No volcanoes, none of that handy "natural phosphorescence" we get in similar stories, just cold, dank, drippy rock. Voga's stuck in a rut politically, ecologically and mentally; it's sterile and just hanging on, like the Cybermen.

For obvious reasons, the Cyberleader can't be portrayed as a Byronic rebel, so the thought-process that led to this version of the Planet of Gold, fuelling the (well, it's traditional to call the Vogans the "sub-plot", but the Cybermen are almost walk-ons in their own story, like the Daleks last time) Vogan aspect of the story is clear. Tyrum thinks Vorus is vainglorious and that, to some extent, his bid to free his people is egotistical. Holmes notes that he's sort of a union leader and, as we'd seen a lot in the previous two years: miners' leaders were an easy target for *Doctor Who* writers. Holmes was more-or-less sidelined for Dicks's revisions to "The Monster of Peladon" (11.4), and – while it's not much of a stretch to see this story as him saying "no, *this*, is what it would be like" – it's significant that the Doctor doesn't spare any time for resolving this planet's internal political dispute, as Pertwee's would have.

We mentioned it in the last story, but here the debt to *Dan Dare* is too flagrant to ignore. Asteroid miners with bulbous heads and white hair (like insects or fish adapted to life without light) have their own disputes but are briefly united to aid the humans. It's in our solar system, even though the story started far away and a world just arrived in Jupiter's orbit one afternoon. If we take the Cybermen out of the equation, this story belongs in a specifically British tradition of space-opera and even the transmats – which operate point-to-point with designated reception-sites – are less like *Star Trek* than like a commuter railway. The name and uniforms of "Interplanetary Space Command" have a familiar Frank Hampton look too. Not as blatant as the near-contemporary *TV Comic* strip "The Wreckers!" (drawn by Martin Asbury), starting just as this story ended, which briefly brought back the Mekon-like interplanetary venture-capitalists called "Vogans" from the 1971 *Countdown* strip "The Vogan Slaves" (drawn by Harry Lindfield). They also have hooded eyes and bulbous heads, so Lindfield's design may have guided John Friedlander's. Or possibly not. (If you want to join the dots between *The Eagle*, *TV21* and *Countdown*, see **Why Did We Countdown to TV Action?** under 8.3, "The Claws of Axos". For the extent to which the BBC supervised – or plundered, or ignored – the various comics over the decades, see **Are All the Comics Fair Game?** under X4.7, "The Unicorn and the Wasp".)

As many people know, the name "Voga" only cropped up in this story after Davis's original proposal of "Vega" was nixed – partly because it's a real, well-known star, but also because they'd just had a Vegan and he didn't look like that ("Monster of Peladon" again). His idea was, we're told, based on "La Vega", a district of what's now the Dominican Republic, fabled as a mysterious city of gold[19] and mentioned by Columbus. Of course, the plural is "Las Vegas" ("Vega" just means "field" in Spanish), so the notion of a space casino wasn't far off anyway. Davis left Britain shortly after this story was broadcast, eventually working on early episodes of a crime show called *Vega$* ($ic). In keeping with the story's general tone, this resort was abandoned and decaying in Davis's first draft.

Why should gold be such a hassle for the Cybermen? Well, in the prologue to his novelisation of 4.6, "The Moonbase" (Target Books called it *Doctor Who and the Cybermen* and gave a cover using an "Invasion" model Cyberman and Troughton from "The Three Doctors", in that familiar Chris Achilleos manner – in shops from February 1975), Davis makes plain what he'd been thinking all those years: the Cybermen are basically Vikings from Space. For co-creator Kit Pedler, they'd been a moral threat, combining over-zealous medication and bureaucratised

What Were the Cybermen's Daftest 'Only' Weaknesses?

...continued from page 99

A Plastic Sword (X5.12, "The Pandorica Opens")

The sentry who guarded the Pandorica for centuries was dispatched by one who'd shortly take over the job. The former was what was left of a Cyberman. Considering all the silly ways with which to dispatch the Lumic model, this one is a real badass. His disembodied head develops steel tentacles and crawls around after Amy, the faceplate splitting in half to eject the previous occupant. The serrated hatch in the face snaps open and shut menacingly. It also fires tranquiliser darts. The severed right arm flails around shooting plasma bolts. Then, like the Iron Man in the Ted Hughes book, it reassembles itself and sets about trying to replace its human component with the woozy Ms Pond.

Then Rory stabs it. End of. Now, admittedly, Rory's newfound cosplay outfit is, like his new self, a Nestene replica, therefore the weapon he uses probably isn't low-carbon steel – but this is pretty pathetic for what had, up to that point, been the first Cyberman to live up to the hype since "The Invasion".

A Baby (X6.12, "Closing Time")

Spending 300 years in Colchester is obviously not good for anyone (although the further you are from the city centre, the less change you'll notice). These Cybermen are so badly-depleted that they deem James Corden the ideal candidate to become Cyberleader, after rejecting George and Shona and the Doctor and, apparently, three others and after the Doctor says he has an underdeveloped brain. Their conversion process is a lot slicker than when they tried it on Lytton ("Attack of the Cybermen"), but it's the silly Lumic one (see above). Rather than surgically remove glands and bits of the brain, they dress Craig Owen (Corden) in Cyber-rompers over his street clothes and shine a blue light, like a photocopier scan, over his face. And that's it, emotions are "cleansed". Except they aren't.

Stupidly, the Cybermen choose that specific moment to switch on the CCTV monitor *with sound*. Baby Stormageddon / Alfie starts yelling, and Craig reacts by sending the emotion-purge into reverse, making the Cybermen start shaking their thangs and exploding their heads as before. The explanation (it says here) is that humans are hard-wired to respond to their children crying – but, that being the case, it's easier to purge with a few well-aimed microwaves shorting the relevant synapses than it is to block off other emotions with a seven-digit password. But no, Craig emerges from inside his tin hat and is exactly as he was ten minutes before, no drugs, no lobotomy, no nanobots. They didn't even shave him. You call that a conversion?

Chess (X7.13, "Nightmare in Silver")

Single-mindedness comes at a price. This defeat is because the Cyberiad can't multi-task. As you'll recall from above, the Model J Cyberman was faster, nimbler, able to do bullet-time bending and capable of adapting to zap-guns. Their leader, a Cyberplanner, was upgrading the Doctor to their specs. The Doctor used a sheet of gold leaf to press pause while he devised a new plan. That plan was… chess. Well, it worked for Evil Since the Dawn of Time (26.3, "The Curse of Fenric"). The Doctor nonetheless kept secrets from his brain's new lodger, including the existence of a whole incarnation who fought in the Time War and the fact that he was all out of regenerations (since he bluffed "Mr Clever" into thinking that orange sparkly pixie-dust was an option) and so told the Cyberplanner that he had a plan that would result in check in three moves. Rather than increase the power and force an answer out of the telepathically-conjoined Time Lord, or test if he was lying, the Cyberplanner devoted computational resources to figuring out what these moves might be.

About chess: only a finite number of possible moves exist from any given position, meaning a chess-playing app on your phone could probably run through all of them in a few seconds. But no, the Cyberplanner distributes its computational matrix across every Cyberman, making them all stand still and think rather than press home their advantage in an assault they had just about won. Again, distributing the calculation across a number of machines isn't exactly taxing; some distributed calculations have used the collected screensavers of a few hundred computers rather than book time on a Cray. What everyone seems to have overlooked is that, while there are indeed computers inside every Cyberman, the main OS is repurposed human neural tissue. Unless Cybermen are made from people who were literally unable to walk and chew gum at the same time, it shouldn't be a problem for them to shoot people and ponder a chess problem.

continued on page 103...

12.5 Revenge of the Cybermen

thinking, but Davis apparently had simpler ideas. His notion seems to have been that gold will keep them away the way Alfred the Great did to the Norsemen, with bribes to not invade this year (the "Danegeld", England's first income tax). So even though gold starts being to Cybermen what mercury was for 60s Daleks (see **What Planet Was David Whitaker On?** under "The Wheel in Space"), there's a pretty straightforward line of reasoning underneath it.

English Lessons

- *Calendar* (n.): an archaic term for the sum-total of administrative changes made in a fixed period (usually a year) of a legislature. It's still used that way in some American states and the Philippines, but the main judicial use of "calendar" is for what everyone else calls the agenda, the to-do list of things to discuss. Tyrum's use of it in the sense meant here, a statute-book, is odd. It's not even Victorian (the Newgate Calendar was a list of offenders – see "The Talons of Weng-Chiang" – and that's the only way we see it used in British legal circles).
- *Cheerio* (interj.): for the benefit of Americans who think they can do Briddish accents, this means "goodbye" and not "hello". It may derive from the practice of putting your chair away after you leave the table but this is unlikely.

Things That Don't Make Sense The big problem with this story is the Cybermen's motivation. With their ranks so badly depleted, why are they letting Kellman murder potential recruits with such merry abandon? All right, Robert Holmes messed up by thinking the Cybermen were just another type of robot, but nothing in Gerry Davis's earlier scripts indicated the villains were techno-zombies – as the Cybermen's co-creator, he might have remembered that detail. Instead, it's all about an army of four tin men wanting to blow up a planet that gave them trouble in the past, rather than bionic men taken a few stages too far and on the comeback trail.

When a pair of Cybermen transmat down to the planet of gold and stomp about the place massacring everyone, nobody thinks of using gold, which is pretty much literally everywhere, against them. Instead, the Vogans send out wave after wave of soldiers with useless pop-guns, to get cut down like pigeons. Did the Vogans, even during the Cyber-War, never develop guns that fired gold bullets? At the very least, why not try sprinkling the Cybermen with gold-dust, the way the Doctor does? It's doubly strange when you consider that Vogans like Tyrum seem to routinely carry bags of gold-dust around with them. (They weren't expecting visitors, so this is like us usually hefting mud pies in our pockets.) The Cybermat's functional again mere minutes after the Doctor wrecks it with gold pellets, and – stranger still – gold thrown at its exterior stops it dead, but gold stuffed into its venom-snout doesn't do it any harm at all.

The Doctor's trio arrive in a transmat booth, walk right around the station to the opposite end and get to another transmat room. When Sarah's bitten and infected, the Doctor spends a lot of time fixing the latter rather than carrying her to their original point of arrival. Once he's done that, he sends Harry and Sarah to Voga rather than to the Nerva's other transmat booth. Moreover, if the transmat filters out non-human matter from Sarah's body, then not only is all known disease eliminated, but people should be arriving at their destinations stark naked. The Cybermen should just be a few internal organs slopping about on the floor.

The purpose of the Nerva Beacon is obscure at best. It's stationed around Jupiter to warn ships about the Voga asteroid, but the first ship that passes is an Earth-Pluto flight, and why on Earth would a ship heading to or from Pluto bother even going past Jupiter? (Planets aren't fixed like islands and Pluto's not even on the Ecliptic.) The idea that ships this far in the future need beacons to avoid large, noticeable asteroids is also dubious, but that's not as questionable as the idea that an inhabitable asteroid can cross the galaxy, slow down and slip into orbit around a nearby planet without anyone seeing it happen.

The Doctor's overcoat has somehow vanished when the Time Ring activates, but it's apparently back in the TARDIS in time for "Terror of the Zygons". He materialises on Nerva not wearing his hat either. Sarah seems to think that the escapade with Harry and the new Doctor has taken "these past few weeks" – maybe they subsisted on jelly-babies while the Doctor took his time fixing the transmat after defeating Styre, but if "Genesis of the Daleks" lasted for any more than the three days it seems to take, her hair would be falling out from distronic toxaemia. She also seems to know that Nerva was a beacon, then forgets and has to

What Were the Cybermen's Daftest 'Only' Weaknesses?

...continued from page 101

Deciding to be Made of Wood for a Day (X7.16, "The Time of the Doctor")

The Papal Mainframe, despite its name, is a bit hazy on what constitutes "technology" and seems perfectly happy with people building sheds, wearing clothes and so on. They've designated Trenzalore as "Level Two" and so keep everything in aspic. The embargo seems, therefore, to mean "anything that's out-of-keeping with a township from Central Europe 1650-1900", which means that nothing changes in the three centuries the Doctor's stuck there. With an unusually shrewd grasp of genre-logic and twentieth-century Earth Pop Culture, the Cybermen find a loophole to send in a scout so long as it looks as if it was carved by Gepetto. Then, reverting to their usual crass idiocy, they equip the highly inflammable varnished wooden stealth-Cyberman with a flamethrower.

Unlike Cyber-Bill in "The Doctor Falls", this one doesn't get a visit from the Blue Fairy but instead runs into a pile-up of earlier Moffat punchlines. It scans the Sonic Screwdriver (scans aren't technology?) but fails to discover that it doesn't work on wood (word *must* have got out, we've had that gag so often by now), so it... all together now... confuses the polarity, just like in "The Day of the Doctor" (X7.15) six weeks before. That illegal scan tells it that the Doctor's illegal tech has reversed the polarity of the flamethrower (somehow) so the Cuprinol-advert-Cyberman (another retread, from X6.0, "The Doctor, the Widow and the Wardrobe") points the gadget at its own wooden heart and charcoals itself before you can say *G.I. Blues*. If they'd despatched wooden Cybermats instead, skipping the stupid boasting that led to this embarrassing defeat, they would have won. Dammit, Cyber-Shades ("The Next Doctor") would have done the trick.

Leaving aside how a self-motivating marionette *isn't* technology, we heard in the previous line of dialogue that the Doctor's happily equipping anti-gravs to kids' toys, so the Papal Mainframe must be very flexible in its *fatwa* about machinery. Tasha Not-River-Song-Really must be pressing an override switch whenever she thinks it would be funny to allow something like this. In this case, the logical Cybermen aren't to blame for failing to foresee a psychopathic space-pope taking the piss.

Going Goth (X8.12, "Death in Heaven")

A nanotech rain makes dead people turn into Cybermen. Sure it does. Then, for some reason, they get their old personalities piped back from the Cloud so they can start feeling sorry for themselves. This being a Steven Moffat script, things just standing around is considered scarier than things stomping around killing. Sure it is. The terrifyingly large and unstoppable army of the deceased – now equipped with jet-pack heels just like Tony Stark – doesn't get around to doing anything much beyond moping around in cemeteries in a light drizzle before forming a suicide love-pact.

For anyone who was in Britain in the 80s, this is a familiar pattern and the lack of anyone doing their hair like Robert Smith, performing the raincoat dance or drinking snakebite is the only unusual part. The real puzzle is why Murray Gold did the music and not Nick Cave or Bauhaus.

Exploding Holograms of Apples (or something) (X10.12, "The Doctor Falls")

It's not entirely clear what's going on here. We get *two* verbal explanations, then a lot of things happen that don't exactly fit with either. What we see is a lot of explosions sending Cybermen of various generations into aerial somersaults like Stuart Fell in a UNIT uniform. These are triggered by a number of handy things, including rifles, laptops and a kid lobbying an apple. Then the Doctor goes on a killing-spree with his Sonic Screwdriver.

Quite how is anyone's guess. There's a bit of chat about the landscape being just a hologram covering fuel-lines, but unless every square foot of this CG Teletubbyland conceals a gas pipeline the size of the Trans-Siberian one, this is a bit haphazard. And these pipes have to be very thin – as strong as a plastic shopping bag, if that – and right under the surface. If the homesteaders on Level 504 are growing turnips, they'd have trouble uprooting the crops without causing a leak.

But if this is what's going on, the rest of the episode, in which the Cybermen get fried just by pointing weapons or screwdrivers at them, makes no sense. It really either needs someone to reprogramme the computer matrix to act like a minefield or a physical, mechanical trigger (a metal-detector, perhaps – they're unlikely to recapitulate their brief experiment with carpentry from Trenzalore). Instead, we get some cobblers about

continued on page 105...

12.5 Revenge of the Cybermen

be told. Harry sees no signs of injury on the corpses, despite looking straight at the necks where there should be whacking great puncture-marks. All 50 bodies presumably have the same bites, but the Nerva crew continues to think a plague's at work.

The Doctor somehow removes what we are later told were blind-headed rivets with a normal screwdriver. Stevenson then tells us that this is only possible with an ultrasonic device.

For whom, precisely, is the gabby Vogan spy in Part One working? He's got the flowing locks and ankle-length fish-net smock of a "Dove", one of Tyrum's lot, and he's shot by two of Vorus's City Militia. But why would Tyrum, who is unaware of Kellman's existence (let alone any of the rest of Vorus's hubristic Cunning Plan), send a spy to contact any humans who might, for some reason, be listening in on that frequency and let them know that there's life on Voga? If the spy has discovered that Kellman is bumping off the Nerva crew, it's sort of what Tyrum wants (or would if he thought there were any humans in the neighbourhood). So if he's warning the other humans about Kellman's treachery, why hasn't he told Tyrum first? Isn't this what Sheprah's got his own army for?

Then the dead spy is dragged all the way through the city to Vorus's office (not that this would cause the slightest comment), dumped on the floor and removed to be buried in secret. Then Tyrum digs him up to show Vorus. Magrik tells Vorus that the anonymous agent was concerned about Vorus's plan. So it's someone they knew who was in on it all. There are better ways of whistle-blowing than contacting the humans, unless this individual was hell-bent on causing a Vogan civil war. The only parties who stand to benefit from a panicked inter-Vogan conflict, triggered by warning the humans that Vogans exist, are the Cybermen. If so, what did they offer him?

In a nice little design touch, Warner's console includes a monitor relaying a feed from a camera pointed at him, built into the desk. Kellman removes the recording of the mysterious message following Warner's death but leaves everything else alone. So there's presumably CCTV footage of a metal snake giving Warner the "plague", but nobody thinks about this (especially as Kellman has hidden cameras he can tap). Nor were any of the other 50 deaths ever examined on action replay. With all the CCTV about the place, Stevenson and Lester ought to have seen the Doctor's party wandering about Nerva first.

Warner dies, and Kellman tells Stevenson and Lester to come in, because it's "better that you see for yourselves". It's really not: if the plague really were contagious, asking commanding officers to walk into a lethal situation would amount to mutiny and warrant him getting shot there and then. As it is, they prepare to shoot Warner to stop the plague spreading, even though everyone still alive on the beacon is in that room. Mere seconds after apprehending intruders with no reason to be there, Lester is giving Sarah his machine-gun.

Kellman's overpowered and made to relinquish the Pentalion Drive then... what? He's obviously not locked up or bound to a chair. Did Lester and Stevenson let this serial-murdering traitor and saboteur sit in Crew Area 3 reading old science fiction magazines? [Here's where the script trims come into play – Kellman originally went back to his smoke-filled room and told Vorus that Harry and Sarah were on their way, hence the swift arrest.]

Why was Kellman so keen to make sure everyone on Earth stopped calling the mystery moon "Neo-Phobos"? Even Stevenson remembers bits and pieces about the Cyber-Wars, so loudly calling this place "Voga" is likely to stir up a few memories. If Kellman's hoping to make a bundle when a gold-planet's residents thank him for ridding the universe of Cybermen, he'd be best advised to not let on that the legendary planet with more gold than the rest of the galaxy put together is in Earth's neighbourhood – the bottom would fall out of the market pronto.

There must be something other than gold on Voga, if only for the guns to work without melting and for all the things that *are* made of gold to have been manufactured (smelting, carving and so on). However, with most of the planet gone and everyone still breathing, the lack of plants suggests some kind of air-filtering and purification plant. Nothing wrong with any of that, although as with similar set-ups (18.1, "Meglos"; 5.4, "The Enemy of the World"; 8.4, "Colony in Space"; "Death to the Daleks"), you have to wonder how many centuries'-worth of Cup-a-Soup their ancestors stashed away.

No, the big problem here is that more useful metals will have been at a premium, making it exceedingly hard to procure, or purloin, the materials and parts needed to build a rocket in secret.

What Were the Cybermen's Daftest 'Only' Weaknesses?

...continued from page 103

the Doctor downloading it all into his hand-held gizmo (available in shops now), so he can detonate them by magic. Why not go the whole hog and set the trigger as him pointing his fingers and going *pew pew*?

On the other hand, are the explosions and apples real? If we take the "explanation" at face value, they've been eating holograms for the last three centuries. As things develop, the "weakness" is being blown up by anyone who can press ENTER or wave a screwdriver in a spaceship that seems to have been designed as a Spaghetti Western theme-park.

And the big one...

Their Own Guns ("The Tenth Planet"; "The Tomb of the Cybermen"; "Earthshock"; "The Five Doctors"; "Attack of the Cybermen"; "Silver Nemesis"; X2.13, "Doomsday"; "Death in Heaven"; "The Timeless Children")

A logical, scientifically-advanced army tends to find itself fighting humans a lot. There are more ways to kill humans than to kill Cybermen (despite this list), but rather than have weaponry designed to only work on puny earthlings, they opt for overkill. Why not equip themselves with projectile weapons to which they are immune? There's no reason for a race that prides itself on what it did for survival's sake to have civil wars, bank-robberies or an urgent desire to look tough. Nonetheless, they've each got a heavy-duty zap-gun and, for most of their history, detached these from their metal bodies so that humanoids can grab them or pick them up from where nonchalant Cybermen have left them lying around.

The Mondas model were the most open to this, with a cumbersomely-mounted killer spotlight they have to unhook from their chest-units in a motion that looks very like undoing their flies. (One in Episode Two of "The Tenth Planet" makes a real mess of it, looking as if he's got his zip stuck.) Ben disarms one with the aid of an 8mm projector and shoots the Cyberman with his own blaster; by the end of the episode, Ben and General Cutler have amassed an arsenal. Other hand-held weapons were almost as easy to wrest from the supposedly unstoppable steel giants – even Tegan could do it. The next two stories after "Earthshock" have the Master zap a Cyber Leader and the Doctor mowing them down on Telos. Inevitably, the not-really-Nazis in "Silver Nemesis" have a go too.

This design flaw was, occasionally, addressed and some Cyber-marques have their guns built in, either inside their heads ("Revenge of the Cybermen"), built into their chest-units ("The Invasion") or mounted within their forearms like the Ice Warriors' sonic zappers (the Lumic model and subsequent "Death in Heaven" design). That's no barrier to them getting hoist by their own plasma. Yvonne Hartman and Danny Pink both use the guns on other Cybermen after being ineptly converted. Not once did any Cyber Controller think to install a safety cut-out.

They've only themselves to blame. In "The Tomb of the Cybermen", we see a firing range where they test their weapons on a Cyberman. Admittedly, it's a "fully robotised" one (like using corpses for target practice), but if they hadn't purposely designed their guns to be fatal to *themselves*, they'd have won on at least half a dozen occasions.

Following the Cyber-War, any responsible government would have catalogued space-tech assets once it was clear that they were stuck in the mud for a while. Vorus is obviously not using gold, a metal almost as much used in ICBM construction as chocolate (never mind that a rocket made of gold wouldn't get off the ground – even Elon Musk hasn't tried that). Somehow, he's constructed a guided missile in his shed and nobody's reported their saucepans going missing. The Skystriker must have been made from scratch, the equivalent of those PoW films where they've made mining equipment from pencil-sharpeners and sung Christmas carols to cover the sound of someone spot-welding inside a vaulting-horse. Vorus also kept the fuelling of this beastie quiet (if Harry and Sarah can breathe, this mine-world uses oxygen, so siphoning it off to make the fuel burn was treasonous as well as risky) and presented it as a *fait accompli* – "here's one I made earlier". (He probably *did* use squeegee bottles and sticky-back plastic.) In fact it would make more sense to use the "orthodox" metal Vorus can pilfer to build a big cannon, shooting gold at the Cybermen – who, if they can now do "revenge", could appreciate irony as well.

Why is the signal from one bomb, deep inside the gold-mine, stronger than from two bombs

12.5 Revenge of the Cybermen

heading back to the less-dense rock? Two Cyber-bombs are enough to wipe out Voga (at a specific juncture of the planetoid, admittedly), but the blast from just one Cyber-bomb is so localised and feeble that the Doctor and Harry can survive by hiding behind some nearby rocks.

The Cyberleader only believes Sarah's story about a rocket on Voga after she mentions Kellman's involvement, even though she's already told him that Kellman's a traitor and he didn't react to the news at all. To be even pickier, you can see the space-time telegraph message hanging inside the TARDIS door as soon as the Doctor opens it.

All right… with hindsight it's odd that the Doctor doesn't seem to notice the Prydonian Chapter Seal splattered all over Vorus's chambers and the City Militia's uniforms.

Critique Most of old-skool fandom would have it that the bits with various Vogans venting vociferously are "padding", and the meat of the story is the long-awaited return of the second-baddest baddies. A smaller band of contrarians maintain that, in fact, Vorus and Tyrum politicking away as their embattled world chooses between stagnant safety and an all-or-nothing gamble is the *real* story and the Cybermen are a slight embarrassment. A few hold on to the vain hope that this story and its abrupt, almost sequel-hunting end will be retconned into significance once we find out why the Prydonian Chapter Seal is all over Voga (a hope that the 2020 series looked like fulfilling amid so many other drastic rethinks of 70s episodes). One thing on which everyone agrees is that the music doesn't do the story any favours. Compared to the previous story directed by Michael E Briant – the dreary, shoddy "Death to the Daleks" – an awful lot of this story works, yet the usual question is "what went wrong?"

But, for better or worse, this was a lot of people's introduction to the Cybermen, and it cashes in on their reputation by having people half-remember them within the story. Even the Doctor's hazy on a few details, which is how the public were after six and a half years. Even if this model of Cybermen is sort of the Roger Moore between more popular or "serious" iterations, they made an impression at the time and some people think of all the others as deviations from this design. The "Earthshock" model owes more to these than to the 60s versions.

The Cybermen were, let's not forget, brought back by popular demand – or so Barry Letts insisted when he foisted it on Philip Hinchcliffe – but with a lot of ballyhoo to reintroduce them. That the production team were less enthusiastic about this than their predecessors or the public simply means that there's a lot more effort put into the salvage-work on the script than in any earlier Cyberman story. (Well, almost: "The Invasion" needed a lot of work to get the UNIT format right.)

The Cybermen made sense in black and white, even if their plans and the stories didn't. Their natural habitat was Lime Grove, in op-art sets with a soundscape of Radiophonica, stock music added almost at random and people doing pathetic foreign accents. They hail from a time when simply superimposing an oscilloscope trace on the picture was considered pretty hot stuff. Seeing them on location in London was shocking and, wisely, kept to one five-minute burst per week for two non-consecutive episodes, amid a lot of mollicking around in sewers, labs and boardrooms. Seeing a couple of shiny new ones standing around in a muddy cave just draws attention to the fact that they don't move much at the best of times. The visual gimmick of guns in their heads is fine, except that these are activated by toggle-switches on their chests. They were always a bit strange, but now they're just daft.

What makes this sting is that there's no rationale behind the plan to blow up a planetoid. Gerry Davis knew that the Cybermen were cosmic vampires, hi-jacking humans to recruit fresh troops, but made no effort to disabuse Robert Holmes or Michael Briant of the idea that they were just generic robots. This ought to have been the definitive Hinchcliffe/Holmes "possession" storyline; instead it's a Saturday Morning Serial from the 30s, without even the rousing recycled Franz Waxman score. Plus, Christopher Robbie (the Cyber-Leader) is having way too much fun to be plausible as an emotionless lobotomised cyborg. Especially when it looks as if he's about to do the Time Warp again.

What we see now is Roger Murray-Leach's first go at an alien world: a planet of gold, no less. It makes more of an impact than the rather bland spaceships (although that diamond-shaped scanner and its peculiar sweep are diverting for a few moments) while the costumes and make-up for the Vogans integrate the planet and set out the factions and loyalties efficiently. The masks don't lend themselves to nuanced expressions, but the cast ingeniously avail to distinguish each character by voice or mannerisms. It falls short – and did at the time – but compared to Metebelis III a year before, it's making an attempt. The circular CSO panel for the video-screen is cleverly unobtrusive, and there's that Celtic-looking swirl everywhere. It's pretty enough in colour (not everyone saw it that way on first broadcast), but in front of it are a lot of experienced actors doing their best, not really cutting it. It all looks a bit *Stingray*… until the climax, which is nowhere near Gerry Anderson standard.

The music's as naff as Carey Blyton's previous attempts, but what that accentuates (we almost said "underscores") is the fundamental problem with all of this production: they aren't all on the same page. The music's telling one story, the pictures another and the dialogue a third. The long-term effect of this will be that Baker asserted himself, as part of the efforts to fix things in rehearsals and on location that also salvaged the Sarah-Harry scenes on Voga. Here, at least, he's an asset and redeems a few expository scenes. In a tonal dog's breakfast like this, that's less obtrusive than it will be later.

One thing is more noticeable if you watch the stories in production order; there's a phased progression away from Action-by-Havoc-style choreographed fight scenes with a harmless *Hai!* and Terry Walsh doing a roll on the ground towards something that looks like it might hurt. There are obvious reasons why the Doctor-Styre duel looks so timid, but there's no major physical violence in "The Ark in Space", then we get this story and some downright brutal clobbering and *then* we have slo-mo massacres on Skaro. The series has got real about violence having consequences, rather than it being part of the variety-show package Letts had made it. As with every story so far in this book, it's a struggle to imagine a version with Jon Pertwee in it.

Conversely, though, it's all too easy to imagine Patrick Troughton as the lead. Not the scatty, insouciant Season Six model, but the grimly xenophobic one of "The Moonbase". In this story, reaching out to other intelligent races is considered foolhardy and dangerous; we're supposed to empathise with the insular, paranoid Tyrum. There's a bit of debate about whether humans can be trusted, but it's largely a retread of "Doctor Who and the Silurians", itself not so different from "The Sensorites" (1.7). The morality of the story is, broadly, everyone knows Cybermen are bad, but nobody's sure of the best way to wipe them out once and for all. Bumping off 50 humans to kill four Cybermen seems a fair exchange, even if a few Vogans get slaughtered along the way. Showing this immediately after "Genesis of the Daleks" makes it even stranger.

Forty-five years on, it's still hard to work out what Kellman was up to – and who, if anyone, provided him with a toxin beyond the ability of the entire solar system's medical facilities to analyse and counter. It's even harder to care. Davis will always be remembered as the script editor who dumbed down the series to keep it going, so it's heartening to look at the paperwork and see him get treated as an embarrassing relic way he treated David Whitaker in 1966. That doesn't make what made it to our screens any better. Holmes tried to brain-up a clunky and obvious storyline, Briant did his best to apply logic and some little visual flair to a pudding of a story with a recycled main set and the cast did their best to make this reworking sing. The effort shows. It's almost as if the whole point of making this story, apart from marking time until the planned season-finale at Loch Ness, was to show people who wanted *Doctor Who* to go back to the old ways why this wasn't such a great idea.

So they've done that. Next.

The Facts

Written by Gerry Davis (mostly). Directed by Michael E. Briant. Viewing figures: 9.5 million, 8.3 million, 9.9 million and 9.4 million. (Part Three was 15 minutes late because the FA Cup Final was that day – Fulham vs. West Ham, so Geoff Noble would have been really confused – and the BBC allowed for any over-run with an episode of what they still called *Boss Cat*.) AIs were 57% for Part One and 58% for Part Four; no record of the other two.

Working Titles "The Return of the Cybermen"

Alternate Versions The very first BBC home video, in 1985 (cost: a mere £34.99 with an "Earthshock"-style Cyberman on the cover); no cliffhangers and clumsily redone titles in red. Some of these had a tracking flaw, so static replaced the last seven minutes (see the end of **The Lore**).

Terrance Dicks novelised this rapidly and

12.5 Revenge of the Cybermen

added a few fondly-remembered touches. In this version, the Doctor's sussed it out as early as when he opens the hatch and Harry sees something scuttling behind him: the line "not a rat – a Cybermat", used in X6.12, "Closing Time", is from this scene. There's also an early outing for "might as well use a peashooter on an elephant". Big Finish tested the waters for the other Season Twelve remakes by performing the original Davis-scripted "Return" in 2020.

Cliffhangers A Cybermat attacks Sarah; the Cybermen storm Nerva and shoot everyone down; Harry's unwittingly moments away from blowing everyone up after a botched rescue.

What Was In the Charts? "The Tears I Cried", The Glitter Band; "Loving You", Minnie Riperton; "Funky Gibbon", The Goodies; "Autobahn", Kraftwerk.

The Lore

This was another of Barry Letts's bequests to the incoming production-team – one he'd announced in a reply to a letter in the *Radio Times* shortly after Jon Pertwee's resignation was made public. A young viewer had asked why the old monsters weren't returning; Letts reassured him that there would be Ice Warriors in a few weeks (spoilers meant little to Letts, who'd sanctioned a great many in the name of pre-publicity) and "a Cyberman adventure in 1975". Robert Holmes was less enthusiastic and Philip Hinchcliffe was frustrated at having this and the bloody Daleks *again* rather than anything that inspired him. Eventually, the director assigned to Story 4D, Michael Briant, expressed a degree of exasperation.

Still, the Cybermen were good box-office and, without any clear idea who'd be playing the lead or how popular this person would be, it seemed prudent to include the two reliable draws. When Tom Baker was unveiled to the press, Pat Gorman had worn an "Invasion" Cyberman costume – but the 1973 Tenth Anniversary *Radio Times* special had shown a composite, comprising that head and chest-unit over a "Moonbase" body with silver Wellington boots. The *Radio Times* special had aroused the curiosity of younger viewers about a popular monster they'd not properly seen.

• Gerry Davis, now associated mainly with *Doomwatch* but working on *Softly Softly*, came back to the office to discuss options. He was pleased to see that his idea of pinning up synopses of every previous story, with photos, to avoid repetition was being upheld. (This slightly confounds the fan-lore that "The Seeds of Doom" was almost given the same title as a Troughton story.) There were exploratory talks and, by early May, a storyline had been agreed. This had plot-beats recycled from 4.6, "The Moonbase" (the first cliffhanger is identical to the second in the 1967 adventure), but set in a space-casino that was over a gold-mine. If you're thinking that this sounds like 4.7, "The Macra Terror", the very next story in Davis's run as script editor, you're not far off. Space Vegas would have to wait until the 2013 Proms (or that episode of *Buck Rogers in the 25th Century*), but the basic shape of a story where the Cybermen couldn't get into the mines under a resort that they wanted to use was there.

Davis was hired because he had co-written many Cyberman stories – but, let's not forget, he was brought in to dumb things down after Donald Tosh, and had written a condescending rejection letter to original Story Editor David Whitaker (concerning the potentially interesting proposal "The New Armada", passed over in favour of, oh dear, 4.5, "The Underwater Menace"). He may well have been the person who finally trashed Holmes's first script, "The Space Trap" (see 6.4, "The Krotons"). Holmes was now on a long-term bid to undo all of Davis's restrictions, but nobody seems to have thought there would be trouble. The formal synopsis was in by the end of May and four episodes were commissioned at the start of June.

Between then and the end of July, when the first episode arrived, it was looking as if the story would be relocated to the setting of the Ark to save money. Letts seems to have been the source of this idea (sets being the single most expensive thing in any BBC production); moving the story to a later transmission slot to hide this made a bit more work for Holmes but not as much as what all the other stories necessitated. Holmes was lukewarm about this opening episode – and Davis's simplistic approach – but waited a month for the rest to come in before listing things that needed rewriting. You will recall that late August 1974 was also when he was babysitting Bob Baker and Dave Martin on "The Destructors" and had just been salvaging "The Ark in Space". The elements we now know were there in the wrong proportions.

Part One, subtitled "The Beacon in Space" begins with a Cybermat attacking a female Warner (the captain) on an old ore-processing satellite converted into a beacon. There's a crusher around for when they need a hazard and it's got traces of gold in it. There are liquid oxygen tanks the right size to hide a Cyberman and a medical officer, Dr Anitra Berglund (someone had been listening to Grieg's *Peer Gynt*). Kellman had done a Klieg-like deal with the Cybermen (as per 5.1, "The Tomb of the Cybermen") and once the first one was revealed, he and it revived others.

Part Two, "The Plague Carriers", included a medical X-ray that can be converted into a radiation weapon. The Cybermen plan to play billiards with the beacon to knock the asteroid out of orbit and into the sun. It's only in Part Three, "The Gold Miners", that we find that the asteroid is inhabited. Gold miners with Welsh surnames have been stranded there for 25 years and regard their new visitors as thieves. Kellman had made contact and lied to one, Jones, about his son still being alive and ready to meet him. The Doctor has to persuade them that they are being duped, but can't find the matter-beam station until the start of Part Four, "The Battle for Nerva", which is just as well as Anitra is held hostage. Kellman's killed and the Doctor offers himself as scientific advisor to the Cyberleader. Harry reprogrammes the Cybermats. Stevenson fills them with gold-dust, saving the day, and also reveals that he put the TARDIS in his cabin, thinking it was a portable toilet.

Aside from Holmes's qualms about women being killed on screen, the problems were fairly obvious. Anitra took up what looked like a Sarah-shaped space in the story, Harry was ill-thought-out (his one moment of consistent characterisation being fleeing in terror when Sarah starts to undress), the Doctor was standing around reading bits from his diary instead of doing much and it was all a bit Saturday Morning Pictures. The main problem was that two stories – a space-battle between Stevenson and Cybermen and the Doctor trying to lead the mine-dwellers to truth and freedom – competed for attention without much to link them. It was studio-bound and needed to establish connections with the Ark storyline. Hinchcliffe wrote to Holmes and Letts about his worries in early September.

• Briant formally started work at the end of September and had four scripts on his desk. He read them and thought they needed even more work. Hinchcliffe agreed. The first concern was that the Doctor wasn't in much danger in the story's latter half, but also that Sarah had little to do throughout and that it was aimed primarily at kids. Hinchcliffe suggested that the humans (and Doctor) are kept alive to physically carry bombs into Voga's core, where Cybermen can't go.

Davis had written the story "blind", unaware that they now had a more active Doctor, so Harry's duties needed refinement. He had also written it with barely any location filming, thinking of this as primarily a way of punctuating studio recordings (as it had been in his day). Hinchcliffe wrote to him in early October stressing the need for more development rather than just incidents happening one after another and proposed that Holmes should add this to the pre-existing story rather than demand last-minute rewrites from Davis.

The all-gold asteroid was called "Alanthea" (an old Greek girl's name now in vogue because of Minecraft), but this was close to "Amalthea", the fifth moon of Jupiter (also the name of an asteroid). Then it was briefly "Vega". Then, possibly looking at that list of old stories on the wall, someone remembered that there was a real, famous star called "Vega" and only a few weeks earlier a space miner called "Vega Nexus" had been zapped for over-acting at the start of 11.4, "The Monster of Peladon" (the one with Ice Warriors, as promised). So it became "Voga". Holmes decided to amplify the dispute in the mines. He took the character of Vorus, until then a stroppy miners' guild leader along the lines of Gebek in "The Monster of Peladon" (or Arthur Scargill in the outside world), and gave him a Davros-like ambition to take decisive action to end a prolonged emergency-measure that had lasted generations. Crucially, the residents of Voga were made alien and motivated by the way the previous Cyber-War had ended.

• Hinchcliffe and Briant had secured more filming days and the money for a location shoot; Briant had visited Wookey Hole with his family and thought it would be ideal. He also contacted the composer for his previous story ("Death to the Daleks"), Carey Blyton. Quite why Briant did this is unclear – he'd worked with Dudley Simpson on 10.5, "The Green Death" and would again on "The Robots of Death" and several *Blakes* 7 episodes. In interviews, he's careful not to say that he thought Simpson was getting stale, but that this

12.5 Revenge of the Cybermen

was a danger if the composer wasn't given a break every so often. Whether that happened is for you to decide, but it means that Simpson, in 15 years on the series, never scored a Cyberman story.

- By now, Letts's original plan to re-use the costumes for "The Invasion" had fallen through – even after repairs, they'd look terrible in colour – and Alistair Bowtell had been commissioned for a new army of four. The style of half-mask pioneered with the Ogrons (9.1, "Day of the Daleks") and developed with the Draconians ("Frontier in Space") was considered a practical way to mass-produce Vogans and differentiate them with the individual actors' faces and performances and bespoke white facial hair. Effects sculptor John Friedlander, who'd made a speciality of this, based them on his assistant, Rhys Jones. The result wasn't quite what anyone expected, causing a bit of merriment when they were unveiled on the location shoot.

- This section's called "The Lore" because a lot of *Doctor Who* stories have accumulated convention anecdotes and yarns in interviews. The main thing most veteran fans know about the making of this one concerns the location shoot at Wookey Hole, so we'll sift through the different accounts.

Let's start with incontrovertible facts: the caves at Wookey Hole consist of a few that are open to the public, commercially administered by Madame Tussaud's, and a lot of underwater chambers and caves only accessible to divers. The public bit is in roughly a reverse 7 or inverted L and is in distinct sections, three main chambers and connecting areas (labelled A-F on the production diagrams). There is a large stalagmite called the "Witch" and two of the chambers are called the Witch's Kitchen and the Witch's Parlour. The third, the Cathedral, was designated A on the production map. Bryant returned to the location for a recce on 11th November and stayed after normal visitor hours to look in detail at his leisure.

His story is that, when left to his own devices, he arranged with the staff to let his party out and, while there, met a diver in wetsuit and breathing gear at around midnight. The other visitor left, but when Briant asked who it was, the staff said they'd not seen him but other visitors said they had – a diver had drowned there some months earlier. Monique Briant, his then-wife and occasional extra, found some interesting stones, possibly arrow-heads, and took them as souvenirs.

The location shoot began well enough, with everyone a bit on edge because of the stuffiness and mildly claustrophobic surroundings. Roger Murray-Leach, assigned instead of Briant's choice of designer, Tony Burroughs ("The Green Death") to ensure continuity with the previous Ark visit, applied soluble gold paint to the rock walls and constructed the rail for the Vogan transit system. They started in the Cathedral with the Doctor, Stevenson and Lester resting on their trek. Joining the cast were Ronald Leigh-Hunt (Commander Stevenson, formerly Commander Radnor in 6.5, "The Seeds of Doom", King Arthur when William Russell was *Sir Lancelot* and the original mentor in *Freewheelers*) and William Marlowe (Lester, formerly Marlowe in 8.2, "The Mind of Evil"). They also shot Sarah and Harry running into a gun-battle between the Vogan "Hawks" and "Doves" (odd names, given that Tyrum's lot, the "Doves" in this schema, have superior weapons and a proper army). There weren't that many extras; the two armies were filmed individually, with the non-speaking guards doubling up. Unsurprisingly, Terry Walsh is on both sides.

- Tuesday 19th was the day Jeremy Wilkin (Kellman) came for the Matterbeam scenes and some of the rockfall. His main starring role had been Drew in *Undermind*, of which more in the next story's notes, but this makes it possible that Holmes suggested him. The spheres from "The Sontaran Experiment" were cleaned up and placed in the Witch's Parlour for all the comings and goings in the story. This cave had a lake and Briant, a boating enthusiast, picked up on the term "skimmer" in one of Tyrum's taunts to Vorus and hired some small speedboats, "Sizzlas", from a company in Henley-in-Arden. They never quite worked right, despite helpful hints about bespoke spark plugs, so were sparingly dropped in when practical (it eventually got into a legal dispute).

The main event that day, however, was the Vogan-Cybermen battle at the stairway and low-roof arch (area E, the "Battle Arch", known to Wookey Hole staff as "Hell's Larder"). The Cybermen had head-cannons (sorry) using photographic flashes, much as the Sea Devils had (9.3, "The Sea Devils", just in case you missed it), while the Vogans had Verey Pistols used to launch distress flares. This meant that nobody could shoot twice in a single shot, but the fight's "choreography" was already more piecemeal than usual, because there was no walkie-talkie signal in the caves. By now the assistant floor manager and armourer had become unwell, partly the bad air but also bad vibes. The rest of the cast and crew ended each day anxious to get back to the hotel in Wells.

The spooky anecdotes mainly centre on the next day, when the crew moved to the Witch's Kitchen. The eponymous Witch was, for a gag, draped in a cloak and given a hat and broomstick. The site staff had specifically asked the electricians who perpetrated the jape not to do anything like that. The day began well, with Sarah and Harry discovered by Vogan guards, Sarah running past more guards back to the Transmat, the Vogan "Dove" being killed (using a prop we've seen before, in Briant's debut story 8.4, "Colony in Space", and will again).

Shortly after three, the Sizzla on which Sladen was riding went out of control and was heading for a crash on a part of that cave's lake with a strong undertow leading to one of the submerged caves. Walsh, who'd expressed misgivings about the scene and insisted on being on hand, jumped in and pulled her off, ingesting several mouthfuls of the stagnant water and needing to have his stomach pumped. A quarter of an hour later, one of the electricians was rigging lights when his ladder gave way and he broke his leg. A contrite crew removed the Witch's garments. Monique Briant decided to return the arrow-heads, just in case. Decades later, Mark Gatiss would rework these convention anecdotes into a sketch in *The League of Gentlemen*.

- The last day (21st) was primarily the Doctor, Harry and Lester attacking the Cybermen and some Dove pick-ups for Part Three, but a local news film crew showed up. (Remember, the public hadn't seen Baker in action yet, so the focus was looking for the new Doctor. The clip, shown on BBC Bristol's *Points West* the following day and available on two different DVD releases, ends with the Cybermen going to the pub.)

- Briant chose to break the studio days up into two per set, one day of camera rehearsals and one of shooting, for the two main settings. Phase One, on Nerva, started with the usual Acton rehearsals from Saturday 23rd ahead of a day of line-ups on 2nd December in TC1 and a couple of recording sessions on 3rd. (In fact, the pre-filmed model effects had already been shot on 12th November at the Puppet Studio and Baker had popped in for a look during recording of "The Ark in Space".)

He brought back a couple of actors he'd used before: Michael Wisher was Magrik in the Vogan scenes, but also a couple of voices Warner picked up on the radio; Warner was Alec Wallis, the radio operator in "The Sea Devils", who'd been in episodes of cop shows Briant had done recently, and was a last-minute replacement. Also joining as the Cyber-Leader was Christopher Robbie, formerly zer Karkus (6.2, "The Mind Robber") and just starting his second career as a continuity announcer. Baker was now confidently adding bits of business, such as the "Three Wise Monkeys" sight-gag, the "Dusty Death" eulogy for a slain Cyberman, whistling to Sarah and the "Fragmentised" joke.

- With all the other CSO at work, the veins caused by the "plague" were instead achieved by Front Axial Projection. The Cybermats were either pulled on wires or CSO rod-puppets (or just the prop being swung about by the victim) – Briant later admitted that radio-controlled ones might have been better. Sladen got the giggles during her assault by one. Kellman's comms include that prop from the Voga location again and an adapted clothes-brush made for *Live and Let Die*. Sarah's reading a phenomenally well-preserved 1974 edition of the New English Library *Science Fiction* magazine and watching a piece of stock footage used in a BBC documentary, *Thanks for the Frying Pan*, revoiced by Briant. Time ran out for all of the transmat scenes, so Sarah and Harry's departure was replaced by the camera staying on the Doctor.

- When the rehearsals for the Voga / Cybership scenes began on 5th, the cast was augmented with David Collings as Vorus, Brian Grellis as Shepmah, Michael Wisher properly and Kevin Stoney as Tyrum. They concentrated on differentiating the characters by mannerisms and voice – Grellis decided to give his character asthma, for example, and Wisher a drippy nose.

- With his debut only a fortnight off, Baker took time to pose for photos, including several with Cybermen, and the recording began with Tyrum's office, as some of this was to be CSO'd into scenes in Vorus's Guild chambers – the same set, redressed over dinner. The majority of scenes were shot in story-order, with seven different bits of the planet built in the studio and used in Parts Two to Four.

- A familiar piece of stock footage of a Saturn V take-off was used, resembling the model built by Jim Ward in that it's a rocket. Added at the end of the day were CSO scenes of the Cybermat pouncing, the "Swiss Roll" Voga surface seen on the Nerva screen and a small effects shot of Kellman's floor smoking. The cast left for Christmas (for

12.5 Revenge of the Cybermen

Baker and Sladen, the last break they'd get until late June). Ten days later, "Robot" began transmission: Hinchcliffe warned Baker that everything was about to change.

• The last piece of this story to be added was a remount of the Time-Ring scene, during "Genesis of the Daleks". However, editing this story, especially Part Two, was a protracted process, partly because Briant was involved in another project (an episode of *Softly Softly*) that was over-running. Carey Blyton had made most of his scoring decisions from the script, before even location filming began, but dubbing was complicated by the delays and Hinchcliffe's misgivings over the score. Blyton reasoned that cave-dwellers ought to sound ancient (as per "Doctor Who and the Silurians"). He wrote about 30 minutes of music for this story. Hinchcliffe called in Peter Howell, then starting his long stint at the BBC Radiophonic Workshop, to punch up the soundtrack a little. Blyton seems not to have held it against anyone and wrote to Hinchcliffe thanking him for the gig. His music for this and "Death to the Daleks" was rearranged into a performance suite and has been re-recorded and released commercially.

• The build-up to this story could be argued to have begun with the 1973 *Radio Times* Special – but the release, in February 1975, of the Target Books version of "The Moonbase" as *Doctor Who and the Cybermen* made a good platform. In April, the Weetabix promotion began, with a one in 24 chance of there being a Cyberman in your three pasteboard figures – they advertised "a Dalek in every pack", but others included the White Robots ("The Mind Robber"), the Giant Robot (only just on screens when there were made, as were the "Robot"-costumed Sarah and Doctor), Linx (11.1, "The Time Warrior" and identified as "Linx" and not "Sontaran") and a Yeti (5.2, "The Abominable Snowman", in the same pose as the cover of the Target book of that story released shortly before). This model of Cyberman proved more popular after the broadcast than others, popping up on *Crackerjack* (see next story) and *The Generation Game*, but it was another eight years before *Doctor Who* went near them. Baker and Marter were especially unimpressed and started pondering how they'd do it if they had a chance. (The "Cyberons" in their abortive film proposal, *Doctor Who Meets Scratchman*, seem to be a reaction to this script's deficiencies.)

• During this story's broadcast, between Parts Two and Three, BBC2 ran a documentary about the bits of Wookey Hole inaccessible to anyone without breathing apparatus, *Worlds Without Sun* episode 3, transmitted 23rd April 1975. On the same day, news broke that William Hartnell, the original Doctor, had died at home, aged 67. With President Ford announcing that America was done with Vietnam (triggering the fall of Saigon), a forthcoming referendum on Britain staying in the EEC, Patty Hearst driving the getaway car in a robbery that left one person dead, Pol Pot executing his predecessor, the first free elections in Portugal for a generation, the continuing fall-out from Denis Healey's controversial budget (see the essay with "The Ark in Space") and unemployment in Britain passing the one million mark, it was a busy news day. And yet, the story still made a splash.

• According to legend, the choice of this story as the test-run for BBC Video's domestic *Doctor Who* releases was because they asked around at the 1983 Longleat event (see **What Happened At Longleat?** under 20.6, "The King's Demons") and under-informed *Doctor Who Magazine* readers said they wanted to see the then-missing "The Tomb of the Cybermen" (5.1). This isn't entirely plausible, but the then-recent "Earthshock" (19.6) had rekindled interest in these adversaries and, with Tom Baker still head and shoulders ahead of other Doctors in public estimation, it was a sound decision to start with that combination of Doctor and Monster – so long as one had not seen the actual story. As evidence that this was the thinking, the original cover combined an "Earthshock" model Cyberman with Baker in a later costume.

As was the custom in those days, the cliffhangers were removed and the whole thing brought in at 90 minutes for a mere £39.95 (that's about £133 now, or $64 in 1985 and $165 now – the idea seems to have been that these were for rental rather than retail). Then a slightly cheaper version as rush-released with a better cover. Once this story was again legally available, the Vogan Guild symbol's later life as the Prydonian Chapter Seal ("The Deadly Assassin", et seq.) led to more and loopier fan-theories than almost any other aspect of the series. Also coming back to haunt us, one of the guards' tunics was recycled for the penultimate episode of *Blakes 7*, although it's easy to miss amid so many other stupid costumes and hairstyles.

Season 13

13.1: "Terror of the Zygons"

(Serial 4F, Four Episodes, 30th August – 20th September 1975.)

Which One is This? Well, Target Books, whose mid-70s novelisations tended to cut to the chase, called this one *Doctor Who and the Loch Ness Monster*. Those of you watching since the 50th Anniversary may also have surmised that shape-shifting aliens are involved. These ones pretend to be Scottish.

Firsts and Lasts Evidently, it's got the Zygons in it, making an impressive debut. They won't be back until 2013, looking a bit different. More pertinently, it's the last "proper" adventure for Brigadier Lethbridge-Stewart as head of UNIT's much-put-upon UK division. He'll be back under very different circumstances. It's the last proper outing for Harry Sullivan, too, but he'll be back as a supporting character ("The Android Invasion") almost before you notice he's gone.

This was the first of two stories to have music by future big-name Geoffrey Burgon. But it's the last time the Doctor wears that overcoat. Plus, this is the first story for a while directed by Douglas Camfield; as usual, he puts his own stamp on things.

Four Things to Notice about "Terror of the Zygons"...

• They make heroic efforts to pass off Bognor Regis as Scotland, but it doesn't entirely ring true. The thatched rooves of the houses are a dead giveaway, for starters. Nonetheless, with a guest-cast who've at least *heard* a real Scottish accent (one of whom even brings his bagpipes), they have a good go at selling a script that starts with "*can you no send over a few haggis? The chef we have here disnae ken the first thing...*" and proceeds to run through all the *Doctor Finlay* clichés. Even the Doctor and Sarah go native, with phrases such as "better keep his recovery dark" and "for why?" Meanwhile, the Brig dons *White Heather Club* mufti, but spares us his rendition of *A Scottish Soldier*. (Confused by these references? Gang awa' doon tae **Where Does This Come Frae?** below.) The cast includes precisely three genuine Scots, one of whom is playing an English soldier.

Season 13 Cast/Crew

- Tom Baker (the Doctor)
- Elisabeth Sladen (Sarah Jane Smith)
- Philip Hinchcliffe (Producer)
- Robert Holmes (Script Editor)

• As the script swings from spooky yarn to space-opera to spy-caper, John Woodnutt (as the Duke of Forgill) gets to deliver some astoundingly hokey dialogue in a dry, educated Edinburgh drawl, alchemically transforming many lines into comedy gold. Everyone has their own favourite, but the most amazing thing is that he also (SPOILER ALERT) plays a stereotypically stage-whispery alien warlord under half a ton of latex, and makes the routine "ssso, Doc-torr" / "puny Earthlings" lines seem fresh too.

• Amid all this Caledonian kerfuffle, Tom Baker keeps all eyes on him, not least in a bravura sequence where the Doctor hypnotises Sarah into surviving hypoxia in a decompression chamber. He now owns this series outright and the UNIT regulars seem to know it. So does the director, Douglas Camfield, who more-or-less invented the Brigadier and UNIT, so see how many ways this story seems to mirror "The Invasion" (6.3), especially in the final episode. This story seems like a tug-of-war between what the series was and what it's becoming.

• Although the build-up made a lot about this being the Doctor vs the Loch Ness Monster, they get coy about this in the finished episodes. Any guesses why? After January's first faltering steps into *Godzilla* territory ("Robot"), we get a stop-motion dinosaur leviathan chasing the Doctor across the glens of Sussex (with mixed results, but a great cliffhanger). We also have one of the best pre-CGI spaceship take-offs and a similarly satisfying explosion. There's an exciting Glam Rock *Top of the Pops* transmogrification effect for the Zygons turning into fake humans. None of these is the effect everyone comments on, though. The story's climax entails as bad a CSO shot as anything from the 70s, featuring a sock-puppet monster well away from where everyone's eye-lines seem to be directed.

13.1 Terror of the Zygons

The Continuity

The Doctor hasn't forgotten how to drive, nor where the bonnet-release catch is on a Land Rover. He's switched from that cardigan to a tweed waistcoat, yellow with a brown houndstooth cross-hatching and, to begin with, adopts a tam o'shanter and matching Royal Stewart tartan scarf [the latter about as long as his usual one].

As with last story, the scuffles with aliens make his shoulders look like his weakest point. [The reason being: the script mentioned the Zygons as having a scorpion sting in one of their hands, but this was downplayed on screen.]

• *Background.* The Doctor's local knowledge of Inverness and environs seems more detailed than he'd get from his visit in 1746 [4.4, "The Highlanders"]. He's attended at least one Scottish funeral [probably as part of UNIT duties].

• *Ethics.* The Brigadier easily manipulates the Doctor into active investigation, despite the latter's qualms about the oil industry, by mentioning how many deaths have occurred already. While initially just curious about the Zygons and their technology, the Doctor abruptly – upon learning a whole lot more of them are coming – goes on the offensive and rather callously locks the rest of the crew inside the control-room before activating the ship's self-destruct. Nonetheless, he seems compassionate towards the Skarasen.

• *Inventory*

– *Sonic Screwdriver.* It can heat up organic fronds / polyps [delete according to if you think the Zygon ship is more plant than animal] and set off a fire-alarm.

– *Other.* That space-time communicator he gave the Brigadier looks vaguely like the communicator the Vogans gave Kellman ["Revenge of the Cybermen"]. To home in on it, the Doctor has a small hand-held boxy thing with a bleep and an extendable aerial. [Perhaps it's the same gadget he uses as a robot-detector in "The Android Invasion" or the radio telescope from "Pyramids of Mars".]

The TARDIS The Doctor homes in on the Brigadier's signal with reasonable accuracy, a few miles away and in less than a week from the first message. He is confident that he can get Sarah to London 'five minutes ago'. [An unbroadcast scene, available on the DVD, features a return of the glitch in the materialisation circuit ("The Invasion") that turned the Ship transparent shortly after arrival. This will become a feature rather than a fault (X6.1, "The Impossible Astronaut").]

The Supporting Cast

• *Sarah* finally seems to be filing a story! She types two-fingeredly; it's the only time we see her doing any reporting other than just asking plot-relevant questions while holding a notebook.

She expresses doubts about her ability to read mediaeval Latin. [In the light of "The Masque of Mandragora" and subsequent indications that the TARDIS can translate text, this suggests that she's not read any text on her travels. This is odd, as she opened a magazine from the twenty-ninth century, as far into the future as eleventh-century monastic records were in the past and didn't react. Perhaps she just looked at the pictures. Anyway, as we saw in "Revenge of the Cybermen", not only was it a well-preserved publication from 1974, but she barely saw anything before a Cybermat bit her, which fuzzied her memory. We have two essays on this topic, one in this book (**Does the Universe Speak English?** under "The Masque of Mandragora", plus **Can He Read Smells?** under X2.9, "The Satan Pit" and subsequently confirmed by X6.7, "A Good Man Goes to War").]

• *Harry.* [With hindsight (X9.7-9.8, "The Zygon Invasion" / "The Zygon Inversion"), the attention Lt. Sullivan pays to Broton's corpse is intriguing.] He takes the initiative in investigating the medical records of the riggers [rather as Martha Jones would when working for UNIT or Torchwood]. He's much more professional [even compared to "Robot"]. He can drive, has a Naval uniform handy somewhere [he seems to change on the plane from Inverness]. He finally loses the duffel-coat [see **The Lore**].

• *The Brigadier* is having an attack of roots. We know he was with a Highland regiment [5.5, "The Web of Fear"], his middle name's 'Gordon' and he pronounces 'vehicle' in an idiomatic way [7.3, "The Ambassadors of Death"], but this time he spends much of the first episode in a kilt [a Stewart tartan, of course], long woollen socks with garter-flashes and a tweed jacket and waistcoat. He salutes the Duke of Forgill. He is as diplomatic as ever with the pub landlord and the Duke, assures the Prime Minister that a crisis will be met with 'discreet but resolute action'.

• *UNIT.* The Brigadier twice specifies that he's withdrawing to 'London HQ'. [So they still have a base in the Capital despite all the rural locales

September or January?

Since 2005, the start of a new series has usually been on Easter Saturday. It's common enough for the years when it wasn't the case to look like "experiments", and the October 2018 launch of Series 11 to be downright confusing for many. In fact, the start of September is thought of by older fans as the natural place to begin a new year (in spite of the relatively few years in which this happened). Similarly, January was often thought of as a sensible place to begin a run of new episodes. Closer examination shows that it's a lot more complicated than that, for reasons that tell us a lot about how BBC Television used to work.

The first thing to understand is that the notion of a US-style "season" didn't take hold until fairly late on. Programmes were scheduled as and when they were ready. *Doctor Who*, being pre-recorded, had a bit of an advantage for planners – a great deal of the usual nightly output was live. The first episode went out on 23rd November 1963 (we trust you knew that), rather than 7th September (the first available Saturday, had they done it the way that would later become standard), and was slotted into a pre-existing line-up, between *Grandstand* and *The Telegoons* (and replacing *Deputy Dawg*).

Once the series was established (in no small part because the start-date meant that the first cliffhanger of 1.2, "The Daleks" was the week before Christmas) and production became methodical, the plan had been to run for a year then take a break. That was exactly what happened with regard to the making of the episodes, but – with their five-week head-start on transmission diminishing and the BBC hierarchy's clever plan for bringing back the Daleks in time for Christmas 1964 and a toy-sale bonanza – Verity Lambert and the planners determined that a pause in transmission might be handy. But it wasn't a break for the summer, it was a hiatus in mid-September 1964. The Olympics was a handy excuse, but – those being in Tokyo and satellites being new – the late-night sports coverage wasn't ever going to interfere with the late-afternoon / early evening line-up.

Nonetheless, with a lot of other series intended for later on Saturdays timetabled to start a new run as soon as the live feeds were done with, the return of *Doctor Who* on Hallowe'en very roughly coincided with a number of other series coming back or starting. (It's notable that many of these series ran as normal over the Christmas and New Year period as if nothing was happening, and that the main Light Entertainment shows of the era took turns to get a Saturday Evening slot once every four weeks.) If there's a recognisable start to the US habit of getting all the hit shows (or promising new ones) to start in the first week of September, it's 1965, and mainly because ITV was doing it.

… sort of. We'll elaborate on this in a bit, but thinking of ITV, the commercial rival, as a coherent, unified entity before the mid-80s is unhelpful. By design, they were competing with one another as well as with the BBC. Part of that arms-race was that some regional franchise-holders adopted American tactics while others didn't bother, as they enjoyed what amounted to a monopoly of advertising revenue in a fairly remote bit of the UK. This was especially true if that company had the rights to broadcast all week, while the first four regions to be granted ITV transmitters (the big population centres) were split into weekday and weekend licence-holders.

September 1965 saw the start of many very successful ITV series, but you can't really put a definite date on them because the 14 separate regional ITV channels rarely synched-up for anything other than the news. A popular show made by one of them might well get the best slot on that specific station, their "patch", but a rival might put on one of their own shows or an imported film then, showing the other station's thing in a different slot on a different day (if at all). Had (to take an example from that month) the first few episodes of ATV's *Thunderbirds* been networked coherently, *Doctor Who* might have ended around the time John Wiles left. The ITV companies were promoting their fresh new seasons as bids to steal a march on their rivals rather than to compete with the BBC, who weren't actively competing with them.

No, in the mid-1960s, the BBC's best sales-tactic was reliability, continuity and being responsive to viewers' needs rather than mere trends or gimmicks. When they imported hit shows, it was usually to offset one of their own – *The Man from U.N.C.L.E.* was on just after *Top of the Pops* and *Doctor Who* in the 60s was usually framed by something like *The Monkees* or *The Munsters* and its own poptabulous stable-mate *Juke Box Jury*. The one time it was matched with a home-grown drama, it was one already under way. (*Quick, Before They Catch Us* – long since wiped, so we have no

continued on page 117...

13.1 Terror of the Zygons

we've seen. "Planet of the Spiders" (11.5) led straight into "Robot" and neither was anywhere near London. That base did have an airstrip nearby so, despite the radar jamming, it's possible that they flew there from Inverness and then drove to London. Presumably that's when Harry changed back into his uniform after nine months in the same shirt and slacks.]

The troops have switched to DPM (camouflage) combat jackets (Denison smocks) with the loose-weave olive scarves.

The Supporting Cast (Evil)

- *Broton, Warlord of the Zygons*. [For a generation of fans raised on Weetabix and Target books, that's his official name.] His plan to enslave humanity as a workforce, and to reverse-terraform Earth for the fugitive Zygon fleet over the coming centuries, doesn't seem to be vindictive, merely practical. And yet, as his plans collapse, he makes a determined attempt to continue even if he dies, especially if he takes the Doctor down with him. While some Zygons grumble about the limits and aesthetics of human form, he appears as the Duke even when it's completely unnecessary.

The Non-Humans

- *The Zygons*. As the nation's children spotted, they do look awfully like giant, grumpy jelly babies. They are roughly humanoid but orange, with a bulbous cranium and a thick neck to support it, so that the head seems to grow into the shoulders. They have no visible ears. They seem not to need or want clothing but are covered in suckers, like an octopus. They have visible ribs. As they feed on the lactic fluids of the Skarasen, Harry hypothesizes that they're mammalian [but they don't seem to be]. They have harsh, sibilant voices, rather like the Ice Warriors, even in their own ship.

Zygons can take 'Body Prints' of captured humans, and thereby transmogrify into their form. The human must be unconscious in a booth, as both the physical appearance (down to clothing) and memory-traces are copied. [It's possible that the body-print technique allows some degree of personality-seepage; when impersonating the Duke, Broton shares the man's dry, sardonic turn of phrase and recondite vocabulary.]

In human form, Zygons are vulnerable to bullets and their blood is indistinguishable [at least, to the naked eye] from those they imitate. This technique, along with the augmentation of the Skarasen and development of the Reciprocator upon which it homes in, seems connected to their advanced organic technology. Their spaceship is tuberous; its controls look like nodules growing out of the surfaces. A pressure-lock for a door has a plant-like stalk to seal it. The self-destruct is operated with transparent tubes that fill with a liquid very like blood.

The six Zygons seen here seem to be centuries old and have been laying their plan since the ship crashed. Since they started waiting for a rescue, a supernova destroyed their home planet; a fleet of ships will arrive in Earth's solar system in a few hundred years. [Interesting wording here: Broton says they 'recently learned' that a 'stellar explosion' destroyed their home world, and the fleet will take 'several centuries' to arrive. This all suggests that they can't travel faster than light and relied on radio for news from home. Subsequent appearances don't tally with this impression – one of the Doctor's grannies accused another of being a Zygon (X11.9, "It Takes You Away") and they were apparently active in the Time War, when their world was obliterated, and able to use Gallifreyan technology (X7.15, "The Day of the Doctor"). All of that may have *become* true as a result of the Time War, but the Doctor here seems unaware of the Zygons' existence. See **Has the Time War Started?** under "Genesis of the Daleks".]

When one dies, the ship detects a lack of a 'syncron response'; the commander can disperse the remains by remote control, leaving no trace. A transmission blankets all local radar and allows a spaceship to travel in stealth mode, even on half power. They seem to measure the amplitude of the Reciprocator signal in 'remars' but use 'Earth Miles' as the standard unit of distance. [Unlike – say – the Daleks, they have a good reason for going native, to not let slip that they're alien doppelgangers.] The engines cannot return the ship to their world, but on 'dynacron thrust' can travel in a planet's atmosphere and gravity-well.

- *The Skarasen*. Despite appearances, this too is a mammal [at least, technically], so we'll use female pronouns. In appearance, she's a hundred-foot-long reptile, with the head of an iguana, a turtle shell and claws. She has fearsome teeth, although the Doctor intimates these may be dentures, as the entire creature has been artificially weaponised. Although primarily brought along

September or January?

...continued from page 115

idea if it really was, as the theme and all available photos indicate, the most 1966 thing ever. It was *in media res* when 4.1, "The Smugglers" began.) The emphasis was on "flow" rather than razzmatazz. So despite 1965 looking like the start of the "natural" broadcasting pattern, it wasn't.

Once again, the production-break and transmission-break were five weeks out of alignment, so what seems to us to be "Season Three" (fandom adopted the US-style designation in the late 70s; we've elected to use it in *About Time* to denote what viewers saw) starts with the last five episodes of the second production-block (recorded two whole months beforehand) and carries on seamlessly to an episode recorded six weeks after the previously shown one (and seven weeks after the regular cast had been in front of the cameras – 3.2, "Mission to the Unknown", the ultimate "Doctor-lite" story). Admittedly, an international swimming contest meant that 3.1, "Galaxy 4" began on the *second* Saturday in September, but a great many other popular family shows had resumed the previous week.

The BBC's Saturday night line-up had many series that all came back after six to eight weeks away. So did a lot of other weekday "hardy perennials". The strange thing, looked at today, was that they all fizzled out or ran skeleton services for July and August. When kids played outside, a family had better things to do than communal televiewing, but that doesn't explain why something like *Nationwide* (a sort of TV tabloid, yoking regional BBC news programmes together around a hub in Lime Grove with items on homelessness, the Jarrow March or a snail drinking beer from a pint-mug) also contracted to a perfunctory 20-minute version rather than the full hour and a bit as normal. The network bosses' hunch – that nobody watches much television in summer – became self-fulfilling by them putting on repeats and filler shows.

But why does September seem like such a logical and aesthetically-right start? It's partly a northern European thing. The agricultural cycle starts with preparing the soil after harvest, the days appreciably shorten and the summer birds leave for Africa. As late as the 1980s, these things always occurred abruptly, within two or three weeks of the start of the equinox. Even in France, toward the lower end of the latitudes where this is clear-cut, the French Revolutionary Calendar picked what we call 23rd September as New Year's Day. Back when everyone had to buy fruit and vegetables in season, the year obviously started when the greengrocer suddenly had full shelves again.

In 1970s Britain, it meant not having to make do with Cyprus or Jersey potatoes when proper mashable, chippable varieties (King Edwards, Maris Pipers and so on) were available. Apples were ripe. Historically, this was when the harvest was in and all the remaining agricultural work was the stuff of big adult menfolk; since mid-July was when small fingers were more useful and shorter people didn't have to bend down as far, schools historically bowed to the inevitable and let the kids have those six weeks off. With the available daylight hours contracting, the cricket season ended and the football and rugby seasons started. This last was especially noticeable on Saturdays at tea-time, when it seems like *Grandstand* will never end. The score-results that people tuned in for went back to normal after the Pools companies had fobbed everyone off with Australian Rules.[20]

More recently, summer was when people went to the seaside or even, if they were rich, abroad. In theory, the weather was better, so people were assumed not to want to watch television so diligently. (That was a relatively novel turn in itself: in 1953, when the habit first started, the BBC put out a technically-advanced serial in August, *The Quatermass Experiment*, and it had received unprecedentedly favourable feedback. Well, it *would* be unprecedented, if three-quarters of the viewers hadn't had tellies until six weeks before, wouldn't it? See X2.7, "The Idiot's Lantern" and the essay with 15.3, "Image of the Fendahl". Nonetheless, the notion that showing anything for which you had high hopes in summer was a waste of time and resources wasn't immediate or obvious back then.)

All the subsidiary activities latched on to this idea: the adverts for the *TV Times* try to match the trailers for forthcoming ITV debuts or return. BBC television did something similar, although the *Radio Times* promos were more about the feature articles. Each new season gave the graphics departments of both halves of the duopoly a chance to show off and try to "theme" each new season. (A particularly ripe example was September 1978, when they cashed in on the Space Opera theme of the summer – disco and bandwagon-jumping films – to present "The

continued on page 119...

13.1 Terror of the Zygons

on the mission as a food-supply (the 'lactic fluids' being vital to Zygon health), she has been adapted to follow instructions delivered to her from a control on the flight-deck until she's close enough to home in on a 'Reciprocator' (a semi-organic bait adhering to the target). She also relays video feed of such a hunt, so that she can be guided by remote control. [The images seem to come from her head, but as the Skarasen's eyes are on the side, the camera must be up her nose or mounted between the orbital arches.]

Planet Notes Apparently the Zygon home world was largely aquatic, with big lakes filled with minerals and a mean temperature above that of Earth c.1975. Then came a stellar explosion. [This lot only hear about it second hand, so don't specify if it was natural – a later set of Zygons attribute their world's destruction to the Time War, possibly to gain the Doctor's sympathy.] This was some time back, possibly around 1500 A.D.

History

- *Dating*. [It can't be any later than 1980, or the Skarasen's swim to Westminster would have run into construction work on the Thames Barrier (see X3.0, "The Runaway Bride").

[Even though everything from the Woolworths torches to the chocolate bar Benton eats in Part Four (a Cadbury *Wombles* bar, on sale 1974-6[21]) just screams '1975', there are institutional reasons why this isn't exactly right. North Sea Oil production is up and running which, in our world, wasn't until around 1977. "Tooth and Claw" (X2.2) seems to confirm that Margaret Thatcher became prominent in 1979 (although the dialogue doesn't actually say she was Prime Minister), but with a PM called 'Jeremy' in "The Green Death" (10.5) shortly before all this, all bets are off and any number of possibilities are opened up concerning the authority-figure who here calls the Brigadier (see **The Lore** for who they were thinking of). The military vehicles don't have tax-discs, so they're no help. UNIT's change to a more contemporary-looking uniform and fatigues indicates that it's after 1972.

[As this is supposed to be Scotland, the way the real Duke and Mr Huckle from Canada wrap up in fur coats and people's breath visibly mists is absolutely no guide to the time of year. There are more deciduous trees than one might expect (funny, that) and they look like early spring. It's a full moon when the Bonnie Prince Charlie rig is attacked. All in all, we're tempted to place this a month after "Robot". So, May 1975, but in a gloomy corner of Scotland.

[That North Sea Oil anachronism? Maybe the secrecy surrounding the destruction of so many rigs meant that the first *reported* oil to be piped ashore was in 1977.]

Forgill Castle is on the site of a Monastery dating to the eleventh century [i.e. the time of the real Macbeth]. A Zygon scout-craft crashed and awaited rescue, later discovering that their home world was destroyed and many more of their people would be coming to Earth. An embryonic Skarasen was released into Loch Ness and adapted into a cyborg. [It's strongly hinted that every reported sighting of the Loch Ness Monster is really this creature, which would place the crash at some time in the sixth century, when St Columba's biographer reports a nasty death and the Irish saint calming the beast and sending it back into the water. If Zygons were all that long-lived, then the whole business with "Cup-a-Soup" and Time Lord Paintings ("The Day of the Doctor") would be redundant.

[Broton speaks of 'centuries' since the crash, during which their milch-cow grew to its present, impressive size. The earliest incident we are told about in this narrative is 1870, when Donald Jamieson was killed in such a way that his brother went insane. In 1922, someone from the Black Isle disappeared. Then, as is well-recorded, sightings of 'Nessie' began to increase after 1933.

[Perhaps the Time War changed things, but the Loch Ness 'gambit' was still part of recorded history as late as "Remembrance of the Daleks" (25.1) and Rose has certainly heard of the Monster in "School Reunion" (X2.3). Yet there are Zygons at work at the Savoy in 1890 (X7.4, "The Power of Three") as well as a scouting party in 1562 who skip to 2013 inside a painting ("The Day of the Doctor"). It's improbable that the Loch Ness ones were unaware of the ones posing as hotel staff in *fin de siècle* London, unless the latter didn't want to be found. Or maybe it's the same ones trying to persuade Karl Benz that petroleum is the fuel of the future as the start of their fiendish long-term plan – perhaps they moved their ship to Inverness after meeting Amy Pond. Occam's Razor leaves us with the ones who operated the Skarasen either arriving after 1562, and thus denied their chance to while away centuries in the bloodiest battle in

September or January?

...continued from page 117

Future" with a star-field turning into words as radiophonic burbles issued from the telly. It made selling the Key to Time storyline a bit easier, even if they only had clips of the first two stories of Season Sixteen to play with, and the graphics look curiously like the Season Eighteen to Twenty-One titles.) Not every season of *Doctor Who* was this amenable to such tactics and not all of the effects of being part of a solid mass of programming were what producers wanted. Philip Hinchcliffe hoped that the start of "The Masque of Mandragora" would be delayed by a few weeks, so he'd get a *Radio Times* cover with less competition from all the newcomers. (It didn't work: he got lumbered with Gemma Jones in *The Duchess of Duke Street*.)

Once again, the context in which *Doctor Who* was being shown helps to explain seemingly odd decisions. In the 1960s, the big day in early autumn wasn't always the start of the school year. In 1967, for example, the main event for the BBC was 30th September: the day BBC1 started 625-line transmission, BBC2 went over to colour transmission (after a taster with Wimbledon in July) and the time-honoured three radio services were reconfigured into four, on new frequencies and with wunnerful Radio One starting its swinging, with-it pop service (see **Did Sergeant Pepper Know the Doctor?** under 5.1, "The Tomb of the Cybermen"). Thus all the new – or moved – Saturday shows (Simon Dee's chatshow, hitherto on Thursdays, *The Monkees*, the return of *Dixon of Dock Green*) debuted that evening with *Doctor Who* starting a new adventure, 5.2, "The Abominable Snowmen", after a four-part story had begun at the start of the month.

Late summer was a risky time to schedule new things on Saturday; *Grandstand* covered live Test Matches that could over-run (1967's solution was to end *Grandstand* at a regular time, with the various results, go and show something else and come back to the cricket after the news). In 1966, sport dominated the summer schedule as never before (the World Cup was happening in Britain, mainly London, and the BBC was both showing it to the world and showing off its technical prowess), so it made sense not to start *Doctor Who*'s new run until 10th September and even then at a later time than usual. What nobody knew when they made "The Smugglers" was that the lead actor would change almost immediately after, so the story started with the two new TARDIS travellers learning the programme's premise – it was made with the third block but always planned to start the fourth, hence the extensive location-work further afield than ever before – as if this status quo would last. When they introduced a new Doctor, they did so with barely any publicity at the end of that year's second story: trailers were made for the third one, but it was all about the Daleks' return just in time for Christmas.

The impression that all this and the commentary in the *Radio Times* and press gives is that one should welcome the new series with "relax, *Doctor Who*'s back" rather than "Wow! *Doctor Who* starts again in just one week… six days… five days…" In 1968, this was taken to extremes as – to work around the Mexico Olympics – the run of episodes was almost continuous, with a repeat of 4.9, "The Evil of the Daleks" treated as though it were a new adventure (*Radio Times* coverage and all) then an actual new story starting in mid-August. Both 6.1, "The Dominators" and 6.2, "The Mind Robber" were made at the end of the marathon production block that had begun with "The Abominable Snowmen" and concluded nearly 14 months of continuous transmissions. Then, after the Olympics (which didn't disrupt any other long-running Saturday staples), they picked up again with "The Invasion" (6.3) and only minimal publicity (showing the "surprise" return of the Cybermen six weeks in advance). The main concession to the publicity machine was the usual debut of a new companion in the last scheduled story of a year's run, allowing for a new set of adventures to start with a brief exposition scene (or a seven-part rerun with a scripted reason for doing so).

The BBC's gradual acceptance of the idea of a New Season as an excuse for a coordinated campaign like the ones they did for Christmas or big sporting events really solidified into a plan when *Doctor Who* had its biggest shake-up ever. Typically, it was after the rest of BBC1 had undergone a huge change, with the start of colour broadcasts in November 1969, but January 1970 was, for the network as a whole, the start of what's now thought of as normal and natural. BBC1 usually dominated Christmas television, but this time – instead of reverting to usual after this interlude – they capitalised on the end of a decade that had seen a lot of changes, almost all of them recorded, and made "The 70s" a bigger thing than they had

continued on page 121…

13.1 Terror of the Zygons

Gallifrey's history, or long *before* then and hibernating while the Skarasen grew big enough to feed them. For there to be any under the Savoy, a well-populated and much-built-upon bit of London's shoreline, they have to have arrived before the Romans. (We can't rule out hibernation in this case, either.) Nonetheless, it would seem that the events of "Terror of the Zygons" are still in play, otherwise Harry Sullivan would not have engineered a virus for UNIT in case these particular aliens showed up ("The Zygon Invasion"). The later-seen ones appear more advanced than the Loch Ness lot; they certainly don't need to keep humans in tubes to maintain their body-prints.]

The Analysis

Where Does This Come Frae? It's an odd thing, but almost every fantasy franchise before the 1980s had a go at doing the Loch Ness Monster, regardless of how well it fits inside the premise of the series. Even *Lost in Space* did it. It allows has-been character-actors to dust off their Groundskeeper Willie voices and the set designers to do ruined castles, pubs and tartan kitsch. The further people are from Scotland in all its complexity and detail, the more probable this is: look at *Brigadoon*. (Or rather, don't. *Song of the South* got suppressed, eventually, but these things are still considered acceptable.) The BBC, being by and for Britain (and Scotland's still part of Britain, pending yet another referendum) has, on occasion, pandered to the sentimental expat Scot demographic, but is more aware of the variety of different Scottish identities and subcultures. They are also more able to make programmes actually in Scotland rather than in a studio with a smoke-machine and a few swords on what look like stone walls.

Whether those programmes get a network showing or not was a decision for people in London. The first national (i.e. pan-British) hit was *The White Heather Club*, a weekly session of piano-accordions and people going *yee-hew* when poncing about in kilts and frilly shirts. It was occasionally ridiculed, not least in Scotland, but it provided the template for decades of New Year's Eve entertainments. (The nearest US comparison would be *Hee-Haw*, but that never resulted in things like *Donald, Where's Your Troosers?* or *The Bluebell Polka*.) Meanwhile, dramatized versions of AJ Cronin's *Doctor Finlay's Casebook* moved into new stories with the same characters and setting (pre-war Highlands, but often shot in actual Scotland – mainly Stirling – with old cars and lots of people in tweed), but oddly, was more popular in black and white than in colour. The barely-suppressed anger of the source-text was decompressed into folksy nostalgia; it was hard to avoid a sense that many London-based TV executives thought that visiting Scotland was like time-travel.

That's not unique to television: since the Highland clearances, there were efforts to reclaim an identity from the remaining fragments and early nineteenth-century writing about rural Scotland (as opposed to Edinburgh's much-vaunted status as "the Athens of the North") was about recovering something on the verge of going. Even as the Celtic Fringe was being dismissed as just the bits the Romans didn't bother with, a huge Enlightenment / Romantic movement was inventing a heroic past for it. A Scottish scholar, James MacPherson concocted a Gaelic poem-cycle of the mythic past with the "Ossian" hoax. Robert Burns wrote poetry attempting to convey a dialect (some might say this justified shameless sentimentality by making it "exotic"). We may quibble about Queen Victoria (and, more especially, Prince Albert) exercising what we now call cultural appropriation but being appropriated was a confection, in part, ascribed to the present generation of Scots to fill in gaps where their devastated former culture had been. Sir Walter Scott's novels were based on history as dodgy as *Braveheart* but gave a tenuous idea of identity beyond mere location and accent. This was what was carried with the Scottish Diaspora.

It has to be said, from a train window, as most visitors to Scotland would have seen it, the journey from overdeveloped Victorian London to wild-looking Scotland was visibly like delving into the past. A lot of affluent native scots would only return from London for grouse-shooting in August, expecting things to be exactly as they left them. If there was a remote area for a real-life *Lost World* in Britain this, or Dartmoor, were good candidates. (Although Conan Doyle, a Scot, elected for the latter for *The Hound of the Baskervilles*, but note how often Holmes observes to Watson that leaving London is like a trip into the Id.)

Therefore, of all the places to claim to have seen a prehistoric monster, the Highlands was the most plausible within easy reach of a hotel with a phone. Nessie-spotting really starts in 1933, but

September or January?

...continued from page 119

bothered doing with the end of the 1950s.

So 3rd January was the day for a lot of high-profile new series, with a new Doctor at the heart of it. It's the first of a run of five new series starting that day (plus one returning after a month off for Christmas) and it got a *Radio Times* front cover, the first since "The Enemy of the World" (5.4). Season Seven has many new features, notably that it's the first time since 1963 that the transmission-run and production block were in synch and that it was a mere six months long. Six months, however, was a long time to be doing so many similar types of story now that the programme was reconfigured from being Adventures in Space and Time to Adventures in Gasworks and Government Offices. As summer approached the ratings – now considered more important – dwindled.

This mattered to many television executives, including some at the BBC, but the most anxious was a relative newcomer. For most of the 1970s, Saturday night was the BBC's personal property, which somewhat rankled with the newly-formed London Weekend Television. We've told some of this story before, and the whole shambles of the 1967 ITV Franchise Auction is a huge topic, but the whole *raison d'etre* of LWT was to be a global player, serving the South East of Britain almost as a side-effect. Many ex-BBC staff and stars had thrown in their lot with this project, but had found that it was harder to make a company from scratch (even hiring engineers and building a studio out of an ice-rink) than just issuing memos as they'd done at Lime Grove or Television Centre. With the weekday London franchise going to a company built out of two unsuccessful bidders and outstripping them in international sales, LWT needed the big money from advertising in hit shows on a Saturday to survive and it simply wasn't happening. With only a few tweaks, the BBC's line-up for Saturdays had gone from a string of broadly-acceptable offerings that needed a good reason to switch over from to an unmissable sequence of hits, each leading logically into the next, to which ITV had no answer.

A glance at the ITV listings magazines, *TV Times* and *TV World* (the ATV mid-60s rival to the national title – yes, Lew Grade was *that* arrogant) shows that by 1968, the various independent stations had more or less given up on Saturday evenings between 5.30 and 8.30pm. However, the BBC were taking no chances. Everything on Saturday nights on BBC1 had been road-tested, even apparent innovations such as *The Two Ronnies* relied on the most experienced writers around all pitching five-minute sketches rather than one writer for the whole 45 minutes. Unlike the comparable CBS Saturday night line-up, it wasn't wall-to-wall sitcoms but meticulously-chosen family material (feature films, comforting police drama, song-and-dance shows, the endless string of puppets and often a US sitcom as the "disposable" item for when mum went off to cook). Even in that six-week desert, they never let up. Look at what was on in autumn when *Doctor Who* was January-June and it's a similar story, but with *The Pink Panther* or *Mary Tyler Moore* filling a Pertwee-shaped hole. Even with Christmas becoming more of a television event, the year ran from September to mid-July on television as it was in schools.

America, mainly too far south for the differences in daylight hours to justify it, also used this pattern. They began it early and applied pseudo-scientific analysis of Nielsen Ratings (the preferred system back then) to work out how to deliver audiences to advertisers. The results were skewed towards New York and LA, where the money was, but seemed to work across the board. The CBS Thursday Night schedules were roughly analogous to BBC1 on Saturdays, but they built up to September relaunches from late June.

It's been speculated that this was a legacy of the period when most television was live and the major stars and executives took summer holidays. Most of it, once the shift to filmed series got under way in 1955-6, was made in Hollywood and looked the same if made in November or May. None of the advantages we've just listed for behaving like this in Britain really applies to America, but they stuck with this way of doing things, largely through the inertia that comes from having a continent-sized landmass. As younger British television executives looked at America as the source of all wisdom about marketing (just as the US networks looked to us for the same thing), moving towards "new season" promotions to match the new football season and school year looked dynamic and "now". (See 16.2, "The Pirate Planet" for LWT screwing this up big-time.)

As we elaborate in **The Lore** section of "Terror of the Zygons", Philip Hinchcliffe killed several birds with one stone by holding over the last story in the 1974-5 production block from May until

continued on page 123...

13.1 Terror of the Zygons

five years later, the rediscovery of the Coelacanth in the waters off Madagascar made throwbacks and "living fossils" that bit more credible. The first film about the alleged monster (*Secret of the Loch*) was made in 1934 and plays up all the notions of stepping five years further back with every ten miles north of the capital. The *Inverness Courier* carried the 1933 sighting by a local doctor, but a tourist from London got national coverage in the *Daily Mail* the following year. This Depression-era link between people with cars and cameras (who could afford motoring holidays) and the publicity around the fearsome beastie in the semi-wild is hardly a three-pipe problem. What's interesting is that the accessibility of that bit of Scotland to visitors with disposable income combined ancient and modern; cameras, film and, later, sonar and radar gave a patina of science and civilisation to the supposedly primordial, just as dressing up to go hunting or fishing allowed people to think they were taming a wilderness even if they had Thermos flasks. The easier it got to travel between Inverness and London, the less alluring the Monster-hunt became. By the mid-80s, it was pretty much over, like the Bermuda Triangle or Ley Lines.

There's a counter-myth to all this: the canny Scots who seem simple but are a step ahead of the supposedly-wily outsider. British films do this more often than American ones; from *I Know Where I'm Going* and *Whisky Galore* to *Local Hero* and, to some extent, *Shallow Grave*, it's almost a given. One curious addition to this roster is Terry Nation's only feature film script, *What a Whopper!* In this, Adam Faith (a savvy Londoner who parlayed brief pop fame into business deals, occasionally financed by acting) plays a savvy Londoner down on his luck who teams up with old con Sid James (who else?) to fake a Nessie sighting in order to sell his book about the monster. The locals can see right through it, but as long as the tourists come, they pretend to be fooled and the hoax spirals out of control (then the real Nessie smashes the fake). We'll come back to this in a tic.

Shortly before "Terror of the Zygons" was aired, a crew connected to a more solemn team endorsed by Sir Peter Scott (see 10.1, "The Three Doctors") released a sonar shot of what looked like the fin or fluke of a large sea-creature in Loch Ness. This was significant as, not being like a plesiosaurus fin (spatulate, with vestigial fingers) but diamond-shaped, it earned the putative creature a Linnean species-name. *Nessiteras rhombopteryx* (as Scott named the creature, all the better to get it listed as an endangered species) was back in the public eye. The shot was, unbeknown to Scott, augmented by a computer (in 1974, nobody really got the idea of computer imaging or PhotoShop). The photos leaked in the Scottish *Sunday Post*, a paper based in Dundee and best known for two vernacular comic strips almost unchanged since the 1930s, *The Broons* and *Oor Wullie*.

We'll not even attempt to explain those (if you've ever wondered why David Tennant says "Jings" in interviews, it's part of the dialect these strips still use and often displayed by Scots as a semi-self-parodic Scottishness), but will mention a different strip from 1975, *The Big Yin*. Artist Malcolm McCormack based this around Billy Connolly's stage persona. It articulated yet another available idea of Scottish identity (or created a new set of clichés): the working-class Glaswegian with occasional bouts of insight or violence. (*Monty Python* fans will recall Terry Jones attempting this accent in the episode "The Golden Age of Ballooning". Amazingly, his was one of the more successful efforts.) There had been gags about Glasgae Patter, the dialect and accent, for decades, but now it was added to the widespread rejection of inherited authority that had been bubbling up in the 60s and 70s. For the first time since the Jacobites, the idea of Devolution was back on the agenda. It had looked like financial suicide for the five million Scots relying on the taxes of the 50 million non-Scots in Britain, but then came oil.

We discussed North Sea Gas under "Fury from the Deep" (5.6), but the prospect of a significant oil reserve closer to Scotland than to London (albeit closer to Norway than to Edinburgh) started getting tantalisingly close just as the 1973 oil crisis raised the price of crude. Britain briefly reintroduced petrol rationing for the first time since World War II. It seemed you couldn't turn on the telly without seeing BBC Energy Correspondent Michael Buerk looking intense in an anorak with a helicopter nearby. It provided a respite for all the shipyards threatened with closure and boosted Aberdeen's economy no end. The BBC had done a sort of update of *The Troubleshooters* called *Oil Strike North* (with some of the same cast) just ahead of the *Doctor Who* tale, but in the real world the emphasis was still on exploration and potential. The emotional and

September or January?

...continued from page 121

September. This was, as we saw, usual practice except for Pertwee's first two years, but it hadn't been planned upon when this story was commissioned. The abrupt end of Season Twelve after a mere 20 weeks hardly seems to have wrong-footed the BBC1 programme-planners as much as it did Elisabeth Sladen: *Dixon of Dock Green* ended the same night as "Revenge of the Cybermen".

What it meant longer-term was that the schedulers (and trailer-makers) had a ready-made four-part story to promote for a 30th August launch, the week after August Bank Holiday and the Doctor's in-character appearance as host of *Disney Time*. What happened next is that, as might be expected, the ratings improved as the nights got longer and tailed off again as Easter approached – but not as drastically as with a January-to-June transmission pattern. September to Easter, punctuated by Christmas, seemed intuitively right as to how *Doctor Who* should be broadcast. (That punctuation was sometimes a long while. A six-week break occurred between "The Deadly Assassin" ending and "The Face of Evil", even though they both counted as part of Season Fourteen and production was almost continuous. We'll pick up that part of the story under **Did Familiarity Breed Respect?** under 17.1, "Destiny of the Daleks").

A very obvious practical effect of this move is with the location filming. Look at a Pertwee story and, like as not, it's drizzly. In extreme cases (8.3, "The Claws of Axos"; 11.3, "Death to the Daleks"), the weather almost becomes a minor character. Available daylight hours have to be grabbed with both hands when shooting in December or January. Using OB location crews slightly offset this ("The Sontaran Experiment" and accompanying essay, plus "The Seeds of Doom"), but with the majority of location work being on 16 mm film, the logistics and the look of the finished product were more satisfying in summer. When the Doctor's connection with UNIT caused him to spend a lot of time in cement factories and quarries, the weather gave it a look of grubby *verité* – but as the TARDIS took him into picturesque villages, mansions and cow pastures, we got something that people wanted to see as they huddled around the telly in a dark November. (The last week of October was usually the occasion of the *Radio Times* doing a "fireside issue"; you will observe a trend for ratings to improve once the clocks go back an hour.)

Between 1975 and 1980, the presence of *Doctor Who* as the opening salvo of BBC1's Saturday Night assault was accepted as almost a no-brainer. Some years, the producer barely needed to promote the series (1977 and, to a lesser extent because of Daleks, 1979, then the almost apologetic 1980 launch). Then the series returned to January but in a twice-weekly weekday slot like a soap, and, despite the new Doctor, as just another show in a whole lot of debuts. Not everyone could be in front of a telly both nights and, despite apparently maintaining the ratings, the series wasn't in the forefront of people's minds as it had been. ITV was providing credible alternatives (notably *Crossroads*). Nobody wants to say it out loud, but scheduling is mainly guesswork backed up by flukes and more prey to circumstances beyond the networks' control than they seem to realise. Saturdays in the 1970s had people coming back home from football or shopping and wanting to see odd-looking adventures with a few scares; weekdays in the 80s had homework, scouts, band-practice or something good on the other side. Nobody knows what the weather's going to be like six months later. We'll pick up on this in **What Difference Does a Day Make?** under 19.1, "Castrovalva", but there's another aspect to scheduling we've not touched on: timing.

As we know from Series 8 and 9, the idea of a series a fair amount of adults only watch because their kids like it starting after the kids' bedtime is idiotic. Yes, there are catch-up services for licence-fee payers in Britain, but not everyone has fast broadband and not everyone wants to faff about with a computer when the whole point was sitting in front of the telly as a family. Historically, the most common time to show *Doctor Who* was 5.15pm It was an *aperitif* before *The Generation Game* and all the rest. When Season Fourteen began, the episodes were either at 6.05 or 6.10. Season Fifteen moved it to 6.20, but some parents deemed this too late (it was part of the over-reaction to Mary Whitehouse; see "The Deadly Assassin", itself delayed until an almost-unprecedentedly-late 6.45pm start).

Nonetheless, the ratings began high and improved, as if to reinforce the idea that people want to wait until dusk before watching. We're so used to the term "Saturday teatime" that its full meaning, especially in Britain in wintertime, is half-forgotten. Perhaps the word ought to be "crepus-

continued on page 125...

13.1 Terror of the Zygons

cognitive linkage between the stultifying version of their identity sold back to them by the media (and, it has to be said, a lot of older Scots who went for this sort of thing, the people Connolly called "human shortbread tins"), the political marginalisation and the prospect of economic and cultural liberation was made explicit in a play from 1973, *The Cheviot, the Stag and the Black, Black Oil* (televised by the BBC in 1974 in a production by Graeme McDonald, of whom more later in this book).

The centre of gravity in UK politics was perceptibly moving from the Home Counties and towards what had been treated as the periphery. Scotland had formally been part of Britain since 1707 (although once the King of Scotland, James VI, became King of England as well in 1603, it was pretty much a done deal: James tried to popularise the word "Britain" for his dual realm, but it was as popular as his bid to ban smoking). As we saw in **Why Didn't Plaid Cymru Lynch Barry Letts?** under "The Green Death", the generation born after World War II were more assertive about cultural identity, especially when that culture had its own (endangered) language and could make a claim to be older than the dominant one. Scottish Nationalism wasn't as violent as the IRA's mainland bombing campaign (notwithstanding a brief fad for "tartan terror" thrillers, notably *Scotch on the Rocks* by future Foreign Secretary Douglas Hurd, adapted by the BBC and then wiped as unrepeatably crass), nor as pointed as Plaid Cymru's tacit support for arson attacks on holiday cottages in Wales. A referendum on Scottish Devolution took place in 1979, although it had been unimaginable ten years before.

As some commentators noted, the Doctor's long tartan scarf was on-trend for late summer 1975: Scottish boy-band The Bay City Rollers were in the charts with three singles, notably their biggest hit "Shang-a-Lang". This, like "Remember", was about how pop music wasn't as good as it used to be. The irony was lost on the nation's 12-year-old girls, who adopted the band's look (oddly like the Tharils from 18.5, "Warriors' Gate", but with tartan trimmings) and screamed mightily. (Luckily, their dodgy manager got it into his head that they could conquer America, leading to a Syd and Marty Kroft show more even embarrassing than any of the others, as well as oblivion for the bouffanted neds.)

A production such as "Terror of the Zygons" would have been unlikely before 1975 but impossible to get on air – let alone for viewers to take seriously – any later. When BBC Wales brought back the Zygons, there was no trace of Scotland, Nessie or oil-rigs. Even their distinctive look changed from angry baby to Spongebob-on-steroids. Not all of these aliens' original appeal was as perishable, though. The first episode clearly invokes werewolf stories (the opening shot even has a full moon). That vaguely ludicrous scene with Angus telling old stories makes a serious point – tales of that kind aren't out-of-keeping with the locale, nor with the sort of paranoid 50s shockers the later episodes evoke. It worked again in 2006 ("Tooth and Claw") with a more orthodox werewolf. (Indeed, the moorland setting and visitors from the big city – with foreign accents – was the start of *An American Werewolf in London*.)

Doppelgangers, fetches (as per 15.3, "Image of the Fendahl") and shape-shifters are the raw material of many Scots folk-tales. Silkie-folk, the seals who occasionally become human, crop up as often as faeries stealing human children and replacing them with changelings (see also 18.3, "Full Circle"). So taking the 50's paranoid SF standby of aliens impersonating your friends (*I Married a Monster from Outer Space / Invasion of the Body Snatchers / They Came From Outer Space,* et al) and placing it in the Highlands was a canny move. And an uncanny one. (We can't forget, try as we might, the stagey 1954 version of aliens in Scotland, *Devil Girl from Mars*, nor its 2013 sort-of remake, *Under the Skin*.) Robert Banks Stewart had staked out this territory before in a serial from 1965, *Undermind*. This had almost the same premise – except that it was a disembodied force brainwashing people prior to an invasion and a couple rather than one man alone (per Quinn Martin's *The Invaders* two years later) whose attempts to warn the authorities were perpetually thwarted – but was almost ostentatiously British about it, basing episodes in country churches, Parliament and the IRA. When the series was cancelled, a promising newcomer called Bob Holmes was given the task of wrapping it up (other episodes were by David Whitaker and Bill Strutton).

The Doctor speculates on the Skarasen's homing signal being a "primitive mating call". It's rather lost in the film adaptation, *The Beast from 20,000 Fathoms*, but Ray Bradbury's story "The Fog Horn" has a sea-monster falling in love with a

September or January?

...continued from page 123

cular". September to March in a country as far north as Canada or Siberia means the sun sets as early as 4.00pm at the Solstice (see our comments on the Russell T. Davies Christmas episodes).

BBC Wales established a regular start-time of 7.00pm, but in Spring. People started missing episodes when this was messed with, but fear of a powerful ITV rival dominated the thinking (Simon Cowell's bafflingly popular *X Factor*). When they hit upon the idea of 7.00pm starts in Autumn (X7.1, "Asylum of the Daleks"), there were records broken left, right and centre – but they'd only made five normal episodes that year, so couldn't build on it (the precise reasons for this can wait for another volume).

The shockingly poor results when they did it "properly" in 2014 were mainly because they put it on at 8.00pm, disrupting the familiarity (in both senses, the "family-ness" and known, comfortable nature). On the BBC's own figures, fewer than half a million people under 15 were watching in 2017 – a year when the content of the episodes was retooled to make it explicitly child-friendly and amenable to new viewers. Overseas, this is less of a problem; BBC America targets 18-25 year old viewers rather than children and parents, so they put it on at 9.00pm for first runs under Moffat and 8.00pm for Whittaker's first two years. Something similar happens in France and Germany. (Japan was very confused and thought it would appeal to horror aficionados, then got complaints that it was too infantile for midnight. They just stopped importing it.) Nonetheless, the majority of viewers are in the UK and they believed that broadcasting it any later than 7.30 was a grave mistake. It broke the habit of watching more abruptly than five-episode seasons or a year off did. Not even the usually on-message Steven Moffat could avoid sounding bitter about it when talking to the press.

The solution was obvious with hindsight: put it on a different day at a reasonable time, hence the Sunday 7.00pm (ish) routine for Series 11, nestled between *Countryfile* (gran-friendly features about farming) and the results show for *Strictly Come Dancing* (which, that particular season, had become newsworthy). All the talk about "Saturdayness" was hastily forgotten and a new set of quasi-nostalgic folk-memories were invented by Chris Chibnall and others.[22] Paradoxically, the ratings, initially favourable, dwindled as Christmas approached – but not just for *Doctor Who*. Television was no longer primarily a broadcast medium.

With the Easter Saturday starts, one advantage the new series had was that the exciting new monsters in the first few episodes were familiar in time for merchandising manufacturers to get them into the shops before Christmas. This ought not to have been a consideration, but it was, especially under Russell T. Davies. Once again, the new format doesn't help as much as it could: an old-fashioned four parter, even if the new monster's kept until the first cliffhanger, has a month or so to bed-in with the public. A one-off appearance in a one-episode story doesn't make the new (or radically rethought) monster "take" as readily without a reappearance.

With merchandising so much a part of BBC Worldwide's game-plan, this aspect of the series has been downplayed (not helped by the similarity of so many recent monsters to one another) and the sales-pitch has been the Doctor's clothing and TARDIS toys. There's never been as much merchandising (and never as expensive) as the stuff on sale now – but, paradoxically, Chibnall's team were less concerned about this than any since John Wiles or Derrick Sherwin in the 1960s. It makes no odds to the BBC Wales execs whether an episode goes out in November or March from the commercial perspective, nor whether the public takes to one spooky man in a top hat over another. Series 11 was noticeably light on monsters and didn't debut a new design of Dalek until a week after Christmas (X12.10, "Resolution").

If you're reading this in the Northern hemisphere, try a small experiment. These stories are best watched an episode at a time anyway, so try just watching a Tom Baker story at roughly the time of year and time of day it was shown – or as close to sunset as it would have been in Britain the day of first broadcast. (Antipodean readers can try it with a six-month shift.) It might have a noticeable effect on your engagement with what's happening on the screen.

---

lighthouse because it mistakes the horn for such a call. The film made the idea of a defrosted plesiosaur one of the front-runners for "explanations" of the Loch Ness Monster and popularised the use of stop-motion monsters trashing cities as a box-office draw. The brief shots of the Skarasen animated by this technique wouldn't give Ray Harryhausen any sleepless nights, but that's what

13.1 Terror of the Zygons

they're aiming at (Tom Baker had, as we've noted, a bit of Harryhausen in his CV). We'll get a vague hint of this story again two years from now (15.1, "Horror of Fang Rock").

There's a possible intermediate step, the 1959 oddity *Behemoth – the Sea Monster* (released in the US as *The Giant Behemoth*, rather redundantly, with all the scenes of non-American people being heroic cut out). This had Willis O'Brien doing the animation under straightened circumstances and Andre Morell (3.5, "The Massacre") warming up for *Quatermass and the Pit* by being unflappable as some random yank took the starring role and tried to sell us on the idea of something from the Pacific coming to London via Cornwall.

English Lessons

- *Your Grace* (hon.): The correct term of address for a Duke or an Archbishop. In his absence, the Brigadier accurately calls him "his Grace".
- *Leicestershire* (n.): A county at the exact centre of England, but not of Britain, so known to rail travellers from London as where "The North" starts. A few semi-industrialised towns (Lutterworth, Leicester, Hinkley) aside, it's solidly agricultural and was famous for foxhunting. The towns went for textile manufacture in a big way, hence the current ethnic diversity. Melton Mowbray is home to the best pork pies on the planet. It's pronounced "Less-Ter-Sheer" because it's been around since before the Romans: the main town, Leicester, was home to King Lear (hence, "Lear Caster", the suffix being what Romans called towns they occupied). Anyone who has a problem with the spelling and pronunciation not matching should consider "Chicago, Illinois" or "Des Moines, Iowa".
- *Chatham* (n.): A town on the Kent coast, at the mouth of the Medway (the river that divides the county in many ways) and at the time home to the main Naval dockyard. It's about 30 miles from the Thames Estuary's southern shore.
- *Brentford* (n.): Technically, it's in Middlesex rather than Central London, but it has a lot of tube stations and bus routes. What it doesn't have is quarries. Draw a circle of a mile radius from the railway station and it goes anticlockwise through Perivale, Ealing, Hounslow, Richmond and Chiswick. In 1975, the name was synonymous with nylon bed-sheets advertised by excitable DJ Alan Freeman.
- *InterCity* (n.): British Rail's main service, even though the commuter lines got more traffic. By 1975, they were promoting their new diesel-electric rolling stock, the 125s, which were technically capable of travelling at 125 mph but rarely got the chance. These came into service in 1976 and many are still running, although the privatised companies try to downplay the BR heritage for fear of unfavourable comparisons and dropped the "InterCity" label. There wasn't a direct line to Inverness until the 80s, but the London King's Cross service might have allowed for a change at Edinburgh Waverley. (This could get really trainspottery, so we'll leave it there.) Before you ask, they were using a medial capital in "InterCity" long before it became hip.

Scottish Lessons

- *Ghillie* (n.): Strictly speaking, it's an outdoor factotum, usually for hunting, and therefore often a gamekeeper and estate manager. In practice, unless it's a very large estate, the ghillie is more or less the butler and major-domo. The most famous is, of course, John Brown, Queen Victoria's suspiciously-close chum. The word's derived from a Gaelic word for "lad" or "boy" – with Forgill Castle being in the Highlands, it might have been more accurate to call the Caber the Duke's "tail", but you can see why they didn't. Talking of him…
- *Caber* (n.): Apparently, not everyone knows this. It's a big log, like a telegraph pole, and one of the characteristic events of the Highland Games is "tossing the caber". Braw laddies compete to chuck these things over distances.
- *The McRanald* (n.): The Clan system is essentially patrilineal; the family's uppermost senior member is the chieftain of a vast set of relatives. Therefore, we have good grounds to suppose that the Duke's family name is also "McRanald" and Angus is related, if only distantly. Such a paterfamilias gets to use the definite article – so, for example, anyone called Campbell is probably technically a member of that clan, but despite the 27 distinct branches, only the present Duke of Argyll is considered "head". If you've ever come across the term "… of that ilk", this is where it comes from: it's usually for such a person who isn't also heir to a title and estate.
- *Waverley* (n.): It's the breakthrough novel of Sir Walter Scott, perpetrator of most of the clichés about Scotland and chivalry that dominated early Victorian pop-culture. Thus, it's the name of Edinburgh's main railway station. It's one of many

off-the-shelf Hoots Mon-style names used for the oil rigs ("Prince Charlie", "Ben Nevis") and exactly what real US companies were calling their drilling platforms and putative oil-fields. (The script called the company "Hibernian Oil"; there's an Edinburgh football team called "Hibernians", but they got their name because they were originally Irish expats – "Hibernia" being what the Romans called Ireland. The opening scene echoes this with "Hibernian Control"; they were to have been the more clichéd but more sensible "Claymore Oil". The sign outside the Sick Bay says "Hiberian".

• *The Black Isle* (n.): It's no more an island than the Isle of Dogs or Rhode Island but is a peninsula just north of Loch Ness (between Dingwall and Cromarty, roughly). Wherever the Forgill estate is, it can't be more than 20 miles from there. Angus calling the visitor from there "a foreigner" is a joke about parochial Scots, but whether it's Angus making the joke or Robert Banks Stewart is for you to decide.

Things That Dinnae Make Sense A generation of schoolkids questioned this before Osgood ("The Day of the Doctor"): a disguised Zygon's body-print seems to be based on the human original and his / her clothing at the time of capture, but as "the Laird", Broton keeps putting on and taking off clothes that seem to have been part of the initial impression and adds others. Specifically, he dons a bowler hat and a camel coat, and changes his cardigan for a waistcoat. Is the cardigan part of his own flesh that reverts to being orange and lumpy when placed in a wardrobe? Does he have to throw it an oat-cake every so often? When he dies as "a Scotsman", then reverts to his naked alien form, is part of his corpse a pair of leather driving-gloves left on a table? (One possible option is that they dress the sleeping human according to how the Zygon impersonator wants to look. Yes, that sounds silly, but it would also explain why, after abducting the pyjama-clad Harry from his sick-bed, they dress him up and drag him to the spaceship... but not why Fake Harry hasn't got a bandage on his head.)

Broton's plan seems a bit Underpants Gnomes-ish. He's going to attack the World Energy Conference *while he's in it*, demonstrate that he has a big milk-lizard at his disposal, do something or other, and then announce a series of demands. What's the something-or-other? They can't intend to secretly replace world leaders, if Broton's scheme entails them being eaten live on television for maximum publicity and terror. Even if it went to plan... what came next? Broton and company want to raise Earth's mean temperature and flood the land, making everything more Zygon-compatible. All right, but wouldn't *not* killing all the oil-producing big-shots and just abducting / duplicating a few world leaders to sabotage any international agreements on pollution or CO_2 emissions be a quicker and stealthier way to do it? Instead, they intend to intimidate humanity into doing so via the threat of being stamped on, individually, by one large milk-producing reptile. Even with more of them on the way, it's improbable that the six Zygons in the ship can enslave humanity.

Actually, how long *have* they been hatching this specific plot? The Zygon home world was destroyed (somehow) a few centuries ago; the dialogue suggests that these aliens have been lurking for all this time, growing a sea-monster from a packet of Sea-Monkeys. Angus's spooky tales with the Jamieson Boys et al imply Skarasen involvement, as do the Nessie-sightings. So did the Zygons secretly nudge humanity into developing petrol engines simply to achieve a World Energy Conference and sudden interest in North Sea Oil around the time their food-supply was fully-grown?

Broton says that they brought the Skarasen to Earth as an embryo, and also that they "depend upon its lactic fluid for survival". So how did they cope for all those centuries without a full-grown Skarasen? What did they feed the calf-Nessie? (This, of course, opens a whole can of worms – perhaps literally – about what Zygons eat while passing for human. Based upon "Nurse Lamont", their blood also turns humanoid; if this change happens at a cellular level, they might ingest human food while in that state. Of course, being both aliens *and* Scottish, they could be capable of eating things most humans would think twice about.) And if Zygons rely upon Skarasens for their very survival, how do the ones in Truth or Consequences, New Mexico (Series Nine, if you've already forgotten) get by? Is there a hundred-foot-long cyborg sea monster hiding in the basement of that block of council flats, being milked surreptitiously by the bloke from the newsagent's?

When exactly was the secret tunnel leading from the Duke's library installed? Have they just been waiting for the Forgill estate to be inherited by a sarcastic Laird whom Broton might enjoy

13.1 Terror of the Zygons

impersonating? Were the previous six Dukes all aliens? All the same alien? (The more one thinks about this, the more it seems that later writers, notably David Fisher and Russell T. Davies, saw this story and thought of ways to make it work. See 16.3, "The Stones of Blood" and X1.4, "Aliens of London" specifically.) And, if a book on a really high shelf triggers the secret door, do Zygons have body-prints for basketball players?

Bagpipes have a reservoir of air that goes through the chanter (the bit that plays the tune) and the drones (the bits that, er, drone) regardless of whether the piper is blowing at that moment. So for Angus's playing to just suddenly stop as if someone switched off a recording is impossible. It'd slowly deflate through the drones, sounding like a beehive dying. Precisely why Angus is so enthusiastic about having a bed-warmer supposedly owned by the Duke of Cumberland is also puzzling: Butcher Cumberland led the forces of his dad, George II, at Culloden and caused the Highland Clearances (see 4.4, "The Highlanders" and its associated essay). It's as likely as a Georgia hotelier proudly showing off a relic of Ulysses S. Grant, or someone in Lyon displaying Klaus Barbie memorabilia.

Plaster of Paris takes a long time to cure, so the trip from the sick-bay to the pub must take all day. That messes up the time-line of the story considerably. (Not as much as Part Four, though.)

The cloud of knockout-gas that incapacitates the entire glen doesn't affect the oil company official, Huckle. On first viewing, this can mislead you into thinking that Huckle is really a Zygon. When it turns out that he *isn't*, many first-timers wonder why the Zygons didn't just copy him and save themselves a lot of hassle? (A Zygon plant in the oil company must stick Skarasen-nip on the rigs. Let's take this as Olra's reason for dressing up as a nurse.) The other problem with the gas sequence is that if the Skarasen walked from Loch Ness to the Moray Firth, we have to surmise that a giant monster stomped through Inverness with no damage.

Benton claims never to have seen injuries like those of the hapless Skarasen-trodden squaddie. "Robot" was only months ago; "The Daemons" (8.5) wasn't that far back either. Our speculation in Volume 3 about the Brigadier having a mind-rubber, or the Tea Lady being a Torchwood agent dosing them all on Retcon, still holds good. (Sarah, mere hours after seeing Nerva Beacon's hefty airlock seals, forgets how sliding doors work.)

Sarah rouses armed UNIT troops to hunt the infiltrator by just saying "It's Harry – we have to stop him!" Presuming they actually know who she means, why would they lock and load on zero evidence to hunt down Lt. Surgeon Sullivan, the base MO? What do they think he's done to deserve this? Besides, she just saw her chum acting grumpy (as you might, with a head injury). Nobody's mentioned shape-shifting aliens yet, just very huge beasties walking the moors and exuding knock-out gas.

Why do the Zygons move the stag's eyes at the precise moment they know that (a) the Brigadier is looking for monitoring devices and (b) Angus is looking directly at it? Maybe they just wanted an excuse to bump him off, but then they take the eyes, as if to say *The Duke's an alien, dummy!* Everyone yelling about looking for bugs was equally subtle.

Broton seems to expect Sarah to find the hidden tunnel, as if it was part of his fiendish plan. The cell door she opens to release Harry takes its time shutting, compared to all the others. This looks as if the Zygons planned to abduct and duplicate the Doctor – what were they planning to *do* with him, given that the Brigadier knows that the Zygons can replicate people and knows they've got him?

Harry and Sarah go from Forgill Castle to the Fox Inn and grumble about the long walk; everyone else uses cars. Yet somehow Zygon-Nurse Lamont can get there instantly when injured.

Something that, with the novelisation and the Capaldi-era beefed-up Zygons as evidence, might *almost* make sense is why the Zygons-as-humans change back when they attack anyone. It's not just the usual alien ability to detect impending cliffhangers; the book version retains a detail cut from the broadcast episodes that the Zygons have a "sting" with which to knock people out. BBC Wales upgraded this, along with the general steroids-and-pointy-teeth alterations, so that they can kill humans and leave those sparking, smouldering piles of horse manure for the Doctor to find ("The Zygon Invasion"). What that *doesn't* cover is why Olra stays disguised as a heavily-bleeding nurse and resorts to hitting a soldier with a rock. Never mind that the naked Zygon colour-scheme is less obvious in woodland than a starched white nurse's apron and hat against a navy-blue dress.

UNIT stage an "immediate" withdrawal which (from Harry's comments about how long it took to walk from the castle to the pub) took hours. Despite the radar block, they seem to fly to London (you could never drive that far in under eight hours) and Harry changes. Broton, meanwhile, shows off his disco transformation effect and puts on a hat then waits. The Doctor rigs a brief signal but, as he underestimates the power of organic crystallography, it knocks him out for an indefinite period while Broton, who's been disguised as the Duke for quite some time now, finally leaves for Central London from this mysterious "disused quarry just beyond Brentford". (We'll assume that the same body-print magic produced enough change for a tube ticket.) The Skarasen was '50 Earth miles' away from its target, even though it had no idea what the target was as Broton hadn't activated the Reciprocator. Brentford's within walking distance of Chiswick (see Volumes 8 and 9). It's unlikely to have had a quarry at any time, as it's so close to Kew Gardens and a number of parks and exclusive golf courses. The District Line will get them to Millbank in fifteen minutes. (Or if the Brig was really on the ball, he'd lay on a speedboat and they'd go up the Thames in the opposite direction to Nessie.) Ergo, the Skarasen negotiates that fifty mile distance in under an hour. Without making any wash or capsizing the hundreds of boats plying the busiest stretch of river in the world (especially when the Dockland area was used for actual docks and cargo-loading).

As the Brigadier has finally encountered an alien that dies when shot with a pistol, the small matter of alien blood spreading pathogens might have to have been addressed. Nevertheless, it's 70s Britain, so everyone gets the idea of terrorism. They'd have a Plan B venue ready while Stanbridge House was fumigated and samples taken.

The Skarasen has yard-long teeth; the Reciprocator is the size and shape of a rubber handle from a bicycle. How does anything with a mouth like that chew such a tiny morsel without an oil-rig to wash it down? It ate an oil-rig but left the thing it was hunting uneaten, for Huckle to find. We never really get any hint about what usually it feeds on, considering the fragility of the eco-system in Loch Ness (something Nessie-hunters have remarked upon), but if it was the Zygons chucking it the odd jolt of energy, that handful of circuits and rubbery flesh is its last proper meal. (Unless, of course, the Doctor's calculations are wrong in 22.5, "Timelash" and there are lots of Karfelon agitators and the Borad being delivered.)

A couple with hindsight: all of this has been happening for centuries within a few miles of Inverness, the original location of the Torchwood Institute (X2.2, "Tooth and Claw"), and nobody there noticed any of it. Nor did the Zygons take any notice of a monastic order harbouring a werewolf, even with their base attached to the nearest monastery. (Not for the first time, we are led to wonder how many times the aliens planning a long-drawn-out conquest must have felt *really* cheesed off when some other lot just showed up unannounced with war-machines, killer shop-dummies or whatever.)

Jings, Crivens and Help M'boab, what is going on with that tag-scene? The Doctor and the Duke need to be back at Tulloch Moor after being dragged 600 miles by aliens, but apparently Harry and the Brig go all that way by rail (a nine-hour journey, so an overnight sleeper – Sarah didn't get a chance to pop home and change, so it must have been the same day or she'd be aye clatty), only to announce that they don't want to go in the TARDIS after all. So what did they talk about over kippers and porridge? The main reason we can see for Harry being on this trip is to run tests on people who've been held by the Zygons, just in case he's thinking of going into biological warfare as a side-line, which is even more reason to ferry him, the Duke, the Caber and Nurse Lamont by a secure, sterile military plane. We have little idea of how long has elapsed or whether the real Duke managed to hold his own at the Energy Conference once it reconvened – assuming that this vitally important meeting didn't just descend into chaos when everyone wanted to see the giant thing in the Thames. The Duke's ethnic-stereotype thrift is supposedly funny, but Inverness has an airport, which had two commercial flights a day from Heathrow and could accommodate a military light aircraft. British Rail, for all its many virtues in those days, was about the most costly and cumbersome way to do this trip.

As it's the last time, we can finally ask about this: originally, a "Brigadier" was someone in charge of a brigade, i.e. a minimum of 3,000 personnel but in the British army. After 1947, it was a refinement of colonel, a field-officer rank in charge of logistics, strategy and so forth. So, while our Brig has the status to order air-strikes,

13.1 Terror of the Zygons

D-notices, etc., UNIT ought to be a bit more puissant than Benton, a borrowed Navy doctor and half a dozen expendable squaddies. Moreover, the Brig got promoted while gaining command of the UK contingent of UNIT even though, within a UN body, this would be confusing; the UK definition of the rank is different from the American, French or Argentine notions. They aren't regular army – why not either keep him as a colonel or make him a general? Admittedly, it's embarrassing to have a general with such a paltry staff and a shoddy HQ, but after so many mad generals pulled rank on him and came unstuck, threatening the end of the world, promoting him would have made sense anyway. The only way that what we see could possibly work is if the French, Argentine and Botswanan divisions of UNIT have even more frequent invasions and environmental crises and the UK is the runt of the litter, bumping along on the scrapings of the UN budget alongside relative backwaters such as Finland and the USA, so UNIT follow their rank designations and protocol.

Critique Behold, the triumph of atmosphere over plot-logic. It's a trick they've pulled off a few times before but never as (seemingly) effortlessly. The script's a bundle of clichés and borderline-offensive stereotypes. If anything, it's best approached as a sort of anthology, with a different mood and sub-genre each week, but at least that means it seems to be going somewhere.

Where it's going is *The Man from UNCLE*, with a tweedy Scottish aristocrat's evil doppelganger trying to take over the world by threatening various delegates at a global summit with a bizarre weapon. How it *got* there was a spooky werewolf tale in Part One (and we concede that it does this better than "Tooth and Claw" by withholding the alien's full face as long as possible and playing with generic expectations rather than confirming them), then a sort of 50s pastiche, mixing Ray Harryhausen and Jack Arnold, then Pertwee-by-numbers for Part Three. All of these are comfortably within Douglas Camfield's range and he puts more care in than the puny-humans-kneel-before-us script requires. Seen an episode a week, with no idea how it's going to pan out, this was more than enough.

The trouble is that it's written by someone who seems never to have watched *Doctor Who*. We'll get that problem with his next script but this, at least, has an experienced cast and director papering over the cracks. This unfamiliarity helps in some ways (Sarah, following the character notes rather than anything we've seen on screen, actually does some journalism). In other ways, it's a drag as the dialogue re-invents the wheel and makes the Zygons trot out some of the most generic nasty-alien lines imaginable. It helps that sometimes they say this crap while in-character as human shortbread tins (a character is called "The Caber", for crying out loud) and they're inside the most interesting-looking spaceship we've seen for a while. It, and much of the plot, resembles 8.3, "The Claws of Axos" more than is perhaps sensible, but it's nice not to have sheet-metal and blinking pea-lights again. Organic spaceships were still a novelty and this fleshy design, with tubes of coloured liquid instead of read-outs, still looks better than some modern takes on the concept. If you can keep a straight face as the Doctor fondles the controls in Part Four, you may have missed the point.

There's a lot of tried-and-tested action serial material here, albeit sometimes made to look fresh by a seasoned action-serial director who's gone away and done *The Sweeney* and recruited a cast who trust him. Some set-pieces look like well-regarded *Doctor Who* scenes of the past (a pitchfork in the hay-loft, like "… and the Silurians", a rig under attack almost identically with the opening of "The Sea Devils" and, in theory, the TARDIS becoming invisible as with "The Invasion" – see also Benton manning the radio during a long wait in the last episode of both stories), but they look and sound different. Geoffrey Burgon (composer) and designer Nigel Curzon were real finds and the Acheson/ Friedlander team are at the top of their game. This is a self-confident production team and design staff giving a fine ensemble cast all the help they need. The Doctor hypnotising Sarah in Part Two is salvaged from a daft premise by music, direction and the way Baker and Sladen play it, and that's just the most obvious example.

What connects all the stories we've seen so far in this volume – and most of what follows – is that most of the key elements are better than they needed to be. That's why the storyline, the alien dialogue and one memorably off-target effect at the end are such let-downs. Everything around them is more-than-serviceable and, as we saw in "The Ark in Space", if the basics are sound, a few small lapses in technical matters can be indulged. When in-character as the Duke, Broton is an

Terror of the Zygons 13.1

entertaining villain and can pull off some quotably daft lines. (All together now: "I underestimated his intelligence. But he underestimated the power of organic crystallography" and of course "You're all utterly unhinged! Must be! Aliens? With wireless sets?") As with the local humans, he's been written with a degree of charm and quirkiness and John Woodnutt (as Broton) is relishing the dry irony.

Once he's revealed as a bulbous-headed alien, it's as if everyone thinks the visual impact of the Zygons can do all the heavy lifting. Their words become perfunctory info-dumping, despite the cast's best efforts. Harry gets their planet's history in under 20 seconds – and when the Doctor ridicules their dull plans, it's hard not to agree. Woodnutt stands out from the English-accented goodies and off-the-shelf aliens. (Consider this: had Barry Letts got his way and cast either Fulton McKay or Graham Crowden as the Doctor, the story might never have been attempted, but the whole series would have been like that.)

And so the Brigadier lays on his last jeep. There will be three more attempts at shoving *Doctor Who* back into the old UNIT format, two of which will reach the screen, and one more outing for Benton and Harry Sullivan in a story even more wilfully "typical" than this (and so similar, pubs, replicants and all, that they might seem to future scholars to be corrupted texts of the same story). But they've gone for the big one, the Loch Ness Monster, making any future attempt at this type of story redundant. Time for something new.

The Facts

Written by Robert Banks Stewart. Directed by Douglas Camfield. Viewing figures: 8.4 million, 6.1 million, 8.2 million, 7.2 million. (The last episode was transmitted 20 minutes earlier than the others, as the Last Night of the Proms was to begin promptly at 9.00pm and they'd opted to lead into it with the epic *How the West Was Won*. A logical sequence.) AI's 59% for Part One, 54% for Part Three. Part Two roughly coincided with LWT showing the debut episode of *Space: 1999*. You can see from Part Three's ratings what everyone thought.

Working Titles It started as "The Secret of Loch Ness", and nearly reached the screen that way. Other titles have been posited but don't appear to have been attached to the scripts, only promotion.

Alternate Versions The DVD has the option of watching the first episode with a restored and re-graded version of the excised TARDIS arrival scene.

Cliffhangers Sarah's phone call is interrupted by a Zygon pouncing on her; a hundred-foot monster is about to step on the fallen Doctor; the spaceship, containing the captured Doctor and the surviving Zygons, blasts out of Loch Ness to start operations somewhere else.

What Was in the Charts? "Barbados", Typically Tropical; "Summertime City", Mike Batt; "Shang-a-Lang", the Bay City Rollers; "Scotch on the Rocks", the Band of the Black Watch.

The Lore

Terrance Dicks had half-heartedly mused upon a Loch Ness Monster adventure but strained to see a story's-worth of idea in the premise. Robert Banks Stewart latched on to North Sea Oil as a topical twist when his former protégé, Robert Holmes, asked him for a script in March 1974. Once the backlog of scripts commissioned under Barry Letts's producership was finished, Holmes contacted many former colleagues who'd given him work in the 1960s or had worked on the same shows as him later. Stewart had "evolved", as the end-credits have it, a paranoid thriller series called *Undermind* about aliens manipulating key figures and recruited Holmes to end his intended long-running series in two episodes in Spring 1965. Stewart's being a Scot made him a go-to writer for *Doctor Finlay's Casebook*, the nostalgic Highland-set A.J. Cronin adaptation that was television comfort-eating for decades. One might think, from this, that the story we landed up with more-or-less wrote itself, but Stewart struggled with the original six-part script and withdrew to a cottage in the country, only delivering the last episode just before 1975 started.

The rewrites began almost immediately. Stewart had delivered a very *Avengers*-ish script with many long chases and action scenes in the Highlands, but the production team could not possibly go to Scotland for that long. The Doctor, Harry and Sarah were more like *Department S* than their characters as developed on screen. Moreover, even with "Robot" in the can since April, the production schedule for the remaining 22 episodes was tightening – it looked as if the last episodes

131

13.1 Terror of the Zygons

would still be in post-production a week before transmission, rather than the two weeks' minimum BBC management would normally insist upon. The budget was also being squeezed. Making this story a four-parter seemed like the first precautionary measure; trimming the location-filming costs for even these was the next step. Holmes also asked that the people behind Nessie's activities should come to the fore. Philip Hinchcliffe was also concerned about the emphasis on a giant monster – it was giving a hostage to fortune if the effects weren't up to it. The next step was more radical and will affect everything else in this book...

- As you will have observed, the usual start of a production year had been late August, early September. Since "The Invasion" (6.3), a story to which we'll be referring a lot, the routine had been to finish the big location-filming sessions over two weeks, then get into the rehearsal suite and get ready for studio. As we saw in Volume 3, this led to many delays for bad weather, or attempts to work around it, and occasional difficulties matching shots when the sky had changed. The 1974-5 production block was no different: however bright the VT footage of Dartmoor looks, recording "The Sontaran Experiment" in October had been miserable; luckily the rest of the filming had been in a hole in the ground ("Revenge of the Cybermen") or a quarry *intended* to look forlorn ("Genesis of the Daleks"). Hinchcliffe bit the bullet and changed things so location filming would happen in summer. As a result, transmissions would begin in autumn. He had few problems pitching this idea to the schedulers, who'd noted a drop-off of over a million viewers after the clocks went forward. A possible concern was the perceived threat of ITV finally putting on a networked blockbuster, the much-hyped *Space: 1999*. Holding over "The Secret of Loch Ness" (as it was then called) for a debut as the school year began might steal a march on this, as well as keeping the momentum for the new-look series rolling for three months off-air rather than six.

- Selling this to the production team and cast was harder. It meant, in effect, starting production on the next stories almost before they'd finished with this one. Elisabeth Sladen had booked a holiday. Worse news arrived: however much the cast and crew liked Ian Marter, or Harry seemed to be working with the viewers, the writers were finding it hard to avoid him being the third wheel.

Meanwhile, Hinchcliffe had given interviews saying that UNIT was getting tired and it was time to move on. Nicholas Courtney took this news badly. Holmes, as if he didn't have enough on his plate, was finding the next story on the roster – the one about mummies – increasingly hard to fix and rewrote it from scratch, under a pen-name, to accommodate an April shoot.

- Among the script elements, everyone was excited about the villainous aliens. From the small detail of them needing the Skarasen's milk (it was "Skarsden" for a while), the costume and monster-make-up designers spun a striking visual conceit. As the director, Douglas Camfield, joined the project, he latched on to the idea of the Zygons as zygotes, semi-developed foetuses, and gave James Acheson and John Friedlander the job of making this work. They took the idea and added octopus-suckers (as much as anything else, a good way to conceal joins). The legs were, in essence, latex pantyhose, held up with braces; over this was a body cast from a mould built around a wire frame.

Only three were made and one of these – for Broton – had a built-in button-mic to pick up and electronically process dialogue in real-time. (The others were voiced off-screen by the actors playing the human versions of those characters, with the suit-actors lip-synching.) The microphone is in the first sucker on the chest, near John Woodnutt's mouth (and is reproduced with absurd fidelity on the chest of the Character Options action-figure). In early drafts, the Zygons' heads were to glow, as were the ribs on the chest-piece – but this would have needed a lot of remounting so the idea, and the "sting" concept, fell by the wayside.

- Camfield, warned off working on *Doctor Who* after the debacle of "Inferno" (7.4), had been in constant work since then. As Holmes and Hinchcliffe increasingly slanted stories to suit particular directors' habits, Camfield seemed a natural fit for this one. As before, he refined the script to suit him, and directly approached actors he'd worked with – bypassing the usual booking procedures. And, as before, he made sure the military details were spot-on. In rehearsals, Camfield identified misfiring bits of the script and split the cast into teams to handle each one independently. Baker was very unenthusiastic about the second cliffhanger, with the Doctor rowing a boat into the Loch and being capsized. The replacement, a chase across the moors, emerged as it became clear where the shoot would be happening (Sussex), even though it required additional model-shots.

• Three things required model-work: the assaulted oil-rigs, the Zygon spaceship (which needed to fly, lurk underwater and explode, plus one for the forced-perspective shot of everyone escaping) and the Skarasen. Pushing the hexagonal end of a Bic biro into the clay created the scaly skin of the Skarasen models. One of these was a two-piece puppet, with a head and neck component and a clawed foot. The other was a complete model – an early experiment with stop-motion. The series had previously made no attempts to use the technique for models, save for the Medusa (6.2, "The Mind Robber") and the Doctor's SOS (6.7, "The War Games"), but here they went full Harryhausen.

As it turned out, the rig's destruction was filmed without a hitch (using a camera set to overcrank, resulting in a slow-motion playback that makes the water less obviously a small tank and helps give size and weight to the collapsing rig). This meant that one of the spares was available to use in Huckle's office instead of a painting or photo. However, Hinchcliffe and Camfield's qualms concerning the Skarasen model-work led the producer to request a fresh caption, after one had been made for "The Secret of Loch Ness". On 27th February, the story got its current name.

• On 21st March, the long-running kid's show *Crackerjack* (oh, all right… *Cra- Ker –Jaaaack!!*) did a spoof wherein goofy-toothed comic Don Maclean simply needed a curly wig and a scarf for everyone to get the joke. The one gag everyone recalls is that former Sensorite Peter Glaze (1.7, "The Sensorites") came on as the Brig and, when asked where Harry was, replied that he was in hospital "having his duffel-coat surgically removed". We mention this because this was the weekend in the middle of the location filming and – almost as if in response – Harry is wearing the duffel-coat when he finds Munro but is then shot and sent to hospital and we never see the garment again.

• The locations selected to pass for Scotland and Brentford were all in Sussex, mainly between Littlehampton and Bognor Regis. (These are both real places, honest.) These had woods, lakes, a coast and what could generously be said to resemble moors. The beach was at a golf course. A hotel in the seaside resort of Bognor was available, out-of-season, for the nine cast-members and a small crew taken on the shoot, plus a couple of rooms for costumes and make-up.

That beach sequence had been the first to be shot, on Monday, 17th March, followed by the TARDIS materialising. Camfield rejected the original idea of our heroes' arrival sending sheep scattering and used a split-screen to revisit the invisible-TARDIS gag from "The Invasion". The lighting conditions changed between shot set-ups, which necessitated cutting the final result when studio recording was underway. The weather was a problem the following day: although everyone recalls 1975 as blisteringly hot, as it was during the summer, it had been snowing that day. Just to make it awkward, it didn't snow all the time – that would have made things easier – but intermittently with strong sunshine every so often.

This was also the day of the quarry sequence: the escape from the spaceship was, as we hinted, done with a model close to the camera and the actors jumping off a platform a long way away. During this, the first mention of a female Prime Minister was made: the idea had been floated that this story (said in promotional material to be set ten years in the future) could be when current Labour minister Shirley Williams was in Number 10, as the press kicked around the notion that Harold Wilson's government was in trouble. The idea was vetoed because it looked like political favouritism, but then the Opposition leader – Edward Heath (see **Who's Running the Country?** under 10.5, "The Green Death") – lost a vote and was replaced by Margaret Thatcher. With a plausible female leader from either side this was, by the BBC's lights, balanced.

• During the two weeks of rehearsal for the first recording days, the cast worked on the details. John Woodnutt, in the dual role of Broton and the Duke, devised with Angus Lennie (as the imaginatively-named "Angus") a backstory explaining why a Duke would have a slightly refined Edinburgh accent rather than the anglicised drawl of someone educated at Fettes, Gordonstoun or Eton. They surmised that he had been the second son, less expensively-educated, and inherited the title after the older brother died. Woodnutt had also worked on the alien voice with Dick Mills of the Radiophonic Workshop at a meeting during rehearsals (2nd April). Lennie (who was currently in *Crossroads*, the notoriously rapidly-made ITV soap, as Shughie McFee, the chef of the motel) had just enough bagpiping experience to make the fingering look plausible as he mimed to Bob

133

13.1 Terror of the Zygons

Murphy's pre-recorded pieces.

- They were in TC3 on the 7th and 8th of April. This story was recorded more or less in episode order, the episodes in set order but with the added complications that some scenes had people looking at screens seeing things that had to have been recorded before and Woodnutt needed to change from the Duke to Broton. The most technically demanding parts came last, with the Body Print effect and the Skarasen appearing briefly through the window. The Body Print was almost the same technique as the Anti-Matter Scout in "The Three Doctors" (10.1), refined through years of use on *Top of the Pops*. The actor is on a blue-screen and the image is turned into a black and white picture, then the grey-scale is exaggerated. Different levels of light or dark are assigned arbitrary colours as the image is degraded further by the camera deliberately going out of focus. Then you mix to an out-of-focus image of the Zygon, also fed through the colour synthesiser, and that comes back into focus and you switch back to natural colours. Place all of that over the image of the set with the same actor ensconced in a sconce and you're away.

This was Nigel Curzon's only *Doctor Who* credit as a designer. This is probably because set design was usually allocated on a taxi-rank basis as – apart from the occasional ribald giggles caused by using Zygon control-panels – nobody had any complaints with the finished look. However, the two "arms" of design, costume and set, miscommunicated on one detail: the doors on the Zygon ship were too narrow for husky-shouldered Zygons to get through. In Part Four, Broton sidles into the cell with the Doctor, or comes as a human, but watch the two carrying Harry from the control-deck at the start of Part Three. (They also forget to operate the palm-print lock before it opens.)

- A second fortnight of rehearsals began – Camfield inspired his "troops" to come in on a Sunday bringing food of their own, as the canteen was shut. The cast refined the climax; Broton was to have attached the reciprocator to the Doctor's jacket and Harry got it off with a thermic lance (the one he was carrying at the quarry). That was a lot of faff to do in the studio at the end of a recording and made little sense. Marter and Sladen also fixed the way a UNIT trooper was just left there in the cellar.

- In TC4 on 22nd April, recording resumed. Then Duke returned to the library to meet the Brigadier and the Doctor, offer his opinions on aliens with wireless sets and show Sarah his library. (An elaborate gag about Sarah trying to get the Caber to climb the steps so she could see if he was a true Scotsman was curtailed). The last day, 23rd, included an R/T room where John Levene's bit of business with the chocolate was another "Invasion" call-back. The scenes at the terrace with the Doctor throwing a treat for the Skarasen came last, with a complicated set-up for the puppet. (You can tell they were in a hurry.) Camfield consulted with Bura and Hardwick, names to make middle-aged British viewers glow with nostalgia for *Trumpton* and Schools television. The animators advised on how to move the puppet within a single plane, something they'd been doing at the time with a reboot of *Captain Pugwash*.

- The decision to move the thirteenth season of serials to a September launch meant that the production rolled on after this with "Pyramids of Mars", starting location shooting on 29th. The twelfth run ended prematurely with "Revenge of the Cybermen" (in mid-May). The former UNIT regulars had been subdued during the recording. (Two of the UNIT regulars, Levene and Marter, came back almost immediately in "The Android Invasion", but neither of them is in any of the filmed sequences. Courtney, who'd already turned down work for "Terror of the Zygons", had a play on, *The Dame of Sark*, which transferred to the West End from Oxford – meaning he was unavailable as the Brigadier.)

- Four days before Part One of "Robot", the BBC's then-traditional Ghost Story for Christmas series had included *The Treasure of Abbot Thomas*. Music for this was from a young-ish composer, more used to composing concert-pieces, Geoffrey Burgon. Due to a complicated misunderstanding during the making of "The Crusades" (2.6), Camfield had decided never to use Dudley Simpson again and approached Burgon to score this story. The brief intrigued Burgon, as did the potential of the recording techniques (ring modulators and varispeed in particular), but he was unimpressed by the acoustics and other facilities at Riverside studios. The music for this story impressed everyone involved; Burgon would be back, with Camfield a few months later for "The Seeds of Doom".

- Over that summer, the series's profile continued to grow. Nestlé launched a chocolate like the fabled *Masterplan* Q with just six wrappers to collect, with character-profiles of the regulars (we're fairly sure this wasn't out when the story was recorded, but if Benton's eating one that had shown himself on the wrapper, that would be a second reason not to show the paper wrapper on screen). Wall's ice-cream, rivals to Lyon's Maid (see Volume Two), had launched the *Dalek Death Ray* ice-lolly with TV ads (voiced by Kenny Everett); these lollies were chocolate fudge encased in mint ice and had wrappers with boasts about Dalek abilities worthy of the 60s spin-off books ("infra-green" rays as the source of Dalek invisibility and, rather less plausibly in a scorching summer that helped sales, flooding London on a whim). Terry Nation was definitely behind the serial about the Daleks in the London *Evening News*.
- On 20th August, the compilation repeat of "The Ark in Space" was followed by a trailer for the forthcoming Saturday line-up ("Terror of the Zygons" and *The Generation Game*, *Match of the Day* and *Parkinson*) and the following Monday, August Bank Holiday, had the Doctor present *Disney Time*.[23] That ended with him getting handed a note that the Brigadier wanted him to go to Loch Ness. The new *Radio Times* came out the next day, with a feature about the Monster by Anthony Haden Guest, memorably illustrated by Frank Bellamy (thereby raising expectations that no model, even today, could match as to what the Skarasen would look like). On the Saturday page was a black and white Bellamy illustration. The Disney connection was maintained as, instead of the usual puppets, BBC1 provided a buffer between *Grandstand* and *Doctor Who* with an unmemorable import, *The Mouse Factory*.
- After the first episode, BBC1 unveiled a regular Saturday summer feature: a variety show done on VT inside a circus tent, *Seaside Special*, with a theme song by Mike Batt that became a hit. One episode – not this pilot – had Baker, Sladen and Marter driving Bessie along Blackpool's Golden Mile. They were there on 5th September (just before finally getting that holiday) to switch on the Illuminations and performed in a short skit involving the Daleks, a lot of *Kiss Me Quick* hats and to Doctor's previous visit to see the Tower being opened in the 1890s (see "The Android Invasion" for more).
- The second episode had competition, but not as much as expected: London Weekend Television showed the glacially-slow pilot episode of *Space: 1999* directly opposite *Doctor Who* but nobody else dared (ATV, for example, thought it would fare better against *Jeux Sans Frontieres* on Wednesdays). Target Books expedited *Doctor Who and the Loch Ness Monster* for a January 1976 release with a striking cover again showing how we'd like to think the Skarasen looked, alongside Broton and the Doctor's head in a *Merrie Melodies* tunnel. The Zygons proved to be more memorable than this incarnation of Nessie and received the accolade of a figure in the second Weetabix set of pasteboard figures in 1977. There was talk of one guesting as one of the incarcerated time-criminals in "Shada" (17.6), but the costumes seem to have been destroyed or perished by then. One did exist for a while longer: the Blackpool *Doctor Who* Experience, re-opened shortly before the episodes aired, later had a Zygon-in-residence to scare kids.

13.2: "Planet of Evil"

(Serial 4H, Four Episodes, 27th September – 18th October 1975.)

Which One is This? For newcomers via the BBC Wales series, this is the one that Chris Chibnall's debut story (X3.7, "42") most closely resembles (the way "The Brain of Morbius" "closely resembles" James Whale's film of *Frankenstein*). For anyone else, it's a bit like *Forbidden Planet*, a bit like *Dr Jekyll & Mr Hyde* and briefly like the video for "Bohemian Rhapsody" – but with more tracksuits.

Firsts and Lasts For the first time, the Doctor admits to having met Shakespeare. Significantly, it's the first broadcast story completely planned and commissioned by Holmes and Hinchcliffe. It's also the first time we've seen this Doctor operate the TARDIS controls, and the last time we see or hear from character-actor Michael Wisher. For the first time, someone other than Dick Mills or Brian Hodgson provides "Special Sound".

It's farewell to the corduroy jacket, but hello to Sarah's groovy leather watchstrap. It's the start of a couple of related staples of the Baker years: desiccated corpses and spooky-sounding gibberish about "draining the life-essence". The repeat was the last time Frank Bellamy provided an illustration for the *Radio Times*.

13.2 Planet of Evil

Four Things to Notice About "Planet of Evil"...

• Not that they've stinted on the dialogue, story or music, but the main point here is the visuals. Specifically, they've opted to blatantly pastiche the two films they were thinking about (see **Where Did This Come From?**) rather than leave it as a little gift for the more astute adult viewer. This gives us a first cliffhanger that, if anything, looks better than the original. (A rather Disneyfied red outline of the Id-monster is replaced by a genuinely weird Anti-Matter monster done by deliberately doing something most CSO line-ups tried to avoid.) Later, we get a werewolf/Jekyll transformation, complete with a not-so-groundbreaking smoking liquid, that's nonetheless better than 7.4, "Inferno". We had moments before where a bit of film-buffery was an overlay on a preconceived script — but here, even more than "Robot", the starting-point and the plot-logic and world-building are subordinated to it.

• We've had space jungles before, especially when Terry Nation was doing Rider-Haggard by way of *Hell in the Pacific*, but never one like this. Even David Maloney's attempt to put some colour into 10.4, "Planet of the Daleks" opted for different shades of green. Even in 1975, enough people were watching in black and white to justify efforts to make the leaves and vines look interesting without any chromatic cues, but they've inverted the natural order to make the plants various reds and purples. (This is where the set budget went, so the spaceship's a bit less whelming — it's flats from Nerva Beacon upside down, for the most part.) This jelly jungle's lurid palate allows them to use a negative of a wildlife documentary for aerial shots of this foliage, conveying the story's basic idea of this world being both "natural" and "wrong".

• The other big visual impact is the costume design. It's Andrew Rose, so shoulder-pads and padded piping are the order of the day (see also 21.6, "The Caves of Androzani" and 23.3, "Terror of the Vervoids"), and he makes sure that all the chaps (except the Doctor) get to air their manly chests. One slightly peculiar costume element is that the Doctor's retained the sartorial clairvoyance of his previous incarnation, and sensibly discards his scarf long before any hint comes that he'll be on an inter-dimensional trip using Kirby wires (see Season Ten for his ability to predict when he'll unexpectedly land somewhere requiring long boots rather than shoes). However, the big consideration for costumes in 7/8 stories is avoiding the CSO colour chosen for that production. As we've noted, there's a lot of red and blue around — so, if you're on the ball, the obvious key-colours are green and yellow. Nobody wears green, but if you (correctly) guessed that everything "not really there" is in yellow this month and have figured out how they did the Anti-Matter creature, you *might* surmise why Sorenson is the only person with a mustard track-suit...

• Imagine that you are a huge fan of actor Prentis Hancock (there must be some) and living in the London area. This story might have presented a problem, as Hancock's here and in *Space: 1999* (which London Weekend have chosen to show at the same time). Both productions have men in velour standing around in futuristic Formica-themed control-rooms (with the same L-shaped table-lamps) talking bollocks about anti-matter and fuel reserves. Hancock gets more lines in these four episodes than in the entire series, though, and seems to relish getting a character who's consistent from one week to the next. Across the board, this story's cast combines old *Doctor Who* hands in odd ways. Michael Wisher, fresh from his barnstorming turn as Davros, is stuck behind a desk for most of the story and does a cringe-inducing voice-over as an unseen crewman. Ewen Solon (Chal in 3.9, "The Savages") is the voice of reason, Louis Mahoney (a newscaster in 10.3, "Frontier in Space", the older Billy Shipton in X3.10, "Blink") is cannon-fodder, as is Graham Weston (6.7, "The War Games"). Max Faulkner and Terry Walsh fall off things. But the guest star, also returning from "The Savages", is Frederick Jaeger as Sorenson; he gets to do "proper" acting *and* be a monster. In fact, the only noticeable cast-member not to have a *Who* under his belt is Terence Brook[24] (as Braun), who dies in the first scene. In short, everyone here knows exactly what they're doing.

The Continuity

The Doctor is remarkably blasé about arriving 30,000 years later and on the other side of the galaxy when trying to take Sarah to London. He responds to a distress call almost instinctively [see 15.2, "The Invisible Enemy", but contrast with 17.3, "The Creature from the Pit"]. He can knock Salamar out with a punch.

He knows a great deal more about the other

What Does Anti-Matter Do?

You know the drill: the people who wrote these episodes took any real-world science they needed from freshly printed newspaper articles. Those articles, while admirable in their concision and accuracy (most of the time), were based on what researchers at that time were telling the reporters. As the years pass, it's harder to relate what went out on BBC1 on a Saturday teatime to what's being taught in schools today (if at all) or what you'd find if you looked it up online. Trawling back through dusty copies of *New Scientist* from the 70s, online scans of the *Sunday Times* magazine or the occasional school textbook with a Saturn V on the front and Glam Rock lettering – in an attempt to make Young's Modulus seem to be somehow connected with *Lift-Off with Ayshea* – it's possible to get a handle on what the misplaced cop-show writers paying bills by attempting science fiction thought the scientists of their time were saying.

In *Doctor Who*, we've had stories based around various different things called "anti-matter", each of which was based on physics as it was understood when each of those scripts was written. This means that they all contradict each other. Any attempt to account for this runs into the problem that describing these discrepancies doesn't oblige us to resolve them – how could we? – nor does it really help as much as we'd like trying to compare it with what's known now. But it's better to try and see what it does help with than just shrug or ignore any real-world science that contradicts fan-fic pet theories.

Let's start with the state-of-the-art account given to us in "The Tsuranga Conundrum" (X11.5). There, as you'll recall, the "iPhone version of CERN" is a diddy particle accelerator to smash up atoms and produce positrons; these are then stored (somehow) in electrical and magnetic fields until needed, then mixed with normal matter and used to propel the space-ambulance. Fine, they "produce" positrons, just like that. Positrons do definitely exist. PET scanners in hospitals are built to detect them; PET stands for Positron Emission Tomography. If you've had one done, the resulting image is a map of the anti-matter your body gave off.

… but you obviously didn't explode, so what happened? Well, you sort of *did* explode, a tiny bit. A positron is an anti-electron and these two have a tendency to part company for a while, fly around as separate entities for a split second then reunite, giving off energy – but they're really small, so the energy they give off is usually a few photons. (We're used to photons being just light waves/particles – because they're the ones we've got organs to perceive – but they're anything on the electromagnetic spectrum, from heat to radio-waves. The dim-bulb twins, electron and positron, annihilate into low-intensity gamma-particles, heading off in opposite directions, and *they're* what the scanner detects.) As most people know, matter and anti-matter annihilate each other and release energy, but if, as we just said, positrons and electrons are doing it at random all over the place, how is anything we touch or see not going bang all the time? Why aren't more massive particles being destroyed by their counterparts? Why is there anything in the universe at all?

A lot of theories concern that last question; the more lurid ones (which made better stories) have made their way onto television shows where old actors try to look comfortable in velour. The easiest way to account for the huge imbalance between things we can touch or see – and things that ought to make them disappear in a flash – is that anti-matter is somewhere else. The bias towards matter is a local habit rather than a universal law. The most story-able version of that is that the missing anti-particles have got a whole universe to themselves – just like ours, but with the film developed wrong.

It's not as wildly divorced from the physics of the time as all that – people seriously posited pretty much the same solution that the Doctor whimsically proposes in "The Mutants" (9.4) about "un-people un-doing un-things untogether" (but with better maths and more circumspection about the term "un-person"; dissident Soviet physicist Andrei Sakharov was a specialist in anti-matter). It's not an idea that's entirely gone away, but current cosmology has rather bigger fish to fry concerning Dark Matter (see **Why Hide Here?** under X3.11, "Utopia") and there are other possibilities that have come along. We'll get back to this in a moment, because we've wriggled out of clarifying what exactly anti-matter *is*, and what makes it so anti. That needs a rethink of a few basic ideas that people still use in conversation, but which research physicists dumped in the era of biplanes.

It's a lot easier to imagine an atom as like a lot of coloured snooker balls glued together with ping-pong balls whizzing around them in circular orbits, like tiny sputniks, than to conceptualise the reality. The "orbit" thing's almost right, as far as distances from the nucleus is concerned, but they

continued on page 139…

13.2 Planet of Evil

universe than he wants to admit. He gives his 'word as a Time Lord' to the entity in the Pool that balance will be restored. Upon exiting the Pool, he mumbles 'Van der Veldt's Equation of Knowledge... quite wrong', as if this were relevant. He spends a lot of Part One staring blankly into space, unconcerned at all the people who want to execute him.

• *Background.* The Doctor has met Shakespeare; 'charming fellow, dreadful actor'. [So much to say here, but it can wait for 17.2, "City of Death".]

• *Ethics.* With two universes at risk, the Doctor confronts / harangues Sorenson on the point that scientists only earn the right to experiment 'at the cost of total responsibility'. [Did he try that line on the relatives of Professor Clegg?; see 11.5, "Planet of the Spiders".] As such, he tactily endorses the notion of Sorenson committing suicide to resolve the situation. The Doctor only picks up a handgun once he's been stunned with one himself, by Salamar, the person on whom he might have to use it [the Anti-Man doesn't notice such weapons].

• *Inventory.* His hand-held tracker homes in on the distress call. [It looks very like hand-held devices in the next two stories, but we don't get a good look at it.] We do see the spectromixer, apparently handy for estimating star-patterns and working out where they've landed; it's a red plastic object roughly the size of an old cassette tape, with a metallic side that has three sliders on it [Sarah can slip it into the locket of her tight jeans, if that's any guide]. The Doctor's bag [see **The TARDIS**] also holds the Etheric Beam Locator. In the Doctor's pocket is a metal tin formerly containing Farrah's Harrogate Toffee, used to contain some of Sorenson's crystals [a cut line has him call it his 'passport' with the Pool Being].

The TARDIS Sarah can let herself in with the Doctor's key. [This is almost unprecedented (5.3, "The Ice Warriors" and 5.4, "The Enemy of the World" had the Doctor sending Jamie and Victoria to wait for him) and is a complete change from the Hartnell days, when the complexity of the lock was a running theme. In 7.1, "Spearhead from Space", the Ship had a 'metabolic detector' to keep humans out.]

The Doctor keeps his spectromixer (a sort of astrolabe) in a Gladstone bag with a few other familiar-looking objects. This is somewhere in the console room, which is much as we saw it in "Death to the Daleks" (11.3). He also has bondage equipment just lying around: a set of four manacles on a metal frame to bind a humanoid hand and foot.

The Console Room is still white but with the zig-zag door-hinges on exterior and interior doors. These are now a dark blue, not quite the same as the police box exterior. The roundels are less deeply indented than before; no scanner is evident. The ceiling is in triangular sections meeting above the console.

The Doctor can pick up distress signals on leaving the space-time vortex and can instigate an emergency landing that seems slightly smoother than normal. [We've mentioned that there's been no chance to go back and update Vira on Earth's status since "The Ark in Space"; the TARDIS apparently going astray at this precise point may not be a glitch or the Doctor's ineptitude, but a hint to her operator that he's forgotten something. By the way, a few hours seem to elapse between the end of this story and the start of the next. Anyone wishing to also squeeze in the backstory for "The Face of Evil" in this gap is welcome to try.]

The light on top has changed again and keeps flashing after they leave the police box exterior.

The Supporting Cast

• *Sarah* is oddly tech-savvy this story; she can identify the sound of the ship's compressors firing up prior to take-off. [Was this relevant to an unseen adventure?] She also guesses (correctly) that power-outages mean that the window locks won't work. On the other hand, she assumes that anywhere with a sun is our solar system and that anything that makes tools must have human-like hands. She's more acutely aware of the presence of the anti-men, stopping still and reacting as if mildly electrically-shocked.

The Doctor trusts her with a TARDIS key and assumes she knows what a spectromixer looks like and where he keeps it. She mocks him mildly but, when alone with Sorenson, tells the professor that the Doctor is 'brilliant' and specialises in 'everything'.

She's changed her clothes since dematerialising in Scotland, adopting a denim look (jeans and waistcoat) with a slightly flouncy gingham top and cork wedgies [so she obviously thinks she's bound for 1975]. She's adopted a flamboyant braided leather watchstrap which will be back a lot.

What Does Anti-Matter Do?

...continued from page 137

are only possible at specific values, unlike real satellite orbits. An electron can no more be between these distances than you can get loose change from an ATM; it's clearly-ascribed values (like banknotes). The electron that gets a bit more energy doesn't shift orbit by widening the circle gradually, it stops being in one and simultaneously starts being in another – the famous "quantum leap".

Using the term orbit as a noun implies the verb "to orbit", angular momentum, direction and so on, and that's wrong. (We'll return to this neck of the woods in **How Do You Transmit Matter?** under 16.6, "The Armageddon Factor", **How Hard Is It to Be the Wrong Size?** under 15.2, "The Invisible Enemy" and **Why is Matter So Weird in Space?** under 22.2, "Vengeance on Varos". You may also want to look at **What Makes the TARDIS Go?** under 1.3, "The Edge of Destruction" and **What *is* the Blinovitch Limitation Effect?** under 20.3, "Mawdryn Undead".) When speculating on what's keeping the electrons in place, Paul Dirac, puzzled that the equations made it just as plausible for an electron to have the opposite charge to that of every electron ever observed, proposed a sort of "sea" of negative-energy states: a field of possible-electron-ness rather than a solid miniature ping-pong ball. (To disambiguate, a little bit, "negative" in that last sentence was the traditional misnomer used in batteries and circuits, not anti-anything.)

It's in keeping with the whole idea of "particles" as hazy possibilities until directly observed. (Schrodinger's Cat, the Two-Slit Experiment, the Many Worlds Hypothesis yadda yadda – this is well-trodden ground these days, but less so in 1928.) A gap in that field, a hole in the fuzz, an island in the sea, could be considered as more than the absence of possible-particle-ness and treated as (drumroll) an anti-particle. It sounded absurd, but it made the sums come out right (much like Copernicus's heliocentric universe and Max Planck's "theoretical" quantum, two other "just suppose" heuristics that turned out to be true), but where were these notional entities?

As chance would have it, there were anomalous results in cloud-chamber traces of gamma-rays: they acted almost like electrons but moved in the wrong direction when encountering magnetic fields. So, very crudely, when an electron "distils" itself from the "cloud" of possibility to become an observable particle (sorry about the scare-quotes, but we're very crudely summarising an analogy), where it *isn't* simultaneously becomes a similar particle of identical mass and opposite charge (plus spin of ½ – what particle physics calls "spin" is as much like axial rotation as an electron's like a cricket-ball). At least, that was the initial idea, but it's been refined into something a bit odder and even less easy to imagine as a picture. We'll stick with the hole-in-a-field thing until we have to drop it, because we're talking about TV writers in the 1970s who probably couldn't rewire a plug.

Just in case that lot hasn't given you a nosebleed thinking about it, that other quantum-mechanical showstopper, Heisenberg's Uncertainty Principle, comes into play here. The reason being: if the nature of the universe prevents anyone from knowing everything about the state of play in any particle interaction, then empty space can't be entirely empty (or we'd at least know everything about that). Nature abhors a vacuum so much, electron-positron pairs have to be summoning each other into existence at random all the time, anywhere – even billions of parsecs from any other particles. But, once again, if it's possible everywhere, and if positrons are just the start and there are anti-protons, anti-quarks and what-have-you, why is observable space so singularly lacking in any of them?

An early front-runner for the most sensible answer was that anti-particles are "normal" ones travelling backwards in time. (That this was "most sensible" gives you an idea of how vertiginous 1930s physics was.) We perceive a one-way directional passage of time (for some reason – the equations on that were equally supportive of the opposite), so anti-matter's beyond our ken. Maybe every electron and positron in the cosmos is just the one particle shuttling back and forth like a bobbin, weaving the universe together.

This poetic-if-scarily-deterministic notion was considered one of the most likely explanations when *Star Trek* used it as a reset-button for an early episode, "The Naked Time" (intended to segue into their first time-paradox story, "Tomorrow is Yesterday", until someone thought better of it). There's a ghost of this idea in *Doctor Who*. As mentioned under "Inferno" (7.4), material from other universes has almost always manifested itself in a way which "undoes" evolution – Professor Sorenson's devolution into Anti-Man is entirely consistent with similar events (e.g. X2.2, "Tooth and

continued on page 141...

13.2 Planet of Evil

The Non-Humans

• *The Pool Being*. When it appears – only at night – the being that comes through the Black Pool is an outline of red energy. It seems to be about three metres tall and vaguely resembles a bipedal catfish with bulbous eyes. On contact with most humans, it removes them from the scene (painfully, it seems), depositing a dried corpse a few moments later. Sarah describes close encounters as being accompanied by a sense of dislocation, mind and body separated. The ship's force-field, when augmented by the atomic accelerators, fends off the creature.

The Doctor, aided by a toffee-tin full of the Sorenson's refined positronic matter, can enter the Being's domain and commune with it.

• *Anti-Man*. When anti-quarks contaminate Sorenson, he downs a drink that slows but doesn't eliminate his bodily change into the bestial Anti-Man. Unlike the Pool Being, this occurs independent of circadian rhythms. It begins with a glow where his eyes ought to be, but the effects become more pronounced as the ship recedes from Zeta Minor [possibly in synch with the pull from the planet on the anti-matter in the hold]. Eventually, Sorenson transforms into a hirsute, toothed, snarling beast with claws [see "Inferno" for a similar bizarre side-effect of a strange powersource]. Oddly, the unrefined ore from the planet repels this werewolf-like creature, but it can still suck the life from someone in seconds [these bodies don't vanish and come back, it seems]. Exposure to the Neutron Accelerator causes Anti-Man to undergo a sort of corporeal fission, whereupon multiple energy-beings – outlined like the Pool Being but otherwise modelled on modelled on Anti-Man – roam the ship. These are able to walk through walls and doors. Once Sorenson is purged of anti-matter, these copies abruptly cease to exist. He seems to revert to how he was before the story started (more evidence, perhaps, of a temporal distortion caused by these crystals) and has no memory of any of the events since his first day on the planet.

Planet Notes

• *Morestra* is the centre of a mighty empire but orbits a dying star. This curious arrangement has led to any scientist with a plausible new powersource getting a lot of political clout; the military grudgingly acts as back-up or search-and-rescue.

• *Zeta Minor* is, apparently, on the edge of the known universe. It's 'as distant again from the centre of the Artoro Galaxy as that galaxy is from the Anterides', if that helps. Beyond Cygnus A at any rate. [Cygnus A is a real galaxy, 600 million light years from Earth's. The jets from its interior black holes were the first extragalactic radio source, discovered in 1951.] Returning at the end, the ship has to cross a 'galactic frontier'. [As we see no stars in the many shots of space, we conclude that it's also at the edge of whichever galaxy they're in. We'll look into this further in a story set at the supposed dead centre of the universe, 20.4, "Terminus", but the idea of an 'edge' is a bit weird in a universe where time travel can happen. As it's the 'known' universe, there seems to be a lot more space to come. This story's essay will elaborate on what people thought about anti-matter but, when compared to 9.4, "The Mutants" and 15.5, "Underworld", we're not so much at the edge of creation as the start of the place where all the anti-matter went. See also 10.1, "The Three Doctors" and **Why Hide Here?** under X3.11, "Utopia" for what else might be going on.]

Professor Sorenson calculates that their home world could run for three centuries on the energy produced from six pounds of the crystal ore from Zeta Minor. (As their sun is dying, we don't know how much power it would put out in that time, but that much "conventional" anti-matter wouldn't match 300 years of an orthodox star's total output.) While they are on Zeta Minor, the crystals merely glow in different colours. However, as the ship gets further from the planet's surface, the presence of the ore (and Sorenson, who is contaminated) makes the planet pull harder the further they recede.

[All right, this makes a sort of sense if the crystals, and by implication the entire planet, are a sort of conduit between dimensions rather than being anti-matter in and of themselves. If Zeta Minor is not so much the end of the physical universe as the hinge-point between overlapping ones – like the Arc of Infinity or the Charged Vacuum Emboitments (20.1, "Arc of Infinity"; 18.3, "Full Circle" et seq) – then the two forms of matter might coexist there without discharging. We now know from the whole Flux storyline that anti-matter from another universe reacts differently with our matter, annihilating without discharge (at least, that's the only way to make sense of what Kate Stewart says in X13.6, "The

What Does Anti-Matter Do?

...continued from page 139

Claw", the Primords in "Inferno" and, implicitly, X3.6, "The Lazarus Experiment"). The hint seems to be that time runs differently for things affected by peculiar forms of matter.

The USS *Enterprise*, of course, has matter-ant-eye-matter reactors (as they pronounce it) using the magical dilithium crystals and, in this instance, they're not too far off-beam (if you'll forgive the phrase). Radiation annihilation is about as good as it gets for powering spaceships: a star releases energy by atomic fusion (usually hydrogen into helium) and is about 7% efficient; fission, as seen in mushroom clouds that used to be cities, is 1% efficient. Annihilation of matter and anti-matter is 100% efficient. (Well, sort of: half of it's usable energy, the other half's neutrinos, particles consisting almost entirely of spin and nearly impossible to detect or engage with in any way.)

That's good news if you've got a way to create or store anti-particles, but this bit's proven to be a bit tricky. Since the first anti-proton was made/released in 1955, the sum total isolated (and FermiLab's been putting them out at 300,000 per annum since the 90s) wouldn't release enough energy to power your television for all of Part One of "Planet of Evil". Last time we did this essay, in 2004, the cost of a trillionth of a gram of antimatter was $20 million. It's come down a little since then but storing it in magnetic "bottles" still takes a lot of energy and cash. (There are 600 *trillion* protons in a single grain of sand.)

There's a method using liquid helium at close to absolute zero to lengthen the wavelength of anti-protons, so that they bounce off the container walls but don't annihilate it or themselves. That's also costly (and liquid helium's a bugger to keep in place). It could be worth it if they even could get amounts measured in micrograms, but at present rates that's going to take longer than recorded history so far. The Dan Brown idea of blowing up the Vatican with a spoonful of it isn't going to happen any time soon. Underlying all of this is a simple fact to be borne in mind throughout the rest of this piece: anti-matter is the best energy *storage* method ever thought of, but creating it from scratch takes at least as much energy as it can release.

We'll give *Trek* this much: they read up on it enough to know that the standard way to obtain it then, as developed at FermiLab and Berkeley, was to zap lithium with protons; in "The Naked Time", they even said "lithium". Then the things they started doing with the engines in later stories went off the deep end, so they had to invent "dilithium" and have it occurring naturally on planets with inconveniently un-American societies. The current preferred real-world methodology is Sodium 22. Check your Periodic Table for why that's replaced lithium.

It could be possible to harvest it from space: there seems to be more of it close to the galactic core. At least, there's *something* giving off the precise 1.02 MEV associated with big-scale electron-positron collisions (or was 50,000 years ago, the time it took for us to get news of that region). Great – let's go there! Once again, we've got a solution that needs us to have already found another solution to take advantage of it. But if we're invoking faster-than-light space travel anyway, what about those imagined far-off anti-matter realms away from our rather pedestrian portion of the universe? So far, no dice there either. It's matter all the way down.

What's now presumed to have happened (Sakharov worked it out in 1967) is that there was a tiny imbalance in charged particles right at the beginning of time. Had there been a 51/49 split between matter and anti-matter at the start of everything, before even hydrogen got its act together, it would have been annihilation city and the remaining 2% of matter would have been all that was left. The released energy would have followed suit, distilling into particles and anti-particles, and the process would be repeated until near enough everything was matter.

Of course, what's now thought is that recognisable matter is only part of the story and there's 96% of the universe we can't see or know anything about. *Doctor Who*, in common with most physicists and almost all science fiction, is guilty of a sort of "matter chauvinism" and has only mentioned Dark Matter once, in "Utopia", as a throw-away detail. If the people who'd made "Planet of Evil" had only thought to call what Sorenson was trying to exploit "Dark Matter" or, better yet, "Dark Energy" instead of "Anti-Matter", we could gloat about this for the rest of recorded history when arguing with Trekkers – but they didn't, hence this essay. Whatever Dark Matter and Dark Energy are, they're considerably weirder than common-or-garden anti-matter.

Be of good cheer, though. If anti-matter's not elsewhere in this universe it must be… (another

continued on page 143…

13.2 Planet of Evil

Vanquishers"), so these crystals might still be a way to access energy without blowing up the user.

[Removing matter in the anti-matter realm or vice versa seems to increase the annihilation energy flowing through, the crystals acting as a sort of "throttle" to increase the amount of energy pouring in from elsewhere and being opened up as they get further from the Pool. Matter and energy being equivalent, the ship's mass increases as it gets further away – thus the planet's gravitational pull, instead of decreasing as the inverse square of the distance, seems to at least increase to match. (This sort of matches the behaviour of the nuclear Weak force, speculated upon when this story was written but partially confirmed since.) Then, as the engines run out of power, gravity takes over and the ship accelerates towards the planet at a faster rate than the mass decreases. Or something like that.

[Alternatively, if we go with the minority idea c.1975 that anti-matter was regular matter travelling backwards in time, Sorenson's atavistic tendency – and his reversion to normal when his dark red fuming drink takes effect – is part of a wider pattern of localised spacetime disturbance. The crystals are literally warping space around the ship. Thus, the further they get from the planet, the more powerful the crystals are because they are inverting entropy. Again, it's not an ideal way to synch the script and what genuine scientists now think is plausible, but four decades ago it was acceptable. Or at least tolerable.

[Nobody's been there for long enough to establish local time-intervals, so the duration of daylight is measured in degrees; Braun told Sorenson it was '15 degrees to full night' and therefore time to start back to base. So, if we take 15 degrees as under an hour and note that the sun rises early in Part Two, we can at least explain why Sarah doesn't seem to need to sleep for the duration of the story. (Vishinsky is happy – so to speak – to count down to impact in 'minutes', so the 'degrees' thing isn't a standard time-unit for Morestrans.)]

By day, the planet is inhabitable, although the mineral strata seem to move, apparently "hiding" from the humans. Sorenson claims that the planet is alive and aware. Seen from space, the planet is maroon; close up, this is augmented by plant-life in similar colour-schemes. No animal life is evident, but the jungle makes odd noises [for once, not the same as every other jungle planet from 1965 to 1980].

History

- *Dating.* Egard Lumb's tombstone says '7Y2 in the year 37166', which sort of fits. [Remember, the press-release for "The Ark in Space" said it was 'the 300th Century', so the production team obviously saw this as roughly contemporary – saving a bit on sets.] The Doctor says it's 30,000 years after they left Loch Ness ["Terror of the Zygons"].

The Morestrans have heard legends of Earth and know its location relative to their home world and Zeta Minor. Earth's been abandoned, as far as they know or care. [This matches the scenario of "The Sontaran Experiment" well enough to be deliberate.]

The Analysis

Where Does This Come From? There's a word that's bandied about when discussing this year's episodes without anyone really checking with anyone else if they're all talking about the same thing. We all sort-of know what "Gothic" means... until anyone asks for a definition. At that point, people start making lists, mumbling about "tropes" and linking the architecture of the Houses of Parliament, the career of Monk Lewis and typography. There's a handy repertoire of visual cues from earlier iterations of Gothic fiction, some of which relate to where it was set or when it was written, but these are symptoms rather than a cause. Just drenching a conventional story in those doesn't make the work "gothic" any more than setting a Western in space makes the result anything like proper SF (see the essay with "The Face of Evil").

The easiest way to get a handle on it is to forget about parameters and think about tendencies; very broadly, if the author and readers agree that the world-view of the work is from a bygone age and nobody seriously believes it any more, the work is Gothic. That approach to deliberate non-realism started out with a lot of books written in the Enlightenment that purported to have been found and translated by the author but written in the Middle Ages. (Or, very rarely, in a country that nobody reading is likely to have visited but of which odd things are said. Gothicism and Orientalism were cousins. In a lot of ways, Edgar Rice Burroughs was a sort of gothicist.) These told of curses, statues coming to life, labyrinthine secret passages in castles – you can make your own check-list. None of these things really makes

Planet of Evil 13.2

What Does Anti-Matter Do?

...continued from page 141

drumroll please) in a different one. And everyone knows that a different universe is sideways from ours, so no tedious long journeys are needed, just a complete rupture in conventional physics. The usual candidate, in the 1970s, was a black hole and, for once, *Doctor Who* got there first. The downside of this is that the ideas people had about black holes in the early 1970s were garbled and contradictory. (See **What's With These Black Holes?** under 10.1, "The Three Doctors" for a round-up of what the *Sunday Times* said in 1972 and other contemporary accounts. See also **Did Rassilon Know Omega?** under "The Deadly Assassin".)

"The Three Doctors" began with the idea of a force equal and opposite to the Time Lords occupying a Realm of Death (probably something to do with Milton, when we get down to it) and Omega had begun as "OHM", i.e. "WHO" upside down and back-to front. Anti-matter was hitched to this story as a shorthand for Omega's realm to be Bizarro-Universe on a BBC budget.

In 1972, that probably sounded reasonable and in keeping with a vague tradition in SF of "contra-terrene" matter (a 1930s term for it with the strong hint of being against nature) as a moral force. The concept of a black hole, still conjectural physics and probably unfamiliar to most viewers before this story, was spot-welded to that – but, as the decade progressed, it became rather a familiar set of associations. You don't go "down" a black hole in these stories, you go "through" it. (In reality you do neither, but most of your particles get layered *onto* it, adding to its mass or giving off hard X-rays as they are stretched and distorted by the runaway gravity. If the ex-star is toroidal, as some might be, somehow, there might be a way out.)

More practically, the associated idea of "white holes" spewing out the matter that had been funnelled through a gap in the continuum after being ripped apart in slow-motion brought with it the idea of equal-and-opposite. It seemed as good an explanation for quasars as any then available. That the term "black hole" is misleading and these things are dense knots in space-time rather than gaps in anything was no problem for the lazy hacks writing *Space:1999*, Disney's *The Black Hole* or *Into Infinity* (AKA *Gerry Anderson's The Day After Tomorrow*), although they were all doing so in the 70s when nobody really knew any better. (X3.13a, "Time Crash" has no such excuse.)

As we'll see, using a black hole as a short-cut to cross a galaxy was being promoted in pop-science books of the time (sneak a look at 15.4, "The Sun Makers" and 17.5, "The Horns of Nimon") and the similar-sounding term "wormhole" is still doing the rounds, now bound up with String Theory. One earlier term for wormholes was "Einstein-Rosen Bridges", which makes it seem as if the issue is all settled, like Relativity. But black holes as a way into anti-universes were uncommon, even in effects-led films, for the simple reason that the protagonists would explode as soon as they drew breath. Omega developed a *Top of the Pops*-style visual effect blob to effect a conversion and relay the Doctor (and assorted supernumeraries and items of furniture) to his quarry-like environment. Is this at all likely?

It's down to quarks – the sub-sub-sub-atomic particles, not the cute robots from 6.1, "The Dominators". There are six "flavours" of quark, plus so-called "strange" quarks which are something like anti-quarks. Put one particular kind of quark together with a strange quark, and miraculously it makes a particle which "mixes" with its anti-particle. The resulting particle is called a "kaon". The crystals Sorenson finds on Zeta Minor are potentially something like this strange matter, neither matter nor anti-matter but made from mixed-up bits of both. They aren't nearly dense enough, though, as in theory a sugarlump-sized piece of strange matter should weigh a few hundred tonnes. It does, however, take something pretty extraordinary to create this kind of strange matter.

The chirality ("handedness") of every subatomic particle right down to quarks would have to simultaneously change. Indeed, as presented in the script, Omega has created an entire realm, particle-by-particle, from scratch, through the operation of his will on the Singularity. Whatever he did to a star to make a black hole made him convert into anti-matter – so, obviously, everything else he made for his own use had to be that way. This was not, however, a pre-existing anti-matter universe (except when it was – the dialogue vacillates on the topic).

In fact, if we're to take the dialogue at all seriously, they were beyond the event horizon of a black hole after being summoned by tachyonic "space lightning" that was somehow visible to a camera on a balloon. Once you've brought tachyons into the picture, all bets are off – they sound like science and pop up in textbooks, but they've

continued on page 145...

13.2 Planet of Evil

any story Gothic, it's the dream-logic connecting them that matters. There's a pre-existing "natural order" that's been disrupted, usually by greed or murder, and the imbalance causes increasingly bizarre and unnatural symptoms until some kind of restitution is made.

Stories later in this book will plunder the dressing-up box of the later Gothic books and the film versions thereof, but are firmly within a twentieth-century worldview of science, democracy and exactly those Enlightenment values the original Gothic stories tried to sidestep. Most of the Sherlock Holmes stories do this too – The Hound of the Baskervilles really lays on the family curse elements (and we'll be back on this trail in 16.3, "The Stones of Blood"), but reveals it to be an elaborate hoax. "Planet of Evil" is almost the opposite. Most of the science-jargon is off-the-shelf, or at least within touching distance of what was assumed about anti-matter in 1975 (see this story's essay for a glance back at what otherwise sensible physicists said). The rest is bog-standard cinema space-opera, albeit nestled inside a conception of nature that's straight out of Macbeth.

There are three separate problems following Sorenson's transgressive researches, but they're presented to us as causally related. The planet's nature is such that removing anything from it gets harder the further you go from the surface. That's a straightforward inverse-gravity, in keeping with the idea of anti-matter we're given. There's also some entity consuming the "life-force" of humans on the surface. It's systematically picking them off, apparently to feed (we have no other explanation) until the Doctor asks it nicely to stop. There is also a sort of hybrid of this and Sorenson; the scientist starts out shambling and hairy, then multiplies into versions of the being in the Black Pool. In some scenes, the attacks on humans are related to attempts to stop Sorenson – rather as the Id-creature bumped off anyone who opposed Morbius in Forbidden Planet – but in others it's the Black Pool being, a sort of manifestation of the planetary "soul". There's no attempt to link these, even if one glowing red outline-monster looks pretty much like the other. Instead, the sequence of events follows the set-pieces of the two most obvious source-texts *as if* one makes the next happen.

It barely needs saying that those two texts are the film versions of The Strange Case of Dr Jekyll and Mr Hyde and the 1954 MGM extravaganza Forbidden Planet, itself a Freud-inflected retread of The Tempest. In both cases, there's a rational, fairly benign researcher whose darker impulses emerge, embodied, and attack any threat to the scientist or the means by which he's become something else. The fall of night is significant in both cases as a prelude to the Sleep of Reason bringing forth a literal monster[25]. An everyday "self" not being the sum-total of what's inside someone's mind is one of the terrors that the Enlightenment had to face – we've said a lot about Mesmerism and Possession already in these books, and they're about to come back big time. Here, despite the temptation to link the Pool-Being's activities to the lack of ultraviolet light or something to do with the star the planet orbits (see, for instance, 15.3, "Image of the Fendahl"), it's just a fact that the anti-man is nocturnal because it's not like us. It's literally anti-human. The samples "want" to be on Zeta Minor in accordance with Aristotle's idea of how gravity and other forces function – each of the four elements belongs with its own kind, so stones are drawn to Earth, fire to the sun and so forth. As we'll see in his next story ("The Masque of Mandragora"), Louis Marks was very familiar with the Quattrocento world-view pastiched in the early Gothic works – so making up this planet from a mix of old films and recent science was (in a very literal sense) second nature.

Note, though, that despite Marks's Rachel Carson-inflected first Who story (2.1, "Planet of Giants"), not *all* of nature is in revolt against Sorenson's hubris. This isn't a terribly well-worked-out ecosystem, because it doesn't need to be. The plants, striking as they were to look at, aren't significant in the script. That's the key to this story: they thought of the visuals first, *then* proposed a superficially-convincing rationale for them. Stevenson doesn't describe the Jekyll-Hyde transformation in much detail, but it's the familiar set-piece of each film adaptation and the way each iteration is judged. The "before" and "after" is how each film is evaluated by critics (which is why they are, unusually, identified by actor and not director, even in the era of auteur theory), but the "between" is what kids loved.

Stevenson's idea of a dual personality is offloaded onto the entire planet here; Sorenson's transformation isn't revealing anything latent inside his mind, it's just an infection caused by magic rocks. That shift from textual inspirations to filmic ones, albeit instigated by very bookish men, has been

What Does Anti-Matter Do?

...continued from page 143

less chance of being caught in the wild than an anti-cricket-ball. By definition, we couldn't know about them directly if they existed (as we mentioned in their big *Who* moment: 18.1, "The Leisure Hive").

If Omega's got tachyons to engage with the outside universe, it's possibly the same method he used to convert anti-particles and might be a side-effect of life in the ultimate cul-de-sac. It's not anything to do with time, apparently, although an outsider might perceive that time had stopped for everyone in close proximity to a singularity – if that outsider had magical scanners that operated beyond an event horizon. (See X10.11, "World Enough and Time" for a version of this basic notion.) The Time Lords are getting updates via the stranded first Doctor (apparently by telepathy, which seems not to obey physical laws in this story), but it takes as long for them to perceive a change in the situation as it does for the Doctors, Jo or us.

The current idea on this is that three aspects of a particle's chirality can be altered: charge, parity and time. Charge is familiar, although electrical charge is only one version. Parity, a sort of chirality in one spatial dimension, is apparently constant – you'd think that the universe wouldn't care one way or another, but a bias seems to exist even within leptogenesis (the making of photon-like particles out of more massive ones). A universe with atoms of reversed charge could work, a reversed parity one couldn't on its own – but one with all three is a goer, in some models. If charge, parity and time are kept in balance everything seems to work, but to alter parity, you have to sling time into reverse. This also applies to individual particles within our universe. (Beta decay inside a kaon retains parity even when you mess with the charge, which ought not to happen. We'll expand on this in a tic, so you can sound knowledgeable at parties.)

It's down at the quantum level, of course, but weak-force interactions don't quite behave themselves when it comes to chirality the way electromagnetic ones do (anti-neutrinos are all stubbornly "right-handed", neutrinos are "left-handed", regardless of what's been done to them in particle accelerators). It would all have to be kept symmetrical overall.[26] Lots of fun theories abound about what's happening, but at the moment not a lot of evidence. So far, no left-handed antineutrinos have shown up (although given how hard it is to detect the normal kind, that's less of a surprise than it could have been), but neither can they been made to occur by changing the charge, as the earlier theories indicated was possible. To do that, you need to faff about with Strange quarks (see 24.1, "Time and the Rani") and there appears to be a Conservation of Strangeness principle like so many other bits of physics. We can't blame anyone writing *Doctor Who* in the 70s for not getting this bit exactly right when Nobel Prize-winners haven't got to the bottom of it, but hang on two paragraphs for an (accidental) example of internal consistency between stories.

We mentioned beta decay. It's the "middle" version of radioactivity, less alarming than gamma radiation, and caused when an unstable nucleus chucks out particles, mainly electrons (you get positrons every so often). Those particles were summoned into being by a neutron abruptly opting to become a proton and the leftover energy/mass resolving into an electron. How does this neutron achieve this? By the down quark becoming an up quark, obviously. This process occurs naturally and involves a peculiar transaction involving bosons and the weak force. A boson is a sort of freight-particle for force, in this case the misleadingly-named weak force. It's only weak at distances above 10-17 metres; closer than that it's stronger than electromagnetism, the strong force or (relatively puny) gravity. Alas, the bosons needed to do this are W and Z bosons and they're a lot bigger than neutrons. A neutron emitting W+ bosons has to obtain mass/energy from the outside universe to convey this weak force. Obviously, that's not tenable long-term, but they have a sort of cosmic overdraft facility that lasts about a trillionth of a trillionth of a second before more orthodox particles absorb the bosons.

Despite the slightly anthropomorphic terms we used, this is a spontaneous, natural event – but, given the apparent role of consciousness in subatomic activity (and how often we've had to fall back on this to account for things in *Doctor Who* that conform to the then-current understanding of quantum physics – see also X3.10, "Blink" et seq.), the presence of immensely powerful beings where such weirdness occurs on a bigger scale in 70s television makes it more likely to be directed.

In both "The Three Doctors" and "Planet of Evil", immensely powerful beings supervise the transi-

continued on page 147...

13.2 Planet of Evil

coming since Holmes took over from Dicks. (Although, oddly, it was Dicks's desire to redo *King Kong* that over-rode Holmes wanting to make "Robot" a thoroughgoing Asimov *homage*.) Now that the backlog of Barry Letts projects has been worked through, it's going to be this way until 15.5, "Underworld". Some of the ideas being explored here were purely procedural – with the advances in CSO and inlay made over the last ten years, was a wholly-electronic monster possible? Could a space-jungle set take advantage of colour rather than evoke South-East Asia as usual? Could they make a third story using the sets from "The Ark in Space"?

It's hypothetically possible that you may not have seen *Forbidden Planet*. It's 1954's idea of state-of-the-art and holds up better than the hitherto-dominant (and increasingly formulaic) invasion-of-suburban-America/ giant-insects-in-3D Hollywood attempts to catch up with printed SF. It's got blue-collar astronauts, a rarity in Hollywood until *Alien* (1979), a lost race whose inner demons became real (but, being pure energy, couldn't be stopped by zap-guns or force-fields), a scientist called Morbius whose mind was the source of this malice, electronic music/ sound effects and a fabulous buried city-machine. We'll see entire scenes lifted from this here and in "The Face of Evil", not least when the invisible being collides with a force-field and when the "grunt" labour grumbles about the repetitive nature of their work. (That last bit is a less-acknowledged debt to Shakespeare, with Trinculo from *The Tempest* turned into a ship's cook.)

Without that film, there'd be no model for *Star Trek* to have pointed at for how to do space opera on screen without looking like Buster Crabbe' *Flash Gordon* (or for later directors to say "don't do that"). However, "Planet of Evil" is written by someone more familiar with *The Tempest* than the film's rejigging of the set-pieces in a 5 cod-Freud version where twenty-fourth-century tech looks like a Californian split-level lounge. What's missing from the film is Shakespeare's occasional doubts about the ethics of colonialism (and the play's true nature as a wedding-feast masque). When Altair 4 is set to self-destruct, it's because the Krell technology can't be allowed to fall into the wrong hands (i.e. anyone human enough to have desires), but there's never any doubt that going there in the first place was right. Marks takes a less Eisenhower-era view of such matters.

For what was believed at the time about anti-matter, see this story's essay.

English Lessons *Harrogate* (n.): a spa-town in Yorkshire, mentioned in passing in 11.2, "Invasion of the Dinosaurs" as a possible emergency bolt-hole for the government if London were to be evacuated (on the model of Vichy France). The toffee – actually more like lemon-tinged barley-sugar – was sold as a way of coping with the foul-tasting spa-water and has been in production since 1840. They still use those tins.

Things That Don't Make Sense Sorenson's miraculous recovery is manifestly a change of plan by the writers, in the face of the logic of the previous three-and-5/6ths episodes. He's been irradiated and every cell contaminated with anti-quark penetration, his brain's turned to soup and he's devolved to bestial fury and fangs, then the antidote he made runs out and finally he's exposed to a neutron accelerator and runs off a dozen copies of himself. But once the crisis is over, he's back to normal, with mild amnesia and a nice clean tracksuit. The most sensible remedy here is if the Pool Being reversed time for him, but if it could do *that*, the rest of the story goes from being nature-out-of-balance to malicious-forces-arbitrarily-jerking-around-humans so everyone changes the subject.

And, what becomes of the dead astronauts? Not their bodies – which are canned and shot out into space – but the cause of death. The Doctor vacillates between the victims being rapidly freeze-dried, with all their fluids drained, and that their "life essence" has been removed/ transferred/ stored (see also "The Talons of Weng-Chiang"; "Image of the Fendahl"; 17.5, "The Horns of Nimon" and others). So this mysterious *mana* or *pneuma* is warm water? Why didn't Magnus Greel get himself a tea-urn? Moreover, what happens to Ponti's body? Did it get pulled back to Zeta Minor to add to all the junk the Pool Being has to remove?

The Morestran home world is both the seat of empire and orbiting a dying sun. It's 30,000 years in the future but their ancestors came from Earth. The sun's decay isn't at the massive-expansion-and-explosion stage, it's just losing a lot of power. Stars take a while to die, so they must have colonised that planet knowing full well it had a best-before date. It can't have changed much in 30.000 years. (If it had, everyone would have noticed the

What Does Anti-Matter Do?

...continued from page 145

tion from matter to anti-matter – but, while Omega can't leave, the entity on Zeta Minor seems able to come and go and allow the Doctor in for a chat. Apparently having a toffee-tin of glowing gemstones gives immunity from exploding to anyone who leaps between continua. Conveniently, for us, a line in the Doctor's diatribe against Sorenson mentions "an oral vaccine to prevent antiquark penetration" – which, despite being like having a pill to avoid being blown up by a grenade, offers a hint. If these crystals are different from normal matter at a level beneath electrons and protons, but just one quark's been altered and the others rearranged to match (because quarks have fractional charges, 1/3, 2/3, -1/3 and – 2/3, so getting one on its own is like finding a rope with only one end), they might – at a pinch, and with a bit of as-yet-undiscovered chicanery with the Higgs Boson or whatever – be able to exist for more than trillionths of a second. It would be ridiculously dense and getting the ship into orbit would be even harder than shown in the latter half of the story, but in *Doctor Who*, there's dwarf-star alloy you can hold in your hands (18.5, "Warriors' Gate"; X6.2, "The Day of the Moon"; X9.2, "The Witch's Familiar"), so at least that bit of made-up science is consistent.

The entity on Zeta Minor is playing entirely by the story's rules. The whole equal-and-opposite notion extends to forces of attraction getting stronger as the distance increases, rather than diminishing as is more common. In keeping with Sorenson's theories, the crystals become more potent as they move further from their origin – the one thing that does that is the kinetic energy of a dropped object near a larger mass (such as a cannon-ball dropped from a table-top as opposed to from a balloon). Instead of the usual inverse-square law, we seem to have a straightforward square – the pull gets greater as the square of the distances, because it's all upside-down and contra-terrene-y.

In relativistic physics, of course, acceleration makes your mass increase fractionally until you approach light-speed, when it gets asymptotically greater. Eventually, your mass reaches near-infinite and so does the amount of energy needed to accelerate any more, but time outside your ship almost stops and you get close to becoming a singularity. Lots of 70s pop-science documentaries tried to explain this, but the best bet for what Marks was half-remembering here is Dr Jacob Bronowski's tram-ride through Zurich in *The Ascent of Man* in 1973.[27] So you have a choice of whether you account for the pull on the ship increasing with distance by an inverse of an inverse-square law, by very localised ramping-up of relativistic effects, *or* by the quarks getting stranger as they leave the influence of a giant-sized weak force.

We can even try to make sense of the similarly-baffling situation at the start of "Underworld" where "the edge of the known universe" is, once again, just the perimeter of the galaxy. Matter is coming into being fully-formed as rocks and dust rather than stray electrons and protons. This time, there's no presiding mastermind pushing the spontaneous generation of matter in any particular direction – but luckily for the Doctor and the Minyans, it all seems to be matter rather than anti-matter.

As we saw, the rules of quantum physics make electron-positron pairs pop up and annihilate in empty space, but if one Edge-of-the-Known-Universe is producing anti-matter exclusively and a hybrid form on Zeta Minor, another edge might take on the counter particles and make matter. Maybe wherever the P7E landed up was the flip-side of Zeta Minor, albeit right at the other extreme of the cosmos. Perhaps it's significant that both are at the start of intergalactic space, as the expansion of the universe seems to be more pronounced between galaxies than in streets or star-systems. (The way space stretches means that energy has to expand commensurately to make the sums come out right and, as with most things to do with particle physics, the sums tell the universe how to behave rather than vice versa. We touched on this in the essay with "Utopia", but the topic's got sexy again with recalibrations in 2019 of the Hubble Constant showing that the acceleration has itself accelerated over the last few billion years.) Whatever force is driving galaxies apart – the current best-guess has to do with Dark Energy, but that's almost like giving up on explaining it in our lifetimes – also seems to "fix" the brief lives of electrons and positrons and other such virtual particles.

The legitimate physics being worked on here allows us to make up some almost-plausible rules for these two stories: if the mysterious being on Zeta Minor is somehow harvesting virtual posi-

continued on page 149...

star's erratic behaviour and evacuated.) So, why is everyone acting as if this will trigger a crisis in their lifetimes? And if this empire's so extensive, with Salamar talking about galaxies the way pedestrians talk about cities, why is the sputtering-out of one star such a crisis? In fact, if their home world runs exclusively on solar, why can't they charge up the spaceship with the abundant light from Zeta Minor's sun?

If the ship can refuel on returning across the galactic frontier, what's stopping their command-base from sending a tanker or somesuch, or depositing fuel supplies at dumps along the route? It was good enough for Amundsen, after all. Instead, Salamar refuses even to take a quick look at the planet before landing, because fuel is so critically-limited. (The script seems confused about whether spaceship fuel is the same as power for a planet, let alone whether other planets in this supposedly-vast empire are also running on fumes. Unless this ship is being powered directly from Morestra, by extension-leads or something, there's no connection between these two facts.)

And what was Sorenson planning to *do* with anti-matter if he'd got it home? If the idea was to recharge their star, they'll most likely accelerate the supernova part of the story. If not, could they replace the star with his little stick of Black Pool rock?[28] (It's especially weird as the Doctor sells Sorenson a scheme to harness the planet's kinetic energy, which rather implies they already have a lot of miraculous abilities and can move whole planets if they so desire. Of course, doing that to excess will make the planet fall into the sun, after causing disaster for calendar manufacturers ...)

We've got a whole essay on what people in 1975 thought anti-matter was like but should add that within the space of two scenes, we go from a sensible comment that a collision between matter and anti-matter will cause explosive annihilation... and then a man whose cells are steeped in the un-stuff avoids exploding by drinking smoking Ribena and "merely" reverting to a savage, unreasoning predator. This is all because the planet lies on the boundary between two places of existence. Why is there a planet at all and not a lot of gamma-rays and heat? What has "life-essence" got to do with any of this? How does sunlight make the Pool Being go away (especially in a jungle where little light reaches the ground)? It's not as if a whole planet, or different time-zones of it, can be on a time-share/s between being matter and being anti-matter. (A few pages back, in **Planet Notes**, we tried a clever pseudo-science account of what could be happening here, but don't recommend running it past any actual physicists. And it doesn't account for a lot of what we see in this story.) If the Pool Being is pure anti-matter – and it can't be impure because *blam!* – what's going on with the desiccated corpses in their nice uniforms littering the place?

This brings us to a big problem with the story: that both the Pool Being and Sorenson (when he's under the influence) absorb the life-essence from hapless blokes in low-cut tops as if this is somehow vital for their survival. If that's the case, what did the anti-matter creatures feed on for the previous few billion years? If, on the other hand, this is the Pool Being's way of saying "get off my lawn", why has the massacre been so slow? Killing seven people in three months is really dragging it out, if the humans weren't taking the hint. Sarah's keenly aware of the presence of the Anti-Matter creature *and* can tell when Sorenson is about to transform. If this transformation is caused by his cells being blasted, why is Sarah's reaction so intermittent?

How long is a day on Zeta Minor? The spaceship lands before nightfall, but barely any time elapses before the Doctor quotes *Romeo & Juliet* on the topic of daybreak. Then the ship has to take off pronto because night will fall "soon". At what point did Sarah find out what the compressor units on a Morestran star-cruiser sound like? How does she know what they're called and that they presage a take-off?

Oh all right, the short-eared elephant in the room: everyone else in this story has gone for the mix 'n' match approach of surnames and accent, so Ponti is obviously Jamaican, Vishinski is very un-Russian and so on. And yet, Crewman Ranjit remains the complete Peter Sellers ethnic stereotype Indian.

Critique A new planet, at last! One that's neither a quarry nor a familiar world revisited. With the contentious exception of post-apocalyptic Earth, we've not had a genuinely fresh one since Metebelis III in "The Green Death" (10.5) and not a lengthy visit to a non-quarry world since "Planet of the Daleks" (10.4). That yarn gave us a studio-bound jungle, a Formica-flatpack spaceship and a lot of other things that made very little sense together. It was also directed by David Maloney and he's learned a thing or two from that experi-

Planet of Evil 13.2

What Does Anti-Matter Do?

...continued from page 147

trons and discarding the virtual electrons in some far-off mirror-image, we don't need a local immensely-powerful-being acting like Maxwell's Demon to make matter distil itself and form rocks and stuff in the Badlands where the Minyans land up. The Zeta Minor being's doing all that's necessary and the freaky action-at-a-distance of quantum entanglement allows the rest to happen. We're going to pick up on that in **How Do You Transmit Matter?**, with special reference to Coco Pops and Kate Bush.

One more bit of oddness from "The Three Doctors" worth mentioning... despite his prowess at making anti-matter objects that can exist in the UNIT drains and travel faster than light, and rendering people summoned this way capable of sitting on chairs he summons into existence by effort of will without chair and occupant annihilating each other, somehow Omega is draining energy from our universe instead of adding to it. He's draining energy on a cosmic scale, even threatening the Time Lords, wherever and whenever they were that week (see **Where (and When) is Gallifrey?** under "Pyramids of Mars"). This seems oddly one-sided, given that the Time Lords consider him an equal-and-opposite force – shouldn't he also be suffering a bit of a power-loss? (Maybe he is: the palace he's built to while away eternity in while making the Gel-Guards from willpower and positrons looks increasingly shabby as the story progresses.) Or, if energy is a constant and doesn't respond to what kind of universe it's in, wouldn't Omega have a lot more power to play with as things proceed in his favour?

Either way, his influence on the Time Lords isn't matched by any significant change in the nature of his realm. That energy isn't being rerouted to anywhere we can see, it's just being lost. Admittedly, this isn't an unexpected consequence of a black hole showing up in the neighbourhood, but this particular black hole's been there for a while and only now started to be a problem – for the last umpteen-thousand years, it's been the primary power-source for time travel. Power from black holes isn't unexpected either, for reasons we sketched in earlier, but that haze of X-rays is ultimately the result of electron-positron pairs happening and one half of the couple being beyond the event horizon, thus unreachable when annihilation-time comes.

Perhaps whatever Omega's up to involves nudging this process away from what the Time Lords have been exploiting. He's somehow made the black hole go on strike and cause power-cuts. (Seriously, how much more Ted Heath-era could this story have been?) The Chancellor and the President are still on the story's first draft when they make these comments, but in the finalised story, Omega uses Singularity effects to override popular and important laws of physics.

In the first iteration of this essay in 2004, there looked like a way out. In 1999, researchers at CERN and Fermilab came up with one possible answer. Bosons, as we've just indicated, are particles that imbue other particles with mass without actually "carrying" mass themselves. (As always, attempts to explain it clearly lead to more complications.) They have all sorts of other odd features, including the ability to "stack" in the same space the way particles can't usually (hence the superfluidity of liquid helium). The transition from anti-matter to matter is easier than the reverse. The agency of the "reverse" transition might be a theoretical particle called an X boson (which sometimes includes both X and Y bosons), but the universe is now too cool to allow many of these to exist even if they ever did.

So, maybe Omega's got some kind of deal going with these X Bosons. In our universe, you might see one created every (tight squeeze here) 10,000,000,000,000,000,000,000,000,000,000 years. But we're talking about someone who used to redecorate stars for a living, so this might not be a problem for him. In fact, if he's in a tiny universe with more energy per square parsec than ours, he could be onto a winner, so long as he keeps his quarry-like living-space at room temperature somehow.

In "Arc of Infinity" (20.1), something called quad magnetism allows both matter and anti-matter to coexist, and allows the Doctor to "bond" to Omega. As standard-issue magnetism involves forces connected to photons, maybe this mysterious "quad" variety is related to home-brewed X Bosons instead. It's supposedly the product of collapsing Q-Stars (like Q-cars and Q-planes, custom jobs?) and the "only" force which can shield anti-matter within our cosmos. (But "Arc of Infinity" later has this colossal cosmic force bound to the Doctor by faxing his medical records to Omega, so let's not rely on it for a tutorial on high-energy physics.)

Of course, if Omega's universe is reversed from

continued on page 151...

13.2 Planet of Evil

ence. Not, perhaps, as much as he could have – he's once again cast Prentis Hancock as a hothead who thinks he knows better than the seasoned and cautious old hand, rather than cast against type. Still, Maloney's doing better with those ingredients than before.

Two things often discussed as problems are, in fact, assets. On the one hand, the Morestran spaceship looks like what it is: a retread of Space Beacon Nerva. With so much dialogue about Earth being forgotten and this story being 30,000 years in the future, that's what would get praised as good continuity in any later story where continuity is the main selling-point. The casual viewer accepts a spaceship that isn't quite the USS *Enterprise* (especially with the camera angled through the Perspex work-surfaces) and the more committed kids would grab its semi-familiarity as a sort of Easter Egg. It does the job and quickly sketches in an idea of where and when we are, who these people are and so on. The script doesn't give much help in that regard, so we take what we can.

The other issue is more closely bound to the story's premise. They're trying to do gothic (as we discussed earlier, a wilful blindness to what we know now, in order to allow older types of story), but within a positivist science fictional setting. It wants you to try to make sense of it while telling a story about things not making sense. That's almost unprecedented. ("Planet of the Daleks" entailed a planet that the author *thought* made sense; the least said about the Festival of Ghana in 2.8, "The Chase", the better...) There is little plot-logic or aesthetic unity between the various symptoms of anti-matter saturation. Part of that is a desire to crib as many cool shots from *Forbidden Planet* as possible, even though that story was predicated on the id-monster resisting interpretation or consensus about how animals work. It's a sort of collage, like most of the best bits of *Doctor Who*.

Another reason was the idea of a Jekyll-Hyde planet and its effect on someone exposed to it. Maloney's at risk of falling between two stools paying lip-service to both of these source-texts, but it just about hangs together. We could be smugly 90s and note that these discontinuous signifiers, along with the mix-and-match surnames and accents, suggest a world just slightly out of our comprehension, but with nothing irrecoverably beyond our frame of reference – like the way a Russell T Davies story set in the far, far future had everyone wearing Top Shop clothes in a strange combination. Or, more sensibly, we can follow the script's lead and say that the Doctor's right about this world reacting to humans in ways he can understand but not adequately explain.

What does cohere is the way the jungle looks, as a deliberate un-Earthly, anti-natural locale with complex lighting effects, and the way the anti-matter being from the Pool seems to be in it but not entirely of it. Placing a prosaically functional base-camp and spaceship within this is – if anything – a step ahead of the original, where Leslie Neilsen landed a bleedin' flying saucer in a painted desert landscape. What's coming to get the Morestrans is the very definition of irrational, so it needs a doggedly prosaic spaceship and crew to offset it. Here, for once, the script helps by having Vishinsky dispassionately conduct a space-funeral and the below-stairs griping of Ponti and de Haan punctuating the big speeches the way Trinculo did in *The Tempest* and the cook did in *Forbidden Planet*. The astronauts have a context, of sorts, at odds with where they are.

Again, the comparison with "Planet of the Daleks" is in this story's favour. The more significant comparison is with the stories either side of it and, here, again, it scores just by not looking like them or anything else around at the time. (Well, maybe, *Space: 1999*, but that was all-film and a lot duller. And Hancock had a moustache, so you can tell his characters apart.) The anti-men are, like the Dalek extermination or the first three title-sequences, made of television, of accentuating what would normally be a malfunction. It couldn't have been done better by anyone at the time, and now it looks unique.

One thing we'll see more of in the near future is the mix of one human spokesbeing and a few more non-speaking unstoppable aliens. This time, we get Frederick Jaeger as both; his performance roots the baffling train of events in a reasonable facsimile of reality. Here's where a sustained rehearsal period comes in handy. Compare this to X3.7, "42" (a bid to make a "standard" spaceship by using yet another closed-down factory, the way they did then) and the way that story's guest-cast seem to have been parachuted in is obvious. That's not entirely a bad thing, as they got a longer shoot on location in 2006-7 and there's no opportunity for a cast-member to do a funny voice (remember, this is Michael Wisher's first gig after playing

What Does Anti-Matter Do?

...continued from page 149

ours in every respect including time, then the problem becomes one of narrative logic rather than physics. He chucks material into our universe that drains energy rather than adding it; the Doctors and objects are in reverse time compared to in UNIT (except for that recorder, which is getting younger inside the force-field) and everything happens on the same day on Gallifrey as on Earth, because, err, because it does. However, that would mean that Omega was sent on his mission several thousand years into Earth's future and spent a minus amount of time in exile before finding the Doctor in 1970s Britain, but we'll get to that in the next essay.

Davros). But here it looks as if the characters are listening to each other (except when they're not supposed to be) and a lot of the key moments are conveyed entirely by performance and not effects or music. Maloney's all over the electronic effects and models, but he's as good as anyone at relying on acting. (Yes, even Hancock is doing what the script requires and at least seems committed.) Even if the storyline seems like the author made it up as he went along, the cast try to find some truth in it.

There's something valedictory about this story. Even though we now see the inside of the TARDIS again, and Sarah seems more at home there than anywhere else, it ends with a "let's try to get home" line like the old days. We've had a lot of spaceships like this in the recent past, but we won't for a while. There's a sense of resisting the obvious – to the extent of letting Sorenson live at the end – but in ways that would, in time, become obvious themselves. It's going to be a while until we see Tom Baker so prepared to go along with a script he thinks is beneath him. He simply stares into the distance when he hasn't got any lines worth his time. Because of the transmission-order differing from the production timetable, we are going to see the story they made beforehand *after* this, so the regulars know where this is going and what's coming next.

Simply dismissing this as a palate-cleanser between the Nessie-in-the-loo spooky fun of "Terror of the Zygons" and the horror-movie pastiche of "Pyramids of Mars" is misguided. This is as legitimate a way to make *Doctor Who* as any other. It requires a different skill-set from the costume-drama-gone-rogue formula or UNIT, but that doesn't make it less worth doing. It could have been done better, with time and resources for a second draft, but it's an option they needed to keep open.

The Facts

Written by Louis Marks. Directed by David Maloney. Viewing figures: 10.4 million, 9.9 million, 9.1 million, 10.1 million. AIs unrecorded, 56, 57, 54. The repeat the following summer (5th-8th July, 1976) got 5.0 for the first two episodes, 4.9 for Wednesday and 3.9 for Thursday.

Alternate Versions The novelisation reinstates a few scenes cut for time.

Cliffhangers The energy-being that's killed so many people approaches the Doctor and Sarah; the Doctor freeze-frames in mid-fall into the multi-dimensional pool; the unconscious Doctor and the terrified Sarah are strapped into space-coffins to be ejected from the ship.

What Was In the Charts? "SOS", Abba; "Pandora's Box", Procol Harum; "Love is the Drug", Roxy Music; "Do It Again", Steely Dan.

The Lore

With Barry Letts's backlog of commissions and story-ideas depleted, Philip Hinchcliffe started from scratch on the sort of project he wanted to see – and avoided things he found cumbersome. After so many Earthbound stories using UNIT and latex-faced monsters (especially green or brown ones), the idea of a truly alien setting was appealing and a purely electronic creature seemed like a break from the norm. Before any script ideas were settled on, Hinchcliffe consulted with Roger Murray-Leach, set designer for much of Season Twelve, on how far they could push the look of a planet without having to cut corners.

• Robert Holmes, meanwhile, was getting in touch with his former mentors from the 1960s (see last story) and found that Louis Marks, with whom Holmes had worked on *No Hiding Place*, had a gap in his busy schedule. After script-edit-

13.2 Planet of Evil

ing *The Stone Tape* (see "Image of the Fendahl"), he was working on an anthology series of unusual ghost stories and was thus a BBC staffer. This required Holmes to get a special dispensation before any script they devised could be formally commissioned. (Hinchcliffe had also worked with him briefly in the late 60s, on the London-based soap *Market at Honey Lane*, for which Holmes also wrote at a different time. See "The Talons of Weng-Chiang".)

In the meantime, Hinchcliffe, Holmes and Marks kicked around ideas: Hinchcliffe got the ball rolling with the notion of basing a story around *A Tale of Two Cities*, but eventually the idea of a Jekyll-Hyde planet – alive but only benign by day – took hold. With the talks on the look of the story progressing, Hinchcliffe found himself gravitating towards a favourite film of his youth, *Forbidden Planet*, and liked the idea of a single, altered human as the menace rather than six blokes pretending to be an alien race. Marks had written two previous *Doctor Who* stories (2.1, "Planet of Giants"; 9.1, "Day of the Daleks"), so needed less babysitting than, say, Lewis Greifer (see next story).

• David Maloney was contracted in late January 1975, just after completing work on "Genesis of the Daleks" and as "The Ark in Space" was being broadcast. He said later that he specifically requested Murray-Leach for the production, but it seems likely that the designer was always part of the mix. Either way, set elements of Nerva Beacon were earmarked for re-use in the spaceship sets, the better to put time and effort into the jungle. Murray-Leach, who'd been working on Spike Milligan's *Q6*, opted to redress pillars generally used for Greek temples or Roman villas as alien tree-trunks (some of them were less usable afterwards). With such an effects-heavy story, the Visual Effects Department wanted a long lead-in time, so delays in the script (and the official clearance) caused small ructions (there was a memo from Bernard Wilkie in mid-May, just ahead of the all-clear). The final scripts are dated the day of the first film rehearsal, 10th June. One late change was Hinchcliffe's request that Sorenson didn't deserve to die at the end.

• One other small hint of things to come was that the July edition of *World of Horror* magazine contained a small ad for a magazine called *TARDIS* edited by Gordon Blows. People replying to this became the nucleus of the first organised fandom

for the series, with all that this entails.

• Being an all-studio production allowed one other obvious change. As the previously made story had been a period-piece, and Sarah had – conveniently – found appropriate clothing just before landing in 1911, the character's overall look was only now getting rethought. Maloney wanted her to "look like a girl" after the practical work-clothing of Season Eleven (punctuated by Sladen's trips to Bus Stop, her favourite boutique for "off-duty" dress) and the functional look of Season Twelve (dictated at least partly by the grubby weather on location in late 1974 and January 1975). Her hair was softened, with less of a sculpted fringe, and Sladen brought in a watch she'd obtained with a braided leather strap.

A practical reason existed to opt for light blue as the story's predominant colour (all the reds and dark blues in the jungle sets and the yellow for CSO precluded anything else, but the dull greens they were trying to get away from after last year), so faded denim was a good option and in-character. To stop this being too monolithic, Sarah's blouse was a loud tartan with the red trimming that would become a regular feature in her look. Sladen recalled the waistcoat restricting her breathing at times. Baker reverted to the corduroy jacket one last time, partly because of the practicalities of flying-harnesses, but also to contrast with the Morestrans who were mainly in the same blue as Sarah. We can't say for certain that it's a coincidence that the uniform was so similar to those of the C57D's crew in *Forbidden Planet*.

• Rehearsals at Acton started on the 19th; studio recording began on 30th in TC6. In the script, it's "Edgar" Lumb who died, not "Egard". The Anti-Matter creature effect was relatively simple, using CSO and deliberately emphasising a side-effect that had caused problems in 11.5, "Planet of the Spiders" and "Robot". In those, you may recall, a silvery object (the Whomobile and the eponymous robot respectively) reflected the yellow backdrop and thus bits of the metallic item vanished or got fuzzy. Here, a silver-grey suit with bulging, frog-like eyes and various dangly bits and pipes was lit in harsh *chiaroscuro*, in a strong red, against a yellow background (some of which was reflected on the suit). When keyed into the background image (usually a jungle or corridor), the yellow-less signal was dialled back so only the red-lit edges came through.

• In Part Two, recorded on 1st July, there was a

brief clip from a BBC2 wildlife documentary about orangutans shown the previous March; it was an aerial shot of Borneo that the *Who* team showed in negative as the Tracker's view of the jungle on the monitor. An idea of using titanium tetrachloride to make the crystals fume was abandoned as it reacted with the metal toffee-tin Baker was holding. As usual, Terry Walsh did the majority of the stunt-falls, but Max Faulkner was on hand for a couple. It's Walsh in the freeze-frame at the end of the episode, with Faulkner doubling for Louis Mahoney. The hand-guns and side-arms had photographers' flash-bulbs installed, as did the bits of the set hit by stray gunfire. Although animation had been ruled out for the Anti-Man effect as too costly, one brief piece of cel-animation was matted in as the creature hit the force-field (the only direct visual "quote" from *Forbidden Planet*).

• The complicated third day of recording was 14th July. One hold-up was the make-up for Sorenson's various stages of atavism. The easiest way was to shoot out-of-sequence and use a double. As the jungle was no longer in use, and the production had moved to TC3, more sets were possible, including the redesigned TARDIS interior. One complication was the make-up for Sorenson's various stages of atavism; the easiest way was to shoot out-of-sequence and use a double. Moreover, to avoid a delay, one scene was rethought to indicate Sorenson's transformation without make-up simply by showing his feet and changing Frederick Jaeger's walk. The transformation was split into four stages by the make-up designer, Jenny Shirecore (her only story). Stage one was just the eyes glowing, a simple enough CSO trick. Stage two was fingernails and a wig. Stages three and four were more complex and Jaeger had earlier had a face-cast made (presumably before he grew the stubble). For most of Part Three, the devolved Sorenson was in fact played by Mike Lee Lane, who had been inside the silver anti-matter suit. The TARDIS scenes for Part Four, however, had Jaeger act opposite Baker in Stage Four make-up. Baker, by now a drinking buddy of Jaeger's, cracked up when confronted with this sight.

• Sorenson's multiplication in Part Four was a fairly straightforward combination of CSO and howlround, replacing the backdrop with the same image as the camera was feeding into the mix. (As we've mentioned, this was on air the four weeks when the video for *Bohemian Rhapsody* was being shot; nobody's ever denied any influence, but it had already become a common *Top of the Pops* technique.)

• Michael Wisher thought that "Morelli" suggested a gangster, so tried to persuade Maloney to let him put on a Brooklyn accent. This was declined, but Wisher was fond of saying that his character's funeral was the most interesting bit of the story. Melvyn Bedford was told he'd got the part of Reig, his first big speaking role, while playing a Mummy in "Pyramids of Mars": his under-powered scream was enough for Maloney to suggest he do it as if he had just been told he'd not get paid.

• Between 19th and 25th of July, the episodes were edited (Part One needed two sessions). Hinchcliffe recommended the design for industry awards and wrote memos commending various technical aspects for recognition by heads of department and Bill Slater. The lighting crew also thought this story was something special and asked Hinchcliffe if it were possible to get a mention along with the cast and designer in the *Radio Times*; the producer made the suggestion, but it didn't happen. (For the summer 1976 repeat, they had Frank Bellamy provide a pen sketch of Vishinsky – the last such commission before Bellamy died.)

• One unforeseen consequence of moving the start-date of the new series to late August was that Dick Mills was on holiday when the dubbing was done. Peter Howell, who had already helped out with the soundtrack of "Revenge of the Cybermen", stepped in to do "Special Sound" (as they still called it) and got his first on-screen credit. Most of the music was added in the last week of August and the second week of September, just ahead of broadcast, with Radiophonic elements added after each session. A bit of Part Four's music was a sneak preview of the already-recorded score for "Pyramids of Mars" (and the last shot was from there too).

• Part Three was shown later than usual, at 6.05pm, because the Saturday afternoon live sport magazine *Grandstand* was celebrating its 1000th weekly edition with an extended programme. As we mentioned, this was the first story since "Spearhead from Space" (7.1) to be re-serialised on BBC1, stripped across Monday to Thursday 5th to 8th July, 1976 (Friday having a compilation of "The Sontaran Experiment").

13.3: "Pyramids of Mars"

(Serial 4G, Four Episodes, 25th October – 11th November 1975.)

Which One is This? Sutekh, mummies, a Victorian priory, a pyramid-shaped guided-missile, a church-organ with a rear-view mirror, a force-field, a fez… what could possibly link all of these? The Doctor has a suspicion, but it's (all together now) "almost too horrible to contemplate".

Firsts and Lasts This is the first story to start with an immensely powerful force penetrating the TARDIS while it is in flight; it's here described as "inconceivable" but will happen with increasing regularity henceforth. This is the story where the "binary" coordinates for Gallifrey and the name "Kasterbouros" are rattled off (recurring any time a writer wants to show off fannish credentials). We have the first mention of the TARDIS controls being "isomorphic" (ditto), the Doctor's first on-screen trip to Mars, the first time Gabriel Woolf does a spooky voice for a daemonic alien, the first on-screen attempt to resolve UNIT dating (oh dear) and the first time we get a physical trip into an alternate future to show why they have to go back, stand and fight. It's also the last instance before 2005 of the TARDIS doors opening directly onto whatever's outside.

The Doctor finally gets the velvet frock-coat we all think of as his look. Plus, this is the story where slightly moth-eaten Victorian manor houses become the natural setting for Tom Baker fighting eldritch horrors. Oh, and the Doctor has a respiratory bypass system he'd neglected to mention until now (but see 6.6, "The Space Pirates").

Four Things to Notice About "Pyramids of Mars"…

• As this is another of those stories that Russell T. Davies and Steven Moffat strip-mined for ideas and in-jokes, the fact that the guy in the fez (Namin) is a baddie and gets killed by another baddie might confuse younger fans. His main role is to establish that the sound of a church-organ lets us know that aliens pretending to be Egyptian gods are doing something. As is increasingly the case, the music's almost a character here. Sutekh's punishment seems to have entailed four bars of music playing over and over for 5000 years. When we cut from his chamber to someone with whom he's communicating (usually his leg-man, Scarman), the music stops. Then when the camera cuts back, it resumes where it would have been if playing continuously.

• There's absolutely no reason for this story to unfold in the English countryside. As it is happening there, we get a poacher (who'd be a comic-relief character in a Pertwee UNIT story) chased around the estate by giant mummies with magnificent pectoral development and brutally murdered in a memorably unique way. He's garrotted between the protuberant chests of these pharaonic assassins in a manner that also ought to be amusing but isn't.

• As the scale of the crisis emerges, the Doctor's flippancy fades and Sarah starts getting all the funny lines. This, more than any other story, cements the character (and Elisabeth Sladen's performance) as the benchmark for how a female companion ought to be. Except, however, that she proves proficient with a gun. The director insisted upon this, despite everyone else's objections.

• When the Eye of Horus is destroyed and Sutekh is released, that music finally ends, and another aspect of his torment is revealed. As every fan knows, he's been sitting on someone's hand for all this time, and it finally gets to leave once he can stand up.

The Continuity

The Doctor is in a right old strop today.

This week, he's 750 years old. He doesn't debate Sarah's claim that this is almost 'middle aged'. He's tweaked his look, adopting a silk cravat and a velvet frock-coat that's either brown or plum depending on lighting conditions. On his first inkling that the Osirans are involved, he intones 'I've a suspicion, but it's almost too horrible to contemplate' and spends much of the next two episodes telling us about the terrible price if Our Heroes fail, his usual bonhomie almost extinguished.

1911 is 'one of his favourites'. [That's entirely apt. Entire books are devoted to that summer, culturally and historically significant in many ways in Britain and Europe.]

• *Background*. Intriguingly, he claims to have 'renounced the society of Time Lords' and is now a wanderer. [The precise nature of the Doctor's parting of ways with his people changes almost from story to story, and this account is partially to mislead Sutekh, but it's plausible enough for us to

Where (and When) is Gallifrey?

If you want a smart-alec answer, Gallifrey is – subject to confirmation by the IAU – on Pluto, between Skywalker and Vulcan. Whether the Doctor knew this in "The Sun Makers" (15.4) is beside the point. If you want anything more definite than that, based on evidence within broadcast episodes, it's a bit tricky. Anything that looks like a direct statement is almost immediately contradicted by events.

These days, we're told it's inside a separate bubble of space-time, one that the Doctor can visit in the TARDIS (X12.2, "Spyfall Part Two" was the last on-screen occasion – we'll get to X12.10, "The Timeless Children" and that "Boundary" in a bit). The relationship of this bubble to our universe is, apparently, negotiable (X9.12, "Hell Bent" opaquely has them move it to "the extreme end of the time continuum"). So our first question is: when was it ever *not* in its own bubble? We get mixed signals on this even within a story (15.6, "The Invasion of Time"), where Rodan announces the TARDIS's arrival and she's asked for an ETA in "relative time". Then, a week later, a Vardan fleet comes in spaceships and lands troops in the Capitol. "Transduction barriers" surround the planet; in the context of the story where these are first mentioned, "The Deadly Assassin", the verb "to transduce" seems to be a specific form of spatial relocation (people shift the TARDIS after a command to "have it transducted").

For time (or Gallifrey, at least) to be invaded, it needs to be physically present. The Vardans come and go via broadcast emissions, but the Sontarans must show up in person with spaceships – both the transduction barriers and the quantum force field must be perforated or removed. That being the case, the transduction barriers aren't just *Star Trek*-style "shields", but a physical dislocation between the outside universe and the planet. (Or, more likely, the entire planetary system, as they need to get sunlight from somewhere. Apart from Gallifrey's brief irruption into our solar system – X4.18, "The End of Time Part Two" – there's always been sunlight when we've been outside the Capitol "in person", the only night scene being a questionable memory of the Master being initiated via the Untempered Schism.)

Once within this, there's a second, more orthodox force-field ("orthodox" insofar as generic convention goes, if not physical possibility), but one that can't be dismantled without evaporating the planet. In "The Day of the Doctor" (X7.15), there are "sky trenches", which we can only imagine are more temporo-spatial discontinuities, but these can't keep out the Daleks (who are by now up-to-code on Time Lord-like abilities; see **What Happened to the Daleks?** under X1.6, "Dalek").

What made the multi-Doctor operation to squeeze Gallifrey even further out of spacetime any more complex or intractable for beings that got to Arcadia without much bother? Why did the next batch of Daleks all conclude that there wasn't a Gallifrey waiting to cause them more trouble? Well, eventually the penny dropped and we had that whole business at Trenzalore, but why the Time Lords, now somehow out of stasis, chose *that* place and time to manifest is unclear (as is how it related to the earlier crack in space that dominated Series 5). However, the return of the planet occasions the only reference of it moving around in time like a giant TARDIS ("Hell Bent"), so, perhaps this wasn't possible before.

However, the Doctor doesn't react to this announcement, so we may be none the wiser. We have the Doctor's reaction to seeing Trenzalore from space in "The Time of the Doctor" (X7.16) as proof that it's not the same system as Gallifrey used to be in. It's apparently a very long way from Earth or anywhere else the Doctor's been in the fifty-first century, otherwise the Kovarian Chapter would have been known to the Cybermen et al in "A Good Man Goes to War" (X6.7). Lots of places are a very long way from Earth, though, so this tells us very little in itself. Ko Sharmus (X12.9, "Ascension of the Cybermen") is on a different very-far-away planet and has a Boundary taking people to a random place, different each time but all as far away from Cybermen as possible (apparently – nobody seems to be able to report back). One of these is the dead world Gallifrey, whence the Master rejigs things to make it stick to one destination. So we have two or three places that are very distant from each other and from Gallifrey. Is the Time Lord base therefore equidistant from everything?

In storytelling terms and as a matter of policy, this would make sense, but the planet they're on must've had a location before they abstracted it from orthodox reality. Right back in the very first episode, Susan was cheerfully lecturing her science teacher about five-dimensional spacetime. Later (1.8, "The Sensorites"), she's mentioning her home planet and it matches what we've seen of Gallifrey (a planet she recognises in 20.7, "The Five Doctors"). In the context of someone who lives in a TARDIS, there's no reason to assume that there's

continued on page 157...

take it seriously.]

He was blamed for starting the Great Fire of London, which he thinks is a bum rap [but see 19.4, "The Visitation"]. He's acquired a picklock from Marie Antoinette and talks as if he met her [it was her hubby who was into locks and gadgets].

He's obviously preoccupied, as he muddles up Vicki and Victoria [two separate companions from separate Doctors] and thinks that Miss Waterfield wore this Edwardian-looking white lace outfit Sarah's picked. [It's manifestly not anything like what Victoria was wearing in 4.9, "The Evil of the Daleks", which was brocaded satin and had a crinoline, multiple petticoats and a décolleté neckline, nor is it at all like the various minis she improbably took to wearing or the tweed "Practical" cyclist's outfit she wore for two straight stories. The latter is at least the same period as Sarah's posh frock (i.e., 35 years after Victoria's native time). If you want to clutch at straws and use this to support the "Season 6B" theory, go ahead. See **Is There a Season 6B?** under 22.4, "The Two Doctors".]

• *Ethics*. The big picture here is so terrifying, he doesn't spare time to mourn Laurence Scarman's death even in passing. He facilitates an 'abomination' such as Sutekh aging to death, remaining deaf to all the deals the pleading Osiran offers. He shows Sarah the world in a post-Sutekh future, demonstrating the cost of their just up and leaving, rather than merely pulling rank [as in X7.9, "Cold War"]. When confronting his opponent, he condemns him 'in the name of all nature'.

• *Inventory*

– *Scarf*. He uses the stitches as an ad hoc tape-measure when comparing the designs on the wall to find the anomaly, inches one side, centimetres the other [he's used to being in 1970s Britain].

– *Other*. His waistcoat pocket contains a parallax coil that he chucks into the time-space tunnel, with a big bang, after it activates the sarcophagus. He uses a mechanical picklock rather than his screwdriver. He has two devices with telescopic probes: one is a portable radio-telescope [looking a bit like the 'Android detector' in the next story], the other is a well-insulated pointer, extending to about a metre, handy for detecting electrified door-handles.

The TARDIS is penetrated by a psychic projection of Sutekh – something that, by rights, shouldn't be possible. It causes a small explosion in the console and a localised wobble, plus a failure of the relative continuum stabiliser [see 17.2, "City of Death", for a lot more about those]. This guides the TARDIS to a spot in the priory on which UNIT HQ would be built, but in 1911. [Logically, the absolute coordinates in spacetime for the lab in, all right, let's call it '1980', would be altogether different from those of the same piece of Earth in 1911 because the galaxy's revolving, Earth's orbiting the sun, the universe is expanding and so on. Taken with similar mistaken landings in the Hartnell years and in, for example, the next story ("The Android Invasion") and a gag about fog in 15.1, "Horror of Fang Rock", it's looking as if absolutes don't apply in the vortex and the Ship takes bearings from local conditions. This accounts for the convention of showing the police box spinning in space and such otherwise inexplicable events as the start of 2.5, "The Web Planet".]

With a few simple controls, the Doctor takes Sarah and Laurence to the 'wrong' future on the same site. He then opens the doors, to let them directly look at this uninhabitable world [prefiguring the way this has been routinely done since X2.0, "The Christmas Invasion"], so there must already be a life-support shield in place [see 17.5, "The Horns of Nimon"].

On leaving Mars, the TARDIS seems unable to return to the priory any earlier than it left; the Doctor must rush about while he's still ahead of the radio signal. He lands in the same spot on both returns. [Even though materialising in the parlour would have saved valuable seconds. Maybe he's fixed the Fast Return switch from 1.3, "Edge of Destruction". See Part Four of 15.2, "The Invisible Enemy" before you decide.]

The Supporting Cast

• *Sarah* seems very proficient with a 1911-vintage shotgun. As if aware that her usual fashion-sense would give the lie to her claim to be from '1980', she has picked this of all days to select an Edwardian lace frock and accessories to wear.

Sarah's Improbably Detailed Knowledge this month is remembering about the 740 Gods whose names are recorded on the walls of the tomb of Thutmose III. Her odd blind spot is how gelignite behaves.

Where (and When) is Gallifrey?

...continued from page 155

any link between these two facts, but a home in another dimension isn't ruled out either. However, the planet can't have started out there.

We know that some Gallifreyans pre-date the Time Lords, and these pioneers were active and powerful within the cosmos a very long time ago. When intimidating the Racnoss Queen (X3.0, "The Runaway Bride"), the Doctor is careful not to mention being a Time Lord, but names his home world and gets a response from someone who's been planning a comeback since the Earth first formed. Taken at face value, this indicates that the ancient Gallifreyans (the Shobogans, as we finally get to call them) were fighting cosmic wars 4.6 billion years ago and removed Huon particles from the universe (relatively) soon thereafter. The start of "Genesis of the Daleks" indicates that the Time Lords' ancestors mastered teleports "when the universe was less than half its present size". As we've suggested elsewhere, that's not necessarily the same as half its present *age* and the huon-hoovering might have been connected with an abrupt change in the acceleration-rate (see **What is the Blinovitch Limitation Effect?** under 20.3, "Mawdryn Undead" for more on Artron energy and red shift). Nonetheless, we've got a definite date for a significant intervention by Gallifreyans, and it's before there was an Earth.

Even in the series' most geocentric phase, the Time Lords' only real interest in Earth owed to the Doctor and the Master being there ("The End of Time Part Two"). Gallifrey manifested in our sky as a big orange lump half as big again as Earth. It might still be possible to account for all of these differences and argue that Earth will become Gallifrey, but it's a much harder sell now. There's also the small detail of a whole extra star – back in 1973, Barry Letts had decided that the Doctor was from somewhere with three stars (as depicted on the astonishingly period design for the new TARDIS key debuting in the same story – 11.1, "The Time Warrior", which coins the name "Gallifrey"). However, it's only relatively recently that the binary system we now accept as standard was revealed (X3.12, "The Sound of Drums").

So now that reason has prevailed, where was this big orange planet before it was evicted from the continuum? Co-ordinator Engin refers to Earth being in "Mutter's Spiral" ("The Deadly Assassin"), which became the standard name for our galaxy (especially in other Robert Holmes stories). The conversation has been taken to mean that wherever Engin and Castellan Spandrell are, it's a long way from Earth. That could mean a different galaxy or, more obliquely, that these days all galaxies are equally distant from whatever dimension they're in. Leaving aside "Mutter" being German for "mother" (which could be recruited for arguments that Gallifrey started out in our galaxy), the main reasons for assuming the Time Lords to be relatively local and visitable by normal means are other Robert Holmes scripts[29].

Gallifrey's dislocation could just as easily be temporal as spatial and, to be consistent, possibly both. We know that moving things a second ahead in time makes them inaccessible ("The Face of Evil" made the first mention of this), but we have a precedent of 27 worlds being hidden inside the Medusa Cascade (X4.12, "The Stolen Earth"), a famous beauty-spot the Doctor was taken to as a kid. Something along those lines is at least a conceptually simple enough explanation for why people don't just wander in.

"Pyramids of Mars" named "Kasterborous" as the district where Gallifrey is to be found (although, this being a Holmes script, it says "constellation", which might – at a pinch – be interpreted as meaning "star-system", i.e. two or more stars as we've just established) and the direction, sort of. Whatever "binary coordinates from galactic zero centre" means (and if there's a 2 in it, this isn't "binary" as we understand it), Sutekh recognises this string of numbers and not the name "Gallifrey", which is odd. If the starting-point for this celestial zip-code is the supermassive black hole at the centre of Mutter's Spiral, it's at the middle of a bulbous disc, so requires at least one other datum point to give direction in at least three dimensions. (And both the Time Lords and the Osirans need to have agreed what that point is, even if it's what the "zero two" at the end denotes.)

If, on the other hand, the "zero centre" is the middle of our local cluster of galaxies, it's even harder to work out what any of this means. If one or two of the numbers are distances from whatever this datum-point is (and if it's really binary, the "ten" and "eleven" are in fact "2" and "3"), they seem a bit imprecise. Seven numbers to specify a single planet out of the whole galaxy is pushing it a bit – for the entire universe, and possibly all of history as well, it's absurd. It takes about as many numbers to pinpoint Des Moines relative to the

continued on page 159...

13.3 Pyramids of Mars

The Non-Humans

[NB: the script wavers between 'Osirian' and 'Osiran', the former a term used in genuine archaeology.]

• *Osirans* were formidably powerful aliens with advanced psychic powers and technology based on the planet Phaester Osiris. Their brains were arranged in a helical manner within their domed skulls. They were a major cosmic power until one of their number, Sutekh, declared war on all life and needed 740 of them to stop him. Because of their moral code, they did not execute him but left him paralysed in a tomb on Earth for 5000 years or more. The Osirians vanished, possibly as a result of this devastating conflict.

Egypt, the chosen burial-site, adopted Osirian ways and worshipped them as the gods seen in pyramids and statues. The prison was secured by a force-field generated on a different pyramid, on Mars, protected by booby-traps and robot mummies and broadcasting a recorded warning. Oddly, their technology is keyed to human posture and gesture: making the Sign of the Eye opens doors and overrides security lockouts. The Eye of Horus symbol [see also 25.4, "The Greatest Show in the Galaxy"] is somehow invested with literal power.

• *Mummies* are, in this case, servo-robots with a lightweight tubular frame encased in chemically-impregnated wrappings. The chests are inhumanly extended and the eye-sockets are more like large ellipses 10cm by 5cm. The hands are like mittens or over-gloves but seem dextrous enough to install components of a missile guidance system.

The wrappings impede scans but allow the radio signals from the relay in the ring; Namin (and Sarah) use this to enforce verbal commands, but Scarman, as Sutekh's vessel, doesn't need it. Oddly, the robots have no recognition-signal, so the Doctor can pose as one unchallenged and one set of mummies loyal to Osiris defend the Pyramid of Mars against Sutekh's robots.

They seem to draw power from a relay in their backs: this is a red glassy tetrahedron used for 'cytronic induction'.

Planet Notes

• *Mars* seems disappointingly like Earth; same gravity and atmosphere. [Admittedly, we're inside a pyramid made for aliens, so we have more excuses than X10.9, "The Empress of Mars" could muster.] The sudden end of a radio signal takes two minutes to reach Earth, so it must be *really* close [see **Things That Don't Make Sense**]. Inside the Pyramid are a number of traps for the unwary [as if anyone would just wander in], most of which have tropisms activated by gestures, such as the Sign of the Eye [a sort of *mudra*] and the arm-waving done by the Doctor that Sarah calls 'triobyphysics'. [So, as well as giving Sutekh an Alexa, Horus had a Wii built into the trap.]

History

• *Dating*. We're told it's 1911, and the leaves make it look like late spring or early summer. [That year was rather hot, so it's unlikely to be any later than June.] For the details on the Osirans containing Sutekh and massively influencing Egyptian civilisation, see **The Non-Humans**.

The Analysis

Where Does This Come From? We were talking last story about the premise of Gothic fiction being that "the past" or "abroad" allows stories not fitting the predominant world-view, and ancient Egypt fits this perfectly. (There was a curious idea that travelling east was going "back" in time and west was, obviously, progress: Virginia Woolf and Mark Twain fell for that too, but there's a whole subset of Orientalist Gothic, such as *Vathek* by Beckford, that use "Arabia" the way the others used the Middle Ages.) The practical difference between 'Gothic' and 'Romantic' was that the latter took Greece as their model, the former everywhere else in antiquity.

Stories about the events common in stories from other belief-systems taking place in the world of the reader were a popular way of – as people say now – checking your privilege. Victorian Britain was sustained on a notion of the Empire being as far away cognitively as geographically, but as well as the practical, real-world reminders of the global reach of imperial economics and militarism, a constant supply of creepy stories involved aspects of the "exotic" being brought to London or the Shires to wreak mayhem.

This is going to come up again in this book, but what's interesting here is that, beyond the basic incongruity of mummies in the English countryside and a pyramid missile aimed at Mars, there's little time to pause and make any sort of critique of museums collecting artefacts from Egypt, India

Where (and When) is Gallifrey?

...continued from page 157

Greenwich Meridian and the Equator.

These coordinates could feasibly lead you anywhere in the universe (*except* the centre of the galaxy). The Doctor needed more numbers to make a simple spatial trip from Earth to present-day Kastria in "The Hand of Fear". Besides, in the 5,000 years that Sutekh's been sat on his scatter-cushion, the galaxy has revolved a bit (0.00001125°, since it takes 12 billion years to do a single rotation – extended over a parsec, that's the distance from here to Pluto). Eldrad states a location that's 150 million years out of date and the Doctor needs an expansion factor that's at least two phone numbers long. Stars and planets alter their relative positions, so you *could* argue that, for this data to have any validity to Sutekh, the direction must be towards another galaxy. Another odd thing about it is that, if Gallifrey is one of the oldest, most firmly-established and powerful civilisations in the entire universe, they ought to have been the ones laying down whatever conventions are being used here so the coordinates ought to be just a string of zeros. Whatever the case, in "Death in Heaven" (X8.12), those coordinates didn't work.

The other odd thing is that these spatial coordinates seem to apply for the Doctor whenever the TARDIS goes home, regardless of what year he set out from or from where. The next time we hear those numbers recited is in "Full Circle" (18.3), just after returning the Earthling to what we have to assume was the late 1970s or early 80s – but uniquely here, there's a CVE in the Doctor's way. (That could have been awkward for Borusa in "The Five Doctors" or the various bits of ancient Gallifreyan tech sent home in Season Twenty-Five. A CVE in or near our galaxy would be a bit obvious, as it spews energy into N-space to avert universal heat death.)

In "Terror of the Autons" (8.1), a bowler-hatted Time Lord popped in on the Doctor to tell him that there was a new regular villain – by "popped in" we mean just that, with a sound effect accompanying his arrival and departure in mid-air, and then on the gantry (there had been a sped-up TARDIS sound before he arrived to impersonate a Magritte). When apologising for manifesting a hundred feet off the ground he says: "my coordinates seem to have slipped a little – still, not bad after 29,000 light years".

This looks at first sight like a definite distance from the then-anonymous Time Lord world to Earth, and it's conveniently close to the distance between Earth and the centre of the galaxy. "Twenty-nine thousand light-years" isn't the sort of figure you automatically pull out of the air. Was Holmes seriously trying to suggest that the Time Lord world was at the centre of the galaxy? So did he deliberately pick this as a good central spot from which the Doctor could be "watched"? Holmes's scripts tend to regard Gallifrey as being a great all-seeing lens at the centre of galactic events, hence terms like "Eye of Harmony" and "Panopticon".

But if we've got someone dressed as a civil servant, the implication is that the Time Lords are Whitehall writ large – and, if we look at other situations like this in other series (asking a former agent to do "one last job to get rehabilitated"), the implication is of MI6, with all that this implies about field agents. This suggests a lot of Time Lord Embassies and consulates and rather undoes the centralising metaphors. (Think of later Holmes scripts or his stint as script editor; the idea of the Time Lords as a former imperial power makes this analogy compelling.)

To be fair, nowhere is it said that the messenger has come straight from Gallifrey, and Time Lord HQ didn't even have a name when the story was written. For all we know, he could have come straight from another "case", or from some sort of local monitoring station. This Time Lord "handler" might not have that much else to do in the outside universe, and his appearance *does* suggest that he's been "transported" to Earth from a fixed base of operations. If somebody more science-orientated had mentioned the distance to the galactic hub in Holmes's presence, or if he remembered it from a book he read, then it's at least feasible that this was his intention. It has a sort of pulpy, comic-book logic and makes the Doctor's home world somehow "special". Being at the focal-point, the hub, the still point of a turning galaxy, appeals to an idea of being both physically real and supernaturally different.

All right, so we *now* all know that this would put Gallifrey in the middle of a supermassive black hole that bends the stars orbiting around it, but Holmes didn't. (Neither did Isaac Asimov, who put Trantor, the hub of the Empire in the *Foundation* trilogy, in a similarly awkward spot and spent the 80s writing prequels and sequels saying he didn't mean it, honest.) Supposing for a moment that it was just space and the rest of this galaxy spun

continued on page 161...

13.3 Pyramids of Mars

or anywhere else. In contrast to the 1959 film, we've no hint that the dodgy foreigner installed at the Priory has a point. Neither do we have any concept that the old gods were genuinely powerful, beyond the standard panoply of psychic powers and weaponry given to aliens in *Doctor Who* – the Erich Von Daniken aspect of the story dissolves the Gothic *frisson* of uncertainty by positing an off-the-shelf space opera rationale. It's almost the last time they can do this.

Before all of this, there's the mythology itself. Horus was associated with the Lower Nile and Set (AKA Sutekh, a later name) was up-river (noted by the costume-designer using a mitre-like hat with a spherical knob on the top). The story is that Set and Osiris were brothers who fought; Osiris was killed but Isis, his sister-wife (the Pharaohs did things that way too) impregnated herself with bits of him and bore a son, Horus. Horus overthrew his uncle (losing an eye in the process) and became a sky-god, represented by a falcon, and supervised the living pharaoh's affairs. Set lost a gonad in the same fight (there's a lot more, involving an unpleasant salad dressing, but it's not strictly relevant here).

As a way to explain seasons and why the Nile floods and makes things fertile, it's at least as good as that stuff with pomegranate seeds the Greeks used (see 15.5, "Underworld") and prefigures a lot of other similar myths (Odin's eye, the Fisher King – the original, not the shouty alien from X9.4, "Before the Flood" – and various notions of an all-seeing eye overlooking the world independent of any owner). Set, Seth, Sutekh, Typhon (the Greeks took over and added it to their own myths) or whatever is represented by a... well, nobody's sure what the animal called the "sha" is meant to be, but the thing Scarman turns into at the end is a pretty good rendering. (Jackals are more Anubis's thing; some say it's an okapi or antelope, others a very thin pig or maybe even an aardvark that crossed an entire continent somehow.) The earliest images of these figures is from the First Dynasty, about 3100 BCE. The majority of the stories we now have about a war of the gods come from around 2040 BCE, when an environmental collapse devastated Egyptian society.

As we mentioned in Volume 2, Mars being a rocky desert planet was a shock to some, but the NASA probes allowed other writers to go to town on "lost civilisation" stories. The previous idea had been the whole canals thing – which, to many people, suggested Egypt anyway, so there was a pre-existing link between Pharaohs and Mars. The idea's first articulation was in November 1934, "The Valley of Dreams" by Stanley Weinbaum (sequel to "A Martian Odyssey"; see **Eldrad Must Live – But How?** under "The Hand of Fear"), in which the silicon-based Martians visited Earth in the past and inspired Egyptian mythology.

After a decade, the idea was a given, like space-pirates or asteroid miners. A good example is *The Sword of Rhiannon* by Leigh Brackett, written in 1949 and published in book form in 1953, but often reprinted. It's got the lot: possession by ancient artefacts, time-travel to when Mars was an oceanic world with galley-slaves and serpent-people, but also a *femme fatale* and an ambiguous protagonist that make it obvious that Lauren Bacall's character in *The Big Sleep* was Brackett's work. That sort of Planetary Romance was still being written in the 70s (Jack Vance was doing it in industrial quantities), but no longer on Mars. (A valedictory story by Roger Zelazny, "A Rose for Ecclesiastes", from 1963, starts with the idea of High Martian as the Hieroglyphs but veers off onto Islam and predeterminism.)

Aside from NASA and the Soviets getting photos, the main thing that changed was the fundamental idea of planetary formation. The original idea of worlds congealing slowly and relatively peacefully (as seen in *Fantasia*) led to an assumption that the outer worlds were made first and the hotter, denser rocky worlds were newer. This, and a rather Whiggish (or Hegelian if you're trying to dignify it) idea of development following pre-set patterns, meant that Mars was older than Earth and thus all the heat and civilisation had come and gone (conversely, Venus was a few million years behind us so was steamy and populated by dinosaurs).

We spent a hefty chunk of Volume 3 discussing Theosophy, Erich von Daniken, archaeologists partially substantiating ancient myths and so on, but this story in particular shows the tension between this school of thought and more orthodox pop-culture. For most of the period between the Renaissance and the Industrial Revolution, the concept of "Egypt" around in Europe was sort of like how Westerners considered India between 1950 and 1980. It was a source of ancient wisdom, now declined into abjection, where so much thought unbelievable had been proven true, anything was now plausible. Napoleon's expedition in

Where (and When) is Gallifrey?

...continued from page 159

around it, with Gallifrey there, the events underlying Season Twenty-Three (notably 23.1, "The Mysterious Planet") would have been a lot harder to hush up – Sol wouldn't quite be naked-eye visible from that distance, but a solar system moving two light years would be detectable and eventually observable. Light would take 29,000 years or so to get to Gallifrey, but we gather that the event was quite a while in our future and that might be significant.[30] However, by that time the Valeyard claims the Solar System is in the "Stellian Galaxy" and, two stories later (or eight episodes into the same story, if you insist), the Doctor simply calls it "the Milky Way" and everyone knows what he means.

In "The Brain of Morbius" the Doctor lands on Karn and says that he was born nearby, which apparently means that Karn is in the region of Gallifrey. In "The Creature from the Pit" (17.3), the Doctor indicates that he *was* born on the Time Lord home world, something which was by no means certain in the 1970s (see **The Lore** of "The Invasion of Time", but also Series 12). And there's an Earthman living on Karn, implying that it isn't *too* far from human space.

Of course, we have a bigger definition of "human space" these days, with three entire galaxies populated by the forty-second century in David Tennant stories. By a thousand years later, things have got even more anthropocentric (see **What's So Great About the 51st Century?** under X1.9, "The Empty Child"). Karn was conveniently near a crashing spaceship in the "Night of the Doctor" online mini-episode. While the human pilot knew of the Time Lords, there wasn't any talk of popping to Gallifrey, but – as before – a spaceship could crash right next to their neighbours, the Sisterhood. This gets around the fundamental problem some people were having, a reluctance to accept that the Time Lords are from just some planet somewhere and not, metaphorically or literally, Olympus/ heaven. There was a simple physical planet once, but it somehow transcended this sordid materiality and refined itself right out of space, accessible only to those who belong (which is why humans can't be allowed there).

Even if we accept this as valid, we have the problem of "when". The series never makes up its mind about this. The unaired pilot episode from 1963 had the Doctor claim to be from the forty-ninth century, which might explain how he knows so much about the run-up to the age of Magnus Greel ("The Talons of Weng-Chiang"), but the idea was dropped from the finished programme. Apart from one jokey, throw-away line in "Nightmare of Eden" (17.4), there's no real evidence that Gallifrey is literally ahead of us. If it *were*, there'd be a perpetual risk that events in our present might affect the development of the early Gallifreyans, another potentially interesting thought not backed up by anything on-screen. "Frontios" (21.3) opens up the idea again by stating that events after Earth's last days are somehow beyond the Time Lords' ken; the "Gallifreyan Noosphere" has limits.[31]

Even after Russell T Davies spent four years setting stories in the absurdly-far-future, demonstrating that the TARDIS (and the Doctor) were up to speed on events and could get there without too much difficulty, this idea has merit. It looked at the time like an attempt to resolve the matter, as well as leaving the end of the story less certain. ("Frontios" flirts with the idea of the TARDIS's obliteration, as the producer had been threatening.) If the Time Lords were from whichever destruction of Earth this was (see 3.6, "The Ark"; X1.2, "The End of the World" and others) then subsequent events were unavailable to them and all of human (and everyone else's) history was visitable by them in retrospect.

Once again, the idea of Gallifrey as an Eternal City and our problems looking smaller *sub specie aeternitatis* has religious overtones, especially if the word "noosphere" meant what Teilhard de Chardin, the coiner of the term, intended. (See **What Were Josiah's 'Blasphemous' Theories?** under 26.2, "Ghost Light", **How Does 'Evolution' Work?** under "Full Circle" and 17.6, "Shada".) It hints at a moral and physical purpose behind the Time Lords' activities, rather than just playground supervision.

A lot of writers assume that today on Earth and today on Gallifrey are the same day. This is especially noticeable in "The Three Doctors" (10.1), where an energy-drain affecting the entire universe coincides with an anti-matter incursion at UNIT HQ and both problems end at the same time with Omega's realm being blown up. It's an extreme version of a phenomenon we called "Gallifreyan Mean Time" (see **Why do Time Lords Always Meet in Sequence?** under 22.3, "The Mark of the Rani"), cited in the occasional Big Finish audio. The Time Lords seem to experience time passing for themselves, personally, at the same

continued on page 163...

13.3 Pyramids of Mars

1798 was sort of the Enlightenment's version of the Moon Landing, a military escapade justified as a scientific investigation "for all mankind" and he took 150 scholars to systematically catalogue and survey everything. A trip to London's Embankment tells the next part of the story: all of Europe went hog-wild for Egyptian-style furniture and clothing, if they couldn't get real artefacts sent. About a generation later, Champollion got a toe-hold on translating hieroglyphics and the real work began.

Nonetheless, the older ideas of what the ancients could do and how they did it persevered – that same patronising assumption that underlay von Daniken's crackpot books was at work, that looking at present-day Egyptians (or Peruvians or Greeks or Mexicans…), it's "impossible" that they could have achieved anything impressive, ergo mysterious powers from the skies helped them. As the nineteenth century ended, two equally simplistic models of history came into conflict, either linear progress from caves to skyscrapers or cyclic catastrophes and reconstructions. Which version one plumped for was down to temperament and – crudely – nationality. Ireland and Germany opted for tragic falls of mighty cultures, England, France and America for heroic marches into the sunlight. It's not as simple as that, and it was a radical English poet of the pre-Champollion era, Shelley, who connected the idea of egocentric rulers and oblivion in *Ozymandias* (quoted by the Master in X12.10, "The Timeless Children"; see also X12.8, "The Haunting of Villa Diodati"). As with Troy and Knossos, the disjunction between the bombast of the monuments and how long it took for anyone to find them again, or connect them to a fairy-tale, was a sobering thought for Europeans currently acting as if they were perpetually on top by right.

So when the Carnarvon Expedition of 1922 found an undisturbed mastaba with a boy-king somehow ignored in the bulk of the documentation they had, and interest in the background to Tutankhamun turned into feverish speculation and folklore, the world was ready to slot it into pre-existing stories. The Universal horror cycle adopted the Mummy as a natural follow-up to Dracula and Frankenstein (and the play that started it was adapted from Bram Stoker's story *The Jewel of Seven Stars*), because the dead returning was the whole point of mummification. The plot of *The Mummy* was straight out of a late eighteenth-century Gothic thriller, a curse making the dead stick around until balance is restored umpteen generations later, a young girl chased by inanimate objects because she looks like one of her ancestors, mesmerism, tunnels etcetera. (Universal made the link between mummies, the Enlightenment and Romanticism in *The Bride of Frankenstein*, in which Mary Shelley does a recap with Lord Byron at the start then continues her tale – apparently set in the 1930s – with a mummy-like Bride given a hairdo like Nefertiti's hat.)

But, as the public got used to invisible rays in their everyday lives, the more *outré* bits of Theosophy came back and, post-war, there were endless half-baked ideas about mental powers and Earth Magic kicking around. These attached themselves to the older ideas of Egypt. By the early 1970s, people were discussing "Pyramid Power" and making wild claims. Unlike many such ideas, the supposed powers of a pyramid aligned to the Pole Star were easy to test, so schoolkids did exactly that: leave a tomato in such a construction over the school holidays and it's supposed to stay fresh (they never did); razorblades placed in one would self-resharpen (they never did) and so on. However, grain seeds found in a pyramid were made to germinate after four millennia.

When the Tutankhamun exhibition came to the British Museum in 1972, all of this stuff came to a head. The fact that Egypt is in Africa had been conveniently forgotten until then; the story of the boy-Pharaoh's (probable) father Akhenaton (see X7.2, "Dinosaurs on a Spaceship") had been comprehensively obliterated from the record until relatively recently; the craftsmanship of the remaining temples had been brought into focus by the moving of Abu Simbel in the 1960s and colour television revealed the true power of the grave-goods as art. Just as the original story of the discovery, then the press stringing together various illnesses and accidents as a "curse of the mummy's tomb", sparked the Universal film, so this exhibition, the Pyramid Power stories and the remarkable similarity of Dogon lore and what modern astronomy revealed – Sirius having a twin star invisible to the naked eye – all fed into the burgeoning of what we now call Afrofuturism. This story went to air at the same time that George Clinton's Parliament released *Mothership Connection*. (Of course, Sun Ra had got there first, but he was still considered "fringe".)

Setting the story in the past was initially a way

Where (and When) is Gallifrey?

...continued from page 161

rate as the Doctor.

We say "seem to", because there's a lot of odd anomalies when the background details of "The Three Doctors" and "The Deadly Assassin" are held up for comparison. Nobody in the latter seems to have any idea that the Omega crisis took place, which is weird. One final oddity about the former is that Omega, a figure from such a remote time that the Doctor has only heard of him as a heroic legend, speaks about spending "thousands of years" in exile. If this is the case, and the Time Lords owe their entire role as cosmic arbiters to him, then the Doctor can only have been born around the time the Earth was formed and must be spending most of his career in the far future relative to his people.

Yet in "The Invasion of Time", it turns out that Rassilon, founder of the Time Lords, died "millions" of years ago. If time works differently in this other universe then perhaps, the Doctors were only in Omega's world for seconds (from the perspective of the Time Lords monitoring his situation). That's not how it seems – everything synchs up in real-time on both sides of the event horizon – and that, as we saw in the last essay, puts the kibosh on the idea that an anti-matter universe is running backwards relative to a matter-dimension. (We're going to dig into this contradiction and others like it in **Seriously, Did Rassilon Meet Omega?** under "The Deadly Assassin".) The power from the star is being directly ducted to Gallifrey somehow, whenever it is.

Returning to "The Trial of a Time Lord", we get a figure of "ten million years" for how long the Time Lords have been lording it over time in the Doctor's era. Gallifrey is the one world whose past and future are of no interest to them, it would appear, but perhaps this is a side-effect of being in an odd relationship with time – why else build the APC Net to predict forthcoming events, unless they can't observe those the way they can everything else? Rassilon's intervention in external cosmic events, in the war against the Great Vampires (18.4, "State of Decay"), is known to a few archivists and fans of spooky stories on Gallifrey, but nobody in the rest of creation seems to be aware of it. This seems to mark the end of the Time Lords' direct intervention and the start of their rather more obscure machinations which everyone seems to agree was A Very Long Time Ago.

Over all of that time, the number of active Time Lords might well have been vast, but we never get much indication that they're any more numerous than our House of Lords. The Doctor only ever seems to meet those he knew at school or former mentors. The big exceptions to this are Omega and Morbius, both exiled but on the comeback trail, and Rassilon (first as a very powerful corpse then revived, like all the previous generations – we're told – in the off-screen Time War).

Nonetheless, the Doctor seems to know Morbius's mind-aroma, perhaps a sort of all-points bulletin issued with all time capsules and never revoked because – as a Time Lord at large in the cosmos – his execution isn't a Fixed Point and running into him might undo that bit of history. Of course, that adventure also provides the first indication that the Doctor's previous three lives aren't the whole story – so this, and Omega being aware of the Doctor from way back even if the Doctor thinks of Omega as a legend from the far distant past, now fit a larger pattern.

If ancient Gallifrey existed in the distant past (as we see it) but removed itself from normal history when Rassilon balanced the Eye of Harmony and turned his society into a culture of "galactic ticket inspectors", then everything locks together neatly. Gallifrey has a physical location, but isn't "there" now. It's reasonable to suppose that events on Earth and Gallifrey might appear to happen "simultaneously" while the Doctor's larking around in England, because as much time has elapsed for the Doctor as for his people. ("The Deadly Assassin" casts a little doubt on this by showing us a President who's been in office for centuries, but who succeeded the one in "The Three Doctors" who seemed to know the Doctor. The Doctor never met the later President so, it would seem, hundreds of years pass on Gallifrey between Benton and the Brigadier getting a ride in the TARDIS and Sarah packing her goodies and going home.) Stories like "The Brain of Morbius", in which a planet in Earth's future seemingly has an ongoing relationship with Gallifrey in the Doctor's time, indicate that Time Lords have no trouble temporarily "tying" their own present to other points in history. It happens to twentieth-century Earth quite a lot, but twentieth-century Earth is by no means alone.

Paradoxically, the one occasion where humans get to go there was at a point in the very far future. Precisely what occurred to have the ruins of the

continued on page 165...

13.3 Pyramids of Mars

to sidestep the real-world detail that Egypt had placed an embargo on removal of artefacts from tombs. As we'll see in **The Lore**, Lewis Griefer was veering towards the idea of reviving seeds from the Pyramids as a starting-point for a story set in the British Museum, but Robert Holmes asked specifically for iconography from old films. He had in mind mainly the 1930s Universal cycle of horror-films, but was aware of the colour remakes / rethinks of these from Hammer Studios in the 50s and 60s. Holmes is credited with suggesting Bernard Archard to play Scarman after seeing him as Dr Heiss in 1970s *Horror of Dracula*, and many have cited the 1959 Hammer version of *The Mummy* with inspiring specific scenes and characters in this story. (See also 5.1, "The Tomb of the Cybermen", where two of the film's cast show up in almost-identical roles.)

Hinchcliffe always downplays the Hammer connection, but the semi-comedic poacher (inevitably played by Michael Ripper in the film), the scene where the villain survives being shot at point-blank and the concerned friend of the missing archaeologist confronting the mysterious Egyptian now residing in the mansion all fit this rather than the 1931 film (which was set in present-day Egypt). However, by casting Archard, who looked even more like Boris Karloff than Holmes did, they are linking back to the 1931 film – in which the resurrected High Priest adopts the persona of "Ardath Bey" and kills by remote control using a pool that permits him to see and affect distant events. Once the first death has happened, Karloff doesn't wear swaddling. As such he prefigures Scarman, the Mummies *and* Sutekh, while the 1959 story restricts the killing to Christopher Lee in bandages (and as normal in the flashbacks to his being cursed to protect the buried priestess – sort of like Rory in X5.13, "The Big Bang"), but has George Pastell in a fez ordering it about. That's when Pastell's character isn't shipping the relics to England, lecturing the English on their hubris and generally being sinister enough for even the local constabulary to get suspicious (eventually). Until the last scene brings back the "love over death" aspect from the Universal film, Lee's mummy is pretty much a robot anyway. However, while the stock characters and setting look vaguely similar, the logic connecting the set-pieces is radically unlike that of "Pyramids of Mars" and there's not much in the finished story that couldn't be seen in the trailer for the film.

[This is probably the best place to point out that the Hammer influence is rarely even this overt. The studio's reputation was at its peak in the mid-70s, although by this stage the horror cycle was almost played out and they fell back upon desperate gimmicks to stay current (see, for instance, *Dracula 1972*, which we'll mention again in 17.6, "Shada", or *The Legend of the Seven Golden Vampires*, to which we'll return a few times). However, fans of these films who formed the core of the nascent *Doctor Who* fandom of the era, which led to them judging the series by slightly off-kilter criteria, as we'll see in Season Fifteen. The earlier Hammer films were starting to become television staples – shown after 11.30pm, so teenagers felt daring even being up to watch them – while the 30s Universal ones, when shown at all, were in bad prints and dismissed as "for kids" because there wasn't much on-screen blood or nudity.]

English Lessons

• *Priory* (n.): A small monastery, but not so small as to lack a prior. This building is evidently not old enough to pre-date the Dissolution of the Monasteries in 1536, but could be on the site of one (see also 15.3, "Image of the Fendahl" and 16.3, "The Stones of Blood").

• *Priest-hole* (n.): After the Reformation, some old established families retained Catholic priests but knew better than to advertise the fact. Once Pope Sixtus V had issued the *Regnans in Excelsis* Bull of 1570, Catholics were considered a threat (an opinion which became fact after the Spanish Armada and the Gunpowder Plot) and many large houses had secret chambers into which one of these "terrorists" could be bundled at short notice. These got further use during the Interregnum, when anyone suspected of not being Protestant enough got the same treatment (as in the children's rhyme *Goosey Goosey Gander*).

• *Folly* (n.): After about 1780, a lot of people redesigned their gardens to suit a new idea of "natural" and "picturesque". Some new-built houses even had artfully-constructed ruins with hired "hermits". Victorians continued the trend, added affectations from other centuries or abroad and made out that their freshly-minted manor houses were inherited. The "gothic" fad in architecture led to things like the Houses of Parliament and the Natural History Museum and has links to

Where (and When) is Gallifrey?

...continued from page 163

Capitol visitable by a big pink portal, and used as a sanctuary for fugitives from the Cybermen, was never stated – nor is where the previous asylum-seeking humans were hiding when the Master was ranting about the Doctor's forgotten past – but it's never stated as being a space-time tunnel, just a Boundary ("Ascension of the Cybermen"), as if there's a difference.

Let's assume that it wasn't a coincidence and that the Master stage-managed it all for the Doctor's benefit and to lure Ashad, the Lone Cyberman, to the ruins. Whenever it is from his perspective, it's after the Doctor's previous visit, which was after he'd trashed the place – but "after" covers a long period. The technology still works as it did for ten million years, so just because it's clearly after 4000 AD as far as Earth history goes (assuming that this Cyber-War is the one mentioned in X7.13, "Nightmare in Silver", although in detail it's massively different from that conflict and the one just before "Revenge of the Cybermen"), it doesn't necessarily follow that "The Deadly Assassin" was in our present or future.

When he became producer, Graham Williams suggested that the Doctor's home world is somehow at the "centre of time" – so Gallifrey becomes a kind of eternal watchtower, overseeing all of history from somewhere beyond / within / separate from the normal course of events (much as the idea of locating a world in the axle of a galaxy made sense once). In "Shada", we see the Time Lords' prison-world, and it apparently can't be reached by normal means but only through the TARDIS, again suggestive of a culture existing outside time as we know it. The odd spaceship in "The Trial of a Time Lord" is definitely external, which is how the paradoxes of the Valeyard trying to kill his younger self can be resolved.

[Then again, that "centre of time" idea takes on a very different meaning if you look at it in terms of hard/er science. If you assume that the universe is currently expanding, but will eventually stop and begin to contract, then the "centre of time" is the apex of the expansion. However, in some models the contraction is accompanied by the same history going in reverse, meaning that the "centre" is the halfway-point between the Big Bang and the uttermost expansion. If it's at the apex of expansion, time travel in either direction is into the past, but it might be easier going with the flow of entropy than against it. See the essay with "Mawdryn Undead". And this is going to need a lot of rethinking now that we've been there.]

This gets us closer to comprehending the apparent contradiction in "The Invasion of Time". Rodan's in charge of Time Lord Traffic Control, monitoring space-fleets as they pass close to the planet. In purely physical terms, this makes no sense. The universe is so immense, even the busiest parts shouldn't have anything comparable to "airspace". But if the fleets in question have some form of time-travel capability and pass close to Gallifrey's "centre of time" region while in transit, then it all seems more reasonable.

But the real giveaway – the only definite, absolute summary of the Doctor's point of origin and therefore our best evidence – comes in 16.3, "The Stones of Blood". The Doctor is asked whether he comes from outer space. His reply, which seems quite serious, is that he comes from *inner time*. It seemed at the time like a glib non-answer but, given this Doctor's fondness for dotty old ladies, it could be the one time he's being absolutely honest. Coming at the core of the season when Williams was laying out his notion of *Doctor Who* cosmology, it has to be taken as seriously as any of the other statements about the location of his home.

---

the spooky tales popular during the 1790s and the later Romantic fad for historical novels about the Middle Ages and the Celtic Fringe (or both, if it's Sir Walter Scott – see "Terror of the Zygons").

• *Lodge* (n.): Traditionally, a lodge was a cottage set up in the middle of woodland or fields for hunting parties to rest in and prepare for the early start of the expedition. In an estate as small as this one, though, it mainly houses the gamekeeper, the person who makes sure there's enough wildlife to slaughter and keeps out poachers. That Laurence Scarman is living there suggests a really compli- cated backstory about his brother, a scientist and scholar who's a Fellow of All Souls (see below) and got to keep the whole house and the gentleman inventor out in a tiny hut festooned with pictures of prize-winning bulls. It's not that the agricultural signifiers are out-of-place among the scientific gubbins and chinaware, just that they tell us that we're on an estate that has farms, never mentioned in the script, so this isn't a typical landowning family of 1911. If Laurence is running the estate from the Lodge, rather than the Priory, and doesn't entertain hunting parties, where is Marcus getting all the money for expeditions to Egypt and the upkeep of this whole demesne? It's not quite incomprehensible enough for **Things That Don't Make Sense**, but everything about Marcus says wealth and status (just getting into All Souls took that) and everything about Laurence says a family fallen on hard times but not prepared to sell its biggest assets. The photo in Part Three would seem to remove the obvious explanation: a third, eldest brother who lives somewhere even more palatial and lucrative, but even then it's strange that Laurence is neither in the military nor the clergy.

- *"I heard him fishing"*: Before World War II, supplies of gelignite were relatively unregulated. Alfred Nobel invented the stuff in 1875, then developed the less volatile dynamite. After around 1900, newspaper reports started circulating of people literally hoist with their own petards when taking gelignite on fishing expeditions and mistiming the fuses or just being unlucky with the sweaty explosive.

The principle is simple: a detonation in or under water sends shock-waves that concuss or kill the fish and send them floating to the surface. During the Blitz, many families used this side-effect of the bombing to supplement their meat ration. Serious anglers frown upon the activity, especially when it's done during spawning periods. It also stirs up too much mud and slime for rapid harvesting. It still sporadically occurs in parts of India and Australia: survivors are severely fined.

- *Fellow of All Souls* (n.): A unique distinction for the Oxford postgraduate college is that all who pass the stringent examination and interview get to be on the board. They don't all become career academics, although Scarman clearly has. He's also a Fellow of the Royal Society, therefore a scientist as much as a linguist or historian.

- *Triobyphysics* (n.): A lot of people, including Russell T. Davies in his book *Damaged Goods*, claim to hear "tribophysics". This is a real science, the engineering of lubrication, although Davies stated that it occurs when two realities intersect (from the Greek for "rubbing", as in "tribadism").

But that's not what Sladen says here. As with "Ebullience Griss" (3.4, "The Daleks' Master Plan") and "sexual air supply" (5.7, "The Wheel in Space"), some people just hear what they expect to hear. Uncle Terrance's Target novelisation spells it the way we have but gives the line to the Doctor; that's how it was intended (and not the even less comprehensible "trial by physics"). So if it's not dimensional frottage, what is it? From the context in which it's used, it must have something to do with making things by drawing shapes of them in the air, in this specific case a doorway. This is obviously nothing to do with ball-bearings or 3-in-1 oil, so "tribophysics" is clearly not what's meant. The cut shots of the previously-flat wall creating a doorway in response to the arm-waving help us less than might have been hoped.

Things That Don't Make Sense The Osirans really have the whole "moving in mysterious ways" part of the deity portfolio down pat. Thousands of their number restrain Sutekh the world-destroyer, but then they imprison him on Mars – an uninhabitable world *that looks it* – in a giant sodding pyramid. It's not the best means of subtly conveying "nothing to see here", is it? It's against their moral code to kill one of their own, but the prison they gave him has wi-fi and the power-source is guarded by riddle-me-rees and not heat-seeking missiles for any lower life-forms Sutekh might press into serving him.

They've set up a warning to give interlopers pause. They do this using radio waves, meaning a large number of nearby civilisations could easily pop over to Mars with their FTL-driven ships and barge into the interesting-looking anomalous object on a desolate dead world before the message reaches them. (Anything that "Marconiscope" can detect will just about be reaching Algol by now, so if the signal's triggered by the Mastaba being unsealed, anyone there will get the warning a century after they're all killed. If it's *not* triggered and was running for 5000 years, it'd be like those car-alarms everyone ignores – so why would the various visitors to Earth between 3000 BCE and 1911 even bother? Maybe Tesla set it off; X12.4, "Nikola Tesla's Night of Terror".) Then the Doctor uses cryptanalysis straight out of Conan-Doyle to translate it. Even in 120 years since "The Adventure of the Dancing Men", the relative frequency of letters in English has changed and this presupposes that the Osirans wrote everything in English (as we later see, they don't and this message was written 5000 years ago). As directed, there isn't time for any repeated message more complex than "Beware Sutekh", and 12 letters isn't enough to make an informed guess, especially as K and U are relatively uncommon (see the scores on Scrabble tiles). Apart from E, every letter in this signal appears once and is thus equally likely. It's very hard to guess "Sutekh" without context and he's known by a lot of other names. This is Horus's idea of "making it easy".

Indeed, why did Horus use radio signals to keep Sutekh in his chair? Sutekh and Scarman teleconference in real-time in Part Four. They have space-time corridors. (That's a point: Sutekh knows about the Time Lords, but doesn't think "AHA! I can travel back in time or cross the universe in an instant" and just uses the TARDIS as an Uber for one brief journey, then kills the one person who can operate it.)

Whence do the Mummies get their missile-building material? The obvious answer – that the components were in the pyramid and Scarman shipped them back – is so ludicrous as to be almost plausible. (Why would the Osirans supply Sutekh with an Ikea pallet of heat-seeking missiles, for assembly by any lower race he might enthrall?) But even if you assume that it's Sutekh-via-Scarman giving instructions, we're back to the problem of there being robot mummies at all – were *they* in the tomb for 5000 years, or did possessed-Scarman pick up electrical equipment and light engineering facilities in Saqqara in 1911, build robots from everyday household items, then programme the Mummies to make missile components? If so, why not give them more nimble hands? And, he'd have precious little time to do it, because Dr Warlock's only just noticed something's up, Namin only arrived a few days ago and Scarman's not been seen for "weeks" rather than months.

We can sort of work out a timeline of Sutekh sending Scarman out to dig up mummy-parts and missile components in a nearby tomb while Namin supervises delivery of the previously-unearthed bits (perhaps key components – like the sarcophagus serving as the terminal for the space-time tunnel – were already en route to England, making it easier to set up operations in a secluded priory than in downtown Cairo), but it's still a stretch. If Scarman is Sutekh's eyes, ears and legs, then it's Sutekh who sees a dismantled mummy in the Lodge but fails to note that he's back to the full complement when the missile's being built. (Like his robot servants, he has hands like oven-gloves, so maybe counting to four is a bit beyond him.)

Scarman's artefacts are in a wing of the house that's supposedly locked and secret, but the window's already open when the Doctor and Sarah pop out. Everything else Sutekh sends to the Priory by space-time tunnel comes out smouldering (Scarman needs a protective suit), but the Doctor is perfectly unsinged. And what's that green slime on the wall of the tomb? In the opening scene, the Egyptians run away and Scarman tries to open the tomb alone. The wall slides open, because it was built by aliens – but did he really think that he, a thin middle-aged man, could wrest blocks of sandstone as big as a 70s television from the wall and not land up with a hernia and mashed toes?

Ernie the poacher is *very* trigger-happy... he only heard screaming after some mummies went in to the Lodge, but jumps to conclude "murdering swine!" with no evidence, and only realises whodunit after he's shot his landlord, Scarman, in the back. Then he heads to the Priory and shoots the next person he sees. Why not try shouting "hands up!"? Then, when things don't go to plan, he runs back to the Lodge – where he knows the Mummies were – and gets himself Jane Russelled to death. The Doctor, Sarah and Laurence all snuck past the Mummies because Scarman recalled them, but two of them are nonetheless at the Lodge, as if forecasting an incoming cliff-hanger and the need to besiege a cottage.

Nice as the idea of the Doctor having a scarf in metric and Imperial is, the measurement thing really doesn't work. He claims that a plastic strip about the length of his finger is 120.3 cm (that's about the length of Deep Roy), then multiplies it by "the binary figure ten zero zero" (which is, um, eight). That would be 962.4 cm, or thirty feet. Not 162.4 (i.e., as tall as Sarah). What any of this has to do with the "spot the odd-one-out" puzzle resembling an optician's test for astigmatism is anyone's guess. And, besides, Sarah never went inside the City of the Exxilons (11.3, "Death to the Daleks"), so why does this remind her of it? Why is the Decatron crucible the only thing to have gathered dust in 5000 years? The Doctor is stumped by that dilemma, then a brace of bling mummies and a voice-over make it easy for him.

Earth and Mars orbit the sun at different speeds, so the distance varies between 78 million km (both the same side of the sun) and 337 million km (at opposite sides). The length of time it takes a radio signal, travelling at light speed, to reach us from a probe or some hypothetical Osirian artefact therefore varies between the length of Part Two of "Pyramids of Mars" (24 min-

13.3 Pyramids of Mars

utes) and an absolute minimum of four minutes, not two. Maybe the Doctor wanted to impress upon Sarah the need for haste.

What *was* the apparition Sarah saw in Part One? The most likely explanation is that the TARDIS intersected with the time-corridor from Part Four, providing a sneak-preview of the solution to the problem yet to start. Okay, provided one can overlook this otherwise being a story where futures and pasts are contingent and fluid, and yet the ending is apparently set in stone. Had the Doctor left for 1980 and not returned to 1911, this manifestation would have never occurred, so the story would never have started. Yet no other explanation is available: Sutekh couldn't project himself before the climax of Part Four. So the Doctor risked a temporal paradox potentially more devastating than Sutekh just to prove a point.

If Sutekh can send his mental force from the time-corridor, as well as his voice, and is visible, why isn't he trying to blow up the Doctor's machine or kill him and Sarah instead of just ranting and pleading?

Critique While *Doctor Who* had never been shy about acknowledging its sources, this one was way more obvious than anything hitherto. It was downright shameless, the way the Haunted House scene from "The Chase" (2.8) had been. Some people took this as an admission of defeat, that they'd finally run out of ideas. After doing the Loch Ness Monster, it seemed as if they'd only got blatant generic pastiche left.

We now know that this was to become the first resort. There hadn't been many stories even slightly like this before: 4.9, "The Evil of the Daleks" mixed Victoriana with space-monsters and took place mainly in an old house in the country; "The Time Warrior" (11.1) had a stranded extraterrestrial messing with the past; "The War Games" (6.7) seemed to be bits of history colliding because of manipulative aliens, but that was about it. After this, it would almost be compulsory to have a story of cosmic forces in a manor house once a year, and ancient myths would usually be involved. It also became a lot easier to identify which old film was being riffed-on in any given story.

Even if you accept this as a legitimate way to do *Who*, if not the "best", it's hard to think of a better example among all that bandwagon-jumping.

And that's with this story falling apart in Part Four. And giving us a sneak preview of the problems people have with "The Talons of Weng-Chiang" in Part One. Another thing taken as waving a little white flag and giving in is the almost minus-quantity of motivation for Sutekh, Horus and (more regrettably) Namin. They leave a gap where reasons to be doing things ought to be, a botched attempt at being enigmatic that amounts to shrugging and saying "well, they're like that". Plotting had never been so schematic, even in the darkest days of Innes Lloyd. "Your evil is my good" is, according to your tastes, "mythic" and "sweeping" or "pathetic" and "amateurish". As Sutekh, Gabriel Woolf sells the line, but even he struggles with some of the others. Given a less proficient cast or a shoddier production, this new recipe for the series would have been ditched as a failed experiment. Instead, it became the template for the next four years.

So why has this become so seminal? The regulars are self-confident enough to move the characters on a little, but that's true of "Revenge of the Cybermen" as well. What they do here is redefine the Doctor's obligations to humanity and their limits. The opening TARDIS scene as good as tells us that UNIT's a busted flush, and the alternate future sequence in Part Two sets the tone for practically all BBC Wales stories set in history (shamelessly in X1.3, "The Unquiet Dead"). Sarah's reactions to this indicate that she still doesn't know the Doctor that well. The premise of an almost unimaginably potent alien being unshackled was best used sparingly. To defeat this demigod, the Doctor must draw on more than just his guile and tenacity – yet, for any future story to work, he can't be revealed as equally powerful. It needs to be carefully judged and, despite the riddles and corny tricks when we actually get to Mars, the Doctor does appear out of his depth for much of the story. We'll never get that again with this Doctor and had only really had it in regeneration stories.

This situation's presented to us as unprecedentedly dangerous for the Doctor and all of the cosmos. That sits oddly with the specificity of the source-texts: Universal's Mummy films and the Hammer retreads. These start with the idea of an immortal servant kept alive by love for a present-day woman who resembles the lost bride of the High Priest who was entombed. Devastating planets isn't on the mummy's agenda. Tapping into the film-iconography while raising the stakes way out of proportion is typical of *Doctor Who*. They don't do it wholesale, though, but hint at the old films without mimicking any specific scene or shot. That's why showing the mummy-robots in broad daylight isn't a problem – we need to see the setting clearly for the sheer incongruity to sink in. Incongruity is closer to the heart of the series than simple "scariness".

The *real* heart of the story, though, is Michael Sheard as Laurence Scarman. He's been reliable support in *Doctor Who* before and will again, but this is where he earns the affection he received. He's as fully-rounded a character as the series allows, struggling to adapt to the situation and – at a crucial moment, to "save" his dead brother – making a misguided but fully human choice against the Doctor's advice. Even with the story's high body-count, this character is the focus, and his death tests Sarah's faith in the Doctor. Even though the story's set in a year when we know the world didn't end, having someone like that around makes it matter. The past isn't safe, nor is it even past in *Doctor Who*. That needed saying in 1975 and it still works.

Something else we have to note here for later: the seamless way the music and sound-effects sustain the sense of this walled-off estate running on its own rules. There's a brazen breach of internal logic when Namin's organ music carries on after he leaves to bow to Sutekh, but that was set up by the scene when the space-time tunnel first activates with a rising chord on the same church organ, apparently revving up (with help from Dick Mills). Namin hears it when we do, so it's not a piece of narrative commentary (or not simply one). We've had music as a real-world feature creeping into the dramatic conventions before, notably in "Terror of the Zygons" with Angus's bagpipes, and it's going to be more pronounced later this season with the Sisterhood of Karn and Chase's synths. After this story, it becomes part of the fabric of the series.

The Facts

Written by "Stephen Harris" (i.e. Robert Holmes revising a scenario by Lewis Greifer). Directed by Paddy Russell. Viewing figures: 10.5 million, 11.3 million, 9.4 million, 11.7 million. A compilation repeat on 27th November, 1976 got 13.7 million and was the 7th most watched thing that week. AI's Part Four got 60%; no others are available.

Alternate Versions A one-episode one-hour version was shown a year later. The original VHS and Betamax video was edited to remove the cliffhangers (they thought this was a good idea back in 1985) and trims some of the poacher's scenes. Time-Life, as usual, cut bits out to allow time for Howard da Silva to explain what happened in the bits they cut out, or something. The novelisation has Ahmed, the first speaking role in the story and – as broadcast – the only non-regular to survive, murdered by Namin's cult in a flashback. It removes the "1980" lines and adds a prologue about the Osirians, plus an epilogue of Sarah looking up the press version of what happened to the Priory.

Cliffhangers The being that came through the space-time tunnel in the sarcophagus kills Namin by laying smouldering hands on the Egyptian's shoulders and turns out to be... Professor Scarman; the Mummies attack the cottage and advance on Sarah; Sutekh focuses his lethal glare on an agonised Doctor, vowing to kill the Time Lord for his interference.

What Was In the Charts? "I Only have Eyes for You", Art Garfunkel; "You Sexy Thing", Hot Chocolate; "I'm on Fire", 5000 Volts; "Feel Like Makin' Love", Bad Company.

The Lore

As Robert Holmes was commissioning story ideas from his former mentors Louis Marks and Robert Banks Stewart, so Philip Hinchcliffe – formerly a script-editor at ATV – got back in touch with Lewis Greifer. As one of the most experienced script-doctors in television, Greifer was exactly the sort of person who'd cope with the abnormal briefs given by *Doctor Who* – he'd helped out on *The Goon Show* – and the abrupt changes of plan that came with the territory. (Hinchcliffe recalls Greifer driving him around Birmingham in a car given to the veteran by Patrick McGoohan, payment-in-kind for script changes after the money had run out on *The Prisoner*.)

Greifer's story idea was about Egyptian gods and spaceships but is otherwise unrecognisable as what we landed up with. It showed a great deal of the mid-seventies fascination with "Pyramid Power" (see **Where Does This Come From?**). He'd done his homework on the mythology, but

13.3 Pyramids of Mars

not on *Doctor Who* – it's possible he'd never actually watched it. The story was mainly a power-struggle between Shebek, Seth and Osiris about how the dying Martian race we recall as the gods of Egypt ought to handle the problem of the humans already developing on their intended refuge, Earth.

Various permutations were tried with pyramid missiles sending seeds to the Moon (Egyptian grain being more useful for terraforming a desert-planet), then terraforming Mars, then UNIT trying to find the Eye of Horus. Along the way, the idea of the seeds being sent *from* present-day Egypt was dismissed (the Egyptian government doesn't allow that any more, since Colonel Nasser's time), so seeds in the British Museum from 80 years before became the starting-point for a draft from July 1974. This was a bit more Hammer Films-ish, with treasure-seekers, guards at the museum killed in mysterious ways (hence UNIT investigating). The surviving Martians tried to reseed their world with the seeds in the Museum, trapping either the Brigadier or Sarah in their rocket, with the Eye of Horus to become sort of what the Key to Time would be a couple of years later: a fetch-quest linking further stories. (All of this in single-spaced, close-typed purple ink from a faded typewriter ribbon.) It still wasn't quite what was asked for. Holmes wanted more mummies and more of the Doctor.

However, it wasn't possible to ask for rewrites, as Greifer went in to the hospital and – once he'd been released – a new job came up: Chairman of Television Studies at Tel Aviv University. By late November, it looked as if Greifer would never find time to visit London for script meetings or rewrites. Under the circumstances, Holmes got permission from Greifer's agent for a root-and-branch rewrite, with the option of taking the author's name off if it deviated too far from this notional next draft. By the start of March, Hinchcliffe and Holmes deemed Greifer's submitted scripts unworkable, and began a fresh story using the ideas they had kicked around over the previous year. Hinchcliffe sent copies of the first two episodes to Greifer's agent, with a note accepting that he might to decline credit for these. Shortly afterwards, Hinchcliffe contacted Graeme MacDonald, designated as the next Head of Serials at the BBC, for permission to use Holmes (pseudonymously if necessary) twice a year as he kept performing salvage jobs like this.

- By now (we're in early April 1975), "Terror of the Zygons" had been delayed to a September transmission slot and production on the next few stories moved forward. As director Paddy Russell started work, she found the scripts (such as they were) full of holes and fuzzy characterisation, so collaborated in refining it. To get slightly ahead of ourselves, this continued in production – the poacher's singular death was improvised on location, because the character just vanishes halfway through Part Two. Hinchcliffe had already decided to show Louis Marks's "Planet of Evil" before "Pyramids", to vary the pace.

- The thinking behind the Mummy costume was that the real ones were desiccated and hollowed out, with the bodies within eviscerated to separately keep the organs in jars like the Canopic one. Thus real mummies have bigger chests than waists and caved-in eye-sockets – but also have their legs bandaged together. On location in woodland, the mobility of the Barbara Kidd design was almost as bad as that, with slippery surfaces and restricted vision.

- As the script took shape, reasons were found to phase out UNIT and move beyond the routine Yeti-in-the-loo stuff. Holmes conceived of the "alternative time" scene as a way to raise the stakes in historical stories. In the phase when this was a UNIT story about a rocket to Mars, Holmes and Hinchcliffe asked Barry Letts (see next story) about the near-future dates; Letts responded that he and Terrance Dicks assumed they were usually about five years in the future (despite that cut line from 8.3, "The Claws of Axos" making UNIT contemporary). So in the final script, Sarah states her year of origin to Laurence as "I'm from 1980".

- Although Highclere, former home of Lord Carnarvon (leader of the expedition that had found Tutankhamun's tomb) was considered, someone in a pub in Newbury tipped off the production assistant, Peter Grimwade (see Volume 5 and "The Robots of Death") that the optimum site for a Priory and woodlands was Stargrove, in East Woodhay, Hampshire. Mick Jagger had bought this estate for his parents and as a recording facility, but – apart from its use as a base for his mobile recording studio (it's part of the backstory for *Smoke on the Water* by Deep Purple[32]) – only the parents and staff were usually there (although on the week of filming, four-year-old Jade was around). However, getting hold of a Rolling Stone in 1975 was tricky, and permission was only finally obtained on 23rd April, just under a week before the crew and cast were to start work there. (Normally, the owners of locations get a fee from the BBC, but Jagger donated it to a school for visually-impaired children.) Paddy Russell road-tested the mummy costumes herself for visibility and traction, finding the experience helped her gauge what she could ask of the drama students from Guildford playing the monsters (one of these was Melvyn Bedford; see "Planet of Evil"). This was on 29th, when Russell improvised Ernie's death-scene. If you guessed that the silvery interior component was of the Canopic Jars was the guts of a Thermos flask, give yourself a jelly-baby.

• Sladen had asked for the collar of her Edwardian outfit to be lower than was entirely authentic. Russell seemed very insistent that Sarah would be a crack shot, despite Sladen's questions and lack of experience. (She had ringing in her ears after the first report from the shotgun, because nobody had mentioned the need for ear-plugs. In the three-sided brick courtyard, the echo was deafening.) As Stargroves is a Grade Two Listed Building, there was no chance of really blowing up a pyramid there, so this was added to the list of models. The local school took a few children to see the filming – Baker was unrecognisable as a Mummy (Russell insisted he do it himself, in costume) but emerged for the usual autographs later.

• The script was still a work-in-progress. Greifer got back in touch to say that this script was no longer his and, with clearance from the Writers' Guild, "Stephen Harris" came to be credited. Holmes was stumped by the last episode's need to be all-studio and cheap, but in keeping with everything so far (abrupt changes of mood, location and story were one of the problems with Greifer's last episode). Hinchcliffe remembered an old logic puzzle from Kafka's *The Castle* (but a lot older than that) which became the Riddle of the Osirians (or "Osirans", as some of the hasty amendments to the scripts had it, hence the variable pronunciation). As the "Acton Hilton" was fully booked, rehearsals were at the Greater London Sports Club, Airedale Avenue, Chiswick, a venue used by the BBC in the 50s with a handy pub for lunches (it looms large in stories about Tony Hancock).

• The cast was an interesting mix. A couple were veterans of the series. Bernard Archard (Professor Scarman) had been Bragen in 4.3, "The Power of the Daleks", and Michael Sheard was making the third of six appearances in the series; Grimwade may have recommended him after they worked on *The Five Red Herrings* (in that cast was Russell Hunter; see "The Robots of Death"). Vic Tablian (credited here as "Vik"), playing Ahmen, was just getting started, but would become sort of the Tutte Lemkow of the 80s.[33] George Tovey played the poacher; his daughter, Roberta, was the big-screen Susan in the Peter Cushing Dalek films.

• As always, there are alternate-universe possible versions of the story with different casts, according to the notes. Namin might well have been Renu Satna ("The Hand of Fear"), although he was probably busy with *It Ain't Alf Hot, Mum*; Scarman could hypothetically have been Christopher Benjamin (7.4, "Inferno" et al) or Leonard Sachs (3.5, "The Massacre"; 20.1, "Arc of Infinity"); Dr Warlock notionally may have been John Baskcomb (8.1, "Terror of the Autons"); Collins theoretically Arthur Hewlett (18.4, "State of Decay"; 23.3, "Terror of the Vervoids"). One other possible Scarman, Peter Welch, will be along as the pub landlord in "The Android Invasion". In the frame to play Ernie were Mostyn Evans (10.5, "The Green Death"; 11.3, "Death to the Daleks"), Freddie Earle (18.5, "Warriors' Gate") and Chubby Oates (11.5, "Planet of the Spiders").

• Russell's brisk style or rehearsal made some of the cast, especially Archard and Peter Copley (as Dr. Warlock), rebellious. Baker took to calling her "sir", but their working relationship was better than on her next story (15.1, "Horror of Fang Rock"). Peter Mayock, as Namin (one of the last parts cast after a long search), would have to mime to the organ music in the first episode, so Simpson pre-recorded that part of the score. The rest of the organ music was played by Leslie Pearson and recorded at St Augustine's Church, Kilburn, later in the month. (The organ in the studio wasn't real and had cardboard pipes). Copley celebrated his 60th birthday during the rehearsals.

• Into TC3 on 19th May for the first session, and, where possible, Russell tried to stay in story order. The main set for both recording sessions was the Organ room, which Christine Ruscoe had partially sourced from stock and hire companies. The TARDIS console was refurbished and the walls around it built from scratch; this is the only Console Room set lacking a scanner. Russell had been in touch with Ian Scoones, the effects

13.3 Pyramids of Mars

designer for the story, almost before she started casting and had tried to find relatively simple ways to do everything in the script (a great deal of it is straightforward editing, roll-backs and playing video-discs in reverse). John Friedlander had built a fibreglass Sutekh head to Scoones's design to be superimposed on the POV shot of the walls and ceiling. The ring had a light inserted in resin but was otherwise a cheap thing from Woolworth's. The Marconiscope was built by the special effects assistants, Mat Irvine and Peter Logan – Scoones had found a "Marconi" brass plate from an old radio.

- There was an unexpected development with the main Sarcophagus having blue stripes almost the same colour as the CSO key-out colour for the story. This allowed an extra effect not anticipated for no extra cost or time. Archard, on arriving at the Organ Room, had to tread where the smoke-holes were concealed in the stair-carpet. His other unusual walk, in Part Two after Clements shoots Scarman, was delayed until the second block when time was running out. The first half, the shot exploding in his chest, was the point where the recording paused on the second day. All of the conversations with Sutekh were recorded with just Archard listening and saying the "I obey" stuff.

- By now, Russell had filled the villain's part with veteran radio and schools-television performer Gabriel Woolf, although Hinchcliffe had misgivings at first. The Jackal-mask didn't fit him; when rehearsals resumed (on the 21st), he stood by as a dummy was sat in a chair with this object on its shoulders. Once it was apparent that the role was more or less a voice-over until the end, he was released until recording. The helmet added resonance to his voice, which was the main reason for keeping him sat there in costume and was mic'ed up carefully to aid this; Woolf had to enunciate clearly, to avoid "popping", and this was factored into his delivery.

- The second pair of recording days were in the smaller TC6 on the 2nd and 3rd June. A lot of Part Three was already recorded or on film. To save a little more time, the scene of the Doctor dressed as a Mummy in the Cottage used one of the "normal" mummies; Baker, off-screen, added the voice. Russell and the lighting supervisor argued over whether the lighting in the cell was too low. (This is a recurrent problem between now and 1989, as the BBC and the transmission engineers have automatic cut-outs if a picture is too dark. The broadcast might have been halted and replaced by a "Technical Fault" caption and music.)

- Scoones supervised the shot of Archard recovering from being shot (walking backwards and then having two charges go off in his jacket, all of which had to look convincing when played in reverse). The sight-gag of the Doctor writing "relax" was, apparently, ad-libbed, but the arrival and departure of the Decatron crucible was tricky to line up – when the resulting roll-back proved to be exactly right, Sladen got a round of applause from the crew. The Marx Brothers-derived sight-gag of the Doctor and Sarah simultaneously turning as the Mummy swings round was added in rehearsals and vetoed by Hinchcliffe and Russell, but they went for it. Baker added the "1666" joke.

Neither Woolf nor Archard wore the Jackal-head mask, which was put on costume-wearing dummies. The effect of the doors sliding open to reveal the TARDIS at the end of the corridor was, as you probably guessed, a model, but... you might not have realised that it was recorded as dropping the doors shut and run backwards on the VT. The flame effects for the end were unprecedentedly ambitious for Television Centre and contributed to the quarter-hour over-run of the last session. After a mishap with a live *Blue Peter* girl-guide camp-fire in TC1, the rules said that they needed trained professionals on hand just in case.

- Baker returned to Television Centre the following day to appear in *Jim'll Fix It* and Russell booked a brief gallery session on the Saturday (10th) to finish the end-credits. This was rare then (see 15.5, "Underworld"). A couple of the roll-Russell edited out the TARDIS's arrival in Alternative 1980, to make Sarah's first glimpse of it more dramatic.

- Terrance Dicks resolves a few remaining anomalies in the novelisation, but the one that caused Holmes most hassle was later, when the "isomorphic" line (already a problem as the word doesn't mean what they say it means) was contradicted on screen in "The Invisible Enemy" (15.2). Holmes responded to the many letters by arguing that the Doctor had good reasons to lie to Sutekh, an excuse that Steven Moffat re-used a few times – along with the troublesome word itself (X6.0, "A Christmas Carol"). Russell T. Davies reassigned Woolf's spooky voice-over in X2.8-2.9, "The Impossible Planet" / "The Satan Pit".

The most flagrant re-use of this story wasn't broadcast, though: both the Marconiscope and the glimpse into "alternate time" had they left at a key moment were scripted in X1.3, "The Unquiet Dead", but dropped. Mars having a pyramid was the source of a gag in *The Sarah Jane Adventures* (Mr Smith blocking a NASA rover's signal at a key moment).

13.4: "The Android Invasion"

(Serial 4J, Four Episodes, 22nd November – 13th December 1975.)

Which One is This? It's "Terror of the Zygons" redone in the style of *Midsomer Murders*, but with bits of "The Ambassadors of Death" (7.3) pasted in where the big scary lizard-cow was. And lashings of ginger pop. Astronauts, village post-offices, eyepatches, rhino-men in chunky boots and Harry Sullivan getting replicated *again* form a fiendish alien masterplan of quite breath-taking stupidity.

Firsts and Lasts Well, it's the final appearance of Ian Marter as Lt. Sullivan (and his evil twin) and of John Levene as Mr Benton (and his sinisterly-competent double). It's the last story directed by Barry Letts, so a few other familiar faces are back one last time. One isn't, so we get the first use of "the Brigadier's in Geneva" to mean "Nick Courtney's got a proper job". Stuart Fell gets dialogue as a Kraal and Max Faulkner gets whole scenes with lines and falls off a cliff (but gets better) as a UNIT corporal. Dave Carter bows out by getting an entire episode as a main character: the technician Grierson.

It's a summer location shoot, for the first time since 5.1, "The Tomb of the Cybermen" (technically, the shoot for 10.2, "Carnival of Monsters" was late spring). The Doctor's got a tweed frock-coat, matching his trousers, that he'll be wearing on and off until "The Sun Makers" (15.4) two years from now. Nearly two years before K9 shows up, we've got the first robot dogs in the series (a potential spoiler, except that the story's title blows the surprise ending of Part Two).

And, as this story's essay explores, it's the last straightforward alien invasion of Earth for 30 years...

Four Things to Notice About "The Android Invasion"...
• If you're coming to this from a post-Moffat world, this is essentially "Extremis" (X10.6), 1975-style. None of yer poncy computer simulations here, matey, this is a physical fake village populated by android replicas of UNIT regulars and rustic stereotypes straight out of "The Daemons" (8.5). Instead of a same-sex date being interrupted by the Pope, we have Benton arranging to pick up his kid sister by the Chinese take-away to take her ballroom dancing. The return of Barry Letts as director after such a short time – making as big an impact on the finished story as Terry Nation, the accredited author – means that this is still thought of as a viable way to make *Doctor Who*. Don't forget that it's only been seven months since "Genesis of the Daleks" was broadcast and we're still in the same calendar year as "Robot", so this isn't so much "retro" as "belated".

• And although it's space-suit-wearing robots with finger-guns rather than Yeti, and a picturesque village rather than Tooting Bec, the domestic details are laid on thicker than normal. The pub and the village shop are so lovingly recreated, it's a perfect time-capsule of 1975 England. Too perfect for anyone who was there to buy the notion of this being "the future", even despite the British Space Programme sending people to Jupiter before Concorde had its maiden commercial flight. Mission Control, Devesham, is as mid-70s as a cheesecloth shirt. As the story spends so much time making us look at people's shoes, the fashion-dating-data is especially evident.

• Between Nation pulling the story in one over-familiar direction and Letts pulling it into a compilation of his favourite bits from when he ran the show, we see what happens when Tom Baker decides to salvage bland dialogue. In one scene, in the Disorientation room, he ramblingly conflates the Dormouse's story from *Alice's Adventures in Wonderland* and Chekhov's *The Three Sisters*; earlier he has the Doctor reminisce about a trip to Malplaquet. The one line everyone remembers from here – *is that finger loaded?* – was his too.

• Letts made his directorial *Who* debut with "The Enemy of the World" (5.4), a story that ended with the Doctor fighting his lookalike. Now that we've seen it again, this tussle isn't as bad as Letts had led us to believe, but the eager way this story's last episode has Baker and Terry Walsh slamming each other around Mission Control seems to confirm a widespread belief that Letts

13.4 The Android Invasion

fancied a chance to do it again "properly". It's such a big set-piece that Part Four is unbalanced by trying to fit everything else around it.

The Continuity

The Doctor now has a salt-and-pepper tweed frock-coat with several pocket-flaps, elbow-patches and a darker collar. He can do that thing with a reed as a snorkel [always shown in adventure serials, but physically impossible for humans]. He likes ginger beer [see X4.7, "The Unicorn and the Wasp"] and can drink it faster than we can without burping or hiccoughs. He has an unorthodox darts style, but it seems to work [although he's apparently not watched it on telly, so doesn't go for 180, but instead aims all three at the bullseye]. He's worried about his memory [see also "Revenge of the Cybermen"] and thinks he'd have recognised the re-entry pod 'like a shot' 300 years before. Once again, his shoulders seem to be remarkably tender.

• *Background.* The Doctor apparently knew the Duke of Marlborough and was at the Pyrrhic victory at Malplaquet. He recognises a DM bomb and knows that you don't get oak trees beyond Earth. [So no alien has tried to plant acorns, despite the number of other strangely-familiar life-forms around and extra-terrestrial visitors picking up curios on their travels.] If we're to believe his burbling when regaining consciousness, he was around when Lewis Carroll was making up stories and may have contributed.

• *Ethics.* None of that equal rights for robots stuff here; he treats these androids as weapons. Still, the signal-blocker he rigs up just stops them in their tracks. The Doctor's reprogrammed duplicate ends up causing Styggron's death (from the virus), seemingly by accident.

• *Inventory:*

– *Sonic Screwdriver* pulls bolts out of the floor. Setting Theta Omega burns through plastic vines tougher than steel. Sarah uses it on both occasions.

– *Other.* What he claims is an 'android detector' looks very like the pocket radio-telescope he showed Laurence Scarman ["Pyramids of Mars"], but without an extended aerial. He has a Victorian earthenware pop-bottle for his ginger beer. The radiation meter he whips out is the same device he had in "The Web of Fear" (5.5) to measure electrical current without touching the third rail [it may even be the one from "The Tomb of the Cybermen"]. There's a steak-knife in his pocket, next to the sonic screwdriver. And, just for once, he's got his UNIT pass handy [perhaps he got the ID photo changed in an unseen moment at the end of "Robot"]. And there's that magnifying glass again.

The TARDIS behaves very oddly indeed. It lands a long way from UNIT HQ but close to where Harry and Benton are. Before that, it lands in an identical spot on Oseidon right smack in the middle of a replica of the same establishment. Then, when Sarah pops the key in the lock, it starts up and heads for the real Devesham, right across the galaxy, stranding her and the Doctor. The Doctor thinks it's time for her 500-year service.

The Supporting Cast

• *Sarah.* [For all that 'I'm from 1980' bosh last time, she's here dressed as if she expects to arrive in 1975-6; those shoes would have been the butt of jokes any time after 1978.] She's picked up the scarf-wearing habit and is carrying a box of matches in her pocket. [Maybe she had a gas cooker at home or was expecting power-cuts.]

She doesn't like ginger pop. Oddly, her android duplicate loves it and has a scarf despite Sarah giving hers to the Doctor. [The logical inference is that Sarah's so used to being possessed and mind-probed, and met so many doppelgangers, that she's got into the habit of concentrating on possible anomalies for her friends to spot. This may also be why robo-Sarah's first move is to tell the Doctor that it's a fiendish plan to replace everyone with android duplicates.]

For her, two years have elapsed since she went to Devesham to report on Guy Crayford's disappearance. [Let's step back a bit: the first time we heard her discuss Harry with the Brigadier, she asked if the Lieutenant was up to the job, as if she'd encountered him before. Admittedly, the first we hear his name is in "Planet of the Spiders" Part Two (11.5) but we never see a first meeting between Sarah and Harry and she's teasing him almost from the start of "Robot". Similarly, Mike Yates knows who she is in "Invasion of the Dinosaurs" (11.2), even though we missed them meeting, and Benton can identify her from a photo. The impression is that the Doctor is the one prominent UNIT officer she'd not run into before "The Time Warrior" (11.1), and she's more

The Android Invasion 13.4
Why Does Earth Keep Getting Invaded?

(… and why do aliens always pick such daft ways to do it?)

At time of going to press, aliens in *Doctor Who* have attempted to invade Earth 54 times. This isn't counting all the intelligent visitors hanging around in large numbers observing, such as the Silence (X6.2, "Day of the Moon") or the Thijarians (X11.6, "Demons of the Punjab") and scammers such as the Slitheen, who were more interested in the planet's scrap value.

Exploitation, if it's not significant enough for the general public to notice, isn't the quite the same thing, so we're not counting the Krillitane (X2.3, "School Reunion") or Chameleon Tours (4.8, "The Faceless Ones"). Nor will we count harvests of humans, such as the Weeping Angels (X3.10, "Blink"; X7.5, "Angels in Manhattan"), the 456 (*Torchwood: Children of Earth*, although they were less discreet about it than usual), the Vespiform Scout (X4.7, "The Unicorn and the Wasp") or Tim Shaw (X11.1, "The Woman Who Fell to Earth").

Neither can we count people coming for things left on the planet – as we'll discuss in a moment, the sheer unobtrusiveness of this world was the attractive feature a great many times. Silurians, time-shifted dinosaurs and trapped aliens trying to get home don't count either (unless, in the latter case, they decide to take Earth instead, as with the Terileptils (19.4, "The Visitation") or, er, the Sheriff of Nottingham (X8.3, "Robot of Sherwood"). In short, we can count 18 honest-to-goodness invasion bids between 2.2, "The Dalek Invasion of Earth" and 25.3, "Silver Nemesis" (that includes the commando-raid by Gel Guards in 10.1, "The Three Doctors"), a further 29 in *Doctor Who* between X1.1, "Rose" and X12.2, "Spyfall Part Two" and, in *The Sarah Jane Adventures*, another five among all the harvests and bids to find lost alien devices and fugitives.

You may have been expecting more: the "lost property" stories where something has been mislaid on Earth amount to 51 in *Doctor Who* (including humans from the wrong time such as Magnus Greel in "The Talons of Weng-Chiang" and Krasko in X11.3, "Rosa"), 15 in *SJA* and 18 in *Torchwood*.

You can check our numbers and add *Class* if you really want to, but the point stands. Actual invasions (or attempts) are few and… well not really far-between because there's a cluster between 1968 and 1971 and another with David Tennant as the Doctor. (Oh, and it appears that three unbroadcast ones took place some time before 2008; the flashback reel the Atraxi cycle through in X5.1, "The Eleventh Hour" features the Ood, the Hath and, er, Proper Dave).

Apart from confirming that the 26 years of the series made during the Cold War by people who could remember the Blitz are considerably less xenophobic than the 12 years of Russell T. Davies and Steven Moffat (see the essay with X1.3, "The Unquiet Dead"), what does this tell us? Well, the first thing to observe is that the Shadow Proclamation aren't taken very seriously. We've been hearing since 1979's "City of Death" (17.2) that Earth is a "Level Five" culture and, latterly, that these are off-limits to alien contamination or exploitation. The number of alien assaults ought to be either zero (if the Shadow Proclamation were any use) or one (if a successful assault happened while the Doctor wasn't around and put everyone else off). The most effective measure we ever see this august body make is to declare Earth "Terminal" and put up detour signs (X3.13, "Last of the Time Lords").

That said, the number of hoops potential invaders must jump through has always seemed a bit silly. Apart from the *fait accompli* of the Yeti taking London apparently overnight and almost by accident (5.5, "The Web of Fear"), everyone goes all around the houses to set up fiendishly stupid over-elaborate plans. Someone other than puny humans and a passing Time Lord must enforce such circumspection. Trouble is, once an alien slips in under the noses of the Judoon, someone coming in to stop them is more disruptive and potentially damaging (X3.1, "Smith and Jones", X12.5, "Fugitive of the Judoon", X13.0, "Revolution of the Daleks").

We'd never heard of the Shadow Proclamation before "Rose" (X1.1), so it's sometimes assumed that the Time War spurred their creation, just as World War II prompted the UN. But, maybe they were always around. We discuss (in **What Happened in 1972?** under "Dreamland") how cosmic supervision was apparently withdrawn once humans developed enough awareness and firepower to see off the majority of interfering aliens without a covert alien force getting in the way. They seem not to have discussed a phased withdrawal and just legged it. Yet something seems to have happened to prevent any attempts at troops-on-the-ground conquest between the Kraals in 1975 and the strangely nostalgic Nestene bid 30 years later. (That assumes the Kraal one still persists in the timeline; see **Was There a Martian Time Slip?** under X4.16, "The Waters of Mars".)

continued on page 177…

surprised that UNIT employs someone like him than that they exist and are investigating missing scientists. Note that in "The Android Invasion", a corporal asks for the Doctor's pass, not hers.

[However, she asks the Brigadier for a pass to Think Tank because she's bored with the sort of articles she gets given. If she was covering the Crayford story before she met the Doctor, what happened at Metropolitan to move her onto "women's angle" stuff? Nonetheless, this is the one story that makes a bit more sense after *The Sarah Jane Adventures* than before, since the spin-off suggests that she was always a UNIT associate, if not officially on their books, and well-in with their recruitment staff.]

• *Harry*. Well, here's a turn-up for the books: Lt. Surgeon Sullivan is, apparently, the planet's leading authority on space-medicine. He seems to be a long-term fixture at the Defence Complex and has a briefcase of all the 'tools of the trade' ready in case of unexpected return visits by lost astronauts. His 'imbecile' credentials are presented to us by his inability to comprehend aliens making a duplicate of him despite his having seen the Zygons do exactly that. He doesn't get a formal goodbye with the TARDIS crew, and his last word in the series is 'twin?'

Harry's duplicate calls Sarah 'Miss Smith' [indicating that Crayford knew Sarah even if he didn't recognise the Doctor] but messes up the safety procedures for the virus. [So obviously Crayford's got him pegged as an imbecile, too.]

[Subsequent episodes paint a much more interesting future for Lt Sullivan. "Mawdryn Undead" (20.3) mentions him doing secret stuff at Porton Down, the government's main biological research station – back in the news after Putin sent intelligence officers to spread Novichok around Salisbury. Ian Marter picked up on this in his novel *Harry Sullivan's War*. Much later, X9.7-9.8, "The Zygon Invasion" / "The Zygon Inversion" hinges, as far as we can work out, on Harry having developed a gas that would viciously 'turn every Zygon on Earth inside out'. Maybe. Possibly. (As the Doctor confiscated the material, we've no idea if it does what it says on the tin, or was ever intended to.) However, in *The Sarah Jane Adventures*, he's spoken of in the past tense (*SJA* 4.3, "Death of the Doctor"), although Sarah mysteriously has a photo of him from "The Sontaran Experiment" in her attic.]

• *Benton* has a kid sister who needs him to take her dancing at the Palais. [If it's the Hammersmith Palais, the most famous ballroom-dancing venue, he's got a long drive to pick her up.

[There's a theory that Benton dies when his evil twin knocks him out, but his eyes move and the Brigadier says he's still rattling around in "Mawdryn Undead". Of course, that could be a side-effect of removing this story from history – see **Was There a Martian Time-Slip?** under X4.15, "The Waters of Mars".]

• *The Brigadier* is 'in Geneva'. [He must do that a lot; this is true both in the real Defence Complex and Crayford's two-or-more-year-old memories and again in "The Seeds of Doom". He has an office with his name on, though, so he's obviously on-site a fair amount.]

The Non-Humans *The Kraals*. Broadly speaking humanoid, with the requisite number of hands, feet, eyes and so on, but facially like a ceratopsian (Protoceratops, Triceratops, that lot) with grey-brown skin, a beak-like mouth and what's either a nose or a horn. We see three and their frills and crevices are all subtly different.

Their planet, Oseidon, has become so radioactive that they're looking for a new home and seem to think Earth fits the bill. [It can't be *that* badly irradiated, if Sarah's hair doesn't fall out and she seems pretty fit even after being exposed to g-forces supposedly beyond human limits, but prolonged exposure might be a different matter. The Kraals seem to live in bunkers or burrows, to the extent that we can tell, so this is possibly a matter of incremental increases in surface exposure causing crop failures as much as radiation sickness.]

Planet Notes
• *Oseidon*. The Doctor claims that it's 'the only planet in the galaxy' with a 'natural radiation' level that high. Oseidon seems, from the brief view we get of it, to be a blue-white wilderness with dark scrub vegetation and a blue sky, orbiting a star apparently like the sun [so either the same size and distance, or much bigger and further away]. The Kraals seem to be the only remaining animal life. [Ergo, it's an Earth-like planet that developed life but finds radiation inimical, then got a big dose of it.]

• *Earth*. Apparently, we currently have the galactic monopoly on oak trees. [This raises a lot of questions about the furniture on Peladon.]

The Android Invasion 13.4
Why Does Earth Keep Getting Invaded?

...continued from page 175

The only aliens to invade sensibly (aerial bombardment, plagues, *then* armed assaults and labour-camps) were the Daleks, defeated by getting exactly what they wanted (first time we saw it), then by having history rewritten so it never happened (second time). Their most recent on-screen invasion, chronologically first and seemingly removed from history, is odd because it's so perfunctory – it's not for show, because the Shadow Proclamation only know that the planet's gone. It seems that the Daleks pottered around for an episode (X4.12, "The Stolen Earth") to stop any chums of the Doctor's from destroying the planet before they'd used it, then left when they'd collected the set.

Nobody else ever tries the direct approach, even though slinging a hefty asteroid and causing a mass extinction event would be easy for anyone with a decent spaceship and made to look like an accident. If Earth no longer has a civilisation, it's no longer Level Five and thus fair game. Instead, we have the umpteen faffy con-tricks pulled on Britain and, thereby (somehow) all of Earth. Can every single advanced-but-needy species in the universe really be keen on pranks rather than shock-and-awe? What are they really after?

Back in the 1960s, there were attempts to work out how many intelligent, technological species were around and the SETI people made a case for listening out for possible signals (deliberate attempts at contacting others or just ambient radio communications between themselves). Even since we revised Volume 3, the situation's moved on a bit, but the majority of discussions start with a statement made by American astronomer / astrophysicist Frank Drake.

In this, the number of stars was whittled down to fit assumptions of how many would support life, what proportion of that life would make machines, how long they'd stick around and so on. There's not a set number for any of these figures or percentages, so the "equation" is more a heuristic or methodological hint than a reliable guide. Recently, using more refined statistical techniques, the various terms of the equation were re-evaluated and a top limit of 15,785 was put on this galaxy's possible number of civilisations enough like ours to be worth talking to. Without magical faster-than-light spaceships, they'd be out-of-contact with each other, or us – provided they were spaced out evenly, an average of 30,000 light years separating them all.

This number was only slightly less arbitrary than any of the others, but it gives a shape to the argument, a starting-point. But both Drake and the rival "Rare Earth" calculation make a lot of assumptions on the requirements needed for planets to spawn life, and what life has to be like for us to acknowledge it as such. While the telescopes and probes have changed our ideas about what a planet can be like, the close examination of bits of Earth thought unlikely to sustain life have altered basic tenets about what can live where.

The current best-guess, pending the James Webb Telescope getting actual proof, is that about one sol-type star in five has an earth-like planet somewhere in its orbit. Similar ratios apply to planets of all sizes in the "Goldilocks" zone of acceptable solar radiation, from current observations. Therefore, even if only this one kind of sun and this one kind of planet is suitable (a debatable proposition), slow radio conversations could be feasible one day. Just this one galaxy ought to be enough to keep *Doctor Who* writers busy for decades to come (unless actual aliens show up and make the series' assumptions about extraterrestrials look silly).

The Drake Equation was mainly a way of getting conversations started, but it's cited often enough for us to use as a benchmark of what was accepted then. People writing *Doctor Who* in the 1970s made one of two basic assumptions: that Earth was so run-of-the-mill that you'd never notice it in the vastness of space – or, more jingoistically, that Earth was unique and vastly superior to any other world.

The first batch of writers barely knew the difference between a galaxy, a constellation and a solar system. Terry Nation's early drafts in particular assumed that our sun and its neighbours were about all there was. (Skaro was, in one version of 1.2, "The Daleks", the twelfth planet in our system. Later, even when five or more other galaxies were plotting against us in 3.4, "The Daleks' Master Plan", the Solar System was the lynchpin of our galaxy's defences and wealth.)

Once script editors got up to speed on both proper science and written science fiction, a more reasonable scale became the norm and the Milky Way (or "Mutter's Spiral" as it's known hereabouts) was one of thousands of galaxies and itself consisted of hundreds of thousands of stars, many of which had life nearby. *Doctor Who*, for the most

continued on page 179...

13.4 The Android Invasion

History Apparently, XK5 went missing two years ago in the vicinity of Jupiter. Astronaut Guy Crawford was presumed dead.

- *Dating*. Just going by the visual evidence, a strong case can be made that it's September 1977 at the *very* latest. The fake village is constructed from Crawford's memories and he disappeared 'two years' before, and almost every detail of the pub, the shop and the Space Defence Centre is accurate for mid-1975. Specifically, the unfaded poster in the shop window promotes eight regional British cheeses, part of the original 'Cheese It' campaign from 1974 and the copy of *Whoopee!* – an IPC kid's comic of the era – has the original masthead (June 1974 – May 1975). We can't read the newspaper headlines, but the *Daily Express* went from broadsheet format to tabloid in 1977, yet it's still big here. The design on the boxes of Cadbury's Milk Tray was phased out from 1974 to 1976, but the shop might be stocking them past the sell-by date (not unknown in such village shops). The Doctor never pays for his two pints of ginger beer, so we can't estimate the date from what he's charged.

Every sheet on the pub calendar says it's '6th July', a 'Friday' – that could indicate the invasion as occurring on that date, meaning we might go for the story starting on 5th July 1977. (Maybe 'in Geneva' is UNIT's euphemism for "been sacked", and the Brigadier's already installed at Brendon School; "Mawdryn Undead".)

[Sarah's reference to her visiting Devesham as a journalist 'two years ago' must refer to her own, subjective time; after all, she hears nothing about the date when they land. Either way, it's the fall-out from something Sarah reported on before she asked the Brigadier for help getting into Think Tank ("Robot") and probably before she met the Doctor. If Sarah-time and chronological time *are* almost in synch, Crawford left in late 1973 / early 1974, making this either July 1975, a few weeks after "Terror of the Zygons", or July 1976.]

Sending an Englishman to Jupiter during Ted Heath's petrol-rationing is somehow easier for some people to believe than the obvious alternative: that this story happens, for everyone except the Doctor and Sarah, *after* "The Seeds of Doom" (or "The Hand of Fear"). Yet, for Sarah to still hold down a job, there can't be long gaps when she's incommunicado and milk-bottles accumulate outside her door. Sir Colin, in "Seeds" (and indeed the people on the Antarctic expedition) seem to be expecting UNIT's boffin to be a white-haired dandy but can get in touch with him and Sarah fairly readily. If we make this July 1975, Harry and/or Benton's lack of a rapturous welcome for the Doctor and Miss Smith might well be because the time since they last saw the TARDIS travellers is shorter for them. However, with UNIT installed at the Defence Centre apparently for some time, and Harry Sullivan now the country's leading authority on space-medicine, we can make a good case for them to have experienced a much longer gap after "Terror of the Zygons" than the Doctor and Sarah. (See **Things That Don't Make Sense** for more.)

Of course, 6th July wasn't a Friday in 1975, 1976 or 1980, but dates in "present day" stories haven't matched since "The War Machines" (3.10). [Although there's a school of thought that the switch to the Gregorian Calendar never happened in the *Doctor Who* universe (25.3, "Silver Nemesis"), it's not much use looking for it to start now.] The lack of any concern about the US bicentennial, at least, is entirely in keeping with real-world England. Besides, if this is all from Crawford's memory, then the calendar might be on 1973 time (the 6th was a Friday in that year).

The "brand new" money in Corporal Adams's wallet includes Series C pound notes (phased out from early 1978 and not legal tender after May 1979). And Sarah is wearing the most 1975 twin-set and shoes imaginable.

The Analysis

Where Does This Come From? Terry Nation had been thinking about android duplicates for longer than most: one of his first television writing gigs was on ABC's *Out of this World*. (This was an anthology series, intended as a summer preplace-ment for *Armchair Theatre* but manifestly looking at American models such as *Alfred Hitchcock Presents* and *The Twilight Zone* – hence Boris Karloff wandering around space-stations or laboratories in a dinner-suit to introduce each story.)

Nation's task had been to adapt "Imposter" by Philip K. Dick, stretching the premise for an hour, but only with the facilities of an electronic studio c.1962. You know the story: someone gets a tip-off that an android duplicate of an agent seeks to commit an act of terrorism, and agent Olham is sent to track it down. On finding the real Olham's dead body, the story's protagonist says: *but if that's*

The Android Invasion 13.4
Why Does Earth Keep Getting Invaded?

...continued from page 177

part, concentrates on a teensy fraction of this amount of real estate and takes a rather parochial view of the cosmic immensity. (See **How Many Significant Galaxies are There?** under 2.5, "The Web Planet".)

Nonetheless, the problem remains that statistically, there's a lot of worlds with resources and a biome like Earth's and, equally probably, there'll be rather more of these than are currently inhabited by aggressive aliens enough like us to want our goodies. Beings from a planet enough like ours for Earth to be attractive would only evolve on 4% of exoplanets. If they've got the tech to come here, they could exploit any of the other 96% with less effort. If we're sticking with the Principle of Mediocrity, as those 70s telly hacks were, then *Doctor Who*'s internal logic with so many almost-human aliens making a grab for Earth's resources falls apart. Either there's a *lot* of alien life and this is because there's a heck of a lot of good planets, or we're pretty much unique and so there are hardly any aliens and all those other planets are unusable because... er...

That's been the problem since 1964. Aside from the issue of everyone on Earth ignoring the increasing number of nearly-successful alien invasions since 1970 (see **How and Why is the Doctor Exiled to Earth?** under 9.5, "The Time Monster" and **Why Does Everyone Forget About the Aliens?** under X3.1, "Smith and Jones"), each one has to be sold to us as if it were the first and therefore increasingly strained explanations have been offered. They were in the neighbourhood (3.2, "The Tenth Planet"); we stopped them from invading so they're cross with us (4.6, "The Moonbase"; 5.9, "The Wheel in Space"; 6.3, "The Invasion"; X13.2, "War of the Sontarans" and implicitly 9.1, "Day of the Daleks"); the Master thought it would be funny (8.1, "Terror of the Autons"; 8.3, "The Claws of Axos"; X8.11, "Dark Water"; X12.1, "Spyfall Part One"); their own world is destroyed, but was so unlike Earth they have to wreck it for humans (6.5, "The Seeds of Death"; "Terror of the Zygons"; 4.8, "The Faceless Ones"; X4.5, "The Poison Sky"); they felt like it (X2.0, "The Christmas Invasion"; X2.12, "Army of Ghosts"; X4.14, "The Next Doctor")...

Logically, if Earth is so banal and hard to conquer, it must be low on anyone's to-do list. One possibility is that it's in demand simply because earlier, bigger cosmic powers conquered / played out all the better planets, so now all the wannabes are fighting over Earth because it's the last reasonably rich world left in this area. This has its problems, mainly that if they're all fighting *each other*, they wouldn't have the wherewithal to invade an ice cream van. We now know that the Sontarans and Rutans have been at each other's throats (figuratively speaking) for 50,000 years, during which time the Rutans ran this galaxy for a spell, then lost it ("The Poison Sky"; 15.1, "Horror of Fang Rock"). We also know that there were cosmic wars in the past, including the Osirans' attempts to stop Sutekh (13.3, "Pyramids of Mars") and, at roughly the same time, the Dark Empire of Horath removed all but the most insignificant intelligent species from this galaxy (*SJA* 2.11, "Enemy of the Bane").

If most of the cultures in this galaxy are roughly the same age as ours, the big question is why we're so slow in building starships and what have you. Even if every other nearby species gets to the point of making invasion fleets for other worlds at roughly the same stage (and none of them develops a technology for efficient recycling and living within their means instead), the odds of all of them running out of nearby empty planets to exploit within a 50-year period – and all being at the stage when Earth looks like the logical next destination – are incredible. (For best effect, say "incredible" like Liz Shaw when she ridicules the Brigadier for believing in bug-eyed monsters.) The older species that come with malice aforethought all seem to be from further away.

What we now know about humans is that most of the rest of the history of the cosmos has them in: the timeline now extends as far as Ten Trillion A.D. On the other hand, the number of human-looking aliens is down a few notches from what we were led to expect in the twentieth century (see **Is Kylie from Planet Zog?** under X4.0, "Voyage of the Damned"). If that's the case, we have to wonder why Earth's so much more attractive now that the number of species that look exactly like humans has been whittled away; it's harder for any fugitive to pass unnoticed.

Two motivations stand out from these as at least in-story logical. Humans are conscious, so getting their respect, awe or obedience is somehow necessary to beings that live for (or on) such things. We had this in the flimsy attempt to make "The Mind Robber" (6.2) less of an abstract threat, but it's there in various forms in stories as different as 8.5, "The Daemons"; X9.5, "The Girl Who Died"; "Pyramids of Mars" and X10.7, "The Pyramid at the

continued on page 181...

13.4 The Android Invasion

Olham, I must be... (which is the trigger-phrase for the bomb inside the android; see X5.3, "Victory of the Daleks" for a less sensible version). So even before "The Chase" (2.8), Nation had to work out how to do duplicates on not-quite-live television.

The Dick story was from just before the glut of doppelganger films we mentioned with "Terror of the Zygons", and has, as was his wont, the main emphasis on an individual doubting something very fundamental: his sense of self. We don't have Nation's rough notes, but this was likely in the mix of the story surrounding Crayford's eyepatch originally. That plot-element is presented to us as going somewhere then, after what's made to look like a big reveal... nothing. It's hard to see why this story-strand exists unless something along the lines of "Imposter" was planned and then forgotten – along with the plague, the radiation-hazard and the reason everything pauses just before 6.00pm.

Nation had been thinking a lot more recently about the ways the authorities would react to pandemics or environmental hazards. The Doctor introduces the idea of a plague or radiation-leak when looking at the new-minted coins in the pub's till, and the "mechanics" wear suits exactly like the sort used in this situation in that era. When the Windscale nuclear power station had a leak in the 1950s, the news footage was of people in white wellingtons and disposable overalls pouring possibly-contaminated milk away and hosing down the cows. (A similar scare in the 80s resulted in more drastic action – renaming the plant as "Sellafield".)

Something similar happened in the Foot and Mouth outbreak in 1967, but it was familiar to the *Doctor Who*-watching youngsters from the scary Public Information Films about what would happen if you brought a pet through customs without a six-month quarantine (*ans.*: rabies – everyone terrified of small yappy dogs) or what might occur if Colorado Beetles ever established themselves in these isles. Nation, as we mentioned, started his dystopian drama *Survivors* with a scant handful of people in the Home Counties coping with the sudden deaths of 95% of the population. A lot of what happens in his scripts for the series (from which he was more-or-less ousted by Terence Dudley – see Volume 5) combines wartime precautions and the 1950's Civil Defence provisions, plus a generous proportion of the latter half of *Day of the Triffids* (local militias, hanging looters, that sort of thing – we'll return to this book a couple of stories from now but note that David Maloney produced the BBC's adaptation after he and Nation finished with *Blakes 7*). There's also something of this in that other cited key text for Nation, *Things to Come* (and this time, what he remembers is actually there – see, "Genesis of the Daleks"). As with 1.2, "The Daleks", the idea of how a society copes with atomic fall-out is introduced, then left to one side once it's done its work. Instead, Nation's arranged all his chess-pieces and then started playing draughts.

The visual conceit of a deserted English village with space-suited malfeasants is oddly common in 1960s British fantasy. Quite aside from the film *The Earth Dies Screaming* (where they were robots who look like 1966-model Cybermen), there's an ITC precedent in *Department S* ("The Pied Piper of Hambledown") and another episode where stolen spacesuits are used in a bank-job and a trial run leads to a dying "astronaut" in a London street ("The Man from X"). Moreover, Nation himself did it in *The Avengers*, in the messed-up episode "Invasion of the Earthmen". This turned out to be a training-ground for infiltrating Nietzschean military types, with a quarry to keep out visitors.[34] (The similar conceit of being drugged and placed in a facsimile of the sets for the series, in the pursuit of information, was so regular that Nation commissioned it twice in three episodes, "Pandora" and "Requiem", making it seem as if Tara King spent most of 1969 off her face.) This juxtaposition aside, the idea of rural England being infiltrated is so obviously a legacy of WWII precautions as to have almost stopped being noticeable as such – consider *Went the Day Well?* as the most obvious starting-point for this whole subgenre, then watch a few episodes of *Dad's Army* (if you haven't already). Then go back to the Napoleonic equivalent in Jane Austen.

In an early draft, the Doctor spotted robo-Sarah as a ringer because she had buttoned up her jacket the wrong way. Visiting a mirror-image world is an idea even older than Lewis Carroll's definitive work on the topic, but there was a 1969 film by *Thunderbirds* creators Gerry and Sylvia Anderson called (in the US) *Doppelganger* and elsewhere as *Journey to the Far Side of the Sun* – yes, it's that idea that dogged David Whitaker's stint as original script editor in 1962-4. Having Bizarro-Earth as a physical place rather than an alternate dimension is so common an idea that only Innes

The Android Invasion 13.4

Why Does Earth Keep Getting Invaded?

...continued from page 179

End of the World". Implicitly, it's the main object of the exercise for the Great Intelligence – or at least one of them (see **The Great Intelligence or a Great Intelligence?** under X7.6, "The Snowmen"). As we suggested in Volume 3, the very act of placing the Doctor in 1970's England made Earth more of a target than it had been, especially once the Master was twirling his moustache.

What this doesn't cover is why so many alien species thought Earth was such a primitive backwater, they could hide something there and nobody would think to look at such a humdrum and remote world. Each individual story that does this (let's take 20.3, "Mawdryn Undead" as an example) is possible to accept *if* there isn't another such story, but the stats we gave you earlier make nonsense of this. Even "Mawdryn Undead" relies on two separate alien races using the same school as a hiding place (by another astonishing coincidence, the Brigadier's there too).

Our count of lost-property stories wasn't terribly specific and lumped together a number of possible sub-genres for anyone interested in categorising stories like a Stanley Gibbons stamp album. Said stories include the Morax, imprisoned in microbial form under a tree (X11.8, "The Witchfinders"), Azal the Daemon and Sutekh the Destroyer ("The Daemons","Pyramids of Mars"), the Worshipful and Ancient Law of Gallifrey (17.6, "Shada") and Magnus Greel ("The Talons of Weng-Chiang").

We could subdivide them into stories where A) someone's picked Earth because the Doctor comes here a lot, B) someone's picked on Earth because humans will be troublesome at some time in the future, and the aliens want to alter things (not just Time Lords on the make, but the Mandragora Helix from "The Masque of Mandragora"; Scaroth from "City of Death" and others) and C) Earth really is the back end of beyond. If nothing else, this finally gives us a way to differentiate between "Silver Nemesis" (an object approaching Earth prompts a large Cyber-fleet to show up) and 25.1, "Remembrance of the Daleks" (the Doctor left an object on Earth to tempt a small incursionary force, but two showed up).

Perhaps the ultimate lost property is the planet itself, formed by the Racnoss Queen as a camouflage for her brood-ship (X3.0, "The Runaway Bride"). In the process, the buried spaceship became the last place other than a TARDIS to have huon particles. Whatever these were, they draw similar particles toward them – so there might be a reason for so many Time Lords to have hidden on Earth beyond the obvious ease of their passing for human. Whether any spaceships less than four and a half billion years old would also be pulled to Earth is open to question; no other story mentions such things.

One other thing that's changed lately is our idea of the scale of the cosmos: you may have seen that Deep Field photo from the Hubble Space Telescope, with 10,000 galaxies in a tiny portion of the sky as seen from here. From this and other such observations, the best estimate is that there are 170 billion galaxies all told. (This may, of course, be another mistaken extrapolation – but if so, the universe is unutterably freaky and all lined up in a row in the one direction the telescope was looking.) That estimate's simply from observing what's observable, with light taking billions of years to get here from the earliest formed galaxies but newer, closer ones still being out of sight.

A model based on current thinking of the content of space, the processes of star formation and galaxy-accretion and the age of the cosmos gives a figure of two trillion. You read that right: those 170 billion galaxies are the 10% we can see today. If we assume our own galaxy and those in the Local Group to be typical, then each of these galaxies has a hundred million stars in, give or take. Of course, not all known galaxies are the same size: Segue 1 and Segue 2, in our Local Group, are a lot smaller than ours and Andromeda is slightly bigger. The oldest ones in the Hubble view formed 800 million years after the Big Bang, so were smaller than those formed more recently (such as ours) and – at the time their light left for us to see – had fewer big atoms formed. First generation stars only bequeath us the first half-dozen elements in the Periodic table. *Doctor Who* is full of miraculous crystals that are fantastic power-sources with wondrous properties – but that, despite having a three-figure atomic number, can be hefted around by actors as if they were lumps of plastic with small light-bulbs inside. Nothing like any of these seems to come from Earth (the Crystal of Kronos in "The Time Monster" is debatable), because Earth's the result of a second or third generation star formation process. Even gold needed a couple of neutron stars to explode, and the 92 naturally occurring elements are the limit of what

continued on page 183...

13.4 The Android Invasion

Lloyd ever thought it was original (see 4.2, "The Tenth Planet"). This idea obviously persisted long enough for the whole subplot of the TARDIS getting confused to be woven inextricably into the finished version, but the original idea is more familiar still and came up when Nation was script-editing the final season of *The Avengers*.

Fake towns used for training come in two varieties: the real ones used by Britain's armed forces for combat practice and the fictional exact replicas used in Cold War paranoid fiction to train *speznatz* to pass for English, only to give themselves away by ordering red wine with fish (*From Russia with Love*), talking to strangers (*Danger Man* "Colony Three"), not knowing the right "top" universities (*Blackadder Goes Forth*) or some other *faux pas* that betrays foreign-ness. (Luckily, the real-life Russian operatives on social media never get any such training, so they make quite a lot of crass errors. They think the plural of "Lego" is "Legos", for heaven's sake.)

The *Mission: Impossible* take on this had an American small town used as a test-bed for a lethal virus, but a more useful comparison is the first Emma Peel *Avengers* episode, "Town of No Return". In this, a slow trickle of well-trained agents replace the local population of a remote village one by one, turning it into the bridgehead for an invasion. This rendering of the idea is especially pertinent, as it's slowly revealed that the rural mistrust of outsiders and the odd emptiness of the village except for a few "residents" in the pub are more than just how any English village was when townies showed up. In Nation's story, Corporal Adams comes out with it and says, "We don't have strangers here", as if it's a law and not a tendency.

In American cinema, the most famous version of that idea is the community that gangs up on an outsider because that's what they're like there – *The Texas Chainsaw Massacre* can stand for dozens of other examples. However, the US idea of ghost-towns isn't far from this either, nor is the "bridgehead" motif of paranoid invasion films. Here we must re-mention *Invasion of the Body-Snatchers*, because there's no other reason for the Kraals' re-entry capsules to look like warty marrows. However, most writers, especially in television and film, live in cities and a fair percentage of them fled stifling small communities. The idea of tightly-bound rural populations rejecting outsiders was far more common than the obverse, the loving, folksy band of neighbourly eccentrics who accept newcomers after a few (comic) misunderstandings. That set of clichés recycles every so often in economic downturns (when "city folks" get blamed for whatever is thought to have gone wrong) and usually in sitcoms or feel-good dramas.

In Britain, this is a bit less benign, as there's less of a reason for anyone with any gumption to stay in a decaying, toxic community when there's a rail service and nobody is more than ten miles from a reasonably-sized metropolis. Ergo, small villages are intrinsically full of people who've chosen to stay and resent anyone intruding. The 1944 Education Act led to a lot of people who might otherwise have drifted into the same job as their fathers – or become a housewife through lack of options – going to university and getting the hell away. Drama and novels in the 1960s are full of that generational urban / rural or industrial / metropolitan conflict, but the most famous example is the story of someone who thought he'd got out, just popped back to see his folks in December 1960 and has never left. Ken Barlow, in *Coronation Street*, is the flipside of all the working-class hopefuls who went to Oxbridge and That Lunnon and wrote about it for half a century. (See Dennis Potter, Alan Bennett, Margaret Drabble, John Braine, AS Byatt, David Storey, David Lodge...)

One other aspect of this not commented upon much: post-war road-building and relatively cheap petrol meant that people went off for "a drive" with no clear destination and, in the 1950s, petrol companies and advertisers hired people to recommend possible places of interest. John Betjeman became a public figure by doing this for Shell-Mex in the 1930s, then again for the Wartime Ministry of Information then most prominently, as he was now a television personality, for a set of what we'd now call infomercials (how he'd hate that word) starting on the second day of commercial television in 1955. Until a new set of adverts in 1974 recommended that people only drive if they had somewhere to go, and the new motorways and A-roads got clogged with everyone having the same idea at the same time, people were routinely spending their Sundays semi-lost on rural back roads, wandering into pubs full of surly, suspicious regulars and generally being made to feel unwelcome unless the pub had (overpriced) food for sale and depended on tourist revenue. Many towns had spent the era of

Why Does Earth Keep Getting Invaded?

...continued from page 181

can be found on a planet like ours.

It's true, some worlds might have exotic alloys or allotropes: the result of vulcanism or meteoric bombardment (some might take diamonds for granted but be amazed at what we do with graphite). But on any world roughly this vintage, what you see here is what you'd get there. Contrary to what *Sapphire and Steel* told us in the titles, trans-uranic, heavy elements will only be found in places likely to have had organic life a few billion years before. Of course, for there to be such wondrous crystals within the vague timescale of human activity in which most of *Doctor Who* takes place, several generations of stars will have been born and died in the 13.6 billion years that this universe has been a going concern, a slightly accelerated version of what's been observed so far. If that's the case, and there's been more time for intelligent life to develop and build spaceships than is usually accepted, the numbers look slightly more favourable for even this galaxy, but so do the numbers for uninhabited-but-tasty worlds.

To reiterate, the number of Earth-scale worlds that *aren't* inhabitable by things like us, either out of the Goldilocks Zone or just lacking atmospheres, water, magnetic shielding or whatever piece of luck was needed to start life off, is estimated at four out of every five. That's a lot of potential *lebensraum* without needing to trick the peoples of inhabited worlds by making plastic daffodils or putting hypnotic devices in transistor radios.

Looking over the last half-century of stories about Earth nearly being invaded, a huge logical flaw emerges. As we discuss in **What's Happened to the Monsters?** under X3.6, "The Lazarus Experiment", a close match for human is biologically and statistically unlikely, but only marginally more so than an air-breathing biped of any other kind. All the invaders-*manqués* that came for our atmosphere and gravity seem to look more like humans than not, but this planet can – and does – sustain an awful lot of other forms. If Earth is at all representative, a lot of conquerors should have six or more limbs, maybe two specialised for tool-use, but the only beetle-like visitors have been psychic menaces (X4.11, "Turn Left"; X10.4, "Knock Knock") and the spiders causing trouble developed from our very own (11.5, "Planet of the Spiders"; X11.4, "Arachnids in the UK"). Moreover, the most persistent humanoids with designs on our world – the Sontarans, the Ice Warriors and the Cybermen – all have trouble with the local gravity at some stage.

If we take the Kraals out of the equation, the only significant invaders-of-the month from the first spike are the Cybermen and the Nestenes. The Master brought the Axons and the Keller Machine's occupant to Earth to annoy the Doctor, ditto with the Nestenes second time around. Yet what they were doing on Earth in the first place is puzzling. Channing, in "Spearhead from Space", says that the Nestenes "have been colonising other planets for a thousand million years". The ninth Doctor tells Rose that they want our atmospheric pollution, "toxins and dioxins" because they lost all their "protein planets".

Our solar system has a lot of potential sources of these less troublesome than Earth, so Channing's word "colonise" indicates something more appeals to them about this planet. Given that they are disembodied mental forces emanating from cephalopod-like giants, it could be our big oceans, but the talk about protein and dioxins slightly contradicts that. If you're close enough for this to be known, assuming you find it an attractive feature, you already risk alerting the Shadow Proclamation. That might not worry the Nestenes, who seem pretty powerful, but their simply *being* that powerful make their stealthy infiltrations look absurd. A lot of the time, the risk of infiltration or domination by aliens through our consumer culture or ecologically-unsound practices seems almost like a form of aversion therapy. Benign aliens inveigle less-benign ones towards Earth expressly to (unwittingly) shock us out of bad habits.

This drags us to an awkward point about Yeti-in-the-Loo and Base-Under-Siege *Doctor Who* stories: they usually rely upon aliens wanting to behave as badly to us as humans do to each other, as if motivated by the same needs and desires as Nazis, Soviets or the British Empire. It's actually improbable that they'd be enough like us to acknowledge us as a threat, just as we disregard 95% of species on Earth because they're too little. If we look at even the simplest and, supposedly, most basic and universal need for raw materials, what does Earth have that other, easier planets lack? Well, obviously, there's life, but humans are a lot more trouble than they're worth. Enslaving humanity should be remarkably low in the list of reasons aliens have come calling.

Apart from the Daleks (2.2, "The Dalek Invasion of Earth"; "Day of the Daleks", both of which we'll come back to as they're deeply strange), the only

continued on page 185...

13.4 The Android Invasion

railways gearing the local economy to tourism, but now anywhere with a road was being treated as a photo-op. We've already seen the condescending, supposedly amusing way this was handled in "The Daemons" (8.5), a story that's never far from view when discussing this one. For a more realistic version, try *The League of Gentlemen*: an entire sitcom about how these places seem to anyone under ten.

The Central Office of Information, heirs to the Ministry, made several scary short films about what can go wrong if you wander around a farm without knowing how farms work and there was a set of guidelines, "The Country Code", for townies to follow. The CoI made films about that, too. And the terrible consequences of polishing a wooden floor and putting a rug on it. These were all on the same 16 mm stock as location filming for BBC dramas, using similar modish tricks such as freeze-frames and slow-motion for the horrifying car-crashes (often with the same cast and stunt crew). The entire style and content of the first two episodes was thus deeply familiar to casual viewers in 1975 Britain. Just as *The Omen* looks, to anyone from that background, like a montage of Public Information Films about the risks of raising spawn of Beelzebub as your own child, so "The Android Invasion" mainly seemed odd because it didn't have a voice over (someone familiar and authoritative, like Donald Pleasence or Patrick Troughton) asking "are you *sure* your friends aren't androids?"

It's not unknown for fictional astronauts to land up in a town looking oddly like their childhood home towns. Nine times out of ten, it'll be deserted until a familiar face shows up, unchanged. Roughly half the time there will be anomalous details. The daddy of that kind of story is Ray Bradbury and *The Silver Locusts / The Martian Chronicles* (pause here for anyone who endured Milton Subotsky's disco-era mini-series to adopt a spooky voice and say: *The chocolate pudding was drugged*). In this, all-American boys land on Mars and find it's just like Green Bluff, Illinois, because telepathic Martians don't want humans lowering the tone of the neighbourhood. Our Hero realises with his dying breath that the air on Mars is thinner than at home (the 1/3 gravity didn't occur to him because it's Bradbury; we're supposed to think it's an allegory and admire his use of adjectives). Being a cheap way to do SF on backlots, this became a regular storyline in American anthology shows.

[Can we pause here and get something clear? There's a tendency to cite *The Twilight Zone* as a "source" for a lot of the ideas used in *Doctor Who*, but it's not as simple as it seems. The 1959 series was shown on some ITV stations in 1963-4, but not completely. The first was Border Television, a small station serving – as the name suggests – the top of England and the bottom of Scotland, so not terribly lucrative and not making many series for the rest of the country. Shortly thereafter, the London-based ABC bought it as another summer filler for *Armchair Theatre* but seem only to have shown the first half dozen episodes before live coverage of the Tokyo Olympics took up that slot. This means that Terry Nation *could* have seen the pilot episode, "Where is Everyone?". So, notionally, the idea of an isolated astronaut reconstructing a deserted town from his memories *might* have come from there, but it's not a compelling resemblance. It's unlikely that anyone in the UK saw any later episode of *The Twilight Zone* before 1983, when BBC2 got it cheap. However, arch-rival *The Outer Limits* was shown in Granada and a few other ITV regions, so is more plausible as an inspiration for 60s / 70s *Doctor Who*.]

The other sort of fake village was the one used to train British soldiers (or agents) for duties overseas. In real life, a couple of villages were evacuated in World War II, converted by the War Office and maintained by the Ministry of Defence throughout the Cold War and beyond. Imber, on Salisbury Plain, is the most famous of these "temporary" evacuations (if you get a chance, see John Boorman's first film, *Catch Us If You Can* for this getting a rare moment on film, never mind the ostensible stars) and was expanded in the 70s to look like the Bogside in Belfast. There's also Tyneham on the coast of Dorset and a village in Norfolk that now resembles Afghanistan.

In all three, the Victorian churches have preservation orders on them, so they look quaintly rural when there's no shelling. The *Doctor Who* team used a purpose-built village near Sennybridge, in Powys, for X7.16, "The Time of the Doctor" as the Christmas village on Trenzalore. This one pre-dates World War II and was hardly kept secret, although what happens there is, for obvious reasons. The idea was revisited in X9.4, "Before the Flood", which foregrounded the sort of detail that might have been included in 1980. In fiction, the clearest example is in *The New Avengers* ("Target",

The Android Invasion 13.4

Why Does Earth Keep Getting Invaded?

...continued from page 183

significant attempt to use humans as forced labour as an end in itself is the Usurians in "The Sun Makers". Broadening the search to include *Torchwood* and *The Sarah Jane Adventures*, it's more often crashed alien spaceships or other misplaced objects that bring people (or people-oids) to our shores. It's remarkable for such objects to remain intact – but, compared to the statistically much more probable fate of falling into the Sun or Jupiter's thick methane atmosphere, it's marginally preferable. The presence of intelligent, inquisitive and acquisitive locals concentrates such *objets trouvés* in museums and secure facilities. Nonetheless, people are a nuisance if you're planning to strip-mine.

It's usual to hear that the invaders want this planet because it's "strategically important" or somesuch. That raises a lot of questions but is usefully vague. The logical assumption is that, as with human military planning, it's either a supply-route or a potential base of operations. One side wants it while another wants to get it first to stop them. However, while this solar system might be logistically handy, the choice of Earth out of all the available planets, moons, asteroids and other objects is odd. Unless the aliens are so exactly like humans that no other spot is congenial to them, it's really too much bother conquering an indigenous lifeform when near-enough places are so abundant.

Earth has several unusual features compared to the rest of the Solar System, but they are more likely marks in the "against" column than "for". The planet's density is a snag if you are landing and taking off regularly: for its size, Earth has a pretty stiff gravitational pull. Beings capable of crossing intergalactic space might scoff at such things, but if the margins are so tight as to make them appropriate this specific planet, it might be a cost. There's a thick atmosphere that rubs against anything making planetfall – shields are possible but are A) another energy-cost and B) a dead giveaway if you're trying to sneak around near a Level Five planet in a war.

It's a planet with two natural satellites (one of which we all see, the other is tiny) and thousands of man-made ones, raising the risk of collision and it being noticed if they abruptly went out of commission. If you're trying to stay off the radar (or equivalent) by coming in on the plane of the Ecliptic, there's a nasty asteroid belt. Quite honestly, unless you're from a planet exactly like Earth and hoping to romp around naked, you'd be better off with the moons of Jupiter. (And if you *are* from somewhere that much like Earth and can eat the food, your odds of catching something nasty jump through the roof. Any number of bacilli, viruses and airborne infections might afflict you, not just the ones that make humans or frogs sick.)

What, though, does any military power have to gain from sticking a base in the arse end of nowhere? Earth's about 2/3 of the way out on one of the spiral arms, so neither a border between this galaxy and others nor especially handy for anywhere else. All the juicy stars producing the useful stuff and about to explode and shower exotic elements are in towards the centre. The distance between stars starts to get greater once you're out in the sticks like us.

Possibly, the idea that nobody else lives nearby might be attractive, although we've got grounds to doubt this from 9.2, "The Curse of Peladon" and the presence of delegates from Mars, Alpha Centauri and Arcturus, plus one from Vega in the sequel (11.4, "The Monster of Peladon"). Add to this a fairly busy spacefaring society around Tau Ceti as recently as 3,000 years ago (16.3, "The Stones of Blood") and Earth looks like the only populated planet *not* currently home to a starfaring society in this section of the galaxy. (Except maybe those around Sirius, which get colonised by humans later so must be undesirable to all these others: 10.3, "Frontier in Space"; 21.6, "The Caves of Androzani"; X7.0, "The Doctor, the Widow and the Wardrobe").

Logically, all these powerful neighbours would make Earth almost the last place to put a base if you're fighting a war. The other point is, for a space-fleet, actual planets are less useful than safe stable berths. Trojan points or spots with gravitational equilibrium – such as the Lagrange points – would make more sense for mustering and refuelling. A solar system with one big planet and a small star would be better for this. Why invade Earth when you can drop anchor at Luhman 16b, just around the corner?

As real-estate, the main bonus seems to be Earth's mineral resources. Again, a lot of the ones aliens try to stake claims on are more common elsewhere. Silicon (19.2, "Four to Doomsday") is much easier to mine on Mars or the Moon. As Earth has been volcanically active for a while, there are odd combinations of elements, such as

continued on page 187...

185

13.4 The Android Invasion

shown after this but made around the same time) which, like many earlier versions of the idea, played with the way we're supposed to accept film sets as reality. (This one used a backlot at Pinewood that often posed as real towns; the police box that blows up when a booby-trapped pram hits is, however, not the same one in which Peter Cushing travelled to Skaro – A1, "Doctor Who and the Daleks"; A2, "Dalek Invasion Earth 2150 A.D.".)

A more pernicious idea of the mock-up town is in the Frederik Pohl story "Tunnel Under the World" (1954) adapted as an episode of *Out of the Unknown* in 1966. This has the *Groundhog Day* aspect of the Nation story, with every day being 15th June and only one person noticing, but it turns out to be a test-bed for advertisers and literally a table-top model. The protagonist, a miniature android, has a faulty reset button. Nation also wrote for this series: another episode was "Andover and the Android".

That kind of television fairly commonly used the word "Android", to the extent that even *The Goodies* had nonchalantly tossed it around in the episode with Patrick Troughton (TX 14th January 1972) that this story closely resembles. Jack Williamson (who also coined the term "genetic engineering") had brought the word into popular use in 1936 to differentiate human-looking creations from robots that looked like petrol-pumps or whatever, but it had been kicking around since the Enlightenment, the heyday of automata (see X2.4, "The Girl in the Fireplace"). It crops up a lot in *Star Trek,* to the embarrassment of anyone coming to the original after seven years of Lt Cmr Data. It's safe to say that the bulk of *Doctor Who*'s target audience knew what the word meant and guessed the big plot twist as quickly as working out what the "them" referred to in the first episode of any Nation story with "Dalek" in the title. Nonetheless, the Doctor gets a line in the Village Store scene to explain it to their parents.

Now that we're back to android duplicates, we ought to mention *The Stepford Wives* – but, as the film didn't open in the UK until 1978, it's only tangentially relevant. The book had been talked-about, though, as it confirmed a lot of British ideas about America. We sort-of knew it before it had been written and the film took off in the UK much more than it initially did in the US. (Director Bryan Forbes applied an outsiders' view of New England and thus delineated just such an insular community as we were discussing a moment ago, albeit one that seemed normal to most Americans.) There isn't a face-removal scene in the actual film, just the poster. The face-off is, however, a key moment in the original *Westworld* from 1973 (and that film's poster) and the use of androids to replace key figures was the plot of the less-fondly-recalled sequel, *Futureworld,* in 1976. However, we got the imagery second-hand via *The Six Million Dollar Man.* Once a year, the evil Dr Dolenz announced that he'd fixed whatever glitch or giveaway wrecked his last scheme for Total World Domination via Fembots, only for Steve Austin (and / or Jaime Sommers) to find a new one. Apart from the obvious shibboleths, these include exploding when trying to digest food and what became a regular lead into advert breaks, the face falling off just like Sarahbot's does at the end of Part Two here, revealing circuitry.

Which brings us to the key point, something we ought to mention more in these pieces: most of the time, *Doctor Who* is under orders to respond to whatever else is on telly at the time. At any given moment, the Head of Series is looking at what the people paying the Licence Fee are watching on ITV or at the cinema, or what the BBC's paying to import from America, Australia or Europe, and saying "do that but cheaper". It's as true of Steven Moffat looking enviously at Christopher Nolan films or Russell T. Davies filling a *Buffy*-shaped hole as it was for Innes Lloyd making 60s London almost the only place the TARDIS could land after three years of space-age costume dramas. Such abrupt shifts in role-model often mean there's a wrenching handbrake-turn on screen (3.10, "The War Machines"; 7.1, "Spearhead from Space"; 10.2, "Carnival of Monsters" and "The Ark in Space" so far, lots more to come) and then a testing of how far they can go in this new direction (4.8, "The Faceless Ones"; "The Ambassadors of Death"; 11.1, "The Time Warrior" and "Genesis of the Daleks" as outliers each case). Then the letters start coming in from people who want the same-old-same-old and the production team tries to wring the last drops out of the old format and sometimes (4.6, "The Moonbase") it comes off, but often ("Invasion of the Dinosaurs"; "Planet of the Spiders") it's a curate's egg and in this instance, as with "The Seeds of Doom", putting Tom Baker in a Pertwee-era story seems almost like a rebuke to people who wanted to regress.

Why Does Earth Keep Getting Invaded?

...continued from page 185

quartz (16.2, "The Pirate Planet"), but that shows up in asteroids too. Making it without volcanoes and centuries would be simple for anyone who could zoom between planets. Methane (X1.1, "Rose") is ludicrously abundant in the gas-giants (see again "The Invisible Enemy"; more recent probes to Titan indicate that this would be a more convenient fuel-stop than people thought in 1977). Moreover, there are vast clouds of it in interstellar space.

The one idea in cheesy media space-opera that *Doctor Who* has reserved as a throwaway was aliens wanting water (X1.5, "World War Three") as most notoriously expounded in *V: The Mini-Series*. Apart from those Jovian moons and Saturn's rings, how about the Kuiper Belt or the Oort Cloud – three billion comets milling about a third of a light year from the sun with nobody that we know of to say no. (If recent *Doctor Who* yarns featuring the Ice Warriors had paid as much attention to what's known now as Brian Hayles did in 1967, not only could we have avoided acute embarrassment – X7.9, "Cold War"; X10.9, "The Empress of Mars" – but we'd have a way to resolve continuity problems from the Troughton and Pertwee stories by having the exiled Martians sleep away millennia at the farthest edge of the solar system.)

One unique resource we have is mud. Soil with up to 25% bacteria is essential if you're planning to grow crops, and takes centuries to make from scratch by conventional methods. So far, nobody's come to steal our topsoil or asked to be paid in mud as a form of danegeld. It's very odd, when you consider that we named the planet after it. They don't even come with writs claiming legal title to DNA patents for things like oak trees, diphtheria or fingernails.

Evidently, beings who come armed and in force have little concern about the Shadow Proclamation or other intelligent species who might also want Earth. Even the sneaky ones who try tricking humans with consumer goods and hypnosis act as if they are the only ones currently in the market for this planet. Nobody seems to notice brief visits – either tourists (24.3, "Delta and the Bannermen"; X4.0, "Voyage of the Damned") or collectors (18.2, "Meglos"; 10.2, "Carnival of Monsters"; "Four to Doomsday"). Invasion might not actually be the most profitable or useful thing aliens could do with Earth.

Another advantage Earth has over a lot of other worlds: a magnetic field traps a lot of the solar radiation. Admittedly, this was a snag for the Daleks, but that raises the obvious question of why they bothered coming to Earth instead of so many more useful rocky planets nearby. They bust a gut weakening humanity's defences rather than, as one might expect, exterminating the species outright. Maybe they get off on humiliating anything that looks like a Thal, but that's militarily absurd when there's so much to lose from coming to the worst planet possible to turn into an aircraft-carrier. Other putative invaders might find this to be an advantage, though, so let's not discount it. For the Kraals, the lack of radiation was a definite plus. With solar flares such an issue in *Doctor Who*, the presence of a viable magnetosphere could well be the most attractive feature of our planet, and the reason so many species go to so much effort to invade by stealth.

The other odd thing about that Dalek plan, and this isn't something anyone would have foreseen in 1964, is that having dense rocky planets so close to the star is a lot less common than the other way around. Apparently, it's an atypical solar system (see **Why Are Elements So Weird in Space?** under 22.2, "Vengeance on Varos"). The remarkable success of the search for exoplanets has, in under 30 years, produced over 3,000 planet-bearing stars in our neck of the woods, nearly 500 of which have more than one confirmed planet.

Worlds as small and dense as ours are the hardest to spot using the techniques available, skewing the results in favour of things like Jupiter or Saturn (but bigger) but, oddly, the majority of these are in close orbits around the star rather than exiled to the depths. This has messed with both the accepted theory of planetary development and the assumption of our system as bog-standard, and therefore a good model from which to extrapolate. If you went to school more than 20 years ago, anything you learned on this topic is doubtful. Earth may be a humdrum planet, but this solar system is weird.

Luckily, it's weird in a way that reinforces a wild speculation we made in the first version of this essay in 2004. There's still room for debate, but it appears that Jupiter is the mysterious factor that made our solar system the way it is, hurling smaller bodies inward toward the sun and flinging the other gas giants out. Other big planets in other

continued on page 189...

13.4 The Android Invasion

We'd already had a story subverting the UNIT "family", with Mike Yates working for the baddies, the Brigadier giving orders to shoot the Doctor on sight and a deserted London used for a hide-and-seek with soldiers. In many ways, "Invasion of the Dinosaurs" was itself a re-tread of "Inferno" (7.4), so trying it again – right down to the eyepatch – would only have worked with something so new as to make older viewers (i.e., those over 11 when it was shown, so too young to recall Evil Parallel Benton first time around) forgive the repetition.

Because, when it comes down to it, most of this is a blend of Terry Nation's Greatest Hits. Philip Hinchcliffe's Scenes We Would Like to See and Barry Letts's Favourite UNIT Riffs. Thereafter, Hinchcliffe could, with a clear conscience, tell prospective writers who sent in a generic script like this or "The Seeds of Doom" that they'd just done something very like that, whatever "that" was.

English Lessons

• *Ginger Pop / Beer* (n.): there are two terms and two broadly similar drinks, but not an exact match. You get the fermented yeast-and-ginger thing brewed by people in summer with self-replicating balls of slime (which can be split up and given away to friends) and commercial stuff in bottles or cans. The latter is even less alcoholic than the properly-diluted home-brew (the stuff the *Famous Five* supposedly drank "lashings" of), but tastes more ginger than beer. Jamaica makes the best of these, but the ones used as mixers with rum or whatever can be drunk neat, as the Doctor does in the pub. The stuff he's carrying with him is more likely someone's domestic version. (See also X4.7, "The Unicorn and the Wasp".) Which you call "pop" and which you call "ginger beer" is as much regional as anything. ("Pop" is the all-purpose onomatopoeia for fizzy drinks in the entire English-speaking world – except bits of the US where, for some reason, they call them "soda". Everyone else thinks "soda" is what you use to get rid of funny smells in the fridge. In the 70s, these drinks were also called "mineral water" and sometimes just "minerals", bewilderingly to many.)

• *Devesham* (n.): as it's a Barry Letts story as much as anyone's, the habitual use of a real-life town with one syllable or letter changed is back. Just as with "Tarminster" (8.1, "Terror of the Autons"), clearly meant to suggest "Warminster", "University of Wessex" and "Minsbridge" (10.1, "The Three Doctors") hinting at "Essex" and "Slimbridge" and "Stangmoor" Prison hinting at either Dartmoor or Broadmoor, so "Devesham" is, in most regards, supposed to suggest "Evesham". That's in Gloucestershire, so on a train-line from Paddington if you start from London towards Wales. (We'll look at the real-life geography of Gloucestershire when we get onto "Leadworth", home of Amy and Rory, in Volume 10.)

• *Nanas* (n.): chumps, charlies etc. It's baby-talk for "bananas" in the traditional Music Hall pronunciation ('ave a banaaaaanah).

• *Horse Brass* (n.): a late-Victorian affectation used on the dray horses (usually Shires) that pulled the wagons with the beer-barrels. They got hung in pubs as a sign of "authenticity" from around the time US servicemen were billeted in English villages (so are as "traditional" as a ploughman's lunch). But they were, at least, brass.

• *Palais* (n.): a popular name for a dance-hall from the 1920s – as in *Come Dancing* by The Kinks – but the most famous was in Hammersmith and had different types of dance-music on offer at different times. You may know about The Clash celebrating the reggae explosion of that era, but in context and with the way Mr Benton's talking about "going dancing", it's probably the venue's association with formation dancing that's being evoked. Ballroom dancing was popular with older people even as Punk happened – *Come Dancing* (the 1950s TV ballroom competition) continued on BBC1 into the 90s – but Benton's "kid sister" would already have been in a competition team, if that's the sort of dance he means. (As with "Planet of the Spiders", Letts seems to think that popular culture and entertainment in Britain haven't changed since 1956.) It could be any Palais in Britain, but with Sarah talking about getting a taxi from Devesham to South Croydon, it seems that people thought this story was set somewhere close to London.

• *Chinese Takeaway* (n.): classic 1970s fast-food. There had been sit-down Chinese restaurants since the 1920s, but the Long March in 1949 led to a lot of Hong Kong residents with UK passports joining established communities in Britain's ports and then the rest of the nation, sometimes adapting pre-existing chip shops to do food to go. The language barrier was, initially, eased by printed menus with the set dishes numbered. These were often by bus stops (like all the best order-and-go establishments), so were handy (and well-lit)

Why Does Earth Keep Getting Invaded?

...continued from page 187

solar systems are close to their stars and in groups of two or three; some are up to a dozen times the mass of Jupiter (after that it's not really a planet any more, but a dwarf star). Jupiter's significantly more massive than anything else – except the sun – but it and the other three gas giants are out in the chilly murk beyond the asteroid belt.

Combining models of planetary formation with the observed exoplanets makes it seem that something unusual happened four or five billion years back. (The most accurate computer model, i.e. the one that lands up producing something like what we've got, needs a fifth gas giant to come out exactly, something at least the size of Neptune. If it ever existed, it's probably way, way out beyond Pluto, which was found when people went looking for something bigger. See "Silver Nemesis".) The Nice Model (named after the town in France, like the coconut biscuits) attributes the current configuration of planets to a lot of swapping. Jupiter, it seems, started out close to the sun, but then somehow planets started playing Carrom. Theoretically, it might have absorbed the other big planets and become a huge one like those we know are there because they make their suns wobble. For some reason, it didn't.

There's a lot of comfort for old-school *Doctor Who* fans in the Nice Model, as it allows exciting space-opera speculations back into the district of proper science after decades of sneering. Patrick Moore (notably X5.1, "The Eleventh Hour") declined an offer to write for the series when Innes Lloyd pitched him the idea that became "The Tenth Planet" (4.2). It was, he said, scientifically preposterous that a world could fly out of the solar system, let alone an inhabited one. Well, habitable or not, extrasolar and even extragalactic planets are back on the table. So are lots of wild and exciting other types of planet that would have been dismissed as comic-book crap even in the 90s (see X4.10, "Midnight").

But the idea we floated in 2004, based on stray comments in "The Android Invasion", "Revenge of the Cybermen" and the "Remembrance of the Daleks" novelisation, was that Jupiter seemed to be host to some kind of spacetime anomaly that made this system easily accessible from long distances. It was speculated that Jupiter was as big as a planet could get before becoming a star, but lots of super-Jupiters exist in close proximity to their parent suns. Again, present observations are far from complete, but anything Jupiter-sized would make a detectable wobble in its sun's orbit and, so far, there are lots of planets smaller than that, quite a few significantly bigger but none the same mass. (There *are* failed stars called Brown Dwarves that have more mass but the same diameter, plus such peculiar properties that anything living on a planet nearby would be bizarre indeed.)

If Earth's main appeal is that it's handy for the commuter rail, so to speak, why did the Alliance of Shades withdraw and leave it all to UNIT? Did the anomaly just stop one day? This is more plausible given Torchwood 3's odd behaviour: patrolling Cardiff for strays then just shutting the time-rift (somehow) when Jack's ex and kid brother destroy the city (again). Time-rifts seem to be mobile ("The Unquiet Dead" is set about two miles from the Torchwood Hub) and finite. However, the existence of a hyperspace bypass near Earth illuminates another series-cliché.

It's looking as if Earth's big asset is easy access via some Jovian time-rift. Location, location, location. If this isn't the case, it's a lot more puzzling than it used to be. If access to Jupiter's what matters, the Jovian moons might be a better bet, but that very accessibility rather negates everything we heard about this system being nowheresville and a good place to hide powerful artefacts.

A weird thought arises: what if, with the Shadow Proclamation watching Earth and the Doctor notoriously protective of the planet, the sheer impracticality of conquering us is the appeal? What if it's some kind of status-symbol or cultural initiation-rite, like killing a bear/ lion/ pike to be a tribal warrior, or an agreed goal that nobody's done yet, like running the four-minute mile was or making a supersonic car is now? The Sontarans in Series 13 were keen to attack Earth to settle old scores about Linx (11.1, "The Time Warrior") as much as to eat chocolate or ride horses. The opportunity came when Tecteun made Earth the focus for the Flux for reasons of her own. There, a contingency plan involving billions of Lupari ships was dusted off, so evidently someone had their eye on Earth from way back. (X13.1, "The Halloween Apocalypse" alerted the Lupari – apparently, previous calamities weren't on their radar, possibly a Bad Wolf thing.) If the eyes of the cosmos are on us, that could be why so many species with the ability to overwhelm any other world go through such absurd rigmarole and invent soft drinks, car-exhaust filters, fake package holidays and rubbish snowmen. It's an initiative test. Conquer Earth and the rest of the galaxy will take you seriously.

13.4 The Android Invasion

places to meet after dark.

- *Rhubarb and Custards* (n.): The jar of sweets next to the scale when robo-Sarah emerges from hiding are instantly recognisable to any 70s kid. Traditionally, rhubarb is served stewed and is too tart to eat alone, so comes with custard. By "custard", we mean what the French call *crème anglais*, made with cornflour and milk rather than eggs (see X5.1, "The Eleventh Hour" et seq. ad nauseam). This sweet-and-sour school dinner classic was also available in confectionery form. Not all sweets sold in quarter-pound bags were boiled sugar (consider Jelly Babies and Liquorice Allsorts), but a lot were. Rhubarb and Custard was such an obvious combination that the cartoon *Roobarb* (which started about this time) inevitably had a dog of that name and a cat called "Custard". By the way, the white lenticular objects on the shelf to Sarah's right, at the back of the shop beside the Milk Tray boxes, are Liquorice Torpedoes.

- *Village Store* (n.): We checked; the dialogue says "store". It's an oddly American term for Sarah to use (even if we're correct in our conjecture that the real Sarah thought very hard about her android double making mistakes). Note that the shop has got a post-box built into the exterior wall: the majority of shops in villages like this were the local post-office. Selling newspapers, sweets, tobacco and groceries was a side-line. According to popular memory, they all had faded jigsaw-puzzle boxes in the window, unsold for decades. Thus, for people in 60s-70s Britain, the term "post office" covered this sort of shop as well as the Post Office Tower (3.10, "The War Machines"), an avant-garde film-unit and prototypes of cable television and the internet. Oh, and they ran the entire phone service (2.1, "Planet of Giants").

Things That Don't Make Sense (Conventional) Never mind that this story's version of spaceflight contradicts not just any BBC Wales story (including *The Sarah Jane Adventures*) and all other UNIT stories except "The Ambassadors of Death" (see **Was There a Martian Time-Slip?** under X4.16, "The Waters of Mars"), it isn't even consistent with itself. Sarah covered Guy Crayford's disappearance "two years ago"; Crayford expects that everyone on Earth with a telescope will fixate on his return. So far, so good, but then we get to Mission Control Mummerset and… no press corps, no journalists other than Sarah (so alone, she can walk into the capsule un-noticed by any UNIT personnel, android or real), no television news-readers, no photographers, not a sausage. It's bizarre, considering that a vagrant found near a meteorite needed a press-conference (7.1, "Spearhead from Space") and John Wakefield was embedded at the previous interplanetary manned mission base ("Ambassadors").

The Kraal androids are so remarkable, one bleeds when its face is scratched and can sup ale. Shame about the faces falling off after a light tap.

We discussed problems with the "two years" date in **History** and **Where Does This Come From?**, but Crayford vanished en route to Jupiter, probably colliding with an asteroid. Even with the British Rocket Group's magical spaceship engines, it would take two years to get that far anyway. So if he disappeared "two years ago", he's actually been gone four years; all of the shop products should be well past the sell-by dates (even for a rural post-office). Never mind that he can stand up after a supposed four-year stint in microgravity (about three times longer than anyone's managed, to date: current record-holder Valeri Polyakov needed six months in hospital afterwards rather than just Harry Sullivan hitting his knee with a hammer or whatever – and Polyakov was himself a doctor). [Quick aside: as we discussed in **How Plausible is a British Space Programme?** under "The Ambassadors of Death", the main thing either story needs that we don't currently have is expertise in anti-radiation treatment for prolonged space-flights. Isn't that something Crayford has in his brain – and bloodstream – that's of more immediate practical use to the Kraals?]

This, of course, brings us to the, er, glaring problem that *everybody* notices: Crayford apparently has not, in two to four whole years, looked under his eyepatch and discovered that his "missing" eyeball was still there. Nor does anybody ask him "what happened to your eye?" (Perhaps they're too polite: it's the *Ridiculously*-British Rocket Group. Certainly nobody in the cast could figure out what that aspect of the plot was about; if the interviews are any guide, everyone thought someone else understood it.) His obliviousness about this raises all sorts of red flags about how he washed himself, shaved and so on – indeed, it throws up a lot more questions than his spending years on a radioactive planet of rhino-men in chain-mail, and building a village with a sweet-shop but no children – but it also gets us into topics best not explored in a family show. Let's just accept the presence of a small and very specific Perception Filter, one that didn't affect the bits of his brain they needed for their giant Hornby model railway.

Why is there a landing-pod in the fake village's surroundings? Are they testing how well androids react to discovering that androids are planning to invade? Why is there a tyre next to it, except when there isn't, and a car-seat, except when there isn't?

That virus is so pathetic it doesn't infect people in the same room – but kills Styggron on contact. (Did he devise a plague that works on his own species but not humans? Keep reading.) The one chance he has to test it on a human results in… Sarah being perfectly fit and well next time he sees her. Ought this not to have caused a rethink? The android of Corporal Adams is malfunctioning but doesn't even do that consistently. In one scene, he's hiding quietly in the woods until the Doctor and Sarah pass, then he goes off for a quick limp and twitches his way off a cliff. The "mechanics" fix him and bring him back to the pub in time for 6.00pm, but this glitch isn't explained and Styggron doesn't ever comment on the potential flaw or its impact on Chedaki's strict timetable.

The Kraal ship is such cheap rubbish, its main exit hatch has a serrated edge, meaning it can never be an airtight seal. Plus it's usually left open, presumably allowing the background radiation on Oseidon to get in. Worse, the controls seem deliberately made as cumbersome as possible and even a simple thing like a drinking-glass is all knobbly and awkward… even though there are no alien claw-like hands to justify this. And somehow, they hid it inside a privet hedge.

Sarah ambles up the gantry of a spaceship that's just arrived back on Earth, which tend to be pretty hot. How much fuel did it take to launch this rocket, considering that there's a control module and a separate living area the size of a bungalow? Then again, if it landed on a gantry with that much precision, there must have been retrorockets and a lot of fuel on board during re-entry. And Crayford no longer has any depth-perception – another way that the business with the eyepatch is just adding risks to an already dicey plan.) She also seriously believes she can get a taxi from Devesham to South Croydon; does she have a substantial sum on her person? There aren't any ATM's in Britain at all, and certainly none out in Pigbinshire.

Isn't the fact that it's still broad daylight something like six hours after the pub clock struck 6.00pm a bit of a giveaway that this isn't England? One of the robots left on "pause" pending the abrupt start of "normality" at 6.00pm audibly clears its throat in the silence. We never get an explanation of why everything is quiet until the clock chimes six.

How many times is the Doctor shot? Crayford seems to achieve a direct hit at point-blank range, then Adams looses a few more rounds into the Doctor's back. At the start of Part Three, robo-Sarah adds another five bullets. Real Sarah's experience of being mind-probed somehow cures her wrenched ankle, and also (presumably) her being shot nearly a dozen times.

And… why *does* the TARDIS land there, and then relocate to the identical spot on the real Earth? Does the Ship really navigate by sight? If she wishes to give the Doctor a bit of excitement by alerting him to an invasion of his *pied à terre*, why vanish as soon as Sarah pops the key in the door?

Things That *Really* Don't Make Sense How did this plan get green-lit? We can't avoid it any more: this is an invasion force of precisely three aliens. And they've chosen the most cumbersome and obvious method of infiltration we've seen so far (except the Loch Ness Monster, which the Zygons *intentionally* used for maximum publicity).

The plan is to send a flurry of "meteorites" down at exactly the place and time as Guy Crayford's long-awaited return, so that every radar rig (and every conventional telescope on Earth, Crayford believes) will be pointed at his part of the sky. Then a Space Defence base, staffed by the most experienced invasion-stoppers and alien-spotters around, will be infiltrated by a pub's regulars (students, farmers and a grumpy landlord) as a prelude to releasing an untested virus. The simple fact that a Space Defence complex exists in England – unlike anything in real life, even if you count the semi-mythical Area 51 (A7, "Dreamland"; X5.2, "Day of the Moon") indicates that the locals have some form on this. Among the professional space-watchers, the arrival of a swarm of meteorites that change direction would probably trigger a lockdown.

As with Styre ("The Sontaran Experiment"), Davros ("Genesis of the Daleks") and, to a lesser extent, Vorus ("Revenge of the Cybermen"), we have a scientist with his own pet-project using the

13.4 The Android Invasion

military funding to sate his own curiosity. When the Doctor arrives, the justification of "science" and "testing our defences" allows a whole extra episode of self-indulgent tricks, including letting robo-Sarah spill the beans just to see how the Doctor reacts. (Unless the real Sarah, maybe, created these daft reactions for her android duplicate by thinking really hard while being mind-probed.)

Styggron's motive in Part Two seems to be, quite simply, that he loves his toy village and wants to play with it for as long as the military will let him. As soon as Chedaki starts asking why they've spent so much time and resources on the androids and the model village, suddenly Styggron presents the virus. Not a terribly sensible way to behave, when your planet is doomed and your species faces extinction.

Making the most charitable assumption possible: if Oseidon is close enough to get our television a few years out of date, we could rationalise a lot of Styggron's loopy behaviour if we assume that Chedaki is a big fan of Department S, The Prisoner and The Avengers, and his heart is set on doing a 60s ITC Adventure-style invasion of England (fake village, lookalikes, attacking a remote and picturesque spot rather than, say, knocking out early-warning radar). Styggron, knowing his virus is a better bet and far more cost-effective, humours him. For some reason, the Kraals were around to ensnare a passing astronaut en route to Jupiter, but they didn't monitor television broadcasts to get the gen on English villages and how dogs work. Did they have someone waiting for a specific astronaut or was this pure luck when they were in the Solar System house-hunting? The odds on them simply stumbling upon an English astronaut in that neck of the woods are too absurd to count, so we have to assume that they already knew that Earth was a likely prospect and had a space programme that advanced when the Daily Express was still a broadsheet. Why was Crayford picked if they had info already? His main contribution seems to have been the (anomalous) smell of England just after a shower.

If we're trying to salvage the plan as presented, this comes very close to working *except* that no reason exists to have humanoid robots in spacesuits wandering around a village pointing exploding fingers at strangers. They aren't in Crayford's memory, and an invasion-force isn't likely to encounter them. They remain a glaring anomaly only useful if, against all odds, a passing humanoid time traveller pops in unannounced. And the entire village is wired up for CCTV *as well as* all the cameras fitted inside the androids themselves. Which are rarely used – Styggron prefers to break cover and yell over the intercom for Crayford to deliver info-dumps or gets hands-on and peeks out from behind secret panels. These supermarket own-brand Autons aren't even the only robots to function when the rest of the village is "asleep".

An alternative, floated in X10.6, "Extremis", is that, for once, an alien invasion-force has decided to road-test their fiendish plan and iron out snags *before* it matters. The whole "infiltrate and kill" thing is androids reverting to type (because that's what androids do in Doctor Who), but the real reason for Styggron to build Lego Village is to test Crayford's utility as Typhoid Mary. Except, they don't inoculate him. And he's unlikely to go into the village after landing. (The pub landlord, Morgan, tells the Doctor that nobody from the Space Defence Centre ever goes into the village, except on Darts night. So why isn't Crayford's memory of the Fleur de Lis filled with scientists and UNIT troops playing darts?)

The trouble with using Crayford's mind as the source of possible unexpected snags is that, by definition, they aren't unexpected. It's especially daft when, against the odds, they capture Sarah, but *don't* feed her data into the plan. (Certainly, they sift her brain-scan fast enough for Chedaki to warn that the Doctor's got previous, and that more usable planets exist with less-experienced anti-alien task forces.) Given that, as we've just seen, a lot of Crayford's data appears to be what he expects rather than what he knows, isn't having external confirmation or asseveration handy?

This brings us to the fuzzy thinking behind the androids themselves. In some scenes, they are entirely run from Styggron's desktop, like a real-life Sims game. In others, the androids seem programmed from "birth" and react for themselves in real-time, in-character – presumably the whole reason for building an entire village for them to learn *in*. Each and every one was made by Crayford getting his brain probed in Top of the Pops style (even the rottweilers?). If Crayford's input into individual androids was at all necessary, what use is the village? If Crayford was pumped for information on what Earth's like, why not hardwire it into the androids and skip the "training"?

This highlights another odd aspect: for all the

years of training and rehearsal that went into the model, the actual invasion "plan" seems almost to be improv. Chedaki (credited as "Marshal", but not in the dialogue) doesn't know about the virus, the DM bombs or even the anti-android gun. Unlike Styggron, he seems to be a last-minute inspector from the Oseidon Ministry of Defence rather than warlord of a fearsome military machine.

Sometimes Crayford or Styggron can send out a command that the Doctor and Sarah can't hear and, in one peculiar incident, Bentonbot reacts by keeling over rather than blinking and droning "I obey" or whatever the sensible thing to do would be. But at other times, the orders go out over the PA, enabling the people being chased to hear orders given about them. The untested virus on which this all hinges is finally given a workout and – apparently – fails, but the launch-window is so tight that they must leave within minutes and Styggron doesn't even look in on Sarah to see if she's dead / escaped / bored. He just plonks her on a bench, not even handcuffed, and explains the plot to Chedaki, leaving her to escape and complicate matters for her duplicate.

It almost seems as if they are trying to future-proof their plan to allow for their information being a bit out of date when they arrive. Almost. As luck would have it, they guess correctly that Benton was promoted to RSM (sad, because Nation wrote him in as "Sergeant Benton" and Holmes went and fixed it), that Cadbury's would change the packaging for Milk Tray to *that specific design*, that the Brigadier would be in Geneva on 5th and 6th July and that McEwan's Export (hitherto a regional brew within Britain) would become nationally popular between 1974 and 1978 after a new brewery complex was opened in 1973. And yet, the way calendars work, the tendency of coins to grow dull and worn and the idea that you pay for things in pubs somehow eluded Styggron's brain-reader.

One last thing… is Chedaki still in orbit waiting for Styggron's report?

Critique To the extent that a tale about androids infiltrating the bucolic Mission Control of a British ship to Jupiter launched before pocket calculators went on sale can be called "banal", this is. It looks like a story from a World Distributors annual they accidentally commissioned as a script, although it has nice half-timbered houses in between the ugly spaceship interiors. (They're at least *uniquely* ugly.)

You'll remember that we praised "Robot" for daring to be a gaudy pastiche of Steed and Mrs Peel saving the world (i.e., England) from humourless nerds. That was because it was a combination of the usual elements of present-day adventures that they'd not tried before. We can't really say the same for this mix of space-monsters and "picturesque English village gone wrong". With the possible exception of "Revenge of the Cybermen", each Tom Baker story so far has stretched the series's parameters in one way or another, but this one's a slump back into the clapped-out formula of British Space Programme, ballroom dancing and bad CSO.

This effort to put a genie back into a bottle has a certain perverse charm; "The Daemons" (8.5) didn't have Baker ad-libbing his way through otherwise routine filler scenes. It looks better than a lot of the yeti-in-the-loo tales simply because of the locations. Above all, they have the advantage of film locations we've not seen before, and a summer shoot rather than the dismal early spring of "Terror of the Zygons" (and all colour stories hitherto).

Absurdly, because of the same change in broadcast and recording schedule, we're now halfway through Philip Hinchcliffe's three seasons as producer and it's still 1975. It's a measure of how far *Doctor Who* has evolved in under a calendar year that this story seemed so retro at the time and more of a period-piece than any other Tom Baker story. For viewers under ten, it was fresh because "The Time Monster" (9.5) was about the last time they tried this mix and that wandered off to Atlantis after a fairly perfunctory battle between UNIT and Roundheads. The Autons were ancient history for much of the target audience. Space-suits without humans inside were, at best, a few tantalising photos in the 1973 *Radio Times* Special (of unused effects from "The Ambassadors of Death") and were deemed to be ridiculous rather than intrinsically scary.

The absurdities of the Terry Nation Set-Pieces have never been so starkly revealed and, rather than spout clichés and non-sequiturs with grim determination (as with, say, 11.3, "Death to the Daleks"), the cast seem to be working overtime trying to make it all work with charm and conviction. Here's where casting Milton Johns as Guy Crayford pays off. Ludicrous as it seems in principle, he is exactly right for the self-deluding, sycophantic and grievously wronged astronaut where the bland space-blokes of "Ambassadors"

13.4 The Android Invasion

wouldn't have been. Nation obviously wrote with people like that in mind but could any of them have come as close to pulling off that daft eyepatch subplot? Similarly, and in keeping with Nation's stint in the dying throes of *The Avengers*, Patrick Newell (Colonel Faraday) is dropped into a Brigadier-shaped hole and plays it almost like he played Mother. Apart from reminding us all how good Nicholas Courtney is, it shows up the inherent silliness of the premise that someone with no idea about the Doctor or various previous invaders is overseeing security.

However, where this story comes good is the non-plotty scenes of pure creepy mood and anomalies. There's no reason *at all* for that scene of the pub almost literally coming to life on the stroke of six, but those scenes strike a chord with anyone who's walked into a shop or pub in a rural settlement and felt the temperature drop when a stranger arrives. We never find out why there's an alien landing-pod on the outskirts of a picture-postcard village. There's little logic to the various mistakes the Doctor and Sarah find (at least, within the terms of the offered explanation: in a computer game these things would make a sort of sense, like text adventures where only certain objects are usable). These scenes give a mood and *frisson* of almost-right-ness (like the Uncanny Valley for places rather than faces) that have no bearing on the ostensible plot (either Nation's or Styggron's). Abruptly reverting to duplicates on the prowl – re-using the "Who's Who" joke from "The Chase" (2.8) for heaven's sake – inside a government facility seems to let the air out. Just like it did at the end of "Zygons", oddly enough.

The really silly thing is the idea that abruptly reverting to how *Doctor Who* worked five years before, when warmed-over *Quatermass* disguised as an ITC series was the only game in town, constituted a return to "normal". Hindsight tells us they were misguided and that "normal" now was "Pyramids of Mars". The ratings and AIs indicate that the viewing public were perfectly happy with this story, if not excited. For a lot of casual viewers, just seeing The New Doctor Who let loose in a picturesque village with odd aliens and familiar faces was enough (see also X5.1, "The Eleventh Hour").

In some ways, it still is – especially as a time-capsule. The hardcore *aficionados* may have spotted how much of the story they'd seen before (or, this being the mid-70s, had read Target book versions of recently) and found it wanting when compared to the last time Harry Sullivan was replicated, a few weeks before, but what makes this over-familiar and nonsensical story watchable is we have two leads trying their damnedest to make it fresh, and a director who knows exactly what he's doing. We might not agree that it's worth doing, but he's put his stamp on it and saved us from a worse waste of four episodes.

There are robot rottweilers. This story is fractally stupid, getting more so as one examines the tiny details that themselves have idiotic consequences. Androids with "hostility circuits", spaceships landing in Devesham with no press coverage or complaints from the pub darts team, plastic trees that smell of damp earth, that same Apollo launch footage from "Revenge of the Cybermen"... it's all there to accept or ridicule as you see fit. This is the price you pay for having odd combinations of ideas, which is usually where the series shines.

If nothing else, respect to Nation for at least trying something other than Daleks – last time was the hubris-adjacent "The Keys of Marinus". After the response to "Genesis", it would have been tempting to strike while the iron was hot and deliver the same again. Had Letts been equally as keen to step out of his comfort-zone, this story might have been special. Today's hardcore *aficionados* have all of that lore and a detailed knowledge of other stories Letts directed or produced and can spot little touches, not least casting Dave Carter in a role that gets more than three lines for once. They might have meagre fun ticking off the familiar Nation set-pieces as they arise. That sense of a repertory company and everyone doing what they do best might be cosy, but the days when that was enough to make a story function had gone.

Realistically, they were flogging a dead horse trying to do this after "The Green Death" (10.5), but by now this type of story was so outdated it almost seemed fresh compared to the stories on either side of it. Any type of story was now one colour in the palate and variety – switching between Horror-movie retreads, space opera and this sort of thing – was what the public wanted. It was, on balance, worth dancing this dance once more just to see what sunshine, Oxfordshire and Tom Baker add to the mix, then dropping it and doing something else.

The Android Invasion 13.4

The Facts

Written by Terry Nation. Directed by Barry Letts. Viewing figures: 11.9 million, 11.3 million, 12.1 million, 11.4 million. (Part Four went out ten minutes later than the others; there seems to be nothing different about ITV scheduling on 6th December compared to the Saturdays before or after.) AI's 58% for Part One.

Working Titles "The Enemy Within" (arguably the most frequent almost-used title ever and perhaps a different story); "The Kraals".

Cliffhangers The intercom on the wall hinges back to reveal alien eyes watching the Doctor and Sarah; Sarah turns out to be a robot; the g-force in Crayford's palatal capsule threatens to crush the Doctor and Sarah.

What Was In the Charts? "Space Oddity", David Bowie (yes, really: the reissue got to Number One that month[35]); "In Dulce Jubilo", Mike Oldfield; "I Believe in Father Christmas", Greg Lake; "All Around My Hat", Steeleye Span.

The Lore

Terry Nation's agent, Roger Hancock, had negotiated an informal-but-binding arrangement for Nation to write a Dalek story once a year. However, with "Genesis of the Daleks" raising the bar somewhat and *Survivors* reminding the BBC hierarchy that he had other strings to his bow, Nation proposed doing something else. He sent in ideas called "Return to Suknan" and "The Enemy Within" (sometimes cited as a working title for the one eventually made), but an idea about a training-ground for alien invaders was picked up. He had script-edited the last year of *The Avengers* and fancied doing something in that idiom.

Meanwhile, Philip Hinchcliffe was increasingly interested in a story about robots, specifically about how an intelligent-but-inhuman being would react to situations. (We'll see ghosts of this idea in "The Brain of Morbius", the final version of "The Hand of Fear", "The Face of Evil" and, most overtly, "The Robots of Death".) In late November 1974, as the last tweaks were being made to "Genesis of the Daleks", Nation was commissioned for "The Kraals" proposal for two weeks later (it arrived a week after that, of course).

• After officially leaving *Doctor Who*, Barry Letts had spent some time attempting to make a drama-documentary series about Marie Curie. As a hybrid science / drama production, it was the subject of one of the inter-departmental turf-wars that were so much a part of BBC internal politics in this era. While people decided who'd pay for it and what facilities were available, Letts was left cooling his heels. He was still listed on his contract as a director, so he gained permission to stay on the payroll in that capacity and, as luck would have it, a present-day *Doctor Who* story was coming up. Letts was signed up for Story 4J at the end of January for a stint between June and mid-September.

• With Robert Holmes up to his eyeballs in fixing "Pyramids of Mars" and "Terror of the Zygons", the formal commission for scripts didn't come for a month after this. In early March, Hinchcliffe wrote to Nation offering more cash than most writers got but with strings: for any last-minute changes, and with Nation being so busy, they reserved the right to amend things and tell him about them rather than ask for him to fix details and wait. One change they mentioned up front was that, since he'd written "Genesis", Harry Sullivan was being sidelined and should appear here as a UNIT staffer rather than aboard the TARDIS. Nation was also advised that, as a BBC production, the amount of filming allotted for the story was limited, so location scenes in the village weren't to be as extensive as, say, *Department S*. Nonetheless, there was rather more in this story than usual.

Nation's script was substantially what we saw, but the insectoid aliens were briefly called "Oseidons" and their android duplicates were mirror-images of the originals. One of the many red-herring theories the Doctor proposes for what's going on is a race called the Dominators (not, presumably, the ones who had Quarks; 6.1, "The Dominators"), or just "Doms". Letts had written an audition piece for potential Sarahs in early 1973, about a tech-tycoon being interviewed and accidentally revealing a forked tongue (see 11.1, "The Time Warrior"); he thought elements of this could be reworked. Holmes was less sure. Smaller tweaks included the number of G's in "Styggron" and the number of Kraals involved – Chedaki got dialogue (most of it "this is a good plan") and even the "Chargehand" got a line.

A larger change was that Oseidon's radiation belt was at the limit of what even the Kraals could stand, causing them to erect a holographic force-

195

13.4 The Android Invasion

field around the fake village; the Doctor and Sarah would walk through this, once they've worked out that it's not Earth. The script uses the term "biomagnetron" for the entire training area, beyond which is a fiery wilderness. At the end, the Doctor discusses with the Brigadier whether detonating a few atomic warheads beyond the Van Allen Belt would keep these putative invaders out.

- In early July, Production Assistant Marion McDougall went on recces in Oxfordshire. One obvious requirement was the Defence Complex, so the atomic defence research station at Harwell was a good place to start. It was complete but as yet uncommissioned, so they had the run of the place for a day (within reason). Nearby picturesque villages were auditioned; Didcot wasn't quite right, but East Hagbourne was. Three days after visiting that village, the filming began at Harwell on 21st July.

- With a summer shoot making the Doctor's heavy velvet jacket and tweed waistcoat a bit much, Barbara Lane made Tom Baker a lightweight oatmeal tweed coat with several pockets and a velvet collar-patch.[36] Stuntman Terry Walsh got one too. Baker, as usual, wanted to do as many stunt falls as possible; Walsh sustained a slight injury doing the really tricky jump in Part One. Oddly, when the next day's shooting moved to the woods and quarry, Walsh had been due to double for Max Faulkner, himself a stuntman of some years' standing and cast as Corporal Adams for that very reason. Instead, Peter Brace fell off a cliff.

- The quarry was near Witney, Worsham Quarry, near the Berkshire border. In climbing a tree in Tubney Woods, Elisabeth Sladen split both the costume trousers and the spare pair, so the rest of that day's scenes were shot so as to avoid revealing the safety-pins. Baker's commitment to realism made him hide underwater himself, in the brackish water, with a cold already. He needed a trip to hospital en route to the production's HQ, the Crown & Thistle, Abingdon.

- For the last two days, the filming was centred on East Hagbourne. The red phone box in the market square was, in fact, a BBC prop (which confused a couple of tourists). For this part of the shoot, radio actor Martin Friend played Styggron. His mask was more mammalian than the scripted insectoid and based on the same skull-model used for the Sontarans. John Friedlander was about to go freelance, partly because of the amount of paperwork required to liaise with the costume and make-up departments and the general infighting, but spent some time on this design, articulating the mouth of one mask for Styggron to speak (with small pegs attaching it to Friend's jaw) and allowing the eyes to be seen.

- Baker's voice was now almost back to normal and he was, predictably, mobbed by children between takes. The extras playing robot villagers were mostly people who'd been in similar roles before; the prosperous farmer is Walter Goodman, who was in a prominent non-speaking role in "Robot" as Chambers. Two of the white-suited androids were Henry Lindsay and Alan Jennings, who also handled the robot rottweilers in UNIT costumes. The helmets for the fingerbang robots were familiar stock ones.

- The last piece to be filmed was a return to Tubney Woods for the scenes with the android Sarah. Baker had just bought himself a flat in Notting Hill Gate, then a rather low-rent, bohemian area: Letts's main memory of the star he'd cast was of Baker collecting seeds in a plastic bag to partially re-wild the concrete jungle around Ladbroke Grove.

- Rehearsals began on the last day of July. Ian Marter was a little put out to find Harry reduced to ancillary status; John Levene accepted that the threatened phase-out of UNIT was happening, but Nicholas Courtney had a stage-play on that was likely to tour Canada. Nonetheless, the authority-figure in the last episode was scripted as "Brigadier" on the off-chance.

- With Part Two under-running, Holmes added the subplot of the Android built just to demonstrate the anti-Android weapon on 7th August. Roy Skelton was cast as Chedaki, the mask hurriedly altered. This change wasn't mentioned to the set-designer, who had built the Kraal spaceship on the understanding that they were insects and walked hunched over, so didn't need high ceilings of the kind humans would have preferred.

- The first recording session was on Monday, 11th August in Studio 3. It was Part One: almost entirely in story-order, with the long filmed inserts being committed to tape (nine of them counting the credits and titles), then several scenes from Part Three. The first ten minutes of Part One are on film, with another four minutes'-worth out of 23 minutes and three seconds barring the credits and titles. One scene not shot that day was 6a, where Crayford and the robot Grierson detect the TARDIS arriving on the

Defence Centre radar. This was to be shot with the remaining Mission Control scenes in Part Four, but Dave Carter is credited in Part One even though this scene was cut from the broadcast version. The scenes in the Disorientation Chamber (on 12th) entailed the familiar *Top of the Pops* technique, starting with a strong blue spotlight pulsing and then using a colour synthesizer as we outlined in "Terror of the Zygons" – it was used a lot in the Glam era, but revived for New Wave.

• Rehearsals resumed on the Thursday of that week and the production moved to the considerably smaller TC8 on August Bank Holiday, Monday 25th. (Baker was on screen as the Doctor that evening, presenting *Disney Time* in character.) In fact, even with the model of the rocket only 14 of the 27 scenes in the third episode were performed that day, with much of the session given to taping the pre-filmed material. The majority of the scenes acted on 26th (the last day) were in the Scanner Room, including the complex fight between Baker and Walsh as the two Doctors. The last scenes performed for the cameras involved Harry and the Colonel being freed and the robot Doctor killed as Styggron (Martin Friend) dies. Friend's prosthetic head affected his weight and he landed up executing a somersault rather than just falling; Stuart Fell commended him on this.

• You can't have failed to have noticed that the same clip of a Saturn 5 used as Vorus's sky-striker in "Revenge of the Cybermen" doubles for Crayford's obviously-different-looking ship. You may also have spotted that the caption-slide for the "real" Oseidon was the same one the Brigadier thought was Cromer (10.1, "The Three Doctors").

• After an almost-continuous production schedule since mid-September 1974, the leads got a month off, although Sladen, Baker and Marter popped to Blackpool to switch on the Illuminations on the Golden Mile for that year and shoot a brief cameo for an edition of *Seaside Special* (as we mentioned in "Terror of the Zygons"). Then Baker and Marter went to the pictures for a private showing of the Cushing Dalek films, as a pointer for whether their idea for an original feature film could work. With a revised start-time for the new run of episodes, nobody else was taking time off. Six editing sessions were needed, ending just before Letts's contract for the story did, but he had signed up Dudley Simpson to do the music and trusted him to get on with it. The score was recorded in two-episode blocks on 20th and 25th of September.

Marter later returned to the fold as a writer for the Target novelisations, starting with *Doctor Who and the Ark in Space*, then added an original novel during the 1985 hiatus, *Harry Sullivan's War*. He also, under a few pseudonyms, novelised feature films (*Splash* – yes, the mermaid romance flick with Daryl Hannah and Tom Hanks – by "Ian Don" was a bestseller for a while). His diabetes caught up with him while completing a last Target book and he died in 1987, on his 42nd birthday.

13.5: "The Brain of Morbius"

(Serial 4K, Four Episodes, 3rd – 25th January 1976.)

Which One is This? The *Frankenstein* one, at least superficially. The bits-and-pieces monster has a plastic see-through head and the obligatory "angry mob of villagers" strikingly resemble one of those "mass Wuthering" record attempts where everyone re-enacts that Kate Bush video.[37]

Firsts and Lasts This was the first story not to have pre-filmed inserts; thus, it's the first made *in toto* in Television Centre during the recording sessions ("The Ark in Space" was entirely made in the Concrete Doughnut, but that included pre-filmed 16mm Wirrn). It's the first (and, for a very long time, only) appearance of the Sisterhood of Karn (see Series 9 and "Night of the Doctor"), the first broadcast hint that the Doctor's lives didn't start with the ostensible first Doctor (see 4.3, "The Power of the Daleks"; **Who are All Those Strange Men in Wigs?** and Series 12), and the first time the companion was temporarily blinded (see 15.1, "Horror of Fang Rock", also by Terrance Dicks).

In its odd attempt to present the Sisterhood as equal-and-opposite to the all-male Time Lords, this is – curiously – our first hint of Gallifrey getting its hands dirty with direct intervention in cosmic affairs (although the real reason the High Council redirected the TARDIS might just be because a normal chimney-sweep wouldn't live long enough…).

And, after the experiment in "Day of the Daleks" (9.1) and the memorable first flight of the TARDIS in "An Unearthly Child" (1.1), we get the title-sequence used to represent a Time Lord's mind (see also "The Deadly Assassin"). Precisely *which* Time Lord, however, is debatable…

13.5 The Brain of Morbius

Four Things to Notice About "The Brain of Morbius"...

• By 1976, over half the population of Britain had colour televisions; this story might have prompted them to ask for a rebate on their licence-fees. It's not just that the colour-schemes are unrewarding (when they aren't downright ugly), it's that the story genuinely looks a lot better on a monochrome set. The opening scene, in particular, actively resembles the 1930s Universal horror films they are pastiching / parodying / plundering – but, in colour, you get a brown cyclorama sky and an unconvincing wooden rock, like one of those naff *Star Trek* planets. In the 1980s, fandom fell prey to a rumour that the production team asked for this story to be transmitted in black and white. You can see why people believed it.

• In the red corner, we have the Sisterhood of Karn: like the Giant Spiders of Metebelis 3 (11.5, "Planet of the Spiders") in many ways, but in flouncy red frocks and Roy Wood make-up. They dance around a fire hissing *deathdeathdeathdeath*, do strange hand-movements while exercising their fearsome mental powers and say everything as if it were of the utmost solemnity and urgency. They therefore get away with some potentially hokey dialogue, allowing everyone to keep a straight face when releasing the ultimate Bob Holmes fart-gag about "the Silent Gas Dirigibles of the Hoothi".

• And in the murky-green corner, Mehendri Solon (Philip Madoc) and Condo (Colin Fay). They have rather better lines, including some memorable Basil Fawlty-ish insults from Boss to Help ("I can see that, you chicken-brained biological disaster") and Madoc sonorously delivers these with relish. Since "Planet of Evil", they've been trying to make the human underlings more interesting than the powerful aliens they serve, and this is where it peaks (although Holmes will persist until 15.4, "The Sun Makers"). As we'll see in **The Lore**, they arrived at what now looks like inevitable casting after considering many other performers. It's hard to imagine how Peter Cushing, Vincent Price or even Freddie Jones could have made as much with the part as Madoc did.

• But the real villain is Morbius, whose voice is that of Michael Spice (see also "The Talons of Weng-Chiang"), but whose body… well, once the glowing green brain is decanted, the evil Time Lord seems a lot less sinister since the voice now comes from a rag-bag with a claw, a glass skull with googly eyes and Condo's arm (which now gesticulates in an appropriately emphatic Hitler / Mussolini style – even pointing at the fishbowl when talking about how powerful his brain still is).

The Continuity

The Doctor hasn't mastered backward double-loops. He can tell star-patterns even in a thunderstorm. [That suggests either good infra-red vision on his part or that the lightning, which doesn't disperse the mist rising from the ground, isn't coming from clouds (we're veering toward the former, but see **Planet Notes**).] He's truculent when he suspects the Time Lords sent him to Karn.

• *Background*. After ID'ing the insectoid alien as a race 'well established in the Cyclops Nebula', the Doctor muses that this is why he finds the local star patterns familiar and that he was 'born in these parts' (i.e. near Karn).

He can identify a bust of Morbius and recognise a telepathic trace of him. Morbius, conversely, needs to be told that the Doctor is a Time Lord and apparently hasn't heard of him. The Doctor is *au fait* with Solon's paper and subsequent reputation but didn't recognise him when they met.

[For a very long time (43 years, ten months and 23 days), it was uncertain whether the faces who appear in the climactic mind-bending duel were pre-Hartnell incarnations of the Doctor. On balance, they were (this clip is among the many memories of past stories in the Matrix meltdown in X12.10, "The Timeless Children" – as big a clue as anything we've ever had about anything). See, of course, the related sidebar.]

• *Ethics*. He's not big on immortality as an end-in-itself. He tells the Sisterhood's leader, Maren, that death is the price of progress. [She appears to take heed and immolates herself in the flame.]

• *Inventory:* He left the sonic screwdriver behind.

– *Scarf*. It's apparently flame retardant.

– *Other*. He's got quite good with his yoyo (a blue one now) and has a telescopic umbrella for unexpected downpours. There's a set of secateurs in his pocket, which we'll see again. He's carrying fireworks on his person [see another Terrance Dicks script, 20.7, "The Five Doctors"], two in his

The Brain of Morbius 13.5

Who are All These Strange Men in Wigs?

In "The Power of the Daleks" (4.3), the Doctor had woken up with a new body and personality – to the outrage of a small but vocal contingent of the viewers. The idea that William Hartnell's was only the latest of a number of faces the Doctor had worn before we got to see a television series about the character was first floated by David Whitaker, the original script-editor. In his over-long screenplay for Episode One, along with a lengthy reprise of the Food Machine scene from "The Daleks" (1.2), the Doctor claimed to be 750 years old and to have worn an earring prior to the "renewal" before the one we'd just seen. Nobody watching knew that, though, because Dennis Spooner was called in to get the episode in at under an hour.

Ten years later, producer Philip Hinchcliffe tried to hint at something similar. This *did* reach the screen and, on 24th January 1976, 10.2 million people wondered whether they were seeing what they thought they were seeing. The set-up: the Doctor, engaged in mental combat with Morbius, rewinds through his previous lives and lets us see them all on a handy piece of nearby apparatus. And there are more than three of them. You can imagine the debates that followed in school playgrounds and university common-rooms; if Hartnell was the original Doctor, then whose were the faces "before" his? Another small but vocal contingent, the new *Doctor Who* Appreciation Society, grumbled that Hinchcliffe and script editor Robert Holmes "didn't understand" the series. There were maybe 200 of them. By the time 10.9 million people watched a garbled repeat, the production team had unleashed "The Deadly Assassin" and the entitled fans were sourly wishing for a new producer.

Eventually, the idea bedded-in among anyone who cared that much and the public just shrugged, as they did when "Mawdryn Undead" (20.3) nonchalantly undid the DWAS orthodoxy on when UNIT stories were supposed to be set. (That story also demonstrated that Artron Energy, the power of regenerations and time-travel, is transferrable, something that kept coming up when River Song was in the mix – bear this in mind for later.) Later stories made the Doctor's lifespan more convoluted (see **Why Does the Doctor's Age Keep Changing?** under 16.5, "The Power of Kroll") and things like Lady Pienforte, the Valeyard and the apparently easy donation of a fresh regeneration cycle were chucked into the mix (25.3, "Silver Nemesis"; 23.4, "The Ultimate Foe"; 20.7, "The Five Doctors".) Some people just pretended that these on-screen hints never happened; some squirmed and found excuses for them and some devised convoluted explanations tied up with the alleged "Cartmel Masterplan" (see **Did Cartmel Have Any Plan At All?** with "Silver Nemesis"). Here's what they came up with...

1. They're Morbius. The one "recognisably" non-Doctorish face we see is that of Michael Spice, who's also, supposedly, the model for the bust of Morbius in Solon's living-room. We may see the eight unknown faces immediately after the Doctor's, but in fact the Doctor gets the upper hand after Hartnell's face appears. In the end, it's clearly the Doctor who wins the contest, as Morbius's head starts to smoulder while the Doctor only collapses after the link is severed. So, the Doctor forces his way back through Morbius's previous selves and eventually batters his opponent by being the hero (although in fact, as it's written in the script, Morbius's head explodes because of the strain of combat rather than because he loses).

The big drawback with this theory is the fashion-sense of the people we see on the display, and the idea that Morbius was attempting cosmic domination whilst parading about in fancy dress from Earth history. Then again, Chancellor Goth's nightmares all come from twentieth-century Earth, so it can't be as obscure a planet as we were led to believe ("The Deadly Assassin"). Besides, how many *Doctor Who* planets have we seen where people wear versions of historical Earth costumes?

On top of that, you have to explain why Morbius is shouting "back… back to your beginning!" while the mysterious faces are appearing. Perhaps he's confused, or simply ranting. But doesn't he say, "back to *the* beginning…"?[38]

2. Fakery. The Doctor's winning the contest all the time, and the faces seen on the display are figments of his imagination, dredged up out of his psyche in order to fool Morbius. A reasonable explanation, but ultimately disappointing. A lot of continuity hassles were "fixed" in the tie-in books and comics by just saying "he was lying" after Holmes used this to get out of dull conversations about "Pyramids of Mars", and broadcast episodes in the Matt Smith Era made it the all-purpose get-

continued on page 201...

13.5 The Brain of Morbius

waistcoat and one behind his ear. Sarah finds a tub of smelling-salts from somewhere.

The TARDIS Gallifrey can apparently steer it by remote control [see 10.3, "Frontier in Space"; 9.4, "The Mutants"; 23.1, "The Mysterious Planet"]. The Doctor can distinguish this from other faults. On departure, he accelerates the take-off to create a bang and a flash, reinforcing his point about fireworks. The light on top's changed again. The calibrators are on the blink, apparently.

[At story's end, he tells Sarah, out of the blue, that they have an urgent appointment. At the start of the next story, "The Seeds of Doom", the World Ecology Bureau has somehow called in the Doctor to look at photos of gourds. We might surmise that the Psionic Beam is back in use and that Major Beresford's allowed to play with it when the Brigadier's in a touring production of *The Dame of Sark* – but we'll address a small problem there in that story's **Things That Don't Make Sense**.]

The Supporting Cast
- *Sarah*. Another day, another salmon-pink outfit. This one's got a quilted waistcoat and trousers with drawstrings at the ankles. There was a jacket, but that got rained on. She seems to have preferred the previous Doctor's looks.

Relying on other people doesn't suit her; she's more than usually prone to yelps when Condo manhandles her. Her instinctive reaction to a tiny ventilation shaft is to think the Doctor wants her to crawl through it.

The Non-Humans
- *Kriz*. An insectoid alien beheaded early in Part One. [It's identified by the Doctor on screen as a 'poor Mutt', and only named 'Kriz' in the novelisation. Many fans assume this being hails from Solos (9.4, "The Mutants", script-edited by Dicks) – partly because the mildly racist 'Mutt' was what human colonists there called the Solonians' larval stage, mainly because the costume is obviously recycled from that story. Dicks's novelisation, however, includes background details for Kriz (see **Alternate Versions**) that bear no similarities to that story. Without any other connection to Solos, we should entertain the idea that it's a different insectoid mutant race that happens to resemble the Solonian chrysalis, the way Humans look like Time Lords.]
- *The Morbius Creature* is made from whatever creature Solon could salvage. It is bipedal and has Condo's right arm, plus a sizeable claw in place of a left hand but is primarily a dark green body stitched crudely together, with patches of hair (notably at the joints). The neck is thick and wrinkly. The only internal organ we know anything about is the methane-filtering lung-system of a birastrop [it's unsaid what they look like normally]. The brain is attached to this body and encased in a transparent spherical case with two metal eyes on stalks. When the brain was in a tank, a membranous vocal arrangement provided a voice for the disembodied tyrant's rants; the same voice is heard here, but with no visible means of production. The brain no longer glows when in the headcase. There seems to be an auxiliary brain (or, at least, motor cortex) in the headless body before Morbius is installed.
- *The Sisterhood / The Time Lords*. Ohica deems the Time Lords the Sisterhood's 'equals in mind power'; they are the only race the Sisterhood cannot 'destroy from within' by placing 'death in the centre of their beings, [sending] them mad with false visions'. The Time Lords have a non-aggression pact with the Sisterhood, apparently only visiting their neighbours when a regeneration goes wrong. Maren seems to think that they're all male.
- *The Time Lords*. Morbius had ambitions to use the Time Lords' powers for military conquest, something that has made his name notorious. The Doctor seems to be able to identify his mind as well as a bust of him. [Two possibilities arise: the obvious one is that, contrary to everything we learn in later stories, all Time Lords of every era know each other and operate in an eternal "present" – see **Why Do Time Lords Always Meet in Sequence?** under 22.3, "The Mark of the Rani" and **Is There a Season 6B?** under 22.4, "The Two Doctors" for all the evidence against this, but **Has the Time War Started?** under "Genesis of the Daleks" and **Did Rassilon Know Omega?** for arguments that back it up. See also **How Can Anyone Know About a Time War?** under X4.13, "Journey's End" and **Where's Susan?** under X4.17, "The End of Time Part One" for complications. Less melodramatic but more practical; with Time Lords gadding about in the history of the outside cosmos, anyone with a TARDIS might get a sort of "most wanted" list of other Time Lords at large that includes pictures of each known regeneration and a sort of telepathic mug-shot. The

Who are All These Strange Men in Wigs?

...continued from page 199

out clause. The Doctor making stuff up, to the extent of inventing earlier lives and memories, was a lazy retcon (retroactive continuity, not the memory-wipe in *Torchwood*) but covered things like this scene, pieces of collective childhood memory that get in the way of pet theories. It was popular in certain drab sectors of fandom during the late 80s and early 90s, before a *much* more complicated theory turned up...

3. Disguise. A subsidiary theory is that along the way the Doctor has "projected" versions of himself, as he does in "Logopolis" (18.7) and K'Anpo does in "Planet of the Spiders" (11.5). This will come back to haunt us in the scene in "Destiny of the Daleks" in which Romana "tries out" various bodies before plumping for that of Princes Astra, but it also covers these odd-looking specimens (and the menu presented in 6.7, "The War Games") while keeping faith with the Chancellor's statement in "The Three Doctors" (10.1) that Hartnell was the earliest model. It was worth a try.

4. It's neither the Doctor nor Morbius, but some other Time Lord. This has been most clearly stated in the last-but-one novel in Virgin's *New Adventures* line (or at least, the last-but-one *New Adventure* to actually have the Doctor in it), *Lungbarrow*. Since this was a reworking of Marc Platt's unused script from the late 80s (see 26.2, "Ghost Light"), and since this was one of the key texts of the so-called "Cartmel Masterplan", it had to be taken seriously, back then. Not that everyone could – even before it was thoroughly contradicted by a whole new series, *Lungbarrow* was one of the most unbearably fannish things ever written. But then, it was the near-conclusion of a six-year-long novel line which took an approach to the *Doctor Who* mythology quite unlike that of the TV series and, in context, it didn't seem so unreasonable. However, if you *aren't* the kind of reader who realises that "even a sponge has more of a life than I", then look away now:

Back on ancient Gallifrey, Rassilon and Omega (who were contemporaries, apparently – see **Did Rassilon Know Omega?** under "The Deadly Assassin") had a mysterious collaborator called "the Other", whose origins were unknown (of course) and who disappeared from Time Lord history when regeneration replaced the ability to reproduce. He told his granddaughter that he'd eventually return, then threw himself into a Loom, which is where new Gallfreyans are "spun" (they don't have parents because that's too icky for 90s fandom). Millions of years later, bits of his identity resurfaced in a no-mark called Theta Sigma, who unexpectedly became a Time Lord and found that age-old technology – like the Hand of Omega (see 25.1, "Remembrance of the Daleks") – "recognised" him. This enabled him to nick an old TARDIS and revisit the Old Times, where the Other's granddaughter Susan took advantage of his befuddled state and left with him to explore the universe. The Doctor, for it was he, forgot all of this until mind-duelling with Morbius. Whereupon he suddenly recalled his earlier lives and started getting involved in Time Lord politics, ultimately becoming (all together now) "more than just a Time Lord".

Well, you were warned.

5. The Doctor is older than claimed and older than the other Time Lords seem to know.

This was clearly the idea Hinchcliffe was getting at, as the "costume" found in the old console room in "The Masque of Mandragora" wasn't supposed to be recognisably like anything we've seen before (but, in practice, they just used a Pertwee-like shirt). This line of thinking is why Runcible's question about face-lifts wasn't met with the originally-scripted "three, so far", but the meaningless and clumsy "several, so far" ("The Deadly Assassin"). The original plan was to have fairly distinguished actors represent "unseen" Doctors – but nobody was interested and the production team stepped in (see below for a factual list). It's said that they asked Peter Cushing, which would also have made sense but opened a can of worms about canonical status (see A1, "Doctor Who and the Daleks"). It would have been really confusing if Cushing had accepted the part of Solon, so we think that this is an instance of wires getting crossed.

This was, of course, before any mention of a limit to how often a Time Lord could regenerate or any hint that this limit was more legal than biological ("The Deadly Assassin" again, plus "The Five Doctors" and X7.16, "The Time of the Doctor"). It was also long before X7.14, "The Name of the Doctor" showed us an elderly-looking Hartnell and a teenage Susan stealing the TARDIS, but that whole episode messes up the Doctor's timeline – twice – so isn't entirely reliable as evidence of what's happening here. The trail left in the ruined

continued on page 203...

13.5 The Brain of Morbius

Doctor's inability to recognise the Master in 8.1, "Terror of the Autons" may be a side-effect of that block on his memory.]
- *Hoothi* travel in silent gas dirigibles. They may also be deadly [see X5.4, "The Time of Angels" for discussion].
- *Birastrops* have lungs capable of surviving cyanide gas, but also crash their ships in these parts. [Quite why a methane filter confers immunity from cyanide is a matter for biochemists – there's a number of possibilities, depending on whether the methane is filtered out or kept while everything else is excluded.]

Planet Notes
- *Karn* apparently isn't a planet anyone would visit by choice. It's a 'thousand parsecs' away from wherever the Doctor was going. Most of the ships that land up there are drawn off-course by the Sisterhood, to make them crash. The Doctor hints that it's near the Nebula of Cyclops; Solon suggests that Dravidian slavers pass by.

It seems to be stormy every night but, by day, has clear blue cloudless skies. Solon claims that there's a belt of 'magnetic radiation' [probably hogwash, but that might account for the ionisation effects that resemble lightning but aren't always accompanied by rain]. It seems (unusually) to be thundery and misty at the same time.

History
- *Dating*. It's 'considerably after' Sarah's time. [If Kriz is from Solos, the most likely dates for someone looking like him rather than resembling a Viking or a hippy are 2,000 years apart, starting A.D. 4900-ish.] Solon is from Earth.

At an unspecified time in the past, the cosmos was convulsed by Morbius leading a band of fanatics to conquer the universe with Time Lord technology [and other things, also unspecified]. He offered immortality to his Cultists, a move that made the Sisterhood of Karn, custodians of the Elixir of Life, paranoid about visitors. Karn was devastated in the last conflict. Upon Morbius's capture, the Time Lords chose – for some reason – to execute him on Karn and scatter his atoms to 'the nine corners of the cosmos'. [This is, we assume, the one and only execution of a Time Lord mentioned in 20.1, "Arc of Infinity".]

Morbius was thoroughly disintegrated. [See X9.11, "Heaven Sent" for how hard it is to completely kill a Time Lord. The traditional Time Lord punishment in a Terrance Dicks novelisation would be a reversal of Morbius's life-stream so that he had never happened, but perhaps the Cult of Morbius' impact on history was too great to remove.] One of Morbius's followers – disgraced surgical genius Mehendri Solon – somehow saved the brain and kept it alive in a tank in a disused Hydrogen plant on Karn. [Solon acts as if his prowess is unprecedented in human history, suggesting that the Time Lords were similarly thorough after Crozier's twenty-fourth-century activities (23.2, "Mindwarp").]

The Analysis

Where Does This Come From? Old films, primarily, but the connection between the borrowed bits and pieces is very 70s. We've mentioned Nazi war criminals already ("Revenge of the Cybermen"), but it's worth repeating that the return of this particular bit of "the repressed" had a good window of opportunity between 1974 and 1980. It was the era of Détente (see, for example, 9.1, "Day of the Daleks") and US-Soviet rapprochement, so plots that had hitherto been easy to sell TV audiences as the results of fiendish Russians became plots hatched by ageing SS officers on the comeback trail.

Lord Olivier seemed always to be doing his comedy German accent, as a fugitive Nazi in *Marathon Man*, then a thinly-disguised version of Nazi-hunter Simon Wiesenthal in *The Boys from Brazil* (and Neil Diamond's *The Jazz Singer*, but that's not strictly relevant) before getting to play a real-life Nazi, Rudolf Hess. The pulpy bestselling novel *The Boys from Brazil* (which, you might be surprised to find, came *after* "Genesis of the Daleks") tied resurgent Nazis with a new form of ickiness, cloning. In the popular imagination of the 1970s, anything that created a visceral repulsion was, ipso facto, a short step to the Third Reich.

In the early 60s, there had been a notoriously botched attempt to spot-weld Fascism and Frankenstein: *They Saved Hitler's Brain* (see also 22.6, "Revelation of the Daleks" as it wasn't so much the brain as the head on a table-top, much like the dummy Davros in that story). You see where we're going with this. More obvious, and better-received at the time and later, was *Donovan's Brain*, rediscovered when the leading lady, Nancy Davis, became First Lady and the idea of a mil-

The Brain of Morbius 13.5
Who are All These Strange Men in Wigs?

...continued from page 201

TARDIS was unequivocally stated as being the Doctor's tracks through time, stopping (or starting) with the Hartnell incarnation and Clara, on a *different* journey into his past, got as far back as a childhood in the same shed we saw in X7.15, "The Day of the Doctor" (also in X8.4, "Listen"). Why should the same person's time-line have a gap marking before and after what that person remembers? Presumably, the same way that person has a gap in own life where he decided in retrospect that one of his incarnations "didn't count" despite being played by the most distinguished actor ever to have taken the role, Sir John Hurt. (See the previous episode, X7.13, "Nightmare in Silver", for even the Doctor not knowing about this incarnation – he was being mind-melded by the Cyber-controller at the time.)

But now it's the 2020s and the idea's come back with renewed force. "The Timeless Children" (X12.10) cemented the idea of pre-Hartnell Doctors, and while it didn't directly include the "Brain of Morbius" faces among their ranks, said blokes reappeared in a memory-orgasm designed to overwhelm the Matrix's paralysis field. Then again, their inclusion there might simply owe to the fourth Doctor having mentally witnessed them while cerebellum-wrestling Morbius (although that obviously wasn't Chris Chibnall's intent). Going strictly by what's on screen, we're now in the awkward position of accepting pre-Hartnell Doctors within the programme's set-up, but were these they? If there's any connection between these faces in the mind-duel and the surprise bonus Doctor(s) we're just learning about, the Doctor was unaware of it and, by implication, of ever having had a moustache or cornrows.

Either way, Jo Martin, the new earliest-known Doctor, is conspicuously absent from the "Morbius" line-up, so was either before Christopher Barry's Elizabethan Doctor or in a *different* forgotten past altogether. By March 1st, 2021, all bets were off as the full story of how regeneration came to Gallifrey was told from the Matrix. This new version, however, came after a lot of very strong hints that Time Lords have families more or less like we do (with, perhaps, more grannies – X11.9, "It Takes You Away") and the Doctor had a childhood (X3.12, "The Sound of Drums"; X4.12, "The Stolen Earth"; "Listen" on top of 19.5, "Black Orchid"; 9.5, "The Time Monster"; 15.3, "Image of the Fendahl"; 17.5, "The Creature from the Pit" and many others).

It also comes as the notion of regeneration being a knack that is instilled in those few Gallifreyans who ascend to being Time Lords has become more complex (e.g., X6.8, "Let's Kill Hitler"; X3.12, "The Sound of Drums"). All that 90s "Loom" stuff (itself very heavily indebted to *The City and the Stars* by Arthur C Clarke) is right off the table. The Time Lords didn't know about the Timeless Child, so perhaps whatever happened at the end of "The Time of the Doctor" entailed them working on the assumption that the Doctor was born a Gallifreyan and had used up all 13 lives. (Or 508, according to the Doctor in *SJA* 4.6, "Death of the Doctor", likely as a joke.) For all we know, the Doctor was born with a seemingly endless reservoir of regeneration energy, but got reduced – as part of their post-Division disguise (unending regenerations would be a bit of a giveaway) – to the bog-standard 13 incarnations. That would explain any occasion when the post-Hartnell Doctors check to see how many lives they've still got in the tank (the scan performed in 20.3, "Mawdryn Undead" immediately springs to mind).

If it's any help, the 1975 paperwork for paying these non-Equity on-screen cameos listed them as earlier incarnations of the Doctor. Tantrums aside, this is probably the one to go for, pending further evidence.

6. As for who those extra faces *really* were..:

George Gallaccio (Moustachioed Victorian), production unit manager (sort of like a line producer, getting the show made rather than worrying about publicity, casting, scripts, admin and overall policy). He was later tipped to become producer of *Doctor Who* (and was de facto producer of this story). Instead he worked on several high-profile drama series, notably the 80s *Miss Marple* adaptations and *Bergerac*.

Robert Holmes (Lemuel Gulliver), author, script editor and half of "Robin Bland".

Graeme Harper (General Zod), production assistant, later director of "The Caves of Androzani" (21.6) and "Revelation of the Daleks" (22.6), plus 11 BBC Wales episodes, the only director to work on both iterations of the series. (See **Who Were the Auteur Directors?** under 18.5, "Warriors' Gate".)

continued on page 205...

13.5 The Brain of Morbius

lionaire having his brain removed and kept cut off from the world in a fishtank was a handy anti-Reagan metaphor.

The 1958 flick is the second of three films of Curt Siodmak's novel (it was *The Lady and the Monster* in 1942 and *The Brain* 20 years after that). Orson Welles did it on radio, but the thing to mention here is that, despite these being black and white movies, the posters and the reprinted novel generally depict glowing green brains. The mind-controlling brain in a glass jar isn't novel in *Doctor Who* (see 1.5, "The Keys of Marinus"), but rather than have Morbius's mental prowess demonstrated before the climactic duel, it's downplayed to make the Sisterhood more formidable. Instead, the most overt visual quotation from any film here is when the brain slops onto the floor, as per the 1931 *Frankenstein* film, and that wasn't scripted.

Universal's film, which derives as much from other films as from bits of the novel, is where we get the idea of the obsessive scientist's lab in a ruin, the continual thunderstorms and the slovenly servant. Due to umpteen sequels, the pop-culture folk-memory is that this guy's called "Igor" and a shambling hunchback: that's a conflation of various similar-but-different characters, as is Condo here, but in 1931, he was called "Fritz" and played by Dwight Frye. The "Ygor" most people recall was Bela Lugosi in 1939's *Son of Frankenstein* – he, like Condo, had a vested interest in helping the brilliant surgeon who'd promised a restored body as payment for services rendered.

Not an arm, though: a more direct precedent for that might be the Hammer film *The Revenge of Frankenstein*, in which Peter Cushing is an undercover Baron trying to complete his research in a hospital specialising in poor patients. His not-at-all-shambling sidekick (played by Captain Scarlet, AKA Francis Matthews) identifies an arm from a former patient because of a distinctive tattoo (see X6.4, "The Doctor's Wife"). In most such films, the scientist's motivation is pared down to egotism, hubris and so on, as it's not what the punters paid to see. This allows Mehendri Solon's obsession with restoring Morbius to be slotted in where Frankenstein's now-routine sketchy motives would be, but there's a different surgeon / assistant dynamic at work here.

The Doctor's abrupt recollection of where he'd heard of Solon before is just one aspect of the story echoing *The Island of Doctor Moreau*. The novel makes more of a point of raising beasts to something like humanity by grafts and implants – something to which Holmes would return in "The Two Doctors" – rather than the way the various films had him playing Mistah Kurtz. It's less like Shaw's *Pygmalion* or any critique of vivisection or obscure racial/class allegory than it's been made into by Hollywood. Condo talks like Tarzan – or Karloff in *Bride of Frankenstein* – as much to give Solon bits of Basil Fawlty dialogue as to make a moral point about anything. Given the haste with which Holmes cobbled together this subplot to replace Dicks's first go (see **The Lore**), this aspect is more a matter of instinctive associations than detailed research.

Talking of Peter Cushing (as we'll do again in **The Lore**), BBC2 started a season of Hammer films on Saturdays at midnight on the night of Part Four of "Robot" (12.1). Most of them were selected to show the range of genres the studio covered, but they kicked off with *Frankenstein Created Woman*. That was 18th January 1975, around the time Terrance Dicks was putting this story together. However, Mel Brooks and Gene Wilder had pastiched the Universal films in one handy bite-size package just prior to this story being written, so we'll point you in the direction of *Young Frankenstein*. And *The Rocky Horror Picture Show*, also in cinemas then.

There's a tick-box approach to the set-pieces from the various 30s films common to both of these and "Morbius", and, of course, *Carry On Screaming*. Here it's most obvious with the monster's claw catching fire, the brain slopping onto the floor with a BBC Comedy Sound Effects "slop", blazing torches as the locals hunt for the killer, a dead girl carried slowly to the authorities – even Condo's shooting resembles Basil Rathbone and Bela Lugosi at the end of *Son of Frankenstein*. In case you failed to spot it, there's even a character who's blind for two episodes (c.f. either O.P. Heggie or Gene Hackman, according to generation or taste).

What we're getting at is that the story's a beast cobbled together from disjecta membra, just like the Morbius Creature. As we've examined elsewhere in these books, the body-horror of the late 70s / early 80s slowly supplanted the existential fear of mind-erasure / possession / duplication as the main subject for films and TV. However, what's being worked on in any permutation of

Who are All These Strange Men in Wigs?

...continued from page 203

Douglas Camfield (Regency Buck with buckled hat), director of the next story (and more 25-minute episodes than anyone else) and tipped as either future producer or future Doctor. The unquestioned *auteur* director of *Doctor Who* and with a better claim to have invented the Brigadier than the writers. His face had appeared before, clean shaven back then, as the third possible Jamie in Episode Two of "The Mind Robber" (6.2). A version of his version of the Doctor appears in the "flashback" sequences of the Missing Adventure *Cold Fusion*.

Robert Banks Stewart (Renaissance Man) author of "Terror of the Zygons" and the next story, "The Seeds of Doom". Later created the series *Shoestring* and *Bergerac*.

Christopher Baker (Flemish, in lacy collar with Van Dyke beard), production assistant (sort of what a 1st AD is in film).

Philip Hinchcliffe (Restoration fop), producer (and therefore responsible for this entire row).

Christopher Barry (Elizabethan), director of this story and several others from "The Daleks" to "Robot" and later "The Creature from the Pit".

Frankenstein is the polar opposite: rather than the viewer / reader's corporeal integrity being ruptured by chainsaws or sharks, it's simply irrelevant. It seems weird now that transplants and implants are relatively commonplace, but the idea seemed blasphemous ("hybrid" and "hubris" coming from the same root, crossing boundaries set by the Gods of Olympus or whoever). Even as late as the 1970s, this was the basis for horror movies (see 4.2, "The Tenth Planet").

The point about *Coma* et al was that rich or powerful people could "harvest" fitter, less well-connected ones; it was predation, but on a more permanent basis than just eating the poor. Thus the egomaniacal tyrant Morbius isn't just described to us as a would-be dictator, he's physically encased in a body he believed he had the right to, stolen from others and put together in a way that wouldn't just happen in nature. Just as the majority of *Doctor Who* aliens are sort of visual metaphors for human moral lacks or excesses (see **Who are You Calling a Monster?** under X3.6, "The Lazarus Experiment"), so this rough beast looks like unfettered ego and appetite taking anything it can get. Appropriately, such an unstoppable body and will can only be defeated by what's presented to us as a battle of souls.

In case you didn't already know, the original idea of this story was to have a robot surgeon with no aesthetic judgement compose a monstrous body that worked more efficiently but looked wrong. This has a vague echo of *Star Trek* (specifically "The Menagerie"), but it's also a comic inversion of the more recent trend to have Frankenstein aim for perfection and fall short (as in the peculiar 1974 *Frankenstein: the True Story*, in which Tom Baker played a version of Walton, the obsessive polar explorer whose narrative frames the novel). It was a legacy of Philip Hinchcliffe's desire to do a story exploring robots as beings with a sort of intelligence unlike ours.

That had to go, for various reasons, but the planet Karn was a pre-existing setting from Dicks's stageplay *Doctor Who: Seven Keys to Doomsday*, as was the idea of a being with a giant claw hand. The Clawrantulars were servants of the Masters of Karn, who stood very still and very tall. Unlike most of that play, these were created by young entrants to a competition, so Dicks couldn't steal them outright – but their bosses, the Masters, did fight the Doctor in a sort of mind-bending duel.

Occupying the planet this time were a Sisterhood whose main features owe a lot to another Late Victorian critique of Imperialism, Sir Henry Rider-Haggard's *She*. (Again, film versions soft-pedal the book-aspects that complicate a seemingly gung-ho adventure story, especially the way Ayesha constantly undercuts Britain's claims to moral superiority and has a prior claim on the other Queen Empress's signifiers of advancement. She knew Jesus personally, for example.)

Two films of *She* did the rounds; one, from Hammer Films in 1965, featured – or course – Peter Cushing and Bernard Cribbins (see A2, *Dalek Invasion Earth 2150AD* and Volume 9), but ostensibly starred Ursula Andress. Before that was a weird one from RKO in the 1930s, starring Randolph Scott and set at the North Pole rather than somewhere in Africa, with memorable Expressionist sets if nothing else. The other film versions were all silent. For once, we can't point to a then-recent repeat on BBC as a prompt for

13.5 The Brain of Morbius

Hinchcliffe and Holmes. (The Cushing film wasn't on between 1971 and 1982, and the botched sequel – featuring Derrick Sherwin in a small role – was only shown between recording and broadcast of "Morbius".)

Something Jeremy Bentham said in an early edition of *Doctor Who Monthly* has led people to think that Gaudi's various Art Nouveau buildings in Barcelona influenced the entire set design. That was Christopher Barry's suggestion, but while it may be true of one or two of the kidney-shaped stained-glass windows, Barry Newbery more gravitated toward the script's claim that Solon's lair was an old power station. The Sphinxes and staircases might not seem in keeping with this, but there's a precedent in a ruin of more recent vintage than the pyramids – the park where the Crystal Palace was relocated to after the 1851 Exhibition has a lot of such items lying around after the Palace itself burned down in 1936. As far as cathedral architecture goes, Newbery was thinking less of the Sagrada Familia than of Chartres or Notre Dame, but with the flying buttresses on the inside instead – and inversion of old styles he'd try again with the columns in 15.2, "The Invisible Enemy". He took the script's hint of a devastated planet and reasoned that only an articulated building with ball-and-socket joints would be left standing. He also plundered the set store for any odd-looking heads he could find. The exteriors are modelled mainly on the Giants' Causeway, a basaltic extrusion in Northern Ireland.

An earlier Solon, the Athenian administrator / tyrant, was said to have used the supposedly reduced brain-size of women as a reason to keep them away from law-making – but as so many people claim so many things about him, it's hard to draw a bead on what he really thought. The name's now fairly common across Europe, so even with the other Greek references in the works of Dicks and Holmes, we can't say it was a deliberate reference or just a cool-sounding villain-name. Ditto "Morbius" as in *Forbidden Planet* (see also "Planet of Evil"; "The Face of Evil").

English Lessons

- *Matron* (n.): the senior nurse in an old hospital. Several *Carry On* films have cemented the word's association with Kenneth Williams (see X2.1, "New Earth").
- *Luv'ly violets, guv*: The idea of winsome blind girls selling flowers (usually in London) is so ingrained, there *has* to have been a real-world referent once. However, apart from Charlie Chaplin's *City Lights*, the most famous we can find in writing is Nydia in Bulwer-Lytton's *The Last Days of Pompeii* (see Volume 3 and X4.2, "The Fires of Pompeii"). Most professional flower-sellers were married to the growers. Disadvantaged girls selling flowers in town squares were once common enough, but they were usually disabled in other ways. The ones at Farringdon Market were sometimes in pairs, one blind and one with crutches, to avoid theft or other hazards. John Groom organised these and other at-risk girls into a systematic Mission that Lord Shaftesbury supported; see below.

However, we've got this folk-memory of lone blind flower-sellers in rags. There were specific songs associated with different flower-selling pitches. Vaughan-Williams used the famous *Who will buy my sweet lavender, one bunch for a penny* in the second movement of his London Symphony and Noel Coward did so in *London's Pride*. It was, supposedly, the basis for the Thames Television ident (you have to use a bit of imagination to hear any resemblance). By World War II, the girls who'd taken up permanent spots around Piccadilly Circus were all old ladies and the last retired around 1950.

- *Piccadilly* (n.): The one in London, not the Manchester one. Until 1959, the main traffic hub, Piccadilly Circus, was the red light district and the nexus of the dance-halls, cinemas and so on in the West End. Before that, around the time of Oscar Wilde, all the exclusive clubs with leather armchairs (and the Café Royal) were there. It was one of the first places to have electrically-lit advertising. Today, it's normally filled with tourists wondering why they're there, because they'd heard of it from people who had heard about it during World War II or recalled its reputation for exciting and exotic delights from when talkies started (or before – see Anna May Wong in *Piccadilly* in 1928). It's still as hard to cross the roads as when it became proverbially busy (see 5.5, "The Web of Fear"). Homeless orphans and the like used to congregate in the region until the Earl of Shaftesbury supported more humane support systems, which is why he is commemorated with the statue on the fountain – erroneously called "Eros". Hence the presence, once upon a time, of girls selling violets or lavender.
- *Mr Allsorts* (n.): as well as Jelly Babies, the

Bassetts company made Liquorice Allsorts, a variety of soft sweets disguising the main ingredient with coconut, fondant or sprinkles. You will see the Doctor offer these in lieu of Jelly Babies in 15.3, "Image of the Fendahl"; 15.4, "The Sun Makers"; and most obviously 16.2, "The Pirate Planet". To advertise these, they invented a character called Bertie Bassett, an anthropomorphic agglomeration of the various varieties. In 1975, the idea of a *Doctor Who* monster resembling this was vaguely ludicrous, but see 25.2, "The Happiness Patrol" for a borderline copyright-infringement.

- *Milliard* (n.): a thousand million. The American "billion" took a long time to become accepted elsewhere, since most countries used that for a million million. (Ergo Gallifrey, Karn and Solos aren't as close as modern viewers might think, but still astronomically adjacent.)

- *Stewed apricots* (n.): a throwaway gag with a lot behind it. In Victorian nursery parlance, "ambrosia" was stewed apricots with a bit of vanilla and maybe cardamom. In Greek mythology, it was the Elixir of Immortality brought to Olympus by doves. In America, apparently, it's something involving tinned pineapple and coconut and that's the definition dominating Wikipedia and the like. Just to add to the fun, the Doctor then comments "no custard". If you were making a Victorian kid's tea or a pre-war school dinner, you'd serve stewed fruit with custard made from powder (op cit), but in the 1970s lazy people got their custard (or rice pud) out of a tin and the best-selling brand was called, of course, "Ambrosia". (Explaining why this might make a more recent British viewer shout 'Oo-arr' to the tune of "Go West" by The Village People is more complicated.)

Things That Don't Make Sense Why exactly is the Doctor sent to Karn? To clear up the Morbius situation, fix the Sisterhood's small plumbing problem or just to make everyone act scared and make silly mistakes? If the High Council have got wind of their greatest criminal staging a comeback tour, sending another Time Lord in unbriefed is asking for trouble. If it's to help the Sisters, then sending a disgraced amateur rather than a formal delegation is a calculated insult. All the cloak-and-dagger stuff just annoys Maren, dragging out the story for two episodes longer than necessary.

With their mental reach, the Sisters can perfectly tune in on the Doctor eating seaweed at Solon's, so they must know that Solon keeps a big bust of Morbius in pride of place. Plus, they definitely know Solon only came to their planet when the warlord was executed *and* that he's been conducting "unnatural experiments"... and yet somehow they've failed to add all of that up to figure out that he's labouring to resurrect their deadliest enemy. Ohica is also a bit thick, in that she loudly discusses that the Flame's pegging out in front of all the other Sisters, despite Maren ordering her not to.

For his part, Solon has been providing the Sisters with "treatment" of some kind. As Karn became the health resort of the cosmos, the elixir must be most efficacious in every case – Solon thinks so. The only reason they'd need him to put their arms in splints after over-energetic dancing or whatever is if the elixir is running out. He's not deduced that either. [There's a school of thought that Solon blocked their flue specifically so that the Time Lords would send someone to fix it, thus providing him with a donor, but that raises all sorts of questions about Condo's ability to shin up onto their roof without them knowing.]

The Sisterhood's boiler-room only seems to have one entrance, but somehow Sarah got in despite Solon and Condo spending that entire scene blocking the doorway. Maren and Ohica would've spotted her using any other entrance.

When the fuses blow, Solon switches to candles because he has a load of them (and big chandeliers in the ceiling, candlesticks left, right and centre and sconces). He therefore seems prepared for random power-cuts, and yet he's apparently planning to do brain-surgery without a back-up generator. Solon's pad seems designed as a theme-park, hence the sphinxes and stone staircases, not for generating power. On the outside, it looks like a beige wedding-cake. Whatever the "Scott Bailey principal" was (and ITV cop-shows aside, the name sounds like they might have been on *The Old Grey Whistle Test*), it seems to require buttresses on the inside *and* outside of a wall and a cellar that's lockable from the outside. How is this of any use to a hydrogen plant?

He has an operating theatre in the attic, a dining-room at ground-level and a lab in the cellar, all connected by big concrete staircases. Bear this in mind when we see Solon decant the squidgy brain from its green goo, accidentally drop it on the floor then, next time we see him, install the brain inside the glass case atop the patchwork body. Condo's bleeding to death at the foot of the stairs,

13.5 The Brain of Morbius

remember, so Solon must have carried the brain under one arm, the glass case under the other, stepped over Condo and climbed two flights of stairs before starting surgery. All while guiding a blind girl up those same stairs (had there been a dumb-waiter, the Doctor's home-brewed Zyklon gas wouldn't have been necessary).

Quite apart from the appallingly unhygienic operating theatre, this place has cobwebs and random junk scattered around [insert "Marie Condo" joke here]. If you care to glance at the table near the pedal-bin where the glass head was kept, next to the mind-bending equipment, you'll see a glass bell-jar containing a fluffy pom-pom and two bath-sponges. What unspeakable evil was Solon planning with these?

Why does Solon even *have* mind-bending equipment? Any two of the three people living there would be a short contest. Condo is tasked with cleaning up the place, and he's been actively looking for his arm. Apparently, he never thought to vacuum the operating theatre, or he'd've seen it grafted onto an assortment of other body-parts.

Why doesn't Solon use Condo's head? An operating assistant only seems necessary because there's been a power-cut. Condo otherwise serves little purpose beyond menial household chores, and we know that tissue rejection isn't a problem, because his arm's already part of the monster. Why does the head need to be from an oxygen-breather (as the opening scene suggests) if the body has birastrop lungs? More to the point, why does Solon worry about the Doctor's brain getting damaged if he's going to bin it and fill the head with Morbius's giant, glowing brain?

Why does all Morbius's brain pulse in time to his spoken dialogue? Do Time Lord brains naturally do that in their skulls? Does this explain why the miniaturised Doctor and Leela can see when they're in his brain in 15.2, "The Invisible Enemy"?

We've got a whole essay about the newly-urgent topic of whose faces we see in the Mind Duel, but a question for here is why Sarah can see any of it and, after a moment's thought, we're curious about precisely which images are chosen. (Consider it this way: if you think about yourself at age 13, or five, or whatever, do you imagine an old photo of yourself? A specific old photo in each case?)

These days, though, the big question is: who the hell is Ohila ("Night of the Doctor" and Series 9)? Her name brings to mind Ohica, who's second-in-command and fairly young-looking. If, for some reason, she went undercover during the Time War by changing one letter of her name (an even less imaginative nom-de-guerre than Obi-Wan Kenobi's), how does anyone with free access to the Elixir of Life hit middle-age if they weren't that way to start with? It can't be the Time War, because Karn's such an obvious target it's as improbable as Skaro being left untouched (yes, all right, Skaro *was* in X7.1, "Asylum of the Daleks" but we weren't supposed to remember that in X9.1, "The Magician's Apprentice") and the whole point of "Night of the Doctor" (A10) is that Karn is in hiding. What reason could Ohica have for not taking the daily recommended dose for 30-odd years, then resuming (she's outwardly the same age when dealing with McGann and Capaldi)? But very well, let's assume that Ohila is Ohica. Again, what purpose does changing one letter serve? Even if it's somehow a fiendishly clever hiding-in-plain-sight thing, the fact that she's boss of the Sisterhood of Karn is something of a giveaway. [Perhaps her name really was "Ohila" all along and Maren was just forgetful. If you live as long as they do, things like that will get annoying. Sarah eventually thanks Ohica by name – under the circumstances, a mumbled "actually, it's Ohila, I didn't like to keep correcting the High One" would have spoiled the mood. Besides, Ohila's name is never spoken aloud in any of the broadcast or online appearances, so it could equally be "Mary-Sue" or "Moffa".]

If, on the other hand, Ohila was a totally different older Sister, and really was there right from the start as she claims in "Hell Bent" (X9.12), where was she when Solon was living in her own backyard? She taunts Rassilon with all sorts of knowledge about the Time Lords and what the Doctor was like as a kid, so her presence when Morbius was marinating in a nearby fusion-plant and would have made the plot of "The Brain of Morbius" go very differently (she'd be over-ruling Maren and helping the Doctor at every turn). Of course, as only five of the Sisters are allowed the Elixir during the drought, Ohila might have got old while they were waiting for normal service to be resumed. So what happened to the favoured five (or three, as Kelia gets strangled and Maren gets sooty committing sutthi)? Was there a coup?

Oh yes, one last thing: every November, we got Public Information Films (see Volume 3) about "The Firework Code" as part of the BBC's public service remit. Yet they let Terrance Dicks do this and 20.7, "The Five Doctors", where the Doctor's carrying fireworks in his pockets and letting them off indoors. Maren's really lucky the Doctor's planned execution was interrupted with bangs and flashes and everyone going "Oooh!"

Critique Perversely, let's start where traditional reviews fizzle out: the sets and costumes. What immediately strikes one is that the exterior set, the rocks and bamboo where the TARDIS lands, is stagey and unimaginatively-lit. This isn't as trivial a point as it seems: everyone involved in this production knew that the first and third scenes would happen on the cardboard-looking Giants' Causeway, punctuated by a short scene with the (better) set of Solon's parlour mainly unshown as we focus on faces. After all of the care lavished on the last studio-based planetary exterior, Zeta Minor, this seems clumsy.

Yes, we've also had purely functional planet-sets recently, but those occurred for plot reasons and, crucially, we didn't see them until we were already invested in the story. (Assuming that we *were* invested, that is – either way, a lot of plot happened before this change of locale.) One could argue that this decision to trust the storytelling and acting to hook the casual viewer is a sign of growing self-confidence, but it could equally be the return of "it's only *Doctor Who* and kids will watch anything". Knowing what we know of the personnel and this story's difficult gestation, the latter is entirely possible. The uncommitted viewer, in 1976 or today, needs a better reason than the visuals or such dialogue as those first three scenes provide to stick around.

Anyone who does gets a reward later, but there's something off-key about the costuming too. The Sisterhood look interesting and it takes effort to see the cheap improvised jewellery as such, but Sarah, Condo and Solon are all in drab muddy greens and browns. The fan-theory that they wanted to show this in black and white is superficially plausible but would have squandered the attention paid to the three good sets, which read a lot better in colour. These three, the laboratory, the parlour and the shrine of the Flame, are busy, with lots of detail and crinkly surfaces, but all made to seem like extensions of their occupants. It's nice, in the abstract, to see a scientist who doesn't occupy a space with gleaming metal and shiny white surfaces, but this is the second matte-brown asymmetrical workshop in a row after Styggron's low-rent lab.

Enough thought has been put into how they work and what they've been converted to do to make the Doctor, Sarah and the Creature look out-of-place. Even Sarah's horrid waistcoat contrasts with the Brain's lurid orange when Morbius is ranting and the sombre olive-green of everything else. None of it is accidental; almost any shot is composed to give maximum information if you've just tuned in. That's why the exterior set is so glaringly bad. It looks as if they deliberately chose to give us something from a school play.

On top of this, it feels like a deliberate policy decision to let the viewers know "we're doing *Frankenstein* this month" even before the first episode's big reveal. All these factors draw a line in the sand, inviting everyone watching to decide if they're "in" or not. The viewing figures, especially for the Christmas omnibus repeat (when most people knew what they were in for) indicate that a lot of the British public had decided that they were. These days, it's very unlikely that anyone will simply be in front of a television and impossible that this would be one of only three options. The story's subsequently been made to bear more weight than it, or any story before "The Curse of Fenric" (26.3), was designed to carry. Developments in Series 12 put this story back at the top of the To Be Watched list for anyone newly joining the series. Does the story-as-made reward anyone who decides to watch it now?

Apparently, yes. As well as providing us with as good a cross-section of all the things Baker and Sladen do well, especially the rapid switches of mood, it's plotted well enough to work as a movie with three hinge-points (and, yes, they're all Sarah encountering parts of "Mr Allsorts"), an atmospheric, internally-consistent whole. Not every old story can be taken in total like that.

For a modern viewer, one scene dominates and distorts what was made in the 70s: the Mind-Duel. It was just an interesting set-piece, but came as the culmination of hints that the Doctor's relationship with the Time Lords is no more comfortable than those of the Sisterhood or Morbius. The story was heading that way anyway, so they added a tiny grace-note of other faces, cameos of the behind-the-camera staff. That in-joke was a sign of how self-confident Philip Hinchcliffe had become, but it was a caprice. This wasn't an "arc episode"; it was one of a number of entertaining escapades the Doctor had. Barely one viewer in a hundred gave that scene a second thought until

13.5 The Brain of Morbius

the repeat showing.

As we've said, this story was a big step in making escapades that regular viewers would get more out of than (hypothetical) newcomers stumbling across the series, but it makes fewer demands on the public's collective memory than the previous most-exclusive adventure, "Planet of the Spiders". Treating the story before and after that one scene as negligible surrounding material is as wrong-headed as the Omnibus edit that reduced it to an hour of memorable moments sans the plot or character-delineation to justify them. The plot and character-delineation are, however, what kept people watching a week at a time in January 1976.

The transition from Solon to Morbius as the Doctor's antagonist, and Maren from inconvenience to ally, is a scene-to-scene negotiation that's actually *more* impressive if you watch the story in one go rather than week-by-week. As we've indicated in other reviews, that's rare. It took years for the story's nature as a hastily-cobbled-together fix by many hands to emerge, because it doesn't look like one. There's a clear, methodical progression following the initial (rather absurd) premise. That ought to be a minimum requirement but, in Season Thirteen so far, it's been treated as negotiable, if not dispensable. There are many reasons to relish "Pyramids of Mars", but rock-solid plotting and character motivation aren't prominent among them. What's engaging about "Terror of the Zygons" or "The Android Invasion" are aesthetic moments and mood; they are watchable almost despite the scripts. "Planet of Evil" runs on pure audio-visual chutzpah. This time, we're given a few deft touches of those bonuses, but not anything extraneous. The story copes without such peaks, but sometimes it's a struggle. When it works, it's because everything's pushing in the same direction; they're willing us to believe that a story made from such disparate – and flagrantly-pilfered – materials might actually hang together through sheer artistic consistency.

This is especially true of the music. The score, as with "Pyramids", occasionally seeps into the storytelling and on one or two occasions does the work that the direction can't manage, notably with the Sisterhood. Dudley Simpson's choice of a marimba and bass trombone for "organic" leads and a very 1976 electric piano setting seem like the sort of thing he always did but, going back over his earlier soundtracks, in fact he's innovating. In this regard, he and designer Barry Newbery are on the same page. These tonal colours are the auditory equivalent of the matte earth-tones of the sets and costumes, with the female vocal as the scarlet of the Sisterhood. None of this is what any director, composer or designer would give us today, but that doesn't make either team wrong.

It's cast ingeniously, sometimes against type, and hindsight makes nonsense of the idea that anyone but Philip Madoc could have played Solon. (Or, at least, none of the names put forward could have got away with what he does.) That character gets a lot of good dialogue, but the decisions on which lines to do as throwaways and which to emphasise all seem to have been based on what Madoc could do with them. The jokes seem to be Solon's, not those of whichever writer devised them, and the asides show a brilliant mind at work but not in control – distractedly calling Maren a "palsied harridan" or telling Morbius that Condo has to be "put down". If they'd got Peter Cushing, this character might have landed up as a cut-rate Zachary Smith.

However, Colin Fay does the real heavy lifting as Condo, a character who overlaps the Ygor/Karl assistant and the Karloff version of the Monster, and who responds to Solon in subtly different ways as the story progresses. It could have been easier to do this relationship as Basil Fawlty and Manuel, but Condo realises that he has options. A lot of that's scripted, but less than you'd think – read the script or a transcript and compare it to what's on screen. Solon, as a monomaniac, has less of a "journey" (as the Hollywood script-gurus would have it). Madoc finds ways to make Solon seem to be making second-by-second adjustments to his plan. His most characteristic moments are rapidly back-peddling to please people he needs, even Morbius, and Madoc varies these to suit each interlocutor.

A performance such as this might have distorted the production, but it's needed because Tom Baker is so securely in control now. He needs a firm base to push against and Madoc, Fay, Cynthia Grenville (as Maren) and Michael Spice (the voice of Morbius) give him it. Elisabeth Sladen finds new ways to suggest a rapport with the Doctor, but not without a tiny bit of needling on both sides. However, the real strength of this is an ensemble cast; Big Name Stars would have been a massive miscalculation. All of this is best appreciated as a whole and wallowed in, not cherry-picked.

The Brain of Morbius   13.5

The Facts

Written by "Robin Bland" (Terrance Dicks, overhauled by Robert Holmes). Directed by Christopher Barry. Viewing figures: 9.5 million, 9.3 million, 10.1 million and 10.2 million. AIs, err, only Part Three has a recorded figure, the now-usual 57%. The December repeat got 10.9 million and caused a lot of trouble, as we'll see.

Alternate Versions Hinchcliffe supervised the one-hour omnibus, shown over the following Christmas. Barry objected, but it was also released on VHS and Betamax, later laser-disc as well. This odd edit, which made even less sense than the original, was the only version of this story Australian viewers got until the late 80s because the standard edit got an A rating, unsuitable for children.

Dicks's novelisation claims that Kriz stems from "the Race", "a mutant insect species widely established in the Nebula of Cyclops", and which seeks to conquer *lebensraum* on behalf of "the Great Mother", their "Goddess and Queen" (all in all, then, it's incompatible with "The Mutants"). Noticeably, it makes no mention of the "extra faces" in the mind-duel, but includes passing reference to the Pertwee, Troughton and Hartnell Doctors. There was also a *Junior Doctor Who* edition of the novelisation.

Cliffhangers Sarah finds a headless body made of bits; Sarah (now blind) stumbles upon a disembodied brain; Sarah stumbles around, her sight returning, as brain and body, united, get up off the table and the nation's kids shout *BEHIND YOU*!.

What Was In the Charts? "Wide Eyed and Legless", Andy Fairweather Low; "A Glass of Champagne", Sailor; "Forever and Ever", Demis Roussos; "Forever and Ever" (a different song, different silly clothes), Slik.

The Lore

After "Robot" and some time off, Terrance Dicks pitched a story to Robert Holmes. It was, in many respects, "State of Decay" (18.4). He submitted "The Haunting" as an outline just before Christmas, and by Twelfth Night was told it wasn't quite "there" – but the idea of taking folkloric villains and riffing on 30s Universal horror films wasn't a bad one (we'll pick up on this with 15.1, "Horror of Fang Rock").

Philip Hinchcliffe wanted to do a robot story, a proper one like all those Asimov puzzle-tales where the precise interpretation of the Three Laws was making a robot act oddly. Dicks came back on 1st May with just the thing: a tale of a loyal but literal-minded robot building a functionally-better body for its master (a fugitive criminal, currently just a head in a box) that was a rag-bag of mismatched body-parts. The war-criminal master, being somewhat vain, couldn't get his robot to see that having a giant claw and the lungs of a Birastrop (or whatever) was no substitute for regaining his former physique – until along comes the Doctor, and the penny drops about what humanoids ought to look like.

Dicks added a subplot about a witchy cult and a restorative elixir and recycled the mind-duel and claw-monster from *Doctor Who and the Seven Keys to Doomsday* (see **Can They Do It Live?** under A6, "The Music of the Spheres"), but kept to the other restriction placed on this story: absolutely no pre-filming. This was, apparently, always the plan, but Terry Nation had made it a priority (see last story).

• With the stars contractually owed a break and every studio in Television Centre booked over September for the umpteen Christmas Specials, this story would have to be made in October. Christopher Barry was attached to the project. He was unexpectedly free after only directing the first four episodes of *Poldark*, but after creating Skaro at Lime Grove (1.2, "The Daleks") and learning CSO ("Robot" but also 9.4, "The Mutants", much of which worked better than expected), he was an obvious choice. Another Hartnell-era veteran, Barry Newbury, was given the set-design brief. The scripts were commissioned in early June: Holmes received the first on 1st July and accepted it as is, the rest were all in by 4th August. Dicks then went on holiday.

• By now, Holmes was encountering a problem Dicks must have warned him about – Bob Baker and Dave Martin's "Hand of Fear" outline had metastasised into something like how Michael Bay would have approached the 1979 *Quatermass* (it ends rather like *Armageddon*, but with the Brigadier as Bruce Willis). Even with savage cuts, it would have to be rethought and moved into the next financial year (we'll pick this up in "The Seeds of Doom" and, of course, "The Hand of Fear").

Even with only 22 episodes actually made for

211

13.5 The Brain of Morbius

what we think of as Season Thirteen ("Terror of the Zygons" was sort of a freebie, a legacy from last year), the inflation-rate for 1975 was biting. The front-runner to replace it was looking like a big-budget affair with lots of location-filming. Thus, Story 4K, always intended as the cheap one of the year, got a lot cheaper. The big above-the-line cost looked like being the sleek-looking robot. The cost, in man-hours and material, was unacceptable, but beefing up the role of the assistant surgeon into a vain genius who was himself attempting a comeback and giving him an Ogron-like sidekick (10.3, "Frontier in Space" in particular) would justify making the guest star role a bigger draw (and upping the fee if they got someone big enough).

Holmes, who'd hoped to spend August working on his pet side-project, *Aliens in the Blood*, set about replacing the machine (Dicks later said that the Raston Warrior Robot from "The Five Doctors" is roughly what he had in mind) with a more traditional Mad Scientist and his lumpen assistant. Ideally, Dicks would have been kept in the loop, but he was still on holiday. Also on holiday, at last, were Tom Baker (off to Italy with Ian Marter to write *Doctor Who Meets Scratchman*) and Elisabeth Sladen, who was now planning to leave.

- Now that the ironic inversion of *Frankenstein* had itself been inverted, it left a decent guest-role that was easy to sell. Barry aimed high, contacting Peter Cushing and Vincent Price. (Yes, an international movie star was more affordable than a BBC-quality robot.) Cushing was committed to a theatre run; Price had been London-based and recently hosted a cookery show on Thames Television (introducing the British to Cajun cuisine), so was more available than might have been thought. (Remember, we're not so long after the *Dr Phibes* films and *Theatre of Blood*, in which he met his future wife, Coral Brown.)

Marter, who'd been in *Dr Phibes Rises Again*, seems to have proposed Price as a possible co-star for *Scratchman*. Another veteran considered was Freddie Jones, who also had Hammer credentials, but most recently been in *Juggernaut* and (oh dear) *Never Too Young to Rock*. Philip Madoc hadn't been short of work since his previous *Doctor Who* (6.7, "The War Games"), but had yet to get a starring role. If you asked the British Public, they'd know things he'd been in (say, that *Dad's Army* episode with the U-Boat or *The Goodies* taking a pop at Apartheid), but not put a name to the face.

- Geraldine Stephenson, a choreographer with the Royal Shakespeare Company, had recently worked with Barry on the gavottes and suchlike in *Poldark*. Barry's reasoning was that having one actual dancer and a number of tall-ish women as the non-speaking Sisters would cut costs; as it turned out, some of the Sisters were dancers, recommended by Stephenson, but willing to work for Equity standard rates as walk-ons. The one who doubles up as young Maren is Martine Holland, last seen as a robot student in a pub in "The Android Invasion".

Cynthia Grenville (older Maren) was cast less formally. She'd worked with Sladen in rep – when she was in the BBC canteen one day, Sladen went up and asked her if she could play an old lady, then turned to Hinchcliffe and introduced her to him. Colin Fay had written to Barry asking for small television roles to help him break out of opera. Other candidates had been Bernard Bresslaw (5.3, "The Ice Warriors"), Michael Kilgarriff ("Robot"; 5.1, "Tomb of the Cybermen") and Stephen Thorne (8.5, "The Daemons"; 10.1, "The Three Doctors" and he'll be back soon – "The Hand of Fear").

- Dicks, after years of doing it to other people's scripts for similar reasons (including Holmes's and especially Baker and Martin's epic first drafts), was peeved at what had happened to his story. It hadn't happened to him before – the changes, he thought, removed the core logic of the situation and made everyone act weirdly. He said so, volubly, to Holmes on 15th September. After a few days he simmered down and accepted the rationale, but thought so much was now unrecognisably his, it would be professionally damaging to leave his name on it. He and his agent agreed to the use of a bland pseudonym (maybe "Stephen Harris"). Later that week, on 24th, the last few tweaks made Solon know that Sarah wasn't permanently blind and resolved how long he'd been on Karn (i.e., before Morbius was executed). This was just as rehearsals started: Fay recalls Baker coming to one session on roller-skates.

These days, we're so used to the names of writers and directors being announced months in advance – and famous writers' participation being part of the publicity build-up – that the idea of keeping it under wraps until the last minute seems odd. Barry occasionally asked to talk to the author, but got fobbed off with Holmes instead and didn't comprehend why until later. Baker sort of guessed and teased Holmes about plundering old films instead of thinking up new ideas.

- The designers were L. Rowland Warne for costumes, Newbery for sets and John Horton (Visual Effects), all of whom had previous. Newbery had last worked on *Doctor Who* in 1969, for "Doctor Who and the Silurians" (7.2), but had been the go-to guy for Hartnell historicals. As with most BBC designers in the 1970s, he was allocated on the taxi-rank system and at very short notice. As we mentioned in **Where Does This Come From?**, he approached the Solon Castle sets pragmatically, thinking of an earthquake-proof building using a different methodology from Mediaeval castle design, and took the Sisterhood to be space-Buddhists with temples like those in China. Maren's throne was a stock chair covered with a Renaissance Italian pelmet. Warne gave the Sisters Tibetan-style hats, but their necklaces were plastic spoons, donated by a BBC tea-lady he named as "Winnie", sprayed gold. When the amount of naked flame in the story was assessed, Warne had to fireproof the latex detailing on the hats, using a substance that irritated the skin of some of the cast.

- Apart from an overlay of stock-footage rain and a 35mm clip of Maren's ring firing a ray (made by the BBC's graphics department), there was no film in this production and it was entirely executed in the two biggest studios in Television Centre. Barry asked Baker to demonstrate a trick with the yoyo, which resulted in Baker's beak getting bonked. He wrote this up in his occasional column in *Reveille*. Barry took the idea of Kriz being an insect (the stage directions described his demise in loving detail) and opted to re-use the Mutant masks from one of his earlier stories; John Scott Martin was recalled to inhabit the costume. The mask was stuffed and given to Madoc to act with later, another rejigged with radio-controlled mandibles and eyes. Joining the cast for the second batch of rehearsals was radio actor Michael Spice as the voice of Morbius. He had a number of TV roles under his belt, but Barry's view was that the voice had to tell the entire story.

- Recording resumed in TC3 on 20th. Before Sladen's stumbling on those stairs, the BBC's inspectors decided that the lack of a handrail was a problem. Sarah's fall on those same stairs needed a stunt performer, Jenny le Pre. In this block they also recorded the sped-up shot of the chandelier falling in (Barry was dissatisfied with this, as the technician letting it fall kept the tension on the chain after it had hit the floor). Barry says he added the shot of the brain slopping onto the floor in rehearsals. Spice was on set to read the lines into a ring modulator, to which the light inside the brain and the membrane for the larynx on the table were slaved. Steve Bowman, on Horton's team, had made the brain from layers of mastic, as used in plumbing and grouting, with small lights inside.

- Notes from the Production Office state that the faces seen in the Mind Duel are indeed the Doctor. They initially thought that famous faces would be amusing, then considered the costs of clearances from Equity and the actors themselves. Behind-the-scenes staff were given costumes by Warne and the photos were taken the day before. (As it happened, Equity got wind of non-members getting work and wrote to Hinchcliffe, so they made a payment to the Actors' Benevolent Fund.)

The last official day of recording included all the tricky scenes of things being set on fire. Fell, in the Monster again, had to carefully wave around a claw coated in flammable gel with a low flame-point; once this was extinguished, they used the real smoke for the subsequent scene of smouldering. Baker's *auto da fe* went wrong first time – Grenville saw that it was out of control and shouted at him to jump.

- Editing took a while, over November and December; the final music dub wasn't completed until 29th December. Dudley Simpson was sufficiently pleased with this story's score to use it as a demonstration, requesting an undubbed copy for use in his talk at the Television and Film School. (Oddly, an undubbed copy of Part One was given to PBS stations when the story was exported, robbing that episode of sound effects and the music. Ten seconds of music from that episode also went AWOL when the story was released otherwise unedited on video and was redubbed from a fan's audio-recording on the DVD.)

- The story went out at a marginally later slot than usual, either 5.55 – 6.20pm or 5.45 – 6.10. When the *Radio Times* revealed the author to be "Robin Bland", Dicks chuckled and relented.

The Times ran interviews with Baker, Holmes and Douglas Camfield, director of the next story (and one of the "Doctor" faces). Mary Whitehouse wasn't best pleased (or so she *said*: a chance to get headlines slagging off one of the most popular shows was exactly what she wanted for her tiny organisation). Many letters to the BBC, *The Guardian* and elsewhere, said that she was wrong

13.5 The Brain of Morbius

again. (One 11-year-old wrote to Bland and got a letter back from Holmes. Aiden Carlyle said it ought to be on at 11 at night, because it was like a war or horror film. Holmes replied, saying that "scary" was another way of saying "exciting" and pointed to the best-ever ratings for the series.) The *Evening News* followed this with a trip to a school in Tooting; of the 385 kids asked, only the youngest would admit to having been scared (nobody asked about Yeti in their loos, though). This seems to have been, as much as anything, knocking-copy by one tabloid against a rival that was trying to stir up anti-BBC feeling for its own ends.

- Hinchcliffe supervised the one-hour edit almost a year later, using the script as a guide for what was needed, rather than rewatch a story he felt had slipped from his control (he wasn't a fan of the gothic sets). Barry offered to assist, but was rebuffed – he hated the finished version, as do many others. *Daily Mail* professional controversialist Jean Rook ran a hatchet-piece on this, slagging off Holmes and claiming her child had been traumatised. This came shortly after broadcast of "The Deadly Assassin", adding to the problems that Whitehouse caused with that story.

- Dicks wrote the novelisation and fixed some of the things he thought were wrong with the broadcast story; he then rewrote that as the second and final "Junior *Doctor Who*" book. (Bizarrely, this kiddy version and the risible illustrations were also the focus of a scare-story from Whitehouse and her stooges.) It was the second story to be released on VHS and Betamax (see "Revenge of the Cybermen") and was originally released in the one-hour edit. They eventually reissued it properly in 1989.

- An 80s Goth band named themselves after the story, and London's LBGT fandom have their own Sisterhood of Karn. Colin Fay went into production after a spell in *All Creatures Great and Small* and worked on the Victoria Wood *Doctor Who* spoof with Jim Broadbent, Crayola and the Ming-Mongs. Dicks re-used ideas from this in his Virgin and BBC books, notably *Timewyrm: Exodus* and *Warmonger* (see **Why Not Mention the War?** under X3.13a, "Time Crash"). Steven Moffat resurrected the Sisterhood for the Fiftieth Anniversary and Series 9. It is unclear, at time of writing, whether Kate Bush in 1978 or the 2009 Armenian Eurovision entrants were consciously mimicking the Sisters. The Sybils in X4.2, "The Fires of Pompeii" definitely were, though.

13.6: "The Seeds of Doom"

(Serial 4, Six Episodes, 31st January – 6th March 1976.)

Which One is This? An alien gourd sprouts, embeds itself in human flesh and grows, spreading carnage. Twice. A plant-obsessed wannabe Bond Villain and his hired muscle labour to ensure that there's six episodes'-worth of mayhem.

Firsts and Lasts Douglas Camfield, who oversaw the filmed inserts of cavemen fighting in August 1963 – so was, technically, the first director of *Doctor Who* (as well as the most prolific), directs his last story. The police box prop, also a veteran from the first story, needed replacing after this, and we won't see UNIT again until 26.1, "Battlefield". We have the last instance of that 70s method of showing a PoV shot of someone looking through binoculars as it would really be (an ellipse with the long axis horizontal) rather than a masked shot with a sideways figure-8 as children expect.

For the first time, the word "possessed" is used on screen for this increasingly common plot-device in Baker's stories.

Six Things to Notice About "The Seeds of Doom"...
- As most people know, deep down, four 25-minute episodes is the ideal story length. As you may have gathered if you've been reading these books from the start, six episodes was, financially, the optimum for something that doesn't look too cheap – thanks to the unique way the BBC is funded, the cost-per-episode actually comes down, but the allotted money remains constant or goes up. Robert Holmes worked on the assumption that a six-parter is a four-parter with a coda and, when Robert Banks Stewart ran into trouble scripting this one, Holmes suggested bolting on two weeks of Antarctic malarkey to the front of his *Avengers*-esque storyline. It's not the most obvious portico or loft-extension on a script (see 7.4, "Inferno"; 15.6, "The Invasion of Time"; X4.16, "The Waters of Mars"), but the others at least stayed in the same genre with the same characters and set-designer.

- Our fun-lovin' criminals, giving the Doctor someone to lob one-liners at when a giant vegetable becomes too abstract a threat, trail clouds of associations for UK viewers. On the one hand,

The Seeds of Doom 13.6

Tony Beckley plays Harrison Chase much the same way he plays a number of effetely thuggish crime-bosses (most famously Camp Freddie in *The Italian Job*) and makes the most of peculiar lines such as "I could play all day in my green cathedral". On the other hand his hired muscle, Scorby, is written – and played – as a terrifying and cynical mercenary. Hindsight makes it hard to see John Challis as anything other than Boycie from *Only Fools and Horses* and *Green, Green Grass*.

• Into all this come a Doctor and Sarah combo (pretty much) written as Steed and Mrs Peel, then lightly amended. Sarah's fields of expertise include botanical fine art and explosives, but then they remember her character-notes and give her a few tirades against macho gun-culture. Tom Baker's performance is definitely a two-speed affair. In Parts One, Four, Five and Six, the Doctor's like a bear with a sore head, occasionally forcing himself to be sort-of-charming but generally snarling at everyone. In Parts Two and Three, he's fluffy and spontaneous, even more like Eric Morecambe than usual – except when it's a scene recorded on location. There, the Doctor is unprecedentedly violent, using physical force and hand-weapons as a first resort (he claims that he's only bluffing about holding people at gunpoint) and not in a tidy, non-imitable "Venusian Karate" sort of way like his last self. Even a punch-up in a quarry, directed to avoid showing the Doctor actually hitting the chauffeur, results in the guy being hospitalised. One especially out-of-character moment has the Doctor immobilise Scorby by twisting his neck. It's not fatal (as it would have been in any other circumstance, or if kids had copied it).

• But what's weird is that this incident, and the *Scooby Doo* chase around the grounds, that the score is like "Terror of the Zygons" but more so. Camfield's petulance towards Dudley Simpson even extends to Geoffrey Burgon doing a parody of synthesiser music of the era and having the Doctor gripe about it on camera.

• As if to offset all the Howard Hawks blokishness, we get the first full-blown example of the Dotty Old Lady. Maren, in the last story, was a faltering first step – but in the flower artist Amelia Ducat, we have the archetype. This cigarillo-smoking old ham is the template for the one-story companions who will dominate this phase of *Doctor Who* the way blimpish military types, harassed managerial men with northern accents and "comedy" yokels on the make did earlier stages. (Stretching a point, elderly women could have played Coordinator Engin or Organon –"The Deadly Assassin and 17.3, "The Creature from the Pit". The Doctor treats those characters with exactly the fond indulgence he normally reserves for such daft old bats as Miss Ducat and Professor Rumford from 16.3, "The Stones of Blood".)

• With the location work done on OB, there are a few odd details. Everyone's breath mists in the grounds of Chase's mansion, but not in Antarctic wastes; the World Ecology Bureau looks suspiciously like Television Centre; Amelia Ducat's studio is gloomier than Chase's garden at night. On the other hand, the main location, Athelhampton House, looks sensational in this format. (You can compare it to a near-contemporary appearance on the usual BBC standby of 16mm film in the 1975 *Morecambe and Wise Christmas Show* or *The Goodies Rule, OK?*.)

The Continuity

The Doctor has started wearing golf-shoes [see Sylvester McCoy's three seasons], but leaves the studs out when in England. He identifies a Krynoid pod on sight from a photo sent by phone [using 70s tech]. Here he's very short-tempered and prone to violence as a first solution, but he can occasionally turn on the charm (often when there's a gun trained on him).

He lets Sarah claim that he's not a medical doctor [see this story's essay], and acts as a backseat driver when the other scientists seek to perform surgery on Winlett. He says, in all seriousness, that: "nothing's hopeless – you just have to think". He also introduces Sarah as "my best friend".

• *Background*. He identifies Scorby's 'When it comes to money, Mr Chase and I are of the same religion' as a quotation from Franklin Adams but cites the author as if he doesn't know him personally. He's President of the Intergalactic Floral Society, naturally. He may have met Mozart.

• *Ethics*. He doesn't want people depending on him for solutions, hence his apparent squeamishness about amputating Winlett's arm. After everything Chase has done, the Doctor still tries to save him from the crusher.

• *Inventory: Other*. He picks up a pistol from a guard he's marmelised and – even though he tells Sarah he'd never use it – looks as if he means business. He brandishes a red toothbrush as proof that he's ready to leave at a moment's notice. His yo-yo's yellow this time.

215

13.6 The Seeds of Doom

The TARDIS It seems the Doctor planned to travel to Antarctic Base 5 by his usual method, then thought better of it. In Part Six, he winds up there because he didn't cancel 'the coordinate programme'.

The Supporting Cast

• *Sarah* likes brandy now [c.f. "The Ark in Space"]. She dresses for Antarctica by adopting a long(ish) stripy scarf and matching bobble-hat, with orange dungarees (compared to the vertical stripes two stories from now) and a long-sleeve T-shirt almost matching the hat. When back in Britain, she's got a brown *faux* dirndl [really a Batik-print waistcoat and almost-matching baggy shorts], a hooded raincoat and boots. She's heard of Amelia Ducat and corrects the Doctor's [accurate] pronunciation to the *ersatz* French way the artist prefers. She tears Scorby off a strip for, well, for being Scorby (cowardice, bullying, pointless sexism, selfishness, unthinking violence…). It seems to her that calling someone 'cloth-eyes' is sensible.

She still hasn't learned that putting on a swimsuit aboard the TARDIS is asking for trouble [11.3, "Death to the Daleks"].

• *UNIT*. The Doctor's still readily available, as an advisor, when anyone needs an expert opinion on weird plants. People know of him, but don't seem ready for the guy with the scarf and jelly babies [supporting the idea that this is shortly after 11.5, "Planet of the Spiders"]. The Brigadier's in Geneva, again [or perhaps has just left but was there in the possibly-later story, "The Android Invasion", if that's the line you want to take].

The Doctor seems to have previously met Major Beresford, the Brig's stand-in. Sarah acts as if she also knows this chap, as well as the doomed Sergeant Henderson. He comes armed with a defoliant that's still on the secret list [possibly a dioxin derivative like Agent Orange]. Beresford packs a heavy-duty laser. [It's less effective than the Disintegrator Gun from "Robot". Possibly, the Think Tank escapade led to a redrafting of arms limitation talks to include that doohickey as well.] They use the radio call sign "Scorpio Sector", rather than all that Greyhound / Trap stuff.

The Non-Humans

• *Krynoids* are repeatedly spoken of as plants but behave oddly compared to terrestrial flora. They grow remarkably fast, from a tendril inside a coconut-sized pod to roughly the size of St Paul's Cathedral in under a day. This, despite very little sunlight and no watering; the roots never get into the soil but, instead, embed themselves in the flesh of humans and achieve a form of symbiosis. [What they would have turned out if the host had been a cow, a cactus or just rock is unclear.] As it grows to the size of a house, the plant can access the human host's memory and vocabulary. Thereafter, it can direct the movement of any other plant within a two-mile radius. Those plants also exhibit rapid growth-spurts and activity, pulling out phone lines and ensnaring fugitives.

There's few eye-witness accounts, so a lot of what the Doctor tells us is conjecture. They seem to have originated on a planet with extreme vulcanism and eject the pods into space; pods travel in pairs, 'like policemen'. After this maximum size is reached, the plants germinate by binary fission, ultimately engulfing entire planets.

History

• *Dating*. The Antarctic base is in touch with London via Telex and gets ten minutes of satellite-phone use per day. [This makes it very obviously the 1970s, even if the "Javlin" logo on the cold-weather wear wasn't more flagrant than the BBC would have liked.] The limitation suggests an era before the Space Shuttle put up big comsats. Sarah is asked for 2p for the phone [so it's before 1980]. Chase has an H-reg Daimler. The classified UNIT defoliant seems to be Agent Orange or similar, so we're pretty much contemporary – Chase even says that it's autumn in Britain [see **Things That Don't Make Sense**]. People still have Trimphones. [Amelia Ducat's mental arithmetic (750 guineas plus inflation equals a grand) works when inflation's running at 22%, strongly suggesting 1975-6. Chase doesn't question this.]

If Moberley's right, the ice-layering indicates that the Krynoid pods landed about 20,000 years before. [However, we're talking about something that came from space, via Earth's atmosphere, so they were probably quite hot when they landed and may have arrived more recently, melting their way down to Pleistocene layers. (Although if Moberley can date it from ice-layers, the infill can't have been that substantial. Maybe the pods parachuted down and had time to cool, before gently settling on the surface of the ice and being buried. Or, Moberley's a lousy palaeontologist.)]

Chase Manor was built just at the end of the

Doctor of What?

As has often been pointed out, if the series had been called "Professor Who", we'd not have warmed to the central character quite so quickly (or often). In Britain, the title "Professor" means, among other things, attachment to a specific university and faculty. It's also a term more commonly associated with supervillains of various descriptions, from Moriarty to Chaos, or ineffectual bunglers and gadgeteers such as Tournesol / Calculus in *Tintin* or Professor Branestawm. "Doctor" suggests a more practical, worldly sort of protagonist, more likely benign than not.

Our Doctor occasionally professes to not being medically-qualified, despite considerable evidence to the contrary. That's been a source of confusion, especially in English, for a very long time. Sometimes, the Doctor claims to just have an honorary doctorate; other times, it turns out they have a PhD. in a specific subject that – what luck! – is exactly what's needed. As most of these conversations take place among humans with English accents, it's logical to start on Earth, specifically Europe, then worry about other planets and times.

"Doctor" comes from the Latin *docere*, meaning teacher (the "do" beginning, common in Indo-European languages, hints at a core meaning of giving something). The traditional process of higher education is to get good at something by sequestering yourself at University ("Bachelor" of Arts or Science), get completely on top of the subject ("Master"), then get so good you can teach it.

Universities really got going in the late eleventh century, as law schools attached to the cathedral cities of Italy. Before long, they were licenced to teach medicine, and not long after that, the practice was restricted to graduates of these institutions, but law came first. In fact, if you look at the curriculum of the first recognised med-school, Salerno, it's initially the same as the legal training, three years learning logic (broadly, book-learning and dialectic), then another five years of poring over Galen's remaining works and dissecting pigs before a public examination by one of the heads of faculty and a year's internship under a practicing graduate. Lawyers and medical practitioners were, in essence, priests who'd added to their studies.

The next development, apart from all the practice people got in wound-dressing and amputation after the Crusades, was Bologna's law school adding a *collegia* formed from lay-students, mainly via the trade guilds. The Holy Roman Emperor Frederick II formally recognised this body. A good reason existed for this: he was trying to sue the Vatican, so an ecclesiastically-based law school was no help to him. Bologna's "commune" also added a medical school at around this time. Anyone who went through any of these could add "La Dotta" (the learned) after his name.

But university wasn't the only course of action to be considered a Doctor. If you look in the 20-volume Oxford English Dictionary, the earliest English use cited is 1303, applied retrospectively to the "fathers" of the church: St. Ambrose, St Jerome, St Gregory and St Augustine. You could say these were the first honorary doctorates, except the work they undertook for their faith took even longer than graduating from Salerno. Becoming a doctor takes time. These days, a medical qualification requires a three to five-year taught course and four or more years in a hospital, and that's before picking a specialised area of expertise.

A PhD. in a different field needs a good first degree, ideally an MA and then a seven-year "research" period, often with a job at the university to keep body and soul together while doing it, and a defence of your thesis (a Viva Voce, as they call it in some fields) against antagonistic examiners (once again, the model was Catholicism, specifically the original "Devil's Advocate" opposing a canonised figure's claim to sainthood). You have to pick a subject almost nobody knows anything about, *then* find a supervisor who knows more than you working in a university and not already supervising someone else. Then you have to publish your work. To keep that university gig that was paying the bills, you'd need to have published a lot, in peer-reviewed or suitably scrutinised journals. You need a track-record (especially now, in the publish-or-perish culture of universities). It's not something you do in an afternoon without people knowing who you are.

Apart from Series 9, when the twelfth Doctor maybe-possibly spent a century or so at St Luke's University, Bristol (this whole storyline will require a lot of careful examination on several fronts), it's hard to imagine any incarnation voluntarily staying put anywhere for that long or making that much of a splash. Being exiled to Earth and serving as UNIT's unpaid scientific advisor rather got in the way of any sustained research programme, unless we count the peculiar unspoken backstory to "Planet of the Spiders" (11.5). Here, the Doctor's

continued on page 219...

13.6 The Seeds of Doom

Wars of the Roses [c.1480]. The corridor with the suit of armour from that period was, however, added in the seventeenth century. Sir Bothwell Chase was executed in 1587.

The Analysis

Where Does This Come From? What you see is what you get: an episode of *The Avengers* directed by someone who'd rather be doing *The Sweeney*. It's barely worth arguing about which specific episode, because it's pretty flagrant – see later if you don't know – but let's dig deeper.

There's something amazingly 1970s at work here. It's a freakish phenomenon that, almost on the stroke of midnight 31st December 1979 / 1st January 1980, was abandoned with such speed, it's as unbelievable as *The Partridge Family 2200 A.D.*, *Fear of Flying* or sales figures for *Jonathan Livingston Seagull* to anyone who wasn't there. If anyone's heard of *The Secret Life of Plants* at all, it's because there was a film of the ludicrous book and a double LP of the soundtrack got into the charts – but even that's been air-brushed from the public memory and never comes up in the context of Stevie Wonder albums. A blind man doing a film soundtrack is actually the most sensible thing about the entire enterprise. The film, directed by Walon Green, used the same cheap tricks as the better-remembered *Koyaanisqatsi*, time-lapse photography, crash-edits and synthesizers (rather weakening the anti-technology argument in both cases). Paramount released it around the time people were being exhorted to simultaneously meditate to psychokinetically prevent Skylab from crashing (yeah, that worked).

The book was co-written by an advocate of dowsing (water-divining with twigs) and took the stance that if conventional science said something was wrong it *must*, ipso facto be true. Except when science provided evidence for their loopy theories, then scientists were visionaries. (Their selection of "outsider" scientists was curious, as George Washington Carver and Jagadish Chandra Bose were employed by universities.) By the end of their book, the authors (Peter Tompkins and Christopher Bird) were claiming that plants produced electrical fields that were detectable by fairies. One of the more reliable bits of research they cited was a project to test pot-plants with polygraphs – one Cleve Backster had been getting funding for this since the 50s – and they leveraged this as proof of Kirlian Photography (see 3.4, "The Daleks' Master Plan") and that plants were telepathic.

With Erich Von Daniken topping the bestseller lists as well, this might seem like the entire decade was a "Just Say No" campaign, but what's interesting is that it was deemed worthwhile to test such remarkable claims. Michel Gauquelin devised a methodology to test one specific assertion made by astrologers; psychology departments whipped out the Zener Cards to try out anyone who claimed to have ESP (see "Planet of the Spiders"); archaeologists pored over satellite photos of Mount Ararat, desperate to see traces of Noah's Ark. (If you're interested, the results were all negative. Still, at least they weren't rejecting these ideas out of hand as the zonked-out loons who wrote that book claimed.)

Plants are alive and obviously grow and change – the Greeks contended that there was a growth-principle, the "vegetable soul" (mentioned by Andrew Marvell in *To His Coy Mistress*), common to all living things but subsumed by the animal soul that makes creatures walk, fly or swim (literal "animation", as possessed by animals but not inanimate stones) and that in turn is behind / beneath / within the psyche. Mediaeval travellers claimed to have encountered halfway-animated plants.

However, humans and animals stop growing eventually. Various earlier philosophers speculated on the cause and what would make it otherwise. As always, we have a residue of these earlier notions in folklore and pop culture (as well as in sinister pseudo-science such as Lysenkoism). In the next story, we'll pick up on what people used to think about mandrake roots, but plant-like men (Dryads in Greek myth, the Green Man in early European art – those Arcimboldo paintings that were so popular in the 1990s, for example – the Scandinavian Skogsra and the souls of suicides in Dante) are found across the West.

Much later, mainly in the 1880s and 1890s, stories of blood-sucking African plants and more aggressive versions of the Venus Fly Trap or Pitcher Plant did the rounds, sometimes reported as news but usually – as in H.G. Wells's short story "The Flowering of the Strange Orchid" – as amusing vignettes. One story, "The Man-Eating Tree" by Edmund Spencer – offered as fact in 1888 – details a newly-discovered plant *Crynoida dajeeana* from Malaya (there's a real genus of plant

Doctor of What?

...continued from page 217

been using UNIT facilities to investigate ESP in humans despite now possessing a repaired and relatively cooperative TARDIS. Before anyone can question this, we've had our first death and a teleporting tractor to deal with. But, why would the Doctor be on hand when the Metebelis crystal is sent to his lab, *unless* all the jibes from government scientists over the last five years have finally got to him?

Throughout the UNIT years, we've had a lot of accredited doctors and professors all calling this bloke "the Doctor" – even Liz Shaw (whose own multiple qualifications are overlooked and is "Miss Shaw" despite having letters in front of her name as well as after). He was challenged precisely once, by Winser (8.3, "The Claws of Axos") and admitted to not having published anything in the UK. Winser, who called the Doctor "you stupid quack", then conveniently got himself killed by a plasmid duvet. Nobody else questions the Doctor's credentials until Martha Jones takes umbrage at her own studies being devalued (X3.1, "Smith and Jones"). Maybe the Doctor's been stung by other comments and sought to get a twentieth-century British qualification under his belt.

In fact, he had one on the books already: an honorary Doctorate from St. Cedd's, Cambridge, in 1960. Unfortunately, it was a different-looking Doctor and – from his perspective – hadn't happened yet. The same scene in "Shada" (17.6) has the Doctor tell Wilkins that there was another visit in 1958, but "I was in a different body". Other than that, there's the muddle over whether he has a medical doctorate from Victorian Scotland. Whereas England only had two universities for centuries (because of the "Stamford Oath", not repealed until 1827), Scotland was an early adopter, with St. Andrew's in 1413, Glasgow in 1451 and three more by 1590.

In "The Moonbase" (4.6), the Doctor claims to have sat for a medical degree in Glasgow in 1888 under Joseph Lister (pioneer of antiseptic surgery). Yet this is impossible, according to the history we think we know. Lister had moved to London in 1877, to lecture at King's College Hospital, only leaving in 1893. The Doctor's reminiscence is couched in at least three "I think"s. Yet the Doctor's clearly been to Scotland several times in unrecorded adventures, can recognise "The Flowers of the Fields" as a lament for the dead ("Terror of the Zygons"), knows his way around Aberdeen (15.5, "Underworld") and has picked up a couple of tartan scarves (as well as an accent from somewhere: 24.1, "Time and the Rani", et seq. then X7.16, "The Time of the Doctor" et seq.). Clara, pretending to be the Doctor and presumably with scraps picked up when she went around his timestream like an antibody (X8.12, "Death in Heaven"), claimed that he "accidentally graduated in the wrong century" in Glasgow. So there is at least one extant medical qualification on the books, from a while back.

We'll come back to this in a moment, but let's here ask why someone so keen to impress everyone with all of their *other* qualifications steers clear of admitting to any medical training. The circumstances under which the Doctor gets put on the spot and mumbles about only having an honorary doctorate seem to coincide with people needing to take responsibility for whatever intervention happens. In "The Ark in Space", he wants to let Vira make the decisions and offers the outrageous excuse "Harry here's only qualified to operate on sailors". Something similar happens in "The Seeds of Doom", when Sarah claims that the Doctor can't help.

Legally, anyone professing to have a medical qualification is responsible for the lives of anyone in that situation, so he could just be avoiding awkward questions and inquests (although, as UNIT had already entrusted to him the safety of the Earth, notably in a plague in 7.2, "Doctor Who and the Silurians", this ought not to matter). In other circumstances, notably when trying to reassure Rita (X6.11, "The God Complex"), he cheerfully admits to being an MD as well as umpteen PhDs.

We've never seen the Doctor perform surgery, but that's not entirely unexpected – apart from this being a family show, there's a traditional distinction between a surgeon (from the Greek, and originally chirurgeon, someone good with his hands) and a book-learned Doctor, originally a priest who specialised and did diagnoses with the aid of horoscopes and colour-charts for urine. (In Britain, senior surgeons have to earn the title "Mister".) The Doctor's medical knowledge impresses Professor Marius, the fiftieth-century's pre-eminent xenobiologist (15.2, "The Invisible Enemy"), but going native in more primitive times, such as ours, might not appeal. After all, imagine anyone before Pasteur or Fleming explaining how bread-mould could make amputations safer, or

continued on page 221...

13.6 The Seeds of Doom

called "crynoids", as we hope you knew). The locals worship it and have a ritual wherein a girl dances around it, cuts into the bark and drinks the sap, which makes her oblivious to the tendrils engulfing her to crush her and drink her blood. This tradition continues with John Collier's 1930 story that inspired the 1959 cheap quicky *Little Shop of Horrors*, then the 80s stage musical, then the film version of that with the revised ending. As it was, it took until 2019 to find any evidence of plants eating large numbers of vertebrates (Canadian "Turtle Sock" pitcher-plants ingest rather more salamanders than thought) rather than this being a sporadic side-effect of insectivorous activity.

Admittedly, plants-that-are-more-like-animals isn't unprecedented in *Doctor Who*. Terry Nation did it almost as often as he had characters with names like "Tarrant". In "The Chase" (2.8), we get a spectacularly silly comment by Ian, a science teacher, that the vegetation on Mechanus looks "just as though it were alive". The first time is the most detailed (as usual): in "The Keys of Marinus" (1.5), Nation had Darrius, the doomed botanist, devising a "growth accelerator" to affect both the balance of nature and the tempo of destruction. (That caused a ruckus because someone else had submitted a similar idea for a six-part story – he complained to the BBC about Nation not having any ideas of his own.) That's interesting, because the most famous real-life active plants – the Venus Fly Trap – works by a furious growth-spurt in just the part of the plant that acts as the hinge, then the rest of the plant grows to re-open the trap. Many of the pop-cultural variations on tropical plants as hazards are based on things British and US troops encountered in South-East Asia, some of which grow at almost-visible rates.

However, the most famous of all, the Triffids, were inspired by the buddleias that sprouted in bomb-sites across Britain in the 1940s. *Doctor Who* adapting a John Wyndham novel is almost too obvious for anyone to have attempted it before – it would have been like *Star Trek* pilfering Ray Bradbury. There have been many screen adaptations of *Day of the Triffids*: a strange film from the early 60s with Howard Keel and our own Carole Ann Ford, David Maloney's 1981 BBC serial (itself adapted without the plants as *28 Days Later*) and a 2009 TV movie. In many ways, Nation's *Survivors* echoes the novel's later stages. The odd thing is that the plants with killer whiplash stings are less impressive on screen because they have to amble about. In "The Seeds of Doom", they evade that problem by cross-pollinating with another 50s British SF classic, *The Quatermass Experiment*. As you'll recall from "The Ark in Space", the infected astronaut's arm is the start of his problems, but in the original 1953 series, and the feature film (which, unlike episodes 3-6, still exists and is shown every so often), he slams his hand into a pot-plant and mixes his genes with its, growing increasingly plant-like and eventually towering over Westminster Abbey like the Krynoid over Chase Manor. The intermediary stages, obviously still a man covered in bark and fronds, has moments where he seems cureable. In the early stages, he is taken to hospital, only to be – well, on television, he's abducted by sinister foreigners who want to know about space travel. On film, he's removed from security confinement by a man hired by his estranged wife. Either way, a contemporary type of mercenary gets involved and Caroon, the hapless astronaut, has his fateful close encounter with a cactus during the mêlée.

Other iffy films often cited as possible influences include *The Trollenberg Terror* (1958) and *Konga!* (1961), although neither is especially compelling as a comparison. The former, a six-part ATV serial from 1956 adapted into an amazingly cheap film (also released as *The Crawling Eye* – see 15.1, "Horror of Fang Rock"), is set on an alpine mountain afflicted by radioactive mist and does, admittedly, feature the then-topical Molotov cocktails (made famous by the Hungarian uprising) and snow and something-on-the-roof. It's mainly a zombie flick, as the big-eyed aliens can't leave the cold, so use reanimated corpses to do their chores. *Konga!* has Michael Gough (3.7, "The Celestial Toymaker"; 20.1, "Arc of Infinity") and a man in a gorilla suit – but for most of the film, it's about the amazing growth-spurts (and mind-control) caused by the sap of unconvincing meat-eating African orchids. It ends as what could generously be called an *homage* to *King Kong*, but with Croydon and a model of Parliament replacing the Empire State Building. Nobody's really inclined to be that generous.

Mercenaries were in the news a lot in the mid-70s. In particular, the Angolan Civil War was a lucrative venue for ex-soldiers looking to support fascists / communists / anyone. (It's the subject of Elvis Costello's *Oliver's Army* and one of the factions, the MPLA, is namechecked in *Anarchy in the*

Doctor of What?

...continued from page 219

why clean-looking knives need to be put in boiling water or spirit alcohol between operations. If a student doctor in Lister's class had mentioned blood-types and Rhesus Factor, it would have been dismissed as gibberish.

Nonetheless, it seems like a prudent precaution for someone spending a while in a time and place where people hear the word / title / name "Doctor" and assume a medical qualification to have one handy, as well as doctorates in other things. Earth did become rather a special case, but the Doctor was a doctor long before then. According to Drax, in "The Armageddon Factor" (16.6), this happened before they both left Gallifrey. The weird thing is that every other Time Lord treats this as unique, as if nobody has achieved a doctorate before or since. This may be for convenience, as there isn't really anything else to call this person (other than "Theta Sigma", as likely a dorm-room address as anything – in 25.2, "The Happiness Patrol" he calls it his "nickname at college").

Let's assume, then, that Prydon Academy awards doctorates regularly enough that someone lacking the right to a name can be called "the Doctor" and forgotten by most of the Time Lords, but not *so* regularly that the title lacks any merit. A stray comment in "Time and the Rani" (24.1) might hint that the chosen specialised subject was Thermodynamics. We mentioned this in the 2004 version of this essay, in passing – however, another comment in the next episode, "So elementary, I broke the Second Law of Thermodynamics", suggests the Doctor knows less about it than your average 14-year-old.

What the Rani-as-Mel actually says was that it was his speciality at University. (They're contemporaries, as is established when they both turn out to be 953.) If the Rani has somehow accurately second-guessed how the Doctor would have explained this usually-obfuscated aspect of his past to a computer programmer from Pease Pottage, then we can take the comment at face value. Given her wrong-headed assessment of his attitudes over the rest of the story, that's improbable. (Still, she worked out how to impersonate Mel, whom she's seen once, when unconscious.) If Gallifrey's at all like Earth, the most likely way for the Rani to have known the Doctor during his studies to become a doctor was if she too was studying – she knows a lot more than him about Stattenheim Remote Controls for TARDISes (22.3,

"The Mark of the Rani") and messing around with mutant brains. If he's a doctor, she probably is too (unless the incident with the lab rats got her thrown out).

No particular thesis title or subject is ever given. The Doctor first admits to any specific doctorates in "The God Complex", where he says he has a medical one and cheese-making. In X11.5, "The Tsuranga Conundrum" we get "medicine, science, engineering, candyfloss, Lego, music, problems, people, hope." "Problems" is the only one too vague to be immediately plausible as a paper (defining the boundaries of "people" is knotty – see **Do Robots Have Rights?** earlier in this book), but the context is yet another attempt to reassure strangers. Obviously, the Doctor knows many subjects to an advanced level, and claims experience and proficiency in them in at various times – from Agronomy to Zymurgy (8.4, "Colony in Space" and, stretching a point, the enzyme-fermentation in "The Power of Kroll"), but spending seven or so years on each to get a bit of paper seems a bit out of character.

Someone with a functioning time machine could, of course, cut out a few tedious stages and simply pop in for interviews a couple of times a year, submitting papers at the appropriate times and maybe using the university facilities for other purposes to be seen to be around. We know from "The Mysterious Planet" (23.1) that the Doctor occasionally published monographs under pseudonyms. The biggest problem is not making a splash and altering history, so finding fiddly little specialisms would be the key (and avoiding accidental plagiarism of people who haven't been born). Other universities on other planets might have different criteria and go in for something like the Krotons' mind-measuring equipment (6.4, "The Krotons"), in which case the Doctor could get a hefty certificate in an hour.

Of course, our assumption about the Doctor's inability to stay put for long enough to do it the hard way could be false. There have been excuses for demonstrations of several other skills that take time to master, from swordplay and spin-bowling to spaceship-navigation and Venusian Aikido. The apparent need to keep studying obscure topics and publishing monographs on these, in local journals-of-record, is a way to bolster up the right to that identity. If we're to believe "Ghost Light" (26.2), every version of the Doctor has at some

continued on page 223...

UK by the Sex Pistols.) In Angola and elsewhere, liberation campaigns became proxy Cold War power-struggles. Even after the original colonial power had been booted, the different factions could call on the leftover commercial interests, neighbouring countries or covert supplies and support from far-off nations. However, when any of these hired guns got caught, their relatives made appeals to their own government to negotiate a release (and thus got into the local paper), since the Geneva Convention specifies that a mercenary is not eligible for the same consideration as a legitimate prisoner of war.

One particularly nasty example was accountant-turned-insurgent-for-hire "Mad Mike" Hoare and his "Wild Geese" (lauded in a film of that name with which Richard Burton and Richard Harris paid their bar tabs), although the press stopped praising them after a disastrous 1981 escapade in the Seychelles. Scorby's boast that he'd worked in Africa and the Middle East is enough background for the viewers. (With this story's author having links to Scotland, note that the name "Scorby" is close to the Scots word for a carrion crow, a corbei.)

But we mentioned a really obvious source for this story, and it's a 1965 *Avengers* episode, "The Man-Eater of Surrey Green". As an example of the series in that year, it's pretty odd – the alien plant *doesn't* turn out to be a hoax engineered by obsessive botanists trying to overthrow the government, for a start. No, this is a genuine, honest-to-goodness extra-terrestrial weed that keeps growing, kills people and possesses the minds of all who come close. Well, almost all: it uses ultrasonic signals, so Steed jury-rigs hearing-aids and rescues Mrs Peel, who helps him dose the thing with weed killer. Noticeably, with Mrs Peel under the influence, Steed's a lot more ruthless and violent.

Most Emma Peel episodes of the series had conspiracies by special-interest groups and / or the Russians, and often had an eccentric millionaire with monomaniacal tendencies – rather as Harrison Chase has here. The majority of the action takes place in a recluse's luxurious country house, as it does here. He has an absurdly loyal butler, as with Hargreaves here. On occasion, the army's called in and their representative(s) will invariably come unstuck, as happens here. There may even be an early scene with one of Our Heroes meeting a different obsessive eccentric for a quick info-dump – but, for once, the formula isn't followed slavishly, as Amelia Ducat isn't bumped off at the first advert break. (That's mainly Douglas Camfield's doing, as she was originally just in that one scene, for Our Heroes to ID the villain, after the Plot Coupon of the conveniently-placed painting in the boot of the Daimler. The novelisation prunes her role back to the original, indicating that Hinchcliffe – who adapted it for Target – wasn't taken with this development.)

In real life, enough eccentric millionaires had pet passions to make any one of these stories superficially plausible. Howard Hughes was nuts about planes. J. Paul Getty was nuts about paintings. William Randolph Hearst was just nuts. Britain still had a few like that, but the majority had sold the family seat to a rock star or lived as tenants of the National Trust. Harrison Chase even has an American-sounding name, but his sealed-off estate and private army is more like a European villain. In the past, however, many such people did send expeditions across the world to collect rare plants. One such was Joseph Banks (to whom this story's author claimed kinship), who was with Cook's expedition to the South Seas (including Australia and Tahiti) and advised George III on the collection at Kew. It's odd that the story doesn't directly name Kew Gardens but (rather improbably) gives the Royal Horticultural Society – now mainly known for the Chelsea Flower Show – a mention at the end.

With all the talk of shape-shifting alien infiltrators in this volume, it's inevitable that we'll get to the granddaddy of them all: John W. Campbell's "Who Goes There?" (and we will, once we reach "Horror of Fang Rock"), but it's the first film version, *The Thing from Another World*, that now commands our attention. Not just for the scenes of hacking a seed-pod out of the ice (Arctic, rather than Antarctic, in the film), but the serial's entire ambience. The film sets up a clear division between rugged he-men who get things done (and makes one of them a hard-drinking she-woman, making the conversations a bit less amenable to *Top Gun*-style gay readings) and effete, morally dubious scientists who are going to get everyone killed if they aren't put in their place. There's no attempt to make the alien adopt the persona of one of the crew and get them paranoid that way – this one's a seven-foot hulking brute that feeds on blood and refuses to listen to beardy

Doctor of What?

...continued from page 221

stage joined the Royal Society, so each face must have a membership and existing members must vouch for each new incarnation.

The Doctor's acted like a published authority on topics from plant-tissue's resistance to being stomped on by giant robots ("Robot") to Elizabethan-era microbiology (3.5, "The Massacre") in each of the most likely periods of Earth's history. If we're to believe Masters in "Doctor Who and the Silurians", the Pertwee Doctor has already got a formidable reputation at the Science Ministry within weeks of waking up with that face. (This spurt of activity seems to have served as a calling-card as late as "The Seeds of Doom", but not in "The Hand of Fear".) This looks like an ability to impress fellow scientists without the aid of time-travel, but in record time. Despite being active and practical instead of sedentary and scholarly, the Doctor must spend a lot of off-screen time in universities.

Hanging around on campus is a good way to meet people before they become famous. In an earlier version of this essay, one social nexus in particular looked like a set of associations made at med school in Scotland in 1888, just not with Lister. It's at least possible that the Doctor's medical training was at Edinburgh University under Joseph Bell. Bell, who could deduce vast amounts about his patients' lives from the tiniest details, is now thought to be the single greatest inspiration behind Sherlock Holmes. Bell's star pupil, Arthur Conan-Doyle, has almost the same circle of friends as the Doctor from this period. Harry Houdini ("Planet of the Spiders"; "Revenge of the Cybermen"; X11.8, "The Witchfinders"); the Prince of Wales / King Edward VII (the Doctor makes frequent references to Belle Epoque Paris – notably in "City of Death" – and there's a direct reference in 7.4, "Inferno"); Sir Arthur Sullivan (1.3, "The Edge of Destruction"); H. G. Wells ("Pyramids of Mars"; "Horror of Fang Rock" and ultimately 22.5, "Timelash") and a whole lot more.

If the Doctor knows all these people, then he surely bumped into Doyle, yet this is never mentioned. He doesn't even wince when Redvers Fenn-Cooper makes a disparaging remark about "young Conan-Doyle" ("Ghost Light"). Either something happened which has affected his memory, or they had a blazing row. Doyle's most famous falling-out was with Houdini, over the Cottingsley "fairies"; fans of the many remaindered films starring Paul McGann will know this as the basis for the film *Fairytale: A True Story* (1997), as well as the other one released in the same month, *Photographing Fairies*. (Plus, if you count it, *Torchwood* 1.5, "Small Worlds.") A Theosophist whose daughters had apparently taken photos of fairies contacted Doyle, who believed in spiritualism. It was a silly joke that got out of hand, but Doyle had too much at stake to admit it. It was 1917, and people needed to believe in life-after-death and other worlds. Still, it seems too trivial a thing to make the Doctor pass up an excuse for a good name-drop.

The odd thing about this is that, on the strength of "The Talons of Weng-Chiang", we might make a good case that the Holmes canon doesn't exist in the *Doctor Who* 1890s – but then, in "The Snowmen" (X7.6), it does and always did (see also 7.2, "Doctor Who and the Silurians"). That story and its immediate sequel and the season finale (X7.7, "The Bells of St John"; X7.14, "The Name of the Doctor") concern a systematic revision of accepted continuity and in-universe history far more drastic than anything ever broadcast (see **Was There a Martian Time-Slip?** under X4.16, "The Waters of Mars" and **The Great Intelligence or Just a Great Intelligence?** under "The Snowmen"). The bad news for those of us trying to make a consistent and coherent account of all televised *Doctor Who* is that Steven Moffat's "head-canon" has overwritten extant episodes; the good news is that we can to some extent account for the anomalies here by suggesting that the Doctor did indeed qualify in human medicine – but only within personal chronology and not that of the outside universe. The Doctor remembers many things that ceased ever to have happened when the past changed. (See **He Remembers This How?** under X1.5, "World War Three" and **Is Time Like Bolognese Sauce?** under X5.5, "Flesh and Stone".) It's not a pretty solution, but it's there if you want it.

The obvious alternative is faking it. The Master seems to have resisted the temptation to outrank the Doctor by legitimate means (9.5, "The Time Monster") and just inveigled his way into two separate university faculties as a Professor without leaving a plausible paper-trail. In "The Mind of Evil" (8.2), he does that without causing any doubt as to his background – he got the Home Office, HM Inspector of Prisons and the Chinese Embassy onside with the bare minimum of mind-control.

continued on page 225...

13.6 The Seeds of Doom

scientists who offer help. It is identified as a plant very early on ("an intellectual carrot", as the audience-identification journalist comments) and plants saplings of itself, but it walks like a human and leaves doors open in blizzards.

One other small detail... that business with the Doctor's toothbrush is a direct reference to Tom Baker's scapegrace lifestyle until shortly before this story was written.

English Lessons
- *Telex* (n.): the 1930s version of the internet. The teletype, a prototype of a fax machine, had previously used telegraphic Morse rather than digital ASCII to connect teleprinters. Telex networked these using dedicated phone lines and, in remote areas, short-wave radio. Although you could use it "live", if you and the other person could type really fast and spoke the lingo (an early version of text-speak), it was mainly for pre-written messages or crude images. One line could carry 25 separate signals, so economically it was an obvious choice for businesses and the military. (America eventually got something similar, AT&T's TWX system and, later, Western Union's version, but who owned what at any given stage is complicated. Just to confuse things more, they trademarked the word "Telex" in the 60s, even though the rest of the world used the word for the older system.) So that's how a photo of an alien seed-pod got from Antarctica to London in under a day.
- *Chilterns* (n.): A small range of chalk hills north of London; the unofficial end of the Home Counties (see 2.2, "The Dalek Invasion of Earth"). They run diagonally south-west to north-east from Reading to Luton, with Aylesbury and High Wycombe either side of the narrow strip. Since the mid-60s, it's been legally designated an Area of Outstanding Natural Beauty, so it can be farmed but not built on too much.
- *Wars of the Roses* (n.): Oh, come on, you did this at school. No? Well, George R.R. Martin certainly did, then added a few dragons and made a mint. Shakespeare did and milked it for a string of hit plays that kept him out of prison.

The quick answer is that it wasn't quite a civil war – because it was fought mainly with mercenaries, and in the peak 30 years, only just over a year of actual conflict happened – but it wiped out several of the major dynasties in the House of Lords. Richard II was considered a bit of a waste of space, so he was deposed and locked up by someone who became Henry IV. Their extended families, the House of York (which had a white rose as their emblem – at least, according to Shakespeare) and the House of Lancaster (with the red rose logo), differed on whether this was a legitimate move.

Victorians liked the story about the flower-selection, and the idea that this was all going somewhere, so they called it "The Wars of the Roses" – even though that's like calling the *Risorgimento* "The Biscuit War". Meanwhile, the nobility were also fighting wars in France (because, being both ultimately French families, they had claims on that throne too), but that's the Hundred Years' War, which had conscripted armies and more glamorous locations. (Hence, in Shakespeare's version, Henry V being a heroic innovator and winning at Agincourt by tactical genius rather than the skill of the peasants he'd conscripted.)

The mess all of that made of dynastic coffers – and Henry VI's marbles – led to further instability; England had five monarchs in 25 years, three of whom died violently at the hands of their rivals. Some of the battles were atrociously bloody – Towton holds the record for being the worst on English soil – but it all came to a head when Richard III's proto-Machiavellian bid to end the bloodshed by grabbing the throne and declaring the only other reasonable claimants (the Princes in the Tower) illegitimate annoyed so many on his own side, they teamed up with their former rivals and fought the Battle of Bosworth. That's how we got a Welsh king – Henry Tudor – instead of all these French-descended northerners.

So, to summarise, Harrison Chase's description of it indicates that he's a major loon.

- *Ack Ack* (n. sl.): Anti-Aircraft guns. "Ack" was militarese for the letter A (AM and PM were "Ack-Emma" and "Pip-Emma" for disambiguation over phone or radio) – but, as it turned out, there was a degree of onomatopoeia about the firing of Bofors or Flak weapons. Women were forbidden to operate the guns directly, but there were three other tasks, just as dangerous and important. Spotters used binoculars to track and identify incoming aircraft; Range-Finders did the calculations on where to point the gun to hit the enemy plane; and Predictors worked out how long to intercept, so they could time the fuses to explode when in range. These last had prototype comput-

Doctor of What?

...continued from page 223

Chronotis, in "Shada" did it the hard way too, staying put in Cambridge for nearly 400 years without anyone noticing anything odd. Yet, as Vorg points out, in "Carnival of Monsters" (10.2), anyone can call themselves "Professor" or "Doctor" in showbiz and get away with it.

As we've mentioned a few times before (notably **Is *Doctor Who* Camp?** under 6.5, "The Seeds of Death"), a lot of the Doctor's methodology hinges on "passing", whether as an English gentleman, a human, a local of wherever they are or an authority on whatever topic is being discussed. Some Doctors (and production teams) make more of this than others, playing up the idea of a fraudulent claim even to the title-used-as-a-name "Doctor". People have a lot invested in the idea of the protagonists being a charming fraud outwitting orthodox authority – it makes the Doctor someone to emulate, even if you're stuck with just the one heart. In other phases and circumstances, an experienced authority-figure who knows more than the officials in charge is someone in whom we can have confidence, especially if that person is using readily available tools such as eyes, ears, a brain and a good memory rather than relying on what other people have said.

It does seem integral to the Doctor's self-conception that "the Doctor" is an example, a teacher. Some periods of the series address this more directly than others, but it seems so important that we now find a whole lot of extra incarnations before the "earliest" version, represented by a woman who calls herself "the Doctor" (Series 12) and has a TARDIS that looks like a police box. In the absence of any hard and fast data on this beyond the scenes in "The Name of the Doctor" of the Hartnell model stealing a TARDIS, we have to conclude that "our" Doctor got a doctorate from Prydon Academy – it was the best way to have the right soubriquet as and when he left and lost the right to any other name (or whatever happened).

One little-noticed feature of the series is a string of what look like continuity errors, where characters somehow divine that this trouble-causing weirdo is called "the Doctor" despite nobody telling that person. Rather than conjecture missing scenes or obscure information-sources, it could be a function of the same TARDIS facility that enables everyone to sound like they're from England unless otherwise specified. There's a sequence in one of the *New Adventures* books (*Cat's Cradle: Warhead* by Andrew Cartmel – and he'd be in a position to know, if this was discussed in script conferences) where someone wonders how he knew that this little Scotsman was called "Doctor", but it never happened on screen.

Yet people from Mavic Chen (3.4, "The Daleks' Master Plan") to Yaz (X11.1, "The Woman Who Fell to Earth"[39]) abruptly decide to call this person "Doctor". Perhaps, like the much-used Perception Filters, it's a mental faculty the Doctor uses to get people's trust. It must be voluntary or "The Invasion of Time" would have ended five minutes into Part Five when the Sontarans look for someone called "Doc-torr" and the Lord President persuades everyone not to let on that they mean him.

So maybe we've got it back-to-front: maybe the title "doctor" means "person who is in some way like the mysterious all-knowing stranger who saved our world" in most cultures and Earth's a tiny bit different. We have, as noted in the introduction, good reason to believe that the English word has very old roots, but the evidence for that could fuel a few theses and papers over the centuries by someone with good reason to obscure the influence of aliens – one in particular – on a Level Five planet. In "A Good Man Goes to War" (X6.7), we are told that the whole universe got the word for healer and wise man from him. Our source is Dr River Song, who's been studying him as her own thesis (so, logically, the one university the Doctor can't have attended is Luna).

The Doctor's knowledge of human anatomy is exemplary. One version can diagnose injuries by tweaking an earlobe in "Remembrance of the Daleks" (25.1); another cures the Silurian plague; he heroically battles the common cold in "The Ark" (3.6). In "Frontios" (21.3), he enthusiastically takes command of a field hospital and saves lives almost in spite of himself. As recently as "Praxeus" (X12.6), we've seen the Doctor do pathology and isolate an inoculation for a space-virus, just as on Sense-Sphere (1.7, "The Sensorites").

Why, then, do so many iterations claim not to be a "real" doctor? We might assume that they just have very high standards.

---

ers, eventually. The women (some of whom lied about their age) were just as vulnerable to attack, especially after the V1 bombers came in – nearly 400 "Ack Ack Girls" were killed.

• **ATS** (n.): the Auxiliary Territorial Service. One of three options for unmarried women between 20 and 30 expected to join the services (the others being nursing or farming). Even in

13.6 The Seeds of Doom

wartime, letting women into the regular army wasn't on, so there was a separate service, originally simply providing infrastructure (telephony, ammunition inspection, radar, searchlights). The most high-profile member was Princess Elizabeth, the current Queen, who drove lorries – they carefully didn't tell anyone where she was until she'd left, but there always seemed to be photographers around. Originally, the women selected to work as military police couldn't legally fire weapons. There was an all-female searchlight regiment, 93rd, and a few mixed units.

- *Folkestone* (n.): A port town in Kent. Together with the distance from London, the speed with which Dunbar gets to and from Chase Manor and his office and the plants painted by Miss Ducat, we're led to believe that we're in "The Garden of England".

Things That Don't Make Sense The Doctor's excuse for only knowing so much about Krynoids rings hollow: for it to be true, his sources wouldn't have lived to provide him with all the convenient info he has at various stages. The only way he can have been right so often is if almost identical circumstances on a different planet led to the *precise* same point where the missile strike happened. Except that doesn't work either, because the Doctor's as sure about that being the point of no return as he is about all the other things he's been right about, so someone must have witnessed a planet being over-run but somehow got away and told people at least once before.

As the Doctor points out, he and Sarah have flown 10,000 miles to Antarctica. In an afternoon. Even if Concorde had run flights from Heathrow to Buenos Aires, it would've been a long journey to such a remote station. Scorby and Keeler just happen to be there, unannounced – apparently, those helpful chaps at South Bend are napping rather than monitoring air-traffic. And you don't just pick up a snow-equipped plane from Hertz at Tierra Del Fuego.

Scorby needs a guide to show him the experimental generator's location, even though dirty great power-cables are running to it to every other building. And how does he know that a time-bomb will set off a chain-reaction from a prototype fuel-cell? (It being the 1970s, "fuel cell" generally means something that recombines hydrogen and oxygen to produce electricity, like on Apollo missions. It also produces water, so even if a fire broke out in a blizzard in Antarctica, it would be put out fairly quickly.)

In as much time as it takes Scorby and Keeler to return to base (i.e. something like half an hour after leaving Antarctica, with no changes of clothing en route), the Doctor has taken Sarah to get changed, gone to see Dunbar, been taken to a quarry for a punch-up, taken the chauffeur to hospital and done all the paperwork and police stuff about duffing the guy up, gone to see Miss Ducat and nipped into Chase Manor – appropriately named, as they spend a lot of time being chased, twice, and threatened with becoming plant-food in two different ways – all before night falls. All of this after the clocks go back. (The chauffeur's breath is visibly misting, in what Chase says is "autumn".) Even if we allow a decent time for a more plausible intercontinental flight after getting checked by the South Bend medics, there isn't enough daylight between meeting Dunbar and nightfall an episode later.

It's late October, so it's spring or early summer in the Southern Hemisphere. Night lasts as long in either continent, according to this story, and Camp Five ("the loneliest spot on Earth") seems so remote that we'd place it inside the 58th Parallel (south) and, to have land under it and not the Ross Ice Shelf, probably well south of that. Ergo, it's far inside the Antarctic Circle and won't *quite* have Midnight Sun for a month, but it's getting there. Krynoid-Winlett leaving the front door open in a howling gale would have been noticed long before Sarah nonchalantly shuts it with her bum. In fact, it's very unlikely that Winlett would roll his sleeves up quite so insouciantly. Sarah would have regretted wearing a metal necklace and rings close to her skin. That ocelot-fur shorty-anorak wasn't the most practical choice either.

Krynoid pods, we're told, "travel in pairs, like policemen". How do they do that, crossing untold reaches of space, while crashing onto the ground three feet apart? They must either have arrived within a split-second of each other (to avoid one being blasted across the continent by the other's impact-crater spray) or a week apart, but on precisely the same spot. Then, they settled onto the ice and didn't germinate. Nor did the heat make them sink into the glacier and mess up all Winlett's careful dating. However, after their long snooze, the pods grew five centimetres in under a day when exposed to ultraviolet light. Given that they were out in space for possibly billions of years, and probably took a while to get pulled into Earth's gravity-well, why didn't they grow while floating round in constant sunlight?

In fact, as the Thing version never lays down any roots, seems happy to run across tundra and – once Keeler's broken free – grows exponentially faster after dark, what definition of "plant" are we using here? Even if it's feeding off the host's flesh, the bulk of a cathedral-sized plant with waving tendrils must get a lot more energy from somewhere. Ditto the terrestrial plants that experience rapid growth-spurts, enough to snap phone-lines and break windows.

If Chase is so against the "mutilation and torture" of bonsai that he complains about it to Dunbar, why does he allow people to prune his hedges into pyramids? Why are there chopped logs and tree-trunks on the grounds? For that matter, why hasn't he replaced all that oak panelling, the floorboards and so on? His supposedly exotic flora seems mainly to comprise a few spider-plants, like you'd get in an office or at a church fete, and potted ferns – surely as big an "insult" as savaging bonsai. (And you'd think that the *Doctor Who* production team, of all people, would know that a synthesizer doesn't make a sound like a record-player being switched off when you cut the power.)

So, there's a World Ecology Bureau – they know the Doctor, and he seems to know Sir Colin. Where were they during "The Green Death" (10.5)? Why weren't they mentioned in "Invasion of the Dinosaurs" (11.2)? Why does Dunbar have *Clive of India* in his bookcase? Above all, what's their connection with an experimental (i.e. potentially risky) fuel-cell in a protected and uncontaminated bit of Antarctica? They sometimes seem to sponsor this expedition, but not much ecological research happens even before the pods show up. And if it *is* them funding it, why is it just three blokes from three of the four nations of Britain, without even a comedy Frenchman, a vaguely-plausible Kiwi or a mad Norwegian? Why such a body would be based in what – from the end of Part Six – seems to be within earshot of Parliament but has no security checks on chauffeurs popping up in Daimlers with easily-checked number plates is another puzzle.

The car might be immaterial, but why *is* Amelia Ducat's painting kept in Chase's car boot? It's fairly valuable, and not exactly handy when replacing a tyre.

The Doctor makes such a fuss about getting the correct frequency to contact Henderson and then, after the sergeant is composted, and without the relevant information, he just switches on an intercom and gets through first go.

How *did* the Royal Horticultural Society hear about this, and why is this not as grave a matter as the earlier security breach? Why do neither Sarah nor Sir Colin know what "Cassiopeia" is? Why is Sarah happy to stand around in an Antarctic blizzard in a swimsuit for as long as it takes for the Doctor to make a lousy joke? And is nobody at the Bureau even slightly interested in what's going to become of Chase's collection?

Critique A lot of stories fall short by one element being slightly out-of-true; this time, though, nothing's quite right and the cumulative effect is dismaying. The last story to have each and every aspect of performance, script, concept and technical matters misaligned in one way or another was "The Web Planet" (2.5) and that was, at least, each department getting a bit giddy with the programme's potential. This is everyone playing safe but not even getting that right.

"Safe" might not be the immediate word one uses for a story where the Doctor brutally mugs a thug, then takes his pistol for most of the rest of the episode. There's a clumsy line of dialogue reminding us that the Doctor doesn't do that sort of thing, but people remember the optics, not a throwaway denial. It's all worryingly generic. Baker ad libs the odd line here and there to remind us this is *Doctor Who*, albeit in a way that makes him sound more like Emma Peel in tweed. In every other regard, he might as well be Bernard Quatermass or one of any number of two-fisted TV Action-Heroes from the 70s. By Part Six, he's the Brigadier in all but name.

Nothing matches anything else: the music runs counter to the visuals in many scenes; the Doctor's level of frivolity (and intelligence) switches between episodes; comedy characters pop in during intense scenes – even the lurches from VT to film are more extreme than usual. Other than Elisabeth Sladen's performance, and that of John Challis (as Scorby), everything about this seems like channel-zapping, or at least a hasty bodge-up of two or three radically different stories. Sometimes, that's a good thing.

So why not here? Partly, because the story's whole thrust is that "gritty realism" UNIT fans say they like – but none of it is even remotely plausible. The "real" here is a multi-bulti-billionaire

13.6 The Seeds of Doom

who's nuts about plants (with an amazingly loyal butler), a dotty old lady who smokes cigarillos, a government ministry nobody's heard of until everyone has and laser-bazookas. Even "The Time Monster" (9.5) kept more of a toehold in the known world, while playing Atlantis and Roundheads for laughs. (What's the opposite of "gritty realism"? Is it like peanut butter or facial scrubs?) By contrast, this one is so lip-bitingly *earnest* about the threat from a cosmic banyan. Any more solemn and it would loop around back to funny. If they'd given this script to Lennie Mayne or Michael E Briant and asked for a comic-strip approach, they might have got away with it. Instead, Douglas Camfield was on the scene before a story or script had formed and got it into his head that he was Howard Hawks. At least he doesn't go full Peckinpah.

He had a point, though, because the anomaly in this script is Scorby, a character from either a better story, or a worse one, who warps the rest around him. Mercenaries in *Doctor Who* are a problem because they have the most linear motivation and least need to stick around once a Doctor-sized menace emerges. Apart from the Doctor and Sarah, he's the main link between the two under-developed plot-lines. He's also the one script-element genuinely plucked from today's headlines, the way the whole story pretends to be. The lack of his character-development over six episodes is only slightly more annoying than the one-note nature of all the others (except Dunbar, which just rubs it in). As virtually the only character written as more than just a plot-function, Scorby distorts the rest of the script and Camfield runs with that. Challis is effective and striking in the role (as long as you're not expecting Del Boy to arrive), avoiding the descent from genuine menace to Muttley-like comedic sidekick we saw in "The Invasion" (6.3) when Camfield downgraded the superficially similar Packer.

More fundamentally than this, the story really doesn't need the Doctor. Tom Baker's always watchable, even when he's persistently grumpy, but if you replace him with Mike Yates and a handy book about alien botany, the story would run almost unaltered. Even Sarah and a manual would *almost* have worked (plus given her a reason to be in the first two episodes). Occasionally, in other stories, this Doctor stands back and lets other people make decisions, or just lets Romana do the Time Lording (or both, in 18.5, "Warriors'

Gate"), but Baker nonetheless commands our attention by offering unexpected sidelights. Here, there's a regulation alpha-male TV action-hero cosplaying as the Doctor while Tony Beckley, (as Chase) as the archest of arch-villains, provides the usual Baker ironic commentary and skewed priorities. He makes the most off-the-peg Bond-villain dialogue chilling or laugh-out-loud funny: even "Why am I surrounded by idiots?" works when he says it, twice in an episode. He and Sylvia Coleridge's turn as Miss Ducat foreshadow what *Doctor Who* will become in a couple of years, but the rest is a rather sad – and dull – attempt to pretend that everything after "Inferno" was a mistake. Resetting to the government calling in the Doctor to deal with a monomaniacal Bond-villain, just because, doesn't work when the TARDIS is functional.

It's not even that it fails at the other basic requirements. The model work is, for its time (and to some extent now) effective at telling the story which is what they're for. The music now works really well as a CD, however little it complements the events or mood on screen; Burgon resisted the temptation to revisit Vaughan Williams and went Debussy-with-a-hint-of-Schoenberg. Even the ITC-variety fights are freshened by VT. Contrary to what's always said, it's not the Antarctica material that's a waste of two episodes – it's all that tedious running around in the garden, beating up chauffeurs and putting people in composters. There are two things *Doctor Who* should never be doing: exactly replicating whatever else is on television at the time and being boring. This does both at once.

If they'd made this as a stand-alone six-part serial, it would be fondly remembered by any ten-year-old boy allowed to stay up late and watch it (sort of like *The Nightmare Man*, which is this story done properly with more commendable bits of "Terror of the Zygons" thrown in). People might say it was a bit like *Doctor Who*, the way they do about Schools Television serials or more adventurous children's television dramas, but any parents watching might be less forgiving of the plundering at work. Moreover, the odd tonal shifts within each episode would be even more alarming if the whole thing wasn't (just about) within a pre-existing series format. Maybe if this had been the first story like that for years, it would have been less stale. Probably not, though.

Glance at **The Lore**, and you'll see that this was

a rush-job made under trying circumstances. We're cutting it a lot of slack for that, because the production never slips below the average with regard to thrills, entertainment or production-values. It's just not adequate as *Doctor Who*. There's a reason that the more slipshod and stagey story preceding it, "The Brain of Morbius", is better-remembered and it's not just the Christmas repeat. Without the emulsifying agent that is *Doctor Who*, this combination of other television programmes is less than the sum of its parts.

The Facts

Written by Robert Banks Stewart. Directed by Douglas Camfield. Viewing figures: 11.4 million, 11.4 million, 10.3 million, 11.1 million, 9.9 million 11.5 million. AI's: only Part One has a recorded figure, 59%. Broadcast was slightly erratic; Part One began at 6.00pm, half an hour before Part Two (brought forward because of the Winter Olympics), then Part Three at 5.55pm and the rest at 5.45pm The theory that Part One's late start owed to fears that it was too violent for small children is slightly doubtful, as the 15-minute gap was filled by a *Tom & Jerry* double-bill. Any other cartoon, maybe they'd have a point.

[What's interesting is that the late start hasn't affected the viewing figures. Until now, any episode starting after 6.00pm was scheduled that late because of Wimbledon or cricket and thus fell into the summer = fewer viewers assumption. The one exception was, of course, "The Feast of Steven" (episode seven of 3.4), shown at 6.35. This story seemed like proof that a later slot wasn't necessarily a disaster, opening the door for putting later episodes out after the very smallest children were safely out of the way. The rest of this book will detail the consequences of this decision.]

The 28th of February was, in many regions, the day on which ITV showed *The Return of the Bionic Woman*, launching the spin-off series. Not every region showed the subsequent episodes on Saturdays, and the BBC1 ratings returned to normal.

Working Titles According to folklore, this would have been "The Seeds of Death" if they hadn't glanced through *The Making of Doctor Who* and found that it'd been done.

Cliffhangers The plant that used to be Winlett strangles Moberley; Scorby's bomb goes off; Sarah's going to be the Krynoid's host; Dunbar gets ingested by a shed-sized flailing blob; everyone's locked out and a huge plant is growling at them from over the roof.

What Was In the Charts? "Sunshine Day", Osbibia; "Squeezebox", The Who; "Jungle Rock", Hank Mizell; "Save Your Kisses for Me", Brotherhood of Man; "Music", John Miles; "S-S-S-Single Bed", Fox.

The Lore

Bob Baker and Dave Martin had proposed a typically grandiose adventure, per Robert Holmes's request to base a story on *The Beast with Five Fingers*. It was a near-future yarn (for the lurid details, see "The Hand of Fear"), but we should mention now that it was six episodes long and involved animals growing to giant size – so would work better with the many location scenes shot on video (because CSO and film don't really mix). This meant the *Doctor Who* team had to book the Outside Broadcast rig for a late October shoot as early as possible (because football, rugby, horse-racing and so on would get priority otherwise).

By the end of June 1975, Story 4L had been allocated to Douglas Camfield, who had just completed "Terror of the Zygons"; he was formally assigned to it until 16th January, 1976. The scripts were intended to write out Sarah and probably the Brigadier. Other projects were in embryo, such as a Borgia romp and a proposal from Eric Pringle (see 21.2, "The Awakening") called "Angarath", in which aliens were behind a human sacrifice cult (see also "The Stones of Blood").

Camfield scouted a few possible locations but, as the scripts came in over August, the story was obviously unworkable. Holmes requested urgent rewrites as Hinchcliffe, who'd been constantly on the go since the shoot for "The Sontaran Experiment" nearly a year before, took three weeks off. He returned on 25th September to find that nothing had improved, so demanded a new script as soon as possible – ideally one using the OB allocation and the personnel he and Camfield had recruited.

Holmes got Robert Banks Stewart in, on a brief to make something involving a constantly-growing antagonist. Above all, it had to be achievable and in quickly. This indicated a present-day British setting and a human villain (possessed by the alien, this being a Hinchcliffe story), plus a

13.6 The Seeds of Doom

blob. Holmes advised, when Stewart floundered a bit at how to stretch this out, to add a two-part development set elsewhere. This led to the idea of two pods.

- Nobody's sure if Holmes, Camfield or Hinchcliffe proposed *The Thing from Another World* as a template – there are various versions of how this four-part idea came to fill six episodes, and the knock-on effect on the production schedule. (Some accounts have this, rather than illness, as the reason Jeremy Bear was only assigned the first block, citing the change in vision-mixer and the decision to do a second location shoot midway through studio recording as evidence backing it up. This being true, was the two-part story leading into Stewart's giant vegetable adventure a separate project, like "The Sontaran Experiment"? It seems unlikely, but things were rather chaotic that autumn. The aforementioned football, rugby etc. is a more likely reason for the OB crew to have been unavailable for the quarry scenes any earlier.) The first script was in by 8th October, the next two within a week and the remainder by 20th.

- Six-part stories have a bigger location budget, so the production assistant, Graeme Harper, looked further afield than the usual Home Counties sites. While around Dorchester, out in the West Country, he scouted Athelhampton – an Elizabethan house open to the public, but occupied by Conservative MP Sir Robert Cooke and his family. It had been used for a few films (notably *Sleuth*), most recently had doubled for Chequers in the climax of *The Goodies Rule, OK?* (so you can see the Pyramidal bushes in the subsequent title-sequences, as a giant Dougal chases them) and would be in the Diana Rigg song-and-dance routine in the then-forthcoming Morecambe and Wise Christmas show. Camfield was very taken with the location and its occupants – and the various ghost-stories and anecdotes attached to it. He was less keen on one other nearby location in Dorchester itself, so the World Ecology Bureau's HQ was removed from that location-session's plan (keep reading).

- With his recent work on ITV tough-guy shows, Camfield cast the story primarily from his own address-book. John Challis had played heavies (police or thieves) since 1969's *Big Breadwinner Hog*; Camfield used him in *The Sweeney* a few months before this story. Harry Fielder, one of his unspeaking *Sweeney* thugs, was given dialogue as the script altered on location (just as John Levene had undergone mission-creep during "The Invasion") but is just "Guard". You may have seen Ian Fairburn (Dr Chester, one of the Antarctica staff) in lab-coats in Camfield's last two *Doctor Who* stories before the director's enforced break ("The Invasion" and "Inferno"). The plum role of Harrison Chase (originally "Harrington") was, shall we say, well within Tony Beckley's comfort-zone. Quite apart from Camp Freddie, he's been Peter the Dutchman in *Get Carter* and various Eurotrash henchmen in ITC shows.

Other cast-members easily slotted into their roles: when not playing Generals, Michael Barrington was behind desks, as he is as Brave Sir Colin here, notably as the dithering Prison Governor in *Porridge*. Alan Chuntz, a licensed taxi-driver when not doing stunts, was obvious casting for the Chauffeur. Camfield had wanted to work with Sylvia Coleridge for a while; he and Holmes appear to have substantially expanded, if not entirely created, the role of her part of Miss Ducat. Michael McStay, cast as Moberley, had been in a car-crash. Camfield's decision not to recast was vindicated, but the false beard needed for the part, which helpfully covered scars, needed extra care to apply.

- The gate at Chase Manor was closer to the house than it seems here, and a long driveway at the back was used to make the drive to the door seem longer. Camfield added shot details and more dialogue with his trusty portable typewriter (see Volume One).

- The dog that Sarah evades was called Tarquin and his trainer, Patrick Milner, played one of the guards. To generate some coverage of the ferocious beast when out of shot, sound recordist Vic Goodrich tried to rile him with his own dog, but Tarquin got *too* steamed and bit through the boot of one of the other actors playing a guard. It being a Friday and Hallowe'en, Camfield arranged a costume ball after the daytime recording and played his guitar, then they told ghost stories. The Cottage, in which Keeler is confined, was used as a green-room and dressing-rooms for most of this location shoot.

- Inside the Krynoid (in both its vaguely-humanoid form – give yourself a pat on the back if you realised that it was a recycled Axon Monster from 8.3, "The Claws of Axos" – and the larger "tent form") was Keith Ashley. He'd recently been a Dalek, a Zygon and the Android with the belted leather mac who kept grabbing Sarah in "The

Android Invasion" and he'll be back as Sir Colin's secretary. Ronald Gough joined him inside the "tent" monster.

• November began. Before returning to work after dark, it being Saturday, Baker popped in on a surprise local family to watch that week's episode of *Doctor Who*. Notoriously, the locked door for the Part Five cliffhanger wasn't locked – the out-take of Challis swearing at this was shown in the 1976 "Festival 40" celebration of BBC Television hitting middle-age *and* on the continuous loop at the Museum of the Moving Image at the NFT in the early 90s *and* it's on the DVD. The last day was marked by Costume Designer Barbara Lane ("Claws of Axos" and many others) obtaining military jumpers for Camfield and Harper – alas, she got them muddled up and Harper outranked the director for a few minutes.

• At the end of the location scenes, Scorby met his waterloo with pond-weeds. John Challis was asked to do the stunt, as he would be identifiable even with a glorified fishing-net on a curved pole. He was assured it would only require one take, but – as the camera tripod slipped in the wet mud – he was recalled after a bath and a shot of brandy. It may not be unconnected that a flu outbreak dogged rehearsals. (Another illness-related problem was that Kenneth Gilbert, playing Dunbar, had caught chickenpox from his daughter and was advised to stay away from the cast and crew, but that was later, in studio.) On the same day, the model work began at Ealing. George Reed, who'd built the laser, made the model of Chase Manor based on photos of Athelhampton. Steve Drewett made the Krynoid, which mainly used wires and piston-rams to move the tentacles. Richard Conway made the model of the Antarctic base, with salt as ice, and added tiny motors for the radio dishes. Those scenes, shot at the Puppet Theatre in Television Centre, were shot at 120 frames per second.

• Studio recording began in the compact Studio 4 on 17th. The dominating concern was Winlett's transformation into a Krynoid, which was in four phases. It seems that they did those in reverse order, removing make-up as they went along. Winlett was John Gleeson, who'd started the year as one of Bettan's rag-tag army in "Genesis of the Daleks". He had developed a hip complaint; Camfield avoided showing Winlett moving too much until the transformation had begun, to exploit Gleeson's noticeable gait.

• As you will have observed, Chase's skylight was sugar-glass and Baker jumped through it, but Terry Walsh landed 20 feet below (the skylight was in a different part of the studio from what was supposedly beneath it). As with Winlett's infection, the shot of the tendril wrapping itself around Mark Jones's arm as Keeler becomes plant-food was achieved with the video-disc used for action replays in sport coverage, playing the whole 20 seconds in reverse. Cuts were made to the scene of Scorby making a Molotov Cocktail, in case it gave too many details to incendiary-minded tots (keep reading).

• Oddly, though, the location shoot wasn't over and a second session began on 7th, during rehearsals, at the Buckland Sand and Silica quarry near Betchworth, Surrey. The first day used the location to represent a quarry, when Chuntz pulls a gun on them (Sladen added the curious line about "clotheyes"). A corner of the pit was transformed into Antarctica for the first two episodes. The Portakabin for the main base may have been the same one as used in "Terror of the Zygons", but the power-plant consisted of one door and a bit of a wall.

On the Sunday, they completed these scenes and borrowed a SnoCat to shoot the start of Part Three. The heavy vehicle was close to the edge of a ridge that was, basically, damp sand and a thirty-foot drop. A more complicated tag scene explained that the TARDIS programming was like that of a lift – once set for Antarctica, that's where it went even though they'd laid in a new course afterwards. Sladen wore a two-piece swimsuit from Bus Stop and, in photos, the ocelot-fur coat used in the first two episodes. However, Camfield shortened the scene. A remount would have been tricky, as the TARDIS prop finally collapsed (onto Sladen) after nearly 15 years' use. (It had been a Police Box prop before it was a time machine.) The quarry staff gave their appearance fee to charity and cleared weeds from the "tundra" themselves before the BBC set-dressers arrived.

• The final day's work began outside, with the entrance to Television Centre fiendishly disguised as the World Ecology Bureau, by sticking adhesive lettering on the internationally-famous doors saying "World Ecology Bureau". Finally, the scenes involving the crushing composter were recorded. Camfield rejected the first design as insufficiently menacing (it was more like a trouser-press). A frequently-reported anecdote is that Baker loudly declared that the script ought to have been composted too – Robert Banks Stewart, in the gallery,

13.6 The Seeds of Doom

overheard and got a shamefaced retraction when the author walked onto the set. Stewart told the story slightly differently.

On this last day for the majority of the cast, Sladen announced that she was leaving when her contract ended; she'd missed one film role because of the reconfiguration of the recording pattern (see "Terror of the Zygons") but would stay to be written out properly. (She may have been thinking of the *Scratchman* film as well as the rumoured juicy story with Renaissance skulduggery coming up.)

- Editing and dubbing began on 8th January, with music for the first two episodes recorded on 15th. Geoffrey Burgon was keen to try unorthodox microphone techniques to make the keyboards sound more metallic. Two days before broadcast of Part One, a minor crisis erupted when the tape was mislaid. It was *just* about possible to have the master tapes re-edited, re-dubbed and generally reconstituted... but they found the misfiled case just in time.

The final dubs and edits were on 2nd and 3rd February, just after the broadcast of Part One, losing a few shots of Chase following Sergeant Henderson, with music added on 12th, including the spoof radiophonic "Floriana Requiem" and "Hymn of the Plants" from Part Three. Burgon's career later took off with *Tinker, Tailor, Soldier, Spy*, and *Brideshead Revisited*, plus films including *Monty Python's Life of Brian*. Some cuts were made when the Krynoid's effect on Winlett's arm was considered too extreme, and when Scorby slapped the Doctor around to get information. Part Three lost a scene of the Doctor gulping whisky when rescued by Dr Chester – it's hard to see why Baker even recorded this, given his concerns about the Doctor's influence on children. Part Four would have included Keeler wrestling with himself about eating the raw meat Chase provided and eventually succumbing. It was, apparently, too well-acted for anyone to be comfortable allowing children to see it.

- Camfield had once before promised his wife he'd give up *Doctor Who* but now, with so many stressful incidents in the two stories he'd done after being beguiled back in, he did so again – driving around East Anglia, he and Sheila (see 3.4, "The Daleks' Master Plan"; "The Invasion") stopped at Ely Cathedral and he swore never to direct it again, in front of the altar. This didn't mean he couldn't write scripts, though, and he had a few ideas kicking around, including a suitably heroic death for Sarah (possibly a legacy of trying to salvage "The Hand of Fear" back in October) and something about another of his pet subjects, the French Foreign Legion. Nonetheless, his 1980 project, Holmes's adaptation of David Wiltshire's novel *Child of the Vodyanoi* (broadcast as *The Nightmare Man*) looks like a composite of his two Season Thirteen stories.

- Robert Banks Stewart worked briefly on another *Doctor Who* idea, but after this he collaborated with Hinchcliffe on *Target*, a cop-show to which we'll return. He was in the frame to take over as producer after Hinchcliffe did two series of that, but instead had to devise a new all-film series and came up with *Shoestring*. After that, he created *Bergerac*, and after *that* he supervised an adaptation of H.E. Bates's books *The Darling Buds of May*. So he made stars of Trevor Eve, John Nettles and Catherine Zeta Jones and provided work for a great many writers and directors mentioned in this book, including Holmes and Camfield.

- BBC1 had responded to the apparent threat of *New Faces* with its own new-to-TV showcase hosted by Cliff Richard. When this ended, they put on *Jim'll Fix It*. Nonetheless, Mary Whitehouse persisted in claiming that *Doctor Who* remained the real menace to small children. Within hours of the story ending, she was making speeches about how terrible it was that kids were being told how to make Molotov Cocktails. After Hinchcliffe's precautions on precisely this score, it seems that someone within the BBC had been leaking her the unamended scripts. Certainly, one school headmaster in Ilkley, Yorkshire, orchestrated a letter-writing campaign, assigning his pupils to complain about the programme. Hinchcliffe kept these and many, many more enthusiastic letters on file for when the Drama heads conducted their inquests. It appears that only one complaint about Part One came in, but a few letters to the *Radio Times* questioned the story-logic – if the Krynoid kills everyone, what will it eat?

- The novelisation came out fairly swiftly, adapted by Hinchcliffe and stripped to the bone. It was the last published by Pinnacle Books in the US, after their odd experiment in repackaging Target books with strange edits, stranger covers and a gushing intro by Harlan Ellison. There was a plan to re-edit the story as a Christmas omnibus; a pdf on the DVDs shows Hinchcliffe's notes on what to keep and how to amend the end-credits.

season 14

14.1: "The Masque of Mandragora"

(Serial 4M, Four Episodes, 4th – 25th September 1976.)

Season 14 Cast/Crew
- Tom Baker (the Doctor)
- Elisabeth Sladen (Sarah Jane Smith, 14.1-14.2)
- Louise Jameson (Leela, 14.4-14.6)

- Philip Hinchcliffe (Producer)
- Robert Holmes (Script Editor)

Which One is This? *Doctor Who: Men in Tights*. Or, for kids who collected the collectables but weren't paying too much attention to titles, it's The One With Hieronymous. The Doctor doesn't dance, he's too busy trying to stop a malignant energy-field's attempts to prevent the Renaissance.

Firsts and Lasts We get the first use of the new typeface for the credits and captions and, shortly after this, a completely different TARDIS console room. Additionally, it's the first time we've stepped out of the flight deck and into the Ship's corridors since 6.2, "The Mind Robber". This is the first Console Room set to have a black "atrium" between the inside and outside, rather than just a door that opens to wherever they've landed. On top of this, we have a new police-box prop after the original collapsed at the end of the last story.

For the first time, Sarah is referred to as the Doctor's "companion" (a term that will become standard later), and will ask a significant question about understanding foreign languages that's been bugging viewers since the Stone Age (well, 1.1, "An Unearthly Child" was in 1963, but *set* in the Stone Age; RADA-trained cavemen elicited the first-ever viewer complaint).

Louis Marks writes the last of four stories, Rodney Bennett directs the last of three stories, and Norman Jones appears in his third and last story as a principal antagonist. It's the last time (at least until 26.1, "Battlefield") that we can legitimately speak of a stunt-crew, rather than one or two performers; there's four besides the credited Stuart Fell and Terry Walsh. The phrase "intensely interesting" gets trotted out for the first time, seemingly to give the Doctor a new catchphrase.

Four Things to Notice About "The Masque of Mandragora"...
- Although the majority of the location filming was done in or around Portmeirion in North Wales, they chose camera angles that, by luck or judgement, stop it looking too much like the Village in *The Prisoner*. The effort of making a plausible Italian principality c.1500 extends to the studio sets. Barry Newbery, who used to do the Hartnell-era historical adventures, knows what's in the Television Centre vaults and modelled his designs on specific paintings from the period (he also had the job of rethinking the TARDIS console from scratch).

- Not all of the design is quite as impressive. The "restored" temple is a theatrical effect and looks it; it gets across what's happening, but it's sadly unimpressive compared to everything else. Similarly, the Helix remarkably looks like a few coloured plastic lumps on a matte black table, with a toy police box fading in and out. One sub-par effect was a last-minute replacement for one that looked worse, as the shot of the TARDIS superimposed on a crumbled-up polystyrene ceiling tile being flushed down the drain was considered better than a giant plastic pastry (see **The Lore**).

- A couple of Pikemen give us a handy info-dump about the Brethren. They're in suitably fifteenth-century armour, but sound like earlier pairs of guards who tell us what the stakes will be when the Doctor lands up there at the cliffhanger (e.g. 2.7, "The Space Museum"; 9.4, "The Mutants"). It's amusingly incongruous to hear someone in what looks like Renaissance Italy saying "I ain't goin' in dere, Giovanni, not fer all ver gowd in Wome. I know men oo've tried. They've nevvah been seen again." The director previously hired Peter Walshe because of his accent ("The Sontaran Experiment") but now does so in spite of it.

- The eponymous Masque has a lot of period details including a tumbler who eats fire, juggles flaming torches and does back-flips. It's Stuart Fell, taking a break from falling off things or having hovercraft driven over him (he also does a somersault when attacking a fireball with a pitch-

14.1 The Masque of Mandragora

fork, as a different character). Terry Walsh does a lot of work in this story too but doesn't break into song when raising a broadsword to behead the Doctor.

The Continuity

The Doctor has taken to whistling when sauntering: this time it's "Yes, We Have No Bananas" [a big hit from 1923, even more amusing because he's eating an orange].

When Sarah asks how she can understand the local dialect, the Doctor describes it as a "Time Lord's gift I allow you to share". Weirdly, he also deduces that Sarah's been hypnotised when she brings the subject up; she's never asked before, so something must be affecting her mind. When the Doctor speaks Latin, both Sarah and the native Italian-speaker Giuliano hear it *as* Latin, rather than hearing a translated version. [This will come back to haunt us in X4.2, "The Fires of Pompeii": we'll discuss where the Doctor picked up the phrase under **Latin Lessons** below.]

Here the Doctor displays the ability to exactly mimic Hieronymous's voice. [The Master does the same trick in "The Time Monster" (9.5), and the first Doctor manages something very similar at the end of "The Celestial Toymaker" (3.7). It's curious that he never uses this skill again, even when it'd obviously be incredibly useful.] He's a decent horseman [see X5.12, "The Pandorica Opens" and X7.15, "The Day of the Doctor", to say nothing of his chats with horses in X2.4, "The Girl in the Fireplace" and X5.3, "A Town Called Mercy"] and fencer [as in "The Sea Devils" (9.3), "The Androids of Tara" (16.4), "The King's Demons" (20.6), "The Christmas Invasion" (X2.0)].

He's dismissive of Astrology [not ignorant, as some claim] but uses the available information in the language of the time when calculating a Lunar Eclipse.

• *Background.* He took fencing lessons from a captain in Cleopatra's army [c.f. X2.3, "School Reunion" and X9.13, "The Husbands of River Song".]. It's unclear whether he's met Leonardo yet [in either his personal past or chronologically], but he says he 'mustn't miss' the polymath [see 17.2, "City of Death" and associated essay, plus 2.9, "The Time Meddler"].

• *Ethics.* The Doctor's insistence on being a dutiful Time Lord enters a whole new phase, as he insists that 'justice for all species' is part of his job.

Interestingly, his gripe with Mandragora is less about altering history or zapping people than because allowing astrology to hamstring science will sap humans of purpose and initiative. He does *try* to stop the villainous Federico from going to his doom by confronting Hieronymous.

The climax, when the Doctor drains the brethren's Helix energy, results in between ten and a dozen Brethren being vaporised. [However, their fates may have already been sealed, if they were more Helix Energy than flesh and blood, so we can give the Doctor a bit of leeway.] It seems as if his ploy results in seven casualties. [The zapped partygoers may only be stunned, but as he's not in a position to blow his cover or intervene, we can't tell if this was part of the plan.]

• *Inventory:*

– *Scarf* acts as an ad-hoc bolas to topple a headsman.

– *Other.* The Doctor fishes a football rattle from out of his pocket. [The only sign of any interest in the game until X5.11, "The Lodger", although he also has a rattle in A7, "The Wedding of Sarah Jane Smith". Of course, in the context of 1490s Italy, the rattle might have been the sort that priests used while leading processions of lepers to a shrine.] He pointedly uses the yellow yoyo to show Hieronymous how long he's been waiting. He leaves San Martino with half a salami.

The TARDIS The Doctor hasn't used the 'second control room' [AKA "console room"] for some time, but the evidence suggests he visited it at various points over the years. It contains a familiar high-back chair [1.1, "An Unearthly Child" and many more], a recorder that smacks of the second Doctor and some dusty old clothes (a frilly shirt and a velvet jacket). There's also a shaving-mirror in the middle of the console. [After Series Five, it's a given that the Doctor *does* need to shave, but we only see John Smith (X3.8, "Human Nature") do it. Then again, there's the stuff in X3.13a, "Time Crash". See also 18.1, "The Leisure Hive"; seasons Six and Twenty and Volumes 7, 8 and 9 for sideboard shenanigans; X6.13, "The Wedding of River Song"; plus X10.12, "World Enough and Time" for the Master's retro look.]

This room centres on a hexagonal console like an escritoire, with hinged compartment-doors that open downwards to reveal either rows of neon buttons and switches or writing implements. One control opens a pair of vertical shut-

Does the Universe Speak English?

One advantage of middle-aged fans writing the new series was that long-standing niggles were placed at the forefront of new plots. In the 2004 edition of this book, we spent pages debating how language works in the old stories – and then, in one scene on "The End of the World" (X1.2), our hard-won conclusion was stated as fact. The TARDIS is a Babel Fish and uses a telepathic matrix to translate things for viewers and companions.

Except when it doesn't.

Almost as soon as the new normal was restated as a plot-point for the new Doctor's arrival (X2.0, "The Christmas Invasion"), things got more complicated. We picked up on this in an essay examining the consequences of this change (**Can He Read Smells?** under X2.8, The Impossible Planet"), but there are a lot of anomalies and further hints of how complicated this process really is in more recent episodes. There are also things in older episodes that make less sense than before, and some that *finally* work, so we're going to have to look at it all again.

Let's pick a recent example: in "Ascension of the Cybermen" (X12.9), Graham bewilders someone with rhyming-slang. Admittedly, the whole purpose of slang is to select which potential listener gets the message and who doesn't, but Graham's not trying to hide anything from her. If the Ship's translation matrix were purely telepathic, the ensuing conversation about *let's have a butcher's* wouldn't have happened. That specific idiom is the only part of Graham's lexus (his personal subset of the language he speaks, in this case East End English c.2019) that causes her any trouble. Nobody has a problem with "glass half full", for example.

(NB: the TARDIS is still back on the unnamed planet and both Graham and the Doctor's groups are in space-time warps flying starships around, so the translation process isn't happening in real time, but was somehow imprinted on one or both parties as soon as they materialised. For most purposes, Graham, the Doctor and the TARDIS are in separate universes until the ships re-enter normal space.)

A year or so before that, an interesting counter-example concerning the TARDIS's absence formed the plot: in "The Ghost Monument" (X11.2), the Doctor's new chums were involuntarily injected with a translation implants and, for the rest of the story, hear Epzo and Angstrom talking with strong-but-variable regional-British accents but using incomprehensible monetary units. As the story's set in the present-day, but across the universe from Sheffield, we might conclude that lots of planets have a Belfast (see also X13.3, "Once, Upon Time" et seq. and 16.4, "The Androids of Tara"). But if what they're hearing is being interpreted, the accents might be rough equivalents to how the space-people conceive of "difference".

The only person speaking with what used to be considered a "standard" English Received Pronunciation is an aristocrat (the Remnants are a slightly different case). The race-competitors are marked as impoverished outsiders both by what they describe from their upbringings and their vowel-sounds. (Presumably they think of Epzo as more like them than Angstrom, because he sounds South Yorkshire.) This might be an odd thing for two people from Sheffield and one from East London to perceive, but it's consistent with a lot of instances of TARDIS-translation. Amy Pond hears Vincent Van Gogh as sounding Scottish, and he hears her speaking Dutch-accented French (X5.10, "Vincent and the Doctor"). Anne Chaplet sounds to us, and to Steven, like someone from the West of England (3.5, "The Massacre").

It seems as if the TARDIS quickly polls who lives in the area and marks out anyone from further away the same way that the indigenous population do, but as an analogy for the Doctor and companions. (Sticking with "The Massacre", Dodo's alarming geographical shifts between episodes might indicate a more fundamental problem.) All of this assumes that spoken English sounds like people from Britain unless otherwise accounted for, and that everything in a comprehensible language seems like it's in English. Logically, therefore, the last few Doctors have been so alienated from the Time Lords as to have what sound like Scottish, Scouse, Mancunian, Estuary, East Midland, Scottish again and Yorkshire accents. (And yet, the one most isolated from them and the other Doctors sounds like Sir John Hurt, an RP overlay of another East Midlands voice.)

What we assumed in the 2004 essay was that deviation from BBC English-as-was – by means of accent, vocabulary or enunciation – is an indication of less-like-standard thought processes and sensory impressions. Daleks sound like Daleks not just because of the crude voice-box machinery that made Ian Chesterton sound like one (1.2, "The Daleks"), but because their thoughts are being imperfectly translated. (That notion is partially

continued on page 237...

14.1 The Masque of Mandragora

ters that conceal a larger scanner-screen (approximately 1.5 metres by one metre) than we've seen before. The console is at the bottom of a short set of steps from the doorway and has three brass railings around it. There are roundels around the room, including some that are stained-glass abstracts, but the overall theme is polished mahogany.

The Doctor states that this was the 'old' console room, and that he can run the Ship just as well from here as from the other one. The power comes on, and the room becomes fully-lit, with one touch of a switch on the console. [We examined this in 22.4, "The Two Doctors" and concluded that, with two console rooms in use – regardless of how many patterns for them are in the Ship's memory (X6.4, "The Doctor's Wife") – we can work out when each was the main one.] Leaving from this room into the outside universe seems a matter of stepping out of the room and turning right into a black "void" that leads to the police box "shell" [18.7, "Logopolis"]. This facility is activated as soon as the Doctor switches on the lights, it seems.

When asked how big the TARDIS is, the Doctor cites 'relative dimensions' and claims there are no constants, 'no measurements in infinity'. Exploring the TARDIS passages in the area of the second console room, Sarah also comes across the boot cupboard. That room's enormous and fully-furnished, with at least one portrait on the wall, though through the doorway only one pair of boots is visible. The corridors have the familiar off-white wall-design with roundels and the familiar engine hum.

The Doctor doesn't know the Ship's locale when it lands in the Helix, because the astrosextant rectifier's gone out of phase, apparently because of the rough journey. [That terminology suggests that the TARDIS steers by the stars. With other seemingly daft comments and peculiar landings lately, it would be wrong to dismiss this out of hand.] The light on the top of the police box has been fixed at last. In fact, the old girl's looking a bit more like a real Police Box these days.

The Supporting Cast
• *Sarah.* She's 5'4", just about. The Doctor, credibly, believes himself to be her best friend. [She now seems to be travelling on the TARDIS just for the sake of it; there's no hint that she's trying to get back to twentieth-century Earth.] She can play a descant recorder. She appears to speak neither Latin nor Italian [c.f. "Terror of the Zygons"] but has seen at least one Marx Brothers film. Under *Sarah's Improbable Skill-Set* this month, she dances with the masquers seemingly without benefit of choreography lessons, even if she's a bit hesitant on some of the tricky bits, and dresses in period garb.

The Non-Humans
• *The Mandragora Helix.* A 'spiral of pure energy that radiates outwards in ways no-one understands' – basically, it's a swirling thing in space. There's a controlling intelligence at its centre, the Doctor stating that it seems more active than usual (suggesting something like a weather-pattern or whirlpool) and vainly trying to 'counter-magnetise' the TARDIS in order to withstand its pull. [Once again, something snares the Ship even though the Ship shouldn't be "flying" in normal space at all. See "Pyramids of Mars" and 2.5, "The Web Planet" for more on this sort of thing. The Doctor doesn't simply dematerialise the TARDIS to get away, either; compare with 5.5, "The Web of Fear". It's possible, given this and the similarity of Mandragora's "realm" to various pocket dimensions – 18.5, "Warriors' Gate" for example – that the Helix exists partly in normal space-time and partly in the Vortex. That might explain its foreknowledge of humankind's development and how it chose such a marvellously convenient spot to rehearse its power-play.] The Doctor describes the Helix as living, but that's all anyone knows. There's some sort of mental turbulence when the Ship enters it.

Arriving at the Helix's centre, the Doctor finds himself in an echoing black space with swirls of something crystalline all around him. There's obviously air here, and an "invisible" ground to stand on. [The Helix seemingly provides them so the Doctor will wander about, giving it a chance to hi-jack the Ship.] A fizzing red ball of Helix energy – an 'energy-wave' – then appears and gets onto the TARDIS, which obviously tickles the Helix's fancy as it starts to chuckle. The energy-wave then forces the TARDIS to land in Renaissance Italy; the Doctor speculates that 'Helix force-fields' distorted the coordinates.

The Helix knows that the 1490s are ideal for its purposes, demonstrating a knowledge of human history. Hieronymous believes he heard the voice of "Demnos" while young, so the Helix has exert-

Does the Universe Speak English?

...continued from page 235

confirmed, then undermined, by Clara Oswald's two stints inside a Mk III Travel Machine. In X7.1, "Asylum of the Daleks", she sounded like a perky lass from Blackpool, but in X9.2, "The Witch's Familiar", the constricted vocabulary available to a Dalek garbles her words and she's unable to say "I am not a Dalek" the way her splinter could.) Alien voices, as distorted by Brian Hodgson, Dick Mills or whoever, sound inhuman because they have the equivalent of accents, as far as this translation-convention goes.

Here's where we have to mention the Fallen Madonna with the Big Boobies. Back in the 80s, there was a sitcom called 'Allo 'Allo, a spoof of the terribly solemn French Resistance drama *Secret Army*. In this, the French characters spoke like Inspecteur Clouseau, the Germans like Schultz from *Hogan's Heroes*, the Italians like Chico Marx and the British like Bertie Wooster. This was, within the terms of orthodox wartime drama, all as it should be – but these cheesy accents were supposedly *the languages themselves*. This meant that when the Resistance contact translated between "languages", she repeated what the French-accented characters had just said in a posh English accent and vice versa. Moreover, when Officer Crabtree – an undercover British operative – tried to pass for a native, he spoke in a garbled English ("good moaning", "I have good nose") to stand in for ungrammatical or badly-enunciated French. As the farcical consequences of this, the café-owner's attempted infidelities and a stolen painting multiplied, so the internal logic of this linguistic convention spiralled away from anything resembling Occupied France. What it *does* resemble is the Radiophonic Workshop's efforts to make voices sound alien in *Doctor Who*.

The Daleks are more interesting, for once, because they were presented to us as having their own language, at least in the tie-in material. In 1965, Terry Nation gave the world *The Dalek Pocket-Book and Space-Traveller's Guide*, featuring a short glossary of the Dalek language. Thus we learned that "Zerinza" was a wish for success, used as a farewell; "Galkor" meant "follow me, I am your guide"; "Clyffil" was a way of saying "I understand you, but I do not agree with you" (very useful for humans, probably less so when talking to Daleks) and the letter J was forbidden, as it was so insulting. Quite why one of the Cult of Skaro had a name beginning with J is doubly confusing. The recurring "Dalek Jast" first appears in "Doomsday" (X2.13), but his colleague, Dalek Caan, comes back in X4.12, "The Stolen Earth" and, intriguingly, still sounds like he's talking through his ring-modulator even though he went skinny-dipping in space-time and has no shell to protect him or translate for him. If Dalek-ness as a mental state and genetic trait is what makes the speech sound gravelly, it ought to have affected Theodore Maxtable (4.9, "The Evil of the Daleks").

Later, we are told in "The Witch's Familiar" that the Dalek word for "sewer" is also their word for "graveyard". This is an on-screen confirmation that their language is not ours, as the books and merchandising told us. Given Nation's debt to Tolkien, and that he grew up in Wales (where a language without the letter J was re-emerging after a century of repression), it made sense at the peak of Dalekmania to keep up the pretence that he was translating their epic history in comics, annuals and occasional TV episodes. What it means *now* is that the Daleks are almost unique in having a spoken language that we know for a fact is being translated. The Judoon, the Sycorax and a couple of David Fisher creations without vocal cords or mouths (17.3, "The Creature from the Pit"; 18.1, "The Leisure Hive"), the Nestene Consciousness, the Jagrafess, most of the Wirrn (see later) and, notoriously, Dor'een (X7.8, "The Rings of Akhatan") are about the only ones introduced to us as needing help with their English.

What seems to be happening, therefore, is that the TARDIS allows the strain to show when allowing languages less like human thought of concepts to be heard as English by the companions and we the viewers. The less human-like, the more it sounds like an actor speaking into some kind of machine to make it sound strange. How does it learn a new language? It's apparently teamwork: the Ship scans for forms of speech, writing or telepathic imprint (it has a catalogue of 90 billion and counting, according to "Spyfall Part One" (X12.1) and a watching-brief for any new ones that might pop up), but it's apparently the Doctor who learns each one from scratch and – if we're to take X1.7, "The Long Game" at face value – makes mistakes at first.

Once they're in the system, any passing humanoid or similar can get the gist once they're in the Doctor's halo. Written languages take a little longer, there being no real mind to read. (See, for

continued on page 239...

14.1 The Masque of Mandragora

ed influence on Earth before. The Doctor suggests a 'tenuous' influence going back centuries, though how is never explained. Once transported to Earth, the energy-wave starts burning up the locals, and anything else in its path, turning human beings into blue crystallised corpses, their tissue destroyed by ionisation. Shrubbery also suffers.

Through a 'sub-thermal re-combination of ionised plasma', this part of the Helix can manifest as a column of light before the Brotherhood of Demnos, speaking to them as if it were a god. [As with the fireball, it seems this energy can restrain itself from the usual dissipation due to entropy and localise itself like an object, emitting visible light as a side-effect.] Only Hieronymous can harmlessly step into the light; even the Doctor's head hurts when he gets too close. When the Helix makes its move, it channels its energy into the Brotherhood members through Hieronymous – who is now a glowing mass of energy (in a cloak and gloves) that can shoot lethal bolts from his fingers. This ionisation is 'molecular' (or so the Doctor claims), so the power's spread thin between the brethren and can be drained; wire and metal can conduct the energy-bolts.

The rest of Mandragora can't manifest itself on Earth unless certain "astrological" conditions are right. In the fifteenth century, it arrives during a lunar eclipse. [Perhaps Demnos, spoken of a real force subservient to Mandragora, told their prepared stooges when to expect it. Or, as plausibly – given that Mandragora steered the TARDIS to the pre-ordained time and place – Mandragora informed Demnos of the time and place while another part of itself hijacked the Doctor's vessel. Or, most probably, Demnos is just a made-up god: a handy source of gullible misfits for Mandragora to exploit, most of whom bought into the idea that the Jubilee Year 1500 would be the end of the world.

[However, with the strong similarity between this energy-field's MO and that of the astrological entity in the *Sarah Jane Adventures* ("The Secrets of the Stars"), it's possible the laws of physics from an earlier iteration of the Universe still constrain Mandragora, which must behave in accordance with stellar motions. See also X3.2, "The Shakespeare Code".]

The Doctor defeats Mandragora by diffusing the field-strength of whatever holds the energy in one place; it 'earths' through the Brethren as soon as it reaches the temple. His only explanation is 'a case of energy squared'. [That sounds like the same garbled version of Coulomb's equation he mentions in 15.1, "Horror of Fang Rock", or rather the other half that he forgets there.]

It isn't destroyed, though, and the Doctor believes that Mandragora's constellation will be in the right place to try again in about 500 years, i.e., towards the end of the twentieth century. [Odd that he uses the term 'constellation' when refuting geocentrism, but that's 70s *Doctor Who* in a nutshell.] The Doctor mentions Helix energies other than Mandragora, though he later refers to Mandragora as a 'them' and it speaks of itself as 'we of Mandragora' [a result of its consciousness being split up into so many pieces, it would seem].

Mandragora controls by 'astral force', aiming to take away humanity's sense of purpose and leave it devoid of ambition. It wants to stop humanity expanding, as it feels that humans might not be contained within the galaxy and could threaten its domain. [It's unclear whether by 'domain' it means the galaxy, or something *outside* the galaxy, but it's probably the latter.] Unsurprisingly, it knows of the Time Lords.

History

• *Dating*. The year isn't mentioned here, but Hinchcliffe's novelisation says 1492. In *SJA*: "Death of the Doctor", Sarah mentions visiting "Italy, San Martino, 1492".

[If the Duke of Milan is Leonardo's patron, it's between 1482 and 1499. His reputation steadily increased over the course of this gig, making the 90s more likely. The later we get in this period, the more remarkable that nobody's talking about Savonarola, so we're probably before 1495. Ferdinand of Naples is on Marco's guest-list, so it can't be any later than that.]

The story ends with the Summer Solstice, so it's June: if they're using the Julian calendar, it's around 9th or 10th and a Full Moon (as it has to be for an eclipse). The oranges are all ripe. [Foodies may quibble at this: the only part of Italy where oranges grow – other than Sicily, which this manifestly is not – is Apulia, specifically the Gargano Peninsula, on the west just above the "heel". Two varieties are grown in commercial quantities: one ripens at Christmas (Durettas) and the other in April / May (Biondos). Although the story makes a big thing of trying to stop the

Does the Universe Speak English?

...continued from page 237

example, the Doctor's problem with written Tibetan in "The Creature from the Pit", even though we've seen and heard him speak the language in 11.5, "Planet of the Spiders" and, presumably, at least some of 5.2, "The Abominable Snowmen" and its backstory.)

There's a small problem with that notion: "The Keeper of Traken" (18.6). For what's probably the first time, we have a TARDIS with no native English speakers aboard. (We'll assume that Steven and Vicki, despite being from The Future, talk like that for real – even if not, we first met them in company with Ian and Barbara. Zoe might also have been from somewhere else, but the fact that Jamie's war-cry *creag an tuire* goes untranslated suggests that he's not speaking Gaelic at any other time. Leela and K9 are complicated, as we'll see, and Romana is a Time Lord. Keep reading.) Nonetheless, Adric and the Doctor sound to us like they always do and a whole planet of BBC/ Home Counties types. (Adric has trouble with the Doctor's handwriting, but can read the logs, so they can't be in any of the three untranslatable Gallifreyan scripts we've seen. More on this later.)

If the viewers at home are eavesdropping on the Doctor's adventures and sharing in the translation, the story's many puns would fall a bit flat. Traken obviously has more than one language, or else the Keeper wouldn't need to translate "Melkur" as "a fly caught in honey". It's entirely possible that almost all of this story is being translated for our benefit, but it's also possible that almost all of *Doctor Who* is. What's puzzling us is: why not all of it?

Obviously, bits of the series where people from different cultures, with different languages, need to not be abruptly able to understand each other need to keep up linguistic barriers. The German officers in "The War Games" (6.7) can, in most cases, speak English when necessary, and probably could before, but speak to each other in German. That's perhaps an early clue of their brainwashing, although the superior officer is an alien speaking German in character.

This odd discretion also applies to Noah in the later stages of "The Ark in Space". There is no reason why a fully-transformed Wirrn queen could articulate human speech, but Noah is comprehensible to the others and knew it. If this was a simple TARDIS translation effect, the other Wirrn and their squeaks and chitterings ought to have been plainly understood by all. It would make sense if the TARDIS had some kind of discretionary filter for when the sudden ability to understand another language would materially alter history or put the Doctor and chums in danger. Quite what was going on when Tegan was, improbably, able to speak the precise Aboriginal language that Kurkudji learned 20,000 years before, out of all the thousand or so currently used in Australia, without the Doctor understanding it first is anyone's guess. (It's in 19.2, "Four to Doomsday", in which an ancient Greek philosopher knows that avocados are called "avocados" and not "river-fruit" or any Greek description of these Mexican pears with a Spanish-derived name.)

We ought to pause here and consider how people normally learn languages, including their mother-tongues. Two main schools of thought developed on this over the last century: neither of them entirely satisfactory, but with so little common ground that it's hard to see any compromise. The front-runner for much of the last hundred years was Behaviourism, the idea that all mental activity results from mimicry and carrot-and-stick conditioning. In this worldview, people learn to speak and write parrot-fashion. Languages change because of an accretion of errors.

As a reaction against this reductive, mechanistic view of human potential, a counter-argument arose that human linguistic ability was a slight variant on innate abilities hard-wired within the structure of the brain. This school of thought was most closely associated with Noam Chomsky, and almost all of the efforts to teach chimps or dolphins some method of communication with humans stem from a desire to prove him wrong. Nobody's quite succeeded, but those experiments, mainly conducted before animal welfare laws, complicated matters somewhat. Chomsky argued that Behaviourism fails to explain how people make new sentences that work, grammatically, but had never been said or thought before. His famous example was *colourless green ideas sleep furiously*, but we could just as easily use *hooray! Pip and Jane Baker*.

Humans, in this view, have an in-built Language Acquisition Device and the main thing it responds to is what's become known as Deep Structure, a grammar-of-grammars, a sense for what's language and what's inhuman noise. The start of a lot of this thinking is philosophy, notably Wittgenstein:

continued on page 241...

14.1 The Masque of Mandragora

Renaissance – usually identified as starting in Florence and Milan – a case could be made that Mandragora picked a more distanced location to draw the "Men of Learning" across Italy. This would make Giuliano and Federico significantly more powerful "players" than they appear.]

The Doctor describes this era as the period between the dark age of superstition and the dawn of a new reason.

San Martino, which seems to be somewhere in northern Italy, despite the oranges, is torn between superstition and science at this point. The young Duke calls a gathering of all the philosophers and men of learning in Italy, including Leonardo da Vinci [inevitably]. An unnamed man in Florence sends him correspondence about ideas related to telescopes. [Though the cult of Demnos appears to slay a number of people at the masque (but perhaps not; we have grounds to believe their firepower is diminished). Some of these are probably important men of learning, but whatever the case, the Doctor acts as if history hasn't been changed.]

The cult of Demnos, Roman in origin, dates back to the third century – so the Doctor's surprised that the current Brotherhood of Demnos is around as late as the fifteenth. Demnos is named as the god of the twin realms of moon-tide and solstice. The Brotherhood follows prophecies influenced by Mandragora, practices ritual sacrifice and uses a surprisingly effective drug that pacifies those who drink it. Hieronymous also brews up a concoction which, once Sarah smells it, makes it easier to hypnotise her into killing the Doctor.

The cult's masks are made out of 'pre-diluvian sandstone with a complex circuit of base metal fused into it'. [This sounds like Pyrovile tech left over from Vesuvius (X4.2, "The Fires of Pompeii"), though its significance is never explained. Why is a mask from Roman times so complex and what has it to do with Mandragora? It stops the Helix energy from burning them up, somehow, so maybe it retains the energy within a localised MHD field, like a fusion reactor. But what does 'pre-diluvian' mean in this context – is it the same as "antediluvian"?] The cult is well-known in San Martino and haunts the old catacombs, complete with secret doors.

The Analysis

Where Does This Come From? The simple answer: on the evening of 12th January 1976, Philip Hinchcliffe got home from a hard day editing "The Seeds of Doom" (13.6), switched on BBC1 for the news and stuck around for the 9.25pm network premiere showing of *The Masque of the Red Death*... then went into work next morning and told Bob Holmes "let's do that". This, and the fact that he'd been re-reading Machiavelli's *The Prince* (after two years working at Television Centre, this seems like locking the stable door after the horse had bolted) were the reasons he gave to the press and the newly-formed fandom.

The more complicated answer: Holmes had voiced a bit of a protest when Hinchcliffe asked why they never did adventures in history and agreed to do it if it was a suitably nasty period such as the Borgias. (He'd had almost the same conversation with Barry Letts and Terrance Dicks and put 11.1, "The Time Warrior" in the era of torture and warlords.) Such a setting had been discussed for some time, and it's cited as one reason Elisabeth Sladen hung on for two more stories after the end of her contract. It became obvious that Renaissance Italy was the place to be, so Holmes got in touch with his former mentor Louis Marks – he'd written a doctoral thesis on the period in the 1950s before deciding that television paid better. Marks, a BBC staff script-editor, needed a special release to work on a series "in-house". This was sought on January 6th, so the "happenstance" of Hinchcliffe seeing the Corman film – while it may have influenced the finished production's tone – wasn't as clear a cause-and-effect as is sometimes suggested. (If you've been reading the **Lore** sections, you may have hit upon the reason why Hinchcliffe might have been watching Vincent Price and Roger Corman more carefully than usual. If not, stick around for the *Scratchman* essay.)

Nonetheless, it's worth looking at why it was a good match. The simplest, most pragmatic reason is simply that the sets and costumes, mainly hired or from stock, made something lavish and colourful easier to realise. It gave audiences a clear idea of what was going on and what the stakes were. Corman came to Britain to make his film and had a young Nicolas Roeg as his cinematographer; a film with a colour in the title justified making the visuals that bit more sumptuous and spectacular

Does the Universe Speak English?

...**continued from page 239**

he once observed: *if a lion could talk, we would not understand him.* Human language, in this view, is ultimately translatable by other humans, but not by any other form because our brains aren't built for it. Grammar is brain-function, made manifest in the outside world. In that case, why should aliens have brains so like ours as to make their thoughts translatable? For example, humans see things in binary oppositions: self-other, yes-no, inside-outside... would a species without lateral symmetry have this ability / limitation?

It's certainly true that the majority of "alien" species in *Doctor Who* are enough like humans in other ways for their linguistic apparatus to be approximately similar – and, thus, translatable without introducing exotic concepts to the viewers and protagonists and thereby inducing nosebleeds and seizures. We covered some of this in **Who are You Calling a Monster?** under X3.6, "The Lazarus Experiment". This suggests that a great many more truly alien aliens are out there, apparently un-noticed, but the TARDIS can't give us any handle on their thought-processes. As with the size of the visitable cosmos (see **How Many Significant Galaxies are There?** under 2.5, "The Web Planet"), it sets an oddly parochial limit to the Doctor's travels.

In the middle of the last century, a third theory did the rounds before falling from favour but provided a lot of good story ideas. The Whorf-Sapir Hypothesis was that the available language of a culture or individuals within that culture actively affected thought-processes: if a language lacks a word for something, there is no corresponding concept. Obviously, in the 1960s, there was no way to measure this – and in the 1970s, it seemed patronising, racist, unscientific and arrogant to call a culture "primitive", because you hadn't comprehensively mined the vocabulary. This is where the factoid about all the Inuit words for "snow" comes in. (The truth, it seems, is that these are languages so inflected that it blurs the boundary between a word and a phrase. Inuktitut has a lot of first-, second- and third-person versions and multiple tenses of the four words Franz Boaz listed in the 30s, so allows up to two million possible "words for snow". It's not helpful to apply an Indo-European category to such a language.)

Vocabulary alone can't condition thought because, if a concept arises, someone will invent or appropriate a word for it (especially in English).

Recent developments in fMRI scanning and suchlike indicate that this concept of language shaping thought as much as it reflects it might still have legs, so watch this space. Lugging around that sort of tech when doing an ethnographic study would be a classic example of observation affecting the outcome, but even with Western languages, there's a lot that can be done – if anyone had the time, money and "uncorrupted" subjects.

There's a ghost of this idea in the payoff to "A Good Man Goes to War" (X6.7), where the TARDIS translation's hint that "the only water in the forest is the river" supposedly explains all of whatever language they speak in the Gamma Forest. (No wonder nothing ever happens there.) It is, of course, easier to suggest a language lacking something than one with features and affordances beyond English or any other Earth language, but in either case it's almost impossible to convey that difference on television. Nothing in Lorna Bucket's dialogue differs from conventional English, apart from her assumption that war is the right place to look for a doctor – which is why the TARDIS foreshadows the idea in X6.4, "The Doctor's Wife". Other than that, there are few efforts to even hint at an alien thought-process through vocabulary; the clearest we can come up with is, Heaven help us, "The Web Planet" and the way speech and light are given the same terminology ("make a mouth of light") and song (or culture generally) is described as a fabric that can be spun, woven or sewn. It's probably significant that this is the one story with absolutely no other humanoids and we're in a different galaxy.

English has a huge vocabulary and an absurdly huge number of ways to customise it, borrowing from earlier source-languages or just being creative. Think of all the different ways nouns can be made plural ("child", "goose", "fish", "cherub", "car", "horse", "medium"...) The Judoon have, as far as we can tell, under 30 possible phonemes, but can sample all of English from a medical student's "Please don't hurt me, I was trying to help, I'm sorry". (X3.1, "Smith and Jones". And three of those 11 words – 13 if you are punctilious – are the same in different cases, two of them the verb "to be" in different tenses.) It may be simply identification as "Earth English" and accessing a bigger, pre-existing file, but the word the commander uses is "assimilated", as if they've learned it all from the

continued on page 243...

14.1 The Masque of Mandragora

and, like the BBC, Pinewood Studios had access to a lot of stripy tights and velvet doublets.

The film has scenes and shots taken almost exactly for the *Doctor Who* romp. The third cliffhanger is especially close, with a tyrant confronting a cowled opponent and removing his mask to find... well, in the film it's Prince Prospero (Price) being confronted with his own face, now blood-red, inside the hood of the red-clad stranger, Death. There follows a scene where the stricken masqueraders dance around Prospero until they fall dead in concentric rings around him in the elegant ballroom set. They're there, as you probably knew, to avoid the Red Death – the castle is fortified to keep it out, as if under siege.

The idea of Italian city-states in the 1460s to 1600 that schools taught in the 1950s (and television promoted) is as unlike what's thought now as differed from what people in 1800 thought. We have an 1860 book to thank for spreading the idea of "the Renaissance" as a discrete event (and a book from five years earlier, by Jules Michelet, for giving us the French word for it). Jacob Burckhardt is largely forgotten now, but his book *The Civilisation of the Renaissance in Italy* fashioned the popular notion of a definite movement. In school textbooks between then and 1980, this syncretic work was simplified and various odd ideas repeated often enough to be treated as fact.

Yes, there was a change in the culture and worldview, veering from received ideas and dogma to fresh insights and an anthropocentric worldview with exciting new art and bold new conceptions. People thought so in relatively close retrospect (Vasari's *The Lives of the Artists*, source for so many peculiar notions about Michelangelo and Leonardo, talks of "la rinascita", re-birth, when looking back from 1550). That's not the same as saying, as self-congratulatory Victorians almost seemed to do, that brave, far-sighted people thought they should dedicate their lives to becoming more like the Victorians. There wasn't a vote to leave the Middle Ages and join the Renaissance.

If anything, the scholars of that time and artists thought of themselves as recovering ideas and information and phrased their notions of what they were up to in Classical terms. Petrarch, as first among these, went to the bother of actually learning Greek and reading old manuscripts for himself. He, like later writers, thought that the fall of Rome in the fifth century was the end of the Golden Age, then followed a long "Middle Age" before the recent moves to restore former glory. (Pioneer historian Leonardo Bruni, writing in 1442, said that this in-between phase ended around 1310 and the first significant use of "middle age" was in 1469, although the term really caught on around James I's reign.)

The school-endorsed version when this story was broadcast came with an idea of junking received opinions and looking for yourself. This is partly true, but even when we can state that this happened, it wasn't always as clear-cut as that. Vienna-based astronomer / mathematician Regiomontanus found that mixing Arabic notation and a better translation of Ptolemy's Almagest (the third-century all-purpose star-guide usually blamed for heliocentrism) got more interesting results (which Copernicus, taught by one of Regiomontanus's pupils, picked up on and used), but his attempt to measure the distance to the new comet of Christmas 1472 was wonky. He had the right idea, triangulation, but was so locked into the Aristotelian worldview that he came up with a far shorter distance to make it fit with the idea that comets were atmospheric phenomena.

Incidents like these furthered the idea that the most significant thing about these years wasn't any one discovery, but a change in mind-set that slotted "discrepancies" into a new model. A book cited by far more people than have struggled to the end of it, Thomas Kuhn's *The Structure of Scientific Revolutions* (1962), cited this as the clearest example of what Kuhn called a "paradigm shift". Something like that *did* pick up momentum in Europe between 1450 and 1600, but it was more about the role and nature of human agency than any conceptual "breakthrough". We'll pick up on this in a tick.

But the idea of the "Medium Aevum" comes with an idea of rejecting accumulated habits in favour of the modern (or ancient). Exactly what's being rejected is harder to define as we get more information. A great deal of what the Victorians said the Renaissance was about is, not to put too fine a point on it, made-up. In "The Masque of Mandragora", Giuliano nervously explains to Sarah that he thinks the world is round and claims that he's not alone.

The second part's right: absolutely nobody in 1490s Italy thought that the Earth was flat. This is a Victorian anti-Catholic gibe from three dubious sources. One is Thomas Jefferson, who claimed

Does the Universe Speak English?

...continued from page 241

student's whimpering.

Most of what we hear them say in English is in the imperative, or devoid of tenses at all and simply declarative statements with few verbs. (Weirdly, though perhaps not as weird as that in this context, they become more articulate without orthodox humans around in X12.5, "Prisoner of the Judoon", even when they think that "Ruth" is only human. But in that story, they describe the language as just "human" after the words "that took me nine weeks" is enough to identify it.) We have to assume that the Judoon language works inbetween the actual phonemes to modify each monosyllable by where it sits in a sentence. Maybe it's the speed that makes a difference. This would make it easier for them to comprehend how suffixes, prefixes and infixes work. (Infixes? When you place a modifier inside another word – "fan-bloody-tastic". Tagalog does it more formally than English.)

We might have suggested that the Judoon only need translating while visiting a Level Five planet that's technically out of their jurisdiction, but they talk in Judoon even on the Shadow Proclamation's asteroid. If it's so easy for their machinery to access English from a tiny set of words and speak to humans in a terse version of English, why is the TARDIS having such a hard time? One possibility, running athwart what the writers were suggesting, is that only the part of their language connected with their workplace practices lacks any subtlety: we hear the barked-out, nearly-ungrammatical instructions in English that come in pre-formed units for all species they might need to arrest, but the rest is beyond human comprehension. Far from being hide-bound (literally) and unimaginative, they are on another plane and can only interact with other species with the equivalent of a phone-menu *press 1 for calls about ___, press 2 for calls concerning ___*. The next time the Shadow Architect's bodyguard speaks, we hear it in simplistic English, with no announcement that they are translating. Apparently, even the TARDIS can only provide pre-metacrisis Donna with shop-talk. Even when they teleport aboard the TARDIS, they talk like that (X12.10, "The Timeless Children"). Yet we have reason to believe that the Ship already spoke Judoon.

This all looks as if there's a once-and-for-all imprint of a whole grammar and most of the vocabulary for any time or place visited by people from "normality" (i.e. Britain 1963-2020 and nearby Anglophone regions), and it continues when the TARDIS is inaccessible or inoperative. That concords with our assumptions about the fates of companions left behind in places very unlike their origins (see **Marrying Troilus: What Was She Thinking?** under 3.3, "The Myth Makers"). Peri (23.2, "Mindwarp") landed up on Krontep with a husband given to yelling untranslatable things like "Gobrom Sabaluna" and who needed "love" explained as a concept – but as broadcast, it seemed to work out for her. Yet she had been on a planet whose inhabitants needed mechanical translators when visiting other worlds (22.2, "Vengeance on Varos") so had, presumably, been getting Sil's words relayed to her accurately on Thoros Beta and inaccurately, via the device, on Varos. Perhaps what we were hearing as "Vorumnik!" was left untranslated, because the Thorosians couldn't understand it before the TARDIS arrived, and that abruptly changing would be a giveaway. Most of the Krontep language, it seems, including some off-piste idioms, was comprehensible to the Mentors and humanoid Thorosians before the story started. From context, we can infer that it's an adjective and a term of approval. Therefore, both things exist in both of their languages. Krontep must, fundamentally, be fairly similar to English.

An unexpected side-effect of the imprinted translation is that it can discriminate between proper nouns and ordinary words. When Donna experiments with talking in what she thinks is Latin when among native speakers, the locals hear it as Welsh (X4.2, "The Fires of Pompeii"). However, many of the characters have names that mean things in Latin. Spurina's name means "smoke woman", Lucius Petronius Dextrus is "Wolf with a stone right hand" (more or less), but we don't hear their names as *Menyw fwg* or *Blaidd gyda llaw chwith carreg* (or however the script-writers' preferred translation software rendered the names) and neither do the Pompeiians. Lucius doesn't respond to the "armless" pun – mainly because he's probably in a lot of pain when the Doctor amputates his petrified member – so we don't know if near-homophones in English are given approximate equivalents in Latin the way that "lovely jubbly" became "quel bon-affaire" when the episode was shown in France. (As we mentioned in **How Does This Play in Pyongyang?**

continued on page 245...

that Galileo was imprisoned and threatened with torture for defying Vatican dogma on this point (it's in *Notes on the State of Virginia* from 1784) – Galileo wasn't ever actually imprisoned, but "confined" to various embassies and palaces, then house-arrest in his own villa for a spell. Despite constant harassment, he had it cushier than Julian Assange. Washington Irving wrote a jokey book about Columbus that was mistaken for a factual text and made the claim, in 1828, that the *Santa Maria*'s crew feared falling off the edge of the world. Columbus made several errors – ironically, he ignored a part of Ptolemy's *Almagest* that was pretty accurate – and miscalculated the diameter of the planet, risking starvation and scurvy if he hadn't run into a Caribbean island where he thought Japan would be.

A less contentious author, William Whewell, wrote one of the first widely-read accounts of the History of Science and the Inductive Method, and cited Copernicus refuting a Roman scholar, Lactanius, for thinking that Earth was flat. But the main "culprit" for this idea, cited by Cyrano de Bergerac and Robert Burton, is St Augustine, and that's a deliberate misreading (he was talking about the challenge of believing in things that can't be seen, such as the antipodes). In most cases, the idea is that the Vatican was the official body reinforcing the ignorance of the public on basic truths, but as later historians have shown, what Giovanni Public thought in 1350 or 1130 was a lot more sophisticated (see, for example *The Cheese and the Worms* by Carlo Ginsberg). The Church was, more often than not, paying for research and investing in innovations. They commissioned Copernicus and built cathedrals that served as observatories, not least to get the precise date of Easter Sunday right.

This highlights another curious omission in this story: apart from Giuliano's father getting the last rites, there's nothing *at all* about religion. A revived Roman cult, based around a genuine stellar force; astrology; a Count with seemingly no fear of eternal hellfire and acts like a *condottiero* rather than a truly Machiavellian authoritarian ruler securing a kingdom – yet only a stray reference to a particularly political Doge reminds us of the close bonds of church and state in this milieu.

This is a view of the city-states that itself leans on Burckhardt. That line in *The Third Man* where Harry Lime compares the Borgias and what they inspired to what Switzerland did in four centuries is a fair synopsis of what the Swiss scholar said about the relationship of violence and progress. This is odd as, if only for his name, Hieronymous was likely based on (or around) the friar / reformer Savonarola (1452-1498). It used to be obligatory, when talking about the Borgias, to drop Savonarola into the mix. He's also slipped off the agenda in the last century, but those same Victorians had him cast as the pantomime villain of the Renaissance Humanist triumph. By his own lights, he succeeded: he was executed for political reasons after an attempt to burn him at the stake was called off because of an unexpected downpour.

In the version usually taught when this story was broadcast, Savonarola was an outlier of the mainstream Catholic view of the revived interest in "pagan" scholarship, more hands-on but pushing in the same direction as the Inquisition and (later) the Counter-Reformation. Marks surely knew all of this but went with Holmes's request for a story about torture, tyranny and tunnels.

The popular idea of the Renaissance came with pretty pictures (partly via more Victorians, the Pre-Raphaelites), because they'd abruptly mastered oil-paints, perspective and directional lighting. A trip to any reasonable-sized art-gallery reveals a distinct change after centuries of more literally "iconic" artwork, representing the idea of the subject and its associations rather than a quasi-photographic representation. Some of this is a development of optics, following Brunelleschi's lead in using something like a pin-hole camera, but it looks so radically different from anything painted in Europe hitherto as to reinforce the idea of a sudden, complete change in worldview.

Such a move, usually identified as "Humanism", was happening and spread faster than previous changes because of printing, but still not overnight. It was, like a lot of these changes, posited as a return to Classical notions of human ability and responsibility, coming from a freshly-translated set of Greek ideas. It wasn't what people have chosen to take away from Kuhn's book, a flip of a switch and suddenly everyone interpreted the world differently. Some twentieth-century scholars saw a link between Humanism and Perspective: both put the observer at the centre of the universe, but there's little evidence of anyone actively thinking that at the time.

[Just a quick aside: with this and the Flat Earth stuff, there's an idea that someone from that time

Does the Universe Speak English?

...continued from page 243

in Volume 9, the programme's title is always pronounced by announcers as "Docteur Ooh" – but when, in the dialogue, someone asks "Doctor who?", it's translated literally. Thus, in X7.16, "The Time of the Doctor" – a story where Clara's Christmas dinner is germane to the plot – we keep hearing "Duck Turkey".) It would be remarkable, and vaguely ludicrous, if the TARDIS had done all of this contextual decision-making in advance, in an instant. It would be, as Rose points out in "The End of the World", a bit sinister and invasive. It also makes less sense when so many stories from that phase of the series rely on people resisting "perception filters" but retaining their ability to follow everyone else's dialogue. Something else must be going on as well.

The perception filter notion does explain one new detail: written text can take a little while longer to resolve itself, but does so before our very eyes. In an extreme case, every form of written script in Shon Shen reworded itself as "Bad Wolf" when the TARDIS became alarmed (X4.11, "Turn Left"). The prayer-leaf in "A Good Man Goes to War" eventually distils the name "River Song" from the concepts of "pond" and "melody" over a few seconds. (We mentioned in **Are Alien Names Inevitably a Bit Silly?** under 9.2, "The Curse of Peladon" that homonyms for "Melody" aren't precisely those for "Song", but even if there's no other running water, what about spit, steam, drinks and so on? The whole point of a pond is that it doesn't run, so we have to conjecture a world where nobody puts river-water in a container of any kind.)

Gallifreyan Script isn't amenable to translation, neither is the ancient language of Krop Tor in X2.8, "The Impossible Planet". Once again, the Doctor's arrival can't translate everything for everyone in the area at once, or a lot of linguists and archaeologists would be out of business in a minute (that would, of course, be a good way to get a PhD. in an afternoon, as we discussed in the last essay). If such translation is difficult and selective, the perceiver must make the choices as much as the writer (whenever that was). Amy doesn't guess that the constricted vocabulary of the Gamma Forests contorts her daughter's name until the TARDIS eventually makes it clear. Even then she needs a visual aid (played by Alex Kingston).

But how does this work in 15.2, "The Invisible Enemy"? Leela's only just learned to write her own name, so why is she (and thereby the viewer) perceiving "Finglish" phonetic spelling everywhere? Well, if the proponents of phonetic spelling are right, this is the obvious way for anything to be written and the alternatives are local aberrations influenced by cultural history. Finglish is Leela's illiteracy made manifest on the walls of the Bi-Al Foundation. It's possibly more acceptable than the alternative: that in the year 5000, everyone's lost touch of the origins and nuances of words and embraced a functional orthography with only one accent. (Fifty years ago, selected schools in Britain piloted a quixotic scheme to teach five-year-olds a 36-letter phonetic alphabet, coming unstuck when two different pronunciations of a word such as "bath" meant two different spellings.)

From these examples, we might conclude that a "true" meaning can be detached from whatever method of conveying that meaning – written alphabet, phonemes and so on – and ferried from brain to brain. Anyone who's tried living in a country where they don't speak your native language can shoot that idea down in flames. Exact homonyms are very rare, even in English.

Supposedly "universal" concepts might be local habits. Take a real-world example pertinent to this series: the majority of Indo-European languages (of which English is a popular example, but they all go back to Sanskrit and beyond) have the past "behind" and the future "ahead". This is so common as to have become almost intuitively true. Other language-groups, however, take the more sensible position that what we know about, in this case the past, is visible and therefore we face it; the things we can't know are lurking behind us and can only be guessed at. Like the Angel of History in that Paul Klee painting, we're being blown backwards into the future. The notion of travelling in time is, therefore, an extension of our metaphors about it. Travel suggests purpose, which in turn suggests a destination (thus "in front of" for most people). In fact, we can all proceed into the future just by sitting around and letting time pass.

There are lots of other seemingly natural aspects of language that are just local customs: Bengali has difficulty with the pluperfect tense and the subjunctive mood. Japanese has no adjectives, as we understand the term. What we're getting at (with so many textbooks listing almost innumerable examples of similar cultural divides, we won't detail any more) is that for the various

continued on page 247...

14.1 The Masque of Mandragora

would *want* to be at the middle of everything. If we're to believe Dante, that's not a very enviable spot.]

By positing a combination of time, place and people that were the only possible locus for the start of the worldview we share, this story accepts an idea of the Renaissance rather at odds with what anyone there and then thought – or, perhaps, what else was possibly going on at the time. Everyone's hazy about where exactly this is happening (probably Tuscany), and the dialogue yields no dates. The novelisation makes a case for 1492 – a year which, for Americans, has obvious memorable features. 1492 was a transitional year because Ferdinand and Isabella expelled Jews and Arabs from their newly-unified Spain – many of them went to Venice, where this printing thing was kicking off, or were accepted in Rome by the new Pope. This was also the year Alexander VI was crowned: as Rodrigo Borgia, he was well-connected politically and his children were destined to become famous – Lucrezia was the poster-girl for poisonings (a bit of a bum rap) and incest (debatable) while Cesare was notoriously ambitious. Savonarola's gripes about this sordid man apparently buying his way to the papacy were one of his selling-points, but Alexander VI is considered to be one of the more pious ones, personal life aside, and he promoted cardinals of whom Savonarola would have approved had he lived. Once again, Victorians have embroidered the grotesque known facts and it's *that* version of Quattrocento Italy we're assumed to have accepted in "The Masque of Mandragora".

Another key event of that year is the French assault on Naples and Tuscany. This partially precipitated the end of the Medici family's financial dominance in the area around Florence, and it's assumed that the death of stellar self-publicist Lorenzo "The Magnificent" that year ended that phase of the Renaissance. "Magnificent" isn't just braggadocio: he was working on Aristotle's theory about what would endure of a man's reputation. We'll just mention that the "Mandragora" design team appears to have taken inspiration from Lorenzo's commissions of idealised and semi-allegorical portraits of his brother, called "Guiliano", who died young. (Not least the screaming mask on the chest-plate of a bust of the lad by Verocchio[40] and the bobbed hairdo.) Lorenzo surviving the assassination attempt that killed his brother seemed to cement the banking family's position even after the bank collapsed. (Part of Marks's doctoral thesis was about this.) Our idea of Florentine art and culture as special starts with Lorenzo's promotion of several local talents we now accept as towering figures (Dante, Boccaccio, Petrarch) and commissioning of living artists and architects whose work endures.

The simplified version people half-recalled from Edward Gibbons in *Decline and Fall of the Roman Empire* was that Arabic scholars had better translations. These drip-fed into Europe and were added to what the Benedictines kept. But what keeps coming up these days is that a lot of newer ideas were circulating in North Africa and pre-1490's Spain mixed in with them (some travellers to Africa got their names attached to what they found there, such as the "Fibonacci Sequence"). Yet even the 1911 *Encyclopaedia Britannica*, the most influential disseminator of the old ideas of "Middle Ages" and "Renaissance", admits that the groundwork had been laid by the previous generation, under Pope Pius II, and that the twin poles of new learning and "reform" (as defined by Savonorola or, later Martin Luther) weren't entirely antithetical.

Some of the big names of the 1450s tried to push both and one, Basilius Bessarion, seems to have inspired the painting of St Augustine's scholarly bachelor pad that Barry Newbery used as the model for Guiliano's rooms. That's why there's that spherical Astrolabe (formerly the property of Regiomontanus) is in the painting and, therefore, the set. Savonarola wanted humanity to clean up its act because the world was about to end and everyone was facing Judgment, but so did Michelangelo. (Italy in this era didn't typically use the "B.C. / A.D." dating convention, but people had noticed the number "1500" coming up soon).

In "Mandragora", the picture is even murkier because the character standing in for the usual depiction of Catholicism is a genuinely powerful Astrologer, and the authority-figure apparently standing between the "progressive" Duke and a happy ending is himself a classic Renaissance man (author of his own fate, until it goes wrong, and beneficiary of the factional politicking between the Vatican and neighbouring kingdoms). We know that the true situation is closer to what would normally be dismissible as "superstition" than to anything reasonable. Guiliano is offered to us as a paragon of the Victorian idea of a Renaissance Man (hence the St. Augustine set

Does the Universe Speak English?

...continued from page 245

Doctor Who aliens to be comprehensible to us and the predominantly Anglophone protagonists, they must think more-or-less like us, and culturally closer to BBC1 viewers than other humans. In the entire cosmos, Earth-humans who have the misfortune to not be from Britain are the exception, it seems. Australians are almost as alien as Daleks and Francophones are off-the-scale strange. How can this be?

We may have an answer right under our noses. Right at the very start of the series, Ian and Barbara invaded the TARDIS just before take-off and, apparently coincidentally, everyone was knocked unconscious by the journey that also broke the Chameleon Circuit. Having humans aboard was evidently stressful and messed up the navigation, the Fast Return switch, the Fault Locator and the door controls. (See, as if it needs saying, 1.1, "An Unearthly Child"; "The Daleks"; 1.3, "The Edge of Destruction"; and 2.1, "Planet of Giants".) So it could well be that 1963 British English became the baseline normality as part of the convoluted healing process, which may partly explain the Ship's strange circumlocutions to warn the occupants about an impending collision with a nova, melting clock-faces and wiping everyone's memories. Had a New Yorker barged in, we'd hear Draconians, Slitheen and Alpha Centaurians as Yanks, Anne Chaplet as coming from Georgia and Doctors 7 and 12 as Mexicans. (That would explain part of X10.0, "The Return of Doctor Mysterio" – see the DVD extras on "The Web Planet" for even more linguistic freakishness.)

Another option is that every alien species that looks and sounds like actors from Britain is descended from people who fled the Cyber-wars via the enigmatic Boundary run by Ko Sharmus ("The Timeless Children" again) and they all talked like the original target audience. That's a lot less probable given that languages change a lot in a short time, especially when new environments require new words and expressions. Small groups in close proximity change it faster than large ones spread out, which is why so many Jacobean names and phrases persist in American English that the mother-tongue discarded or altered long since. Besides, as we saw at the start of this piece, Ravio can't always understand Graham. This may, of course, be a complete red herring, but the statistically-improbable number of humanoids and similarly unlikely number of aliens that sound like they are speaking the Queen's English ought to have some deep connection (not least because we'd've had an attempted explanation at some point in the last six decades).

However, even with all of these incidents and more, the suspicion remains that we're seeing a literal account of what was happening. All of the aliens who invaded Earth, all the ones encountered on their home planets and all the ones who met other aliens in neutral territory were in fact conversing and occasionally writing things down in exactly the language, accent and idiom it seems like: late twentieth-century/ early twenty-first-century British English. There are examples throughout both versions of *Doctor Who*, right from Susan explaining the acronym "TARDIS" (which, as Bill points out in X10.1, "The Pilot", only works in one language) to Peri impressing the DJ on Necros by being a real American (22.6, "Revelation of the Daleks") to the Doctor's oddly-culturally-specific free-association on Mars (X4.16, "The Waters of Mars"). That Doctor tried to loosen up his thought-processes with occasional bursts of tourist-French or restaurant-Italian, and put on fake accents when in-character, so he was apparently defaulting to *faux*-London 20 years either side of 1990 at all other times. Even when alone in the TARDIS, it would seem.

Flip that over and look at it from the other side: when the Cybermen arrived in 1986 (4.2, "The Tenth Planet"), their plan to conquer Earth can't really have hinged on a handy TARDIS being nearby, so they must really have been speaking English. Their leader uses the term "foregone conclusion", so either this not-entirely-intuitive phrase, coined by Shakespeare in *Othello*, was another improbable instance of convergent evolution or they'd been monitoring Earth from afar and learned the local languages. They do, after all, attack an international base at the South Pole and an even more polyglot central control in Geneva, one where we hear other languages routinely spoken (rather than embarrassingly-stereotyped "Mama Mia! Bellissima!" from Tito). Hence Roy Skelton's decision to make the voices sound androgynous and non-specific.

So then, the question is why – if they've learned the language from broadcasts – none of these aliens have American accents. (Given that they're on their slow way to Earth in the 1980s, it's odd that they don't preface every statement with

continued on page 249...

14.1 The Masque of Mandragora

with music, astronomy and a small niche for tasteful religiosity), but he's out of his depth. (As has been commented before, his story's less a cheerier version of *Hamlet* than a prequel to *The Tempest*.)

More specific details are easier to track. The name "Mandragora" is an old term for a mandrake (as in *Othello*:

"Not poppy, nor mandragora,
Nor all the drowsy syrups of the world,
Shall ever medicine thee to that sweet sleep
Which thou owedst yesterday.")

Apart from its tranquilising effect, the shape of the root – like a man's lower half – led to all sorts of beliefs about its semi-human characteristics (see "The Seeds of Doom") and a notion that it was engendered by the last ejaculation of a hanged man on the gibbet. A similarly-named play *Mandragola*, was written by Niccolò Machiavelli and performed in 1504 (indeed, the authors of *Doctor Who: The Unfolding Text* reflexively referred to this story as "The Masque of Mandragola"), but while it's handy to link Count Federico and Machiavelli, there's not much connection. The play's a rather grim satire using a glorified date-rape drug to demonstrate that church and state are corrupt – Ben Jonson was way better at that sort of thing.

The Masque part of the title's picked up by a quick tableau in Part Four, where some of the guests are shown looking like a Breughel painting (and another has a fish mask that's like a more bling version of the ones in the temple of Amdo; 4.5, "The Underwater Menace"). The city most associated with this is Venice and, as in the Poe story that gave Corman a subject, Carnival was seen almost as a way of warding off plagues. Both Lent and quarantine were originally 40 days. (We could further examine this, but we'd land up concluding a deep link between 10.2, "Carnival of Monsters", *The Seventh Seal* and Artaud's notion of the Theatre of Cruelty.)

1970s Britain was rather fond of Renaissance music, especially after the soundtrack albums of *The Six Wives of Henry VIII* and *Elizabeth R*. David Munrow was everywhere for a while (including the disc on Voyager II), introducing audiences to sackbuts, rackets, serpents and crumhorns, and BBC Radio 4 had a spell of re-working Michael Praetorius's *Courante* as call-signs. As we discussed in Volume 2, every British schoolkid was issued with a recorder at some stage in the 1960s or 70s, so Sarah's ability to pick out "The British Grenadiers" isn't unusual.

This being a Philip Hinchcliffe production, the main reason to do something was that... it was doable. Specifically, he had joined ATV as the (ahem) fall-out from *The Prisoner* was netting Portmeirion a lot of publicity. More to the point, as a student he'd worked as a tour-guide there, so knew of a handy location for pseudo-Italian shenanigans. The architectural scrapbook-in-stone was first used in television in the first broadcast episode of *Danger Man* in 1960 (mainly second-unit shooting by future Oscar-winner John Schlesinger – who was fired), but had been a resort since the 1920s. The bulk of the salvage-and-pastiche building was between 1925 and 1975.

The Count's goons had the names of Italian composers (Rossini, Scarlatti et al – the cast added them for all the unspeaking roles as well). As we hinted, "Hieronymous" (usually spelled without the last "O" that makes it seem like an adjective) is a version of the name "Jerome", as in the scholarly saint (see last story's essay). As the Doctor hints, another famous bearer of the name is Bosch. The Spanish version, slightly amended, is "Geronimo" – see Series 5 et seq. – but for scholars of Marks's generation, the most obvious referent was Kyd's *The Spanish Tragedy* via Eliot's *The Waste Land*. (Eliot's pioneering attempt at sampling includes the subtitle to Kyd's play: *Hieronymo's Mad Againe*.) Some have seen similarities between the plot-points and those of *The Revenger's Tragedy* (1606), more in Middleton's play than the film with Chris Eccleston.

And finally, back to Poe: the Doctor's method for coping with the turbulence when Mandragora swallows the TARDIS is remarkably like "Descent into the Maelstrom".

English Lessons

• *Knees-Up* (n.): as in the song "Knees Up Mother Brown". It's a working-class, East End, pre-television idea of a party (in a pub, like as not). As a description of the formal Masque, it's as inappropriate as calling it a "hop".

• *Bosh* (n.): Nonsense. A late Victorian phrase given new currency when the Great War started and British troops were sent to fight the Bosche (the ones with the spikes on their helmets). That's from the French insults for the Germans as block-

The Masque of Mandragora 14.1

Does the Universe Speak English?

...continued from page 247

"Breaker Breaker one-nine".) In the 60s, it was still vaguely plausible that the majority of spoken English voices would have been approximately British-sounding. Some of the alien invaders of 70s England (sorry, that should read "twentieth-century Earth") may have been mimicking John Snagge or Uncle Mac, delayed by how long it takes a radio signal to reach them. Aliens not actively seeking to learn our thought-processes may have had a harder time of it. (7.3, "The Ambassadors of Death" indicates a species whose language and thought is as "other" as their radiation-based biology, which is why four whole episodes are given over to building a translation device.)

On the other hand, to take a clear example, the Ice Warriors disinterred in some Ice Age were frozen a very long time earlier and by the way crashed. They can't have learned to speak English from us: they're more likely to have had a Martian Linguaphone course in speaking Mammoth. They certainly weren't expecting The One They Call Doc-Torr to have a conveniently-placed translation matrix as and when they awoke. (For what it's worth, their sibilant stage-whisper was always taken as their struggling with our air rather than an 'Allo 'Allo translation convention. However, one of many odd features about the one encounter with them on home ground, X10.9, "The Empress of Mars", is that they talk like that at home, among themselves.)

This whole idea may seem absurd, but other, smaller absurdities fall into line behind it. The word "radiation" is visible, in English, on the dials in the Dalek city on Skaro (dodging the first real opportunity to present us with an alien alphabet), but – as the **Smells** essay indicated – if this translation were for Ian's benefit, he could comprehend all the city's dials and readouts and probably the TARDIS controls too. That would explain why the Daleks had a pen for Susan to use. How a Dalek held a pen is another matter, but it may not have been written recently. If Daleks naturally speak English, contrary to what Nation wrote in that book, it might explain why they shouted *Extermineiren* (X4.13, "Journey's End") rather than *Vernicht*. They have dodgy software. (Still, at least it's not Grammarly, which really is designed for aliens.)

This raises a further point: apart from the syntactic and semantic content, a lot of a word or phrase's potential meaning is derived from context and an interpretation of intent. Native English speakers from Britain hear some words differently from Americans or Australians. A lot of what we do in these books is necessary because of this deficit in tacit knowledge. Politicians use "dog-whistle" terminology (and even one's choice of shirt is culturally overdetermined – in their native Britain, a Fred Perry shirt simply means one hasn't turned out one's wardrobe since Britpop, not that one is a militant bigot).

To use Daleks again, the rising intonation at the end of a sentence is, for them, an indication that they're saying a command, not a question. For many people under 30 – and nearly all Australians – "uptalk" invites you to continue the conversation rather than make a declarative statement to end it. It may be a side-effect of conducting the majority of interactions without face-to-face contact (see **RT Phone Home?** under "The End of the World") or, in Britain, it could all be Kylie Minogue's fault. (Listen carefully to Janet Fielding as Tegan in early 80s episodes – you can generally tell if she's playing up Tegan's Australian-ness by how the sentence ends.) Older people trying this sound smarmy and shallow; they also tend to disregard anything said this way by anyone else. It's become stereotypically girly, a display of insecurity to sidestep status-relationships and establish bonds. The point is, there's a generational and cultural marker at work that, somehow, David Graham and Peter Hawkins interpolated into the scripted command to talk in monotones. As a result, the Daleks in "The Daleks" now seem more sympathetic, to some younger viewers, than the rather theatrical Thals. (Although, as with the Sontarans and their pointless videophones, it's unlikely that Daleks need the camera when doing Zoom conferences.) Spoken English has developed since 1963, but the way Daleks speak was set in stone. Any variation suggests they're Up To Something (4.3, "The Power of the Daleks" and various twenty-first century remakes; 4.9, "The Evil of the Daleks").

But the smoking nose-laser for anyone looking to prove that the *real* reason is that all intelligent life off-world speaks English-English is, of course, "The Invasion of Time" (15.6). Maybe all the dialogue in "The Deadly Assassin", was in Gallifreyan, but we had a special introduction narrated for us by the Doctor with a screen-crawl suitable for a 40s pirate movie, so we're invited to take it as read (so to speak) that it's all translated. Spandrel's

continued on page 251...

14.1 The Masque of Mandragora

heads (or cabbage-heads, or wooden-heads, depending which source you go to and when). "Boche" (in various spellings) is a German surname, as in the dishwasher manufacturers. The most famous "Hieronymous" of them all was the artist of *The Garden of Earthly Delights*, Hieronymus Bosch.

Latin Lessons

- *Solvitur Ambulando* is supposedly Diogenes the Cynic's retort to Zeno's Paradox. Zeno was trying to refute reality with geometry, suggesting that if an arrow is in flight, at every point one can halve the remaining distance, and halve that figure and halve *that* and thereby prove that the arrow will have infinitely small "halves" to cross and thus can never arrive (the version usually cited is Achilles and a Tortoise, attributed by Zeno to his tutor, Parmenides). Diogenes, a serious-minded practical joker, supposedly said "you can solve that one by walking".

Why Greek philosophers would be talking in Latin is another matter: the main engine for what we've landed up calling "the Renaissance" was when the likes of Plutarch started going back to primary sources, but by that time (say, the 1460s onwards, the habit really caught on when Erasmus started recommending it c.1500), this handy two-word tag was already in regular use. There were Latin editions of the one-stop guide to Greek philosophy, compiled by Diogenes Laertius in the third century, kicking around Europe three centuries before this story's set. The first printed copy of that was from the 1470s (a copy was presented to Cosimo de Medici). The Latin version of the phrase had taken on a life of its own well before the Greek original was finally published in the seventeenth century. It was often erroneously accredited to St. Augustine.

So, whether or not the Doctor met either of these Diogeneses, he could plausibly have met many people who would have phrased it that way, rather than in Greek or their native language (Lewis Carroll, Dorothy L. Sayers, Isaac Newton, Leonardo...), each of whom would be more on the empirical side of investigation than the purely abstract theoretical. Marco would be one, as the Doctor would have guessed, so for the young Duke it's another way of knowing that the Doctor is a man of letters and on his team. For Sarah, in her drugged state, it's Latin and elicits a significant question. It's the story's thematic battle between reason and faith *and* a significant plot-point done in-character in just two words. Top Marks.

- *Iron Decrees of Fate* sounds almost like Andrew Marvell ("Definition of Love"), but the link between the tapestry woven by the Fates (Clothos, Lachesis and Atropos) and iron keeps cropping up among classically-educated writers – even Max Weber uses it memorably – because Ovid has Venus make a comment along those lines when paraphrasing the *Aenead* in Book XV of *Metamorphoses*.

Things That Don't Make Sense Curiously, in the TARDIS's second console room, only the old clothes are covered in dust. (How does dust form in the TARDIS anyway? Maybe the Doctor follows Quentin Crisp's advice and has it delivered from Harrod's.)

Count Federico, a big-league political schemer who subtly murders the old Duke by poison, then tries to kill the young Duke by shouting *Death to Giuliano!* as loudly as possible and rushing him with a force of over half a dozen fully-armoured men. Can he rely on *all* of them to keep their mouths shut? Or is he thinking that once he's ensconced as ruler, nobody will ask too many questions about how he got there? That said, the number of soldiers who attack at the end of Part Two seems much greater than the start of Part Three.

This highlights a bigger flaw, albeit one the script shares with *Hamlet*: Giuliano is the legitimate heir and outranks his uncle. Even if the new Prince / Duke (it varies from scene to scene) is a tolerant and progressive ruler and opts not to have his rival executed, or even bumped off quietly like his own dad, he can banish Federico or keep him under house-arrest. Giuliano is obviously an adult Duke, not under a regent until he turns 21 (real-life instances exist of this sort of thing, although, for example, Henry VIII ascended the throne at 17 and threw his father's hangers-on to the dogs). In fact, it's odd that Giuliano wasn't married at 14 to a female Medici or Borgia, leaving him with an influential father-in-law. Giuliano does seem to be well-in with all the most powerful men in this bit of Europe, unlike the Count.

It's a weird Quattrocento Italian Principality that appears to have precisely one priest. (Although there's plainsong when the old Duke dies. Maybe the Meddling Monk popped by with a gramophone.)

Does the Universe Speak English?

...continued from page 249

bewilderment at the term "framed" is because aliens speak nineteenth-century English rather than idiomatic twentieth century. The sequel has a lot of idiomatic terms and a human hanging around understanding everything said in her presence, regardless of whether it was for general consumption or, as with the Inauguration, an ancient ritual. The Doctor gets Borusa to understand both UK referents for "tea" – he hears it as a reference to the drink using a plant, genus Camilla, but the Doctor also intends the early-evening/late afternoon light meal. Later, Rodan has to translate *déjà vu*. What's not translated is the Vardan chittering sounds when they communicate with each other electronically. (They also speak to each other, in English, which is odd for telepaths.) Leela has to ask about English words (notably "proficient" and "prodigious"), but most curiously from this perspective, the Doctor talks to himself and explains that QED is Latin. "Sontaran Special Space Service" is four S's in a row in whatever language he and Stor speak. Rodan spells her name to the Doctor. And it's all English English and not American, because the confusion over the word "bathroom" isn't exploited for comedy the way an American would.

Now, it *could* all be a rewrite of the actual events for our benefit (see **Who Narrates This Series?** under 22.1, "The Mysterious Planet"), but everything within the story as we see it tends towards the idea that the Time Lords speak BBC English (see also the odd Earth idioms used by Omega in "The Three Doctors" – "mind over anti-matter", "the Atlas of this world"). Apparently, the language and vocabulary, accents and semiology, spellings and punctuation of Britain 1963-89 were cosmic and eternal, and now, perhaps as a consequence of the Time War, it's the language of Britain 2005 to date. Although seemingly unlikely, it solves problems like the Master's message to the peoples of the universe in "Logopolis" and the moment in "The Two Doctors" (22.4) when Peri points out that she doesn't speak Spanish, and the Doctor – referring to Sontarans and Androgums – replies: 'That's all right, neither do they.'

It may well be that the Doctor's primary task, back before "An Unearthly Child", was to spread the use of a language that the Time Lords comprehend and allows intelligent beings to see the universe in a particular way. This may be how the word "Doctor" spread (see "A Good Man Goes to War" and **Doctor of What?** under "The Seeds of Doom"). Perhaps a side effect was giving Ireland a lot of place-names that can be anglicised to sound a bit like "Gallifrey" (watch X12.9, "Ascension of the Cybermen" before ruling this out).

Maybe it's all the aliens who crashed in Britain before 1922 that led the committee who advised on a "standard" pronunciation to recommend what, cosmically speaking, is the industry standard accent and vocabulary. Might it not be Gallifrey's disappearance after the Time War that makes everyone in the post-2005 stories sound more vernacular? We've explored one odd alteration to Britain's place in the time-lines in **Was There a Martian Time-Slip?** ("The Waters of Mars"), so there may have been others. Perhaps Torchwood 3's main purpose in policing the time-rift in Cardiff was to prevent the whole cosmos from speaking like Talfryn Thomas (7.1, "Spearhead from Space"; 10.5, "The Green Death"). Or is that why Donna quoting Latin at Romans makes them hear her as Welsh?

Sarah is 5'4" in the TARDIS ("just"), but in Italy the Doctor tells the peasants that she's 5'4 1/2", and moments later he tries to tell the guards that she's 5'5". Maybe the Ship has a compression-field, like in 10.2, "Carnival of Monsters". How tall would she have been if this had been a six-parter?

The Doctor really is remarkably lucky to find the abducted Sarah; out of all the hiding-places in San Martino, he takes shelter in exactly the same region where the Brotherhood's gathering. The supposedly intelligent Helix draws attention to itself by wandering around the countryside barbequing peasants and guards, and turning the flesh an alarming shade of blue (which suggests it melted the copper in the brass armour and, somehow, added sulphur). So when it enters the temple, why aren't the Brethren similarly pan-fried? On discovering Mandragora Energy at work, the Doctor tells Sarah "I don't know how it got into the TARDIS". Um, you left the door open.

Shortly before the whole "how do I understand Italian?" thing, the Doctor makes a pun that only works in English: *you can't count, Count*. (Well, probably doesn't work: we tried asking and the suggestion *non si può contare* came from a slightly questionable source. It's more "this is unreliable", using "conte" as Count-the-title and "count" as in

14.1 The Masque of Mandragora

"count on me".) On a similar tack, does the young Duke hear "Florence Nightingale" as someone's name or a small bird from a neighbouring city?

Rossini is told to pick "two of your best men", but he doesn't make any selection: two cocky sods just decide they'll go with the Doctor and the Count. (To be fair, on the strength of the previous three episodes, their definition of "best" is probably "alive".)

Who's this "another", a foretold second Mandragora agent, whom Hieronymous mentions? It's in Part Three, just before Sarah is disarmed, and Hieronymous briefly thinks that the Doctor might be an ally. Is he just stalling for time? This is more important if you combine it with the climax and realise that none of the Brethren infused with cosmic energy can identify any of the others as such without the masks and robes – it doesn't even make their hair stand up (except the deputy High Priest played by Robert James, but he always looked like that).

Luckily, there's a party-frock in Sarah's size (whatever that is by Part Four) and someone to do her hair. And teach her all the dance-steps, apparently. The masque is a bit sparsely-attended, considering how many people we were told would be coming with entourages. Rossini states that Demnos worshippers are coming "out of every street" to converge at the temple, yet there's only around a dozen people there when Hieronymous starts doling out the Helix-power.

What does the Doctor actually do at the climax? Not so much how he defeats Mandragora and evaporates the Brethren with basic school physics, more the whole "glowing like Hieronymous and not being fried along with them" part. He survived the onslaught by draining Hieronymous, but he was earthed with all that copper wire. When he goes to the party and impersonates the mad monk so well, you could read by him he isn't wired. There isn't that much wire in all of Europe at that time. Whatever he's doing still allows him to restrain the energy so that it doesn't set fire to his lion costume or evaporate his scarf, but not so well that any familiar curly hair or boggly eyes are visible. Is he holding a small but bright plasma flux close to his face by wishing really hard?

Judging by the young prince's overall happiness-level at the end, he's now established as the undisputed ruler in San Martino. Okay, but didn't any of the Great and the Good attending his masque start to doubt him after some of their number were brutally killed? After all, the whole point of holding the ball was to assert the security of the realm. Can the Brethren set their fingers to stun? If so, it's hard to see why the Helix or the Brethren would be so merciful – and yet, the people on Guiliano's guest-list are such that history surely would have changed had *any* of them died prematurely.

It would help the Doctor's science-beats-superstition if he didn't utter silly things like "if it's ionised plasma, it's molecular". Ionised plasma isn't even atoms any more. [Our Science-Pedant correspondent would like a word about the term "sub-thermal" as applied to "ionisation", especially with regard to the use of neutrons instead of X-rays for analysis of crystal structures. But it really just boils down to "they're talking bollocks".]

Nitpicking a bit, but the Doctor states that "50 years later", he could have used Galileo's telescope – yet it's the late fifteenth century, so he's about sixty years out. In Part One, Marco is sceptical when Giuliano receives a letter describing the principle of the telescope, but in Part Four, it turns out that there's already a massively anachronistic telescope in the palace.

Anyone who's made a flask of coffee and watched a lunar eclipse knows that they ain't that fast. To get from the first nibbling at the edge of the Full Moon to total obscurity takes at least half an hour – you can't see the darkness move as is shown here.

And, where does Sarah get that very 70s knitted bolero jacket she's got on in the last scene? She also wears it at the end of the next story, but we haven't seen it before this and it's not especially Quattrocento Italian.

Critique Season Thirteen was assured; Season Fourteen has a swagger we've not seen since 1973 and, before that, 1965. We'll get glimpses of it again with the first four Key to Time adventures and Season Twenty-Five, but *Doctor Who*'s not going to be this consistently bold and self-confident again until Russell T Davies.

This is the story that cashes the cheque written by "Pyramids of Mars". There, the idea of a powerful entity blighting Earth in what we think of as the fixed, knowable past and potentially wrecking history was laboriously explained, but it was a side-effect of that period's own history. Something from 5,000 years before was waking up in 1911, and the Doctor just happened to be on hand to stop it. Here, by contrast, the Doctor bears some of the guilt and the entity, even less knowable than an Osirian, is deliberately targeting a sensitive point in Earth's development. That's all we need. The same author laid the groundwork for that concept in 9.1, "Day of the Daleks", but it was a possible future trying to intervene in our present. Instead, and after a half-forgotten proof-of-concept adventure played for laughs (2.9, "The Time Meddler"), a new staple of *Doctor Who* has arrived.

Rather than banking on the incongruity of a *Doctor Who* monster inside a costume-drama setting as the hook, the Doctor's foe is almost too perfectly in keeping with the period's ideas, or our idea of the period at least. When something superficially similar to a fire-demon enters this story, as permitted by the Doctor's use of pseudo-scientific terminology, that iconography can be indulged for four episodes and then put safely in the past with the tights and fish-masks. This is a very mid-twentieth-century version of Renaissance Italy, and the ball of malicious fire from the heavens trying to keep everyone in barbaric, feudal ignorance suits the self-flattering Victorian idea of linear progress. *We don't believe in that stuff any more but it looked pretty* – all very Pre-Raphaelite and patronising.

The source-text for the film they were trying to copy, on the other hand, was a tale of hubris and nemesis. If this production fails to match Roger Corman (the "masque" here resembles a wedding-dance in someone's front room rather than the would-be-decadent production-number with Jane Asher, Vincent Price and a cast of a few dozen more than the BBC could afford or fit in), it veers closer to Poe's theme than *Who* would normally allow. We know (well, we're reasonably sure) that the Doctor doesn't believe in horoscopes, but he's right to castigate Sarah for thinking she's so much better than *quattrocento* scholars. That's the same insularity and arrogance that Poe attacked in "The Masque of the Red Death", where a pampered princeling thinks that he can use his power and wealth to avoid a plague and still throw a party. (Obviously, that would never happen these days...) We'd never really had a rebuke to our arrogance like that before.

In a way, doing a Renaissance story at teatime on Saturday is on a hiding to nothing: anyone who knows anything beyond the basics will find this version a bit timid, a trifle too modern in its attitudes, rather crudely sketched in. We mentioned before that Giuliano's pet theory that the world is round comes from a Victorian nostrum. Anyone who doesn't know the reality, on the other hand, might gripe that the premise and setting are outrageous and luridly implausible. Some did, when not whinging about the violence (such as it was: most of the gruesome bits are just talk).

Rodney Bennett and the production team rightly choose to emphasise the obvious, the visually-appealing (swordfights, horses, alluring locations, young men in tights), but a lot of thought goes into the other aspects. The cast know their way around this period and drop subtle hints of how power-relations inside the court affect posture and reactions: the round of applause as Federico wins a game of chess with a flourish (probably allowed to win); Marco pouring wine for everyone; Rossini's abrupt change of fealty and so on. Barry Newbery's sets and the borrowed or made costumes are as good as you'd expect from a mid-1970s BBC production (when things like *Elizabeth R* were winning awards and ratings then getting exported hither and yon).

The drawback is Bennett's diffidence with special effects. This is especially noticeable in the opening scene. On the plus side, the embarrassing plastic jewels and sparklers are out of the way quickly; any viewer who persevered would soon be looking at grand archways and codpieces. Those early moments involve Tom Baker and Lis Sladen doing what they do best and keeping our attention in the face of lamentable visuals. The "new" console is intriguing in its dusty, abandoned state; it's the first time since "The Mind Robber" that we've seen any other bits of the TARDIS. Most of the rest of the story is well within what Bennett can do, although the stagey restoration of the temple of Demnos was a risk in a colour production. (That said, cutting from the image shaking to Giuliano's reflection wobbling as Sarah chucks a stone in the brook was a neat way to get out of the scene.) Bennett seems aware that effects are hostages to fortune and shies away from them where possible, which makes the faceless Hieronymous cliffhanger doubly pleasing.

And we've not even mentioned the guest-cast. All right, so the two pikemen are a bit underwhelming and Peter Tuddenham's hammy demi-god-laugh fails to convince us that he's more menacing than Norman Jones – come on, it's *Norman Jones*, in peak form – but this is in every other regard perfectly cast and played. Hindsight

14.1 The Masque of Mandragora

makes Marco (Tim Piggott-Smith) more watchable than Giuliano (Gareth Armstrong), of course, but they look like they've been close since childhood. In a just and fair world, the latter would have been just as famous as the former. Not even a fire-breathing Stuart Fell can distract from them. This is a production that can put Robert James (4.3, "The Power of the Daleks") in a subsidiary role as the High Priest without squandering him. However, all eyes are on Hieronymous. Jones became Weetabix-card royalty with this part, taking the place of a conventional monster with the aid of a memorable mask, a few thunderbolts from his fingers but mainly sheer presence (making Stephen Thorne as Omega look a bit sad by comparison).

There's that swagger again: this year, we don't need home-made Frankenstein creatures, Egyptian Gods or stop-motion Nessie, and we certainly don't need Cybermen, Daleks or Sontarans. Kids are lapping it up just because it's a string of good stories with exciting moments and bewildering concepts. Students are digging the ironic humour and performances. Television professionals are impressed that cheesy old *Who* has such production values. Only lazy parents and a few grumpy fans missing the Brigadier had any complaints.

The Facts

Written by Louis Marks. Directed by Rodney Bennett. Viewing figures: 8.3 million, 9.8 million, 9.2 million, 10.6 million. AIs 58%, 56%, unrecorded, 56%. Part One was opposite a thrilling county cricket championship final – well, thrilling for a Northants supporter, as they'd finally got to the last round of the Gillette Cup. ITV stations tried all sorts of things. (A special featuring manufactured band Guys & Dolls with the Biddu Orchestra and Tina Charles – prime reasons why punk had to happen – was London Weekend's weapon, followed by *The Sweepstake Game* and yet another revival of *Candid Camera*. ATV tried Adam West in *Batman*, which makes as much sense as anything.)

Working Titles "The Catacombs of Death". We've also heard "The Curse of Mandragora" bandied about. Oh, and "Doom of Destiny". And "The Secret of the Labyrinth".

Cliffhangers The Doctor's about to be beheaded; the Brethren recapture Sarah; Hieronymous is unmasked – but there's nobody behind it.

What Was In the Charts? "Sir Duke", Stevie Wonder; "Dancing with the Captain", Paul Nicholas; "Howzat?", Sherbet; "Jeans On", David Dundas.

The Lore

Once work on "The Seeds of Doom' ended in December 1975 (barring the edits and music), the two regular cast-members had some time away. Denied Sarah's epic exit when the original version of "The Hand of Fear" had been dropped from the six-week slot for Story 4L, Elisabeth Sladen had already secured theatre and radio work for the upcoming months. Tom Baker, now in-demand as a columnist, guest speaker and for hospital visits to children's wards, took time to try and get his feature film project funded. Philip Hinchcliffe was thinking that the upcoming series would be his last as producer, and he and Robert Holmes had a plan for a new series.

In the meantime, as the next run of episodes started to take shape, Hinchcliffe contacted Rodney Bennett shortly before Christmas about directing a story in late spring and, on the same day, semi-formally commissioned Louis Marks for a script. Marks, a BBC script-editor, needed a special dispensation (as with "Planet of Evil"), but they had a great excuse: this was a story set in the time of the Borgias and Marks's PhD. thesis had been on the economics of late-Republican Florence. An application was made in the first week of January and, as luck would have it, BBC1 scheduled a first showing of *The Masque of the Red Death* a week later, which Hinchcliffe watched diligently. Veteran set designer Barry Newbery was unofficially in the loop for Story 4M before Christmas.

Marks's staff clearance and formal commission came in late January, by which time Hinchcliffe had been touch with the BBC's Copyrights department about the *Scratchman* script, had meetings with Jean Diamond and James Hill about how close to the television series this film would be and – as far as we can tell – sanctioned the production of a long-play record, *Doctor Who and the Pescatons*. (We're unclear on whose idea this was – the name "Don Norman" comes up – how far anyone in the production office was involved or even aware of it, or even precisely when and where it was recorded. Like everyone who's ever listened to it, we keep asking "how did this get made?")

• During this break, Baker took up Ian Marter's suggestion of a holiday in a farmhouse in Siena to write a film version of their rejected script about Scratchman. Baker's then-partner Marianne Ford and her daughter, plus David Maloney and his young daughter, accompanied them. Productivity languished, as they spent much of the time playing cricket, suffering from an infestation of fleas and swimming (Baker nearly drowned, according to legend, saved by Sophie Maloney).

• Scripts for the new series were coming in, although Eric Pringle's "Angorath" seems to have been overlooked during the crisis that led to "The Seeds of Doom" and another, from former script editor Dennis Spooner, was apparently delivered but never read. Holmes was keen on the work of a young comedy writer, Chris Boucher, but none of his story proposals quite met the mark. The most promising, called "The Day God Went Mad", seemed frustratingly close to being workable on its second draft. Douglas Camfield's idea for a replacement for 4L, "The Lost Legion", looked achievable and a first episode was submitted at the start of February. Bob Baker and Dave Martin were still trying to get "The Hand of Fear" housebroken.

• Hinchcliffe was also trying to secure permission to film the renaissance story at Portmeirion, a location he knew well but which had a very protective owner. By early March, permission had come from Sir Clough Williams-Ellis, proprietor, conditional on a credit for the location (the same with *Danger Man* and the final episode of *The Prisoner*) and for external use only, no interior shots. However, as the resort was likely to be free out-of-season, the team could use the self-catering chalets for accommodation and make-up / costume. (It's worth remembering that, while *The Prisoner* was in syndication round the world, it had not been repeated in Britain and wouldn't until a few weeks after this location shoot was scheduled to take place. In an age before home video, nobody had pin-sharp recall of the locations' use in the 1967 series, so it's more luck than judgement that "Mandragora" mostly uses different angles and set-ups from those now very familiar from McGoohan's pet project.)

• In the immediate future, however, *Doctor Who* would continue in sound only. Terrance Dicks approached BBC Radio with a story-proposal. A subdivision, making programmes for schools since the 1950s, had an idea for an Earth Science programme using a time machine and, inevitably, someone had proposed the TARDIS, the Doctor and Sarah. Argo, a subsidiary of Decca Records, had commissioned Victor Pemberton, author of 5.6, "Fury from the Deep", script editor of 5.1, "The Tomb of the Cybermen" and creator of a radio drama about a coastal menace, *The Slide*, to write a sub-aqua audio drama and he'd come up with the aforementioned *Pescatons*. Even Bob Holmes had adapted a rejected Troughton story as *Aliens in the Blood* and had it accepted in late March.

• Sladen, on a new contract taking her up to July, was back in Liverpool on stage at the Playhouse in *Mooney's Caravan* with her husband, Brian Miller (they often came as a set) and in April did a radio play at BBC Manchester, *Bitter Almond*. The Schools broadcast, an episode of *Exploration Earth*, was recorded on 27th April for an autumn transmission.

On Sladen's account, the first she knew about *Doctor Who and the Pescatons* was a script through her letterbox and a note telling her to be at a recording studio in Soho (probably Molinar) the following morning. Until the 2006 CD reissue, under the BBC's auspices, she had believed it to be a BBC project. As this wasn't, the TARDIS sound had to be changed – but, with Brian Hodgson, who'd done the original, now a freelancer they could make a plausible-sounding replacement. The script betrays no sign of Pemberton having watched *Doctor Who* ever, let alone since he left, and has the Doctor carrying a flute as a matter of course. As it turns into *King Kong*, there's nothing about UNIT and increasingly less for Sarah to do, but Baker gamely sells the premise and even sings a snatch of "Hello, Dolly" (God knows whether they got clearance for that). Music was by Kenny Clayton.

• Meanwhile, in 1490s Italy, "The Secrets of the Labyrinth" (as it was now called) was coming together. There had already been a recce at Portmeirion. Camfield's "Lost Legion" scripts were trickling in late and looked less useable as the story unfolded (we'll pick up on this next story). Newbery had a few ideas about the sets, mainly with reference to Vittore Carpaccio's paintings *The Vision of St Ursula* (the death of Giuliano's father is framed to resemble it) and *St. Augustine in his*

14.1 The Masque of Mandragora

Study (which, flipped left-to-right, is the basis for the young Duke's study).

He was also asked to fix a long-standing bugbear: the TARDIS interior is a large proportion of any BBC studio's floor-space – so, if it's needed, the recording schedule has to work around it. A smaller set, ideally one less generic and *Star Trek*-like, could cut down on studio time and be manageable if the recording roster meant that they didn't have TC1 or TC3 to play with (as was increasingly the case). Hinchcliffe had an idea of a more Jules Verne-esque console room with a CSO panel behind sliding screens rather than a TV monitor. The cost would be amortised over the whole production year.

- Various fan groups were by now consolidating into the *Doctor Who* Appreciation Society, based in Westfield College. Terrance Dicks was invited to meet them on 29th.
- On 2nd May, the cast and crew went to Paddington station and got on a train to Bangor, the railway station nearest to Portmeirion. Most of the cast stayed in the main hotel, where Sir Clough entertained them (especially Baker, a connoisseur of eccentrics). Joining Baker and Sladen on the shoot in the surrounding countryside were former RSC player Gareth Armstrong as Giuliano, Jon Laurimore (a last-minute replacement for David Swift) as Federico, Anthony Carrick as Rossini, Jay Neill and Peter Walshe as the Pikemen, James Appleby and John Clamp as the orthodox guards chasing the Doctor through the market and, of course, Pat Gorman as a Guard on the gate.

Although only a few speaking-role performers were on film, there was a sizeable stunt crew and numerous extras in period costumes. (Contrary to what's sometimes reported, one item of costumery is thought to originate with Zefferelli's *Romeo and Juliet*: Rossini's tabard. Most came from a 1954 film of the play and were in stock at Berman's and Nathan's, the main film / TV costume hire company in London, while some were BBC stock. We'll see bits of these again in 16.4, "The Androids of Tara".)

The shoot required four horses and several equestrian stuntmen doubling as guards. There were seven of these in all; to Bennett's amusement, they kept their cigarettes and lighters in their codpieces. Fell's encounter with alien energy was unscripted, but the effect of the Helix energy crossing the millstream was achieved by Ian Scoones laying 20 feet of igniter cable. We could list every shot and where the location was used in *The Prisoner*, but anyone who cares probably already knows.

- Rehearsals began on 13th (also the day Sladen's departure was announced: it made the papers and *Nationwide*). Joining the cast were a few *Who* veterans. Norman Jones, as Hieronymous, had been Major Baker in "Doctor Who and the Silurians" (7.2) and Khrisong in "The Abominable Snowmen" (5.1). Marco was the then-unknown Tim Pigott-Smith, last seen in "The Claws of Axos" (8.3). The High Priest was Robert James, Lesterson from 4.3, "The Power of the Daleks" and the off-screen voice of the "Titan" (Mandragora) was Peter Tuddenham from "The Ark in Space" and, later *Blakes 7*. (The walk-ons also include a few familiar names, such as Keith Ashley and Cy Town.) Baker took to referring to Marco and Giuliano as "Gert and Daisy", after a popular wartime radio comedy starring Elsie and Doris Walters.
- The studio recording days, which included the palace scenes, were all spent in the large Studio 3, starting on 24th. Just over a month earlier, BBC2 had shown a 60th birthday celebration of Yehudi Menuhin, with David Attenborough interviewing him and performances by the great violinist and his friends and family (Ravi Shankar, Stephane Grappelli, people like that). Ken Sharp had designed a set that Newbery thought would make a good State Room for this story, so Newbery and Hinchcliffe asked for it to be kept. Newbery appears to have proposed that the credits for this and subsequent stories ought to be in a Renaissance typeface, Cantoria.
- The music we hear in the finished Palace scenes was from a 1961 German LP, *Tanzmuzik der Renaissance* by Collegium Aureum (the "Programme as Broadcast" document makes a bit of a hash of the track-listing). It seems that these three cues were played into the studio as a guide for Sladen and the professionals.
- To give a visual focus for the Mandragora Energy in the filmed sequences, Bennett arranged for a large sparkler to be shot against a black background in studio, then superimposed on the film to match where the steam had sputtered on the water. For scenes of the energy speaking, an out-of-focus lava-lamp was superimposed, the edges closed off to make the "shaft" effect.
- The Temple was restored by the old theatrical

trick of painted gauzes, illuminated on cue but translucent the rest of the time. In attempting the cliffhanger shot of Hieronymous-with-no-face, they tried another FAP set-up, but the shadow of the monk's hood made it impossible, so they reverted to inlaying the same lava-lamp as before within the cut-out of the cowl. (For all the increasing sophistication of the electronic effects, things like this still amounted to cutting holes in black card, sticking it in front of a TV monitor and pointing a camera at it and mixing it with the other image.) The rapid eclipse was a caption with moving parts, as used on The Sky at Night and Ask the Family in those days – the BBC slightly confusingly called these "animated".

- Finally, the new TARDIS set was unveiled (Hinchcliffe invited a couple of DWAS observers to camera rehearsals). This was mainly in fibre-glass, with ersatz stained-glass windows and wooden stairs. Anne Baugh contributed to the console design. The shaving mirror, only seen in this story, was the one souvenir Hinchcliffe took with him when he left the series. It had cost £14 from petty cash. There was a proposal to add to the mystery of how many Doctors there had been by leaving other items around, but only the frilly shirt and the recorder remained, plus a chair that was last seen in 9.5, "The Time Monster".

- The "Hall of the Titans" was, as might be imagined, a big green cloth with the model superimposed and Sladen and Baker – plus a newly-constructed Police Box (see last story) in front of it. There had been a trial-run for the effects in May, in Studio 4B (the "Puppet" studio), but they looked even worse than what was broadcast.

- Editing began with Sarah's abduction slightly modified (children might have copied the smothering), a scene of Brothers scattering rose-petals on the altar moved to Part Two and a redundant sequence where Mandragora warns Hieronymous about the Doctor nipped off the end of the "possession" scene. Ten days later, in editing, Part Three lost a possibly interesting scene where Federico tells Rossini that Giuliani is consorting with sorcerers and ridding the land of him would earn favour with the Pope. The last line, retained in Hinchcliffe's novelisation, was also cut, with Giuliani watching the TARDIS leave and wondering if, one day, there would be a rational explanation for that. After the experiments of the previous two years, Hinchcliffe committed to hiring Dudley Simpson for all 26 episodes of the new series. His score (recorded 8th and 9th July), sound effects and a final gallery-only inlay day (27th July) were the final components. After Baker and Marter's odd experience, Holmes was also planning a holiday in Italy (see "The Talons of Weng-Chiang" for how that panned out) and Hinchcliffe was off for a few weeks.

- Hinchcliffe hoped that the Montreal Olympics would delay the new run by a couple of weeks, so that all the high-profile series at the start of September would bag their Radio Times covers before Doctor Who, making the coveted cover more likely for "Mandragora" Part One. It wasn't to be, so Gemma Jones in The Duchess of Duke Street was depicted on 4th-10th September issue, but there was a long interview with Hinchcliffe and some whimsical illustrations for this and the Saturday listing. In this piece, entitled Doctor Who's Renaissance, the producer mentioned that the audience was increasingly sophisticated and wanted solid drama with a fantasy setting. His claim that old-style monsters were being, as the interviewer put it, "mothballed" was carefully couched in terms of trying something new to stop the popular baddies becoming stale. Taken with his earlier comments about UNIT, this was bad news for a small but vocal section of the nascent fandom.

The episodes were scheduled to start around 6.00pm, rather later than had been the norm – partly to make it seem that Mary Whitehouse's complaints were being listened to, but mainly because ITV was trying to get a toehold in the Saturday Night line-up.

- In 1981, the first out-of-Doctor run of repeats would have included this story to tick the Tom Baker box had not the then-producer, John Nathan-Turner, decided that three seconds of Peter Davison in the underperforming "Logopolis" (18.7) justified the title The Five Faces of Doctor Who. Hinchcliffe's evident pride in this story extended to writing the Target books novelisation. Marks found that "serious" drama colleagues were congratulating him for the story. He was by now too busy to do any further scripts and landed up becoming a respected producer, working on such dramas as Fearless Frank (almost the last time Leonard Rossiter shone in a "straight" role), Middlemarch and The Lost Boys (directed by Bennett). In 1977, the second Weetabix pasteboard figures set included Hieronymous – wearing the mask, what we'd now consider a "spoiler", had any chance existed of the story being repeated.

14.2: "The Hand of Fear"

(Serial 4N, Four Episodes, 2nd – 23rd October 1976.)

Which One is This? Sarah leaves. There's three and a half episodes of other stuff, mainly a retread of *The Beast With Five Fingers* in a nuclear power-station and a visit to the cheapest planet in the galaxy. And several people say "Eldrad Must Live" – over and over and over.

Firsts and Lasts Well, obviously, it's the last appearance of Sarah Jane Smith (except all the other appearances and her two spin-off shows).

It's the last story directed by Lennie Mayne. It's the first use of the Gallifrey "Is that in Ireland?" riff (back as late as Series 12), the ever-popular "armless" gag and Dave Martin's habit of giving stories slogans. It's the first time we're told how amazingly rare silicon-based life is (see 16.3, "The Stones of Blood").

After a decade of using quarries as locations, it's the first time the TARDIS has, within the story, landed in one. Shortly after this, we get our first substantial hint that the Doctor plays cricket. An alien undergoes gender-reassignment in mid-episode (we're reasonably sure that's a first, but who knows what's up with the delegates in 3.4, "The Daleks' Master Plan"?). We have the first hint of a companion having packed a suitcase and chosen to shack up with the Doctor (or, at least, come prepared for a reasonably long stay). It's the first story to end with a freeze-frame (and the last one planned – 22.6, "Revelation of the Daleks" was a last-minute fudge).

Four Things to Notice About "The Hand of Fear"...
- They say doctors make the worst patients: Bob Baker and Dave Martin play to their strengths in the first two episodes by showing ordinary people at work when something weird afflicts them – and, for once, when a set-piece explosion happens, the Doctor and Sarah are taken to hospital for checks. Seeing the haughty Time Lord receive the same treatment as everyone else at an NHS hospital, as another doctor is condescending to him for once, grounds the later space-opera faff and nuclear power meltdown. It's not so much a Yeti-in-the-loo-style attempt to make the everyday ooh-scary as pre-emptive recognition of how things would really play out, second-guessing sceptical parents in the room.
- That's a real working quarry and a real explosion to make a real cliff-face really fall on the camera. That's a real nuclear power station. That's really Tom Baker, Elisabeth Sladen, Rex Robinson, a few guards and a stuntman inside it. Max Faulkner really falls 30 feet from a gantry, doubling for Dr Carter. The thing Carter swings at the Doctor, er, isn't a real spanner.
- We get three versions of Eldrad. First is Sarah's Pet Rock, a stone hand that controls her mind (even without the ring that hypnotises everyone else, which Sarah uses with merry abandon). At the end we get Eldrad Classic, a huge hulking brick house of a man played with characteristic delicacy by Stephen Thorne (see 8.5, "The Daemons"; 10.1, "The Three Doctors"; 10.3, "Frontier in Space".) The intermediate stage is more interesting. Judith Paris plays a silicon-based being that supposedly modelled itself on Sarah (despite being taller) and she's doing a great impression of Elsa Lanchester in *Bride of Frankenstein*, twitching and strutting and not really believing what the mirror tells her. Look closely and you'll see that she's given this female form a pair of stack heels – even though, for once, Sarah's not wearing any.
- Part Four is a queer beastie: most of it is a rerun of "Death to the Daleks" (11.3) Part Four, even with the frequent cutaways to watching a stone-skinned humanoid in a cowl who turns out to have been dead for umpteen generations. Then it turns into "The Three Doctors" minus two Doctors. Then Eldrad is dispatched with slapstick. Then we get the long-awaited answer to the question buzzing around the media and the nation's school playgrounds: what could be so important as to make the Doctor and Sarah part company for good? The amount of anticipation this generated burdened Part One of "The Deadly Assassin" with expectations no episode could entirely satisfy, but on its own terms, the end of this story is as perfect a companion send-off as we ever get and (SPOILER) the cruellest thing the Master ever did to the Doctor.

The Continuity

The Doctor Weirdly, he never mentions UNIT or claims any official status that would open doors. [His pique at being the Brigadier's errand-boy (see "Pyramids of Mars") is such that he risks being

Eldrad Must Live – But How?

Of the many, many strange aspects of "The Hand of Fear", the strangest is the least commented-upon. Eldrad reconfigured his body using radiation to make a form capable of engaging with terrestrial life and supposedly chose Sarah as a template. Then, when back on home territory, he was installed in a new body like his original form and, we are led to assume, suitable for life on Kastria. The other Kastrians we see (King Rokon, Technik Obarl and Commander Zazzka) all look like this new-old form. Some of them wear eiderdowns against the cold.

What's weird is that this form is bipedal, about two metres tall, has five-digit hands on the end of each of two arms subtending from a torso with a head on top, flourishes in an oxygen atmosphere at a temperature that Sarah can survive by borrowing the Doctor's velvet jacket... in short, is almost exactly like the form Eldrad adopted to survive on Earth. It's also almost exactly like a human, just a bit knobbly and grape-coloured.

Even odder, when in that interim form, it was vulnerable to acid but light enough for the Doctor to lift it. That form could regenerate itself when exposed to atomic radiation, but nothing on Kastria suggests that the planet nourished its population that way. The people of this world have lifts that indicate which floor they're on by roots of three, but Rokon, Eldrad et al have hands like ours. Admittedly, Eldrad claims to have devised a new form appropriate for the change in conditions on Kastria – but that form, as we're told repeatedly, is based on silicon and not carbon. Nothing about Kastria then or now seems likely to favour such a biochemistry.

The idea of silicon-based life is as old as the Periodic Table. Back in the nineteenth century, huge strides were made in the analysis and synthesis of long-chain molecules, and soon chemistry split into two large fields: organic chemistry (fun things to do with carbon) and inorganic chemistry (everything else). Organic chemistry made huge strides, in everything from dyes (the Victorians went hog-wild for mauve, then followed this with fresh new colours and no restraint, making future generations glad that colour photography only came along after World War I) to celluloid and other synthetic materials to working out what Vitamins were.

At the root of it was carbon's helpful atomic structure, bonding well with so many other key ingredients (especially oxygen, hydrogen, sulphur and nitrogen), because of the number of spaces on its outermost shell of electrons. When Mendeleev sorted out the elements into rows and columns based on charges (left to right) with the number of shells as the basis for top-to-bottom place in his grid, it revealed "family resemblances" between elements. (The precise details of atomic theory came afterwards.)

Immediately underneath the starting-point, hydrogen, there's a pile of soft things that go berserk when exposed to oxygen (lithium, sodium, potassium, caesium) on the left-hand side of the table. A lot of odd gases, including those as-yet undiscovered, had no gaps in their outer shells, so didn't react to anything – the noble gases – and they all showed up to fill assigned spaces on the right-hand edge over the next 70 years. That's column 18; over to the left in column 14, the first entry is carbon – so, if you're looking for a carbon-surrogate, it makes sense to look immediately under it and see silicon, then germanium, tin and lead (plus a couple of new ones that haven't turned up in the wild on Earth).

These metals all have interesting properties and silicon and germanium, both semi-conductors, were fundamental to the development of the transistor. Mendeleev predicted the existence of "ekasilicon" and most of its properties before it was discovered by a patriotic German 16 years later. Looking at what would be in the fourth Period (rows top-to-bottom 1- 7) and fourteenth (p) column, there *had* to be something a bit like carbon, a bit more like silicon and a bit like tin and lead. Whatever these elements had in common that differed from the others was worth investigating. (Later on, it would make the slightly faffy process of refining silicon for micro-electronics more economic than looking for the much rarer germanium.)

As with so much of the bedrock of science fiction, silicon-based life was an idea popularised by H.G. Wells. The logic was clear: carbon is fundamental to our kind of life because of what conditions prevail *here*, but other worlds with other atmospheres and temperature-ranges might favour the next similar element and analogous chemical processes with different elements. Wells speculated on beings on a world hotter than a Bessemer Converter, with oceans of liquid iron and a sulphur atmosphere (sulphur is two columns right of silicon, the same way oxygen is two to the right of carbon) and a silicon-aluminium

continued on page 261...

14.2 The Hand of Fear

shot several times when he saunters into a nuclear power station.] He receives NHS treatment. [Well, he *seems* English and you don't need ID or money unless you're trying to park your car at the hospital.]

He can withstand enormous pressure and temperature (twice the boiling-point of water) in a ventilation shaft leading to a nuclear reactor. He's also happy to give his coat to Sarah on the freezing surface of Kastria. He appears to be a decent medium-pace right-arm bowler.

To free Sarah from Eldrad's control, he gives her what looks like a sock to her jaw, then places her (involuntarily) back in a trance to get more information, then frees her of it for good. Neither the Doctor nor Sarah entirely trust Eldrad, but they nonetheless work to save her when she's poisoned by a death-trap.

• *Background*. He's been to much colder planets than Kastria. [Of course.] On receiving a telepathic summons from Gallifrey, he marvels that it's finally come [as if he'd given up hope of such a call]. He knows that non-Time Lords are forbidden entry there. He remembers Sarah's home address but, apparently, hasn't been there.

• *Ethics*. He falls back on a statute concerning the duties and responsibilities of Time Lords in the field towards "lesser" species. [We've not heard this before and were sort of under the impression that any kind of involvement was strictly off-limits – but Eldrad, who knows about Time Lords and TARDISes, seems to think it's legitimate.] Specifically, he is obliged to oppose aggression towards indigenous species, but cannot break the First Law of Time [distortion of history; compare against "The Three Doctors"], so he can return Eldrad to Kastria c.1976 but not intervene in that planet's past. [A cut scene had Eldrad enter the coordinates, a means for the Doctor to establish how trustworthy his guest's sob-story was.]

This arrangement is only stipulated after Eldrad loses the ability to torture the truth out of the Doctor [so any subsequent claims that this is "a clever lie" can be treated sympathetically]. His justification to Sarah is that Eldrad left on Earth would cause more trouble, rather than it just being nice to take a stranded alien home.

He cites speech and diplomacy as 'older weapons'.

• *Inventory:*
– *Sonic Screwdriver*. Handy for TARDIS repairs. Boy, is Sarah sick of it.
– *Scarf*. The Doctor uses it as a Linus-blanket and it later makes an ideal tripwire for Eldrad. It must be fairly durable, as a fast-moving silicon lump doesn't stretch the stitching or break the thread.
– *Other*. He has a telescopic magician's stick but chucks it away on Kastria. His pockets contain a mergin nut, a multi-quantiscope, a Zeus-plug [see X2.4, "The Girl in the Fireplace"] and a Ganymede driver. [The names of the last two suggest some kind of relationship.] And he's replaced the cricket ball Harry blew up ["The Ark in Space"].

The TARDIS The Doctor claims that people aboard the TARDIS are in 'a state of temporal grace'; for this reason, Eldrad cannot whammy him inside the Ship. [This appears to be a function of the Ship's transdimensional nature and not something that happens with a flick of a switch. (See **He Remembers This *How*?** under X1.5, "World War Three"; **Is Arthur the Horse a Companion?** under X2.4, "The Girl in the Fireplace"; **Is Time Like Bolognese Sauce?** under X5.4, "The Time of Angels"; and our comments on noetic viruses with 15.2, "The Invisible Enemy" and 'conceptual geometers' in Season Seventeen.)

[Apart from the possible pun on the word 'temporal', as opposed to "spiritual", this idea has been more honoured in the breach than the observance. In 20.1, "Arc of Infinity", it's claimed that some kind of temporal grace circuit was broken (hence the lethal gunfire in 19.6, "Earthshock"). In X6.8, "Let's Kill Hitler", the eleventh Doctor admits the whole 'temporal grace' thing was a 'clever lie' when Mels comments on it. (Side note to ask: when would Mels have heard of this? Young Amelia can't have told her. Perhaps the Silence explained it – and she remembered, somehow – so this TARDIS-feature must be fairly widely-reported. If, as X6.1, "The Impossible Astronaut" hints at in a muddled way (then immediately contradicts), the Silence are the ones building a TARDIS in Craig's non-existent upstairs room, they'd have ample reason to find out. See **Who's Building a TARDIS and Why?** under X6.2, "The Day of the Moon".)

[The logical conclusion is that telling this annoying kid it was a 'clever lie' was *itself* a clever

Eldrad Must Live – But How?

...continued from page 259

base for their body-chemistry.

Wells and the scientists on whose work he was riffing (Julius Scheiner, Robert Ball, James Emerson Reynolds) assumed that such entities would be inside volcanic planets (this being 1893-4, life inside the Earth was a popular topic – see Volume 3 and 16.1, "The Ribos Operation" for loopy notions about ice and Wagner) and that, with such conditions only lasting a brief time, any such life would be very old or extinct. (They were still hazy on radioactivity. Assumptions about why the Earth's core was still molten mainly hinged on the planet not being as old as we know it is.) With most metals being liquid at these temperatures, albeit under enormous pressure, transpiration and respiration were less awkward than they might be for such creatures. JBS Haldane thought so, speculating in the 1930s on molten silicate beings using the oxidisation of liquid iron to sustain themselves.

This is where we get to the first of the five usual objections to silicon-based life that chemists offer when confronted with the usual television versions. If we assume that these entities (the silicon-based ones, not the chemists) follow some process analogous to breathing, then the obvious analogue to CO2 is Silicon Dioxide, i.e., sand. As we know, sand at that temperature is liquid – blow a bubble in it, then let it cool to room-temperature, and you've made a bottle. At the sort of pressures you might encounter if you're a magma-beast, glass might not behave the way it does up here. Admittedly, these days there are a lot of exotic liquid crystals beyond the ones used to make readouts or tellies, but not much work has been put into how to make such things function as a bloodstream or cell-walls. Of course, the main problem here is that people are assuming that something based on silicon is at all bothered with oxygen. That needn't be the case.

Still, let's stick with the ones that make the best stories, those that can interact with humans and – if necessary – be faked-up in a TV studio. Problem two, as you'll have surmised, is that they can't do much in an environment suitable for people like us. If you need gaseous sulfur (as it's after 1992 and we're talking science and not cookery, we're obliged to use the American spelling), you're already above 444° C and the pressures we were thinking of inside a planet make sulfur at these temperatures act oddly. Even in a lab at one atmosphere, it has two separate liquid stages, one at 115° C and then a darker allotrope at 200° C. (There's an intermediate pre-liquid stage at 95° C where it polymerises, a fact integral to rubber tyre manufacture.) But that was just Wells blowing smoke (almost literally).

There might be other ways for a silicon bio-chemistry to work at lower temperatures. One promising avenue does, as those chemists surmised, entail oxygen. With it, in place of proteins and amino acids based on carbon as a lynchpin for hydrogen, oxygen, nitrogen, sulfur et al, you have silicones. Silicon and oxygen atoms make various types of gel, from the transparent stuff in those exceptionally bouncy balls (also used as fake glass when windows shatter in film – you know this from umpteen editions of *Doctor Who Confidential* where Danny Hargreaves blows things up), to the stuff used to stick real windows in their frames or fix bathroom tiles, to the famous silicone implants of various starlets. Now, for the reason specified in the last paragraph, a silly-putty monster will tend to leave little piles of sand wherever it goes. That's not as big a problem as it being more likely than not to use sulphuric acid in lieu of water.[41]

If that combination of features sounds familiar, you're right. Some of the dialogue in *Alien* makes a good case for the xenomorph to be silicon-based, but then it spends the rest of the film eating carbon-based humans and laying eggs in its leftovers. Human meat may not be toxic to such a critter, but it won't be especially nourishing. A more plausible scenario, aside from the whole room-temperature / one-atmosphere thing, is the notorious pizza-monster from *Star Trek*, the Horta. There, neither side really got the hang of the other lot being alive until Spock did his Vulcan Plot Device without the aid of an oven-mitt.

Both of those cases involve a silicon exoskeleton around a squidgy silicone core, but a biochemistry that doesn't really match ours. Both spend hours at a time in conditions that favour humans. Maybe the external rigidity is simply exposure to oxygen and, in their natural habitat, they lack such plaques. That's not quite what we see on Kastria, but we'll get to that. The Ogri (16.3, "The Stones of Blood") seem more in keeping with what we'd expect, even leaving a sand-trail after they've rumbled past, but the need for globulin is just as counterintuitive as the xenomorphs' taste

continued on page 263...

14.2 The Hand of Fear

lie to cover for the fact that – for reasons best known to Herself – the TARDIS allowed all this to happen. A great deal of what occurs with River Song only works if we assume that the TARDIS is complicit: a high-risk strategy when we consider X5.13, "The Big Bang".

[Temporal grace, if what the Doctor says here is true, would account for the survival of Professor Chronotis in "Shada" (17.6) and Captain Jack every time he dies after X1.13, "The Parting of the Ways". It also looks like the underlying idea of what went wrong for Mawdryn and company in "Mawdryn Undead" (20.3). See **What Happens in a Regeneration?** under 11.5, "Planet of the Spiders".]

The Doctor tells Eldrad that if the coordinates are slightly off, it will set up 'symbolic resonance' in the 'tracoid time crystal' and break the TARDIS. [Another clever lie, possibly. This Doctor tends to use lit-crit terminology when trying to put one over on people (see also 16.1, "The Ribos Operation" for 'dithyrambic oscillations', "Pyramids of Mars" for 'isomorphic' controls). Earlier in this story, he asked the intern whether Sarah showed signs of 'paralepsis' – like "prolepsis" and "metalepsis", this refers to storytelling technique.]

Sarah doesn't think the TARDIS has a bath or any hair-care facilities, but finds a banana somewhere. The cold of Kastria affects the thermocouplings and sends the astro-rectifier out of whack. [That might be why the Ship misses South Croydon – in X2.3, "School Reunion", we're told it landed in Aberdeen instead. Or, after "Terror of the Zygons", the Ship thinks that this is Sarah's home; the time seems to be correct.]

The Supporting Cast

• *Sarah*. Lives in Hillview Road, South Croydon. Although she was apparently intending to pop home at the start of this story, she wasn't exactly dressed for work. [A red and white candy-stripe romper-suit with three red stars on the bib, matching headscarf and Kickers™, long red and white stripy socks and a long-sleeve top (red) – she's described as dressing 'like Andy Pandy'.] Despite her protests, she was undoubtedly planning on more adventures with the Doctor.

Oddly, when overwhelmed by Eldrad she becomes – if anything – more playful and girlish. She disobeys direct orders to stay away from the reactor and tells the Doctor 'I worry about you'.

After the crisis, she resorts to outright carping and lists a number of recurrent gripes such as hypnosis, cold, threats to life and limb and confusion. This looks like a ploy to get the Doctor to take her somewhere fun – but backfires when he has to leave her behind. She takes with her a potted plant, a stuffed toy owl, a suitcase, her raincoat [or one very like the one she left on Skaro in "Genesis of the Daleks"], a tennis-racket, a suitcase with a lot of stickers, the bolero jacket from the end of the last story and what looks like a picture frame.

[In "School Reunion", it turns out that she waited for the Doctor to return for decades (and seems to not remember their meeting again in 20.7, "The Five Doctors"). He claims he didn't come back for her because it's a 'curse' of having to watch people he loves grow old, 'wither and die' (as if humans don't have to do that). Alternatively, fear of paradoxes might be to blame: when they are reunited, in A7, "The Wedding of Sarah Jane Smith", he seems to know a lot about what the future holds for Luke, Clyde and Rani. By the way, Sarah did keep the owl in her attic.]

The Supporting Cast
(conniving and probably evil)

• *Eldrad*. [On Eldrad's rise and fall, see **History**.] Eldrad's ring contains his body-print and emits an actinic flash that renders people susceptible to his will. The phrase 'Eldrad must live' goads those affected onward; while able to feign normality, they behave like addicts. [We speak of possession being a dominant threat in the Hinchcliffe stories, but this is more "obsession", and seems almost neurochemical. With the possible exception of Sarah's abrupt knowledge of nuclear power stations, perhaps owing to physical contact with the hand and the ring, other recruits act as if they only know the name 'Eldrad'. Allowing anything to go against him is akin to withdrawal.]

When unable to force the Doctor to comply with his – or, now, her – wishes, she resorts to cajolery and deception. Once aboard the TARDIS, her mental force fails to coerce the Doctor, and so she must accept a return to Kastria in the present time. Reborn as male (see **The Non-Humans**), Eldrad plans to use the race-banks [presumably a large number of similar rings] to restore his people and reign over them, but they thwarted this by choosing self-immolation over servitude.

Ultimately, Eldrad plummets down a ravine;

Eldrad Must Live – But How?

...continued from page 261

for astronauts and space-monks. Silicon bonds rather enthusiastically with oxygen, making sand unless particular care is taken to make the more interesting polymers such as silicone. With hydrogen, it makes silanes (sort of like methane) and with both together silicates (like carbonates but with carbon replaced).

There is another way for beasties to be silicon-based, with no need for sulphuric acid, and that's if their water-surrogate is ammonia. Can you see the problem there? For ammonia to be a liquid, it needs to be either very cold or under extreme pressure. Cold as in -60° C tops, more likely down at – 100° C. Pressure, though, makes things interesting. If you're on the surface of Venus, ammonia will be liquid up to almost water's boiling point. (Trouble is, the surface's ambient temperature is well above that: say, about 400° C above.) There's also the problem of ammonia being not only devoid of oxygen but breaking down on contact with it and making water. (Water is to ammonia what sulphuric acid is to water, since ammonia has a pH in double figures.) Add hydrogen to ammonia-based compounds and you can get methane, so there's a respiration-analogue available that offers a bit less energy than oxygen. (You could also use chlorine, but that might explode.) It's also possible that polysinanols (the silicon version of sugars) could be dissolved in liquid nitrogen.

You can see why the earliest stories about silicon-based life (e.g., "A Martian Odyssey" by one-hit-wonder Stanley Weinbaum) were about the difficulty of communicating with them or getting them to acknowledge us as alive. Any such being would have evolved on a planet right off the desres list for humans. If we met them on neutral ground, they'd not look alive at first, unless we were specifically on the alert for slow-moving extremophiles in acid-pools, ammonia-swamps, blast-furnaces or mobile thermos-flasks.

There's another reason these guys are traditionally presented as novelty-items in stories: compared to carbon, silicon's quite hard to come by in the cosmos at large. Earth has a lot more of it, proportionally, than the observed interstellar material and we've not come across any silicon-based life. That other abundant element, oxygen, has made all of the exposed silicon take the most obvious and inert form. Whole deserts of it. Out in space, carbon outnumbers silicon 10 to 1, but in the Earth's composition it's 925:1 in favour of silicon. Under different conditions, something might have happened (and let's not rule out creatures at the Earth's Core quite unlike anything Doug McClure encountered), but even then a couple of things make it unlikely that any such life would amount to much.

Carbon's success is mainly because it bonds to so many things. It's a physically smaller atom and its bonds are more durable than silicon's. A quasi-organic compound made from silanes would fall apart fairly easily. (Here's where a learned discourse on pentavalence would go if we were doing this as anything more than background to discussing Stephen Thorne dressed as a Christmas Tree ornament.) Organic compounds have carbon collaborating more than Ed Sheeran.

Magnesium, zinc, phosphorus, plus all the usual suspects we've mentioned, carbon's a good mixer and can enable nice long chains with lots of information. If you're looking to make self-replicating double-helix molecules with silicon, you're in for a much harder time. (That said, it's possible that silicon's presence was vital for the carbon-chains to get into shape to do the zip-fastener routine.) Silicon-based polymers don't have chirality the same way that carbon-based ones can and usually do – there are "clockwise" and "anti-clockwise" versions of sugars, for example. (We can only digest one, the right-handed type, so if making southpaw sucrose were economically viable, we'd have the diet panacea.) RNA and DNA are the most obviously chiral molecules, so a silicon version might not function (another technical digression could have gone here and allowed you to use "enantiomeric" in Scrabble).

By now you could be wondering: if carbon's so promiscuous and silicon's capable of bonding with a select few elements, including carbon, what's to prevent a carbon-based molecule with plenty of silicon in it? The answer is, not much. They haven't been especially abundant in terrestrial biology, but they've been synthesised in labs. Unlike properly silicon-based chains, they don't fall apart in water or turn to stone when exposed to air.

This looks like a safer bet for the supposed silicon-based life-forms we've met in *Doctor Who*. After all, even apparently petrified entities such as the Ogri or the Pyroviles (X4.2, "The Fires of Pompeii") seem to have some kind of relationship with organic molecules. The Ogri feed on the

continued on page 265...

14.2 The Hand of Fear

the Doctor doesn't think he's dead but nonetheless throws the ring down after him. [Sarah is slightly sad that she can't have it as a souvenir, so may still be slightly affected.]

The Non-Humans
• *Kastrians*. In their present form, Kastrians are broadly humanoid but with a blue, crystalline surface texture like fluorspar. The head of each is surmounted with a large pointy octagonal stone [as if an icosahedron had been cut in half and used as a hat, or a large Metebelis crystal – see 10.5, "The Green Death" and 11.5, "Planet of the Spiders"]. When they die, they crumble to sand and shale.

Exactly how they die is unclear. Technik Obarl seems to succumb to sub-zero temperatures [he and his colleague needed quilts to stay 'operational']. Nonetheless, Eldrad subsists as a buried disembodied hand for at least 150 million years. [The 'dead' hand has no internal structure, skeleton, skin, musculature or suchlike, suggesting undifferentiated silicon-based molecules throughout. This would help explain why a hand has as much willpower as a brain.]

Memory and consciousness seem retained within a ring that also contains the entire biological matrix. With the correct technology, a new body containing all the memories up to the previous one's destruction can be generated. Without it, the disjecta membra can regenerate using ambient energy, especially atomic radiation. Oddly, when Eldrad does this inside a nuclear power station (aided by a couple of missiles), he [or the ring] rewrites the phenotype and constructs a body appropriate to new surroundings – close contact with Sarah means that Eldrad manifests as, approximately, a young woman. In this form, Eldrad is bullet-proof and can impose a mental force that overpowers the Doctor. [When restored to his normal shape, Eldrad has good reason to do this again but doesn't, so the ability may be another adaptation and not normal among Kastrians.

[This metamorphic faculty may not be limited to intelligent life-forms. Had the hand been unearthed in a cow-pasture, the ring may have "possessed" a bull, charged into a power-station and created a quadrupedal, horned, silicon-based megalomaniac. What would have happened had a pterosaur found the hand before it was buried is unclear, as are the consequences of it being disinterred before the discovery of atomic fission. The Big Finish audio *Eldrad Must Die!* by Marc Platt (26.2, "Ghost Light") has some fun with the idea that multiple Eldrads could conceivably sprout from different bits of him. Assuming that Eldrad is not unique among his people, the Kastrians would seem ideally suited to spread across the galaxy, not necessarily needing warp-capable spaceships to engage in a form of panspermia (seeding themselves slowly across the stars, taking aeons if needed). Yet they have a sleek ship ready for Eldrad's execution...]

The Kastrian vessel seems capable of crossing a sizeable portion of the galaxy in a short time. The Kastrian survival bunker is deep within the planet, with a geodesic dome on the surface, and warmed from the core [so it seems to be a semi-volcanic world, making the silicon lifestyle an interesting choice]. Their technology functions perfectly when Eldrad returns – including pre-recorded messages and a number of booby-traps. The lift registers descent in roots of three [our only indication of what the Kastrians were like before Eldrad's remodelling].

Planet Notes *Kastria* is perishing cold, but not lethally so for Sarah. The portion we see of it is a small Buckminster Fuller-style surface dome atop a long lift-shaft down at least 306 levels. The surface seems exactly the same in two scenes, 150 million years apart.

[A notional mechanism for this might be a planet with sporadically captured rotation. The solar heat evaporates silicon, which falls as a sort of "snow" on the cold side and alters the planet's centre of gravity so that it temporarily balances and rotates like most worlds do, out of synch with the orbit. This would even out the temperature and slow the winds. Any life that developed from the resultant chemistry might take the "normal" rotation to be an environmental catastrophe and adapt to it under duress. If the subterranean bases were originally the hot side, they would survive if the crisis continued, but not if that spot was once again exposed to perpetual sunlight – especially not if the barriers were destroyed. Millions of years later, the situation might return to the status quo ante, but with nobody around to enjoy it.]

History
• *Dating*. [It's so 1976, you can practically taste the Lord Toffingham ice-lollies: Sarah's clothes,

Eldrad Must Live – But How?

...continued from page 263

amino acids in the swamps of their native world and substitute human or animal globulin when exiled to Earth; the Pyroviles (and, it would seem, the Weeping Angels; X5.5, "Flesh and Stone"; X13.4, "Village of the Angels") convert people into stone incrementally. This seems very like the Petrifold Regression illness from X2.1, "New Earth". In everyday biology, some grasses integrate silicon crystals into their stems, but not at a molecular level. Those lab-grown compounds are the result of complex enzymes but are made at room temperature and without any particularly difficult techniques after the enzymes themselves have been brewed. Is this what's happening with the new model Kastrians?

Let's sift through what we're told about them. Eldrad apparently made a new physical form to help the Kastrians survive an increasingly hostile world. That form has a crystalline matrix, but acid can dissolve its bonds. Nonetheless, a gas that kills Kastrians has no effect on Sarah. The hand survives for hundreds of millions of years, and the corpses remain intact for that long, but the ring containing the information needed to remake Eldrad doesn't seem to be unique. There were race-banks with which the entire culture and population could be reconstituted. Intense radiation helps Eldrad reform from a hand and a ring, but the mild radiation after the barriers collapsed isn't enough to sustain Zazzka. The conditions on modern-day Kastria are the same after at least 150 million years have elapsed. (We don't know how long his fragmented hand floated in space before being caught in Earth's gravitational field.) It's cold and windy, but no more so than Antarctica in "The Seeds of Doom", and the air's breathable for both Sarah and Eldrad. It's also perfectly fine for Eldrad in his revised edition. Sarah's cold, but so were Obarl and Zazzka way back when.

That's interesting, as this is, apparently, what the planet's like when the barriers are down. These barriers are preventing a total environmental collapse due to solar winds "dehydrating" Kastria and cooling it beyond their tolerance. There are thermal chambers and "inexhaustible" energy from the planet's core. This is all a bit self-contradictory, but the main thing seems to be that the belt-and-braces approach, building a barrier *and* redesigning their phenotype around a different biochemistry and, for all we know, different body-shape seems to indicate ambitions beyond mere survival. The most logical motive for this is if Eldrad wants a body-type that can flourish on the large number of Earth-like worlds but isn't susceptible to whatever bugs or weapons those worlds might have.

The business of regenerating with radiation is almost within reach of silicon's known properties. As we said, it's a semi-conductor. Transistors work by using the way an electron added to "doped" silicon makes it better able to conduct larger amounts of electricity, a small input in one wire "switches on" a bigger flow. If silicon's atomic structure is amenable to alterations then, by analogy, some kind of silicon-infused DNA-analogue might self-replicate with gamma particles instead of amino acids.

All of this suggests that we have never encountered a genuine silicon-based life form in *Doctor Who*. Or have we? There's a lot about the Rills from "Galaxy 4" (3.1) that fits with what we were saying earlier. They breathe ammonia rather than use it as we use water, so their temperature range is a bit high for the low-temperature model and way too low for the volcano-resident type. All the same, it was a good early shot at making the universe bigger than just humanoids, clunky robots and biped with animal-heads.

Nonetheless, a genuine silicon-based life-form opens up a lot of possible stories unlike anything we've had. One option is that they come to Earth and, failing to identify carbon-based life as significant (or even possible), attempt to communicate with the cities and roads they assume to be the dominant species – or even cleanse the world of the lukewarm parasites (i.e. us). Another is that the TARDIS could land on a completely alien world for once, rather than a choice of beaches in Wales and beaches in South Africa. A third, in keeping with the way things are being done these days, is that the Doctor is forced to accept that they've been a bit of a carbon-centric.

the ambulances going *nee-nah*, Carter's shirt and tie (and his new P-reg Austin Allegro 2 with round steering-wheel[43]), Driscoll's hair... the one anomaly is a Nunton staffer wearing a tennis-shirt that's more 1968, 1980 or 1995. The stock-footage jetfighters are first-generation Hawker Siddely Harriers (except when they turn into 60's Buccaneers) used by the RAF from 1969 to 1990. The stock-footage ambulance indicates that the hospital, quarry and power-station are all some-

14.2 The Hand of Fear

where near Watford (the first doesn't look like Watford General Hospital, but somewhere smaller) before the M25 was built. Nunton is, for obvious reasons, very like a second-generation Magnox nuclear power station built in the 1960s. It could have been in use up to around 2015, but the early-70s lettering would have gone by 1980.]

A very long time ago, the Kastrians were dying because of their inhospitable planet. Eldrad designed a new body-type, using silicon, and devised shields to protect the citadel from cosmic radiation. Thinking he was owed the people's unswerving fealty and denied his goal of seising the throne and leading his people on to conquest, Eldrad destroyed the barriers in a fit of pique – an act the survivors describe as 'genocide'. King Rokon evacuated the last handful to the deepest level of the thermal caves. Eldrad was slated for execution by ferrying him bodily to intergalactic space and atomising him and the ship. The power-drain in the last stage was so great that Rokon ordered the detonation before the ship had left the galaxy. On the chance that any of Eldrad survived, Rokon then destroyed the race-bank that had been the last hope of his people.

The premature detonation allowed Eldrad's hand and ring to survive intact and eventually reach Earth 150 million years ago, landing in sand that became Jurassic limestone. There is no indication of how long it was floating or how it reached Earth.

The Analysis

Where Does This Come From? It's often been noted that the Baker-Martin scripts are less ambivalent about nuclear power than most. That's not entirely true. Consider, as a counter-example, Malcolm Hulke's script for "Invasion of the Dinosaurs" (11.2), in which eco-terrorists attempt a mass cull of humanity and polluting technology, but cheerfully run an atomic reactor to fuel their timescoop. The Doctor locates them with a Geiger counter through about a hundred feet of tarmac, soil, concrete and electrical cables. Most people accepted this in 1974.

What's been forgotten since the various catastrophic meltdowns and near-misses since the late 70s is that being pro- or anti-nuclear wasn't in any way aligned with any other political beliefs. The 1959 General Election saw the Labour Party (and especially their fresh-faced, pro-technology socialist ex-aristocrat Anthony Wedgewood-Benn) presenting Party Political Broadcasts from in front of a big picture of Windscale power station, talking up the idea of progress and change being inherently Labour characteristics as against the class-bound, stagnant, backward-looking Tories.

Hulke's left-wing credentials are well-established, yet even he thought of nuclear power as less of a worry than coal-powered stations (however much he sided with the miners in the novelisation of 10.5, "The Green Death"). You'll know from **What Kind of Future Did We Expect?** under 2.3, "The Rescue", that enthusiasm for technology and various exciting programmes for education, public health and transport cut across barriers of age and class. Plus you'll recognise from **How Plausible was the British Space Programme?** (7.3, "The Ambassadors of Death") how much government and industrial support there was for staying in the game as a matter of national prestige, job-creation and simply being unable to imagine any other kind of future for Britain.

What changed was a perception that the US profit-above-safety culture and the British hush-it-up-muddle-through-and-rename-everything-afterwards tendencies would start to coincide as and when British atomic power was privatised and our shining gems sold off to unregulated multinationals. Then, just to put the tin hat on it, a Soviet-run generator near Kiev ran amok despite neither of these being in place. Some production companies rejected the script of *The China Syndrome* (1979) as implausible and too anti-business – then something remarkably similar took place at Three Mile Island. Even though it was unregulated Capitalism at fault (in the film and, to some extent, in the real incident), this fed into a pervasive anti-establishment mood after Watergate and Vietnam.

Meanwhile, the official account of the 1957 fire at Windscale was coming into question and, as we now know, a lot was kept quiet because then-Prime Minister Harold Macmillan was trying to persuade President Eisenhower that future missile development should be a joint venture. (Windscale's goal was to generate electricity, but also to make weapons-grade plutonium in case the Americans turned on Britain.) It was run as if Britain were still at war; the local populace and landscape were there for the reactor's benefit, not vice versa. The safety precautions thought "super-

Could *Scratchman* Have Happened?

Without looking it up, take a guess what Hammer Films' biggest earner of the 1970s was. They'd won the Queen's Award for Industry in 1968 for exporting their trademark horror flicks, but the distribution deal with Columbia ate into their profits. Shifts in what was doable dominated the industry in that decade, causing some very odd decisions. But in the early 70s, Christopher Lee was still prepared to play Dracula, Dinosaurs Ruled the Earth and *Moon Zero Two* showed us what life would be like in 2021 A.D. (lots of sitcom stars watching go-go dancers and saying dialogue from old Westerns in regional English accents). So was it *Vampire Circus*, with the future Mrs Richard Dawkins spatchcocked by a crucifix? No. How about peculiar Kung-Fu crossover *The Legend of the 7 Golden Vampires*, co-financed by the Shaw Brothers and shot partly in Hong Kong? Of course not. *Doctor Jekyll and Sister Hyde*? *Countess Dracula*? *The Vampire Lovers*?

If you remembered that Hammer's initial successes were in adapting radio serials and then television shows, and that they moved into horror on the back of *The Quatermass Xperiment* (sic), you might have got it. The mid-70s trend for slightly smuttier, not-quite-canonical expansions of hit BBC and ITV sitcoms was kicked off with a feature film adaptation of *On the Buses*. This, not anything in their blood 'n' boobs franchises, was the company's cash-cow. It didn't get shown in American drive-ins, but it didn't need to be. It took £1 million at the UK box-office, over ten times the budget.

The series was cheerfully vulgar, based on the bizarre premise that two of the ugliest leading-men in showbiz, Reg Varney and Bob Grant, were irresistible to the many mini-skirted dolly-birds they met when working as driver and conductor of a double-decker in London. Their boss, Blakey, looked like Hitler. That's as subtle as it got. The film version was coarser-grained. This, and two sequels that took the story further from the London Weekend original, took enough at the UK box office to offset all the flop horrors that failed to keep pace with *The Exorcist* or *Rosemary's Baby*. Hammer thereafter gave up on films and made cheap television (see 16.6, "The Armageddon Factor" et seq.). *Holiday on the Buses* had the regulars working at a Butlins-style holiday camp after being fired from the job – that was the "sit" of the sitcom in the first place, but the film made more money than the two before.

Once other studios saw the way the wind was blowing, we got *And Now For Something Completely Different*, a mendaciously-titled remake of the best sketches of the first two years of *Monty Python's Flying Circus*, then big-screen outings for *Man About the House* and *George and Mildred*[12], *Are You Being Served?*, *Steptoe and Son* (twice), *Till Death Us Do Part* and (belatedly) *Porridge* and *Rising Damp* – all distressingly lucrative compared to the majority of films made in, by and for Britain. With the television companies not believing in archiving their output methodically, and much of it made in black and white until very recently, early 70's films of hit television shows were a way to expand upon previously-made works (as with the 1972 *Dad's Army* film compressing the first eight episodes into 90 minutes with better special effects and more location work, in colour) or get ruder, rather than rely on innuendo and the studio audience's giggles (such as *Up Pompeii* and its follow-ups). Just to remind you, film versions of BBC series weren't made by the BBC, which didn't get into feature films until 1990.

Established *auteurs* were given almost automatic funding, so Ken Russell, Joseph Losey, Stanley Kubrick and Nicolas Roeg ploughed their own furrows up to a point, but until the rules changed in 1985, it was easier to finance the sequel to a hit than to get that first film made – and much easier to get money if you didn't need it than if you did. Unless it's for kids, in which case there's a whole different organisation and distribution network, the Children's Film Foundation, but then the film had to star child actors, not frighten the horses and not cost much.

There were still people going to see Hammer Horrors, bizarre as these increasingly were, as well as the films from this period that get remembered (although, notoriously, incoming British Lion exec Michael Deeley "buried" two of the acknowledged classics, *Don't Look Now* and *The Wicker Man*, in a double bill on limited release), but the main priority for studios and successive governments was keeping those valued technicians and actors in work by more-or-less breaking even more often than not. There were money-making series of bawdy comedies, such as the sputtering last years of the *Carry On* cycle and its spiritual (so to speak) heir *Confessions of a Window-Cleaner* et seq. and a number of one-off "sex comedies", neither particularly explicit nor especially funny, allowing people to pay their bills in inflation-riven times. Any actual nudity in *Confessions...* is usually undercranked,

continued on page 269...

14.2 The Hand of Fear

fluous" prevented a worse disaster and the clean-up was broadly successful, but this incident was far worse than TMI (if not in the Chernobyl/Fukushima bracket).

What we're getting at is that the apparently small detail in Part Two, where Professor Watson thinks Sarah's a psychiatric patient or cultist rather than an environmental protester, is worth a closer look. In the early 70s, it seemed, from Britain, as if every American or European between 15 and 25 was in either a pseudo-religious cult or a radical political movement. Look west and we saw EST, the Bhagwan, the Moonies, the Jesus Freaks, the Manson Family, the Children of God, the Maharishi, Sullivanians, Dianetics, Patty Hearst, Jonestown and more; some benign, some not, but all creepy-looking to a nation that had trouble taking Lord Longford or Mormons seriously.

Look east and we saw the Baader-Meinhof gang (24.4, "Dragonfire"), the Red Army Faction, ETA, the Black September movement, GARI, OAS, the Red Brigade, Carlos the Jackal, the PLO, Anni di Piombo ... terror attacks in Western Europe peaked in 1979 at 1,019 in a year (of course, that includes the IRA, whose age-profile seemed to be older). Far-left, hard-right, nationalists and nihilists, everyone was at it. Watson assumes that "Eldrad" is a cult-leader, and that the young woman wandering into the reactor is bent on self-immolation to make a statement. It's not about nuclear power – that's just a spectacularly noticeable target that will impact upon a lot more people than a bank or a television studio.

As we'll see in **The Lore**, the original story-proposal was very different. How did we get from a post-apocalyptic scenario – with giant gorillas, prehistoric man living in the sea and warring alien factions coming out of the Sun – to this? The simple answer is that both storylines were consequences of trying to amalgamate three things the writers wanted into one story: silicon-based aliens; a nearby nuclear power station (with a PR man who'd love it if *Doctor Who* was filmed there) and a creeping disembodied hand. To help "sell" the idea to the power-station, the emphasis was on the man whose job it was to stop potential disasters. (After their curious idea of a meltdown evacuation procedure in 8.3, "The Claws of Axos" – saunter downstairs, drive slowly to a spot half a mile away, watch the explosion through binoculars then drive back – the more homework they did, the better.)

We've got a whole essay about the history and probability of the idea of silicon-based life, but here we must note the basic metaphor of "a heart of stone" and "bloodless" as applied to a ruthlessly pragmatic alien. In that bizarre earlier draft, we were back to the idea of Mengele-like experimentation on humans to establish survival capabilities (see "The Sontaran Experiment"), this time with a Dr Moreau-aspect combining human and animal characteristics. An element of this remains in the conniving Eldrad and his / her unswerving zeal to survive, return and rule. Compared to any other well-known stories about silicon-based entities from that period or before, it makes Eldrad a lot less sympathetic.

This being Baker and Martin, we have to assume they knew *Star Trek*'s essay into this field, "Devil in the Dark", almost word-for-word by now. (See also 17.3, "The Creature from the Pit"). Had they submitted such a story to Barry Letts and Terrance Dicks, it would probably have leant towards the "they may have different biology, but they're still an intelligent, sensitive race" line. There's a vestige of this in the Doctor's reactions, but even he is mistrustful of Eldrad once she's capable of speech and, therefore, lying. Until that point, the hand is an unstoppable force rather than an antagonist and – inevitably, given the year in which it's made – able to possess people.

That ought not to be so surprising. The founding text for disembodied hands on the make is Robert Siodmak's *The Beast with Five Fingers* (1943), in which one apparently drives Peter Lorre insane. And, oh, look, it bends him to its will with a ring. Twenty years later, an exploding spaceship leaves a bit of jetsam in *The Crawling Hand* (it's actually a whole arm that washes up on a beach and possesses a surfer-dude, making him go Goth 20 years early). A year or so later, in 1964, Michael Gough ("Arc of Infinity"; 3.7, "The Celestial Toymaker") is an artist who loses a hand just after Christopher Lee slags his work off and so, this being an Amicus anthology (*Doctor Terror's House of Horror*, if you'd not guessed), the hand gets revenge.

Amicus went back to this for a whole film, *And Now the Screaming Starts*, set in the seventeenth century but made in 1973. The genre-logic demands that any mobile hand can mentally overwhelm whole humans. This "rule" dictates how the rest of the story fits together. As the six-episode version demonstrates, there are many ways

The Hand of Fear 14.2
Could *Scratchman* Have Happened?

...continued from page 267

making these films look oddly like the Keystone Kops doing soft-porn.

Welcome to the truly peculiar world of British film in the 1970s.

It's into this context that Tom Baker and Ian Marter stumbled, not entirely blindly, when they proposed a feature film based on *Doctor Who*. It had songs (until Philip Hinchcliffe said otherwise), walking scarecrows (see X3.8, "Human Nature"), not-quite Cybermen rising from the waves like Sea Devils, actual Daleks (with, apparently, Terry Nation's blessing), the Devil (sort of, "Mr Scratch" was an old name for Old Nick), Scottish islands, a giant pinball machine, CIA-style Time Lords with American accents (or not) and a cricket match. How could it fail? We've told some of the story in passing when discussing television *Who*'s production, but there's rather a lot else going on at the same time. The situation we've just sketched in changed with a combination of film industry chicanery, altered corporate structures and revised government legislation. Then it changed *again*.

Had such a film as Baker and Marter pitched been made in 1977, it could have massively impacted on the BBC's "parent" series. Had it happened a year later, it would've had a different impact. And if it had been a hit or a flop in either case, it would have caused wildly different ripples. Where such a film would have slotted into the volatile British film ecosystem would also have varied almost from month to month. At no point was it anything like what would have happened in Hollywood or how things were after 1985. Applying hindsight isn't much help; we have to sift what was going on *at the time* for clues about how things might have panned out at any stage. Our first clue would come from recalling what film Baker and Marter were watching when they had their lightbulb moment.

... trouble is, we're not sure what it was. When promoting the novel he wrote from the surviving script, Baker claimed that it was "a film with Roger Daltrey, which was about monsters", and people have assumed that he meant Ken Russell's *Lisztomania*. The dates don't entirely work for that, as Baker and his agent were in meetings with the BBC three months before that film's release, over a storyline he and Marter had bashed out three months before *that* (rejected by Holmes and Hinchcliffe, probably mainly for cost reasons). We know that the idea was sufficiently inspiring that the two actors-turned writers hired a cinema in Curzon Street to watch the Peter Cushing efforts, but that was in the gap between "The Android Invasion" and "The Brain of Morbius", September 1975. If one of their sorties into Soho to watch films and play pinball really was the starting point, it was around the time they were making "Revenge of the Cybermen" and the only film on release in November 1974 with a mop-haired Englishman and some monsters was *Mutations*, directed by Jack Cardiff (that Englishman was, um, Tom Baker). Of course, the pinball detail might be a hint that Baker was conflating their various trips to the pictures and he's thinking of *Tommy* – also directed by Russell and also starring Daltrey. That was in the cinemas (in London, at least) at the same time as *Young Frankenstein,* March 1975. These are hard films to muddle up, though, despite both being enraptured by pre-war Hollywood. *Tommy* is singularly lacking in monsters (unless you count Oliver Reed), but if we assume that Baker, 45 years on, was a little muddled about the sequence of events, then we might recover the full story.

There are many obvious reasons why *Lisztomania*'s Pop Art sensibility, as applied to the first musician to get teenage girls screaming and Wagner's role in the rise of Fascism, would seem like a good fit for Holmes and Hinchlife's *Doctor Who*. Most glaring is the satirical use of Hammer Horror props and iconography: Wagner's leeching off his father-in-law, Franz Liszt, is depicted as literal vampirism; later, his reworking of Teutonic mythology and Aryan Supremacism (as per *The Ring Cycle*) is performed in a ruined castle in a thunderstorm as he creates Siegfried from dead bodies (it's Prog-Rock embarrassment Rick Wakeman, in a horned helmet, silver face-paint and bolts through his neck, quaffing a stein of lager). Then, Ringo Starr shows up as the Pope.

More generally, just as *Doctor Who* was increasingly doing, it assumed a teenage audience who'd grown up on reruns of old films and accepted collage as the defining art-form of the era. *Tommy* had applied this to Pete Townshend's odd allegory and *Lisztomania* to the mid-nineteenth century and classical music. Goodtimes Productions found the money to do both films exactly as Russell wanted and it worked, the first time. It at least caused a splash on the second attempt. A major studio didn't give Russell this much leeway again until *Altered States*; Terry Gilliam largely filled his

continued on page 271...

269

to combine the three elements forced to work together in this story, but the broadcast one has the least variation from the basic source material.

One of the least noticed aspects is the way the writers and script-editor tried to make each episode within a story different from the others. A change of location, a change of characters even – in this case – one character changing physically from episode to episode, all kept it fresh and in motion. One character hangs around for the start of the next episode (Carter into Part Two, Watson into Part Three, female Eldrad into Part Four), but it's curiously like a 60's story in this regard. In a similar vein, there's an oddly *Quatermass*-like incremental absurdity to the narrative, where each step along the route to the finale is laboriously questioned and proved before they move to the next. Compared to the next script from the same source, this is reassuringly stolid. "The Invisible Enemy" only just allows us time for the Doctor – or Professor Marius – to mention the latest bizarre twist before they set up the next one, with no room for doubt or second-thoughts. This is odd, as that owes more details to the 50s *Quatermass* serials than this one does.

English Lessons

• *South Croydon* (n.): A suburb of a suburb. Croydon, in Surrey, was a commuter town that impinged upon London, or vice versa. It got big enough to have facilities of its own; South Croydon was the first part of it beyond the reach of a standard rail or bus ride in-and-out of the capital. It thus became a standing joke, at least for Londoners (as per Slough, Watford or Romford) and London-hating Surrey residents. Croydon Aerodrome was the precursor to Heathrow and Gatwick (19.7, "Time Flight"; 4.8, "The Faceless Ones") and was where Chamberlain made his "peace in our time" statement ("The Green Death"). These days, it's been granted city status and has a swish tram service.

• *Season* (n.): In the sense that the Doctor means it, he could be thinking that South Croydon is a resort or spa-town, like Bath in Jane Austen's time, a seaside town like Brighton (see 15.1, "Horror of Fang Rock"; 18.1, "The Leisure Hive") or a winter-resort such as Aspen or Grenoble. Or, even more implausibly, he could be thinking of the Society pages and the custom of debutantes to "come out" and be promoted on the marriage market. The cut dialogue indicates that they were thinking of the seaside, as there's a joke about a stick of rock (see 15.5, "Underworld").

• *Ammonites* (n.): Those spiral fossils. Most of England was underwater in the Jurassic era, so sandstone quarries tend to contain ammonites, trilobites, belemnites and the occasional ichthyosaur.

• *Dolomite* (n.): Just to be clear, the current US terminology is slightly different from the 1970's UK categories. The stratum in which Eldrad's hand was found is straightforward limestone without any significant amounts of magnesium.

• *The answer lies in the quarry* paraphrases the phrase associated with Arthur Fallowfield, the fictional gardening expert played by Kenneth Williams in *Beyond Our Ken* (a radio comedy now slightly unfairly remembered as the dry run for *Round the Horne*). He would answer any question at all with "The answer lies in the soil", said in an exaggerated West Country accent. However, Williams was parodying several real ones, including Ralph Whiteman (credited with originating the phrase), Percy Thrower (of BBC Television's *Gardening Club* and later *Gardeners' World*) and wartime "Dig for Victory" radio gardener Mr Middleton (see X1.9, "The Empty Child").

• *Andy Pandy* (n.): Arguably Britain's first "cult" show, along with *Muffin the Mule* (see X2.7, "The Idiot's Lantern"), since it was made on film to be repeated – in an era when all other television was live and repeats meant the cast doing it all again. It was on continuously from 1951 to 1st January 1975, aimed at under-fives. (There was, inevitably, a big-budget stop-motion remake in 2002. It's not nearly as evocative or involving; small children seem to prefer the original when shown both.) There were 13 episodes, over and over again, plus a later four colour ones. It was about a marionette who woke up when the children watching turned up, as did his friend Teddy (a bear in a bow-tie). The postmodern twist was that when these two left, a third character, rag-doll Looby Lou, awoke and danced for our alleged entertainment, but we weren't allowed to tell Andy and Teddy that she could do this. Quite why a teddy bear and a sort of clown / Pierrot / babydoll hybrid had a rag doll to help them sleep was never explored. Like a lot of the successors (in the *Watch With Mother* slot at 1.45pm, just in time for a snack and a nap), it had a piano and a slightly shrill soprano for the music and a crisply-spoken lady narrating and talking to us and the

Could *Scratchman* Have Happened?

...continued from page 269

niche in the UK film-making ecosystem. Russell used fantasy as a tool of personal expression and social criticism, in a way that most older filmgoers didn't get but which spoke to audiences under 30. *Doctor Who* was heading in a similar direction, albeit less "authored". Hindsight, in the shape of Season Fourteen, makes this connection seem irresistible – but, if Baker's memory and the BBC's documentation are right, the plans were firming-up during the hasty rewrites on "The Brain of Morbius", and when "The Android Invasion" was looking like the series' future.

Lisztomania was the biggest box-office hit in Britain, for a couple of weeks around Christmas 1975. Overseas audiences didn't get it, so it lost Goodtimes productions (David Puttnam's company) a shedload of money. They tried to sell it as a hybrid of *Tommy* (Russell's previous film for them, a big hit), *Mahler* (his previous nineteenth-century composer biopic – he did a string of them) and a recent hit they'd not made, *The Rocky Horror Picture Show* (which did for Edgar Lustgarten what *Lisztomania* did for 1960 Dirk Bogarde vehicle *Song Without End* – he played Liszt as more-or-less Elvis – and *Airplane!* did for *Zero Hour!*). It's actually more like Russell's *Monitor* documentary "Pop Goes the Easel", mixed with his films *The Boy Friend* and *The Dance of the Seven Veils* and – although we can't find any evidence of direct influence – the end is remarkably like that of then-current "buzz" book *Gravity's Rainbow*. Anyone familiar with Russell's *oeuvre* would have spotted that he was riffing on bad Hollywood biopics while using mid-twentieth-century popular culture to illustrate what was going on by analogy, in a way we now associate with cartoonish guidebooks. (*Derrida for Beginners* and 80s Biff cartoons are a close approximation.) For a young, cine-literate audience, especially one in Britain well-used to the ironic distance between Hollywood musicals and Music Hall, or our normality, this was familiar territory. The US distributors of *The Boy Friend*, his take on this topic, hacked half an hour out – the ground wasn't prepared for foreign critics to make head or tail of *Lisztomania*.

The most significant reason for thinking of this as the model for *any* 70s *Doctor Who* film is simply that it got made. Russell may have clashed with studio bosses, but things got easier once he'd proved that he didn't need them – he funded *Savage Messiah* (1972) by mortgaging his house.

He distributed it by getting the British Film Institute to include it with some films they were showing in regional theatres (to connect to filmgoers without the usual middle-men). He was, in today's terms, a "brand". Funding for anything as extravagant and fantastical needed a reliable name-brand: a famous director; a hit television series expanded for the big screen or a previous hit from the same stable and with substantially the same set-up. Russell's style was instantly recognisable. You can tell in a moment, often from a single frame, if you're watching one of his films. Even if you only know his name from jokes about his style and obsessions, such as *Monty Python* depicting him doing *Gardening Club* with nuns, Nazis and a Pantomime Goose, once you've seen him in full effect (e.g., *The Devils* or – probably more popular among readers of these books – *Lair of the White Worm*), you'll see why. His work is as authored as that of David Lynch, Federico Fellini or Quentin Tarantino. As we'll see, the main motivation for *Doctor Who Meets Scratchman* is to have made something indelibly stamped with Tom Baker's personality, regardless of who directed it.

This imperative didn't necessarily come from Baker himself, but it's interesting how often his agent, Jean Diamond, contacted the BBC's *Doctor Who* production office to clarify what the film would be like and who'd own it. Even with the precedent of Terry Nation's ruthless exploitation of the Daleks, the BBC's present-day control over the trademarks and rights to the series was a long time coming. BBC Enterprises wasn't as brand-alert as BBC Worldwide became, although they did police use of the images and names more rigorously than, say, Irwin Allen.

The smoking gun here is *Doctor Who and the Pescatons*, from around the same time, which seems to have simply happened without anyone really looking into the details. Obviously, *someone* was given oversight, since they couldn't use the TARDIS take-off sound as-is and had to hire Brian Hodgson to make a new one. Argo, a subsidiary of Decca, must have checked that they were allowed to make this, even if Baker had set it all up over drinks one evening (as seems to have been the case). Letters to and from Decca came in early November 1975, between Diamond sounding out Hinchcliffe about the film and Oscar winner James Hill being confirmed as director. The other key fact we have: Diamond and the BBC agreed in early

continued on page 273...

14.2 The Hand of Fear

puppets. Unlike most of them, it didn't have Peter Hawkins doing character voices as, obviously, puppets can't talk. (See Volumes 1 and 2 for more on why a 60s British childhood sounds like him.) Andy's stripey onesie was blue and white, not red and white, but the original episodes were in black and white. Nonetheless, the dolls sold well, so Dr Carter ought to have specified.

- **WHI 1212** (n.): At one time, the most famous phone number in Britain and possibly the world was "Whitehall One Two One Two", the non-emergency number for the original Scotland Yard. (The last four digits of the current number for New Scotland Yard, and all London police stations, are the same.) Not only was it always used in films and announced to the public from 1934 to the late 60s, but a 50s US radio series with what they assured us was an "all-British" cast re-enacted supposedly real cases (much like *Dragnet*, but with unconvincing Scotsmen and dowagers). Just before this number in the Doctor's string of digits is "999", the standard number for police, fire, ambulance and coastguard. Obviously, living inside a police box has made the Doctor think about such things.

Things That Don't Make Sense This whole thing could have been prevented if Rokon had just confiscated that bloody ring. It's the one bit of Eldrad almost guaranteed to survive even if his entire body were atomised, it could hypnotise anyone who finds it – and, by the way, it contains Eldrad's body print. Like Horus before him ("Pyramids of Mars"), Rokon bends over backwards to set up a sequel and equips the genocidal master-criminal with exactly what's needed to stage a comeback. (And, it's unlikely that removing someone's ring would be considered a form of blasphemy, since Eldrad created the silicon-based bodies and all the technology thereof. Removing his ring should be no more taboo than executing him and committing mass suicide.)

Rokon obviously feared that Eldrad would return, so established automatic defences to kill him. Okay, but allowing for the Kastrian 2.0 genome and those all-purpose rings, why didn't Rokon or his supporters rig up a way to resurrect defenders of the race-bank if and when Eldrad decided to reclaim the family estate? Why not send his ship into Kastria's sun, or at least an orbit where any fragments would eventually land up there?

In fact, it's hard to think of any circumstances where an exploding spaceship could send a fragment to Earth from another star without it being deliberately aimed. If it's being sent "beyond all solar systems" and will reach this point in six "spans" after a journey that's already lasted 19 of these, then Kastria is 25 Somethings from intergalactic space. Even with constant acceleration, that's a bit lopsided. Our solar system is not only halfway from the centre to the periphery when seen from the top, but halfway through its spiral arm when looked at from the side – right on the central plane (that's why we see the Milky Way from here). Wherever Kastria is, you don't just pass Earth en-route to the galaxy's edge after 76% of your journey-time. Never mind that even if Eldrad's hand was sent drifting in the general direction the ship was heading, the gravitational pull of our sun or Jupiter would snag whatever cosmic flotsam came in from beyond the solar system far more than Earth, unless its trajectory was along *precisely* the right approach-path. (The usual temperature of a meteor burning in Earth's atmosphere is slightly higher than the evaporation temperature of silicon – just saying).

The story begins with Obarl and Zazzka wearing white quilted hoodies, apparently to stay warm. Notwithstanding the obvious reasons why a silicon-based life-form might not find this adequate or necessary, when Eldrad returns, she puts the central heating on – within seconds, everywhere is warm enough for Sarah. This is, we're told, an "inexhaustible" source of geothermal energy. So what were the white anoraks for? It can't be to protect them from radiation – unless they fear that they'd grow too big to get out of the door. We're also unclear on how acid would affect someone with putty for blood. Incidentally, a planet conducive to silicon-based life ought not to have an atmosphere humans can breathe – certainly not after however long it's been since anyone used the air.

Nonetheless, the Kastrians are so gloomy that even the ludicrous improbability of Eldrad's return (they can't have planned that s/he would encounter someone with a TARDIS) is enough for them to do a Jonestown rather than use their fairly nifty spaceship technology to evacuate or something. It's not as if the Race Bank takes up that much space.

A final addition to Sarah's Odd Skill-Set: she somehow knows her way around a nuclear power

Could *Scratchman* Have Happened?

...**continued from page 271**

January 1976 that Baker was unavailable for a film until March 1977. Baker is the film's Unique Selling Point.

Everyone agreed that making a film with a different Doctor was a non-starter. By now, Baker was such a hit that use of previous Doctors' faces on the Target novelisation covers of those Doctors' stories was being phased out. We're still at a stage when Baker was amazed at the turn-outs for signings and personal appearances, but he was writing columns for *The Times* and *Reveille* and being profiled by national papers. Eventually he would find ways to capitalise on this, skirting very close to breaching BBC guidelines (see 17.4, "Nightmare of Eden").

The other key elements of the film's storyline were also rigidly-controlled: Terry Nation had become very aggressive about misuse of the Daleks and demanded considerable sums for their appearances in any unofficial capacity; the BBC had secured the copyright for the Metropolitan Police Box after the police had stopped using them, but Baker was keen to use the TARDIS as more than a means of getting in and out of a story. Above all, Philip Hinchcliffe and BBC Enterprises were concerned that any such film ought to be like televised *Doctor Who* but bigger, not just a random fantasy with a police box and Tom Baker. With Baker now ferociously possessive about the character and stipulating do's and don'ts, this was less of a problem than would emerge in the late 80s with the various drafts of the abortive feature film (starring either Rutger Hauer, Donald Sutherland or Dudley Moore). Hinchcliffe was concerned that the Cyberons were a bit close to the Cybermen, that Nation would grumble about the Daleks and that it was slightly more fantasy than the real series. He strove to ensure that everything was run by him and Enterprises' lawyers first.

Money from the British Board of Film Finance was sometimes allotted to international co-productions that looked guaranteed to make it all back and then some, or to films that looked award-winning but which no commercial body would touch – depending on which party was in government and who was President of the Board of Trade that month. Sometimes funding entailed "Front Money" (start-up costs and projected expenses), sometimes "End Money" (unexpected extras, plus post-production, promotion and distribution), as with live theatre, but most of the time no one body would provide both or even all of either of these sums. Sometimes an allocation covered up to a quarter of the projected cost, conditional on private sponsors (banks, corporations or manufacturers) stumping up the rest. The Hollywood model, a studio paying for everything up-front, wasn't really applicable even when companies owned both major UK studios and cinema chains and audiences were gagging to see British-made films. (Whole books examine why Rank and British Lion came unstuck trying it the American way.) Theatrical producers did act as "angels" for films, but Michael White, the Tony Award-winning West End impresario who gave Andrew Lloyd Webber his first hit, lost a lot of the money he made from his low-budget production *Monty Python and the Holy Grail* when he was stitched up over *The Rocky Horror Picture Show*. He later produced many remarkable films, but still died poor.

A tax on cinema seat sales, the Eady Levy, partly-funded many of these films, but the bulk of this – as at 1976 – had gone toward British-made films, using British studio technicians, actors and / or facilities, but ultimately backed by US producers or distributors. It was mainly used to start off projects that would attract other funding and thus guarantee a decent return, as far as anyone could. Thus Eon, and thereby United Artists, would be handed millions for a James Bond film, but a modestly-priced project about something inexplicable to Americans would have to ask elsewhere (almost the reverse of the 1990s, when Lottery-Funded whimsy was almost all that could get made). The definition of "a British film" included *Convoy*, *Superman: the Movie* and *Vanishing Point*.

Sometimes, the film's makers and distributors used proceeds made in another country, but which had been retained by that country's government along similar lines to the Eady Levy or pre-war quota system, so they'd make a film on location using that revenue and just edit it in London. (*Don't Look Now* got "free" use of Venice locations because of this; a different company would have had to pay a lot more.) Other forms of semi-governmental funding were available, albeit with strings and peculiar threshold conditions. In 1970, United Artists snaffled 40% of the available cash while British Lion got 11/2%. US companies liked the (relatively cheap) quality work of the set-builders, gaffers and cinematographers, and always liked getting RADA-trained thesps to add a

continued on page 275...

14.2 The Hand of Fear

station. It can't just be Eldrad sniffing out radiation, as the route to the reactor is too circuitous and involves ladders and staircases. Even if the Doctor's nursing a grudge against UNIT, Sarah – upon recovering – should mention that they have friends in high places. But by the time she can do so, Professor Watson has accepted the Doctor as some kind of expert because, err, he can crawl through radioactive ventilator shafts at 200° C. Five minutes before that, he thought Sarah was one of the Doctor's patients.

The change in attitude comes when the Doctor prevents a meltdown by ... what *does* he do? He knocks Sarah out, and Sarah drops the hand. Breaking contact with Sarah apparently undoes whatever Eldrad did to overload the reactor by opening a door and drumming its fingers. There's no hint of the usual ways to trigger a runaway reaction, nor of the Doctor re-inserting rods to fix it. If anything, the Doctor crawling through the outlet would create blockage that would make coolant-pressure rise, as per Three Mile Island. (Well, sort of: Nunton looks like it might be a Magnox reactor, like Oldbury, and therefore cooled with CO_2. These don't have the sort of steam-pressure trouble as with TMI or Chernobyl, but that makes what caused the overload even more mysterious. It would also pop him into the room like a champagne cork, splattering him against the wall.) As the plans the Doctor punches up on the screen are mainly circuit-diagrams, rather than architectural plans or plumbing diagrams, maybe he faxed himself to the reactor. It makes as much sense as what we're told. It's also notable how little time it takes to get from the Control Room to the main reactor. Only a few fire-doors separate the staff from the R4 zone.

It's also odd that there's a reactor with a door you can open and walk into. Wouldn't the hinges melt? Professor Watson calls his wife and daughter to tell them that nothing is wrong. He'd sound more reassuring if the Radiophonic Workshop hadn't drowned him out with klaxons.

Miss Jackson pops back in Part Three to describe all the scenes they forgot to film. She wasn't in the bits they *did* film of everyone leaving. All the things she describes took place in an action-packed 30 seconds after the Doctor and Sarah left.

That the RAF is so happy to launch an aerial assault on a nuclear power-station is also a little odd. Various contingency plans exist for evacuation, SWAT team assaults and, of course, for SCRAM shut-downs, but it's deeply strange that they have on standby a plan of attack with nuclear missiles, just in case an alien that feeds on energy starts a meltdown. How, in fact, does Watson authorise the attack? One phone call, with no code-words or even ID – not even DoB and mother's maiden-name – and two jet fighters get scrambled for a tactical strike.

Fortunately, there's an "un-explosion" when the missiles hit, so not even the impact of four missiles on concrete is seen – the place is in no worse a mess than when Watson fled. This suggests that Eldrad can absorb *all* energy, even kinetic. Plummeting to his doom would therefore make him bigger, wouldn't it?

The Doctor works out that they're on Level 306 from the lift indicator based on roots of three. That and the set-design, plus Carter's comment about "geodesic" patterns on the electron micrograph indicate that the original, pre-conversion configuration for the Kastrians had three as the magic number. Eldrad was very persuasive to get everyone to become bipeds with a pair of five-digit hands and two eyes. If this wasn't the case, and Kastrians originally looked like slightly different humanoids with fewer nodules, then what was all the stuff about mimicking Sarah's body about? As Eldrad only saw Sarah after leaving a chamber that had been sealed with a thick anti-radiation door, the only reason for looking (vaguely) like her and not Driscoll is if the stone hand absorbed some of her (carbon-based) DNA.

Wherever the TARDIS lands, it's manifestly not Aberdeen ("School Reunion").

Critique Those Hollywood script-gurus who'd be so impressed (we reckon) with "The Brain of Morbius" would be tearing their hair out at this one. That's probably why it's so much more enjoyable than most blockbusters. You really can't see where it's going.

Generally, Baker and Martin arrange their scripts to escalate from a fairly out-there initial premise to something wilder and less achievable in careful increments, convincing the authority-figure of each twist before slamming a further one in everyone's faces. Even something as goofy as "The Three Doctors" (10.1) has a lot of stilted exposition scenes for Dr Tyler's benefit, then he asks "are you saying that...?" and then something explodes and the cycle begins again. Because the

Could *Scratchman* Have Happened?

...continued from page 273

touch of class, but they usually needed at least a token American, often someone that audiences had heard of (but not invariably, and not always anyone who could still get work in Hollywood).

Had this film been solely aimed at the domestic market, TV's Doctor Who in a feature film would have been money in the bank. However, a film with extensive special effects would, of necessity, need a global distribution to break even. Baker and Marter were anxious to get UK funding and backing and made a few script-adjustments to tap into available money. For locations, they envisioned the Canary Islands (paid for by revenue from British films kept by the Spanish government) and the Hebrides. For all that they talked up Vincent Price's interest (exactly when he expressed interest is unclear, but it was probably well before they announced it in mid-1976), the delays grew and Marter, then Sladen, left the parent series. The Companion roles were rethought for bigger stars as a lure for co-production monies.

The plot still hinged on rural Scotland, cricket and Daleks (none of which was automatically catnip for US studios), and it was in between the conventional genres that American audiences wanted. It wasn't horror enough for the drive-in crowd after *The Texas Chainsaw Massacre*; it wasn't juvenile enough to justify being action-fantasy and it wasn't grim enough to match contemporary expectations of science fiction. (This was the phase when Hollywood defined "Science Fiction" as miserable, pretentious dystopias, usually with Charlton Heston and explosions – Britain did a few of this sort of film in co-production with German companies, notably *Who* with Elliott Gould and Trevor Howard and *Rollerball* with James Caan.) As the negotiations between Hill and the BBC were underway, George Lucas was in Elstree committing professional suicide with a pet project and Hollywood insiders were laughing about it behind his back. He could afford it, because he'd just had a runaway hit with *American Graffiti*.

With James Hill now firmly committed, the writers and the BBC had a "name" even if the ostensible star was unknown outside Britain. Hill had his own production company. His track-record is mixed: he had an Oscar (for *Born Free*) but had directed some real drivel. Like many directors in Britain, he took whatever work was around, including a lot of ITC television-on-film, after starting in documentaries. Other that the leonine fluke and some early dramas, his career had been dominated by makeweight faff such as: *Every Day's a Holiday* (US title: *Seaside Swingers*), a holiday camp-based musical that reminds us why British teenagers in 1963 so enthusiastically welcomed the Beatles and the Rolling Stones; *The Home Made Car*, a short wordless film funded by BP, familiar to middle-aged British viewers as a filler on Trade Test Transmissions between programmes on BBC2 in the 1960s; *The Man from O.R.G.Y.*, an early example of the naff "sex-comedies" mentioned above that ended more careers than it started; and 1973's *The Belstone Fox*, his last big-budget feature (sort of *Kes* with fur). After these and the abortive *Scratchman*, he went into television full time, notably *Black Beauty*, *The New Avengers* and – here's irony – *Worzel Gummidge*. Another tenuous future Doctor Who connection is his 1969 *Captain Nemo and the Underwater City* written by Pip and Jane Baker. This and the 1965 Sherlock Holmes / Jack the Ripper pastiche *A Study in Terror* seem like decent enough credentials to do a Doctor Who film with Tom Baker, but once again, this is applying post-Season Fourteen hindsight. Other than "Pyramids of Mars" and maybe "The Daemons" (8.5), nothing in televised Doctor Who could be taken as proof-of-concept for a Hill-directed script about the Devil, a cricket-match and Cyberons.

Last time the BBC danced this little dance, it had been with remakes of broadcast episodes. Baker and Marter arranged a private viewing of the two Dalek films and were unimpressed. This is significant as the instigators of those films, Milton Subotsky and Max Rosenberg, had been the only people able to make big-budget fantasy adventures in the UK in the 1970s. Indeed, once Marter had been away from the series for a while, the Doctor's sidekick became a little less Harry-like. The name usually mentioned to fill this slot is Doug McClure, the Token Yank in *The Land That Time Forgot*, *At the Earth's Core*, *People that Time Forgot* and *Warlords of Atlantis*.

Token Yank Syndrome, a feature of British-made fantasy films that we politely pretend got us Big Name Stars rather than washed-up, blacklisted or unemployable Hollywood detritus, seems to have been a worry even with the talk of Vincent Price as the villain (Price himself never said a dickie-bird about it). A small pack of ex-pat Americans and Canadians keep cropping up in supporting roles

continued on page 277...

14.2 The Hand of Fear

inciting incident is handled like a police procedural, we sort of go along with it; by the end of Episode Three, we'll swallow any old tosh about wrestling a gargoyle. The situation spirals out from something in the observable real world that's not perhaps as well-known as it could be (in that case, black holes and anti-matter – never mind that they aren't the same thing – or, say, nuclear power stations and the idea of silicon-based life) rather than deriving from other television dramas.

This story learned that lesson and makes sure that we end each episode with an arresting image, not a plot-development or change of genre. Unlike "Terror of the Zygons", the other four-parter of this period that can be considered as almost an anthology-series rather than a serial, we don't get phase-changes matched to the episode ends. Those come at different stages of each week's instalment, but they do come. Sarah's adventure inside a nuclear reactor does take the equivalent of a 25-minute episode, but it starts ten minutes before the end of Part One and ends ten minutes before the end of Part Two. The big reveal of Lady Eldrad comes a similar length into Part Three, then Kastrian Eldrad a shorter length into Part Four, so we can have a lengthy coda. This is, in most regards, a lopsided six-parter.

Consequently, a lot of characters are in it for one-and-a-bit episodes, long enough for the Doctor to calmly explain the latest development to them between explosions. In any other story, Dr Carter, Professor Watson or ChicDrad would be the main guest role; in at least one other story, Kastrian Eldrad would be the main antagonist – nobody who remembers "The Three Doctors" can avoid a twinge of nostalgia at Stephen Thorne getting almost the same character and nearly the same dialogue. He does as expected, as does Rex Robinson as Carter, until he goes bonkers in a power station. Glyn Houston gets a tougher task, taking Watson from a manager in a knowable crisis to someone utterly out of his depth and trusting the Doctor without any obvious turning-point.

That's the story in a nutshell: there aren't any save-points in the story, just pauses in the storytelling to break it up into episodes. It's only at the end that it stops looking like an eight-year-old making something up by piling up incidents saying "and then... and then... and then..." It turns out that the whole thing was going somewhere after all.

Well, all right, not *quite* the actual end: there's something else dominating the whole of this story that comes afterwards. Most companion departures to date have followed the Doctor being stoic or getting into a fresh scrape. Only two before this had focussed on what the companion thought or felt. "The Chase" (2.8) was exultant that Ian and Barbara had made it to London, 1965, *then* returned to the TARDIS. The clearer analogue for what we have in this story is Susan being almost forced out (2.2, "The Dalek Invasion of Earth"). Even with six episodes to set up her relationship with David, this seems to come out of nowhere. Sometimes, they've just dumped someone after a few episodes where we'd stopped noticing they were around ("The Faceless Ones"; 3.10, "The War Machines"; "The Android Invasion").

Other farewell stories have, when they could be bothered, tried to set up how close that character has got to the Doctor and whoever else was aboard and, on occasion, established an idea that this one was indispensable (5.6, "Fury from the Deep" is the clearest example, but see also "Earthshock" and 23.2, "Mindwarp"). This is the most successful example. Bluntly, if anyone had somehow missed the advance warnings and interviews on *Nationwide*, they'd still have picked up that Sarah was going from the "I worry about you" scene in Part Three. The costume, the child-like coyness when possessed, the perkiness before and after all seem as if Sladen was being ordered to be as winning as possible. Any cuter and she'd have tipped over into Zooey Deschanel-style ghastliness.

Perhaps if they'd not had to write Sarah out and set up the whole return to Gallifrey for the next story, the journey through Kastria's core wouldn't have seemed as perfunctory. It's hard to see how much more they could have squeezed in, given the amount of vamping going on. It's not even fresh padding: it's recycled from Exxilon via Mars. If the last episode had begun with the Doctor being forced to take Eldrad home, they might have found enough material for a whole 25 minutes on the economy-world, but that might have meant padding in the costlier filmed scenes and the cliffhangers matching the switches in location and style.

The string of surprises, like a magician's scarves endlessly billowing out of a hat, would be a lot less impressive. Judith Paris's astonishing arrival as Gyno-Eldrad wouldn't have been a mid-episode

Could *Scratchman* Have Happened?

...continued from page 275

in British-made films (Donald Sutherland and John Ratzenberger toiled in this field until stardom beckoned, Shane Rimmer and Bill Hootkins carved niches before and after), but lead roles often went to any passing American.

It was often part of the funding deals. Amicus, the main Subotsky-Rosenberg company (they'd done the Dalek films as "Aaru"), were canny at getting US companies interested in films with a lot of British character-actors and these cosmetic transatlantic castings. Subotsky and Rosenberg adeptly saw how the tide turned and, after fruitfully mining the 60s-early 70s horror boom with "portmanteau" films (four or five shorts with a linking narrative, including *Vault of Horror* with then-unknown Tom Baker), jumped ship just before the bubble burst. They moved on to what we'd now call Steampunk-*Kaiju* adventures, usually based on just-out-of-copyright Edgar Rice Burroughs books. With Disney doing *Island at the Top of the World* as well, this constitutes a mini-genre (Hinchcliffe's decision to give the TARDIS a makeover made a lot of sense in that context). *At the Earth's Core* was one of only four British-financed films to make the UK Top Twenty grossing films (in end-of-year round-ups) in the 1970s.

The other three? *Up Pompeii*, *Stardust* and *Bugsy Malone*. *Stardust* was the sequel to surprise smash *That'll be the Day*, a film partly financed by Ronco selling a soundtrack album of it ahead of release. Both were Goodtimes productions. *Bugsy Malone* was co-produced by them and Robert Stigwood, the record mogul moving into movies. It was intended purely for kids, but any parents showing it to their offspring these days would feel distinctly uncomfortable. (We're not suggesting that *Pescatons* was a toe in the water to see if this funding-style could work for a *Who* film – but, as Baker apparently had an "in" with Decca, the soundtrack rights might have been offered to them had the film come to pass. Maybe that's why there were songs until Hinchcliffe said no.) Stigwood was still partly based in London in 1976; for much of his peak film-production, his factotum was Beryl Vertue. Now, here's where it gets interesting as Vertue had been running Associated London Films, a subsidiary of Associated London Scripts (see Volume One) and got *Steptoe* and *Up Pompeii* from BBC1 to the big screen by selling EMI's Nat Cohen on the idea.

Up Pompeii, as we explained in "The Fires of Pompeii" (X4.2), was a bawdy farce ostensibly set in Roman times – but really a vehicle for Frankie Howerd, so not really likely to travel well. Vertue had been his agent and he had been one of the founders of ALS in the 50s. The apparently quixotic decision to give Howerd a key role in Stigwood's car-crash *Sergeant Pepper* movie is about the most sensible aspect of the whole enterprise. In any other big-budget rock musical, it would be the most glaring misjudgement, but we'd bet that half of you had forgotten he was in it – let alone that he becomes Pope. (Perhaps Ringo was unavailable.) But an even bigger mystery is that nobody at BBC Enterprises got in touch with Vertue and that, for all the talk about this film and touting it to various potential backers, she doesn't seem to have got wind of it. At a crucial moment for Baker and Marter, someone who'd been in right at the start of *Doctor Who* and had handled many of Terry Nation's rights arrangements (including Subotsky and Rosenberg) was at the heart of one of the most significant new forces in UK cinema. (That said, she had just been Executive Producer on two major flops, with NFFC backing, including a disastrous second *Steptoe* film.)

As far as making a British film that wasn't soft-porn or a sitcom adaptation went, Goodtimes was almost the only game in town other than Amicus / AIP. The Amicus collaboration with American International Pictures – yes, the people who gave us Roger Corman and *How to Stuff a Wild Bikini* – had been on the skids, but AIP's track record for finding British projects that appealed elsewhere went back to 1957 and *Rock All Night*, a retitling of Anglo-Amalgamated's *The Tommy Steele Story*. They were the culprits for *Konga!* Their most successful recent British enterprise was the *Doctor Phibes* mini-franchise, with Vincent Price and a small part for Ian Marter. Corman seems to have politely declined. (Picking James Hill over Robert Fuest indicates this wasn't the road they meant to go down – a pity, as he's about the only director other than Russell or Gilliam we can envisage getting away with the storyline in the 2019 novelisation.) Anything else of any note was a project initiated in America and made in Britain to capitalise on technical or financial features. What's interesting is that, for all that Baker and Marter were keen to get a British production company, nobody's found any indication that Goodtimes were even

continued on page 279...

14.2 The Hand of Fear

twist, but a closing shot with a week for us to get used to the idea. Each location would only have been in one episode, instead of just the rather pedestrian hospital set, and we'd miss the opening-out from hospital in the studio to a Real Life Nuclear Power Station in Part One, then to a proper look at the new TARDIS set in Part Three, then to a shockingly naff planet. Having the station location-work in the same episode as that remarkable quarry explosion and the closing shot of the hand coming to life pretty much guarantees viewer-loyalty.

In theory, none of this, nor the curious prelude with the quilty-men and the exploding spaceship, ought to fit together. That they seem to (eventually) – along with stolen horror-movie shots, possession and terrorism – is entirely because this is *Doctor Who*. And that, as much as anything, is what the series is for.

The Facts

Written by Bob Baker and Dave Martin. Directed by Lennie Mayne Viewing figures: 10.5 million, 10.2 million, 11.1 million, 12.0 million. AI's 63% for Part Three, none of the others show up (odd that Sarah's departure wasn't logged). Part Two was slightly earlier than the others because of a rescheduling to accommodate the bizarrely-popular *Horse of the Year Show*, which was inserted in a special edition of *Match of the Day* – the football highlights – because it was a "Champion of Champions" trophy and they were competing for £4,000!

Canada edited this into a feature-length episode retitled *Eldrad Must Live!* – which is, let's be honest, a cooler title.

Cliffhangers Sarah's broken into the main reactor – in its Tupperware box, the stone hand has started moving; Driscoll carries the hand into the nuclear furnace; Eldrad's been harpooned.

What Was In the Charts? "If You Leave Me Now", Chicago; "The Light of Experience", Ghiorgi Zamphir; "Blinded by the Light", Manfred Mann's Earth Band; "Love and Affection", Joan Armatrading.

The Lore

You will recall that the first version of this story was commissioned on 20th June 1975 as a six-part story to end Season Thirteen. That scenario has the same title as this story, features a stone hand landing on Earth and a nuclear power-station feeling the effects as the silicon-based alien uses the reactor to regenerate itself. It also (probably) writes Sarah out of the series – but that's about the extent of the similarities.

Elisabeth Sladen had been thinking about leaving for a while, apparently after the change of shooting schedule for what became Season Thirteen had wrecked her holiday plans and cost her a film part. One of the options in the original "Hand of Fear" was that either the Brigadier or Sarah was killed saving Earth: as Nicholas Courtney's availability was patchy, it looked as if Sarah would be sacrificed. The six-part script was – as anyone who read Volume 3 might expect – somewhat ambitious. It was, in fact, stark, staring ambitious, but Robert Holmes persevered in getting it to work. Bob Baker and Dave Martin tended towards optimism concerning what was physically possible, affordable on a BBC budget and comprehensible to viewers – even though they had, by now, become accustomed to making fantasy with much fewer resources at HTV in Bristol.

In some ways, Holmes had himself to blame: Baker and Martin had come to him with a relatively simple proposal, along the lines of *The China Syndrome*, about the possibility of a terrorist attack on a nuclear power-station causing a mass evacuation. They'd even spoken to the PR people at Oldbury, the station they could see from the converted barn in Thornbury they used as an office. But Holmes had gone off on one about scaring kids, and Baker mentioned having himself been scared by *The Beast with Five Fingers*. From that it was a short step to *The Hands of Orlac* and possession. The proposal they sent back to Holmes using a disembodied hand and humans subject to its will went a little off-track.

The outline resembles the later ITV *Quatermass* serial in its near-future dystopia and oppressive back-to-nature Luddite movement and the way an old man blows himself up to thwart the aliens behind this. That old man was the Brigadier, now assigned to EXIT (Extraterrestrial Xenobiology Intelligence Taskforce), and it was the space-shuttle with a warhead that redeployed the back-

Could *Scratchman* Have Happened?

...continued from page 277

approached, obvious as they might seem.

Neither, oddly, was Lew Grade (from what we've been able to discover, anyway – it was rumoured briefly in 1978). British television's one-man Warner Brothers had combined business savvy and a gut instinct for what might work (or who was passionate enough to make a weird project work) and carved out an empire. This had two branches: ATV was the regional television company in the ITV network and ITC was the film-based production company for export-led glossy shows. The boundaries were increasingly porous as overseas networks accepted British-made video-taped shows (notably *The Muppet Show*, made in London after every US network dismissed the idea as crazy), and Grade had repositioned ITC as a feature-film production and distribution company on top of everything else. These days we mainly remember the flops ¬ but, in 1975-6, nothing as disastrous as *Raise the Titanic, Can't Stop the Music, Saturn 3* or *The Legend of the Lone Ranger* had yet befallen them. In fact, with Peter Sellers's triumphant return as Clouseau in *Return of the Pink Panther* and the hit wartime adventure *The Eagle has Landed*, they were on a bit of a roll.

Would Lord Grade have touched *Doctor Who*, the series that almost knocked his various Gerry Anderson shows out of contention? It's not as far-fetched as it might seem. Baker, Marter and Hill believed in the project and, as with Anderson, Jim Henson and Patrick McGoohan, anyone with faith in their own material got a sympathetic hearing from Grade and, usually, hands-off investment. (The jury's still out on whether Terry Nation could have got an ATV Dalek series off the ground if US deals hadn't looked more tempting, but Nation shortly thereafter got a gig as story consultant and lead writer on *The Persuaders!*, perhaps the quintessential Grade-style deal-first-premise-later pitch.)

US tax law changed, so the revenues from overseas productions weren't as favourable as before as the industry tried to avoid any more studio closures and lay-offs of crews. Between 1965 and 1971, the Americans were spending about £19 million a year in Britain (peaking at £31 million in 1968); 1972-9, it's reckoned they spent an average of £6 million (and under £3 million in 1974). Yet what little they had invested was skewed towards fantasy films. Cost-cutting aside, using British film-crews held an obvious appeal, as they knew what they were doing. Apart from theatre-trained, Panto-seasoned thesps who could "sell" a silly premise, the reason so many fantasy films were made in the UK was that the practical effects and post-production facilities were about as good as that money could buy – and often better than Hollywood's.

Ray Harryhausen used Shepperton studios because, apart from being close to the Spanish locations, effects technicians Wally Veevers, Les Bowie and others made better matte paintings and had inlay facilities second to none at the time. Disney had pioneered a yellow-screen using sodium-lamps (a precursor of the blue-screen system developed by ILM for George Lucas, but not of CSO) which Hitchcock availed himself of for *The Birds*, but there were problems in lighting any sizeable screen. Shepperton had ironed out the snags. Large numbers of travelling mattes were also a Shepperton speciality. Harryhausen also found it easier to supervise model-making in English.

In Britain itself, the big buzz was about the possibility of a new funding arrangement. Harold Wilson, partially responsible for the favourable conditions for US companies, had shaken up the moribund distribution cartel that had made Rank and Odeon almost the only games in town in the late 1940s. MGM had come to Elstree in 1953 while Rank, which owned Pinewood and nearly a third of all cinemas in Britain, had tried to take on Hollywood: its television wing was ABC, makers of *Armchair Theatre* and *The Avengers* (see Volume 1), until the weird 1967 ITV franchise auction. In the 1970s, it diversified into photocopying (Rank Xerox) and food (Rank Hovis McDougall, the flour and bread giant) and seemed to be letting film production slide unless it was hiring the Pinewood facilities and staff to other companies.

Wilson, as Prime Minister, had been keen to get the maximum use from the indigenous film productions facilities, as an employer and a way to exert what's now called "soft power" – he preferred more unmistakably British, award-winning films to the semi-Americanised box-office smashes, but accepted the need for both. Then, when he unexpectedly resigned in March 1976, he was appointed chair of an agency to implement the suggested measures of a commission he'd set up in 1974, led by Lord Terry. As it turned out, not much came of this – the inflation spiral and industrial relations made people seek shorter-term

continued on page 281...

14.2 The Hand of Fear

ground research and possible location shoot at the power-station or another like it. Along the way, however, the two alien factions and their differing approaches to the threat of humans getting space travel cause animals in Bristol Zoo to assume gigantic size.

Meanwhile, a mobile stone hand stalks Sarah as she's sent to a Maoist-style labour-camp farmstead. Stone, because – to suggest heartlessness – they've decided on a species made of "the unstable Tellyrium molecule" (presumably not the real element Tellurium, as discussed in 6.4, "The Krotons") and had the beings feed on radiation (that made the nuclear generator handy for them, if not for nearby humans). There are two of these interlopers from the black hole Omega 4.6: a "dove" who's decided to take humanity back to their rural past (there's a whole subplot about palaeontologists finding evidence of "homo littoralis", the notional beach-dwelling ancestor then popularised by Elaine Morgan's popular, if sadly fact-free, books) and is doing a decent impression of *The Man Who Fell to Earth* (without the gin or the multiple tellies) and a "hawk" who's lowering inside an atomic base, regenerating himself before using the weapons to scour all life from the planet. (In some ways, this seems like the last episode of their recent HTV serial *Sky*.) For much of the story, Sarah's subjected to humiliations such as giant gorillas and forced marriage to a brain-damaged farm-hand while the Doctor and Brigadier do all the investigation.

Revisions to this began almost immediately, as you might imagine. Philip Hinchcliffe raised a few concerns about internal logic (why are the aliens using manipulated humans instead of, you know, invading or bombing?), and proposed that Harry Sullivan would be a logical replacement for a similar character in the first draft. The Brigadier's role was now reduced to leaving memos for the Doctor to find. Holmes proposed changing the name of the stone people from Omegans (he remembered "The Three Doctors", but not who wrote it). As a detour, Baker and Martin threw in a spivvy ex-Time Lord called Drax who had his own motives but helped the Doctor: he was essentially a second-hand car dealer but with TARDISes instead of Ford Cortinas or Hillman Imps. They apparently wrote the part with Trevor Ray (see 7.2, "Doctor Who and the Silurians") in mind.

In this version, people started acting oddly when they touched a stone monument uncovered in the dig at the quarry – a detail more than slightly familiar from *2001: A Space Odyssey*, but also the bodged-up new ending to *The Changes* (see "The Sontaran Experiment") replacing the morphine-addicted Merlyn of the original books. They'd suggested a pyramid, but Holmes tipped them off about the forthcoming story involving Sutekh (which had also had the Brigadier dying in a missile, in one draft). The "Dove" alien was also experimenting on animals to make them suitable replacements for humanity, or something, a sort of *Island of Doctor Moreau* subplot (explicitly named as such in the scenario for Part Four).

This was the state-of-play when Hinchcliffe went on holiday in September 1975, with Douglas Camfield already assigned to the story and shooting to begin in six weeks. The Moreau idea seeped into "The Brain of Morbius", also being salvaged at the time. Drax would have to wait a couple of years for his moment on screen (16.6, "The Armageddon Factor"). Hinchcliffe returned and found that this script's problems weren't resolving. The six-part version was knocked on the head in late September and rapidly replaced by "The Seeds of Doom", a curio that used the facilities allotted to the Baker / Martin story (OB for more convincing giant gorillas on CSO was now for huge tent-like plants).

Camfield had a lot of input into the replacement script and, aware that the shambles left Sarah still aboard the TARDIS, proposed a suitable final tale for her. Holmes called his bluff (few options remained) and commissioned "The Lost Legion" shortly before Christmas. This was a sort of *Beau Geste* pastiche in space, telling of a centuries-long conflict between the Sarkel and the Khorians and a galactic Foreign Legion caught between them. The finale was that, on the verge of a truce, Sarah is assassinated by a fanatic and her funeral – with full military honours – becomes the foundation for a millennium of peace.

Or something like that... as it turned out, the final episode was never turned in. The first episode arrived on Holmes's desk in early February 1976 and the next two, belatedly, on 2nd April. At around the time the first Camfield script arrived, Holmes set to work taming "The Hand of Fear" into almost what was made, requesting that Baker and Martin flesh out the treatment, within reason. On 3rd March, the Baker / Martin story was recommissioned as four-parter, with the writers receiving an additional fee for work on this new

The Hand of Fear 14.2

Could *Scratchman* Have Happened?

...continued from page 279

measures, and the 1979 election ended any hope of the Terry Report's bold proposals coming to fruition. But Wilson's clout, as a recent Prime Minister, earned this latest attempt to push British films as a long-term bet rather more credibility. In the context of the BBC's decision to try *Doctor Who* in America in mid-1977 (see **How Does This Play in Pyongyang?** under X4.1, "Partners in Crime") and the noticeable lack of any fantasy films in mid-70's America that weren't dystopias or cartoons, anyone trying to pitch a *Doctor Who* film as a potential export would get a sympathetic hearing. At least in Britain.

So this film looks as if it might have been possible. The timetable for pre-production had been established in the initial talks between Diamond and Enterprises as 18 months, starting 1st January 1976. In spring of that year, Marter and Baker had been on the much-mythologised holiday in Italy but not written much. Nonetheless, contracts were out by the end of April and Hinchcliffe had seen a script and was talking to Hill in September.

The problem, unsurprisingly, was then funding and contracts – especially who got the profits. However, Hinchcliffe was soon out and Graham Williams, his replacement, had misgivings about the script and the production complexities. He'd just been embroiled in a BBC co-production deal that had gone sour and, within weeks of being parachuted into *Doctor Who* as producer-designate, called a meeting to try and get everyone on the same page about *Scratchman*. With six months to go on the initial agreement, Hill was courting Warner Brothers, Universal and Disney while Baker was grumbling to the press about the financial hassle.

Universal had been one of the main US companies to see the virtues of letting British film-makers be British. Apart from distributing Hammer's familiar monsters, it had spread its bets better than the other American monoliths. United Artists had grabbed Eady cash for the Bond franchise but, as part of the deal, were forbidden to cast an American as 007 (watch *Doctor No* and see Jack Lord slowly realise he's not the star). This panned out well for them, so they were pretty hands-off with *A Hard Day's Night* (other than insisting on an August release, in case Beatlemania was over by then). The lesson was well-taken by other Hollywood companies. Universal, with its television production wing firmly established, could allow a British-made film to indulge the home audience and take a gamble on it crossing over. "Gamble" makes it sound haphazard, which is entirely right given that all film-making is based on the idea that 80% won't break even. But in the 1970s, everyone who thought themselves skilled players had been proved wrong, and carefully-marketed product flopped while "accidental" hits abounded. Studio heads either retired or were sidelined after their diligent application of the old rules brought nothing but ruin. They'd lost hundreds of millions on three-hour musicals nobody wanted to see while the indies, most noticeably *Easy Rider* and projects made by that group, made vastly more as a percentage of their costs. The sad and simple truth was that Hollywood had dropped the ball in the late 1960s and, consequently, wasn't really investing as much in any production – cheap British ones or their own – while television was allowing a few of them to tick over. Big corporations bought the studios, who were facing bankruptcy, almost as write-offs. (Paramount was the most obvious as Gulf and Western used them as more or less in-house promotion. Watch Mel Brooks's *Silent Movie* wherein they're depicted as "Engulf and Devour".)

So... a Disney *Doctor Who*? If we're looking at mid-1970's live-action, *The Island at the Top of the World* and *Escape to Witch Mountain* indicate what the company had deemed potentially commercial a couple of years earlier, but neither had set the world alight (the latter broke even eventually, aided by a re-issue and a sequel). Their idea of "British" was *Bedknobs and Broomsticks* or *One of Our Dinosaurs is Missing* (and that animated *Robin Hood* with an all-American cast). *The Littlest Horse Thieves* wasn't widely distributed, even in Britain, but indicates that the company was moving away from fantasy – even their animated output was diminishing.

After *Star Wars*, this changed. However, looking at what was on the blocks in 1976-7, the nearest to *Doctor Who*'s brand of live-action fantasy-adventure is *Pete's Dragon* and *Freaky Friday*. United Artists, in this period, were run by Transamerican, a holding company for insurance and other conservative interests. The owners weren't happy at their tax-loss movie company making things like *Midnight Cowboy* and *Last Tango in Paris*, so something foreign and weird with the Devil and cricket wasn't an appealing prospect. (They later played

continued on page 283...

14.2 The Hand of Fear

storyline. Although Holmes and Camfield got on well (they had both served in the Black Watch at different times), and Camfield had been rewriting entire episodes almost from scratch ever since the debacle of "The Daleks' Master Plan" (3.4), Holmes had learned better than to proceed without a Plan B. Another consideration was that Sladen was reluctant to go out guns blazing, preferring a story that only has Sarah's departure as a side-effect rather than the whole point.

- In April, a stripped-down version of "The Hand of Fear", retaining the Unique Selling Points of a moving fossil hand, a location-shoot at a real nuclear power-station and one of the three plum roles being split between two performers (one male, one female) was bumped up to slot 4N. Lennie Mayne was picked to direct. Since "The Monster of Peladon" (11.4), he'd been working on *The Brothers*, *Softly Softly Task Force* and *The Onedin Line*. Unsurprisingly, he got in touch with Rex Robinson for one of the key roles. An anonymous male technician became "Miss Jackson" and the director's wife, Frances Pigeon, got the gig (as with the thankless role of Queen Thalira's handmaid in the Peladon story).

For the main guest roles, he looked at female leads for ITC series to play female Eldrad: Alexandra Bastedo and Annette Andre. Also on his radar was promising newcomer Rula Lenska (21.4, "Resurrection of the Daleks"). He eventually plumped for dancer / actor Judith Paris who, apart from copious stage work, had been in Ken Russell's *The Devils* and James Hill's *Every Day's a Holiday*. The wish-list for Watsons included Dinsdale Landen (26.3, "The Curse of Fenric"), Stephen Yardley ("Genesis of the Daleks"; 22.2, "Vengeance on Varos"), Anthony Ainley (Volumes 5 and 6) and Patrick Stewart. Seasoned actor Donald Houston got the role, after years of playing policemen.

- The management at Oldbury were, as Baker and Martin predicted, very enthusiastic and cleared with the Central Electricity Generating Board all the relevant permissions to film in the station. They had done things like this before (including, apparently[44], a clip for *Top of the Pops* of Slade performing *Gudbuy T'Jane* with Pan's People in November 1972) and would often be available for *Blakes 7* in years to come. The crew did a preliminary recce in mid-May. The CEGB were given a look at the script and only found two points worth querying: the real Oldbury plant didn't have a fission reactor of the kind specified and the RAF bombing the place concerned them. Reassured that the BBC's budget only extended to stock footage missiles, they approved use of the facility.

- Hinchcliffe, meanwhile, was reconsidering his decision to leave at the end of this run after a talk with Bill Slater. He was taken with the idea of silicon-based life and devised a race with sleek surfaces (this may be the chess-piece-like aliens he was contemplating as a more practical alternative to Daleks) and working on ideas for a fourth year. The current run was shaping up to include a Victorian adventure called "A Foe from the Future" from Robert Banks Stewart and a companionless story on Gallifrey, "The Dangerous Assassin", for which Holmes would need clearance from BBC Drama in order to write it himself.

Tom Baker, meanwhile, was telling anyone who'd listen about his film project. Just before filming for this story started, he was in Blackpool for an event and told Radio One's Tony Blackburn about the possible locations in Lanzarote and the Hebrides. The Blackpool Centenary formed the basis of the edition of *Seaside Special* shown on 19th, mainly featuring the Goodies and the cast of *Are You Being Served?*, hosted by Ken Dodd (24.3, "Delta and the Bannermen"). There was a chat with the Doctor, or Tom Baker – it's hard to tell which – who was claiming to have been at the opening and ridden camels on the beach and a clip of Bessie and the Doctor, with a Kraal and a Sontaran, in the carnival procession. The *Doctor Who* Exhibition had re-opened in Blackpool and the BBC weren't above a bit of cross-promotion.

- The crew went west for the week, based at hotels in Thornbury. The filming began on 14th June at the Amey Roadtone Company's quarry near Crowbury, Gloucestershire. More dialogue was filmed than used, including an idea of Croydon as a seaside resort (hence the "season") and thus having peppermint-flavoured sticks instead of Jurassic rock. BBC designer Barbara Lane adapted Sarah's outfit from a pair of dungarees Sladen bought from her favourite boutique, Bus Stop. On the second day, the main event was the explosion. A camera was placed in a steel cage but was buried when the blast was more successful than anticipated. The lens cracked, but the film was usable (they cut just before the cracks appeared).

Could *Scratchman* Have Happened?

...continued from page 281

safe combining the all-American wholesome topics of roller-skates and cowboys, hence *Heaven's Gate*.)

By June 1977, and the end of the initial contract, Baker dropped himself in it for suggesting – in a newspaper interview – that readers could chip in and cover the cost. This pioneering attempt at crowdfunding broke a few tax laws but indicates that he remained defiant of the intractable negotiations. What finally did it was his trip to the US that summer to launch the sales-drive that resulted in PBS stations buying seasons Twelve to Fifteen. While he was there, and attending conventions, he joined the queues to see *Star Wars*... and got the immediate sense that he'd missed the boat.

There were obvious differences, and a clear space remained in the market for what he intended, but it would need to be more spectacular, with more elaborate (and costly) effects and a faster pace. Obviously, the hype around *Star Wars* made adventures in space and time a lot more attractive to studios, hence the huge number of similar projects either dusted off after years in development hell or simply dashed off in a hurry to cash in. However, the sheer *Doctor Who*-ness of *Scratchman* was, after all that time worrying how little it resembled the broadcast show, a potential liability.

The project never went away while Baker starred in the television series. The National Film Finance Commission (heirs to the BBFF) finally pledged a quarter of a million pounds in September 1977 after the Time-Life / PBS showings of Pertwee episodes had attracted US interest the previous month. By now, the potential big-screen Sarah, Twiggy, had a small child so was out of the running (there was also talk of Susan George – see 5.6, "Fury from the Deep"), but the names Price and McClure were still being waved under the noses of the press. A new phase began with PBS making Baker noticeably popular in America. By October 1978, Hill had finally offered an option to BBC Enterprises. More wrangling over merchandising rights delayed things, and the film – now possibly renamed *Doctor Who: The Big Game* – was again left to die on the vine as time for making it while Baker wasn't at TVC saving the universe (January-March of most years) ran out.

But what if Universal had stumped up the cash in spring 1977? In theory, the film could have been in UK cinemas for Christmas, beating *Star Wars* by a few weeks but suffering a lot of unfavourable comparisons. In America, it would have been ahead of the torrent of wannabes, but by being about England, Cricket and unfamiliar monsters, a hard sell even with the PBS episodes getting a cult following. Still, it might have been a monster hit. What then? Baker was voicing concerns about outstaying his welcome, getting tired of the series and being hamstrung by Williams and the directors. Had the film caught on overseas, he could have starred in the sequels and a new Doctor taken over on telly.

Depending on the timing, 15.6, "The Invasion of Time" could have been a regeneration story. (Would Louise Jameson have stayed on if Baker was going? Who would Williams have cast as the fifth Doctor?[45]) A hit film would have been handy for the BBC when pay-rises weren't matching inflation. Williams might even have secured a decent budget for Season Sixteen, his cherished "Umbrella" series. We might even speculate that the quest for a script editor might have ended with Ian Marter returning in a different capacity. With Baker demanding more input into the scripting process, an ally in the key job might have made him stick around. He could have become unstoppable.

If either Universal or Disney had got behind the project, there might have been roller-coaster rides based on the series. The BBC would have loved that. Disney and the BBC were already old allies (see "Terror of the Zygons"), but this could have moved things into a whole new area, ahead of Disney buying US network ABC. Universal were primarily making filmed shows or TV Movies, so *Scratchman* could have been given cinema distribution in Britain but shown as a made-for-television special in the States. Season Sixteen might have been made on 35mm film to be shown on US television (see **Which is Better, Film or VT?** under "The Sontaran Experiment").

Of course, the film could have flopped horribly. That might have chastened Baker considerably. We know that the next two years brought him and the series unprecedented popularity, strengthening his hand in negotiations with Graeme MacDonald, but a more biddable Baker might have worked *with* Williams rather than against him. Or he could have left, if the film had been the main motive for sticking around. Whether a high-

continued on page 285...

14.2 The Hand of Fear

- No record remains of who played Eldrad in the long-shot in Part Three: the costume was unready so a vague approximation was used (for all we know, Frances Pidgeon may have been in it). The dialogue for the Part Three scene where the Doctor and Sarah march back to confront whatever's in the reactor was largely ad-libbed.

- On 17th June, the team underwent the elaborate safety and security precautions to film inside the Turbine Hall. Half a dozen Radiological Health technicians check all the cast, crew and nearly 200 pieces of equipment before and after. The script had detailed an elaborate fight between the possessed Carter and the Doctor, but scarf-pulling and hanging on by fingertips weren't practical in the location they had available. The signs telling us how dangerous those areas are were added by the BBC to much safer areas where the CEGB was happy to allow filming (if nothing else, actual radiation would have fogged 16mm film). Max Faulkner, doubling for Rex Robinson, executed the stunt fall himself.

- And then... the bit with Sarah leaving the TARDIS. It wasn't Croydon or Aberdeen, but Stokefield Road, Oldbury. Pidgeon acted as dog-wrangler and Mayne provided the whistling. Sladen suggested that the episode should end with a freeze-frame, the way US series such as *Hawaii Five-0* went to advert breaks. The whole thing, building the TARDIS prop, roll-back and mix for the dematerialisation and a couple of takes for each camera-angle, took just under 90 minutes.

- The cast began two weeks' rehearsals on 26th June. The read-through showed flaws in the scripted departure scene for Sarah. It had some merit – showing that Holmes, at least, was aware of the odd way the Doctor's age kept changing (and had a whimsical explanation for it), but it wasn't hitting the spot. Renu Satna, then one of the few actual Indians in *It Ain't Half Hot, Mum*, but before that famous among kids for his dual role in *Cloudburst*, was given lines scripted for the Doctor about pain being useful.

- As so many spaceship models were given exciting crinkly surfaces to maximise the effect of the directional sunlight (see, for example, *Silent Running*), Drewett opted to go the other way and make Eldrad's cosmic Black Maria a smooth, curved vessel (some have seen a resemblance to the War Machines in George Pal's *War of the Worlds*, but Drewett's background in car design may have been a bigger influence). An old photo of stellar nebula M57 was used as the backdrop for the time-lapse sequence.

- A fly got loose in the studio, irritating several of the techs and the actors. During a take of the sequence where Sarah is re-hypnotised to tell the Doctor about Eldrad, Sladen swallowed it.

- Another technician character expanded and got the name "Driscoll" and South African actor Roy Boyd was cast late in the day – his CV had a lot of thugs, assassins and security agents in it, most recently *The XYY Man* opposite Stephen Yardley. The planned shoot needed a hasty revision as, during a break, someone stole one of the prop hands. There were three: the one found in the quarry lacking a finger; the one with the newly-regrown digit (this went missing and was, eventually, recovered when the unnamed BBC staffer was fired for other offences), and a third with Drewett's hand inside it and a black sleeve, for CSO inlay scenes. As you probably worked out, the melting door effect was achieved with expanded polystyrene and a solvent (you can do it yourselves with nail varnish remover, but keep a window open).

- On 15th, an edition of *Tomorrow's World* was broadcast including a couple of RAF Buccaneers on a bombing-run; Mayne obtained the videotape for use in Part Three. During the TARDIS scene for Part Three (19th June), Baker changed the unmemorable string of digits and letters to the BBC switchboard, Scotland Yard and 999. This was our first look at the new CSO scanner, with sliding shutters (given a respray, these will be with us until 20.6, "The King's Demons"). There was a plan to use Front Axial Projection for Eldrad's glowing eyes, but the lighting wasn't quite right, so they resorted to CSO patches.

- Sladen and Baker reworked the material about lucky squirk's foot charms, the planet Berberus being colder than Kastria (see 22.4, "The Two Doctors" for a similar name, hinting this was Holmes's work) and adverts for cheap kilowatts. The main problem was that they got the giggles in recording and kept sliding down the new TARDIS set's polished fibreglass curves. (In a moment, we'll try to explain *Multi-Coloured Swap Shop*, but here we'll mention that the electronic effect of the Doctor's summons was achieved with a plug-in device built for that series by Roy Ellsworth.) This wasn't the end of the shoot, though.

Could *Scratchman* Have Happened?

...continued from page 283

profile failure associated with the series would have dampened viewing figures is debatable. In almost every scenario we imagine after a film with this storyline is released in December 1977, the programme's future after Season Sixteen is radically different. A mid-1978 release changes slightly less, but still offers an interesting contrast with *Superman: the Movie* and *Close Encounters of the Third Kind*. As the US broadcasts bedded in, this could have changed perceptions of the series within the BBC. If a bad film had damaged the programme's reputation in Blighty, this book might not have happened, but a hit could have altered things dramatically. The archives would be complete, for a start.

We can even ponder what could have happened if the project had lingered just a little longer, say 1979, so that Douglas Adams could have put in a word to Eric Idle and handed it to George Harrison's handy new project Handmade Films to handle. All things being equal, most people would rather that *Time Bandits* had been made instead, but it's not too hard to imagine a summer 1980 release, possibly directed by Terry Gilliam. Adams had his own screenplay, *Doctor Who and the Krikketmen*, which muddied the waters in Hill's negotiations and had been the subject of memos from 1977 onward. Here it's worth mentioning that a couple of London-based financial institutions were said to be interested in three-picture deals with Baker, Marter and Hill. If Adams's proposal had been bundled in and a third story thought up, Baker might still have found his missing half-million during Season Fifteen's shoot. (It's entirely possible that these potential backers could have seen the *Krikkitmen* script and called the whole thing off. Adams wasn't a known quantity then and the idea, as we know from the third *Hitch-Hiker's* book, is a five-minute sketch dragged out beyond reason.)

The most important thing following either a hit or a flop would have been a rethink of the BBC's funding arrangements for the series. A big-budget film that didn't hit the spot could have weakened any producer's hand in negotiations – the argument that it could have been better with more resources would no longer wash, even if studio time was the problem. Or it could have led to *Doctor Who* getting purpose-built facilities somewhere other than Television Centre, for better or worse.

One thing to calm down the fevered speculation: there were three film versions of *Doctor Who* and they didn't really change anything. The Aaru Dalek films came and went; not even the prospect of a radio spin-off made anything especially different. Terry Nation was planning to try America before the first of these films so not even that, and the Daleks' departure from the series for nearly five years, was altered. The Paul McGann TV Movie made the BBC take the rights to the novels from Virgin Books, but it just delayed the return of the proper series by a few years while the rights were renegotiated. An apparent "spoiler" film, 1978's *A Hitch in Time* starring Patrick Troughton, is so forgotten that Wikipedia thinks it's an error. (It's real, it was on BBC1 a few days before "The Trial of a Time Lord" started and Michael Pickwoad designed the huge props for the bit that's just like 2.1, "Planet of Giants".) It's entirely possible that *Doctor Who Meets Scratchman* could have caused as few ripples in 1977 as the book version's release in 2019. (See also **What Happened to That Feature Film?** under X6.5, "The Rebel Flesh".)

- The weighty block that falls on the female Eldrad was rather intimidating for Paris, who seems to have narrowly avoided being compressed for real. Mayne rejected an effect of the body (more polystyrene) being pulverised. After directing 10.1, "The Three Doctors", Mayne knew as well as anyone who had to play the restored tyrant – so Stephen Thorne, in a glorified set of fisherman's waders and with crystals in his moustache, replaced Paris for the last few scenes. Also joining the cast was Roy Skelton, voice-man and occasional on-screen performer since "The Ark" (3.6) as Rokon. He also recorded a voice-over for Part One. Six days later, Baker was in another quarry, at Betchworth, for "The Deadly Assassin".

- Leaving the series at around her birthday allowed a joint party for Sladen, but – even if we ignore the various ways Sarah has returned – it wasn't over. There was, to begin with, a photocall to promote the release of *Doctor Who and the Pescatons*. The Schools Radio broadcast came in October – just before that, Sladen was interviewed about her departure and, with Baker, did a phone-in on the newly-launched BBC1 Saturday morning live show *Multi-Coloured Swap Shop*. This was presented as a radical new departure, encompass-

14.2 The Hand of Fear

ing various cartoons and features within a three-hour slot (just like ATV's *Tiswas* had been doing for nearly three years) and with a slightly forced informality, joking with the camera-crew and floor-managers.

The title came from the way viewers were invited to use television as a precursor to eBay and swap items with other viewers across Britain (one of the few episodes not wiped has a collector trying to shift some Nazi memorabilia). Over the coming years, this and similar successors were a big part of promoting *Doctor Who*, and Mat Irvine's demonstrations of special effects were popular (see also Danny Hargreaves in *Doctor Who Confidential*). However, the first edition had Baker and Sladen answering questions from children on 2nd October, the day Part One went out. (You can watch it on the DVD of this story, if you can stand Noel Edmonds.) Part Four elicited favourable letters in the *Radio Times*, but by this stage Leela had been revealed to the world.

- Sladen did indeed keep the yellow rain-wear for gardening (until they were stolen) and the toy owl was eventually given to her daughter, Sadie Miller (who threw up on it). A replica was a set-element in *The Sarah Jane Adventures*. The "Andy Pandy" suit was brought out of mothballs for A3, "Dimensions in Time" in 1993 and Sadie, then about eight, wore a miniature version to a convention the following year. We'll assume you know about 18.7a, "K9 and Company"; "The Five Doctors"; "School Reunion"; X4.12-4.13, "The Stolen Earth" / "Journey's End" and X4.18, "The End of Time Part Two", plus Big Finish's *Sarah Jane Smith* audios and of course *The Sarah Jane Adventures*. We'll pick up on all of this in A6, "The Wedding of Sarah Jane Smith" and A9, "Death of the Doctor". "The Hand of Fear" was repeated on BBC4 in May 2011, after Sladen's death.

- Lennie Mayne died about a year after this story, drowning when his boat was caught in a squall.

14.3: "The Deadly Assassin"

(Serial 4P, Four Episodes, 30th October – 20th November 1976.)

Which One is This? Gallifrey 101. The Doctor finds that "home" is as alien as anywhere he's been, and that nobody there knows much about their own planet. Then he fights for his life in someone else's nightmares before confronting the real forces of darkness (on screen, the Master; off screen, Mary Whitehouse).

Firsts and Lasts It's the first story entirely set on the Doctor's home planet, the first not to have a companion and therefore the first full story (3.2, "Mission to the Unknown" is a special case) with an entirely male on-screen cast (Helen Blatch is credited as a computer voice). Although the Doctor was absent for whole episodes because Hartnell or Troughton got a week off, this is the first time that the Doctor spends an entire episode asleep and dreaming but still present (unless we count 6.2, "The Mind Robber").

It's the first time we hear about the Matrix, Rassilon, the College of Cardinals, the Panopticon, the Castellan, Artron energy, Transduction Barriers, the Prydonian Chapter, the Chancellery Guard or the planet Tersurus. Oh, and there's the first and, for 40 years, only on-screen reference to "Shobogans" (X9.12, "Hell Bent"; X12.10, "The Timeless Children"). It's also the first (and to date only) on-screen mention of the Celestial Intervention Agency, which will crop up a lot more in the tie-in works.

For the first time, we hear the TARDIS described as a Type 40, or a "capsule", with a trimonic lock. Our galaxy's first called "Mutter's Spiral" here. It's the Master's first appearance since 1973, and the plot hinges on a hitherto-undisclosed limit on the number of regenerations a Time Lord can have. The people of Gallifrey all turn out to have pronounceable names, rather than formulae as we'd been led to expect.

It's the first mention of the Eye of Harmony, the Sash of Rassilon, Bio-Data Extracts, the Rod of Rassilon, Gold Usher and stasers; most of the Time Lord costumes in subsequent stories were made for this, including those collars, plus it's the first story to have an opening screen-crawl like an Errol Flynn swashbuckler (or 30s *Flash Gordon*), and the first to have a spoken introduction by the Doctor, or anyone. (The next won't happen until the TV Movie, then X1.8, "Father's Day".) It's also the first of four appearances of Borusa, the Doctor's old schoolteacher (who looks different every time).

Conversely, it's the last appearance of actors Bernard Horsfall (here as Chancellor Goth) and George Pravda (Castellan Spandrell). A design feature we've seen before, in "Revenge of the

Cybermen", here gets promoted to represent Gallifrey. There's also a pair of boots we'll be seeing rather more of in future...

Four Things to Notice About "The Deadly Assassin"...
• Actually, let's start with those boots. The set designer and costumier here planned everything to synch, partly to make the Doctor stand out more than usual. Hence, the Time Lords seem to have some kind of system beyond the colour-coding that Commentator Runcible remarks upon. The working, everyday Gallifreyans employ some sort of dress-code we're left to figure out, while the Chancellery Guards have flamboyant uniforms with big gold boots and scarlet suits that aren't Manchester United track-suits at all, honest. But when the Doctor selects a new outfit after returning his stolen monastic robe, he opts for a heroic shirt, brick-red britches and what are usually described as "buccaneer" boots. All of this makes the attentive viewer more than usually alert to every other character wearing a pair of Hush Puppies, those pig-skin leisure-brogues forever associated with cardigans and easy-listening compilation LPs. Even the resplendent Lord President's got them, as seen when he's lying dead on a dais. It's the one part of the Gallifreyan "look" that won't be back every time we return.

• As we'll pick up in **Where Does This Come From?**, several real-world referents are at work in this story, but the one you'd have to be from off-world *not* to spot is the Kennedy assassination and the endless stories of conspiracy and cover-up surrounding it. (Not the first time they've done this in *Doctor Who*; see 3.5, "The Massacre" and laterally 1.5, "The Keys of Marinus".) There's even a joke mention of a body called the CIA ("Celestial Intervention Agency") pulling strings behind the scenes. For most of the first-night audience, this was only the second-most-obvious "source". So much effort, however, goes into the first cliff-hanger making the Doctor not just the patsy but the *only* suspect, some well-known fans-turned-writers spent decades thinking that the Doctor dunnit.

• Most of the Time Lords we've met have used titles ("the Doctor", "the Master") or let others call them things ("that Monk fellow"). Terrance Dicks and Malcolm Hulke, in *The Making of Doctor Who*, set up the idea that the Time Lords all use cod-algebraic numbers and Greek letters instead of names, following the renaming of "Ohm" in "The Three Doctors" (10.1) as "Omega". Holmes is having none of that and has gone fossicking in old books, disinterring old words and names that elicit the sense of a history behind them instead of space-opera gobbledegook. Some are slightly altered European place-names (wine-lovers know Roussillon, football fans in the 70s all knew Borussia Monchengladbach), but many are English words that have lain unspoken in dictionaries for decades. It gives this planet a texture and is in keeping with the fustian vocabulary of the place. This, of course, presupposes that nobody's going to revive, say, the word "Goth" for anything that'll make the Prydonian Chancellor sound like he drinks snakebite, mopes around in a long black leather coat and nail-varnish and listens to 80s indie music.

• An entire episode is spent inside a computer-generated virtual reality called "the Matrix". This is 1976, when computers still used the kind of paper tape we're going to see spill out of K9, and, instead of bullet-time martial arts faff, we've got biplanes and steam-trains. The fussy old dears at the BBC were strict about scary-looking animals, so the crocodiles and spiders in this look atrocious (but not in the right way), yet the mechanical threats genuinely intimidate. Worse – or better, if you're a kid and not a parent – we have distorted human faces (clowns, Samurai masks, surgeon's masks, gas-masks) and general World War I iconography surrounding a whole episode that's *Hell in the Pacific* filmed in a school playground with buddleias and oak-trees. Mary Whitehouse got het up about the third cliffhanger, but the surest sign that this was conceived with David Maloney as director is the detail of a horse in a gas-mask.

The Continuity

The Doctor has an unusually high level of Artron energy, enabling him to recover from a psychic "death" that would kill most Time Lords. [In light of disclosures about the Doctor's past in "The Timeless Children", this – and Engin's surprise at it – seem more significant than in 1976.] He's cagey about past misdemeanours when talking to Runcible, his schoolmate. He writes Spandrel a note in a version of the Gallifreyan script [never seen before or again]

When Runcible asks if the Doctor has had a 'facelift' [presumably meaning "regenerated"; see "The Brain of Morbius" and accompanying essay], the Doctor admits to having had 'several, so far'.

14.3 The Deadly Assassin

[Interesting that Runcible phrases it this way. The thought of changing his appearance horrifies the Doctor in "The War Games" (6.7) – understandably, as it's the end of that particular consciousness, but 15.6, "The Invasion of Time" treats it as an everyday part of Time Lord life. Prior to "Planet of the Spiders", where the term 'regeneration" was first used, only the Doctor seemed to have this ability and the Time Lord supervising the Doctor's trial in "The War Games" – whom we might assume was Goth – spoke of it that way when passing sentence.] Oddly, Runcible recognises the Doctor despite the physical change, as if by aura. The Doctor can identify [if not pronounce] tricophenyl aldehyde by smell and knows it to be a neural inhibitor.

The majority of Time Lords present don't seem to remember the Doctor. [The upper echelon, certainly, should know all about his role in the Omega crisis, but might feel motivated to keep him, a renegade, out of the public gaze. Or they were persuaded to forget.]

- *Background*. The Doctor, raised a member of the Prydonian Chapter, foreswore his vows. [This is curious, in the light of so many Baker stories where he scrupulously sticks to his oath and upholds the Laws of Time – as recently as the last story ("The Hand of Fear"). It indicates he thinks he's being truer to his world's values by not being there and testing them in real-life situations at ground-level. Bear this in mind for "The Invasion of Time"; 18.5, "Warriors' Gate" and Seasons 25 and 26. Then go directly to X4.18, "The End of Time Part Two", where he champions these values against what his own people have become.]

He asks Engin to tell him about the stories about Rassilon. [Later stories suggest Rassilon is a figure about whom young Gallifreyans can't help but have learned in detail. The Doctor's question could be an attempt to get a fresh take, like asking a six-year-old.]

Borusa tutored the Doctor at the Prydon Academy on Gallifrey, and told him that he'd never amount to anything in the galaxy while he retained his 'propensity for vulgar facetiousness'. Also at the Academy was future newscaster Runcible, 'the Fatuous', who believes that the Doctor was expelled after a scandal of some sort. [Expelled from the Academy or Gallifrey? If he had a doctorate before leaving the planet, as Drax believes (16.6, "The Armageddon Factor"), more likely the latter.]

The Doctor has been to Constantinople at some point [see *Inventory*]. He never met the outgoing President of the Time Lords. [That this President has come and gone apparently since 10.1, "The Three Doctors" might indicate that the old duffer in Part One has a point about 'choppin' and changin'. Alternatively, the Doctors whom the Time Lords briefed on the Omega crisis, the first two, may well have forgotten this meeting per the rules of multi-Doctor stories (see also X10.12, "The Doctor Falls" for Missy's explanation).] The Doctor claims to have visited planets where Gallifrey's technology is almost laughably antiquated. He's word-perfect on Article 17 of the Constitution.

- *Ethics*. See above. He has no qualms about using a staser-rifle [does it have a stun setting?] to shoot someone about to murder the President. He seems almost more concerned with the potential risk to nearby planets [e.g. Karn, we suppose] if the Eye of Harmony detonates than to the Time Lords themselves. He even appears to relish the societal disruption this crisis could bring, even when told that 'countless lives' were lost.

- *Inventory*:

– *Scarf*. It's left in the Museum with his other clothes [and yet, he seems to have them all back next story]. When he dreams about being chucked off a cliff, his dream-self has a scarf to hook around a handy shrub. This scarf is split by a Samurai's sword.

– *Other*. He picked up a hookah, apparently in Constantinople, and keeps it in a Gladstone Bag [traditional for doctors but only used this once].

The TARDIS is a Type 40 TT capsule, one of 305 registered, and the only one not de-registered (it was 'removed from the register') and still in use (Goth calls this 'extraordinary'). Hildred can identify it on sight, it seems, then says that the chameleon circuit makes the exterior 'infinitely variable'. [This puts the notion of a pre-set menu of appearances out of contention – see 18.7, "Logopolis" and 22.1, "Attack of the Cybermen" for more.] The Time Lords can unlock the TARDIS with a 'cypher indent key'. The writing desk has quill-pens, paper and the Seal of the Prydonian Chapter. And wax.

The Supporting Cast

- *Borusa*. Recently elevated to the rank of Cardinal, a senior figure in Time Lord politics, after a long and distinguished career at Prydon

Seriously, Did Rassilon Ever Meet Omega?

Although the wailing and gnashing of teeth among older fans when "The Deadly Assassin" was first broadcast has now become a running gag, used to ridicule similar jeremiads on YouTube claiming that *Doctor Who* is now "broken" because of allowing girls to write scripts (or whatever it is this week), there's one reaction among experienced viewers from the story's first airing that remains pertinent. In the read-aloud scroll of preamble, we're told that "... the Time Lords faced the most dangerous crisis in their long history". Since October 1976, some people have been hearing and reading this and saying "Really?"

We're told about all sorts of ancient crises: the Drornid schism in 17.6, "Shada"; the Matrix Wars from X9.12, "Hell Bent"; the Great Vampire – 18.4, "State of Decay" et al – not to mention the subsequent calamities, including the Fall of Arcadia (X7.15, "The Day of the Doctor") and the Master popping in, killing everyone and blowing up the Capitol (X12.2, "Spyfall Part Two").

Even if you can somehow shrug those off, there's the small matter of "The Three Doctors" (10.1). A complete loss of power, the depletion of the life-energy of the Time Lords themselves and a situation so grave that the High Council agree to break the First Law of Time... that wasn't any kind of problem compared to a TV cameraman being turned into an Action Man and an ex-President having a shorter retirement than planned? Every other intelligent species in the cosmos *has* to have noticed Omega's comeback bid, and the incident can't have passed unremarked-on by all those people on Gallifrey who weren't in the High Council. Or BBC1 viewers. It was a big event, the Tenth Anniversary story of the series and prompted the biggest fan-service ploy since bringing back the Daleks in 1964 and 1972. Yes, this is at least as drastic and – to the everyday Time Lord in the street – noticeable, but somehow it's been brushed under the carpet. Everyone in "The Deadly Assassin" seems to have forgotten the Omega crisis. Regular viewers hadn't. (In fact, we'd just had Stephen Thorne taking us on a trip down memory lane the previous week, playing an Eldrad in "The Hand of Fear" exactly the same way he'd portrayed Omega in 1973.)

Now, forgetting things isn't unheard-of when we're dealing with the Time Lords. They use amnesia the way Hollywood executives and the White House use NDAs or British celebrities use superinjunctions. Right at the start of their impact on the series (6.7, "The War Games"), the Doctor's people blotted out everything Jamie and Zoe remembered after they first stepped into the TARDIS and put firewalls in his head about how to operate his Ship. It came up again in "The Five Doctors" (20.7), when the previous incarnations all went their own ways (and appears to have affected the companions – in X2.3, "School Reunion", Sarah doesn't seem to remember meeting the Doctors on Gallifrey). "The Five Doctors" makes sure we remember Jamie and Zoe's mindwipe by having the Doctor work out that they're ringers because they can identify the Brigadier. (Although Terrance Dicks, who wrote this and co-wrote "The War Games" slightly misremembers it himself, fluffing the explanation.) It'll soon be back in "Shada".

It might be that the High Council put out some sort of blanket "never mind about that" mental field, allowing everyone to shrug off this whole unpleasant interlude, but Spandrell and Engin know something about it because it's there on the Doctor's police record... even though this is the one and only mention on screen of the Celestial Intervention Agency, rescinding the sentence of exile. Clearly, someone remembers Omega. By 1983 (20.1, "Arc of Infinity"), a High Council member wants the Time Lords to acknowledge their debt to him. If we assume that Hedin is motivated by a need to overcome widespread amnesia, to the extent of jeopardising his long friendship with the Doctor rather drastically, some of this story almost starts to make sense.

However, that story rather relied on us remembering "The Three Doctors": few concessions are made to anyone wondering what Hedin's up to or why everyone changes their opinion of the situation in Part Four. One might hope that casual viewers would know the deal with Omega if they'd seen *The Five Faces of Doctor Who* repeat of "The Three Doctors" about 14 months before, but that was on BBC2 opposite the main news. Either way, a decent proportion of the audience who were reading *Doctor Who Monthly* would either be invested from way back, know from plot synopses and handy guides to Gallifrey and continuity or have read the comic strips.

We'll get into that in more detail in a tic but should note that there were two in the early days: the "main" strip, a continuous serial about the current Doctor on screen, with or without the current companions (usually without, thank heavens) and a "back-up" four-page slot for one-off stories using

continued on page 291...

14.3 The Deadly Assassin

Academy. There, he taught the Doctor, Runcible and [apparently] Goth. He used to teach that 'only in mathematics can we find truth', which explains his view of history.

He still acts like a schoolmaster, giving the Doctor 'nine out of ten' for saving the universe, but is oddly concerned with the opinions of others outside the Capitol. He warns that they need a new President soon because they 'must not appear leaderless', and to maintain 'public confidence' invents a story of Goth thwarting the Master.

Intriguingly, he insists on punctilious accuracy during the Doctor's trial, insisting on the letter of the law when the accused runs for the Presidency while Goth – for his own reasons – sticks with the spirit. Borusa plans to make the Master a public enemy after the renegade's apparent death [perhaps he changes his mind after the Master's escape; most Time Lords don't seem to know of the Master in 23.4, "The Ultimate Foe"].

Borusa himself doesn't seem to know of the Master. [The Master, however, mentions hiding from Borusa with the Doctor while truant in "The Timeless Children" – no surprise there, as headmasters remembering all their former charges is unheard of, even the troublemakers. Alternatively, the appellation "Master" might be quite new, as hinted in 8.1, "Terror of the Autons". Nonetheless, by 20.7, "The Five Doctors", Borusa has clearly been briefed or had anamnesis.]

[NB: in "The Invasion of Time", Borusa has apparently been promoted to Chancellor, Goth's old job, and is *de facto* Vice President. In this story, the College of Cardinals seems to outrank the Chancellors of the various Chapters.]

The Doctor reflexively calls Borusa 'sir' [something he only ever does again with the White Guardian; 16.1, "The Ribos Operation"].

- *Engin*. He's identified as 'Coordinator' but he's essentially a librarian, his function mainly custody of ancient archives and data-retrieval. This includes: the care and maintenance of the APC net terminal for terminally-ill Time Lords; analysis and filing of the biog-data extracts of those living; access to historical records and a detailed knowledge of the layout of the Capitol. He seems frail and easily-distracted but knows the intricacies of exitonic circuitry and the medical aspects of mind-transference and Artron energy.

- *Spandrell*. As Castellan, he is – in all essentials – a cop. He is sardonic towards his underlings and a little impatient with Engin. He pops pills [probably antacid tablets for ulcers]. In his line of work, he has to liaise with the higher echelons of the Chapters, but mainly the citizens who aren't Time Lords. He's used to getting his hands dirty (literally and figuratively, this being an ancient and crumbly city with lots of mica dust) and is less by-the-book than the Chancellery Guards. He has an accent unlike any other Gallifreyan. He has occasionally had to run in Shobogans for vandalism and, unlike all other senior officials we see, is armed.

- *Goth*. Currently acting as Chancellor is the ambitious Goth, the No. 2 in the Time Lord Council. [Was Goth one of the Time Lords on the Doctor's tribunal in "The War Games"? David Maloney directed that story and this one, casting Bernard Horsfall in both roles. If Goth and the Doctor met at the latter's trial, it's unmentioned here. Other actors playing Time Lords in that era recur – Clyde Pollitt appeared in "The War Games" and "The Three Doctors", Graham Leaman in "Colony in Space" and "The Three Doctors", etc., so Goth reappearing is at least as consistent as "Arc of Infinity" and "The Five Doctors" having the same Castellan.] He has been suborned by the Master after the outgoing President passed him over for promotion.

The Supporting Cast (Evil)

- *The Master*. Now on his last legs, in every sense. Out of regenerations, he's also at the end of this life. He's in a bad way, resembling a charred corpse with no eyelids. Desire for vengeance on the Doctor and the Time Lords has kept him alive, until he can realise his scheme to reboot his regeneration cycle by harnessing the Eye of Harmony. His level of infirmity seems to change from scene to scene; he ends the story physically active and survives an apparently fatal fall into an abyss. [When next we see him, in 18.6, "The Keeper of Traken", he's got his eyelids back and a different voice, but seems much the same. It's never stated that the Master's degeneration is natural for Time Lords approaching the end of their thirteenth lives; it's presented as if his sins and corruption have finally caught up with him.]

- *The Time Lords*. All seem to be old men. They all have names, unlike the renegades.

Whereas in the past they've been austere immortals ["The War Games"] or all-powerful technicians ["The Three Doctors"], here the Doctor's people are more like the university dons

Seriously, Did Rassilon Ever Meet Omega?

...continued from page 289

old monsters and characters. In the main strip, Rassilon's a constant presence, lurking within the Matrix until the laws of reality break down and hob-nobbing with other "Higher Evolutionaries" in a cosmic council-of-war whenever "all hell broke loose" (i.e. once every nine months). As with the television stories of the time, he's mentioned at least once a year even in non-Gallifrey comic-strips. (Not that there were many of those, as practically the whole Davison era was, in *Doctor Who Magazine*, a constant calamity of encroaching cosmic cataclysm.) The decision to remove the Time Lords from the BBC Wales revival was at least partly to eliminate this sense of a clued-up coterie of viewers who were different from regular ones. The Time War made everyone as fannish (or not) as everyone else.

In reply to a bewildered reader in an early 80s *DWM* letter, the considered opinion of the Matrix Data Bank was that Omega did the hard engineering work, Rassilon supervised and did the theoretical stuff. Again, nothing of this was on screen, where Omega was sufficiently forceful to will objects into existence and Engin talks of Rassilon as "mainly an engineer and an architect". That's a bit too prosaic for a lot of viewers and a backlash ensued in later stories, building up Rassilon's fearsome reputation as either a wise founder who led the Gallifreyans to the Promised Land and / or a stern wartime leader who had to be restrained. Omega, when mentioned, was the necessary sacrifice that allowed all this or one who chose to rule in hell rather than serve in heaven. All suitably biblical-sounding, but at odds with the idea of either of them as a glorified Isambard Kingdom Brunel.

What's especially noticeable, looking at the broadcast stories with this in mind, is that there is a curious gap. Rassilon's come back, three times – twice, as part of the Time Lords' campaign to resurrect their members as soldiers in the Great Time War; Omega's been mentioned, hinted at – see later – and *in absentia* provided the biggest, most literal *deus ex machina* since the TARDIS to absolve the Doctor of guilt about how he ended that war (X7.15, "The Day of the Doctor"), but there's absolutely nothing on screen to indicate that they ever met or were coeval. This, added to the absence of any hint to that effect prior to 1990, is intensely interesting. A halo of fan-lore and assumptions says they must have done, but there's a total lack of anything to that effect within the episodes transmitted since "The War Games" in 1969.

If you weren't paying much attention, it could make sense – in an Occam's Razor sort of way – to assume that they were two names for the same person. Time Lord history was shown to be garbled in the first story to name Rassilon ("The Deadly Assassin") and Omega's debut in "The Three Doctors" indicated that the Time Lords were mistaken – pitching it most generously – when they thought he'd died creating the source of their power: a black hole. They also thought he'd been destroyed when that black hole exploded in a matter-antimatter annihilation. Rassilon, by contrast, came back from a black hole and gave the Gallifreyans time travel by somehow separating the singularity from the rest of it and hiding it under the Panopticon.

Two black holes, two heroes from the distant past, two cover-ups... why not just the one?

Well, because "The Three Doctors" ended with the black hole turning into a supernova (somehow). If a star had exploded underneath the Time Lords' main hall, someone would have noticed. Moreover, as Omega's singularity was destroyed, if it *were* the Eye of Harmony the Time Lords would abruptly lose the ability to time-travel, rather defeating their purpose and abruptly ending *Doctor Who*. (Or forever confining it to the Yeti-in-the-Loo UNIT format, contrary to the production team's wishes and those of nearly every child in the country.)

Ten years later, we saw Omega again, running around Amsterdam after an indefinite spell in a special anti-matter TARDIS ("Arc of Infinity"), and soon after we meet Rassilon, in the Tomb where he'd spent what was probably ten million years posthumously tricking would-be despots into becoming the interior décor ("The Five Doctors"). They were undeniably two separate shouty men in different silly hats and there were two separate black holes. Although "Remembrance of the Daleks" (25.1) says Omega came first, we have Andred's claim that Rassilon died "aeons ago" ("The Invasion of Time") and Omega's complaint that he's been stuck in the anti-nowhere suburbs for "thousands" of years. A black hole is a space-time anomaly – relative to an outside observer, time crawls almost to a standstill, so that's less of a problem than it looks. (We might excuse Andred's comment as hyperbole, under the circumstances.) We've not got anything to absolutely rule out

continued on page 293...

of the cosmos, self-involved old men obsessed with decorum. Those we've seen previously made a point of not intervening in the outside universe in accordance with a moral code; these are insular from habit and a genuine lack of interest in anyone but themselves. The story's tenor is that nothing's changed for millions of years – in Engin's words, the 'barren path of pure technology' was consciously abandoned rather than simply neglected.

Yet, in contrast to the impression the Doctor gave us ('we can live forever, barring accidents', "The War Games" Episode 10), there is a limit of 12 regenerations, i.e. 13 lives. Each of these could be sequoia-length (even in this story, an old duffer speaks as if he remembers Pandak III's inauguration and says that President lasted '900 years'), but nobody gets more. Engin, archivist and custodian of the APC net (thus in contact with most dying Time Lords), doesn't believe that anything can avert the end of this regenerative cycle. The Master hopes to get a new lease of life using the powers of the Presidency. [His original plan was apparently to install a proxy as President and be given a pardon and a fresh cycle. (Borusa plausibly tempts him with this in "The Five Doctors" and the High Council do it for the Doctor in X7.16, "Time of the Doctor".) Or he could simply discard Goth and access the power of the Eye of Harmony as he did the Source when replacing his stooge as Keeper of Traken.] Goth dies, so the Master resorts to theft, using the Rod of Rassilon to unseal the Eye and the Sash of Rassilon to survive exposure to a Singularity (c.f. "The Three Doctors" and Omega's erosion).

[The obvious point here is that regeneration is a knack learned at the Academy rather than simply an innate power in all Gallifreyans. Thus the limit on this ability must also be imposed rather than a biological function. Since 2005, we've seen the same effect used for regeneration and TARDIS energy; many have assumed that there is some kind of "regeneration energy" reserve inside every Time Lord, but there are several obvious reasons why this cannot be the case. First and foremost, Melody Pond could regenerate (X6.2, "Day of the Moon"; X6.8, "Let's Kill Hitler"; X7.5, "Angels Take Manhattan") but was medically human; moreover the body-count of fully-fledged Time Lords in this story and "The Invasion of Time" would have left the Capitol looking like Dresden in 1945 if they'd all died containing the kind of energy we see when the Doctor lets rip these days. For the Master's plan here to work, the regeneration ability must be a quasi-yogic method of accessing ambient temporal energy and re-channelling it. More advanced Time Lords can fashion "avatars" during the regeneration process – Cho-Je in 11.5, "Planet of the Spiders", trial-run Romanas in "Destiny of the Daleks" and eventually the Watcher in 18.7, "Logopolis". The key must therefore be control of the process rather than raw energy or biology. (See **What Actually Happens in a Regeneration?** under "Planet of the Spiders".) The John Simm Master can suspend his own and other people's ability to regenerate, so it cannot simply be autonomic.

[Legally, only the Lord President can wear the Sash so – we might surmise – only the High Council can over-rule the stipulation on regenerations. The ability to regenerate and operate a TARDIS are not lost when one forswears the vows, it seems (just as a defrocked priest can perform sacraments). The limit must be connected to whatever Rassilon did to the genome to allow time travel (although the Doctor later tells Jamie he was lying, the account of the "Rassilon Imprimatur" in 22.4, "The Two Doctors" makes enough sense to be perhaps 80% true). It evidently came into effect after Tecteun's experiments on the Timeless Child ("The Timeless Children"). Whatever nefarious trick the Division pulled once they'd apprehended the Fugitive involved busting the Doctor down to the regulation Prydonian genome, making even the Matrix forget it (cf. "Popplewick's description of the 'primitive phases one and two' in "The Ultimate Foe") and starting again from scratch. Thus every incident where the Doctor and others run a check on how many lives are in the kitty ("The Three Doctors"; 20.3, "Mawdryn Undead"; 23.4, "The Ultimate Foe"; "Time of the Doctor") gave a valid reading based on the assumption that Hartnell was 'the original'. If transferring the "password" to unlock regenerations requires an "envelope" of temporal energy, that accounts for how Melody saves the Doctor in "Let's Kill Hitler" – presumably she removed her lipstick – and why couriering it from a different universe via Amy's Crack needed enough packaging to sink a battle-fleet.

[The less-obvious point is that whatever the Time Lords did to 'resurrect' the Master during the Time War, and the endless rebirths and deaths suffered by combatants, as described in X4.18,

Seriously, Did Rassilon Ever Meet Omega?

...continued from page 291

them starting out at the same time, but nothing makes it rock-solid certainty either.

At this point we ought to note that even between 1972 and 1976, the nature of black holes, as understood by television writers, moved from them being sites where the rules broke down to objects that underpinned the rest of creation. As we'll see elsewhere in this volume, the notion that they could serve as space-time "bridges", inexhaustible power-sources or the nexial points of multiple realities, came in instalments. In "The Three Doctors", Omega has turned an energy-source into a magic lamp (as we explained in **What's With These Black Holes?** with that story, this had been "permitted" by speculation from Steven Hawking, no less, so was legitimate back then).

"The Deadly Assassin" goes even further: this is the source of time travel, regeneration and more. Some of the more out-there physics of that time – which Holmes was reading even before 15.4, "The Sun Makers" – suggested that "nonlocal causality violation" (time travel to the likes of us) was possible by travelling near some kind of orthogonally-rotating singularity that bent spacetime out of shape. But one could only travel back as far as the creation of that singularity. Ergo, the Eye of Harmony was the very first, from seconds after the Big Bang, and artificially preserved by some means to last until whenever the TARDIS can't go. (We now know that's at least 100 trillion years from now, the last years of life-sustaining energy and – if we take X9.12, "Hell Bent" at face value – right up to the end of matter.) The idea is that it's an anchor-point for all time-travel, not just any old black hole, and Rassilon fetching it and bringing it home was the moment when the Time Lords achieved complete mastery of the forces Omega initially provided for them.[46]

The one that didn't blow up, the Eye of Harmony, has caused a few more problems in recent years. The 1996 TV Movie claimed that this was (a) installed within the Doctor's TARDIS (rather like having an oil-well and a tarmac-laying machine in your car) and (b) only useable by people with human eyes. The former was such a silly idea that Gary Russell, in novelising the script, tried to disown it and claim that it was just a link to the real one under the Panopticon. (As script editor of Big Finish, he also oversaw "The Apocalypse Element", an audio story in which Gallifrey's systems are retroactively keyed to accept users with human eyeballs.) When we and the Doctor all thought that there was no more Gallifrey, this idea came back (X7.11, "Journey to the Centre of the TARDIS") – and, lo, it turned out that the only TARDIS in the whole wide wonderful universe had the Eye of Harmony at its core. The previous episode (X7.10, "Hide") suggested it was just a link, but we were all too busy wondering why bringing a Metebelis crystal to 1974 England – where a large number of psychic spiders were looking for just such an object – seemed like a good idea (as well as the whole pronunciation mess) to worry.

The Doctor's TARDIS worked, obviously, so either a functioning Eye of Harmony was out there somewhere or the thing wasn't as important as hitherto stated. That made sense when we were told several times in "The Deadly Assassin" that Gallifrey would be destroyed if the Master messed with Rassilon's Star – but then, one day, it wasn't destroyed at all but hidden (X7.15, "The Day of the Doctor"). Since then, we know of at least four other functioning TARDISes at large in the universe – do they all work because the Doctor's got custody of the Eye of Harmony? How is this possible if Rassilon balanced the mass of the singularity against that of Gallifrey in "an eternally dynamic equation"?

Well, at a pinch, this could be what it took 13 Doctors (technically 14, as the McCoy Doctor seems present twice over) to work out as a subroutine when removing Gallifrey from the line of fire in "The Day of the Doctor". It's no bigger than any of the other continuity or logic problems inherent in that scene and at least allows the TARDIS to have functioned when Gallifrey was in a separate continuum. We also know that, as Rassilon himself was back, he'd conceivably moved it to a safe place to stop the Daleks getting hold of it.

This leaves us with a more complicated problem: what, if anything, did Omega do in the Time War? It's inconceivable the Gallifreyans didn't think he could be resurrected and pressed into service, but – given his animosity towards them and the way the Daleks abruptly upgraded themselves – it's equally possible he would have been an asset to the opposition. Even with the caveats we offered for recruiting every possible Gallifrey native (**Where's Susan?** under X4.17, "The End of Time Part One"), it would have been relatively

continued on page 295...

14.3 The Deadly Assassin

"The End of Time Part Two", isn't the same as regeneration. It clearly left the new-model Master able to turn into a baby (X3.11, "Utopia"), then grow up to look like Sir Derek Jacobi and regenerate more three times so far. It may be the same process that allowed Rassilon to get out of bed after millions of years punishing anyone who got greedy ("The Five Doctors") and turn into 007-playing-Ultron ("The End of Time Part Two") and Mad Frankie Frazer ("Hell Bent"). Weapons-grade regeneration, as seen at Trenzalore, would have been handy, as would unlimited fresh lives, so the limit must have a good enough reason for them not to have broken it even under duress.]

The Time Lords' ceremonial robes, with high, rounded collars are 'seldom worn'. [From this point on, however, they *always* seem to wear those same outfits – including one hilarious moment in "Arc of Infinity" when someone sneaks around committing murder, but keeps his collar on to cast a suspicious shadow.] Ceremonial make-up is also on show, and almost everyone seen here wears a leathery-looking skull-cap. The symbol of the Time Lords, and the Seal of the Prydonian Chapter, is an ornate figure-eight inside a circle, suggesting the Earth sign for "infinity". [It's later called the Seal of Rassilon. In this story, the figure-eight is seen on a slant. In the TV Movie it's upright, like the Vogan symbol in "Revenge of the Cybermen".]

Chancellery Guards, red-uniformed soldiers in shiny white capes, even shinier helmets and gold boots, handle security in the Capitol. They're led by a Commander and under the Castellan's control. Castellan Spandrell acts like a chief of police. [Coordinator Engin notes that Spandrell's duties usually involve more 'plebeian classes', hinting at a Gallifreyan population other than the Time Lords – and near the Capitol – who cause trouble.] There are over 50 Guards at the President's resignation ceremony, all armed. A buzzing 'rogin tracer' lets them follow the Doctor's trail.

The Castellan has never heard of the Master [unlike the high-ranking Time Lords in 8.4, "Colony in Space"]. The Celestial Intervention Agency is said to have interceded to remit the Doctor's sentence of banishment to Earth. Castellan Spandrell, obviously irritated by the CIA's existence, says that it gets its fingers into everything. The biog-data files of CIA agents aren't expected to mention any Agency involvement.

[The Agency is only mentioned fleetingly here and never again mentioned on-screen, but crops up repeatedly in the tie-in works. Fan-lore likes to claim the Agency was behind every mission of intervention the Time Lords ever gave the Doctor, but here the "CIA" reference was only included as a joke. If the Agency wanted to end the Doctor's exile, it must have convinced the authorities to send him the dematerialisation circuit in "The Three Doctors" – but there, it's portrayed as a reward from the Time Lord hierarchy for defeating Omega. This indicates that the Gallifreyan CIA works alongside the President and Chancellor, so isn't operating behind the High Council's back. It's an official Agency rather than a secret criminal group; its status as a recognised body proves that the Time Lords aren't as non-interventionist as hitherto claimed. As the Agency isn't visible here, it's possible it enjoyed a good rapport with the administration in "The Three Doctors", but less so with the recent regime. Given that the Time Lord played by Graham Leaman appears in "The Three Doctors" and in the behind-closed-doors discussion in "Colony in Space" (8.4), we might spin any number of theories for why Spandrell's reading of the records differs from what we saw in 1973 (see **Things That Don't Make Sense**). Series 12 shows us that a special-ops group called 'the Division' was also at work, so secretly that the High Council didn't know about it. One or more of the pre-Hartnell Doctors worked for them ("The Timeless Children"; X13.3, "Once, Upon Time"), as did Gat (X12.5, "Fugitive of the Judoon") and Karvanista (Series 13).]

The unnamed President – regarded as wise and beloved – is assassinated at his elaborate resignation ceremony. [Whether he's a new President or a regeneration of the one in office in "The Three Doctors" isn't clear, but it's probably the latter, as it's implied he's been in charge for 'centuries'.] He's referred to as Time Lord President [not President of Gallifrey or Lord President, as will become customary].

The President dies without naming a successor: Goth – even as Chancellor – does not automatically become President and must still stand for election. [Again, compare the Chancellor's position with "The Three Doctors".] Indeed, the President nominated someone else before his death; the true successor is never named.

Goth found the Master on Tersurus. [So high-ranking Time Lords do sometimes leave the planet, for whatever reason. See also "The Curse

Seriously, Did Rassilon Ever Meet Omega?

...continued from page 293

simple to time-scoop someone dying in 1980's Amsterdam and, at very least, create a pocket universe of anti-matter in which he could design weapons.

He has previous: in "The Day of the Doctor", there was a whole Omega Arsenal of eldritch weapons from the Ancient Times. (How ancient? We have good reason, as we've established in two essays in this book, to make a stab at dating the Dark Times Before Rassilon at least ten million years in the planet's own past and possibly "aeons".) At the very least, he could have been incorporated into the Matrix as part of a Brains Trust. Yet the nearest thing we've had to a mention, apart from this legacy of self-aware ordinance, is when the armies at Demon's Run (X6.7, "A Good Man Goes to War") have what looks a bit like the Greek letter Omega on their hats, but probably isn't. To be fair, that could just be coincidence, like there being a "Jenny" (Jenny Flint, to be specific) in that story who wasn't the Doctor's daughter. But in those days, anything in a Steven Moffat script was potentially Terribly Important, so a lot of people took note. If the First and Greatest of the Time Lords was available for hire by the Papal Mainframe (or maybe vice versa), why wasn't Gallifrey employing him in their darkest hour?

One possible answer is that he'd gone over to the opposition. We know that the Daleks are significantly more advanced, almost supernaturally so, by the time they invade Arcadia compared to their last on-screen appearance ("Remembrance of the Daleks"). In that 1988 story, they're familiar with the Hand of Omega, the remote stellar manipulator used to detonate stars, and hope to use it to become rivals to the Time Lords. In the dialogue for this, the Doctor is very clear that Omega "left behind" technology that Rassilon used when he "formed the basis of Time Lord society". Unbroadcast lines about the Doctor being "more than just a Time Lord" needn't concern us here, but the novelisation, also by Ben Aaronovitch, makes a big thing of the two legendary shouty men being near-contemporaries. Anyone familiar with the broadcast appearances of these characters would be imagining Stephen Thorne and Richard Mathews as supernaturally powerful beings unable to discuss the weather without causing structural damage to buildings.

Inevitably, the idea of them as rivals has come up. It's there from "The Three Doctors" on, Omega believing that he single-handedly is equal to the whole of Time Lord power and knowledge. It's hard to imagine Davros or the Daleks putting up with him for long, but no other explanation has ever been offered for how beings held at stalemate by the Movellans for centuries rose to rival Gallifrey. Nor have we heard anything about why Omega wasn't invited to the eternal battle fought with his leftovers. Omega's operatic self-pity is a good match for Davros's conniving ambition, yet this possibility's been unexplored.

Instead, the broadcast episodes have rested on an unexamined assumption that such rivalry never happened. Off-screen, it's all rather different. These days, the Virgin Books *New Adventures* series is interesting for the quality of the writing, the historical significance of who wrote some of them and artifacts of 90s entertainment. In the interregnum between Season Twenty-Six and Series 1, a portion of fandom clung to them like life-rafts. As we've seen (**Did Cartmel Have Any Plan At All?** under 25.3, "Silver Nemesis"), that contingent invested a lot in the idea that the Sylvester McCoy television stories were going somewhere – that there was a plan, an arc, an objective beyond messing with viewers' heads and removing our collective certainty about who the Doctor was and what he was up to.

A central plank of this alleged plan, and a recurrent feature of these books, was that Gallifrey's distant past included an enigmatic individual called "the Other" (pause for anyone raised on *Carry On* films or *The Two Ronnies* to resume a straight face), who was a contemporary of both Rassilon and Omega. We'll spare you the full detail of this backstory (see **Who Are All These Strange Men in Wigs?** under "The Brain of Morbius" for the specifics), but all you need to know is that (a) in these stories, the Doctor was a reincarnation of this chap and (b) since 2005 BBC Wales has done its darnedest to contradict every iota of the storyline and wreck the oddly prim notion of the Time Lords therein, then replace it with a similar-but-significantly-different new enigmatic backstory for the Doctor (X12.10. "The Timeless Children").

The origin of this influential, if unsubstantiated idea, is *Doctor Who Magazine*. The back-up strips tried out combinations of old characters and *2000 A.D.*-style art. Not all of the writers were entirely up-to-speed with what had happened in *Doctor Who* since they'd stopped watching (they were

continued on page 297...

14.3 The Deadly Assassin

of Fatal Death".] Spandrell indicates that members of the High Council aren't great scientists. Significantly, Goth tells Borusa that 'the Time Lords must not be seen to be leaderless at this time' [our emphasis], suggesting they're answerable to some external power. [Either the plebeian classes, or other cultures such as the Third Zone; see 22.4, "The Two Doctors".]

Time Lord society is divided into chapters, presumably related to Time Lord academies [although admission seems to be by clan rather than academic selection]. Each chapter has its own colours. The Prydonians wear red and orange, the Arcalians wear green and the Patrexes wear heliotrope [or at least that's what Runcible says, but see **Things That Don't Make Sense**]. Other chapters exist, though no other colours are shown here.

The Prydonians, the Doctor's chapter, seem to be considered especially noble and high-class, even though they're notoriously devious. The Castellan refers the case to the Chancellor when he finds out the Doctor's a member, as 'when a Prydonian forswears his birthright, there is nothing else he fears to lose'. Goth, a Prydonian, claims they see 'a little further ahead than most'. Cardinal Borusa leads the Prydonian chapter, which has produced more Presidents than all others combined. Other Cardinals are mentioned. ["Cardinal" may be a title given to the head of a chapter, or the head of an academy, as it's indicated that each chapter has its own.]

A robed figure called Gold Usher, so important that the guards won't bar him entry, performs some unspecified function at the resignation [see "The Invasion of Time"], while the President himself wears white. Before his death, the President compiles a Resignation Honours' List, to be read at the ceremony, and this may well include the name of his chosen successor. [Gold Usher's costume is kept in a display at the Panopticon museum but worn by the Keeper of the Matrix in 23.4, "The Ultimate Foe", suggesting a close link between the President's unique access to the Matrix and this official's everyday tasks.]

The President holds the symbols of office, the Sash of Rassilon and the Key [see **History**]. The resignation is broadcast to a wider population than just the robed types seen here, and the audience seems expected to know / care about figures like Cardinal Borusa. Mention is made of a former President called Pandak III, who lasted for 900 years, far longer than these modern Presidents.

The guard-commander interrogates the Doctor with a gun-like torture device which causes 15 intensity levels of pain. The inquest into the assassination is held *in camera*. [This isn't the formal affair of his malfeasance tribunal in 6.7, "The War Games".] No lawyers are involved, just the Chancellor's judgement; the Doctor is apparently only allowed to speak when sentence is to be pronounced. If found guilty, he's condemned to death in a vaporisation chamber. [How common is this sort of thing? "Arc of Infinity" suggests only one Time Lord has ever been executed – undoubtedly meaning Morbius – but here nobody finds the sentence strange, even if it's imposed for a surely unheard-of crime on Gallifrey.]

The Doctor wriggles out of this by calling on Article Seventeen of the Constitution, which technically allows him to stand as a presidential candidate and says in part that no candidate can be restrained from presenting his claim. Incoming presidents usually pardon political prisoners. [This can't be a reference to the kind of prisoners kept on Shada (17.6), as no President would be idiotic enough to let history-threatening war criminals go free. Besides, the Time Lords have forgotten about Shada. So what kind of political prisoners are there on Gallifrey? Either way, Goth speaks as if not freeing all political prisoners is against precedent.] Vaporisation without representation is against the Constitution. [Probably true, but parodying James Otis, a colonial Massachusetts lawyer articulating the views that led to the American Revolution. So Gallifrey has an agreed constitution with articles, differing from Britain (see **Where Does This Come From?** and 23.3, "Terror of the Vervoids").]

The energy-weapons on display here can kill Time Lords without them regenerating [presuming the fallen can regenerate]. A lightweight rifle-like weapon called a staser causes a lot of damage except to body tissue; oddly, a corpse killed by a staser bolt will be charred beyond recognition within an hour. [In X9.11, "Heaven Sent", it transpires that the individual cells in a Time Lord's body take ages to all die of natural causes, so this seems like a precaution.] Runcible dies without regenerating when he's stabbed in the back.

Planet Notes
- *Gallifrey*. The heart of Time Lord society is the Capitol, a grand, classical-style "city" whose limits

Seriously, Did Rassilon Ever Meet Omega?

...**continued from page 295**

mainly Hartnell kids), but they knew their Marvel lore and – in all honesty – these strips look like auditions to work with Stan Lee on the real thing. So when Alan Moore (yes, that one) was given his first (official) paying gig as a comic writer, it was with Marvel UK on the back-up strips. Most of what he knew about *Who* lore came from the magazine's editor Jeremy Bentham (no, not that one). From Bentham's account, this seems to have involved a few meetings in pubs and a lot of names written on the backs of beer mats.

We may sneer now at what these stories got wrong (angsty Cybermen saying "It is indeed awesome, Cyberleader" and so on), but they gave the impression that Alan Moore knew the score when, in fact, he was vamping on the "you hum it, I'll pick it up" basis. Inevitably, Russell T. Davies helped himself to a bit of this, from namechecking the Deathsmiths of Goth in the 2005 Annual and the recently-published prequel to "Rose" to making the Untempered Schism (X3.12, "The Sound of Drums") look very like the Warp-Gate – both of these from Moore's "4-D War". (It was published in *DWM* #51, April 1981, just after 18.7, "Logopolis" and, perhaps as significantly, 18.5, "Warriors' Gate"). This is the first use of the words "time war" in any version of *Doctor Who*.

That, like a lot in these strips, is pretty off-the-shelf in written SF by 1980, but was enough to fill a four-page strip, especially if the artwork was impressive. The December 1980 back-up, "Star Death", was introduced by the Doctor (wearing his "Terror of the Zygons" scarf) as "...the *birth* of a *legend*" (their italics) and was the old saw of a mercenary from the future causing the thing he'd been sent to prevent (as per 9.1, "Day of the Daleks" and *Terminator*). This temporal menace was called "Fenris the Hellbringer" – all very Nordic and not really much to do with 26.3, "The Curse of Fenric" – and what he caused was the Time Lords. His sabotage of the detonation of a star called "Qqaba" – very Islamic and not much to do with 18.2, "Meglos" – sent Omega into oblivion and caused Rassilon to vent his fury by zapping the guy's time-manipulator belt and sending him into the vortex for eternity (well, five issues; "4-D War" was the sequel) with electrical bolts from his fingers. He was sort of like Spitty Rassilon in X4.18, "The End of Time Part Two", but also like the Emperor in *Return of the Jedi* four years early. The monk's habit completes the resemblance.

And then he looked at the damaged directional control of this future tech and thought *Aha!* (If we're totting up things that twenty-first-century episodes seem to have recycled, our first glimpse of Rassilon is of big eyebrows and a hard stare, just like the sneak preview of Peter Capaldi in "The Day of the Doctor".) The most peculiar aspect is that the "Omega" who dies is only significant to Rassilon because he's a Gallifreyan and killing one of them offends his pride, rather than anything to do with any possible friendship, rivalry or even having been in the same room once or twice. Unlike on television, Rassilon was a presence and Omega was simply a name. On screen, just to make it seem deliberate, the Doctor was that very month looking up old archives of Rassilon's fight against the Great Vampire ("State of Decay").

So there's a paracanonical story where Rassilon and Omega are contemporaries and it's before time travel is controllable, so the balance of probabilities is that Rassilon didn't pop back to ensure that his world's history came out right. It's 1980, one Bootstrap Paradox at a time is enough to bewilder eight-year-old readers. But this version took, where "Day of the Daleks" was only known to most readers from the Target book. The impact is at least as much to do with John Stokes's art[47] as Moore's rather hackneyed script, but when Moore became a Big Name, the strip was rediscovered. (There are no credits on the back-up strips. Some sources name David Lloyd as the artist for this, as he was for other Moore stories.)

Why this made more of an impression on *Doctor Who* fans than "Tilotny Throws a Shape" did for *Star Wars Monthly* readers is perhaps down to the latter franchise being (largely) the work of an overall boss who didn't notice what Marvel were doing in his name. *Return of the Jedi* was the next truly canonical work, and after that most of what was published as *Star Wars* original fiction was redundant. As *Doctor Who* got more comic-like, relying on continuity references and team-ups, and the *DWM* strips that followed matched these earlier back-ups and what was now happening on television, the Moore version was remembered better than the earlier broadcast Gallifrey-based stories – few of which were repeated by the BBC and none more than once. Revisiting the broadcast episodes once home video came in was, for many, slightly deflating, like looking at Episode One of "Colony in Space" after looking at the Frank

continued on page 299...

14.3 The Deadly Assassin

aren't established here. [See "The Invasion of Time", "The Sound of Drums" (X3.12) et seq.]. The TARDIS can land there without difficulty while the Doctor is unconscious, though the landing is unauthorised and the Chancellery Guards are soon on the scene when the alert's sounded. The Doctor lands indoors, yet says he's right outside the Capitol, meaning that the Capitol is just the central area of a larger enclosed community.

Objects can be 'transducted' to and from the Capitol. The TARDIS can't leave again until the transduction barriers are raised. [It might be that he's landed in the city but only as near to the protected part, the Capitol, as the barriers will allow and can only enter when the TARDIS is impounded with him in it. The dialogue suggests otherwise.] Wherever he landed, the sound of dripping water prevails, but the lifts all seem to work.

The Master's attempt to unleash the Eye of Harmony's power ruins parts of the city; countless lives are lost. Gallifrey has apparently never known such catastrophe. Vaults and foundations dating back to the Old Time were found deep beneath the Coordinator's chamber [and under much of the rest of the Capitol].

The President's resignation ceremony is held in a great hall known as the Panopticon and covered for Public Register Video – the Gallifreyan version of television, which the Doctor can watch on the TARDIS screen – by Commentator Runcible. Rather old-fashioned camera technology records the event, albeit with video-discs held within the camera itself. There's a communications tower with 53 stories, close to the Capitol's perimeter, and a Capitol museum not far from the Panopticon.

Co-Ordinator Engin's chamber is equipped with a machine, apparently a computer of some description, which can immediately give the Castellan information on Time Lord affairs. The voice which answers him is female, though no women are seen anywhere else on the planet [the first Time Lady that we see, Rodan, appears in "The Invasion of Time"]. The chamber also contains extracted biog-data on individual Time Lords, the information being stored on what looks suspiciously like microfilm in canisters colour-coded according to the subject's chapter. These are later renamed 'Bio-data' extracts. The biog-data files are also known as data extracts (DEs), and data extraction requires an operating key, only issued to High Councillors and the Coordinator.

Records of data extraction can only be changed by a mathematical genius with a phenomenal grasp of exitonic circuitry. Even so, the Doctor believes the system would be considered primitive on some worlds. [The Time Lords specialise in temporal engineering, so it's reasonable that their records storage technology wouldn't be the most sophisticated in the universe. See our comments on the "files" in "Colony in Space".] The DE on the Master has gone.

The Time Lords measure local time according to the 'time-band'. [Whatever that is. Spandrell's significant use of the phrase '48 hours' might suggest a very Earth-like 24-hour day.] The Co-Ordinator refers to Earth as Sol 3 in Mutter's Spiral. [This has often been taken to mean the Milky Way; Engin would hardly refer to his own galaxy in this way. For all we know, Earth's sun is in a spiral-shaped constellation from Gallifrey's point of view – or our cluster of galaxies looks helical from Gallifrey – but they're hardly likely to impose such parochial standards on every planet in every galaxy across all time.]

At one point, Spandrell says that he has to keep running in 'Sheboogins' [his pronunciation] for vandalism and 'hooliganism'. [The Doctor does likewise when quashing a rumour about himself (X9.12, "Hell Bent"). The only other time the word 'Shobogans' comes up ("The Timeless Children"), the Master uses it to refer to the original Gallifreyans before regeneration and time travel. We might assume a sort of distinction between a city of a few thousand Time Lords and a population of 2.47 billion (X7.15, "The Day of the Doctor") based, we assume, on the Untempered Schism ("The Sound of Drums" again, but see also X8.4, "Listen"). Terrance Dicks assumes in his novelisation of "The Invasion of Time" that the 'Shobogans' (his spelling) are the outsiders and drop-outs Leela joins, but nobody says it on-screen. Indeed, in context it may simply be local slang for tearaway kids – like calling brats 'little monkeys' – the scamps who put glue on the President's Perigosto Stick or lose the Moon (8.5, "The Daemons"; "Hell Bent").]

The Eye of Harmony is kept beneath the Panopticon, sealed with the Rod [identified here as the 'Key', but see "The Invasion of Time"], and is within a black crystal about two metres in length, hexagonal in cross-section and pointed at one end with coolant tubes attached. Disconnecting these tubes (with a conventional wrench) causes earthquakes.

Seriously, Did Rassilon Ever Meet Omega?

...continued from page 297

Bellamy illustration of the opening scenes in *Radio Times*. Stokes and Moore gave us an ancient Gallifrey that was epic in a child-friendly way.

This, rather than anything ever transmitted, embedded itself in the head-canons of the *New Adventures* authors. Subsequent BBC Books picked up on it without overt acknowledgement. Well, *mostly*: we'd be remiss if we didn't mention the extended fugue on this theme by one Lawrence Miles in *Alien Bodies* and the two-volume *Interference*, in which the Order of the Black Sun, Moore's cadre of time-travelling assassins, were linked to Faction Paradox, Miles's voodoo cultist anti-Time-Lord mages. The conclusion of Moore's trilogy is the insubstantial "Black Sun Rising", about a summit conference between various time-travelling powers; *Alien Bodies* does that better too. (The comic's almost the *Star Trek* romp "Journey to Babel" with Sontarans and Moore's own recurring characters Wardog, Cobweb and Zeitgeist – who also pop up in Moore's *Captain Britain*.)

The real cadenza to "Star Death" is *Time's Crucible*, the fifth *New Adventures* book and first in a series called "Cat's Cradle". Marc Platt, the second NA author to have already done a "proper" story (26.2, "Ghost Light"), gave us all his pet theories in novel form rather than as a series of fanzine articles, but his notions about ancient Gallifrey form the basis for all subsequent books until 2005. It again has the creation of the Time Lords as one giant bootstrap, but this time Rassilon's big clue is the Doctor's TARDIS colliding with the prototype Timescaphe.

However, even with Omega mentioned and the Other (stop giggling) a significant player in the flashbacks to the overthrow of the Pythia (a foremother of the Sisterhood of Karn) and the subsequent ascendancy of Rassilon and science on Gallifrey, there's not much to indicate either intense rivalry or close cooperation. One might think that the name "Omega" is a job-description, like "Castellan", for all the similarity between this story's minor character and the fallen angel in "The Three Doctors". Still, the flavour of this version of the distant past was carried in other books in the range and Davies riffed on it in *Damaged Goods*. A version of it persists in the Big Finish audios. The 80s comics, 90s novels and early twenty-first-century audio plays have provided rich pickings for BBC Wales and, with the "shock" revelation in Series 12, this version of the distant past isn't likely to completely go away on screen either.

Yet we've still no indication that Omega was ever around in the Time War, nor that Rassilon was his contemporary. They never mention each other.

Rassilon supposedly set the nucleus of a black hole 'in an eternally-dynamic equation against the mass of the planet'. [That's a neat trick, only plausible if Gallifrey's mass is significantly more than Earth's: the minimum size of a conventional black hole is three solar masses, i.e., about six quintillion kilogrammes. Of course, there are smaller ones formed by processes other than stellar collapse. If, as we've speculated, this is a primordial one from the period just after Event One, the Big Bang, it could be anything over a Planck Mass, about 22 microgrammes, but they tend to evaporate rapidly. By "evaporate rapidly," we mean the way Alderaan did in *Star Wars*, but with backwash of intense radiation that would eventually wipe out life across half a galaxy. A better bet is something like 10^{11} kilos, roughly the mass of the United States.

[If Rassilon got a singularity to exist without the mass that created it, he could have a smaller object, infinitely dense, but still chucking out hard x-rays like nobody's business. It would still distort the orbit and rotation of any planet nearby. Nobody visiting Gallifrey walks or runs differently from anyone on Earth – nor do any Time Lords bounce around like lunarnauts on visits to our planet. So, even with the planet appearing almost twice the size of ours in X4.18, "The End of Time Part Two", Gallifrey's mass can't be much different from that of Earth. Rassilon obviously did something else not even the Doctor guesses to fit an infinitely dense heavy object inside a wardrobe-size fake gem without it being in a separate continuum like a TARDIS.]

History

• *Dating*. [Seriously? See **Where (and When) is Gallifrey?** under "Pyramids of Mars".]

Rassilon laid the foundations of Time Lord society an awfully long time ago, after retrieving the nucleus of a black hole, bringing it to Gallifrey and balancing the mass against that of the planet to allow time travel. Although he was primarily an engineer and architect, later generations revere him as their moral touchstone. The artefacts used to help him withstand the singularity's forces are

14.3 The Deadly Assassin

now ceremonial props of the President, their original function almost completely forgotten. Since then very little has changed, except that the Time Lords have 'turned aside from the barren road of pure technology', forgotten how they do what they do (and why) and generally stagnated.

The Doctor's 'Malfeasance hearing' was at relative date 309,906; the Tribunal's relative leniency is noted.

The current President is considered a bit of a lightweight compared to Pandak III, only in the job for a couple of centuries before resigning.

The Analysis

Where Does This Come From? Once again, Holmes and Hinchcliffe offered a simple explanation that doesn't quite stack up. Holmes said that he was watching *The Manchurian Candidate* on telly one night and came into the office next day saying, "let's do that". True, there's a lot of that film in this story's make-up, but the BBC had last shown it in 1971. (Holmes lived in Hertfordshire, so his local ITV stations would have been Thames and London Weekend. We can't find any indication of them showing the film at the right time either.)

But all is not lost, as the mid-70s was another boom time for paranoid conspiracy thrillers, and Alan J. Pakula's very similar film *The Parallax View* did the rounds at the time. Moreover, its star, Warren Beatty, was the subject of a special edition of *Film Night* in late October 1975. All the reviews agreed that the 1974 film was like a modern version of *The Manchurian Candidate*. But with regard to specific details, it's a lot less like "The Deadly Assassin" than the 1962 film. Both have snipers and brainwashing at their core, but *The Parallax View* is definitely post-Watergate and unavoidably post-JFK.

The Manchurian Candidate is, as much as anything, a dig at McCarthyism (strongly hinting that this ostensible anti-Communist witch-hunt was itself a Communist ploy) and a meditation on how the media needs heroes who seem like establishment figures. Many key scenes have television or newspapers as either a narrative ploy or a topic of conversation. Oddly, the majority of mid-70s thrillers, with the obvious exception of the thriller-like *All the President's Men* (based on a book that uses movie-thriller techniques to relate how the real-life Nixon conspiracy was unearthed), eschew such concerns and have a lone protagonist trying to go off-grid (*Three Days of the Condor* is as good a specimen as any).

"The Deadly Assassin" borrows greatly from this subgenre in the first episode, but also from older forms, as we'll discuss shortly. The story's main similarity to *The Parallax View* is the film's end, where Beatty's character, trying to prevent an assassination, finds himself on a gantry when the shot rings out and sees a rifle at his feet, whereupon people point at him and shout "there he is". *The Manchurian Candidate*, on the other hand, gives us many parallels, from the way Abraham Lincoln is constantly alluded to as an icon of lost integrity and vigour (per the references back to Rassilon), nightmares being used as an investigative tool (the APC net sequence), the way the official record is knowingly tampered with – the Pakula film leaves it open whether the official investigations have been suborned or just missed the point – and the emphasis on what television cameras see.

The camera angles used on the Public Register are very familiar to BBC1 viewers from the State Opening of Parliament. Most of the rigmarole surrounding the Queen announcing the government's legislative package (in a speech the Prime Minister writes, so watching Her Majesty's poker-face lapse is a popular sport) was a Victorian attempt to seem much older, but some is adapted from earlier customs. Specifically, there is an official called "Black Rod" – the full title is usually "Gentleman Usher of the Black Rod", but we currently have the first woman to hold the title – whose main task is the overall security and access to the House of Lords and the Palace of Westminster generally. This person has a ceremonial staff but is also custodian of the Mace used to signify that Parliament is in session. (Legally, it can't function without it, as various firebrand MP's have tried to demonstrate, notoriously Michael Hestletine in 1976.)

At the Opening ceremony, this person is ritually shut out and must ask permission to enter the Chamber, a precaution used to secure Parliament against high-handed monarchs (e.g., Charles I, who sent troops in shortly before declaring war on his own country). On this occasion, Black Rod would be dressed in formal wear from the 1660s, when Charles II renegotiated the role of Parliament (in 1688, Parliament forcibly renegotiated it with his brother, the deposed James II). The Rod itself gets the starring role in this stiltedly theatrical ceremony, knocking three times on the sealed door of the Chamber. Since 1971, the role has been merged with that of the Serjeant at Arms of the Lord Chancellor, so the Lords can't do anything when he (or she) is not present. This person also supervises the induction of new Lords. (As you might imagine, we'll return to this sort of thing in "The Invasion of Time".)

As we've hinted, the encrustation of ritual and circumlocution (with the Government's real motives smothered under euphemisms and given to the monarch to announce, then discussed in more detail when the cameras went away) was part of the Parliamentary "game" being satirised here. Most political journalists had to play along to get any information at all and, when fed stories by Lobby briefings, have to mumble about "sources close to the Prime Minister" as if they'd won this scoop after years of making contacts. Runcible's on-air pablum was shown to be inadequate as he unctuously announces "just a little disturbance" while the Chancellery Guards run behind him. 1976, as we'll see, was transitioning from how it had been done since the early 1960s to a new sort of courtship dance under Thatcher. The public were increasingly under the impression that they had trusted our leaders under false pretences. Now that the proceedings of Parliament are routinely televised, this sense of disenchantment is hard to recapture.

One of the initial beneficiaries of the less deferential style of politics had been Harold Wilson, who became Prime Minister in 1964 and again in 1974. Now, on the receiving end after various scandals caused by his ministers and officials (see **Who's Running the Country?** under 10.5, "The Green Death") and several alleged plots against him by right-wingers and the military, the wily Labour leader had run out of lives and unexpectedly resigned in April 1976, just as this story was commissioned.

It's customary for a resigning PM to hand out knighthoods and peerages, and Wilson's added fuel to wild conspiracy theories on all sides (see **English Lessons**). For all of Holmes's later claims to have been thinking mainly of older universities, Parliament is undeniably the main source for Gallifrey's ceremonial trappings, from the robes and hats (like the ermine worn by Lords as much as the gowns used at university graduations) to the nature of the APC Net. If the Time Lords (let's remember that "normal" peers are referred to as "Lords Temporal" to distinguish them from bishops, who are "Lords Spiritual") are the House of Commons, then the advisory body made up of the pickled brains of dead ones is a wicked allegorical dig at the House of Lords in the pre-Thatcher era. (One significant change since this story has been the shift towards non-hereditary lords, "Life Peers", making the House of Lords more like a Senate than a family business.)

Thus, dead minds rule the planet. It's a slightly watered-down version of a notion in Robert Silverberg's then-recent novel *Nightwings* (adapted from three late-60s novellas) set in a far future where Rome (or "Roum") had a Guild of Rememberers who could access the brains of the dead leaders plumbed into a sort of Wikipedia in the catacombs. The book's atmosphere of crumbling cities, chapters and guilds and half-forgotten abilities is suggestive in other ways, but let's stick with Rome for now and, specifically, the Vatican. That's been the default interpretation of the events in "The Deadly Assassin" among people unfamiliar with Parliament and the use of the term "Cardinals" hasn't dispelled this impression.

As we've investigated earlier in this book (**Doctor of What?** under "The Seeds of Doom"), the oldest universities were attached to the church, but even in the Middle Ages were at arm's length. In Britain after the Reformation, the move towards secularisation was a constant back-and-forth. Both bodies have "Deans" and "Colleges" (and "Chancellors", here a title inherited from "The Three Doctors"). In the Catholic Church, a College of Cardinals elects a Pope – so a strict definition of "Cardinal" can be applied as someone within a hierarchy capable of making such a decision. The Church of England no longer has these but applying the word "Synod" to the Time Lords would have been too specific. ("Cardinal" is also an adjective, as in points on a compass or a really big mistake.) As with other fustian terms such as "Castellan" and the character-names, it establishes a sense of age and authority.

"Panopticon", on the other hand, pushes a secular notion of observation and authority. The term is associated with the founder of Utilitarianism, Jeremy Bentham (whose preserved remains are in a glass case at University College, London). A distant relative of his with the same name was a leading figure in the *Doctor Who* Appreciation Society, so the pun must have been irresistible to Holmes. (The DWAS returned the favour by calling their convention "PanoptiCon".) However, the idea is of a surveillance society

14.3 The Deadly Assassin

where citizens – most commonly criminals inside a specially-designed prison – were observed at all times by one or more warder. For the Time Lords to apply the word to their own ceremonies and society suggests they are themselves on display at all times. Borusa and Goth both comment on the importance of how others will perceive the activities of the Time Lord elite.

We've discussed the extent to which *Doctor Who* routinely examines Utilitarianism (notably **Do Robots Have Rights?** in this volume), but here the Doctor functions as a scapegoat to preserve the smooth running of Gallifrey for appearances' sake. Borusa does the usual British thing of insisting that there's a tradition of justice and fair play while participating in a stitch-up. (Also in the news while this was written: the first appeal against the convictions of the Birmingham Six were considered and dismissed. They were eventually pardoned, while the West Midlands Serious Crimes Squad officers and forensic examiner were encouraged to retire.)

As a former beat bobby, Holmes might have been expected to emphasise the drudgery of police work, but this investigation is from the point of view of the lead officer, the Castellan. He is a very recognisable type from countless US films, the dogged Lieutenant with a stomach ulcer and dim subordinates. (It's so hoary that we can't find a specific original, but let's mention Wilks in *The Big Heat* as a starting-point.) They usually just bawl out maverick cops, but on occasion get their fair share of the action. By 1976, this was enshrined in television, so think of Bernie Casey in *Starsky and Hutch*, Garfield Morgan in *The Sweeney* – or Lloyd Bridges in *Airplane!*

This is interesting, as the usual response to Kennedy-style assassination conspiracy plots focuses on the lone investigator (usually a journalist, as in *The Parallax View*) hiding from every authority figure rather than recruiting them, because the authority-figure is implicated. Had this genuinely been a satire on the Warren Commission – or the recently unearthed Zapruder footage and subsequent kerfuffle – there would have been doctored evidence at every turn and the Master would have suborned Borusa, Spandrell, Engin and Runcible. Spandrell's role is closer to the kind of cop who finds the Mayor's on the take (e.g. Steve McQueen in *Bullett* – we bet that's the first time George Pravda's been compared to him). Instead, the evidence is left to be re-interpreted with a fresh account to link the individual pieces together and all the data on the Rod and Sash is left in plain sight for the Doctor to explain.

That's because this has another set of generic rules at work: the Cargo Cult story of how a society's rituals derived from a logical (and forgotten) set of causes. We'll develop this theme in the next story (indeed, in all three of Chris Boucher's scripts), but it's interesting to see how Gallifrey and the Sevateem both work on rituals derived from lost or misunderstood technology. This sort of thing, as you'll know by now, was very lucrative for Erich von Daniken in the 1970s, but that decade was also a boom time for quasi-scientific explanations of cultural mores, especially if they could get pictures of naked women into it. Desmond Morris, a former zookeeper and TV host, launched a mini-industry of books and specials accounting for human habits via evolutionary biology, while archaeologists were finding relatively mundane-seeming events behind familiar mythology. The granddaddy of this in TV was *Quatermass and the Pit* (1959), hinting at a simple (if bizarre) reason for vast swathes of human behaviour and religion. Within written SF, there's an inversion where a fallen or altered society has quasi-liturgical versions of commonplaces from our time (as in the Silverberg book mentioned earlier). We'll mention *A Canticle for Liebowitz* as the granddaddy of these and move on.

Consensual hallucinations, especially mediated via computers, were just beginning to become commonplace in SF at that time – the biggest one before William Gibson staked out the territory was John Varley's "Overdrawn at the Memory Bank", published around the time this was being shot (and made into a duff TV movie in Canada). Prior to that, Ben Bova had written *The Duelling Machine* about mental gladiatorial combat. What's noticeable is how rule-governed the dreaming in "The Deadly Assassin" is: Goth uses a map to find water rather than thinking "I'd like a pond here" and making it happen. If anything, this is more like a text adventure from the early days of home computing than a nightmare.

It's tempting to claim that this story-element echoes the *Star Trek* episode "Shore Leave", but they're only similar in that both include a biplane, and even that's more overtly *North by Northwest*. Instead, this section takes many features from American films about World War II (in the South Pacific – Holmes served in Burma) and the repertoire of common bad dreams (foot stuck and unable to run from oncoming vehicle, crocodiles, clowns, dentists, falling, World War I) and Saturday Morning Pictures staples.

Apart from the already-mentioned element of *The Manchurian Candidate* where Frank Sinatra's nightmares are the first clues to what really happened before the platoon's memories were altered, there is a simple, pragmatic reason for this episode-long chase: barely any dialogue. The story's *raison d'etre* was Tom Baker's contention that he could carry the series without a regular companion, so the first and third episode are exercises in seeing how far viewers could comprehend matters by other means. The Doctor talks to himself to an unnatural degree in Part One, and that's all the dialogue he gets in Part Three.

English Lessons

• *Pomp and Circumstance* (n): For most people in Britain, this means "Land of Hope and Glory", as sung at the Last Night of the Proms – vaguely jingoistic lyrics to Elgar's "Pomp and Circumstance March No.1". Americans think of the same piece as school graduations. The term is first used in this form in *Othello* but with a comma. Then Philip Massinger grabbed it in 1640, but *Pompa Circensis* was the procession before gladiators arrived in the arena – so maybe "Entry of the Gladiators" ought to be used at Commencement ceremonies.

• *What?* (interj.): An interesting one, because it's a verbal tic associated with retired colonels, magistrates, posh old duffers with military moustaches and the like. It's like the (cinematic) French habit of adding "no?" at the end of a sentence in accented English (recently used a lot online), or the Canadian "eh?" or the London "innit?" However, John Dawson (credited as "Time Lord") was a last-minute recasting and kept the dialogue intact, even though his accent's too Northern to pass for that kind of relic. (For the benefit of American actors reading, nobody in Britain has actually talked like that since about 1950, and even then, just the one "what", not two like people seem to think.)

• *Poltroon* (n.): craven, cowardly imbecile. A lot of people pronounce it as if the first O were a U.

• *Castellan* (n.): literally, the person in charge of a castle's defences.

• *Runcible* (adj.): Made up by Edward Lear, the term "runcible spoon" later became a real implement, a fork at one end and a spoon at the other. So

"dual use", appropriate for a TV reporter specialising in politics.

• *Spandrel* (n.): Cleverly, Holmes has picked on a word used in both clock-making and ecclesiastical architecture, a load-bearing arch in a bracket, for the world-weary cop.

• *Resignation Honours List* (n.): A topical reference to another bit of Parliamentary procedure. Unlike the normal run of honours where cross-party nominations are allocated, a resigning Prime Minister gets to give peerages, knighthoods OBE's and the like to whomsoever s/he pleases. (Theresa May's honours for 1970s cricketers was about the only worthwhile thing of her premiership.) In April 1976, Harold Wilson resigned under mysterious circumstances and the so-called "Lavender List" o' somewhat eccentric choices caused concern and amusement, depending on one's party allegiance. One of the controversial businessmen made a Lord committed suicide while investigated for fraud a year later; another was later convicted and imprisoned. A third, James Goldsmith, was given to suing the press for investigating his dodgy deals and later formed a Eurosceptic party, despite himself being a Member of the European Parliament representing his tax-exile in France.

• *Verisimilitude* (n.): Plausibility, or "Truthiness". It's a perfectly cromulent word, but it's surprising how many fanzine articles stated that Holmes made it up.

• *Shobogan* (n.): not a word in English, but a town in Wisconsin called "Sheboygan" is famous as America's bratwurst capital or the birthplace of E.E. "Doc" Smith (op cit.) and The Chordettes (see 23.3, "Delta and the Bannermen"; X9.9, "Sleep No More"). Australian slang has 'bogans', meaning roughly 'trailer-trash' or 'chavs'[48] but probably later. (We tried various spellings and an English-Czech dictionary in case George Pravda was trying to slip a rude word past the censors, but nothing came up.)

• *Flea-bitings* (n.): We'll assume you know the literal meaning. Some sources say this was a deliberate allusion to Webster's *The White Devil*; after "The Masque of Mandragora", this is entirely possible.

Things That Don't Make Sense [NB: nearly every quibble from the 2004 edition evaporates like hand-sanitiser if we re-evaluate two things. The very first time we heard the words "Time Lords", in Episode Six of "The War Games" (6.7), was during a conversation about memory-editing and

14.3 The Deadly Assassin

perception-filters. This combination of tricks has been their routine method of covering their traces ever since. It's entirely in keeping that the buried truth of Gallifrey's own past and the sources of their power might be staring everyone in the face and they don't realise it. For the plots of "The Ultimate Foe"; X9.12, "Hell Bent" and many Sylvester McCoy stories to function, we *have* to assume that the Doctor was disabused of many of these evasions (after that traumatic childhood encounter with the Matrix) but had told his then-BFF the Master, who followed-up with enquiries of his own.

[To resolve the discrepancy between what the Chief of Police and Head Librarian in this story don't know and what Cardinals seem to half-know in 15.6, "The Invasion of Time", we need only consider that whatever Theta Sigma got up to when playing hookey from Academy was known to his headmaster (the future Cardinal/ Chancellor/ Lord President) hence 20.7, "The Five Doctors". After "The Deadly Assassin", Borusa revealed carefully-chosen highlights as part of the news-management after the earthquake caused by the Master unlocking Rassilon's Star – an event that made people wonder about other things they'd overlooked, such as why there's that hole in the Panopticon floor into which the Rod of Rassilon would slot nicely.]

The Doctor's had this vision and finds himself re-enacting it. We later discover that his idea was to use the rifle to shoot the gun from the real assassin's hand. Later yet, the Doctor tells Spandrell that he knew all along that the sights would be fixed. Why waste time taking careful aim when just shooting into the air would have caused a commotion and wrecked the real killer's aim? Why wait until the President was on the dais?

That dream was a forecast of probabilities from the Matrix, not an example of genuine clairvoyance. (The Doctor doesn't believe in that; well, not this week. And besides, compare the "dream" version's Goth waving his hands in the air when the shot rings out to the real one stealthily firing a staser in Part Two's reprise – without anyone around him noticing.) The Doctor's summoned to Gallifrey but, on arrival, seems wary of the guards. Why slip past them rather than taking the opportunity to say "take me to your leader" and telling someone in authority about the impending assassination? Unlike before, the majority of Time Lords don't remember him (see above). The upper echelon would know all about the incident with Omega, though. This new-style political High Council would want to have the Doctor out of the public gaze – he knows about the embarrassing loss of literal and metaphorical power and the cover-up over Omega's survival – so, once again, he's unlikely to be in the Panopticon in time for the forecast assassination and probably being interrogated by the leading suspects and the intended victim ahead of the predicted murder.

The Capitol's on high alert, so how does the TARDIS get through the transduction barriers? (Goth or the Master popping in on Rodan's little booth would be really conspicuous.) And why park there? Of all the planets the Doctor's visited, Gallifrey is the one place he could be reasonably sure of getting a decent spot.

What else was forecast? Did the Master sieve out any images of him leaving Goth for dead, the Doctor becoming President and leaving the way open for two invasions in a week, a nasty Time War, Rassilon coming back as first James Bond then as an East End crime boss, the Master wiping everyone else out then converting their corpses into Cybermen?[49] And why didn't the APC system predict his tampering, or warn anybody the moment he arrived on Gallifrey? Wouldn't the sudden absence of any information at all about the President's medium-term future be a bit of a red flag to whoever gets these routine forecasts – regardless of what we later discover is the President's main job, being a living search-engine? If Goth *does* get to be President, the Matrix would reject him more violently than it does the Doctor when he's crowned in "The Invasion of Time". In fact, if someone's been busily making a mental play-pen inside the net, just on the off-chance that the Doctor pops in for a nose around, wouldn't the President know?

To reiterate: between his arrest and interrogation, the Doctor is apparently taken to a theatrical costumier's and told "pick anything you want in your size", so opts to be tortured while dressed as Errol Flynn. Were the King of Hearts and Viking costumes already taken? Another confusing sartorial choice: Goth and the Master have a timeshare on a black cotton cloak with a hood. On second viewing (and indeed the third, fourth and nth rewatches), it gets harder to keep track; Goth seems to teleport from courtroom to chambers to dripping caverns but seems to be in two places at once when the cameraman gets killed. It takes intense concentration to tell when the Master's opened a can of spinach and got up from his death-bed to murder someone in person, instead of sending Goth in a stocking-mask to do some of his dirty work. Why is he Golluming around in the shadows shooting Pat Gorman, when there's so much else that needs micro-managing?

There's a Tribunal hearing on the assassination. It's unlike the other two trials into the Doctor's activities. Apparently assassinating the Lord President is less serious than preventing a genocidal war conducted with stolen humans ("The War Games") or "Conduct Unbecoming a Time Lord" (the initial charge against the Doctor in Season Twenty-Three). If being accused of murder isn't enough to over-rule Article Seventeen, what is? With death pretty negotiable on this planet (Rassilon, in his tomb, is still an active player in "The Five Doctors") and time travel a daily practical concern, there must still be some boundaries on who is considered a viable candidate for the presidency.

Borusa is said to be leader of the Prydonian chapter, yet he appears wearing the "seldom worn" heliotrope robes of the Patrexes [see "The Invasion of Time", for more of this]. We don't see any green-robed Arcalians even when Runcible's pointing them out to his viewers. After telling the Doctor that he's waiting for a signal from his camera technician before beginning his broadcast, Runcible almost immediately starts talking to the camera.

If Goth *wasn't* the outgoing President's appointee, was there nothing written down in the resignation speech or the honours list as to the true successor? The President died with the speech on a scroll in his hand, but nobody reads it looking for clues. The President's the one living mind linked to the Matrix. His secret wouldn't have died with him. He talked to other people about his decisions. Even that guy in the lift knew there was something interesting about the list. Goth couldn't have been sure that he'd be able to keep his motives secret for very long. (Let's not forget, he genuinely thinks the Master's plan will leave him as President of the Time Lords for a fairly long time and has no idea about the blowing-up-Gallifrey-next-afternoon part.) He'd need to keep making sure that all the interested parties died suddenly, without benefit of clergy, so to speak. Even if we forget "The Invasion of Time" and every other story with Time Lords in thereafter and follow the story's hint that the APC net is for old, frail Time Lords losing consciousness but not quite dead, just one of these elderly "dormice" popping his Hush Puppies from natural causes would wreck everything.

Goth even found a prediction of the first cliff-hanger with the Doctor on the camera-platform. All that time when the Doctor was on trial and, before that, being tortured or selecting an outfit in which to be tortured, and *now* the Master thinks to pick up the evidence? By killing Runcible so overtly, while the Doctor has an ironclad alibi, it's as if he wants to exonerate the Doctor in front of the local chief of police, a police sergeant and the media and thereby get the authorities looking into possible alternatives. Why doesn't he just hypnotise Runcible, take the footage and order him to forget everything he's seen?

We're also trying to figure out *how* Runcible was spatchcocked by a frail skeleton-man with hours to live. We're forced to envision some kind of rig, a spring-loaded stake-projector or a long piece of rope suspended from the ceiling with a sharpened stake on it, plus Runcible standing obligingly still as it swings toward him. Even by the Master's usual standards (inflatable chairs, a mathematical model of a city, becoming Prime Minister for a day, creating the afterlife, being a Polish hospital orderly for ten years, turning spies into dongles), this is an extraordinarily elaborate set-up for one counter-productive murder. Especially as he's already been identified and has a gun that can shrink people.

Is the Doctor really not capable of recognising Goth's voice when they're facing each other in the Matrix, or indeed, making out his face through that flimsy mask? 'Cos the audience is. For that matter, why (other than concealing his identity from viewers) does Goth disguise his voice when alone with his Master?

Goth's hallucinated fears are all very specific to mid-twentieth-century Earth and become increasingly mundane and realistic rather than having abrupt nightmarish shifts of context. The Doctor may not be able to avert fatal situations by saying "I deny this reality", but Goth can rewrite its rules to his liking. Why should poison, flaming marsh-gas and being hit with sticks make any difference to him? Why bother imagining dead fish, such an obvious giveaway? All of this presupposes that Goth actually constructed the dreamscape – but as he seems as rule-bound as anyone, he may be simply sustaining something the Master tailored

14.3 The Deadly Assassin

to the Doctor's fears. In which case, why keep the Prydonian Chancellor and presumptive President stuck in a cellar playing video-games when there's an election to win? The dreamscape continues after Goth's unplugged, so it must run on automatic when not in use; maybe Academy students grind characters for in-game currency. And nobody notices that the front-runner in the impending election, plus the only other candidate, wandered off at a very important moment. Don't they have hustings?

Engin's office has all the records and dossiers Spandrell needs *and* a slide-out table and APC terminal just in case someone wants to pop in and die. Even with what we now know about the procedure and the Confession Dials (Series 9's big idea), it's like putting a kindergarten in the firestation. Does Engin do dry-cleaning as well? The Doctor's whole goal in entering the Matrix is to identify the hack in the APC net. After spectacularly failing at this, he then just asks if there's another room beneath the one he's standing in and Engin obligingly takes him there. Why not do that an episode or so earlier? The Doctor's party-trick of identifying a neural inhibitor by sniffing the needle ought to have left him unable to speak for a few minutes. As it is, he calls it "try coffinal aldehyde", so maybe it *does* affect him.

Upon learning that the Master isn't dead, Spandrell decides to leg it to warn Hildred rather than using the glove-phone through which he's been sending sarcastic comments and orders for three episodes now. The reawakening Master manages to strangle Hildred into submission before the guard can shoot him, even though the staser's aimed right at his head and ready to fire. Then at the end, Spandrell (also packing a patrol staser) just mumbles "Look – the Master" and watches blithely as the baddie slowly sidles into a grandfather clock and leaves. Just before, the Doctor sees the Master's TARDIS disguised as a terrestrial timepiece but doesn't think to question it; odd in itself, doubly so when you remember that Gallifreyans can apparently recognise disguised TARDISes, as Commander Hildred does in Part One.

Critique The Time Lords were always more potent the further they were from our gaze. When they were noises-off in Episode Nine of "The War Games", they were terrifying; then they appeared and were calm, quiet and dull. In "Colony in Space", they were ministerial types in what looked like someone's patio, wearing silly wigs. In "The Three Doctors", they were ministerial types in drag, wandering around the set from *Top of the Pops*. One also showed up dressed as a Whitehall chap in pinstripes and bowler in "Terror of the Autons". What we're getting at is that the version of Gallifrey in this story is the inevitable end-point of that running-gag. Equally inevitably, any four-part story set on the planet using BBC resources was bound to disappoint anyone who'd invented the Doctor's home world using the unlimited effects budget of daydreaming.

Disregarding the basic joke of the Time Lords being part university dons, part Whitehall mandarins, this story is the logical conclusion of everything we'd seen and heard before. It's a society concerned with observation, so it's only natural that they are themselves overseen and monitored, a society dominated by appearances and visual display. From this, it follows that they would be vulnerable to gaps in their knowledge and things kept from their scrutiny. Their strict non-intervention policy has led to insularity and stasis and the only three of their number who do anything have been outside: the Doctor, the Master and Goth. Previous stories involved the Master accessing a Time Lord file detailing some ancient power, so that data-retrieval system would have to become prominent in a rematch between him and the Doctor on home ground. The precise nature of that archive was a shock in 1976, but now it's almost routine.

We'll never recover the first-night thrill of these concepts being shown to us and the behind-the-scenes glimpse at the Doctor's old life. It rapidly became the template for all stories about the Time Lords (more than was wise). Every script about them refers back to this one, sometimes slavishly. The story's visuals have been replicated so often, it's hard to see why anyone made a fuss. The difference is that, despite all the money and resources now available, none of the people involved is Robert Holmes, David Maloney, Roger Murray-Leach or James Acheson. Two of those four helped to establish the Time Lords in earlier stories, so accusing them of "not understanding" or "betraying" these earlier episodes is downright daft.

The texture of this world mainly comes from Holmes. In giving the apparatus of Gallifrey a vocabulary of dusty words from the recesses of the OED (a trick that won Gene Wolfe numerous awards just a few years later), he established both a sense of great age and a feeling of the world being lived-in. His invented names (remember, "Gallifrey" was from one of his scripts) seem viable rather than the kick-over-the-Scrabble-board technique: "Rassilon" sounds like he comes from an old story and the name immediately "took". It's a testament to his world-building that the planet seems self-consistent and viable, even though so much of it parodies sclerotic British institutions. People have wallowed in the atmosphere, and added details of their own, but it has now outgrown the initial satirical intent and become its own entity, like Lilliput.

Throwing a cynical cop from a 50s film into this might seem mildly absurd, but Spandrel can ask relevant questions and be exasperated with his underling Hildred whenever less-committed parents or small children seem likely to want a bit of a change. Whoever had the nerve to propose George Pravda rather than the usual senior cop actors deserves praise, because it makes enough of a contrast to the blindingly obvious casting of Erik Chitty as Engin. These two are enough to reinforce the basic "heresy" of the story (to some stodgy fans) that, for the majority of the time and for some during even a ceremonial occasion, the Capitol is simply where they work.

There are flaws, of course. The Master's mask makes his dialogue in Part Four hard to hear (there were some lurid mishearings of the word "poltroon" and "in extremis"). All the Part One material where the Doctor talks to himself is forced and rings hollow (perhaps deliberately – see **The Lore**). The shrunken camera technician is flagrantly an Action Man. Goth's office looks like they've dropped a hearth-rug on a swivel-chair in an office-block they're still building. Engin's lair has walls made from tinfoil and bin-liners, it seems. The Doctor describing the Master as "...my sworn arch-enemy, a fiend who glories in chaos and destruction" might have passed muster if Adam West had said it in Commissioner Gordon's office but is glow-in-the-dark wrong in this context. Worst of all, Part Three gets really pedestrian and – literally – mundane after an exhilaratingly unsettling start. Everything from "I deny this reality" to the cliffhanger comes from a less imaginative story. (Granted, it's head and shoulders better than Terry Nation's attempts to do this sort of thing, but that's damning with faint praise.)

But they devoted a full episode to showing the Doctor getting beaten up for real (well, you know what we mean) and shook the police-procedural we were watching up completely. It was a hugely daring move and, with hindsight, the end of an era. We'll never have this many stunts in a story again and certainly not in one episode (until 2005, anyway). We'll not see the Doctor so thoroughly knocked about until another Holmes script, "The Caves of Androzani" (21.6), and he regenerates after all that beating and poison. We joked about Terry Walsh playing the Doctor for most of Part Four of "The Monster of Peladon" (11.4), but here Walsh, Baker, Bernard Horsfall and Eddie Powell spend the vast majority of the episode seemingly knocking lumps out of each other as the two combatants. Baker has never seemed so vulnerable as at the start of Part Four and won't again until "The Leisure Hive" (18.1).

In many ways, bringing back the Master is like admitting defeat: they're struggling to think of a good reason for whatever's happening to be happening, and well-motivated antagonists are an effort. This time, Hinchcliffe and Holmes dodge that staser-bolt by giving him the biggest stakes of all, a wrecked body and no more regenerations, and his solution is suitably extreme. That's the problem. How does he top this in any potential rematch? As we now know, he can't. Neither could anyone really match Roger Delgado, so they don't even try. They use these two problems against each other, just as they used the lack of a regular companion and the need to pit the Doctor against his own people. All of this required nerve. That swagger we were talking about two reviews ago has paid off and, right from the screen-crawl opening, this story's got it into its head that it's a one-off and they can do whatever they like. Even hack up that scarf.

The Facts

Written by Robert Holmes. Directed by David Maloney. Viewing figures: 11.8 million, 12.1 million, 13.0 million, 11.8 million. AIs 59% (Part Two) 61% (Part Four). The summer repeat was less stellar: 4.4 million, 2.6 million, 3.8 million and 3.5 million. *The Whole Universe Show* really was that off-putting.

Working Titles "The Dangerous Assassin". Yes, really.

Alternate Versions The VHS edit and August 1977 repeat had the Part Three cliffhanger edited

14.3 The Deadly Assassin

after Bill Slater caved into Mary Whitehouse. The original ending is lost and was reconstituted for the DVD from a Umatic copy then owned by BBC Worldwide. So on the streaming services, this ends with a close up of Goth saying "You're finished, Doctor", but otherwise it ends as nature intended with a freeze-frame of the Doctor's head under water. The VHS release reinstated the cut shot from a noticeably inferior copy.

Terrance Dicks's novelisation came out just after the summer repeat and introduces a few intriguing details: The Doctor's childhood playing hide-and-seek in the Capitol is mentioned (something picked up on in "Hell Bent"); Borusa's status is clarified, as followed-up in "The Invasion of Time"; the Doctor was apparently being groomed for a seat on the High Council before he fled; the Capitol is dimly lit at the best of times and needs lanterns (and the Eye of Harmony is under a flagstone that generations of junior Time Lords wore smooth by walking on) and there's a Time Lord in a bright yellow robe on the front cover – not Gold Usher, as he looks younger. It's more the colour of the young Doctor-in-waiting we see in "The Timeless Children".

Cliffhangers The Doctor fires the staser-rifle and the President dies, just as in the dream; the Doctor's foot is caught in a railway line as a train approaches; a triumphant Goth holds the Doctor's head under water.

What Was In the Charts? "Couldn't Get It Right", Climax Blues Band; "Under the Moon of Love", Showaddywaddy; "Somebody to Love", Queen; "Sorry Seems to be the Hardest Word", Elton John.

The Lore

With Elisabeth Sladen's departure, everyone working on the series thought it was time for a change. Normally, they'd have crafted a replacement character and cast someone to play her (probably a her, at any rate, and probably from our time and place, i.e. 1970s England). Tom Baker had other ideas. His Doctor was more sympathetic for young viewers than any earlier model. His conception of the role was of someone so far ahead of everyone else, stopping to explain everything needed more than a seemingly stupid person asking questions and continually getting into scrapes – the Doctor seemed daft for hanging around with such a person. In Baker's opinion, the Doctor could manage perfectly well as a solo traveller and only needed a constant supply of newcomers, each a native of wherever the TARDIS had taken him, for exposition purposes. Generally, when Baker voiced such an opinion in rehearsals, the director would patiently explain why it wasn't practical or, every so often, try it and see if it worked. Sometimes, it did.

Philip Hinchcliffe and Robert Holmes decided to call Baker's bluff by writing a story where the Doctor was alone in a hostile world and – not coincidentally – Baker was needed for almost every scene and had a lot more dialogue to remember. As this was an experiment, potentially a drastic revision to the fundamental series-format now going for over a dozen years, Holmes had to get permission from the Writers' Guild to handle it himself. The plan was to end the production block with a string of stories where each new world had a fresh person to whom the Doctor would talk – rather as 2009 Specials attempted – by which time either Baker would see the error of his ways or the public would complain. (Or, hypothetically, the stroppy star turned out to be right, as with Patrick Troughton in Season Six.)

The stories in the pipeline all had young women who weren't like Sarah. Chris Boucher's debut story, by now on its fourth title, had Leela; his proposed Storm Mine Murder story had Toos and Robert Banks Stewart's "A Foe from the Future" had a sort of Eliza Doolittle character who may or may not have been intended to stay on. (As part of the continuing negotiations over *Scratchman*, there had been discussions with Twiggy as a possible Sarah-analogue in the film and possibly as the Eliza figure on television. It's unclear whether this was the same character crossing from small to big screen, as is whether it was either / or. She was doing a variety show for BBC2 and appearing on *The Muppet Show*, so obviously she and her agent were keen to get her out from just being a model who did a Ken Russell film once.)

However, the first trial for this new pattern was the (then) all-male, all-old home planet of the Time Lords, an environment known to the Doctor but only hinted at to viewers. Hinchcliffe was keen to explore this world, Holmes wanted to bring back the Master as a more desperate, driven character and to play with the genre of paranoid political thrillers. Both wanted to move away from rubber-faced alien hordes. Holmes pointed out that, by definition, this character is supposed to be as smart as the Doctor but always loses, which makes for bad drama. So, this story had to focus on something other than just defeating the Doctor or conquering Earth. Hinchcliffe took the idea of a "pupating" Master as a way to keep the next producer's options open, in case they decided not to stick with whoever was cast for this story. The script mentions that the Master is partially rejuvenated at the climax, stands taller, talks more clearly and can fight the Doctor blow-for-blow.

- After the breakdowns in communications between departments during "Terror of the Zygons" (doors too small for the bulbous-headed aliens to get through, etc.), James Acheson wanted to liaise with a set designer to get a unified concept of a planet. In this case, it was Roger Murray-Leach; they shared an office for this production. David Maloney was assigned to this story-slot well in advance (November 1975). The main concern quickly became the story's film allocation in the hallucination scenes... this meant that the city had to be all-studio, despite scripted moments of the Doctor looking out of a window at the rain over the Capitol. Murray-Leach wanted a city with no boundaries, so the struts and doorways had slats revealing dark space behind them and the "walls" were translucent and showed more structures behind them. His idea was to hint at a glass edifice buried within the planet's bedrock, with an open, escape-proof prison cell suspended in mid-air.

- One idea rapidly abandoned was that the Matrix nightmare would include a distorted Victorian London (as per "The Ultimate Foe", also partly by Holmes), but there was another story with a similar setting on the cards and the filming for the Gallifrey story was scheduled for July, curtailing the night-shooting. However, Holmes approached this as a "greatest hits" medley of scary moments from films, including a flagrant steal from *North by Northwest* with the biplane.

With the increased film allocation for the story (eight tenths of Part Three was on film, unprecedented except for 7.1, "Spearhead from Space"), there was a five-day shoot with two actors and two stunt-men. Maloney had cast Bernard Horsfall three times before for *Doctor Who* and was picked for coping with the physical aspects as well as looking like a Senator. He also looked vaguely like Terry Walsh – so, for once, Eddie Powell doubled for Baker and Walsh was Goth in dangerous scenes. (Hinchcliffe states that Holmes suggested the casting and mischievously proposes that the author was thinking of a slightly more conventionally-handsome version of himself.)

- Much of the filming for the nightmare sequences took advantage of the school holidays to use a large park within the grounds of a secondary school – but filming began, predictably, in a quarry. You will recall that the location for this, Betchworth Quarry, had been Skaro in "Genesis of the Daleks", but that was a dismal January and this was in the second consecutive dry, hot summer (many days the temperature got to 32° C, about 90° F). Drought conditions kept showers and laundry to a minimum. Bear this in mind for all of Horsfall's heavy costumes and the stagnant pond for the climax of Part Three.

- The shoot began, on Monday 26th July, with the planned end of Part Two, a cliffhanger where the Doctor plummets after a Samurai severs his scarf. Horsfall was in full costume for this and Baker was provided with an experimental new costume for the Doctor, more swashbuckling than professorial – plus a stunt-scarf. His scrambling up the cliff was simply a shallower incline and a tilted camera, then a dummy made the fall. The costumes had to be carefully supervised as the fight, and the Doctor's increasingly battered and bloody clothing, were shot out-of-sequence. (One script-aspect toned down is how badly a bullet injures the Doctor's leg. In the script, it's practically shattered.)

- On Thursday, Peter Day, the other effects designer for this story, rigged calor gas pipes under the surface of the school's pond as Walsh and Maloney set up for the Part Three finale. Edits covered a lot of the doubling work, but if you look hard, you can tell it's Walsh on fire as Goth. The final shot wasn't done there, though, but in the rather more hygienic school swimming bath. Baker was reluctant, as, on holiday in Italy, he'd almost drowned (and before that he'd caught a bug when submerged while filming "The Android Invasion"), but held on for rather longer than we see in the finished version.

Then the camera crew and Horsfall went to Redhill Aerodrome. Horsfall was in the cockpit on the ground, with camera motion to simulate flight, but a professional pilot flew the Stampe biplane for all the aerial shots. (That plane's been around a bit, most famously *Indiana Jones and the Last Crusade*.)

- Maloney's cast included several familiar actors

who had *Who* credentials and lots of other work under their belts. Erik Chitty (Engin), for example, had been in "The Massacre" (3.5), but subsequently became famous as the doddery science teacher in *Please, Sir*. One newcomer was Llewellyn Rees (the President), later seen in *Withnail & I* and *A Fish Called Wanda*, who'd been General Secretary of Equity in World War II. Peter Pratt (the Master), formerly the D'Oyly Carte Company's comic lead, had worked in radio and done occasional television. He knew Roger Delgado socially and was interested in a new direction for the Master, possibly long-term. Helen Blatch, later Commander Fabian in "The Twin Dilemma" (21.7) voiced the information retrieval in Part One and the "King James Version" account of Rassilon's journey in Part Three. George Pravda was back for a third time (5.4, "The Enemy of the World"; 9.4, "The Mutants") and had just been in *The Duchess of Duke Street*.

- The design work continued, but Acheson concluded that the workload on a stretched budget and brief lead-in time was impossible. With no time to bring on a new designer, the assistant, Joan Ellacott, was tasked with finishing the story and got co-credit. As it turned out, Acheson contracted regular outside designer Alistair Bowtell to make the collars and the Master's mask and gloves, meaning Acheson had work doing the glass-fibre construction of the fan-shaped collars.

- Recording began in Studio 3 with the TARDIS scenes and surrounding set. The transduction effect was based on a signal generator built for *Multi-Coloured Swap Shop*. Overnight, the TARDIS set was struck to allow the giant Panopticon set to occupy most of the studio. The extras were corralled into one section of the set, recorded, then moved to another, recorded and finally the remainder. (Some asked for three fees; others appear to have legged it after half a day in the August heat wearing woollen robes and huge fibreglass collars.)

A CSO shot of Baker falling into the Matrix was attempted, but wasn't quite right, so the spiral effect (from General Screen Effects) was applied to the title graphics instead. Murray-Leach decided to re-use the graphic for the Vogan "hawks" ("Revenge of the Cybermen"), and the script was adjusted to make this, rather than a street-light, the target for testing the altered gun-sights. Following this, he devised an alien "scribble" (including a mouse) as the letter the Doctor wrote – due to a misunderstanding, Pravda was handed this to read from instead of the orthodox note. He was slightly flustered, as he'd not bothered to memorise the message because it was written down.

- Pratt was finding the mask uncomfortable. They hoped to have tubes of coloured fluid visibly pulsing across the scabrous skin, but this didn't show up on camera. Considerable thought went into how decrepit and scary the Master was to look – the consensus became to go ahead and assume that any small child watching would have a parent nearby. A graphic slide for the end-credits for Part Four was prepared for a *Man from UNCLE*-style gag: *We thank the Time Lords and the Keeper of the Records for their help and cooperation.* 1

- Simpson contemplated re-using his Master Theme from seasons Eight through Ten, but Hinchcliffe wanted to move the character away from what he thought was a simplistic notion.

- The *Radio Times* spoilered everyone by listing "The Master" in the credits for Part One: even though this had not been proclaimed to the public, it *had* formed a large part of the publicity releases for the press and Drama department internal use. This version – it was made clear – would be masked, a sort of "pupa", rather than a full-blown replacement for Roger Delgado. Nonetheless, when the episode aired, Jon Pertwee was upset, thinking that the intention had been to allude to Delgado's fatal car-crash by showing a burned Master.

- All four episodes were on at five past six, rather later than usual and an hour after the end of *Grandstand*. There was enough time for dads and lads to get back from football matches, but the intervening schedule was more child-friendly (*Tom and Jerry* and *Basil Brush*, plus news, regional news and a brief sports round-up). The night of Part Three was when BBC1 finally showed *The Author of Beltraffio*, the film Baker had made between "Robot" and "The Sontaran Experiment". It was a nuanced Henry James adaptation, directed by Tony Scott and co-produced by his brother Ridley. Both made more profitable films later.

- The last episode went out on 20th November, days before "The Robots of Death" went into the studio. We're so used to thinking of this as "Season Fourteen" that the fact of a six-week gap between the end of this story's transmission and the start of the next ("The Face of Evil" began on

New Year's Day) seems odd, but that's how it was. The original plan had been to show "The Face of Evil" from 27th onwards but circumstances – including trouble with the six-part Victorian adventure – made this impractical.

Instead, over the next two Saturdays, we were given omnibus repeats of "Pyramids of Mars" and "The Brain of Morbius" – then, on 11th December, a dismal Gerry Anderson pilot for a series that never happened: *Into Infinity* (written by Johnny Byrne of 18.6, "The Keeper of Traken"). The "Brain of Morbius" repeat occasioned a snide hatchet-piece by Jean Rook of *The Daily Express*, a lowbrow paper best known for the twee *Rupert Bear* strip. This piece bitched about Holmes and the series as a whole, adding to the sense that the Series and Serials department had to be seen to do something about the "menace" of *Doctor Who*. After the weird brouhaha over "The Seeds of Doom", Mary Whitehouse and her self-styled "National Viewers and Listeners' Association" were making noises. In a speech in April, she had targeted the series as Public Enemy Number One.

Something rarely mentioned when this topic comes up is that a few days before Part Three was shown, an enormous stink erupted over the end of an episode of *I, Claudius*. On 8th November, Part Eight ("Zeus, By Jove") took an element of the original novel and turbo-charged it. Emperor Caligula (John Hurt), thinking himself a god, starts following mythological storylines. After impregnating his sister, Drusilla, he realises that the spawn of gods tended to kill their fathers – so he decides to get there first and eat the foetus, as Zeus did. The version originally transmitted was the third edit, but this was *still* too shocking for many viewers, so the repeat later that week simply showed Claudius (Derek Jacobi) recoiling in horror from something unseen. The master tapes had been wiped, and the edit now available is thought to be the only one. So there was a precedent for what happened to "The Deadly Assassin". From a BBC managerial perspective, a simple solution presented itself when, inevitably, Whitehouse got on her hind legs about the freeze-frame of the Doctor's head under water.

Hinchcliffe thought an edited version of the shot was acceptable – but, days before broadcast, Bill Slater asked for a trim, so the freeze-frame ending was used. Whitehouse claimed that children aspired to do this to their siblings at bath time (we have no evidence that she knew of any such real incident) and wrote to Charles Curran, Director General of the BBC. He took the unprecedented step of replying to this and claimed that, while he had sanctioned the broadcast as it was, in retrospect he might have been more cautious.

With the press – mysteriously – aware of all of this, she claimed victory. (Curiously, when Hinchcliffe appeared on daytime chat show *Pebble Mill at One* – see "Horror of Fang Rock" – to promote *Whose Doctor Who* just before Easter 1977, they showed the clip uncut just ahead of *Trumpton*, aimed at the under-fives, during a school holiday. Nobody complained.) Anyone thinking that this sort of prissiness wouldn't happen in the BBC ranks now might wish to contemplate how X8.3, "Robot of Sherwood" lost a crucial shot of the android Sheriff being decapitated – without which, the rest of the episode is even more confused – after ISIS executed an English engineer earlier that week. The scene was wiped before broadcast; it's not even a DVD extra.

• Graham Williams, in interviews, said he started shadowing Hinchcliffe in "July" and shortly thereafter attended a studio session. From what other people say, it was likely during this story. Granted, if you asked any two relevant people what was going on, you'd've got three different answers – but, from assessing all the statements made, we've almost got a plausible timeline for how a former *Z Cars* script-editor replaced Hinchcliffe and whose idea it was.

Hinchcliffe once claimed that he was introduced to Williams as his "replacement" backstage at the Panopticon set. This can't be entirely right, as the decision wasn't formally taken until Williams was interviewed and presented his peculiar document outlining the Key to Time concept for a year-long storyline (see 16.1, "The Ribos Operation" and various **Lore** entries for Season Fifteen). During the studio sessions for this story (or possibly the last), Williams was along for the ride – feeling, as he later said, like a visitor from the Stone Age.

We'll enlarge on this as we go, mainly under "The Invisible Enemy", but the thing to note right now is that, contrary to what's often reported elsewhere, Williams *wasn't* parachuted-in as a response to the broadcast of this story. If nothing else, the usual story of how Tom Baker found out is during pre-filming for "The Robots of Death" on 2nd November, the Tuesday after Part One aired. So, unless Mary Whitehouse's claim that children unable to tell a freeze-frame from reality means someone was traumatised by the Time Lord

President hovering in mid-fall for a week, this doesn't tally.

• Meanwhile, another self-important group of viewers was also irate over the story. The newly-formed *Doctor Who* Appreciation Society grumbled about the lack of respect the Time Lords were given compared to how they'd imagined Gallifrey. Jan Vincent Rudski, in *TARDIS*, bemoaned the story's lack of awe (in block capitals: WHAT HAS HAPPENED TO THE MAGIC OF DOCTOR WHO?) and, in the end-of-season poll, it came last. ("The Talons of Weng-Chiang", Holmes's other script that year, came top. Your mileage may vary.)

• James Acheson ran away to join the circus. Or, at least, manage an ice-circus in Spain. He was art director on *Sir Henry at Rawlinson End* (a film with a lower budget than *Doctor Who*), then returned to costumes for *Time Bandits* and subsequent *Python*-related movies, including *Brazil*. He eventually won three Oscars for costume design (*The Last Emperor*, which also got him a BAFTA, *Dangerous Liaisons* and *Restoration*). He worked continuously thereafter, specialising in superhero movies between 2001 and 2015 and retired after one last Terry Jones film, *Absolutely Anything*.

• The repeat, over the following summer, got some of the lowest viewing figures ever for a BBC1 *Doctor Who* transmission. Part of this was the result of the programme on immediately after it, a supposedly child-friendly science series called *The Whole Universe Show* that was patronising and factually wrong. Part Two, only surpassed by an unannounced repeat of "Pyramids of Mars" in 1994 on Sunday mornings, was sandwiched between this and a *Nationwide* mini-episode where Richard Stilgoe did DIY and performed tedious comic songs about it. It was also opposite *Crossroads* in most regions.

14.4: "The Face of Evil"

(Serial 4Q, 4 Episodes, 1st – 22nd January 1977.)

Which One is This? A near-omnipotent computer gets delusions of grandeur – it thinks it's Tom Baker.

Firsts and Lasts Enter Leela, as different a companion from Sarah as could be imagined; for her, "Women's Lib" isn't just theory. Playing her, Louise Jameson breaks the mould of *Doctor Who* girls by being more employable after this than before. Pennant Roberts, the one director to have worked on the series in the 70s and 80s, starts here. For once, he has a script he doesn't need to salvage.

This is the first story where the Inlay operator's contribution is so great, a new credit of "Electronic Effects" is used for Dave Chapman. Mat Irvine is promoted to full Special Effects designer and starts appearing on *Swap Shop*. This is the first story to use a competition-winning child in the cast (cf. X3.11, "Utopia"), thus it's the first use of a non-Equity member in a (scripted) speaking-role (as opposed to random taxi-drivers asking for fares).

We have the last two appearances of a space-helmet that's been a constant since 3.2, "Mission to the Unknown", and the first use of the "move it a second ahead in time to hide it" idea (see, for example, X4.12, "The Stolen Earth").

It might seem like a fiddly point, but it reflects bigger changes coming: the end credits have the date in Roman numerals rather than Arabic (so "MCMLXXVI" rather than "1976"), because it was not shown until New Year's Day 1977, after which all BBC productions were dated thus. The BBC Drama department was about to have one of its periodic upheavals; *Doctor Who* would be caught up in the mess.

Scriptwriter Chris Boucher makes his debut here. Among other things, he is the first writer to have grown up in the 1950s rather than pre-war. Of the key people currently making *Doctor Who*, only Philip Hinchcliffe is approximately the same age. In fact, this story was the last remaining pre-1990 story from which the producer, writer, director and regulars were all still alive.

Four Things to Notice About "The Face of Evil"...

• In his memoir, Tom Baker muddled this one up with "Planet of Evil". There are grounds for this: they both take a lot of inspiration from *Forbidden Planet*; they are studio-bound but set on jungle planets with Formica spaceships; they have similar names. But in that one, the menfolk wore track-suits; in this one, half of them wear Victorian acrobat costumes and the others wear stubble and fake tan (and a bit of chamois-leather here and there). And this is the one with a Mount Rushmore-style Doctor-head carved into a hillside. And an amusing Production-Code.

• But with all the violence going on, the most memorable stand-off is when the Doctor bluffs

The Face of Evil 14.4

Was This an SF Series?

Lately, we've been getting a lot of up-themselves Booker winners and Nobel Laureates writing about clones, self-aware software, dystopias and other planets. When asked, they clutch their pearls at the idea that their novels are in any way "Science Fiction". They're right – their ponderous works that the posh critics say "transcend the genre" are lousy at doing what SF does, despite raiding the toybox of old ideas. Most of their efforts end up with clumsy info-dumps delivering self-contradictory backstories that would be laughed at if submitted to an SF editor under a pseudonym. They get a free pass.

Once in a while, a newspaper columnist will make the breathtaking discovery that things have changed since the 1940s and patiently explain that it's not all superheroes and space-monsters, then things will go back to normal. Every five years, you'll get a similarly breathless attempt to explain Afrofuturism as a breakthrough or that there's a new female or non-cisgender author making a stand against the tired racist, sexist "usual" SF – and then someone will point out how often we've been here since around 1953.

Then the posh critics will drone about how it could never be like "proper" writing because it's a "genre" – although, of course, self-styled "Literary Fiction" is no such thing. Then they'll use some nineteenth-century definition of "good" writing to denounce SF's "typical" prose, on the my-kid-could-do better principle previously deployed against Picasso, Kandinsky or Rothko, as if the same apparent shortcoming wasn't also there as a deliberate choice in DH Lawrence, Samuel Beckett or Gertrude Stein. Not that they ever actually cite examples of these supposed deficiencies – it's taken as read, literally.

This wasn't always the case. In what we'll call, for want of a better term, the Space Age (a subset of the Cold War era also including the Permissive Society, LPs and Pop Art), Britain, France and some bits of America treated SF authors as people with their fingers on the pulse of a rapidly-changing world. Especially those authors with reputable "literary" works in print and Friends in High Places. Kingsley Amis issued a condescending book, *New Maps of Hell*, treating it like a sort of Outsider Art written by idiot-savants – but his chum Brian Aldiss was on *Late Night Line Up* and eventually landed up as a Booker judge. Michael Moorcock's *New Worlds* got an Arts Council grant (outraging Tory back-benchers for the usual Mary Whitehouse reasons), and a lot of American writers came to London and then, eventually, returned and took up University posts – or made a point of not doing so.

A window of opportunity opened, with all those Butler Act students from working-class backgrounds getting into the brand-name universities, when people who'd grown up reading SF were making a case for it as a legitimate approach to fiction. America had a similar, parallel, movement and – although the two "New Waves" started from different places – they cross-pollinated. Publishers took note and (mostly) gave authors the legroom such an approach allowed and usually demanded.

On the whole, within the community of "proper" SF writers and readers, *Doctor Who* was a bit of a joke. Ordinarily, there was a bit of a gulf between the sententious pipe-smoking authors whose opinions were sought by BBC2 or the Sunday Papers, and the kiddy-friendly monster-movies and cartoons. In 1977, things were rather different, though: the *cognoscenti* were, for a while, happy to include a mass-audience family show along with their Terribly Serious Art.

What was going on? Answering that's going to involve most of you forgetting what you think you know about the topic. Forget things happening on screen; forget the confusing use of "science" or, for most purposes, the name "science fiction"; forget "genre". We're talking about a game between readers and authors and how it influenced wider popular culture, culminating in the early 1970s – and how *Doctor Who* briefly became the focal-point.

We'll clarify as we go but we'll start with a practical example. In 2014, Darren Aronovsky put out a film called *Noah* which (as you might expect) is about a bloke who builds a big wooden boat to save all life on Earth from a flood that God's told him is coming. This was soon out on DVD and the majority of shops plonked it on a shelf called "Sci-Fi".

That term was coined by prize numpty Forrest Ackerman, publisher of *Famous Monsters of Film Land*. Most people who write or read SF reject it (and are embarrassed by him and his other activities, which are the source of most media representations of overweight geeks with no perspective or social skills), but it's been handy for people trying to sell junk to a targeted audience (or "demographic", as they call the rubes now). It's also handy

continued on page 315…

14.4 The Face of Evil

armed assailants with a jelly-baby: then someone calls his bluff and he eats the sweet himself, saying "I don't take orders from anyone". This wasn't scripted.

- In the course of four episodes, we get some fairly complex discussions about the nature of faith and the use of religion as a form of social conditioning. This would perhaps have carried more weight if the Tribe of Sevateem could decide from one scene to the next how to pronounce their god's name: "Xoanon".

- Opinions will always vary, but the end of Part Three is a strong candidate for "Most Disturbing Cliffhanger". As the Doctor is psychically cudgelled by the multiple minds of Xoanon, three large images of his own face fill giant screens with a child's voice wailing "who am I?" Not only is it an unsettling image, but compared to someone pulling a gun on the Doctor, it's hard to see either how he'd get out of it or how you'd explain what's going on to a four-year-old.

The Continuity

The Doctor seems to have recovered his old clothes [see "The Deadly Assassin"], but kept the boots he picked up on Gallifrey. He tied a knot in his hankie to remind him to do something [possibly check up on the Mordee expedition], as he finds when he goes to add one to realign the TARDIS tracers. He forgot all about Xoanon [at least consciously: when the name comes up, he asks 'what's those?' as if dimly aware of a multiple entity of that name]. He says he's never met anyone called "Leela" before. He seems to think that Rudyard Kipling and Gertrude Stein are roughly interchangeable. He whistles the same bit of Mozart he hummed when bound up in Antarctica ["The Seeds of Doom"], as well as "Colonel Bogey".

- *Background.* At some point in his current life, the Doctor happened upon a colony ship with a malfunctioning computer and offered assistance. It went wrong because the 'malfunction' was the computer achieving consciousness and his attempted cure was a patch using his own mind. [Precisely when this happened is unclear. Terrance Dicks's novelisation suggests that the Doctor woke up in the night during Part Two of "Robot" and nipped off in the TARDIS while still not entirely in his right mind. It's hard to see when else he was alone and that reckless before his rather chastening experience with the Mandragora Helix.]

Whenever he did encounter Xoanon, he attended at least one dinner party thrown by the computer. He's seen Tri-Psi projections done as a "parlour-trick". He recognises a Starfall Seven space-suit [the helmet is such a regular feature of so many previous costumes, it's possible we have also seen it]. He imprinted his brain-pattern on the computer, something that seems fairly easy in the UNIT period ["Robot"; 10.5, "The Green Death"] and appears to have a ready method for uninstalling this within a few minutes, although that leaves him unconscious for two days afterwards.

He claims he took archery lessons from William Tell. [That's about as likely as meeting Paul Bunyan or Robin Hood; see X8.3, "Robot of Sherwood". However, most of the early efforts to disprove the Tell legend were by Renaissance descendants of the same Hapsburgs being resisted when the Swiss Confederacy was formed in 1291, shortly before the 1307 date usually ascribed to Tell's non-filicide. So if such a person existed, perhaps the Doctor helped foster the legend *and* removed the evidence. (See also **Whom Did They Meet at the Roof of the World?** under 1.4, "Marco Polo" for another instance of a wildly divergent historical record and popular myth.)]

- *Ethics.* Broadly sound, and yet he punishes a stroppy guard who's slapped Leela by flipping a vicious Horda onto the man's shoulder. [Admittedly, he aims for the leather epaulette rather than the abundant flesh on display, but it's a curiously sadistic moment.

[This matters, because the whole situation on this planet results from the Doctor's mind interfacing with that of a powerful machine, so we have to wonder how much of the grim eugenics experiment and mind-control is his doing. Consciously, this Doctor is appalled at the way things have gone, and puts his life in jeopardy to help restore some kind of balance. Yet neither the Tesh's bloodless vivisection nor the Sevateem's barbarity is entirely at odds with things he's done recently to resolve nasty situations. There's no getting around it: everything that happened on this planet, all the death and enforced ignorance, is indirectly his doing.]

At the individual level, he is more his normal self and berates Leela for reflexively killing her own tribesmen. He is appalled when the Tesh want to vaporise Leela for particle analysis. When

Was This an SF Series?

...continued from page 313

for telling whether the person talking knows anything about what they are (usually) dismissing to an equally out-of-the-loop audience – if they call it "sci-fi", they probably don't. These people think about "genre" as a solid entity (rather than as a sales-pitch, which is what those DVD shelving decisions are about) based on content. Some, if they take a second to ponder various examples they've encountered on telly or at the pictures, start thinking about symbols and attempt to systematise those.

Most of the symbols are second-hand and, in other things sold as cinematic genres, come in clusters. A Western can include: gunfights; steam-trains; Indians; cowboys; saloons; stage-coaches; John Wayne; badly-dubbed Italian actors; a harmonica on the soundtrack; horses... but no one film has all of these. Not every film with any one or more is a Western (the 1973 *Westworld* isn't but has as many of these as any "legit" oater). As a rule of thumb, though, it's a good start. Any drama with a handful of these that isn't explicitly a Western is making a point about Westerns or genre-boundaries. (*Westworld* has androids going berserk in theme-park representations of history that are about wish-fulfilment without consequences; the mythic west is a daydream of literally getting away with murder, not having orthodox responsibilities and getting out unscathed because you're the "good guy".) One can argue that Westerns are really "about" the dialectic of frontier values and European ones but giving people Stetsons and Colt 45s makes that somehow different from a similar story set in any other place and/or time (where an identical plot and incidents would be read as "Imperialist"). The iconography alters the reception the story gets. Not every commercial genre is as clear-cut, though.

Whether or not you accept the premise that there are separate things called SF and Sci-Fi, you probably have your own check-list of similar symbolic items to look for and decide how to approach a work with some of them in. Are any of these defining characteristics?

A moment's thought makes that idea look silly. There are few people prepared to expend a moment's thought. Any hard-and-fast content-rule as a way to tell SF from anything else will almost immediately fall apart. "Anything with spaceships in" means that historical dramas such as *Goodbye Lenin* and *Apollo 13* would be SF. A lot of things that manifestly belong in SF have no space-travel. Androids show up a lot in allegories about Civil Rights where nothing else has changed the way it inevitably would, but that's about as close to an example as we can get and it barely covers a fraction of what SF can be. Pop into libraries across Britain or America and look at what pictures they stick on the spines to ghettoise the books – after a while, collecting each goofy graphic and adding it to a pile becomes like stamp-collecting.

In fact, it's ridiculously hard to make any general "definition" stick, and attempting to do it misses the point, for reasons we'll illustrate in detail later. There's another problem we have to wrestle with first, this habit of thinking of SF as a "genre" at all. (That one's compounded by people who do it for a living using the word "genre" loosely to people from outside, although it's less common this century. Aldiss was a repeat offender until someone explained it to him.) A genre, to publishers and motion picture distributors, is a marketing tool. Audiences sometimes follow suit.

Musicals are a genre. Revenge-dramas are a genre. Dramatic monologues are a genre. They aren't mutually-exclusive, and people can take or leave any specimen as they please, rather than thinking they *must* enjoy any example of the form equally (although some people do, apparently). Comedy is a genre, but nobody likes equally all things labelled as "comedy" – if any genre creates things that seem like personal affronts to the people who get off on being affronted, it's that one.

But fundamentally, a genre is about the approach to the subject-matter rather than a tickbox of plot-beats or set-pieces. Whose approach? The people making it may have different ideas about what they're doing than the people on the receiving end (especially if it's a film and the studio interferes). The bigger the audience, the more possible receptions any work can get, not all of them intended. So rather than start with pompous declarations (or quote other people's) about "speculation" or "tools" or "problem-solving", or going in for the usual history-lessons about Lucien of Samothrace or Hugo Gernsback, let's focus on the reception and who's doing it, then come back to this stuff.

The most helpful working description, or at least ring-fence, of SF is "a conversation that's been

continued on page 317...

needs must, he thinks nothing of impersonating a god. When a Tesh guard tries to kill him under hypnosis, he only reluctantly fights back, his technique sending the guy into an electrified wall.

His concern for the planet's population is at least partly guilt at his mistake, partly concern for his own survival, but mainly worry that his return has precipitated a possible massacre. Later on, he also seems worried for Xoanon as an individual in torment.

• *Inventory:*
– *Sonic Screwdriver.* Apart from jury-rigging a mind-wipe, the screwdriver emits a low-frequency burst that, when combined with an icosahedral blue crystal, emits an oscillating tone that overcomes Leela's temporary possession by Xoanon.

– *Other.* He uses a jelly-baby to disarm an attacker and offers one to Leela when they first meet. He has a pocket mirror handy. There's also a clockwork egg-timer, along the lines of an alarm clock but with a four-minute cycle and a loud pair of bells on top. And there's a coin he can chuck at a wall to test for a charge [cf 11.3, "Death to the Daleks"].

At the end, Leela opens a chocolate in a foil wrapper from a sealed plastic tub. [As broadcast, these look like the Doctor's, but see **The Lore**.] When building a Tesh gun for the Sevateem, he produces a variety of tools that he may have found in a box or had on his person.

The TARDIS seems to have taken a shine to Leela. [We'll elaborate in 15.2, "The Invisible Enemy" and 15.3, "Image of the Fendahl", but the way Leela can just run in and operate a control seems, with hindsight, as if the TARDIS "recruited" her. (See also **Who Decides What Makes a Companion?** under 21.5, "Planet of Fire" and **Are Steven and Dodo Related?** under 3.5, "The Massacre".)]

The tracers need an overhaul, as the Doctor thinks missing Hyde Park results from a 'nexial discontinuity'. ['Nexial' suggests the 'causal nexus' mentioned in stories such as "Logopolis" (18.7), so either this is a conjectural future that might not happen – although to the TARDIS, all timelines are potentially "soft" – or there's something timey-wimey afoot. The details of this planet's backstory don't match any story in Earth's far future, so it could be a blind-alley compared to, say, "The Ark in Space" and "Planet of Evil" (clearly intended to be in the same future as each other).

But, as we'll discuss in "The Invisible Enemy", there's a strong hint of a Bootstrap Paradox about Leela's ancestry. In which case, perhaps the TARDIS *needed* to come there to cause this, as with the odd times it chose to deliver messages (X4.6, "The Doctor's Daughter"; X4.8, "Silence in the Library") and the whole business with Wimbledon Common ("The Massacre"). Considering that Leela's ancestors left Earth in the fifty-first century, making them roughly contemporary with River Song, this could be part of something fairly big we're not being told about. See **What's So Great About the 51st Century?** under X1.9, "The Empty Child" and our discussion of Time Agents under "The Talons of Weng-Chiang" in a few pages from now.]

The Supporting Cast
• **Leela** seems superficially like Sarah: the same apparent age and build with slightly lighter hair and slightly darker skin, plus very dark eyes. She is not noticeably more muscular than Sarah [although "The Talons of Wang-Chiang" intimates she has arm-muscles 'like a horse'].

Although she is persistently fearless, belligerent, supremely self-confident and capable, her first scene demonstrates chinks in her armour. She maintains her denial that Xoanon exists, even when it gets her sentenced to the ordeal of the Horda, but immediately recants when her father, Sole, takes the test for her. He dies in agony; from then on, Leela seems to fear nothing. Her apostasy is itself overturned when she meets and aids the Doctor, who looks like The Evil One. She eventually chats with Xoanon himself.

She is proficient with the crossbow and a dagger and carries Janis thorns that at first paralyse her opponents, then kills them slowly. She sees nothing wrong with first-use of weapons. Even after a Janis thorn nearly kills her, she ignores the Doctor's prohibitions on their use.

Her speech is slightly stilted, with few contractions [but has a wider vocabulary than the "Me Tarzan/ Kimo Sabe" stuff one might expect in a different series]. She can use a term such as 'a guarded truce'.

As most people know, she wears slightly more than the Sevateem men, but slightly less than Jo Grant would. Her usual outfit is a sort of suede swimsuit with buskins, plus a few beaded bracelets and a similar necklace. Unlike the only other Sevateem woman we see, she wears her hair loose.

Was This an SF Series?

...continued from page 315

going on since 1926". In 2021, this is easier to use with newcomers, because that word "conversation" currently extends to things like "Me Too" and "Black Lives Matter", but let's stay with the 95-year huddle that people mistake for a genre. People have dropped in, left, come back after joining other conversations and bitched about Those People Over There. The topic's shifted around a lot and split off into smaller groups, some of whose members never rejoin and some of these groups aren't talking to the others at the moment. Nonetheless, anyone who's spent time in the huddle has picked up a few habits of thought, short-hand terms and likes or dislikes and this will carry over into other spaces. Those perspectives and tendencies are what we ought to be looking at first.

[And, yes, this does sound like how communities on social media behave and self-regulate, just with a 70-year head-start and with letter-columns, shared houses, fanzines and conventions instead of digital technology. Most of the house-rules were in place before America joined World War II. Read the various memoirs of the "Futurians", a particularly heated gang in New York in the late 30s, for the first flame-wars. Anyone taking bets on Netflix or HBO doing a drama about this?]

The main thing to bear in mind is that, no matter the medium or technology being used, the whole basis of the conversation is the prose. SF is primarily novels and short stories. This is where almost all of the toybox of imaginary mechanisms or phenomena came from – even if people who now make billion-dollar franchises out of a sort of fair-use policy about robots, time-machines, alternate histories or impossibly fast spaceships don't know this (or pretend not to when any lawyers are around).

That prose was, originally, in magazine form. Not pulps, though: the stuff Gernsback printed wasn't even up to that standard (unless he pilfered it from countries with different copyright laws) and he didn't pay enough. Once there was a market, the major magazine companies raised the bar and his clumsy label "Scientifiction" first became "Science Fiction" and then got retroactively used to identify previous works. Like "Swedish Fish" (a strawberry-flavoured corn-syrup jelly sweet containing no fish, unheard-of in Sweden), this label is massively misleading to the newcomer, but we'll get to that.

The thing is: it was a way for people to join the conversation and, before too long, that meant writing their own stories with more of the things they liked and less of the hackwork done by professional writers more used to Westerns or pirate stories. There was a vocabulary of items (spaceships, robots, time-paradoxes...) and a grammar of how to parse a story with these things in them. The vocabulary is easy to spot – especially on the covers of those magazines – but the grammar took a while to develop and takes each newcomer a while to get the hang of.

But – and this is the root cause of a lot of problems you'll recognise – the cover-art wasn't always such a great help. It's interesting how much crossover there was with musicals in this regard. As we discussed in X3.4, "Daleks in Manhattan", the huge city-scapes are a feature of Fred and Ginger's escapades in Van Nest Polgase's huge Modernist spaces and the sets for *42nd Street* and *Gold Diggers of 1935*; the brass bikinis that exercise Margaret Atwood so often are originally from *Gold Diggers of 1933* ("Petting in the Park" looks like an anthology of late-30s *Amazing Stories* covers); those enormous machines in Frank R Paul's primary-coloured images are suspiciously like the monochrome impressions of steam-ships and their engines in *Follow the Fleet* and *Shall We Dance*.

This, in turn, is out there in the design of the time. Look at Piccadilly Line tube stations and the London Transport posters advertising days out then. Look at seaside towns that had a lot of investment in the 1930s. The four-colour artwork simply exaggerated that trend and put Saturn in the sky over it. What's interesting about this parallel development of iconography and prose is that the former is so much more portable, so it could be collaged by Hollywood in among the other out-there sets, props and costumes repurposed for chapterplays. People who'd never heard of the authors who were rapidly developing a wholly separate set of ground-rules and interpretative habits could cut-and-paste these jumbles and pass it off on kids. That's where Ackerman and his ilk come in and how George Lucas bilked everyone.

Books and degree-courses exist to detail the inner working of the feverish feedback-loop of readers and writers, even as the outside world was watching Buster Crabbe (and, let's be honest, the SF kids were too, even as they were reading

continued on page 319...

14.4 The Face of Evil

The Non-Humans

- *Xoanon* is a freakishly powerful computer, capable of manifesting psychic "beasts" at a distance and materialising chairs and gramophones. It can control the minds of large numbers of people at once. Within the confines of the Mordee ship, it can see everything and manipulate all the systems – but outside the time-barrier, it can override the subsonic barriers keeping its invisible servants from entering the Sevateem village, trap people in shafts of light from above and contact the High Priest, Neeva, via a sub-space radio. The main control, on Level 37, is a seemingly empty chamber with several wall-sized monitor screens in an octagon around a spherical glass terminal.

Unfortunately, the birth of this puissant entity was mistaken for a malfunction. The Doctor, who happened to be passing, "repaired" it by imprinting a copy of his mind as an ad hoc operating system, overlaying it on an already-developing personality. The conflict caused by this created a chorus of Xoanon-voices: one female; one adult male; one a child and one the Doctor. By way of a self-induced therapy, the computer landed the ship on a hostile planet and raised the stakes for the Survey Team and technicians, selectively breeding the former for aggression and physical prowess and the latter for mental powers. These became the Sevateem and the Tesh, hunters in the wild and priests within the ship. The psychic demons sent to harass the Sevateem are invisible but, when hit by ray-guns, look like the Doctor's snarling face.

The healed Xoanon has a bit of a sense of humour, laughing at the Doctor's mock-indignation and providing a late nineteenth-century chaise-longue for the Doctor. It seemingly offers the Tesh and the Seveteem a self-destruct button, to prove its good faith, but they decline.

Planet Notes The sky on this unnamed planet is dark red. The abundant jungle is the usual green, with what looks like Earth-normal daylight. According to Leela, this is the whole of their world: this jungle and the Place of Land behind the mountain with the Evil One's face carved into it. There seems to be some kind of animal life, as Andor speaks of "game" and they've all got leather clothes. [Admittedly not *much* clothing, so it can't be too cold. Without goosebumps, we'll assume an ambient temperature of about 20°C.] It does seem to get misty at night [we'll assume just the one sun although the sky's almost the same colour at night]. The soil's rather sandy, so they probably don't farm much.

Native life includes a nasty sort of land-piranha called a Horda, with a lateral mandible like an insect [i.e. scissors instead of a mouth] but with teeth; this thing 'can strip the flesh off a man's arm before he has time to cry out'. [Not that a Sevateem man would do anything as wimpy as crying out.] These move with a fish-like motion and look like blue and red Cybermats [5.1, "The Tomb of the Cybermen"]. The Janis Thorn, another unpleasant local specimen, can immobilise instantly and is said to bring death within about 30 seconds.

Among the Sevateem, proxies are allowed for those accused of crimes – Sole takes the test of the Horda on Leela's behalf, and when he dies while doing so, she's banished. The Sevateem know how long a second is.

Even when Xoanon is cured, the land is filled with noises and sounds very like every other space-jungle we've been on since Kembel [3.2, "Mission to the Unknown"] except Zeta Minor ["Planet of Evil"].

The Tesh have a story of the Lord of Time returning to free them and bring perfect communion with Xoanon; the Sevateem have an Evil One who imprisoned their god. The Tesh live in a spaceship within what looks like an impact crater, in a zone a second out of phase with the rest of the planet. When making visits to the rest of their world, they wear spacesuits (identified as Starfall Seven model) to avoid infection [so there may be native bacteria and viruses that affected some humans].

History

- *Dating*. ["The Invisible Enemy" stipulates that Leela's ancestors left Earth around 5000 AD, but a few steps seem to exist between The Great Break Out and the Mordee Expedition. There's nothing remotely like Xoanon in any sixth millennium story we have ever seen.]

It's at least three generations since the ship landed [if the record of previous failed assaults on the Evil One is right, seven previous goes, the last remembered by the "old ones", it might mean seven generations or about 200 terrestrial years]. The knives and crossbows indicate some degree of metalworking, although these seem to be heirlooms.

Was This an SF Series?

...continued from page 317

"respectable" fiction and each other's work). The dates of the vocabulary are well-known, but the grammar, and how to apply it, snuck up on everyone. Tracing that process has been tricky.

For our purposes, though, it's quicker if we illustrate with an analogy. Suppose, for a moment, that it were possible to grow up with no idea when Jane Austen was alive, and that there was an edition of her work without any of the shedloads of notes, analyses or pictures from endless film and television adaptations. How would someone in the loop of this 95-year conversation, able to do the SF-habitual interpretation, react to *Persuasion* (1817)? Well, the first thing they'd do that anyone else wouldn't is simply plough on and make mental note of the unfamiliar terms, hoping that context or later developments would illuminate them. They wouldn't flip through an encyclopaedia or use any online trainer-wheels. The characters all seem to know the difference between a *barouche*, a *chaise*, a *curricle* and a *gig* are, so the differences matter within the story's world, and these things all seem to be wheeled vehicles. (Austen omits any mention of what powers them, but when someone sends a "chair" for Anne, other people get involved, not just a driver.) Everyone in this world spends a lot of time either indoors, looking mournfully out of windows, or in enclosed carriages. Anne walking outside in Bath is treated as if she were streaking, and a day out in the country is handled like the Normandy landings.

What's happened to make the world like this? Let's read on and look for evidence that might resolve this. Captain Wentworth made a lot of money out of a war somewhere; he's treated with awe and suspicion alike for having a suntan. Anne is treated as if she's at death's door because she's all of 28 years old. (The place-names are familiar, so it's unlikely to be anywhere that has a longer year than ours.) The book opens with Anne's father reading up on family trees as if they were studbooks. Sir Walter treats freckles as proof of moral bankruptcy and seems more concerned with genetics than income. Yet Wentworth was discarded as a possible match for Anne because he had insufficiently-impressive contacts.

What do people do in this world?[48] Country dancing looms large. Nobody seems to earn money by conventional means, but Sir Walter's difficulty with maintaining Kellynch (apparently a fortress, sans retainers or servants) is treated as unusual. Bath is affordable, more so the further downhill you get, but society judges one by how close the house is to something called a "Pump-Room". (It's possible that our reader might know about that already, if they're British, but it might, at a pinch, be some kind of air-filtration or water-purification).

War is lucrative, but it's over. The only casualty is the wastrel son of a comic-relief widow, but the end of hostilities seems to have adversely affected the economy. Sir Walter is trying to offload his daughters on the open market – not just to cut his own overheads, but to raise his personal kudos. There's a sort of reputation-economy, like Russian *Blat* or Chinese *Guanxi*. The main trade seems to be information, especially (within this community) about potential suitors. However, for plot reasons, Anne bypasses this commerce by an apparent psychic ability to see through people's performance of status to assess long-term worth (in a subplot with a distant cousin, Mr Eliot, who triggers her Spidey-sense three chapters before any evidence arrives). It's like reading the stock-exchange; confirmation of this similarity comes when Wentworth suffers a setback and she starts noticing him again, as if buying low to sell high.

Our hypothetical naïve reader might have a working hypothesis of a post-holocaust world where bloodlines are a commodity, but with an informal social network rather than some sort of DNA-matching central authority. Anne was taken off the market for some kind of mental instability, but the second-oldest daughter let Sir Walter use her as a breed-mare without checking for compatibility and that sort of backfired too. With no information other than the words on the page, it's hard to work out exactly what all the terms mean ("an Admiral of the White"... anyone... anyone...?), but it's possible to derive a good-enough rationale for everything that's there.

Earnest Janeites probably wouldn't accept this as the book's real value, but it accounts for all the character-dynamics (and the ways character is jettisoned once a person achieves the "correct" social status). This "strong misreading"[49] doesn't do violence to the book and, in some ways, gets the reader closer to what people in 1820 would have made of it than simply watching a BBC adaptation and cooing over the crinolines – or watching *Bridgerton* – as though it were historically-based. (If you were studying Austen in the 70s or 80s, you

continued on page 321...

14.4 The Face of Evil

Their ancestors appear to have salvaged some things from the crash, including a pilot's seat, a Starfall Seven spacesuit and medical equipment. [A cut scene includes the survival rations, the "chocolate" Leela helps herself to at the end.]

The Analysis

Where Does This Come From? This is another example of interviews obscuring as much as they reveal. When the makers discuss Leela, we get a lot of chat about Raquel Welsh in *One Million Years BC*, but not a sausage about Linda Harrison. Yet any discussion of this story without *Planet of the Apes* and, more explicitly, *Beneath the Planet of the Apes* is like pretending that "The Brain of Morbius" had nothing to do with Boris Karloff. Even if the basic premise of a hunted man who knows what things used to be like and works out what went wrong isn't unique, the shot of Charlton Heston falling through a hologram wall that seems to be a solid cliff-face might strike you as familiar.

Behind this is a race of psychic mutants who wear tight hoods and monastic robes, using their mental powers to make their enemies fight each other and worshipping leftover technology (in this case, an atomic warhead). This all happens in the "Forbidden Zone" and when the Apes find that Taylor (Heston) got in, they attack en masse, through the ruins of New York. Joining Taylor is another Astronaut, played by James Franciscus, so we get info-dumps galore for anyone new to this and someone other than Chuck wearing a leather loincloth and stubble. There are clear precedents in this film for the Sevateem, the Tesh, the residual guilt over causing this whole dysfunctional world and all the pseudo-religious iconography. So Harrison, as "Nova", the silent love-interest for Heston last time around, is at least as plausible a template for a savage warrior-woman in a leather swimsuit as any other.

But, as we just said, the idea of a ruined Earth spawning religions based on twentieth-century leftovers was hardly novel. We've mentioned a trend in SF novels positing post-apocalyptic societies with garbled versions of our culture treated as religions (and, under the last story, cited *A Canticle for Leibowitz* as the most prominent example). We could also remind everyone that the one SF author everyone had heard of, Isaac Asimov, had reworked Gibbon's *Decline and Fall* into the *Foundation* stories and allegorised the Dark Ages as lots of backwoods planets worshipping leftover tech and a pseudo-monastic R&D department.

The flip-side of this was the anthropological concept of the "Cargo Cult": an isolated community reacting to visits from more technological societies by imitating the "miraculous" aircraft or medicines in hope of a return visit. Enough versions of this idea percolate in 50s books and magazines for it to be almost a given and, when combined with the quasi-religious awe (and very familiar patterns of behaviour) surrounding the whole Flying Saucer mania, looked as if our own culture could have been influenced by something like that and misconstrued as the work of a deity. Erich Von Daniken cleaned up on this, and lots of wannabes got into print with similar spurious notions. One of these, oddly enough, was Andrew Tomas, who proposed that the last Ice Age was caused by Atlantis blocking the Gulf Stream. Leela's ally being named "Tomas" might be coincidence, but with a star called "Tom", you don't arbitrarily put in a name like that.

The idea of aliens posing as gods or being misconstrued as such is almost as old as SF (see the comments on "Pyramids of Mars" about Stanley Weinbaum) and was part of the paranoid appeal of Charles Fort's stories (Boucher would make a return visit to "we are property" territory in "Image of the Fendahl"). Taking an outsider's view of human hubris and belittling our achievements was the downside of the same "sense of wonder" that was the twentieth century's downmarket take on the Romantic Sublime. Back in the 1950s, Brian Aldiss coined the term "shaggy god story" for this sort of narrative.

However, the lost-astronaut-sees-people-worshiping-space-tech thread often turned into a sort of "Connecticut Yankee on Planet Zog" storyline, with the visitor as the protagonist, often tilting the society's motives towards, say, helping him mine copper to fix his spaceship and leave, regardless of the consequences for that culture. You got the occasional *Heart of Darkness/ Wizard of Oz* story (odd that those novels' similarities are seldom noticed), but it was usually a likable castaway doing as well as possible under tricky circumstances.

Here's where we have to mention Harry Harrison, because – when not ridiculing inherited clichés outright – he found ways to re-work such set-piece ideas. There's one book of his that's fre-

Was This an SF Series?

...continued from page 319

may have encountered many interpretations far more bizarre than what we've just floated, with which people got tenure.)

The world our reader's deduced, or created, isn't what real-life Bath society was like then – but that was always Austen's point. The satire came from inverting the priorities of the phenomenal world and omitting a lot of awkward practicalities for clarity's sake. Her readers didn't need the realities explained but measured the world of the stories against this shared knowledge. The working-hypothesis our naïve reader derives comes from real-world knowledge of what's left-unsaid in fiction from our own time and culture, plus a repertoire of possibilities common within SF; both need experience. A seasoned SF reader will quickly pick up on small details and significant omissions to try out such things against the printed text and attempt a general theory, or two. For anyone else, especially A-Level students, reading Austen this century needs a lot of work in thinking yourself into the mind-set of the early-nineteenth-century reader, using all those crib-notes and acknowledging the vast "explanation" industry and those Janeites zealously patrolling "correct" responses.

Above all, you'd need to avoid skim-reading. The inferential process that unblocks an SF text isn't a million miles away from learning to read: working out an unfamiliar word's meaning by its place in a sentence and the work it does (terms such as "noun", "verb" and "preposition" came later). It's a version of what people working in early-reading or remedial adult classes call "syntactic bootstrapping". People later pick up short-cuts and read things with a lot more redundancy, but SF readers keep these skills fresh. (If you recall the stuff about Stanislaus Dehaene's neurological analysis of how reading happens inside the brain, either "dorsal" or "lateral" routes depending on the degree of commitment and attention, in **Why Doesn't Anyone Read Any More?** under X2.2, "Tooth and Claw", so much the better.) Applying the grammar of SF thought to a different vocabulary is more rewarding than taking the vocabulary and slapping it in where it doesn't belong. That process, and the legacy of nearly a century of works with what were once innovations then became stock riffs, makes up the SF conversation. And in the 1970s, the people writing *Doctor Who* were almost all part of that conversation.

Of the four script-editors at work in the 1970s, two had grown up reading SF, one was interested in commerce, technology and Greek mythology... and one was Douglas Adams. In what's the most important eight-year period of the series (certainly the one that, shall we say, "inspired" the bulk of what came after it, especially after the 2005 revival), the decisions were made by men steeped in those traditions and habits of thought, and fully aware of the legacy-codes. Terrance Dicks cut his literary teeth reading *Astounding Science Fiction*, the pace-setter for the defining period of SF's development, then broadened out his tastes and wound up at Downing College, Cambridge (where FR Leavis sternly policed the borders of the accepted "canon", only grudgingly allowing Austen into his charmed circle of morally-serious blokes).

Robert Holmes read pretty much everything but was certainly in the conversation by the time he worked on *Emergency Ward 10* and kept up with what appeared in the magazines during his shift editing *Who*. That's effectively nine years when anyone pitching a story-idea had access to someone who knew how to make a world from peculiar language-use and well-established precedents. As we'll explore when we get to "The Sun Makers" (15.4) and "The Ribos Operation" (16.1), Holmes's preferences are closer to the magazine that supplanted *Astounding* as the Place to Be, *Galaxy*. This publication, launched in 1950, is the source of most of what Kingsley Amis, Brian Aldiss and Robert Conquest claimed to be the more "sophisticated" short stories, many of them written in reply to the previous generation's assumptions and apparent innocence. (If you recall Volume 1 and our very first essay, you'll know that Aldiss was consulted by Alice Frick in the initial talks that led to *Doctor Who*. A high proportion of his picks for the influential Penguin anthology from that time showed up in *Out of the Unknown*.) Whether Holmes was diligently reading works by the *Galaxy* stable of writers or – like them – reacting sardonically to the *Astounding* school of thought, is difficult to judge without him leaving any clues, but it serves as a reminder that this conversation sub-divided and re-merged every so often, like wax in a lava-lamp. By 1968, it was almost impossible for any one person to read everything being printed in a year, and the small clusters developed their own codes and tastes as quickly as the 1930s kids had.

continued on page 323...

14.4 The Face of Evil

quently cited as an influence on "The Face of Evil", another mentioned a few times but a third that plays with the off-the-shelf idea just described. It was eventually published as *Deathworld Two* but serialised as "The Ethical Engineer". It almost killed off this sub-genre of Planetary Romances by asking the questions *Star Trek* was beginning to about altering native cultures (the "Prime Directive" – like this story's original title), then coming to the unwelcome conclusion that two wrongs make a right because fewer people get killed that way. That published title makes it clear that the protagonist was the same one as in *Deathworld*, a story of someone trapped on a planet where practically all the plants and animals were lethal, and the natives had evolved superfast reflexes and instincts. Sound familiar?

Nonetheless, the Harrison novel usually claimed as the starting point is *Captive Universe* (1969), itself a spin on "Universe" by Robert Heinlein (later reworked as *Orphans of the Sky*). In both cases, a repressive religion is keeping the truth from the masses but keeping everyone alive and minimising risks for future generations. A rebellious faction (or in Harrison's take, one teenage boy) breaks out of the small township and discovers the truth – they're on a Generation Starship and the culture's a copy of an old Earth one (in this case, the Aztecs; for Heinlein, it's very like the Midwest c.1907), because it's sustainable if the systems fail. They have failed, and Our Hero must figure out how to steer the ship because the priesthood, whose job it was, have lost the plot.

This was Chris Boucher's basic premise before Philip Hinchcliffe asked to make it a whole planet rather than a ship, but note Leela's remark that "there is no other part" of the planet. Harrison also has the odd eugenics subplot we get here. On the alphabetised paperback SF section of a 70s WH Smiths or John Menzies, Harrison would be next to Heinlein and Frank Herbert. We'd be remiss if we failed to mention another religious-fanaticism-and-hostile-ecology favourite (and the whole "they hunt by vibrations" thing we'll also have in 16.5, "The Power of Kroll"), but *Dune* can wait until next story. We have another novel, *Destination: Void*, to contend with here. In this, a colony ship's been sent to a planet that isn't there, part of an experiment to see how to make a shipboard computer become conscious and fix things. Yes. The version in print now was revised in the 70s to make it read more like his hit and to incorporate developments in AI since 1964, but it still ends with the ship manifesting near-divine agency after a few botched attempts to interface with it.

Still within the corpus of SF lore and practices Boucher had imbibed: the idea of moving a place one second forward in time to create an impenetrable barrier was first articulated in that form in *Stepsons of Terra*, an early novel by Robert Silverberg. The old Greek word "Xoanon" (a wooden religious icon, often claimed to have "descended from the heavens" as per 18.2, "Meglos") pops up as a feeble-but-manipulative alien needing human help to fix his family's spaceship in "Pilot Plant" by Bob Shaw, a writer getting into his stride in the mid-70s. Similarly, Samuel R Delany's novella about a generation starship developing its own folklore, *The Ballad of Beta 3*, has a protagonist called "Leela", but the name didn't start there. Oliver Messien's *Turangalila* popularised the term from Sanskrit, variously translated as "game", "cycle of life and death", "divine dialectic" or "cosmic dance" (and, as you may know, Matt Groenig was a big fan of the Messien symphony).

Another source for the name, discussed more often, is Leila Khalid: the much-photographed member of the Palestine Liberation Organisation and, as a generation of not-really-paying-attention dads noted, the name's enough like "Layla" for the hit song and it's less-well-known source text to get muddled up with it. That might not be accidental, as *Layla and Majun* is both the bedrock of a lot of Sufi texts on divine madness (their unrequited love and her forcible marriage to someone else lead in this direction) and topical, after the gossip about Eric Clapton and Patti Boyd gave it a whole new audience in the west. But "Leila" wasn't that unfamiliar a name in 50s Britain (see the essay on *Blue Peter* with 17.4, "Nightmare of Eden").

After "Planet of Evil", we don't need to elaborate too much on invisible monsters from the Id showing up in the crossfire of zap-guns – except that the Id, and a lot of other dime-store Freud, was a more accessible concept in the 1970s than today, when such notions are increasingly debunked or ignored. For viewers in 1977, the Doctor sitting on a Victorian chaise-longue with a gramophone and being asked "where do you think I started to go wrong?" was a very obvious gag. Also rather period is the association of "schizophrenia" (technically, the inability to differentiate between internal mental states and the

Was This an SF Series?

...continued from page 321

The general public, meanwhile, was getting a crash-course on the vocabulary. Apart from all that colour-supplement stuff and various New Waves, there were a couple of mass media primers for the punters. *Star Trek*, in its original configuration, was a handy *summa* of the state-of-the-art c.1960 and introduced the general public to what had changed since the chapterplays (however much it outwardly resembled them). For its time, it's noteworthy as a highest-common-denominator attempt to show off what was currently in that toybox. As with Hartnell-era *Who*, it had to explain, laboriously, each individual concept or type of story while making some attempt to show regular characters learning from each new experience. (*Who* scores over *Trek* in not being, at heart, an anthology series and in a shorter lead-time between making an episode and the viewers responding to it. They aren't perpetually reinventing the wheel and solemnly discussing a possibility three episodes after dealing with it as a fact, as happens a lot with Kirk and Spock.)

On the big screen, the bigger the better, Kubrick and Clarke were cleverly making a story that had each detail literally what would happen in this situation and symbolically a network of artistic statements... and a lot of pretty pictures and relatively avant-garde music. *2001: a Space Odyssey* matched enough of NASA's work for the people yearning for a sort-of documentary to not find too many niggly details, but to get the Film Studies crowd enthusiastic about what was possible if a major studio funded an art-house flick.

Yet a real-life Moon Landing meant that the news was full of primers on the basics, such as zero-g, the lack of atmosphere, reaction-mass and solar power. SF writers (and most readers) are wary of the press assuming it to be "prophetic" and treating it like a weather forecast, as it's really about what's possible and how people *might* deal with it rather than what's prosaically likely. If anything, the Apollo program freed writers from the need to talk about any of that sort of thing and get on with more interesting stuff.[50] Within the field, there's a lot of talk these days about a "metatext" or "megatext" of SF, a set of basic dance-moves or chord-progressions such as FTL drives, neural jacks, non-violent matriarchies and Bootstrap Paradoxes. For a while, none of that needed to be "sold" to an audience (a reason to lament X9.4, "Before the Flood").

Thus, during this golden time, jobbing television writers stopped submitting proposals about a sister-planet to Earth exactly on the other side of the sun or men forced to wear dresses by evil matriarchies (see Volumes 1 and 2) and availed themselves of the accumulated residue of ideas available for use after 40 years, supervised by script editors who habitually generated these and could always come up with more by the same process. (Here comes another bit of that borrowed vocabulary that gets misused: "Hard SF" is, at its simplest, SF made from fresh ingredients. It's a subset which starts from scratch without any of that inherited vocabulary and looks at the implications of a particular development, often a bit of recent science, which nobody else has used yet. What science they use is down to them: sociology's a discipline with procedures based in all that Karl Popper falsifiability stuff, but you get physicists whining if it's not exclusively physics that makes new stories happen. Microbiology is peer-reviewed and experimentally verified, but somehow not everybody thinks of stories rooted in that as Hard SF. Conversely, fantasy ideas such as Ray Kurzweil's "Singularity" are treated as Hard SF because computers are involved.)

The majority of SF is, as we've suggested by the use of the conversation motif, reactions to other people's ideas on the "no, *this* is what would happen" principle. Ideas generate ideas when real-life experience is brought to bear. Dicks and Holmes were doing this before the rest of their school of writers found out what the clichés even were.

But with an audience of kids and their associated adults, who mainly watch cop-shows or costume dramas, you can get away with rearranging the clichés for a while. If the effects technology keeps improving, it seems fresh. There's now a whole toybox of visual collage and buzzwords you can use to disguise a rewritten Western or police procedural. SF readers and authors use the adjective "skiffy" for this sort of thing but tend to resent the assumption that what they do is more than ancestrally related to it. 70s *Doctor Who* had a lot of writers who did that kind of cut-and-paste, but script editors and producers kept them honest (or tried to, if it was Bob Baker and Dave Martin). Yet by virtue of being television and not print, the series had other strings to its bow. Explaining why gets us back to those wonky definitions.

Take as read, for now, the idea that the SF-ness

continued on page 325...

14.4 The Face of Evil

outside world) and split or multiple personality. The quote from this story that went viral in 2016 ('The very powerful and the very stupid have one thing in common. They don't alter their views to fit the facts, they alter the facts to fit their views'.), is part of that interpretation.

All of this is part of a wider concern in Britain at the time: although the instruments of the state were still notionally connected with the Church of England, Britain was increasingly secular. Religion was something other people did. The BBC was, like many people, obliged to pay lip-service and not actively disrespect and particular faith-group (although the more foreign they were, the less this seemed to matter), but American culture's tendency to drag God into everything seemed weird and backward. The trajectory from Victorian credulity and repression to the present inevitably led to a near future where the West would outgrow such notions. That's not something the current BBC guidelines would countenance (see X3.3, "Gridlock" for the closest they were allowed to get).

It was, however, a commonly-held assumption in the 1970s, not just in Europe but in America before the 1980 election – it's odd now to look back and see how Jimmy Carter's churchgoing was ridiculed before the mobilisation of the Evangelical movement for political ends. The interplay of politics and religion was the stuff of costume dramas (especially Trollope adaptations and biographies of Victorian reformers), but Robert Holmes used it to bulk out stories. In many ways Davros, Vorus and Maren have the same sort of plot-dynamic as fire-and-brimstone preachers in classic serials. As it is, a whole sub-plot about Calib's plotting against Neeva that doesn't go anywhere: if Tomas is Andor's son, it's a straight copy of the Eelek/ Axus plotline from 6.4, "The Krotons", so might not have been Boucher's doing anyway.

John Bloomfield's designs for the Tesh costumes began with the unorthodox colour-scheme and worked outwards, based on the build of the actors they were looking to cast. Although the result looks like a slightly later Moebius design, the similarity of this costume and the Cyclist outfit he gave Leela two stories later is suggestive, as is similarity to Victorian circus acrobats. (The combination of knee-britches and epaulettes and the skullcaps was familiar to viewers from many costume-dramas of the era, notably *The Pallisers* and *A Horseman Riding By*. See "The Talons of Weng-Chiang" for more on *The Good Old Days*.)

English Lessons
- *Colonel Bogey*: As this was still under copyright, the composers get a credit along with Ron Grainer and Dudley Simpson in the paperwork even for Tom Baker whistling it. He *had* to whistle, as the most familiar lyrics wouldn't have been appropriate: it's wartime ribaldry about Nazi genital shortcomings and, as such, a coded message of defiance when used in *Bridge on the River Kwai*. The title's a golf-reference, not nasal.
- *"Over the teeth and..."*, in Britain, usually ends "round the gums/ look out stomach, here it comes". It's either for feeding babies or getting drunk.

Things That Don't Make Sense There's a giant Tom Baker face on a hillside. The Tesh must have gone out and carved it, probably with blaster-rays and possibly with an anti-grav transporter. With the Sevateem around, that's risky, but it's also odd that the Tesh didn't use similar weapons on their pesky neighbours. Of course, Xoanon secretly wants the Sevateem to live, so might place an embargo on such efficient pest-control, but either way, a lot of Tesh with hand-tools must have been chipping away for centuries, somehow avoiding the Sevateem's notice until it was all done.

Once Leela leaves, there's precisely one woman on this planet. This is equal to, or possibly worse than, the gender imbalance among the Thals (1.2, "The Daleks"). [Pennant Roberts was directing and has a track record of swapping character-genders to get a better balance. So that one other woman in the Sevateem war-party in Part Two was probably his idea and compounds the felony, preventing us from assuming that they keep the womenfolk corralled in another part of the village (fearing rampaging Tesh?) as usual.] And how do the Tesh reproduce?

The Test of the Horda is invoked to discover whether the Doctor can be killed: if he survives, he's the Evil One. He survives and... suddenly everyone starts listening to him. Leela – accused of being a blasphemous witch – was to have taken this and her dad steps in and undergoes it on her behalf. She'd've easily proved her innocence and there'd be no story, but he dies and she's banished. Nothing in this suggests that Sole is either a wizard on trial or has expunged Leela's alleged guilt.

Was This an SF Series?

...continued from page 323

of an SF novel or short story is more in the way it allows language to misbehave systematically rather than in any of the stock items such as robots or teleports. Unlike escapist fiction, it not only acknowledges that actions and discoveries have consequences, it starts by working out all of these and focussing on the less-obvious ones, tempting the reader with these as a trail of breadcrumbs back to the root cause. Conjecturing on the world-conditions required for otherwise nonsensical sentence to work and trying to line up all the oddities and unconventional terms – what was once called "taking an inferential walk" – is how readers accept the author's challenge to figure out what's going on before any exposition or info-dumping, and ahead of what may or may not be a surprise twist.

What does it allow the story to do that other types of writing don't? Well, stories about robots or teleports, for one. Quick, easy science or history lessons, if that's what appeals to you. Speculation about society's reactions to developments, how people would behave under different circumstances or if raised in a radically different (and hitherto non-existent) culture or environment, purely ludic wordplay, personal statements impossible by conventional means and – of course, – critiques of earlier stories using the same techniques. In short, all the things you may have encountered in "definitions" of SF but also a lot more.

The basic unit of SF-ness may be the sentence, but the work that the author did and then invited you to do backwards is inductive reasoning at the level of entire societies, worlds or universes. Around the time *Doctor Who* Season Fourteen went out, Robert Scholes – a rare example of a university lecturer on SF who'd voluntarily read some before it became fashionable to run courses on it – suggested that "SF" could just as plausibly stand for "Structural Fabulation". This galumphing phrase at least moves the debate on from whether there's any real science involved beyond the system-making habit. It makes a distinction between other forms of fabulation (Fantasy, Magic Realism, Utopias, Menippean Satire, Fox News...) based on a process akin to Logical Positivism and how science is supposed to work. It's about thinking systemically, rather than treating each anomaly as a one-off. To skip a little ahead of ourselves, this is why Graham Williams's comment about endless discussions on whether green-skinned people need to go to the toilet is significant: if you've been looking at the world of the story this way, rather than just making ad hoc changes to suit a particular story you want to tell, you can adapt to circumstances such as budget-cuts or an unavailable location. As you can see in **The Lore** entries in these books, that skill is a handy one to have.

As we suggested earlier, this description works about as well if applied to interpretations the author may not have intended – it was the 70s and Roland Barthes was still around, so stated authorial intention was no longer taken as gospel anyway. The most important thing about this attempt is that it doesn't negate reading it for fun, whereas "Speculative Fiction" (Robert Heinlein's 1950s attempt at rebranding, borrowed with thanks by Harlan Ellison in the 60s to mark his New Wave, then pilfered, unacknowledged, by Margaret Atwood to pretend that she was Above All That) and "the literature of cognitive estrangement" (use-free pundit Darko Suvin's university-friendly term, less impressive if you recall that he was writing in French and "la science" means "knowledge" or "cognition", so he's defined SF as "Science Fiction" and expects a round of applause) don't seem nearly as entertaining.

So we can slot into that any of the ways people in the field (which is the word most professionals use these days, rather than "genre") have tried to explain what it is they do, then see if they still work. The crudest, that SF is about "the impact of technology on humans", would automatically qualify *Tess of the d'Urbervilles* and most episodes of *Columbo* as SF. *Tess* touches on the effects of machinery on rural civilisation, the way Darwin changed the shape of the world and the nature of humanity in an age coming to terms with entropy. *Columbo*'s simpler; it frequently features characters who use new technological systems or social movements to commit ingenious murders (although the one with Richard Basehart is outright fantasy). Either would seem closer to SF than, say, one of the many "Regular Character Confronts a Member of His or Her Family and Resolves His or Her Personal Issues" episodes of *Deep Space Nine*.

Full-blown SF does this better than most fiction, when it does it at all, but this rules out whole swathes of evidently SF works: some lack all overt technology (post-apocalyptic stuff, the big growth-market of the 60s, is about the very lack of

continued on page 327...

14.4 The Face of Evil

Are there two different tests? This would almost make sense of Leela's detailed knowledge of how to survive the one the Doctor undergoes, but why not put the Doctor through the test she fears?

For that matter, after Leela's shock at seeing the Doctor's features, you'd expect that the Sevateem would be stunned at the revelation of the Evil One when Neeva unwraps him. They're not that stunned, though; it's just a rather muted acceptance. How often does this sort of thing happen? What makes this *really* odd is that Neeva knows Xoanon's voice very well but fails to react when another Tom Baker-soundalike shows up in a silly scarf. Wouldn't mimicking one of Xoanon's voices be further proof of this stranger's bad intentions? Has Jon Culshaw been to their world recently?

The Doctor tells Leela never to be certain in Part One, then tries to get her to be certain that there's no god in Part Two (probably, to be fair, Boucher's joke rather than an anomaly). The Tesh leader knows the Doctor's interested in the sacred heart of Xoanon, but only posts one wet-looking guard outside the door. The Doctor is puzzled as to why Xoanon only electrifies the walls of the ship instead of the floor, and since Xoanon then goes out of its way to kill him, we're as much in the dark as he is. It also takes the most powerful computer ever built a full 25 minutes to overload the atomic generators and make them explode, far longer than it'd take a modern-day human being to mess up a nuclear reactor. Eventually it proves itself capable of controlling the actions of everyone on the ship except the troublesome Doctor, who isn't even immune to the psi-power of Xoanon's servants.

For the geography of this planet to make sense, the mountain has to interrupt the black wall that surrounds the ship, yet apparently no Sevateem has attempted the obvious approach of following the wall and entering the idol's mouth. Even though there's a handy path leading right up to it. Why do the Tesh call themselves the Tesh and not, say, "Tex"? As custodians of the Ship, they ought to know their own past a bit better. Maybe Xoanon thought up the names and invented their costumes for a giggle. The Tower of Imelo was important enough to be one of the story's working titles. "Imelo" is, of course, the middle of "Time Lord", but that only works written down. The Sevateem, as we gather from their inability to read the stencilled clue on their "gong", are illiterate. They can apparently tell the time, though, as Leela uses "seconds" to measure the time a Janis thorn takes to kill rather than "heartbeats".

Apart from all that, the main omission is in Part Four. We spent much of the previous episode dealing with the Doctor explaining to Leela how to get through a Psi-Tri projection, then operating an anti-grav transporter to get them to the ship. Then the Doctor tells Neeva to bring his troops in through the idol's mouth and – lo – they make it all the way to Level 37 with no help at all. Perhaps the Doctor quickly knocked up a set of sketches for the Sevateem troops (possibly laminated, like in X12.2, "Spyfall Part Two"). Likewise, Leela managing to follow the Doctor from the Auxiliary Control Room to the TARDIS is *just* about plausible if she watched him operate the shuttle controls really carefully, but only if there's a second shuttle we're not told about.

One other niggle – apart from a cool cliffhanger, what does the Doctor's visit to Level 37 achieve? It just serves to annoy Xoanon, doubling the story's body-count, and goading the mad computer into possessing every human within coo-ee to stop the Doctor from doing what he could easily have done in Part Three; build an interface and uninstall Doctor-Sim.

Critique After a story where experienced hands went all-out to make a coherent world, arguably biting off more than they could chew, we have a new writer, director, designer, costume designer and co-star. All of them get it right first time. Most, if not all, get it substantially right on subsequent occasions, but they're never used in this combination again. That's a shame.

The weird thing about Philip Hinchcliffe's tenure is that so few of the key personnel were newcomers. Pennant Roberts is only the second neophyte director we've had (the other was Rodney Bennett). His mix of planning-innovation and methodical calm in the studio meant that he drew the short straw in later stories, being expected to bail out a troubled script. That's not needed here, so he learns the peculiarities of this series relatively stress-free. The recruitment for new-to-*Who* writers has been tricky too. Robert Banks Stewart needed a lot of hand-holding and his scripts required fixes on location, but at least two of his three attempts got to the screen without Holmes having to (pseudonymously) rebuild them.

By contrast, Chris Boucher has arrived with a bang – and was the first writer since Ian Stuart

Was This an SF Series?

...continued from page 325

it). Alternate universes, time-paradoxes, psi-powers and anything predicated upon a social change (Malorie Blackman's *Noughts and Crosses*, Robert Silverberg's "To See the Invisible Man", the stories in Thomas Disch's *334* and myriad others) have to be considered breaches to this alleged rule/ definition. They're still SF, though, so that definition's a bust. This also applies to the modification that SF's about the relationship between humanity and its tools or, as Terry Pratchett put it, about the Faustian deal between our intelligence and our ape ancestry. Yes, a lot of it's "about" that but not exclusively, not invariably and there's a lot on that topic that isn't SF at all. Dickens did a few.[53]

Theodore Sturgeon defined a science fiction story as "a human problem, and a human solution, which would not have happened at all without its speculative scientific content", which comes uncomfortably close to reducing the whole thing to a series of sterile puzzles. It also rather limits the subject matter to humans, a subject thousands of other people have written about already. It does, at least, move us away from just technology, making the case that an SF story has to be more than a Western with ray-guns. It still puts "content" at the forefront, but that risks making "style" and "content" separate.[54] But he's on to something with the idea that the story needs a change (the "what if" or "novum") around which the rest of the narrative contorts from what we experience daily. That's a reason why doorstop trilogies are comforting rather than exciting, because the reader pretty much absorbs the implications in the first book, and the rest is relatively routine storytelling unless the author's on the ball and has a surprise ready that was hidden in plain sight (although changes like that often upset the comfort-reader).

But doorstop trilogies really started happening in the 80s, and we're talking about what the viewing public in 70s Britain had in common with the SF-reading community. There was a sort of bond formed by the less-good television options available (*Space: 1999* and various American shows – only *The Six Million Dollar Man* made any headway), but the skiffy cut-and-paste collage options weren't plentiful. There was a commonality in the collective "yeah, right" about *Star Trek*'s basic assumptions. People tended to be suspicious of short-haired Americans in uniform and resented the idea that Earth = USA. (See **Is This Any Way to Run a Galactic Empire?** under 9.4, "The Mutants"

and **Did *Blakes 7* Wreck Everything?** under 15.5, "Underworld".) More fundamentally, the narrative structure of most of the British-made SF-adjacent shows tended more towards a similar interpretative strategy to how readers make SF-ness happen than most other television. The legacy of 50s "Cosy Catastrophe" stories and *Quatermass* left the viewers with a wider range of possible explanations for what was happening than simple space-opera or superheroes, and the means by which those sorts of stories had been told were available to directors and viewers alike.

The basic visual narrative of a *Doctor Who* adventure is towards disruption of something that looks like another kind of television. Key moments in the plot are the image of something incongruous even within the terms of the story up to that point. Not just a Yeti in a loo in Tooting Bec (although the presence of the bizarre within the everyday is a staple) but a furious red outline of a humanoid figure in an alien jungle ("Planet of Evil"). The cliffhanger "money shot" is often the point where we stop cutting between one term and another and show them together in the same shot.

It's a different televisual grammar and, as a glance at, say, 15.1, "Horror of Fang Rock" will show, needs very little in the way of altered vocabulary, i.e. ostentatious special effects, aliens or bombast, to make the more orthodox elements hang together in a different way from superficially-similar dramas (e.g. *The Duchess of Duke Street* later that night). Usually, leading up to that turning-point, a number of incidents make us wonder how different a world would have to be from ours for this to be accepted or even possible. *Doctor Who* had an advantage over other series, because it started again from scratch every few episodes, without recourse to a "reset" at the end of every single episode. Enough time elapsed between episodes for us to work out a rough idea of how this world works, then it gets upset by fresh evidence. The "series of serials" format avoided having to reinvent the wheel the way most six-part SF-like serials did but allowed more time for evidence and conjecture than a one-hour (or 50 minutes and adverts) segment.

If we're taking the position that television and film use the shot the way prose uses the sentence, then we can see a very closely analogous process at work in *Doctor Who* to what we're saying SF is

continued on page 329...

14.4 The Face of Evil

Black (then "Mr Telly") to do two stories in a row. That's one of the things that gives this three-story run at the start of 1977 a feeling of Year Zero. This isn't a story in a recognised groove from earlier in the 1970s. Yes, it's got a jungle and a few visual cribs from *Forbidden Planet* (as did "Planet of Evil") and the main human antagonist is yet another dodgy priest trying to preserve his power-base (a stock figure since Hartnell's day – arguably since the cavemen we met in the very first story), but conceptually and procedurally we're breaking new ground.

Part of that is that, with a few visual references from 60s films to get ideas across to the designers, the bulk of the content is derived from 60s books. Beyond that, though, it's the example of the books as how-to guides for making up planets and societies, rather than as a repository of specific details that can be shoplifted, that makes the difference. Whatever this planet is called, it was conceived from the ground up. The plot-necessities were met by how such a world would work, rather than the usual methodology. In the past, even in stories covered within this book, the thought-processes of previous SF writers were jury-rigged to justify decisions based upon how much they looked like favourite scenes from old films. (Don't get us wrong: there's still a lot of that, but the balance is now 70:30 whole-cloth to homage rather than the other way around.) Or, more usually, they weren't used at all and we got nonsense like "Planet of the Daleks" (10.4) or "The Wheel in Space" (5.7).

Part of it is that, with the obvious exceptions of a police-box, a bag of jelly babies and a bloke in a scarf, nothing here is immediately familiar from "Robot" or even "Pyramids of Mars". It's a back-handed compliment to Barry Letts that it took so long for his legacy to fade, if it ever did. This story is the one where we stop looking over our shoulders at Sarah, UNIT, simplistic morality-tales and contemporary references. The Doctor, while proficient with a crossbow and able to defend himself (and, on one occasion, pull a nasty prank on someone who's offended him), isn't really keen on physical conflict and takes a dim view of Leela doing it. There are onscreen deaths, some spectacular enough for any eight-year-old boy not to feel cheated, but the whole second episode seems to be building up to a set-piece conflict of the kind Letts would build an episode around – and we don't get it. No Action By Havoc five-minute plot-hiatus, just a few people writhing in spotlights and verbal reports of a rout that prompts everything in the final two episodes. The Doctor regrets any death he witnesses (especially the Tesh who's fried after attacking him), but it's more than that – he caused this whole mess by doing what seemed like the nice thing to do, then swanning off like always.

It would be wrong to say that this is unprecedented. The idea that the Doctor's do-goodery has unforeseen consequences goes back to the Ark (well, 3.6, "The Ark"), but the spell when Robert Holmes shadowed Terrance Dicks as script editor made it a feature – the last two Pertwee stories of all had the Doctor face up to what he'd done, and "Invasion of the Dinosaurs" (11.2) involved his "cure" of Mike Yates after BOSS brainwashed the captain (10.5, "The Green Death"), leading Yates to the Dark Side. But this story makes unravelling the cause of the planet's woes a more painful admission for the Doctor, something briefly touched upon in "The Masque of Mandragora" but taking three episodes to piece together here.

Facing up to the reckless way the Doctor's been leaving his mark on whole worlds is a rebuke to earlier stories (and a few formulaic US franchises), but making it the starting-point for a story where we didn't see the original incident is bold. We and the Doctor have to figure it out from the evidence before us. The viewers are trusted to connect the pieces rather than needing spoon-feeding. Leela asks helpful questions just when we have our own theories (or, if we missed an episode, need a quick update). But she listens to the answers and acts on them off her own bat.

And that's the most obvious break from the past. We might draw comparisons between Leela and Jamie (see Volume 2), but she's a lot more consistent from story to story. Within the terms of her own tribe, she's politically savvy and able to see nuance, but then she's shown a wider world where the Tesh are also victims. She reflexively kills to protect, just as the Brigadier did, because – something not every writer really got – her "savagery" is learned behaviour, inculcated for a reason. Later stories make a big thing of her "mindlessness", but what's really going on is very quick thinking. One of the many reasons to appreciate Louise Jameson's casting is that she keeps faith with this idea even when the writers don't. These reviews would get repetitive if we kept saying it, but we were extremely lucky to have her.

Not that the rest of the cast are shabby: David

Was This an SF Series?

...continued from page 327

up to. The biggest difference between prose and television is, of course, the speed with which we get information; you can read at your own pace, but telly goes at its speed. The amount of information (pictures, sound, editing-pace and so on) is also variable and often contradictory. *Doctor Who*, though, had the option of including pastiche and parody of other television; these augmented the available repertoire of possible theories the viewer might form about what was going on. Orthodox thriller elements, "straight" historical drama and outright fantasy were all legitimate possibilities until proven wrong – if they were. (The vexed relationship of SF and fantasy gets its own essay in Volume 5.) Applying the SF methodology to the matter of what rules to apply this month got less important as the series curtailed the other subcategories, but it was still vestigially there. Opening scenes often teased people with the possibility that they were branching out from aliens and time-paradoxes.

The traditional point made here is that the rate at which viewers absorb multiple narrative elements has accelerated since the 1970s – but this doesn't stand up to close examination when it's *Doctor Who*. If you get a chance, look out some of the YouTube channels where various chatty Millennials react to old episodes. It's noticeable how often they miss what viewers at the time picked up on *instantly* about the connections between subplots. (It's the same when watching with teens. Much of the perplexity over Series 13's six-part serial was unfamiliarity with the idea of serials per se – weird, right? – but the lack of instant explication and immediate resolution was a stumbling-block for some viewers, rather than being part of why people would choose to watch *Doctor Who*.) Some of that's just because they're doing reaction-videos and shooting themselves in the foot by talking through the explanations or dialogue-clues, but there might be a deeper reason that goes against the current orthodoxy. Namely, perhaps 1970s BBC1 viewers were better at this (or, if you insist, more "genre-savvy") than today's youth. After all, attempting to reverse-engineer the ground-rules and customs of an alien society was something British television audiences were doing all the time back then...

We mention in the essay on Schools Television with "The Sun Makers" (15.4) how much explanation *Sesame Street* needed, and in **What Was**

Children's Television Like Back Then? (3.7, "The Celestial Toymaker"), we sketched in how much Polish, French and Czech stuff we were exposed to and left to fend for ourselves. But UK viewers were bombarded with so much inexplicable American stuff, it was hard to sort out what was genuinely how they did things there, what was generic convention or network restrictions and what was just made up. *Kojak* was as incomprehensibly "other" as *The Water Margin*. Anyone watching *Dynasty* in the UK did so as if it were very slow, very silly SF.

Consider: the character-names seemed to follow some sort of rule about using surnames as first names if you were posh, using two hyphenated first-names if you weren't. Was that how things were in Colorado then? We had no way of knowing. All four, or five, or however many, of Alexis's children changed their faces, voices and heights without anyone commenting on it – then when her sister turned out to be the Rani with a silly name, an obvious reason presented itself (22.3, "The Mark of the Rani"). Regeneration made more sense than an English mum calling her kid "Caress" in the 1940s. It was evidently something you didn't discuss openly, like divorce in 1950s sitcoms, and politely pretended it wasn't happening. Then the spin-off series *The Colbys* ended with one of these kids abducted by a flying saucer, but she was back in *Dynasty* none the worse for her ordeal (except, you know, looking totally different and having an English accent) and never asked about it (well, once, apparently by public demand). *Twin Peaks* was a doddle after all that.

1970s BBC viewers were forced to do inferential half-marathons to the point that they barely noticed how much interpretative work they were doing. And, as we suggested above, children are doing that with everything they see, hear or read. Teenage brains are built for system-building from limited information, often over-generalising and seeing things in starkly black-and-white terms. SF thinking is a natural progression for them. This is why we spent four paragraphs misconstruing Jane Austen rather than running through a digest of half a century's theses on the topic. It's a skill you can let atrophy through lack of use – but, as we've said, 70s British television gave it ample scope for exercise. And a family-friendly drama series watched by an average of a third of the viewing public is in no way a "cult".

Television's big drawback compared to prose is

continued on page 331...

14.4 The Face of Evil

Garfield, as Neeva, has done this sort of thing before but never in such a state of undress. He retains his dignity and focus in a part that's tricky to pitch right (and thank goodness the usual first-call for these roles, Brian Blessed, was busy playing Caesar Augustus). Leslie Schofield brings a sort of feral cunning to Calib, making an interesting contrast with Philip Madoc as a similar character in "The Krotons" – Calib's very much a street-fighting man, even though he's in a jungle. It's an odd mix of nervous energy and calculation and could easily have backfired. A load of people dressed like Tarzan, but talking as if they're in the boardroom of a multinational in an 80s drama ought to have been absurd.

It's cast to perfection, it looks a lot costlier than it was, none of the effects go massively wrong and it has one of the smartest scripts ever. There's a disturbing cliffhanger, a jawdropping one and the one in between has the Doctor's face killing someone. Whatever the backstage reason, Baker's on top of his game and striking sparks with Jameson from the start. How are they going to top this?

The Facts

Written by Chris Boucher. Directed by Pennant Roberts. Viewing figures: 10.7 million, 11.1 million, 11.3 million, 11.7 million. AIs 61, unrecorded, 59 and 60.

Working Titles "Prime Directive", "The Tower of Imelo", "The Day God Went Mad". (The three other titles sometimes listed are for other Boucher proposals that fed into this story.)

Alternate Versions They wrote a version of the ending where Leela didn't leave with the Doctor, just in case.

Cliffhangers The Doctor is nonplussed to find a Mount Rushmore-style effigy of himself; Andor is killed by Tom Baker's giant poisoned electric head; the Doctor, inside Xoanon's mind when the computer has a mental breakdown, is pummelled into a foetal position by his own face on three screens yelling "who am I?" in a child's voice.

What Was In the Charts? "Isn't She Lovely?", David Parton; "Boogie Nights", Heatwave; "Anarchy in the UK", the Sex Pistols; "Don't Cry for Me, Argentina", Julie Covington.

The Lore

Chris Boucher's television career had been sporadic. He had written quick sketches for Dave Allen and Bernard Braden as a side-hustle when supplementing his income from Calor, a bottled-butane supplier. Then, he graduated to working on an ITV sitcom, *Romany Jones*, which struggled to continue after the original star died.

Following a hint that *Doctor Who* was in the market, Boucher used his background as an SF reader to pitch story ideas and, in early 1975, had an outline looked at by Robert Holmes. This scenario ("Silent Scream") was close to unusable, but Holmes and Philip Hinchcliffe liked the cut of his jib. He offered a couple of ideas about Generation Starships, "The Dreamers of Phados" and "The Mentor Conspiracy" (see **Where Does This Come From?**). Holmes warmly but cautiously encouraged the newcomer (much as Terrance Dicks had with Holmes seven years earlier) and worked closely on turning detailed breakdowns into plausible and practical stories. At least one proposal was a hundred pages long.

Holmes had a notion about a manipulative computer distorting the entire society (apparently like the *Star Trek* episode "For the World is Hollow and I Have Touched the Sky" – see 15.5, "Underworld" for more on that). This touched on Boucher's interest in how religions might form around cultural needs. By August, Boucher had a workable storyline, "Prime Directive", but Hinchcliffe had a couple of suggestions: it should be a whole planet and there might be a Mount Rushmore-style carving of the Doctor's face on a mountain. A version of this, using ideas from his earlier proposals, was in during October and was working reasonably well.

In keeping with the *ur*-texts Boucher and Holmes had in mind, there was a young rebel tribesman, Loke, who was discovering the truth of his world when the Doctor arrived. One of the earlier proposals had a warrior-woman, Leela, who had helped the Doctor and Sarah. However, with Sarah out of the picture, a decision on how or whether to replace the orthodox *Doctor Who* girl was postponed while the "Deadly Assassin" experiment was being assessed. Boucher was encouraged to include a local character who was young and female to plug any gap in this or "Planet of the Robots", the other script they were

Was This an SF Series?

...continued from page 329

that the author can withhold details. One of the key tricks in SF (and it works for most fiction) is to describe in detail the things that scene's viewpoint-character encounters, occasionally explaining how much they mean to that person and why, then leaving everything else to the reader's imagination. A surprise extra, such as the often-cited "the door dilated", can be chucked into make ripples in the pond. Television can't really do that: the sets have to be built, the costumes worn and the number of ears a character has ought to be immediately obvious. We touched on this in **Is Kylie from Planet Zog?** under X4.0, "Voyage of the Damned" and **Who Are You Calling Monsters?** under X3.6, "The Lazarus Experiment", but what is practically achievable – especially on a low budget – means that the most interesting bits of any world are generally off-screen. Matching what we're told about, say, the Battle of Reykjavik, the Ice Age and the Filipino Army with the visuals of "The Talons of Weng-Chiang" is more evocative than showing us anything, even if they could do it – because we did half the work.

The SF conversation began in the letters pages of news-stand magazines; for a while, between 1968 and 1983, it was a public debate. The public then completed a drift away to the skiffy stuff then more readily-available. *Doctor Who* lost its charm (or easy access) for casual viewers at roughly the same time and it, too, sank into skiffy thrills. No conversation with that many people involved could avoid splitting up into smaller clusters. *Doctor Who* got its own fandom and a script editor who wanted to be writing *The Professionals*.

Soon, the books available in mainstream shops were confined to blockbusters and doorstop trilogies, spreading like Japanese Knotweed and increasingly opaque to the novice reader. *Star Trek: the Next Generation* ushered in an actual television genre, with its own rules and customs, which made many printed SF conversationalists huddle together determined to not do what those people were up to. The showrunners of the revived *Who* are, to a greater or lesser extent, conversant with pretty-picture-collage skiffy, but never really got to grips with SF – and, in Steven Moffat's case, actively resisted any association with it, to the extent of distancing the series from a schools science programme (see X5.1, "The Eleventh Hour"). Why expend effort trying to think like Holmes or Dicks when you can just sample their stuff?

It's easy to blame George Lucas. It's tempting to point the finger at Douglas Adams, who made a career from sneering at what little SF he'd read. We could even argue that this was just a return to the *status quo ante* of David Whitaker and Gerry Davis. Instead, it's better to cherish that extended phase between, for the sake of argument, "The Krotons" (6.4) and "Snakedance" (20.2), when the programme's centre-of-gravity was SF-as-written but done in such a way that the public were along for the ride. For many people, *Doctor Who* was the gateway-drug to proper, written-down, grown-up SF. It was also, by popular acclaim, more innovative, more enjoyable and far more memorable during this period. Funny, that.

---

discussing with him. Loke therefore had a sex-change, and Boucher re-used the name and basic character from his earlier storyline (some of his plot-functions went to Tomas, Andor's son).

This caused few problems when the idea of companion-of-the-month was later dropped, and Boucher was asked to have Leela stay for the next story (alongside Toos, the next companion-of-the-month lined up). When Leela stuck around for the Victorian story and the whole year that followed, there was a slight dispute over who owned the rights to the character (never entirely resolved) and the option to bump her off remained. After all the work both sides poured into them, the scripts for "The Day God Went Mad" were all on time or a day early, the last arriving in early April 1976. By now, Pennant Roberts had been commissioned to direct. The projected over-spend on "The Deadly Assassin" and the impending Victorian romp made this and the next story low-cost, studio-bound productions.

• Roberts had directed *Survivors* and *Doomwatch*, as well as episodes of series we'll hear a lot about in volume 4.2: *Softly Softly Task Force*, *Sutherland's Law* and *The Regiment*. Two of his three episodes for the last-named were co-written by Holmes. He had, for another project, auditioned Louise Jameson and kept her in mind, but casting Leela wasn't as straightforward as that. Hinchcliffe had someone else in mind (Emily Richard, later Jim's mum in *Empire of the Sun* and at the time the lead in the Barry Letts *Lorna Doone*) – but she had another role coming up, so the team auditioned 60 women in five batches over August.

With hindsight, the notion of Susan Wooldridge (*The Jewel in the Crown*), Carol Drinkwater (*All*

14.4 The Face of Evil

Creatures Great and Small), Carol Leader (*Play School*, *Chock-a-Block*), Heather Tobias (the voice of Pig in *Pipkins*), Sally Geeson (*Bless This House*) or Colette Gleeson (18.2, "Meglos") as Leela is odd. Most of these were blondes. One front-runner was Pamela Salem, cast as Toos in "The Robots of Death": her agent seems to have jumped the gun and announced her as the new *Who* girl to the press (see "Underworld" for another instance of this). Jameson had been increasingly busy in 1976 and shortlisted to play Purdey in *The New Avengers*. After the second round of auditions and screen tests, she got the *Who* part and was contracted in late August for 14 episodes – but nobody told Tom Baker.

- Roberts and Jameson workshopped the character, deciding that she was a bit literal-minded, didn't – or rather did not – use contractions (see also Jan Chappell as Cally from *Blakes 7*, another role Roberts cast and a friend of Jameson's from RADA) and had a sort of Spidey-sense for danger. This was represented by a habit Jameson had seen her dog Bosie do, tilting his head slightly. Other aspects of the character came from the small girl in the flat above hers. Leela, in Urdu, was supposedly "brown-eyes", so they wrote into her contract that she had to wear red contact lenses to make her very blue eyes brown. To match this, and cover her un-Tarzan-like freckles, the make-up designer Ann Ailes tried various fake tans. In the first publicity photos, Jameson looks perilously like Al Jolson.

- John Bloomfield, an award-winning costume designer, joined the series and devised a soft leather garment for Leela that was more or less a swimsuit. Jameson had to schedule her toilet breaks carefully as it took a lot of getting out of, even after the risk of smearing the make-up on her legs subsided. There was originally a headband. Leela's jewellery was designed with an eye for merchandising to girls – Jameson would offer a set as a prize on *Multi-Coloured Swap Shop* – but this never took off. The boots, if you look closely, have built-up heels.

- It seems that, as Chris D'oyly-John grew ever more exasperated over Hinchcliffe's spending, the production team took a large chunk of September off to renegotiate budgets. (We talk of "Season Fourteen" as a cohesive six-story block, but with the transmission and production suspended ahead of this story, it's effectively two three-story groups. The *Radio Times* certainly thought so, when "The Face of Evil" Part One was advertised as part of the New Year line-up.) Nonetheless, as far as the shooting schedule went, it was almost continuous.

Just over two weeks after the remounted scenes for "The Deadly Assassin", filming began at Ealing on 20th September. The Doctor's stroll around the jungle went well, then Jameson got out of her bathrobe to start work. The lighting crew were enthusiastic, but Baker – usually a staunch advocate of young women not wearing much – was upset. Never mind the Doctor having any sidekick at all, having one so overtly murderous seemed to be a mistake. It took several months for Jameson to establish any sort of rapport with the star.

- With Hinchcliffe away for the 22nd, Baker amended a scene of the Doctor confronting the assassins so that – instead of wresting a knife from one – he threatened Lugo with a Jelly Baby. He was anxious that this deviation would cause problems, but Hinchcliffe was pleased that a potential source of complaints had been defused. Joining for the next day were Leslie Schofield (previously a Confederate soldier in 6.7, "The War Games") as Calib, Brendan Price as Tomas (a last-minute replacement), Lloyd McGuire as Lugo plus Victor Lucas and Brett Forrest.

- For Thursday, the Ealing pit, often filled with water (as per 2.8, "The Chase" or 4.4, "The Highlanders"), was used for the Test of the Horda. One radio-controlled Horda had been used on the Monday, but a large number of rubber ones were made to quiver en masse (Steve Drewett made these, Mat Irvine operated the "performing" one). There was also a glove-puppet with lateral mandible, for the shots of it biting things (and people). On Monday, the shots of tribesmen being chased by invisible beasties were added. (One of these, identified in the script as "Koras", is very obviously Peter Dean made up as Benny from Abba, making a third future *EastEnders* regular in this story's cast.)

- While the precise story-title was being discussed, rehearsals began with a read-through. The recording began on 11th October in TC3 with Part One and the forest scenes for Part Two. During this session, Baker noted that the original pronunciation made it sound like "Janice Thorn", which he said sounded like an out-of-work actress, so that changed. Why "Xoanon" moved the stress to the second syllable at the same time is unclear.

The Face of Evil 14.4

- Scenes were lost for timing reasons: the big gap is that the Doctor saves the starving Sevateem by finding a box of survival rations left by their ancestors. Leela helps herself to these "chocolates" at the end of Part Four, and the shibboleth for Neeva to give Calib was originally "have a chocolate".

- The next lot of rehearsals began on the 14th and recording resumed on 24th. The afternoon session was abandoned for some reason, but the crew had a visitor: the Blackpool exhibition ran a contest to win a day behind the scenes and an Australian schoolboy, Anthony Friese, won. They just so happened to need an extra voice for Xoanon at the third cliffhanger, so he was recruited to scream "who am I?" in between meeting Baker and being shown around Television Centre.

- Baker annoyed Boucher by deliberately misattributing a line from Kipling's *Barrack-Room Ballads* to Gertrude Stein, but misattribution is a bit of a running-gag in this season. Leela's accidental electrocution replaced a more assertive move by the Doctor that Baker was reluctant to use (it could be imitated and it was, in effect, a man punching a woman). With the field rations explanation gone, the Doctor gave the password "I don't believe in ghosts either", referring back to the "rattlesnake" scene in Part Two. Another amended fight, with Peter Baldock as a possessed Tesh, emphasised that the Doctor was trying to keep both parties alive.

- Matters got complicated on 25th... as transmission of Elisabeth Sladen's last episode neared, the press were getting wind of the new *Doctor Who* girl, so a photo-call was arranged. Also, the two leads conducted a deeply strange interview on *Nationwide* with Bob Wellings. For most of this, Baker stayed in character as the Doctor and was a bit surly about his new hanger-on while Jameson was like a shy version of Leela who'd been told to be polite and not kill anyone. Ninety minutes before this, the scoop had been beaten by *John Craven's Newsround* showing the first meeting of the Doctor and Leela just after *Blue Peter*.

- By now, Hinchcliffe had looked at the production schedule for the Victorian adventure and decided to pause broadcasts and show this nearly-completed story in January. It being a slow news day, Jameson got a lot of pictures in the papers on 26th, when the remainder of Part Four was taped. A few scenes were lost, notably the shuttle between the cave and the ship (probably dropped for budgetary reasons), and a couple of small details about Andor's weakening grip on the tribe were edited out. (This includes confirmation that Tomas was his son and that, when they still believed the Doctor to be the Evil One and dead, he launched the attack knowing that Neeva was lying.)

- Part One was shown on New Year's Day 1977, six weeks after "The Deadly Assassin" ended (almost as long as the gap between 2.9, "The Time Meddler" and 3.1, "Galaxy 4"). Newspapers traditionally run a lot of filler in the week between Christmas and New Year, and on New Year's Eve, the *Daily Mirror* ran a Terrance Dicks story, "Doctor Who and the Hell Planet", in which astronauts visit a toxic world and discover that – all together now – it's Earth 7,000 years in the future. (So anyone who griped about X12.3, "Orphan 55" can suck it up.) Part One was shown after the UK TV premiere of *Willy Wonka and the Chocolate Factory*, which is more apt than not, at the new regular time of 6.20pm. After the kerfuffle over "The Deadly Assassin", this seemed like a sensible precaution. An imported cartoon, *Tarzan, Lord of the Jungle* was on in the *Basil Brush* slot and then the sport, news and *Jim'll Fix It*. Part Two was ten minutes later, because they gave Jimmy Savile more air-time.

- Public reaction to Leela was more favourable than Baker's, although the usual tabloid hypocrisy about television showing "near-naked" girls (not at all like the ones they plastered on Page Three) and attempts to whip up outrage over the violence weren't long in coming (see next story). Some wondered whether a woman being violent was more shocking than the stuff in *Starsky and Hutch*, some claimed that Leela was always falling over (they must have seen the *Newsround* clip and nothing else), and occasionally it was proposed that having a "savage" was less feminist than it seemed. As we're going to see, the programme was a Rorschach Test for the commentariat.

- The story was repeated on BBC4 in December 2015, making it almost the only *Doctor Who* on BBC television between Series 9 and 10, other than those Christmas episodes and a mini-scene introducing Pearl Mackie as Bill.

14.5: "The Robots of Death"

(Serial 4R, Four Episodes, 29th January – 19th February 1977.)

Which One is This? It's a country-house murder with a few slight differences. The house is a mobile storm-mine on a desert planet and we see the butler do it – we just don't know who reprogrammed him.

Firsts and Lasts It's the last story directed by Michael E Briant and the first to give the Doctor and Leela a robot chum (with hindsight, D84 is a trial-run for K9 and might have been a better idea). It's the last time we see the classy fake-oak TARDIS console room, although Part One offers an extended look at it. We also get our last view of the TARDIS key designed by Barry Letts for Season Eleven: henceforth it'll be a standard Yale key.

Four Things to Notice About "The Robots of Death"...

• The director, who reluctantly returned to *Doctor Who* but thought he was now better than that, judged the first-draft script as corny and clichéd. He and the designer set about trying to up the ante with the visuals, going for an Art Deco look (because nobody's done a whodunit in a 1930s setting). The astute among you will recall that this almost exactly replicates Raymond P Cusick's thought-process in "The Daleks" (1.2). So they've replaced one cliché with a different one.

• As we've noted earlier in this book (**Do Robots Have Rights?** under "Robot"), America tends to treat stories about robots as race allegories while Europeans, from Capek onwards, treat it as a class issue. Here, to defuse either interpretation, half the crew are from what in 1970s Britain were under-represented ethnic minorities, and the two most obvious suspects have working-class accents. One of the last-named survives, as do the two neurotic posh white characters. To complicate it further, two of the cast are Scotsmen trying to sound English, and they land up trying to kill each other.

• Once again (as in "The Android Invasion"), there's an attempt to preserve a mystery by only showing us certain characters from the knees down in key scenes. And once again, this makes us consider the shoes. This is a shame, as the robots look great from the ankles up and the *agent provocateur* is wearing this year's fashionable Vatican Swiss Guard look (see last story), so has very distinctive trousers. They could get away with this once a week on Saturdays, with no repeats (until a Christmas omnibus), but watched all in one go, it's a dead giveaway. Luckily, most viewers are too busy laughing at the robots' tinfoil shoes to pay attention.

• This is another story that Russell T. Davies *really* liked, especially the robots themselves. Apart from the "please do not throw hands at me" scene re-enacted with suspiciously-similar robots in X4.0, "Voyage of the Damned", consider how the "infected" robots' eyes glow red and think about the other similarities between them and the Ood (notably X2.8-2.9, "The Impossible Planet" / "The Satan Pit" and X4.3, "Planet of the Ood").

The Continuity

The Doctor states that 'to the rational mind nothing is inexplicable, only unexplained'. This makes it more annoying for him when he can't immediately furnish Leela with an explanation of something. He's also peeved when her acute senses detect an anomaly he missed. Once again, his shoulders are his most vulnerable point. He's rather fond of bumblebees.

• *Background*. He's been to other societies where robots were persuaded to turn on their creators, and many others where they were as common as this world. He mentions the Loyeed, who have a term for robophobia, 'Grimwade's Syndrome'. Apparently he knew Marie Antoinette at the time of her arrest [c.f. "The Ark in Space"]. He's also been on a storm-mine on Corlano Beta. He seems familiar with the Laserson Probe, a gadget of remarkable utility.

• *Ethics*. After a few encounters with superficially charming AIs {including Xoanon last story], he finally seems to have taken a shine to one: the undercover agent D84. He asks for D84's consent when doing risky things (as with Leela, Toos and Uvanov), and is concerned about saving him while destroying the reprogrammed robots. He congratulates the robot on failing, as it's 'one of the basic human freedoms'. [We get the distinct impression that he and Taron Capel might've bonded had not the campaign for robot liberty been homicidal. The Doctor would have given any other oppressed group help from the first

Cultural Primer: *Top of the Pops*

As we've been saying throughout these books, simply considering *Doctor Who* as a BBC "version" of any US or home-grown space-epic or time-travel yarn is a category error of the first magnitude. The people making it, and the viewers for whom it was intended, often barely noticed that such things existed and had other priorities. The BBC were making a low-rent family drama with resources appropriated from, and appropriate for, costume dramas and light entertainment. Although you *can* find parallels in the production-techniques and intentions of various BBC dramas over the years (*Adam Adamant Lives!* and *Out of the Unknown* for the 1960s, *I, Claudius* and *Doomwatch* for the 70s, *Blakes 7* and *Tenko* in the early 80s and so on), doing that misses the point.

The simplest one-line definition of how *Doctor Who* was made, what it looked like in any phase of its original format, who they thought was watching and what they thought those punters at home wanted is: *Top of the Pops* with a plot.

Despite a few brief periods of wandering, the fundamental nature of *TOTP* (as it's usually abbreviated) was to be half an hour at 7.30pm on Thursdays on BBC1, just as *Doctor Who* was primarily a method of keeping the audience(s) for Saturday teatime occupied between sport and mass-appeal Light Entertainment or action films. This was television as a communal experience – there was nothing "cult" about either. The ritual was as much part of the experience as the content of any one episode, or the discussions about it on the way to school or at the tea-break at work. *Top of the Pops* was as much about confirming, fuelling or contradicting the preconceptions of grumpy parents (or cynical older siblings into "serious" album bands) as about giving "the Kids" something of their own.

The format was, subject to slight alterations along the way, simple. A studio had three stages on which bands performed versions of their current hits (either completely live, with a studio orchestra and in-house backing singers, or completely lip-synched to the single, or some compromise that kept the Musician's Union and BBC engineers happy). Around these were a studio audience of 16-25-year-olds in modish dress – all supposedly there to dance, but mainly looking up at the monitors to see if they were in shot. It was never the same kids twice.

There was a host who sometimes provided evidence of enthusiasm for every single act or resorted to dad-jokes to keep the momentum up (and occasionally interview artistes or guest presenters). Obvious gaps were filled when the week's big chart-riser was an American who couldn't be bothered to fly over for one spot or was a dead artiste's work re-issued for some reason. And there was the Top 20 countdown (or 30, or 40), the details of which had only just been collated and released on the Tuesday of the week. When *TOTP* was on Thursdays at prime time, the recording was on Wednesday evening. The haste with which an edition was put together added a bit of zing, but frustrated any attempts to make "art".

All of this took place inside a space that was, in many sense, made of pop. That's "pop" as in music and "Pop" as in Richard Hamilton, Eduardo Paolozzi, Peter Blake, Andy Warhol, Jasper Johns et al. The set-design, lighting and video effects were all of-the-moment, made to seem as unlike anything else on television as possible. That's why it now looks so much like the other BBC quasi-disposable "happening", *Doctor Who*. It's not just that the same technicians were working on both series, nor simply that the directors were watching each other's work. Both were facing the same problems and finding similar solutions. As we've said many times before, *Doctor Who* was, for the youngest viewers (and a lot of the oldest) less a story you followed than a place you visited once a week. It was, in the 60s and early 70s, "about" odd noises and strange-looking visuals. Each edition had to be not just unlike (nearly) any other series, but as different as possible from the previous iteration, even if sticking to a certain ritual.

These days, talking about the 42-year run of *TOTP* (1964-2006) presents various difficulties. There are lots of clips online in isolation but lacking the strangeness their original context brought to them (especially as these clips were often from a kitsch rerun show, *TOTP2*, from the ironic 90s, cherry-picked and with smart-alec comments attached). Most episodes made before 1975 have vanished from the archives, if they ever got there in the first place. Some can't be shown now for legal reasons (Noel Edmunds, a key player in the 1970s, has apparently slapped injunctions on his editions). The confirmation of a lot of people's worst fears about one of the early presenters now taints everything (we'll get to him presently).

However, and this is the basic difference American readers will have to get to grips with about this series, it was never about the presenters and never "curated" (as we'd say now) – we're not

continued on page 337...

14.5 The Robots of Death

episode. In a Sylvester McCoy story, he'd've steered the TARDIS there deliberately to overthrow human tyranny.]

- *Inventory:*
- *Sonic Screwdriver.* Handy for jimmying a lock, but – curiously – not used on screen when making an anti-robot device from a comms link and a reprogrammed robot's head.
- *Jelly Babies.* To calm down the hostile Bright Young Things, the Doctor offers them to break the ice. He himself eats two, a yellow and a green.
- *Scarf.* This and the hat are used to confuse a disorientated killer robot by disguising another killer robot as the Doctor, so they keep repeatedly trying to strangle each other.
- *Other.* He lends his yellow yoyo to Leela to keep her out of his hair, and also to discuss why the TARDIS's dimensional transcendentalism isn't magic. He's got a cheap pocket-torch from Woolworths and a blow-pipe of some kind [possibly confiscated from Leela – see next story], through which he can breathe when submerged.

The TARDIS is travelling very smoothly, for once. [In the light of comments in the next script by this author (15.3, "Image of the Fendahl"), it's possible the Ship has taken to Leela.] There seem to be a lot of boxes around the place. There's also an oval marble table on a corner and a rack on the wall holding the Doctor's other jackets, including the corduroy one, and his hat and scarf.

The Supporting Cast

- *Leela* continues to puzzle us over what was taught in that jungle. She seems comfortable with the speed in 'miles an hour' and knows the word 'mechanical'. She somehow gets the concept of 'money'. She can imitate a dowager duchess on being released from confinement, acts like a police inspector when interrogating a robot and seems to adjust to the concept of robots remarkably quickly. On the other hand, she hears that something's wrong with the motors before the Doctor and is alert to Poul's odd behaviour. Her first aid skills seem more helpful than the advanced Kaldor medicine [perhaps some kind of acupressure or shiatsu]. Her people apparently had a saying, 'when you are injured, look for a man with scars' [wise enough, but it contradicts other statements about Sevateem rehab].
- *D84.* An undercover robot agent for the mining company, with Poul investigating the threats made by Taron Capel. In posing as a D-class, he must remain silent in mixed company. Once outed, he reveals something like a dry wit. ('Would you like to use it? I cannot speak') and has an oddly hesitant way of repeating himself when deliberating ('I must have, I must have information'). When the fail-safe switch immobilises all un-programmed robots, D84 – on a different circuit – continues to act autonomously. He can overhear SV7's commands to the rebel machines but doesn't obey them.

The Non-Humans

- *The Robots* come in three categories. Utility androids bear numbers with the prefix D and are black (or a very dark green) with silver trim, Vocs (which can talk and follow complex instructions) are V and are light green with the same trim, and the supervisory hub SV7 is entirely silver. All follow the same basic design of a carved humanoid male face with wavy "hair", a quilted tabard and culottes in the assigned colour and an identification badge [like a car registration number] on the chest and shoes made of something very like cooking foil. Those that can speak have calm RP voices, like BBC continuity announcers of yesteryear. The hands seem to be detachable and semi-autonomous.

[As the robots present as male, we'll stick with that pronoun – nobody seems to have wanted female-shaped machines.] They're sufficiently anthropomorphic to have their primary visual input through the eyes, a problem when the eyes are covered. Reprogramming seems to be via this route too, and Taron Capel hacks his converts first through blipvert-style signals on a screen then a physical upgrade in his workshop. Reprogrammed robots have red glowing eyes. A laserson probe in the forehead causes severe damage. Capel accesses each robot's CPU by removing the face-plate. [In short, they've followed the human model more than they needed to.]

Broken / deactivated robots are identified with a small red disc called a 'corpse marker' (it resembles a bicycle reflector) and kept in a holding-bay. [To forestall a few paragraphs of **Things That Don't Make Sense**, we'll assume that they normally limp there under their own steam and put themselves to bed before Dask shows up to say goodnight and stick a disc on them.]

Cultural Primer: *Top of the Pops*

...continued from page 335

talking about a series with a Dick Clark, a Dan Sugarman, a Don Cornelius or a Casey Kasem. The star of the show was that week's Top 30 singles (or 20, or 40), regardless of perceived "quality". If it was climbing the chart, it was on, somehow or other, even if it was a dreadful novelty single, a controversial song or by someone unable or unwilling to come to the UK to promote it.

[And let's get this out of the way... the collation of which singles were selling best was a bit haphazard. Various trade papers had their own polls with different rankings, as we mention in X3.7, "42". The BBC commissioned their own. Yet none of these was split up like America's *Billboard* into categories: we only started getting those once smaller labels pushed to get an "Indie" chart in the early 80s. Unlike America, with its odd history of radio-station management, outright discrimination and that AM/FM stuff, if it sold, it made the list (even LPs got into the singles chart if they were by the Beatles and selling absurdly fast). There were no genres not counted in the Top 20 (or however many) – until someone noticed that Hindi film-score tracks were being distributed through informal networks in the 90s, but that's a different story for another time. Disco, Metal, Punk, Reggae, comedy songs, school choirs doing treacly songs about grandparents or sparrows and elderly American balladeers having comebacks would be cheek-by-jowl in the same chart and thus on the same edition of *TOTP*.]

Pop music was the demotic art-form of the late twentieth century and attempts by big business to control it often came unstuck. There were other programmes for chin-stroking musos, hosted and curated by the sort of pompous music journalists who preferred reading the sleeve-notes to playing the records. There were other programmes self-consciously trying to set the agenda and present the new acts that they (and the Tin Pan Alley pluggers) thought the public ought to buy. The beauty (if that's the word) of the *TOTP* format was that it followed what the public were actually buying that week and tried to represent it without thought for what future viewers might think. Unexpected wonders, scandalous transgressive performances or sheer car-crash wrongnesses were equally possible, often coming hard on each others' heels. The public got what the public wanted, all at once and right in their laps. You rarely had any idea what would happen next.

The series and its basic premise is harder to explain to a generation who can't conceptualise either the thrill of going out to buy a physical record or the speed of changes in music, style and the grammar of television between 1960 and 1990. Britain was a pop-cultural Galapagos, with accelerated development compared to unwieldy continental landmasses where Dinosaurs ruled the Charts and entire years passed without haircuts significantly altering. An experienced viewer can date a record, dress or visual effect to within six months.

Neither can anyone not raised in the UK really grasp how one three-minute performance on one show could instantly change the whole game. America, in particular, developed its own methods for giving kids a dose of pop on television, but these strange, lumbering beasts were hidden away in an after-school slot away from the general public and drenched in targeted advertising. *TOTP*'s 7.30pm Thursday slot allowed people to just stumble across things without intending or deliberately seeking them out. An appearance on *TOTP* could change everything; the whole country would see and hear something and be talking about it the next morning. (This, of course, gave a bit of a head start to any new band living less than an hour's drive from where the studio was. Shakin' Stevens getting flu meant that a South London band bubbling under the Top 40 were called in at two hours' notice, which is how Boy George became a household name in under a week after Culture Club performed "Do You Really Want to Hurt Me?" almost unrehearsed.)

The whole point of pop music was to be of-its-time. In late twentieth-century Britain, *its time* meant that particular Thursday evening.

Here's the first thing that would strike anyone coming across *TOTP* clips after exposure to *Doctor Who* from the same year: they look almost interchangeable. If anything, the instant-response pop show had slightly better inlay and electronic effects because the technicians had practiced on *Doctor Who* first (even if these trial-runs weren't shown until later). For example, the Eradicator effect from "Carnival of Monsters" (10.2) was worked out in the studio on 3rd July, 1972, but not shown until 27th January, 1973, by which time half the country had seen it when Alice Cooper performed "School's Out" in August. When the story was on air, The Sweet were Number One with "Blockbuster", and the most-used clip uses the same colour-synthesiser as the anti-matter crea-

continued on page 339...

14.5 The Robots of Death

Planet Notes This planet has a desert with ferocious sandstorms and, to judge by the lighting, at least two suns. [Cass says 'where in seven suns is that robot?', so it may be more, but that's improbable – more likely they're on one of a number of worlds, in a small cluster of stars, that trade with each other and don't have much to do with anyone else. The biggest population centre is Kaldor City, leading a lot of people (and the tie-in works) to suppose that 'Kaldor' is the name of the planet. On screen, that doesn't necessarily follow – Kansas City is in Missouri and the planet Barcelona, X1.13, "The Parting of the Ways", isn't anywhere near the city of that name.]

The sand covers most of the planet, apparently, and contains valuable mineral ores (Keefan, Xelenite, traces of Lucanol) which get stirred up by the periodic storms and, if the miners are lucky, sucked straight into the mine's hoppers.

The Doctor and Leela, while exposed to the open air in intake vents, can breathe normally. [Unless there's some sort of environmental filter that we're not told about, that means the atmosphere must be breathable and within the usual temperature range.]

A tour usually lasts about a year: the shipboard recycling seems to work on a monthly cycle.

History

• *Dating*. [Other than the Tchaikovsky and Debussy playing on the soundtrack at the start, nothing connects this story to Earth. If we take these as evidence, then it's clearly far into the future, generations after the Twenty Families arrived.] Chess and physical books are still popular pastimes.

Twenty Families arrived on the planet in the first wave and became the elite. Thus, more recently, they could hush up a case of robophobia-induced suicide.

The Analysis

Where Does This Come From? So much has been written about the way this story's *look* runs athwart the source-material (and commonplace comparisons between this mine and any other in the real world or other television), it's odd how everyone's missed what's under our noses – and, more to the point, under or on the noses of the actors. If you were a kid in Britain in early 1977, the sight of Brian Croucher in eyeliner, lipstick and (taking the school playground taunt literally) a big girl's blouse made absolute sense.

Anyone wondering why the essay about *Top of the Pops* accompanies this story or who skipped our comments on Glam with "Terror of the Autons" (8.1) probably thinks Millennials invented gender-fluidity. Just quickly, between 1971 and 1973, the rapid turnover of styles and movements in UK pop music caused a lot of people to combine straightforward riff-driven blues (a style considered terminally unhip since the mid-60s) with pop-art conceptual performances and lyrics about the mix of high-life and low-lifes. Youth Culture had been around long enough for past styles to be plundered, sometimes ironically.

As performers, men in feather boas outnumbered the raunchy/butch women, but the audiences at the gigs were a different matter. Phase One was when people who were more comfortable not acting macho talked about revealing their real-selves on stage (we're talking Lou Reed, Ziggy-era David Bowie, Eno-era Roxy Music and the pioneer of all this, Marc Bolan); Phase Two was when bands who could sound a bit like that found that putting on make-up and flamboyant clothes made them irresistible to girls (The Sweet, Slade, Mud, Mott the Hoople, Alvin Stardust, Gary Glitter – the "bricklayers in drag"); Phase Three, when the party was more-or-less over, entailed foreigners who'd belatedly jumped on the bandwagon keeping it going (Abba, Alice Cooper, Sparks, New York Dolls, Fox) and acts signed in the Klondike phase developed into something more odd (Brian Eno, Be-Bop Deluxe, Queen) while the earlier models went to America and cashed in. Phase Two had ended about three years before this story was made, but the skills that BBC make-up artists had honed hadn't lapsed. (Sweet's guitarist, Steve Priest, admitted that he'd figured out that the longer he took getting made-up, the more chance he had of being sat next to one of the Pan's People dancers and getting a phone number.)

Just to make the connection stronger, a lot of the set-design for the Storm Mine resembles *TOTP* c. August 1973. That's even less of a surprise if one recalls the biggest design story of the Glam era: Barbara Hulanicki's boutique-cum-theme-park, Big Biba. During the 60s, the Biba look took bits of Art Nouveau and an earthy colour-range into the high street while catering for stars (and, with stars wearing their stuff on television, one

Cultural Primer: *Top of the Pops*

...continued from page 337

ture that ate Bessie and the TARDIS in "The Three Doctors" (10.1) a few weeks before in screen time, but a month earlier at Television Centre. We could argue all night about whether Glam and *TOTP* were cause or effect, but Pertwee era stories have that whole Ziggy Stardust vibe. Check out the last episode of "The Green Death" (10.5) for blatantly *TOTP*-ish visuals applied to storytelling, plus a set for Professor Jones's pad that's a collage of Victoriana and Op-Art.

TOTP was, in some ways, less ambitious with CSO because they were using it non-diegetically (rather than as a way of showing what characters in a story were really seeing), but this means that they got it right more often. By the same token, a lot of inlay effects used signal-generators built by in-house engineers and, after a while, these would be lent to *Doctor Who*. The Transduction effect in "The Deadly Assassin" is a ripe example (that's also in the Alice Cooper clip). Over the 1980s, you can date the development of commercial image-processing as on-screen text, Quantel, Paintbox and HARRY come into use in both series.

Some of *Doctor Who* had an obligation towards a kind of mimetic honesty, looking the way a real place like that ought to (especially in present-day or historical settings), but the whole point of *Who*, from this perspective, is to rupture that familiarity somehow – if only by having people from today playing dress-up the way pop stars did when pilfering historical-looking garb. It's interesting that the peak period for "pure" Historical stories is also when this trend for retro cosplay in pop accelerated (see **Did Sergeant Pepper Know the Doctor?** under 5.1, "The Tomb of the Cybermen"). When Roy Wood of The Move performed "Fire Brigade" in 1968, he wasn't in *exactly* the same Pageboy outfit Dodo had plundered in 3.6, "The Ark". But in both cases, the aim was a striking look that would "read" well in black and white, looking out-of-place and therefore more modern than that week's fashions.

Around this were sets that, for most practical purposes, can be considered gift-wrapping. Indeed, as the series embraced colour, everything got gaudy, shiny and insubstantial – but the series' design had always been playful. Of the few episodes left in the archives from before 1970, almost all go for bold Op-Art sets like giant pinball machines.[55] There's often a giant Eidophor screen as a focal point (as with the Testing Room set for "The Tomb of the Cybermen", Kent's office in 5.4, "The Enemy of the World" or the main hall in 4.7, "The Macra Terror".) The BBC didn't have many of these: some sources say only one was bought, so the two programmes had to work around each other's requirements and share the main one with *Out of the Unknown* and Election Night coverage. Only rarely is there any attempt at *TOTP*-space looking like anything but a TV studio, but the surroundings are intended to be exciting, not overwhelming. These are abstract spaces, only occasionally resembling the lairs of villains in lurid spy series but more commonly resembling the less-mimetic sets in *Doctor Who*. (6.7, "The War Games" has an alien HQ that only needs Pan's People to complete the crossover.) They are also intended to be as contemporary as possible. Again, as with what was happening in fashion and graphic design, there was a bewilderingly rapid churn-rate of trends and styles. These can be used like tree-rings for dating purposes.

The difficulty for anyone attempting to make a thesis of this is that the majority of the first 500 episodes are missing. In fact, there's only five complete editions from the 1960s (one of those is the camera rehearsal, another lacks the studio sound for the links between numbers). However, a lot of backstage photos exist. What comes across time and again – in shots of the sets for monochrome episodes – is how much colour there was, even if the viewers at home couldn't see it. Yet a great majority of sets designs across the decades fall back on a few high-contrast objects suspended from the ceiling and a matte black backdrop. (You'd think from this that Tony Snoaden, designer of "The Sun Makers" and 9.3, "The Sea Devils" would be an obvious crossover, but oddly, he never worked on the Pops.)

This was, it has to be admitted, something of a cliché in 60s set design (to the extent that Sydney Newman issued memos about it when Head of Drama), but it persisted into the Punk era on *TOTP*. Another regular feature was a raised stage with a loud concentric pattern of squares, circles or zig-zaggy explosions, often matched by two flats behind the performer(s) so that they could be shot from two angles, allowing a third camera to cover the presenter and the fourth and fifth to get ready for the next act. Sometimes one of these flats would be replaced by that Eidophor, either projecting film or with a polarised light display (like

continued on page 341...

14.5 The Robots of Death

could create a new fad within hours). It was significantly less expensive than Mary Quant's stuff, but just as desirable to teenagers and film-stars. Everyone from Twiggy to Freddie Mercury wore Biba, so did shop-assistants.

In 1973, they bought the 1930s Art Deco department story Derry and Tom's (famous for its roof-garden) and turned it into what we'd now call a "retail experience". It was purposely like walking into a Fred Astaire/ Ginger Rogers film and their trademark look (metallic decals on dark matte surfaces) was applied to baked bean tins, the lifts, the wallpaper, accessories and children's wear. And, yes, rock stars and the like came to eat there, or browse, but most people came to look around and daydream. Hardly anyone actually bought anything. It was an odd business model, but late 1973 was about as bad a time to launch something like this as September 1939 or February 2020. Our point is: if Biba had sold robots, they'd look like D84. Toos has a bedroom almost identical to the shop's display.

By the time this story was made and shown, the cycle of revived movie icons had moved on to Humphrey Bogart and Lauren Bacall – but, for the original intended audience, this mix-and-match of *Jugendstil*, Bauhaus, Streamline Moderne and RKO musicals was "retro" in as much as it looked like a five-year-old repeat of *Top of the Pops* or *Lift Off with Ayshea*. (ITV's Glam-era *TOTP* knock-off, presented by two puppets and a wannabe pop-star who was – allegedly – secretly married to Roy Wood. Mysteriously, Wood's band Wizzard were rarely not on the show. His make-up was very like Taron Capel's, but he had a wild beard and copious hair.)

The usual pretext given for this trip down Memorex lane was that the director and his designers looked at the script and blenched at the idea of doing an industrial complex where everyone wears overalls. That doesn't bear close examination. The dialogue and setting make a big feature of the divide between the pampered humans and the actual workers – in 70s Britain, it's hard to resist a temptation to make this yet another "Trouble At T'Mill" set-up of exploited workers in cloth caps and posh folks in silk.

The name "Taron Capel" hints at Karel Capek, who gave us the word "Robot" (Czech for "Worker", in case you didn't know) in a satire about industrial relations written (oh, look) in the 1920s. The BBC made a version of it in 1936 and, from the photos, it's the most Expressionist-looking thing ever done in Britain. There's a "Zilda" on the Storm Mine, not too far from "Zelda" (pre-Nintendo, a name associated solely with F. Scott Fitzgerald's wife). If you have people with English accents being waited on hand and foot by people with slightly posher English accents, everyone will be thinking of Jeeves. (The odd trousers worn on the men *and* all the robots look like Plus Fours, compounding the Wodehouse associations.) If this wasn't inter-war British enough, the plot then turns into an Agatha Christie pastiche. We'll talk about which one in a bit, but we'll nudge you towards our comments on X4.7, "The Unicorn and the Wasp".

What's remarkable, therefore, is that there may have been a brief moment when Michael Briant *wasn't* thinking of Lalique, Tiffany, the Chrysler Building interiors and SS *Normandie*. How could this be? Well, the reputation of robots had taken a bit of a knock after Capek and most screen representations were rather lumpen after World War II. We've discussed some of this under "Robot" and "The Brain of Morbius", so rather than hammer it into the ground, the most obvious comparison is British television adaptations of Isaac Asimov stories about robots.

A 1962 ITV version of "Little Lost Robot" is probably the most damaging in this regard, with a walking petrol-pump hiding among lots of other walking petrol-pumps (and Boris Karloff in evening-dress telling us about it at the start). Even though it's on a commercial station and has advert breaks, there isn't enough plot for the slot, so the viewer is left looking at these ugly lumps for ages. That was in the *Out of This World* series, a summer digression from ABC's *Armchair Theatre* and so supervised by Irene Shubik under Sydney Newman's aegis. As we all know, Newman was headhunted to shake up BBC's Drama production and that's how *Doctor Who* happened, but so did a revised anthology series, *Out of the Unknown*, in which Shubik got to do this sort of thing without the need for a Rod Serling-like host. Of the six Asimov stories adapted in the series's three good seasons, three were the puzzle-stories about the Three Laws on which his reputation was founded, and one was a compressed version of one of his detective novels with a human and robot team.

No two of these looked alike or had the same person play Susan Calvin, the expert who deduced the robots' motivation for acting strangely. Three

Cultural Primer: *Top of the Pops*

...continued from page 339

the "targets" in "Tomb"). Once CSO came in, they were allowed a lot more leeway, but the costume designers had to think carefully.

That brings us to the second thing that strikes anyone new to this: as with *Doctor Who*, we have a series designed to allow a much wider range of possible events than any other from the same department, but the full repertoire can never all happen at once in any given half-hour. No one edition of *Top of the Pops* could be as exciting as the series as a concept.

Top of the Pops as a ritual was stronger than any given week's edition, just as *Doctor Who* was. What makes the apparent anomalies interesting is exactly the way they contradict the usual trite histories of pop-culture we get fed – Engelbert Humperdinck was at Number One for most of the Summer of Love, for example. The height of Glam had late surges of hits for Perry Como and Donald Pears. By partially surrendering control of the content to the record-buying publicoid, the BBC allowed people onto their screens and into people's living-rooms that stood little chance of breaking in or becoming mainstream otherwise. Even an edition from a week with an outstandingly great Top Thirty (the remit changed in the early 70s) could only show so many and would, in trying to entertain as many viewers as possible, go for variety over quality and chart-placing over either. As with the charts whence the selection came, any one edition might have one act guaranteed to make the majority of viewers think "what the hell did they put *this* on for?" But no two viewers, especially in a household watching it together, would agree on which. Grannies bought 45s too.

That's a significant parallel to *Doctor Who* that *won't* strike the first-time viewer. As we explained in **Did the BBC Actually Like *Doctor Who*?** (with 3.9, "The Savages"), a tension existed in the Corporation's upper echelons between public service as an idea and the notion of giving people what was good for them. What is usually overlooked or papered-over in the normal account of the BBC's attitude to rock and roll (and then pop) is that they were institutionally obliged to provide a service for everyone in Britain – and, therefore, *had* to allow pop and science fiction a reasonable amount of screen-time and airplay. Over on the commercial side of the fence, the ITV companies had trouble in the 1950s with the common association of rock and roll with knife-gangs and race-riots. Advertisers ran a mile when anything looking or sounding like youth culture was mentioned.

It took a BBC producer to get the music and style onto the nation's screens with *Six-Five Special*. The focus of the first wave of British rock was a café in Soho, the 2I's (as in "two eyes"). Working class lads from across the country flocked there to be discovered and signed up by impresarios based in Denmark Street (as near as dammit the real Tin Pan Alley of London); we'll skip over why so many privately-educated dapper middle-aged chaps were keen on talking to rough young men in coffee-houses and concentrate on the result. By the time *Six-Five Special* ended at Christmas 1958, there were ITV companies keen to jump the bandwagon and a steady supply of moody-looking teenagers with dime-Western stage-names. The thing is, as you may recall, not every ITV company showed everything made by the other ITV companies, and rarely if ever were they all showing one at the same time (except maybe the news). National exposure really needed the BBC. With over 75% of the population having a telly by 1960 (52 million people in total, so about 39 million viewers in theory), and only one genuine network (as opposed to the dog-eat-dog approach of the regional ITV stations), it was possible to reach practically all of Britain in one go, if that was what you wanted.

With hindsight, *Six-Five Special* was to *Top of the Pops* what *The Quatermass Experiment* was for *Doctor Who*: a proof-of-concept and a way to create an audience for something they hadn't known was possible with television. Telly and rock were the two new mass entertainment booms just before Sputnik; in all three cases, the grown-ups had to adjust rapidly. When we see what's left in the archives of these pioneering series, they look creaky and odd, but both acknowledged television-ness in their content – not least because it's the one thing all viewers have in common. Yes, Lonnie Donegan was recycling Leadbelly; yes the plot of *Quatermass* sags badly in the middle when it turns into almost a routine police procedural, but they both showed cameras and backstage areas and made it about "now".

What happened next was odd, but factors into the rest of this story: as the impresarios tried to mould their protégés into All Round Family Entertainers and made more "safe" records, kids at home had been watching Donegan, the biggest

continued on page 343...

14.5 The Robots of Death

were comedies. We know "The Prophet" for providing handy stock costumes for 6.2, "The Mind Robber" and a famous bit of Radiophonica, but "Liar!" had unblinking androids in overalls (you've seen the protagonist being built in the titles for *Malcolm in the Middle*). The story was originally published in 1941 and was the one where editor John W Campbell noticed a trend in Asimov's stories and codified them as the Three Laws, for later use.

The novel the OOTU team turned into a straight detective drama was *The Naked Sun*, one of three Asimov robot stories aired in rapid succession in six weeks. Judging from what's left of it, it was designed and costumed to look as unlike the others in the same series as possible – paisley and chiffon cassocks for the humans (most of whom you'd recognise if you watch seasons Twelve to Fourteen), PVC purple snoods and long hooped skirts for the robots. And those late 60s inflatable armchairs (8.1, "Terror of the Autons") that came back in 1998. Other stories in this series occasionally played with the expectations and design shorthand of earlier robot-themed stories, so "The Midas Plague" went to town on jokey robot psychiatrists and so on. In short, Briant was avoiding a cliché already steadfastly resisted for over about a dozen years even within the BBC, and his "imaginative" solution to the non-existent problem was already close to becoming a staple.

The plot of *The Naked Sun* is about, not to put too fine a point on it, hysteria. It's a sequel to *The Caves of Steel*, which is about what the Doctor would call robophobia, and set in a future New York that's more crowded and busy than the present model. Being by a lad from Brooklyn, that book's warmly indulgent about traffic and population density so the second book – obviously a New Yorker's view of California – has a sparsely-populated planet where people have taken social distancing to extremes. They freak out at the idea of being in the same room as anyone else. They never physically meet but surround themselves with robots and communicate on 3D videophones. This whole situation hinges on a loophole in the Three Laws allowing robots to be used as murder weapons and a roboticist who really doesn't like humans. He's planning something big to remove them. Just to stop this similarity seeming like happenstance, the robot detective, R Daneel Olivaw, was played by here David Collings,

whose character in "The Robots of Death" is the rough equivalent of Elijah Bailey, Olivaw's partner. (Five years earlier, in 1964, there had been a version of *The Caves of Steel* with Peter Cushing as Bailey. Barely any of this survives, but it seems to be all shiny metal and capes. Terry Nation did the adaptation.)

Isaac Asimov and Agatha Christie make appropriate bedfellows, if that's the phrase we want. Both suffered from over-exposure; both became emblematic of their preferred category of fiction (to the detriment of other writers and their own reputations); both innovated early in their careers and (after the innovations became fitted-as-standard by later, better writers) the next generation of readers wondered why the big-name writers were so well-regarded and decided that – if these best-sellers were "as good as it gets" – neither category of writing was much cop. And both got adapted for television rather a lot.

The Christie most usually cited in this context has gone through a few titles but is now called *And Then There Were None*. It's Christie's best-selling mystery (and, by some measures, the world's) – since publication in 1939, it's been adapted left, right and centre, including twice for British television and two English-language films (although most adaptations alter the end to make it less bleak and inadvertently amusing). The adaptations struggle with the problem that a finite number of suspects being whittled down makes sleuthing almost redundant (we'll avoid any spoilers on how the book and most recent BBC version got around this). "The Robots of Death" isn't, when looked at coldly, much like this or any Christie mystery, but the general ambience helps to disguise the more overt borrowing from *The Naked Sun*.

But the Asimov connection (reputedly why "Uvanov" is called that, although another suggestion has merit – see the **Lore**) isn't the extent of the SF legacy being mixed up and served here. As with the hunting by vibration stuff last story, we've got a hint or two of *Dune* in the whole set-up, filtering a precious substance from sand and hoping for a decent storm. There's a whole cliffhanger constructed around the premise of *A Fall of Moondust* (Arthur C Clarke's pastiche of the books that got turned into Disaster Movies), with the sinking into dust when the engines fail. Twenty Families set-up is a bit of a staple, but recently (i.e., the late 60s and early 70s) given a fresh coat

Cultural Primer: *Top of the Pops*

...continued from page 341

star on *Six-Five Special*, and forming Skiffle bands. (See X4.17, "The End of Time Part One" and our discussion of this fad – but be aware that the other exponents of this trend they had on included Jon Pertwee, and a backing band including a lad from the audience called Terry, who was signed up and renamed "Adam Faith".)

Along with Davy Crockett hats, the must-have present of Christmas 1958 was Bert Weedon's book *Play in a Day* – and, if they hadn't got one already, a six-string guitar of whatever quality one could afford with money from delivering newspapers. In the mass media's eyes, the initial burst of rock and roll was replaced with Trad Jazz (people found they could do the Twist to Dixieland), then non-threatening boys (mainly Americans called Ricky or local lads who could rush out covers of the same Brill Building ballads) and instrumentals – a few British acts topped the Billboard chart in 1962 this way. But if you went to see a live band, something else was happening – actually, lots of somethings – but they all honed their craft on local circuits and word-of-mouth bookings. Meanwhile, the residue of 50s rock and roll was allowed onto children's television and some of the first wave performers made excruciatingly wholesome movies. (We refer you to our comments on Cliff Richard films under X2.7, "The Idiot's Lantern". Of Adam Faith's first two films, it's perhaps kinder to say nothing except that even budding screenwriter Terry Nation was embarrassed by *What a Whopper!*) So while The Shadows and their ilk were confined to *Crackerjack* – go on, say it – they were still emphasising two important facts: you could make a living doing this and you could please audiences doing what you liked doing. (And a third fact – Hank Marvin was cool while wearing NHS glasses, years before John Lennon or Michael Caine.)

One of the other somethings in progress was folk music. *Our* folk, not just stuff about railroads and cotton we'd learned from Woody Guthrie on *Children's Hour*. Unlike America, where folk was getting as formulaic as the pop on offer, Britain, especially the Celtic Fringe, had a three-century head-start and a BBC-backed gold-rush to find the rootsiest stuff about press-gangs and failed rebellions. People were aware of Bob Dylan and Pete Seeger, but as with the schoolboys then competing for the most obscure Delta Blues vinyl (watch this space), it was more about finding old songs than about writing new ones in the same idiom.

Here we have to introduce a polarisation that will haunt *Top of the Pops*, between pop as a (potentially tawdry) dream-factory and the (occasionally tedious) quest for "authenticity". Most successful acts included something personal in their output without making it an ordeal to hear, but the line from skiffle to folk to punk to indie is strong, if circuitous. Whenever the public got bored by a trend, the three-chords-and-the-truth DIY mob were always there, waiting for their moment. How a Light Entertainment show accommodated them we'll come to. The other problem the "authentic" lot had was that a lot of the potential audience, especially teenage boys, valued proficiency, "chops", as an end in itself and idolised virtuoso performers. Five years on from *Six-Five Special*, rather a lot of those were on the club circuit.

We can take as read that you know the next bit, those local bands with word-of-mouth live reputations all got recording contracts once one of them broke through just before the Cuban Missile Crisis, blah blah blah Hamburg, blah blah blah Cavern Club, blah blah blah Yeah Yeah Yeah. What's not as widely-reported is the role of Manchester/Liverpool ITV station Granada in promoting an aggressively regional identity while getting their other output onto national television. (The first year or so of *TOTP* came from Manchester, in a studio originally a Methodist chapel and more recently the base of the Mancunian Film Company. They loaned it to Hammer Films on occasion. Manchester, close to Liverpool, was where the action was at in 1964-5.)

Despite being a geographically small set of islands, Britain had extremely localised cultures. The much-vaunted pirate radio stations (see 5.6, "Fury from the Deep") were mainly based on ships just outside UK waters and thus could only get heard beyond London or the Pennines on exceptional days. BBC Radio would occasionally give the big new wave of pop acts national airplay, but the birth of *TOTP* was as much as anything a reaction against the emphatically London-centric Rediffusion show *Ready Steady Go!* (That ran from August 1963 to Christmas 1966. You can see the studio in the "Grimble Wedge" clip from the film *Bedazzled*.) The other ITV stations ran this at various times. (Anglia, the station based in Norwich and mainly concerned with running adverts for

continued on page 345...

of paint in Larry Niven's *Known Space* series. There's even a character named after Poul Anderson. Once again, it's not just a matter of plundering a few ideas here and there but, as with "The Face of Evil", a whole methodology of brewing up worlds from first principles (and following traditions learned from exposure to hundreds of SF paperbacks) that's at work here.

There's also a strong hint of whaling. In Britain, especially in the 1970s, this was a touchy subject, but the whole North Sea Oil business had started a mild interest in the combination of greed, skill, isolation and hunters' instinct associated with the nineteenth-century trade in whale-oil, ambergris and corsets. Trawlermen had a similar mystique but were rarely out for more than three days and everyone (more or less) ate cod and herring. (It's worth reminding American readers that *Moby Dick* isn't really in the Anglo-European canon and is only really known about because so many Americans made jokes about it – the book had rather the same status as *Gilligan's Island* in that regard. Anyone who tries to read Melville without the huge cultural baggage it has in the US sees something not unlike fanfic about genocide. See 23.1, "The Mysterious Planet".)

British pop-cultural ideas about the "romance" of this activity were almost all from second-hand and were oddly mixed with the Gold Rush and slavery. John Huston's film version, seen against the seemingly endless stream of films about all-white cowboys, made whaling seem more racially-inclusive, but that was about the extent of people's knowledge. (Briant claims that the multi-ethnic Storm Mine crew was part of a bid to avoid the off-the-shelf future mentioned above rather than this.)

One odd detail that reveals a lot more going on: the Doctor berates Leela for acting as if she's psychic, then grumbles when she's proved right. It's part of a behind-the-scenes debate where Holmes thought Leela perhaps had a clairvoyant granny, but Boucher opted for highly developed senses. As with the whole "Body Language" thread, it's eating their cake and having it, keeping the shape of various Romanticist ideas about "Noble Savages" attuned with things beyond rational understanding while making a rational case for how it really works. As we'll see again, pop-psychology and "frank" social anthropology was big business, especially after Desmond Morris gave it his air of authority from 50s series *Zoo Time* and his earlier career at London Zoo.

A more fundamental point we need to make: in common with many stories of this era, the Doctor's sticking-point is when people are killed to further a particular agenda, not the agenda itself. This being a story from 1976, there's a lot of that about in Britain, especially when discussing Palestine, Northern Ireland and US Civil Rights. The problem with making aliens or robots allegorical representations of social issues, especially race or class, is that the story eventually has to choose between being rhetorically consistent or logically coherent. Either way, the need to wrap things up in four or six episodes requires a reversion to biological determinism and a sort of essentialist stance at odds with whatever enlightened message the story had tried to convey.

"The Mutants" (9.4) resolved the attempt to satirise Apartheid with the initial idea of an alien species whose larval form looks human-ish by abruptly ending five and a half episodes of showing how Imperialism works on people "just like us" by re-estranging the Solonians. The story concludes by making them first sub-human and then superhuman and turning Ky into an avenging angel, somewhat undermining the various appeals to "universal" human rights in the foregoing episodes. Here, one fanatic tampers with robots and literally converts them to a cause; that same conversion process allows the Doctor to use some unspecified trap-door in the upgrade to target only those robots forcibly made to see things Capel's way. And in both cases, the Doctor and his companion, as newcomers, can see what centuries of social conditioning have made the local oligarchs fail to notice. The next story ("The Talons of Weng-Chiang") tries that again in a real-world historical situation, and the results are a lot messier. But in this story, the Doctor's concern to treat D84 decently is couched in terms of the robot being human-like, not so much the idea that intelligent, aware beings ought to be respected on their own terms. For the story to stop, Capel and the "infected" robots have to be contained with extreme prejudice, if that's the term we want.

And, in keeping with the orthodoxy of the time (and still occasionally heard in political commentary), it needs an outsider to tell the oppressed masses that they're oppressed. This worked either way: right-wing regimes, notably South Africa during Apartheid, blamed agitators for all unrest,

Cultural Primer: *Top of the Pops*

...continued from page 343

silage and fertiliser, put it on at 4.30 on Sunday afternoons while Granada spitefully put it out on Mondays, rather invalidating the show's slogan "The Weekend Starts Here".) All these different bits of Britain started invading each other and cross-pollinating.

There are a lot of stylistic features of *RSG!* that look familiar to anyone who's seen *Shindig!* or *Six-Five Special*: the way the studio-ness of the studio is unashamedly revealed, cameras in shot and scaffolding clearly visible; the way a slightly stiff host keeps things moving and whips up the teen audience rather than trying to keep them in check; the cutaway shots to that audience either screaming or dancing; the professional dancers not looking much more competent than the kids; the schematic set-design. By now, advertisers loved that kind of thing. In fact, the series and the commercials within it began to look like each other. (Another caveat about the available source-material: in the early 80s, Dave Clark got the rights to the archive episodes and re-edited them to make it appear that the Dave Clark Five were the biggest act on the planet. These are the most likely ones you'd find now, but others have emerged, rather more representative of what eye-witnesses recall the series being like.) The fashions of the era were leaning towards stark mono-chrome and op-art, even to the extent of white lipstick (that made teeth look yellow, but this didn't matter on camera). Whether television reflected this shift or caused it is a matter of debate (see also **What Were the Most Mod Stories?** under 2.7, "The Space Museum").

The BBC, with a new television channel coming soon, was retooling and created *Top of the Pops* to cater for this audience and others with a bit less of a skew towards Mods and particular record labels. There had been a lot of short-lived pop programmes, or some with pop in them (ABC's *Thank Your Lucky Stars* responded to viewer-complaints by moving to a broader variety format and losing viewers, *Discs a Go-go* was only really available in Bristol or South Wales), but the only nationally-networked pop-related programme of any duration had been BBC Saturday teatime show *Juke Box Jury*, an American format retooled for mainstream Britain and, by using 59 seconds of a record rather than a live performance or the whole disc, evaded the Musicians' Union's strictures. *TOTP* was different and made no bones about giving the public a visual representation of the record you could buy, sometimes even putting the needle into the groove on camera just before the artist lip-synched, but usually approximating it with a live band and a genuine vocal (for better or worse). The first edition went out on BBC Television (as it still was for the next four months) on New Year's Day 1964.

Yes, that's a Wednesday. And it was at 6.35 pm. They were still working out the formula, but they got the fundamentals right by beginning with the Rolling Stones performing a song Lennon and McCartney had given them: "I Wanna Be Your Man". Five days earlier, the public had seen Daleks for the first time just before a *Juke Box Jury* panel of "experts" decided that "As Usual" by Brenda Lee would be a Hit and "Diana" by The Bachelors wouldn't (wrong on both counts). That panel had included the first *TOTP* presenter – and here comes the snag...

Those US readers still reeling in shock – or feeling vindicated that their gut-reaction was right – concerning Bill Cosby and Michael Jackson have some idea how Britain has been over Jimmy Savile. He was protected by friends in high places, notably Margaret Thatcher (she gave him a knighthood in 1990 and made him the public face of British Rail), and he would humblebrag about his work for charity and religious beliefs – but many, if not most, people sensed Something Not Quite right about this umpteenager. (See the earlier version of this essay in 2004 for our disquiet, without lawyers good enough for us to say more than that at the time.) The extent and depth of his abuse was the shock, not that it happened at all. However, now that this has been revealed, the entire BBC and *Top of the Pops* have been attacked by sections of the media looking for ways to bring public service broadcasting to an end. It's hard to look at the details of Savile's depravity and say that the press over-reacted, but an agenda exists behind their using it to attack the BBC as an institution. Rupert Murdoch hardly escapes blame for the atmosphere of male impunity in that era.

Anyway, an ugly older man with long blond hair was an oddity in 1964, so the incongruity in "The War Machines" (3.10) of the Hartnell Doctor sauntering into a disco in Swinging London came complete with Kitty saying what a lot of people were thinking. But she refrained from calling him a child-molester.

Savile was one of a roster of presenters, another

continued on page 347...

14.5 The Robots of Death

assuming that the people they were marginalising would never think to object. On the left, even Marx assumed that the lumpenproletariat needed to be cured of what would later be called "false consciousness" – and, while people from more diverse backgrounds had been getting into university since World War II, it was generally taken that enlightened middle-class people would show the way. (Consider the career of Tony Benn, who rejected a hereditary peerage, but then consider that anyone from a working-class background who didn't stay true to his or her roots was called a "class traitor", something nobody called the erstwhile Viscount Stansgate.) This line of thinking has cropped up in the series since 1963, but it's about to get more complicated.

However, in the light of the previous story by the same author, the way Capel talks about altering the consciousnesses of his converts is akin to a religious cult. The V-class robot's conversion in Part Three has triumphant music as if this liberation is a form of salvation. The extent to which cults were spreading in the mid-1970 and being reported as sinister (mainly from the viewpoint of relatives who'd been rejected) is something that is often overlooked now. Obviously, hindsight makes the more alarming ones seem like something that ought to have been prevented, but where does this differ from straightforward religious persecution? It's more that an increasingly secular Britain looked askance at American-style charismatic churches while maintaining curiosity about how the under-thirties were looking for a sense of community in Eastern-style retreats.

There remains to this day a sense of unease about anyone who seems too happy and wants to tell you all about it. (The UK Krishna Consciousness movement found a way to defuse this with cheap, tasty food and a more low-key good-humour.) Before Jonestown and the Bhagwan Rajneesh problems of the late 70s, this was generally treated as just US-style smarminess and, occasional family break-ups aside, shrugged off as a fad that other people do. It still made most people uncomfortable, though.

English Lessons

- *Amateurs* (n.): it's more the way Russell Hunter says it than anything – he sounds exactly like Melvyn Hayes in the then-popular sitcom *It Ain't 'Alf Hot, Mum*, routinely attempting to turn lumbering soldiers into a chorus-line and himself probably dressed as Carmen Miranda. Viewers in 1977 would be half-expecting the follow-up line "I'm an *artiste*!"
- *We'll all go together when we go* is a parody Revivalist hymn about nuclear war, written and performed by Tom Lehrer in 1958.
- *Wainscoting* (n.): not a village in Dorset, but a form of skirting-board between the wall and the floor. Traditionally where mice reside and – as you'll know from *Tom and Jerry* – their entrance to the human domestic space.

Things That Don't Make Sense Once you've decided to call a story "The Robots of Death" (actually one of the better choices available), there's no point in hiding it from the viewers. But, for it to remain a shock to the residents of this mobile salon, they can't have any hint or suspicion of it being possible. So that opening scene where Chub relates an Urban Legend about a berserker masseur-bot is weird on many counts. Oddly, nobody jokes that a robot might've killed him for badmouthing them.

For that matter, if we're talking about dialling down expectations of a robot revolution, why would Taren Capel send the Company signed, threatening letters, enabling them to deploy agents to stop him? If, as we're told, Dask is in charge of robot maintenance, he should obviously be the No. 1, Let's-All-Stare-At-Him-Suspiciously Prime Suspect for villainous robot-reprogramming – but that never quite happens, even though this is a man who indulges in Dramatic Cosplay (so much so, he dresses in some sort of golden, hooded cultist robes when he's alone and modifying robots).

Once it becomes clear that the mine can run without human intervention, the script expends a lot of dialogue to justify an organic crew – with instincts and the ability to react immediately to streams that the machines would miss. Okay, but this makes nonsense of scheduled rest-periods where *all* humans are off-duty. And only a select few of the crew have these uncanny abilities (apparently only Toos, Zilda and the Commander himself), making Uvanov's complaints about their being "undermanned" after the first three murders that bit weirder.

We see at least six broken robots in that holding bay with massive head-trauma. Only one was the one Borg beat up. Is this the usual rate of wear and tear on a Storm Mine less than halfway through its

Cultural Primer: *Top of the Pops*

...continued from page 345

difference from the American version of pop TV. The programme was bigger than any presenter or performer – even the Beatles were just wheeled on, when they could make it (see 2.8, "The Chase"). The only differences between him and Pete Murray, Alan Freeman or David Jacobs was that they had a bit of previous; Murray was a *Six-Five* veteran, Freeman did *Pick of the Pops* on radio and Jacobs was the unctuous *Juke Box* foreman. No matter how strange Sonny and Cher looked, or The Kinks sounded, or how hard *Little Red Rooster* was to dance to, there was an old hand taking the edge off it but channelling audience enthusiasm. Viewers had a pretty good idea what these veterans actually liked, and that a record-plugger wasn't paying them to sell whatever they were introducing. (In US terms, they were more Casey Kasem than Dick Clark.) The vexed issue of doing it live led *Ready, Steady, Go!* to rebrand as *RSG! Live* and recruit performers (notably Dusty Springfield and Eric Burdon) to host specials highlighting American acts – notably a Motown launch and a Stax follow-up, then Jimi Hendrix's TV debut. As with a few other ITV pop shows, they thought that a young lady who seemed "ordinary" was a good back-up presenter, but this often backfired. *TOTP* never bothered.

In this arms race, the most in-demand acts sharpened their screen presence to add to their live act, songwriting skill (or ear for a good cover) and confidence. What happened next in America is well-documented, if imperfectly understood by American rock journalists. But with that first wave of Mersey Beat (and other regional "sounds") off invading, Britain had space and demand for the next lot, all of whose wish-lists had an appearance on *Top of the Pops*. This was increasingly practical when the show moved to Television Centre (in defiance of building regulations about loud noises). Most bands had it as almost the reason to get a contract; to get on telly and prove that it was a "proper job" rather than a hobby.

So, like *Doctor Who*, it had its first "Imperial Phase" (to quote The Pet Shop Boys quoting Hegel) when it could do no wrong. Then it started looking staid and vulnerable, and the ITV rivals thought they smelled blood in the water. The obvious next move is regeneration. In *TOTP*'s case, this was forced on them partly by what was happening in the charts and partly by institutional changes. In late 1967, the centre of gravity of popular music started shifting from singles to albums and, while a steady supply of new British bands had fresh-sounding hits, the big names were either in America getting lazy or off in remote farmhouses getting "meaningful".

The government, meanwhile, had finally had enough of pirates jamming the frequencies of emergency services, plus the murders that were becoming a feature of contractual disputes, and shut the whole lot down (except the ones on land in mainland Europe). The BBC, to fill the void as part of their public service obligation, reconfigured their own radio output to include a national pop service, Radio 1, repurposing a lot of pirate jingles and many of the DJs. Some of the most popular of these were filtered into the *TOTP* roster just in time for colour. BBC2, already in colour, took on some of the album-orientated bands and tried out some new visual effects to illustrate the performances. (Despite what we said about *Doctor Who* being a trial run for the Pops, what remains of *Colour Me Pop* looks like a tentative practice for Season Seven, with a host very like John Wakefield from 7.3, "The Ambassadors of Death" introducing the Moody Blues, the Small Faces or the Bonzo Dog Band.)

There were faltering attempts to include album tracks in the weekly chart rundown, but eventually the penny dropped that *Top of the Pops* was freed from the responsibility to represent *all* of contemporary music: just the singles that people were buying in bulk. As a new cohort of pre-teens got pocket-money, that changed. Glam filled the void just as Jo Grant – almost interchangeable with the girls in the studio audience dancing ineptly while looking at the monitors – entered the Doctor's life; it fizzled out when she left to go mushroom-hunting.

That rapid-response approach to light entertainment makes it easy to date a particular clip or episode (and useful as a yardstick for everything else the BBC made at the time). It's also what makes some improvised fill-ins for unavailable artistes so memorably bizarre. There were three basic ways to cover an absentee before the rise of the video clip (the usual date given for that is 1975, but as we'll see, Queen "invented" it the way George Lucas "invented" space opera). One was, simply, to play a particularly rousing one under the chart countdown, cutting between jiggling dolly-birds and photo-captions of the performers

continued on page 349...

mission? If so, maybe this explains why there is exactly one D-class "grunt" robot and something like 20 "white collar" droids in service. (In fact, very close examination reveals a D33 who's there for the first ten minutes – apparently in two places at once – then vanishes.) Either way, why has Dask not fixed the repairable ones? He ought, therefore, to have a workshop better than the pokey little hole Taron Capel has stashed away in secret. Maybe the robots are still under warranty and he's not allowed to repair them, but if that's the case, what's he there for?

Meanwhile, Poul is designated "chief mover", suggesting his expertise lies with the engines (yes, he's undercover, but he still needs to perform his official job; unless the job-term means "coordinator" / "manager" of some sort). So Dask's job is to fix broken robots but he doesn't really seem to do it, and instead he fixes his own sabotage in a way that's (probably) Poul's job. And Uvanov's never wondered "what do we pay you for?" Do Zeta Links break down as a matter of course and need human intervention?

You have to question the company's choice of field agents, as Poul – sent to catch a criminal who reprograms robots – is partnered with a robot and turns out to have robophobia. Did the Company not check for phobias before sending him? (In one of the DVD commentaries, Briant and Jameson rationalised that Poul was trained as a spy and paying more than normal attention to body-language now compared to when he was just a miner. That just makes the Company seem even stupider for not thinking this through.) He's a rubbish detective anyway: he tells Uvanov about Kerril privately, instead of announcing it to everyone over the comms and asking D84 to watch how people react. Then, when Leela's apprehended, he explains Corpse Markers to her; even Uvanov thinks that's counter-productive toward getting a confession. As pretending-not-to-be-a-cop goes, he's a bit too Method. Poul also believes that the Doctor's theory about a killer robot is preposterous, when that's exactly what he's been sent here to prevent (denial?).

This being *Doctor Who*, the robots are even less logical. V5 is fooled by V4 wearing the Doctor's hat, even though the Doctor hasn't worn a hat since he boarded the Mine. Being incapable of taking a hat off is as pathetic as a robot ever gets in this series. SV7 is also on hand but doesn't do anything other than quietly repeat "That is not the Doctor". Typical management type.

Choosing to kill Chub and then Kerril makes a good red herring – but only if Taron Capel knew about Uvanov's past and the Twenty Families hushing up a suicide. Zilda somehow works out the combination to Uvanov's safe, as impressive a leap as Uvanov working out her location when she uses the shipwide intercom. Poul, Kerril and Uvanov all know the real story behind the death of Zilda's brother – and yet none of them put two and two together or noticed the family resemblance.

When a plot-point about voice-pattern recognition is coming, it's odd that Toos asks "who is it" of the Doctor. It's also odd that the Doctor later miscounts the robots marching on the command-deck because one of them is Taron Capel in drag, especially as he omits the sliver-sprayed Marigold gloves (with the very visible logo when V5's being reprogrammed). Why V5 needs a physical upgrade while SV7 can be brainwashed with *Top of the Pops* effects is another mystery, probably connected with the omitted explanation of what the Doctor actually does with V2's head and a comms-link to make all the cultist robots blow up.

Toos's claim that if SV7's gone bad, then all the robots have gone bad doesn't make sense – even if SV7 commands the non-modified Vocs to kill humans, their constrainers should still stop them – and is later proved to be wrong anyway, when Dask turns off all the friendly robots so that only the killers remain functional.

Russell Hunter develops an Irish accent for one single line ("we might get a chance to use one of these"). But then, Tom Baker pronounces "Terran insects" as "Tehran". Leela's Sevateem-educated vocabulary now includes "mechanical", "creepy" and "miles per hour", and she's picked up a regal "thenk-yow" from somewhere (when Poul releases her from the straps – how would a Sevateem warrior have seen Arthur Askey or *The Rocky Horror Show?*).

As in "The Daemons" (8.5), the Doctor claims that it's aerodynamically impossible for bumblebees to fly, which was conclusively disproved by the invention of the helicopter. The Doctor's scarf teleports around between takes, notably in the sequence where he's rigging up the thing that blows up robot brains somehow. More alarmingly, every indication is that, when the Doctor and Leela are locked in the study in Part One and we

Cultural Primer: *Top of the Pops*

...continued from page 347

with their appropriate chart-place. Until surprisingly late, the revelation of who was selling best and who was "the toppermost of the poppermost" ((c) John Lennon, 1964) came at the *start* of each edition rather than being serialised with a cliffhanger and a reveal at the end. The BBC compiled the chart used for most of this period from an average of the other charts, because the other lists were subject to payola – the DJs practically made up those used on the Pirate stations. (One week in August 1968 had three different Number One records, depending on who you asked.)

Another was a specially-made film clip. Some were provided by the record companies, who'd actually been doing that sort of thing since the 1940s, but sped up when the punishing tour-schedules they'd arranged didn't synch with what the public were buying. Some were clips from feature films in which the song appeared – not just people trying to cash in on *A Hard Day's Night*, but the whole sorry parade of acts turned by their managers into the dreaded All-Round Family Entertainers. (And that's just British acts – the use of US bands in the endless Beach Party flicks was a handy source too, as was the increasingly desperate run of Elvis films.) However, the BBC ran a course for would-be directors. This provided a handy stream of young lads, raised on advertising and the *Nouvelle Vague*, trying to get a toe-hold. Illustrating an American record with practically zero budget and less time caused a few memorable incidents – often memorable the right way. However, a clip for "Do You Know the Way to San Jose" involving two seaside donkeys has gone down in legend. Often the Graphics department would bodge up something using either a rostrum camera on still photos or, when needed, a piece of ad-hoc animation. (The 1972 reissue of *Leader of the Pack* had a Roy Lichtenstein pastiche that seemed to have been drawn in felt tip – a trick used again for the earwormy *Johnny Reggae* you'll know from 9.3, "The Sea Devils".)

The third option was to bring on the dancing girls. Originally, there was a troupe called the Go-Jos[56], with the tricky brief of devising a routine from midday Tuesday to early afternoon Wednesday (if the single they'd already worked out a routine to had fallen in the charts) and accommodating the camera crew's requirements. BBC2 had a less chart-driven show, *The Beat Room*, with their own chorines: the Beat Girls. These two troupes show up in various other places and with a few other semi-regular dance-teams on our screens (The Young Generation were regulars on *The Rolf Harris Show*, for example). They slowly swapped personnel and, by 1968, a new set of girl dancers got the *TOTP* gig – the notorious Pan's People. As the archetypal "something for the dads", they had an odd reputation for stimulating corybanting that the video evidence does little to support. They look a bit mumsy.

Flick Colby, the choreographer (and former member) had a tendency to take short cuts, including miming the lyrics (her routine for "You're So Vain" is a masterpiece of charades-to-music). However, at best the collaboration between a sympathetic director and Colby's girls made something that could only work as television, using the sets, costumes, lighting and editing to make the slightly lumpen frugging of Babs, Dee-Dee, Ruth, Cherry and Sue a component in a video installation made in under 36 hours. Following this lot, from 1976 on, there was Ruby Flipper (with a couple of male dancers), Legs & Co and Zoo, after which the need for this kind of fill-in was almost gone.

Later, just before the rise of the pop video, there was a handy source of footage of American soul acts (as is so often the case, more in-demand in Britain than across mainstream America) in *Soul Train*. The studio audience on *Top of the Pops* were occasionally selected for dancing ability, such as it was, but were really there as props. Nobody got on twice, unlike *American Bandstand*. Another beneficial aspect of a national broadcaster in a geographically small area with UHF transmitters was that the sound-quality of the programmes warranted sets with decent speakers, so the US format of virtually looking in on a teen party with the music as the background for the dancers never really took hold (except for *The White Heather Club*, but that's a different thing.) The American "dance party" idea of pop television gave us an idea of impossibly gifted kids (when we saw it) compared to our "ordinary" 16-25-year-olds. (Except when someone demonstrated a new fad dance: 1975 was the year Northern Soul briefly broke out on the series; 1982 had that whole Body-Popping thing.) "Bohemian Rhapsody", being impossible to do live on a small stage with bopping teens, needed a home-made clip that looks, now, pretty basic and very like near-contemporary *Doctor*

continued on page 351...

14.5 The Robots of Death

see a Voc listening carefully at the door, it's supposed to be D84. If the director couldn't get this straight, what hope have we got?

By the time the Doctor leaves the command deck to make his robot-destructor, he's clearly worked out that Dask is Taren Capel. So why did he not impress this upon Uvanov and Toos (who, without this knowledge, must debate whether or not the robots are holding Dask captive)? Why do *they* not figure this out, when of the original crew, there's only the three of them and the incapacitated Poul left alive? Quite why things explode so satisfyingly in a helium-laced atmosphere can wait until we find out how the helium "knows" to stay in the workshop when the doors left gaping open. The Doctor advises D84 to stay in the storage bay, as if his destructor-gadget has a limited range, but it's pretty much assumed that it wipes out every robot aboard the ship. Why should Taren Capel makes himself up as a Voc, i.e. a robot who's technically inferior to SV7?

In the tag-scene, the Doctor blithely announces that a rescue-ship's on its way. When was this sent? How did it know anyone needed rescuing? If Uvanov can contact the head office for back-up, why has *any* of this happened? Yes, he's more concerned about his reputation and income, but even if he survived, something like this on his record wouldn't help him. Yes, the nasty storm might, in theory, have cut them off, but any SOS beacon unable to cope with an emergency is worse than useless. Perhaps the robots sabotaged communications, but that would have been mentioned (and would have helped the general Agatha Christie ambience of the early episodes, like cutting the phone lines). Above all, with a crisis unfolding and two humanoids showing up unexpectedly, only Poul would have known that they weren't Company investigators or the fuzz.

The other thing is, that rescue ship's probably got robots on board. Even if Poul was, for some reason, left unmolested on the command deck when Uvanov and Toos ran out to help the Doctor, he's got a very uncomfortable trip home ahead.

Critique If Philip Hinchcliffe had left *Doctor Who* after "The Seeds of Doom", there'd be a very different collective memory of his time on the series. The ten stories after Barry Letts's last, "Robot", split almost evenly into cheap-but-clever and pretty-but-daft; those who count "scary" as a *sine qua non* will be reasonably happy with seven out of ten productions generally regarded well on that score. His first year was a bold/ desperate (delete according to taste) attempt to shake off Letts's influence and find a new recipe, the second was enhanced/ marred by overt plagiarism of old films. Two of the five stories made in this block were UNIT adventures, two were basically historicals (does anyone think a real neurosurgeon would perform operations in candle-light with cobwebs in the theatre?) and the other one was a sort-of sequel to "The Ark in Space" (as far as a sets went) with the one genuinely alien planet of the 70s so far (unless you count the Time Lords in "The Three Doctors"). That reputation Hinchcliffe has as a "hawk" isn't looking too sharp.

If you're looking for a "typical" story out of that lot, it's probably "The Android Invasion", heaven help us. Given time and options, he was invariably conservative, concentrating on getting a story made *at all*, then doing it on time and on budget. Most of what look like brave moves up to this point were damage-limitation, generally starting with Robert Holmes salvaging a script at short notice. Even the ground-breaking "Genesis of the Daleks" was a Letts commission, with Terry Nation shamed into putting in some work for a change. Anyone else taking over the series at the end of Season Thirteen, with the BBC happily indulging a hit series (so long as it didn't cost too much or tie up resources intended for "serious" drama), could have done almost anything with it. It's the choices made in Season Fourteen that cemented his reputation and curtailed the options open to his successor. On the face of it, commissioning "The Robots of Death" is the safest of these choices.

A story about killer robots isn't exactly breaking new ground, but it's coming surprisingly late in *Doctor Who*'s development. If anything, the series-cliché has been helpful, misguided robots and heavily-armed cyborgs. The bones of the script are sound. If you compare it with the sources, you can see that Boucher's hastily-commissioned story cunningly uses the deficiencies inherent in (a) doing *And Then There Were None* in a futuristic context or (b) doing *The Naked Sun* as television to fix each other. Rather than everyone aboard having an individual secret, each of which requires a detailed knowledge of the nuances of that society to comprehend, there's one connecting scandal underlying the relations of three of the crew with

Cultural Primer: *Top of the Pops*

...continued from page 349

Who. This suited *Top of the Pops*, where the Single was the Star, but it caught on at the roughly same time as another of those DIY have-a-go movements, punk.

Town Councils and Mary Whitehouse may have griped about Punk, and punks might have whinged about disco, but at last there was an alternative to the diet of "mellow" AOR, self-indulgent noodling and novelty hits that blighted the mid-70s. Both movements, and the near-simultaneous reggae and synth-pop booms, brought a fresh excitement, just as the horror-movie retread, base-under-siege and Yeti-in-the-loo phases of *Doctor Who* each finally ended and allowed some fresh air in.

Of course, almost all the bands that made it by acting rebellious started by wanting to be on the show as kids. (The Clash found it harder than the rest to reconcile bringing down Capitalism with signing to CBS and appearing on BBC1, so they made it known that they'd never do *TOTP*. But they made videos, appeared on the cover of *Smash Hits* and cashed in big time when "Should I Stay or Should I Go" made it to Number One on the back of a Levis advert.) None of these movements happened in isolation in Britain, mainly because the singles were all shoved together willy-nilly on *Top of the Pops* – so, despite the ferocious tribalism of teenagers in Britain then, there was a lot of cross-pollination. Everyone knew all of it. And, as a public-service broadcaster, the BBC allowed different voices and opinions on, even if it was a hit single slagging off Radio One or *Top of the Pops*. Even when a single had been banned, there was no way to pretend it didn't exist once it reached Number One. (Although, in the case of "God Save the Queen" by the Sex Pistols, they gave it a good try during Jubilee week 1977. They were less successful with "Relax" by Frankie Goes to Hollywood.)

When, with almost suspicious timing, the Musicians' Union called a strike and took *TOTP* off the air in mid-1980 – just as the New Romantics were getting into the charts and Tom Baker was being forced to wear pedal-pushers – it allowed all the changes that were bubbling under to come at once. When the series returned, just in time for *Ashes to Ashes* to get to Number One, it re-invented itself again. *Doctor Who*'s new look started three weeks later and, as we've hinted in the revised Volume 5, is as much to do with the new camera equipment also being rolled out for *Pops* as any radical shift by the incoming producer. But the trickery possible with the Quantel machinery extended the range of the visual possibilities for both series, just as CSO made them both look new in 1970. Make up and costumes also followed the trends (especially in the run of episodes from 18.5, "Warriors' Gate" to 19.4, "The Visitation"). Similarly, late 1987's much-needed change to Acid House and Balieric beats coincided with Ace showing up in cycling shorts and a bomber-jacket festooned with badges.

As a core-sample through what the public wanted, what the technology was able to give them in a hurry on tight budgets (and how the BBC tried to negotiate serving one section of the public without alienating others), both *Doctor Who* and *Top of the Pops* are invaluable. As weapons in the audience-share combat with the ITV system and then the post-duopoly environment,

continued on page 353...

---

the situation now unfolding. All the dirty laundry being washed helps sketch in the outside world from which they're isolated and makes these characters a little less one-note.

However, the production on top of this script is what makes this interesting: everyone who got involved after the commissioning process had their cliché collision-warning activated and went off in a different direction. That's not always wise. Here, the counter-intuitive casting, idiosyncratic costuming, practical set design and technical wizardry are all pulling in different directions from a central point: the look and manner of the robots. There had never been screen robots exactly like this before and few even remotely similar. Look at old cover-art from 30s magazines: the bots are brassy there. The Moderne hood-ornaments on streamline cars are a closer match, or the long, lean figures on table-lamps, but they aren't quite right either. 1970s movie robots are either massive-and-imposing (*Logan's Run*, for example) or steely shop-dummies (*THX 1138*, *Sleeper*). Many 60s Asimov adaptations simply used pretty actors who don't blink (unless they were making a point – see 6.2, "The Mind Robber"). And, of course, after 1977 the rules of what robots "ought" to look like changed and it took genuine Japanese machinery to reset expectations a generation later (X6.10, "The Girl Who Waited"; X10.2, "Smile").

With that point out of the way, the less obvious,

less commented-upon aspects need to be acknowledged. One we've alluded to is that this story is about a society that makes sense to itself and is told on those terms. This isn't an allegory; critics wanting to shoehorn it into a debate on class pounced on that one-liner about Marie Antoinette, but Brian Croucher (Borg) and Russell Hunter (Uvanov) put banana-skins under that reading every time they open their mouths. The whole Twenty Families subplot moves that aspect of this planet to the fore in an unrelated way, if you want it. Individual scenes might reflect real-world situations, but the story as a whole is self-sufficient. It's available for any interpretation.

If it's "about" any one thing, it's how a culture fails to spot what's under its nose until an alien materialises and points it out to them. That's pretty much universal (the next story will show affluent Londoners failing to acknowledge their Chinese population or underclass; the previous one had two cultures oblivious to their true origins, as did the one before that). The "mystery" element – working out which, if any, of the Storm Mine crew is the killer/ cult-leader – is also available as a way to get to know this world and its inhabitants, but it's only superficial. Hindsight, and enhanced trouser-recognition skills among those people watching now, make it almost redundant.

That's significant, because the rewards of whodunits on screen aren't limited to puzzle-solving or mastery of a set of generic codes; on their own terms, such stories rely on a comprehension of social norms and motivation rooted in knowledge of the story's *milieu* (1930s country houses, 1950s Los Angeles, 1450s monasteries or whatever). Columbo figures out the killer's "foolproof" scheme through tiny social cues and shibboleths, just as Miss Marple does.

On top of this is a network of media semiotics, enabling anyone familiar with the various character-actors or stars to identify the killer just on the basic principle of which non-regular cast-member you recognise first, or who's too big a name (or too identifiable on an "oh, isn't that...?" basis)[57] to be just an info-dump. Or you can simply place bets on who's most likely to do a big confessional meltdown scene or which professions an audience of that time would cheer or boo. (There's a thesis on the popular reputation of Freudian analysis over time, as indexed by whether a shrink is the protagonist's secret weapon or the real killer.)

And on top of this is the basic reward of a threat to an apparently desirable/ idyllic locale being safely neutralised and the reset-button pressed. "The Robots of Death" doesn't do any of this: we can't spot the killer from the cast-list, the plot means that this entire society's on the skids and all we know of this world is what the story itself tells us. Instead, we have to learn to read this world on its own terms, something most children are always doing, and only later measure it against our own.

Chris Boucher gave us a legible world. Michael Bryant and his designers coloured it in. Even if you can't follow the plot, the design (Ken Sharp's horizontal stripes are present and correct in the corridors as per 4.7, "The Macra Terror", but it gets a bit Charles Rennie Mackintosh on the control deck) and how the actors relate to each other do the work for you and lets you just wallow. The production rewards your attention but doesn't demand it. The softness of the menace is hinted at in the music, with a slow heartbeat for the deaths and urgent brass for the workplace. There are goofs and anomalies, but you need to rewatch and pay attention to spot most of those – and for each one you collect, there's usually a connection you'd missed.

One of the fundamental messages of *Doctor Who*, the one most terrifying to authority-figures and Mary Whitehouse, is that the world the viewers inhabit is neither natural nor as-it-should-be; "familiar" isn't the same as "right". We're not normal, just local. Getting to know a different society quickly was always the point and could be done didactically (as John Lucarotti did in Season One) or experientially, with the TARDIS crew using clues to figure out their location and then asking people about it. As the Doctor got more control over the Ship, we needed companions less genre-savvy than the viewer. That's one way in which Leela re-energised the series, but this story's almost the last time we get that incremental piecing together of how a world unlike ours works. We'll miss it when it's gone, just as we'll never see robots like this again – unless it's a deliberate *homage* to this story rather than a side-effect of how people making the series were thinking.

And, yes, D84 should have been a regular, if not a full-blown companion.

The Robots of Death

Cultural Primer: *Top of the Pops*

...continued from page 351

they were flexible and sensitive. Both were, to a certain extent, killed off by chicanery within BBC1 management; moved around from their hallowed spot then – when this caused a rating slide – accused of being out-of-touch and unpopular. With *TOTP*, there's a grain of truth in this, with the move towards counting downloads removing its *raison d'etre*, but putting it on BBC2 on Sundays wasn't helpful. It was finally axed (apart from Christmas round-ups of the year, often presented by Reggie Yates: Leo Jones in Series Three) just after X2.13, "Doomsday". The last single shown was "Hips Don't Lie" by Shakira. In a lot of ways, consensus about pop music in the UK died with it.

But although there were moments in pop-culture when both series seemed in lock-step, such as Season Five, Season Nineteen and Season Twenty-Six, in the 1970s the two seemed like conjoined twins. Just as a black-and-white *Doctor Who* seems to end oddly without the "sting" in the end theme, so a *Top of the Pops* without the CCS version of "Whole Lotta Love" seems like a fake. (There were about seven other regular theme tunes, many with the announcement "Yes, it's Number One, it's *Top of the Pops*", but they kept coming back to the one everyone knew.)

What this all meant was a visual vocabulary for pop that partook of the methods of fantasy television and – at best – made a temporary utopia (or, at least, heterotopia) filled with possibilities. On a budget for fourpence ha'penny. This evolved in parallel with the methodology for British telefantasy and had the same sexual ambivalence, camp hypersexuality, effects technology... and capacity for slipping over into naffness and stupidity. There was the same slight snobbery among 20-somethings towards both, ditto anyone over 30 who wasn't a parent. (There is, when we get down to it, very little to choose between chin-stroking musos, the Frankfurt Group and grumpy grandparents when it comes to sneering at the taste of the masses.)

Above all, there was an air of supreme self-confidence about both series and a public that would let them take us anywhere, so long as it was different.

The Facts

Written by Chris Boucher. Directed by Michael E Briant. Viewing figures: 12.8 million, 12.4 million, 13.1 million 12.6 million. AIs 62%, unknown for 2 and 3, 57%. The two-episode New Year's Eve/Day repeat garnered 11 million and 7 million.

Alternate Versions An edited two-part anthology was shown just after Christmas 1977, ahead of "Underworld" (15.5). A one-part version was released by BBC video in 1985 with lurid title-graphics and some light trims for violence. The novelisation restores "Grimwade" to "Grimwold" and amends "Laserson" to "Laseron" (Boucher seems to have liked the change and used "Laseron" as Travis's gun-hand in *Blakes 7*).

Cliffhangers The Doctor is lured into a hopper and about to drown in coco-pops; the sinking storm mine is about to be crushed; a robot lunges, calmly repeating "Kill the Doctor".

What Was In the Charts? "Knowing Me, Knowing You", Abba; "Sound and Vision", David Bowie ("programmes tonight on BBC1"); "Car Wash", Rose Royce; "(Get a) Grip (On Yourself)", The Stranglers.

The Lore

To recap from last time... after going through all their old contacts (Louis Marks, Robert Banks Stewart, Lewis Griefer), talking to people connected with the series (Barry Letts, John Lucarotti, Douglas Camfield) and sounding out promising newcomers (Douglas Adams, Eric Pringle), Philip Hinchcliffe and Robert Holmes seemed to hit paydirt with Chris Boucher. A year of careful nurturing had resulted in "The Face of Evil", and almost immediately they entrusted him with the sort of robot-themed story "The Brain of Morbius" had begun by being.

It was a bit more complicated than that, though, as they were juggling a few other possibilities for the season's fifth slot. Even with Sarah gone, the Camfield "Lost Legion" was still in contention. By all accounts, it had a sword-and-sorcery vibe that was a new avenue for the series to explore, combined with the author/director's interest (to put it mildly) in the military code. It was just not coming in on time, or in enough time to fix it.

Boucher, by contrast, seemed to be fairly prompt despite holding down a regular job, and stuck to the brief while bringing his own interests to bear. With the six-part tale "A Foe from the

14.5 The Robots of Death

Future" abruptly dropped (see next story) and Holmes forced, yet again, to write a new story from scratch with the same elements, leaving the matter in Boucher's hands was one fewer hassle. Holmes liked the idea of an isolated setting cut off by storms and a prowling killer picking people off one by one (see also 15.1, "Horror of Fang Rock") and Boucher picked up on this, unwittingly pilfering from *Dune* (as he later realised to his mild embarrassment). The Storm-mine helped to avoid yet-another space station. With the Sarah-replacement issue still up in the air, he threw in a capable young woman to eventually side with the Doctor, Toos. The formal commission for the storyline of "The Storm Mine Murders" came in late June. By this time, Hinchcliffe was actively considering the Sarah-surrogate from Boucher's previous story as a potential full-time companion; by the time the second episode of this one arrived (27th August), Louise Jameson had been contracted to play Leela for 14 episodes.

Quite what they were going to *do* with this character after that is anyone's guess. There's talk of plans to bump off Leela, but this mainly focuses on "The Sun Makers" (15.4). If, as is surmised, the early versions of "The Talons of Greel" had a cockney street-urchin who was the next companion-in-waiting, and if, as reported, Jameson was reluctant to stick around for more than those 14 episodes, the only way the story's affectionate, ironic tone would have worked is if, surviving all these threats to her person, Leela abruptly fell in love with PC Quick and chose to stay in this gloomy, crumbling city. But that would be silly. Odds are, she'd be Greel-fodder or rat-chow. That would end the season on a bit of a downer (unless you're Tom Baker).

- As with "The Face of Evil", this had to be a lower-budget story to offset the overspend on "The Deadly Assassin". The final cost was set at around £7500 under the usual amount allocated for a four-parter, nearly a ten percent cut. Hinchcliffe, aware that the story would stand or fall on its visuals, checked that Richard Conway was available to do the models and tried to keep the post-production effects work to a minimum. He persuaded Michael E Briant to make one last return to the series to handle a technically complex studio-only story (models aside – although keep reading). Briant, in turn, attempted to secure the services of a studio team he had worked with before on *Warship*.

However, Briant was not a fan of the basic script. After the experience of "Revenge of the Cybermen" (which he and Holmes thought was about robots), he was reluctant to handle what seemed like an off-the-shelf set of ideas. Between being sounded out and formally joining the production, he contacted set designer Ken Sharp (see 4.7, "The Macra Terror"; 8.3, "The Claws of Axos"; and a sidelight in the notes for "The Masque of Mandragora"). Sharp's enthusiasm was slightly raised by the prospect of working with Emmy Award-winning costume designer Elizabeth Waller.

About six weeks later, in mid-September 1976, Briant officially started work and took Sharp and Conway to a quarry in Cornwall. This wasn't a location recce, for once, but an examination of how open-cast mining works – the jets and Archimedes Screws of the Sandminer were a direct consequence of this, as was the hopper in the first cliffhanger. It was probably around this point that Briant opted to use the Ealing studio to pre-film the hopper scene, as the flow of the cork chips (used to simulate ore) would be more controllable and they easily could do retakes.

- In Briant's defence, the script he had wasn't quite what we saw. Boucher had clearly outlined the sort of character-dynamics and plot-beats but, to get a little ahead of ourselves, the episodes under-ran. With what he had on the page, Briant started casting slightly against this, to avoid what he considered the tiresome machismo and conventional-looking crews of the run-of-the-mill space adventures. (In more recent interviews, he identifies *Space:1999* as everything he was trying to avoid; earlier he cited Asimov adaptations and early 70s Hollywood dystopias.)

Russell Hunter (Uvanov) was at that point best known among adults as the Dickensian informer Lonely in *Callan* – the antithesis of the Alpha Male – and another possible candidate was Ronald Lacey. (For kids and teens, however, Hunter was remembered as the scarily powerful mage Mr Stabs in *Ace of Wands*.) Similar thinking guided the choice of David Baillie as non-ranting, hidden-in-plain-sight Dask/Capel. Briant would later cast him in *Blakes 7* ("Project Avalon"). A future regular in that series, Brian Croucher, was a last-minute replacement for Brian McDermott as Borg. He, like Leon Eagles in the previous story, had been in the ATV children's serial *The Jensen Code*, on which Hinchcliffe had worked. David Collings

(Poul) had been hidden under latex last time Briant used him ("Revenge of the Cybermen"). Rob Edwards (Chub) and Pamela Salem (Toos) had just been voices of Xoanon. Gregory de Polnay (D84) had been a regular in the last series of *Dixon of Dock Green*.

- Waller's starting-point, as with Briant and Sharp in different ways, was the idea of Art Deco. The suggestion of the humans as a slightly decadent elite riding on the shoulders of the mechanical workforce led her in the direction of *Metropolis* and Sharp towards the SS *Queen Mary*. Another slave-based aristocracy, Classical Greece, informed the design of the robots themselves. She hired art students to shape the heads in Plasticine, then developed moulds from which to make masks in three colours. The feet were clad in a lurex stocking; she now admits that the less flexible shiny external coating was an error. The two design wings worked in concert to make a unified world (and note that Chub, killed before the majority of the CSO scenes, gets to wear a blue smock that wouldn't have been practical later).

- Two weeks into pre-production, it was found that Part Two needed a longer ending, so Boucher added the sinking-into-silt scene. He used this to hint that the Doctor had identified the murderer and to lightly skit Holmes's idea that a clairvoyant Leela had inherited Spidey-sense from a "witch granny". Further rewrites came three weeks later, with the TARDIS scene revised heavily and the storage-bank scene from Part Two added. A further addition was Zilda breaking into Uvanov's office. This *still* wasn't enough, so Holmes devised the anomalous scene at the start with Chub teasing Borg about robot masseurs.

- The pre-filming started on 2nd November with model filming at Ealing, directed by the production assistant on this story, Peter Grimwade. As so many times before, Baker tried to add business to the routine action scenes and offered an alternative to the Doctor's simple escape with a snorkel. This involved scarf-swinging, the door-hinges and whatever. Briant was used to this, but the conversation attracted an audience. After a lengthy peroration from the star on how the scene should be played, Graham Williams was introduced to Baker as the new producer of *Doctor Who*. Baker then did the scene exactly as written.

- Yes, a new producer. With the momentum of a hit show, Hinchcliffe had been prevailed upon to stay for a fourth series. Yet by the time he'd made provisional plans to make Season Fifteen, Bill Slater, Head of Series, had changed his mind and sounded out a replacement. Williams was almost the same age as Hinchcliffe and, like him, had been working as a script editor, most recently on *Z Cars*. He had been trying to move into production and had two projects on the go in early 1976: one a prestigious US co-production, the other an all-film police series set in Southampton. We'll develop this in Season Fifteen's write-ups, here it's worth noting that he was supposed to shadow Hinchcliffe but, with the series's semi-permanent state of crisis, was barely kept in the loop. This transition semi-officially started in July but was only confirmed in early December.

Hinchcliffe, meanwhile, was increasingly devil-may-care; he'd been acting as if he was leaving when he encouraged everyone involved with "The Deadly Assassin" to go for broke. After it was confirmed, he undid the savings he had managed on the two consecutive low-cost studio-only stories Boucher had provided. Production Unit Manager Christopher Doyly John was exasperated, as we'll see next story.

Briant suggests he was told about Williams getting the job well before Baker – keep an eye on this as we proceed, especially in Season Sixteen. Baker, not unreasonably, thought that he was at the cutting-edge of the programme's publicity and feedback from young viewers and, again, not unreasonably, that he had as much of an idea about how the part ought to be played as anyone. What this prompted him to do became *very* unreasonable. However, at this stage he's just been overruled about having a regular female companion at all, let alone a savage with a knife, and now he's been shut out of the key decision about the programme's – and his own – future.

- As was his habit, Briant took the first day of each studio session to rehearse and block out every line-up of the complex CSO and inlay effects, while giving the actors one last go and a chance to get used to the costumes. Therefore, the first actual recording was on 23rd November, the second day of the session, in Studio 8. On 22nd they concentrated on the choreography of the robots, who were moving with restricted vision in complicated sets of straight paths. The PA handled this: Baker amended the scripted line about "Grimwol's Syndrome" to "Grimwade", as well as adding the Doctor's line about the rational mind. Leela was scripted to pick up her crossbow, rather than a Tesh Disruptor. After a mishap with the knife-throw almost injured a cameraman, it was decided that Jameson (in contact-lenses, in semi-darkness) ought to be given a blunt prop dagger. The following day, the actors playing robots redubbed their dialogue. There had been a plan to use a voice-effect on set but instead the performers spoke into plastic cups and tried to match what the other actors had heard the in studio.

Rehearsals resumed on 25th (with Baker bigging-up his film for the press), but the big story of the day was that the press got to hear about Leela. You'll recall the details from last story's write-up, but bear in mind what Baker had been like on *Nationwide*. The next set of camera-rehearsals began on 5th December. By then, Graham Williams had done a curious presentation to the BBC Drama heads explaining his ideas for the series. (This was on 30th November, so everyone had already been told he was incoming producer but in most discussions, including Williams's own comments, it's spoken of as a job interview.) However, Williams did get one task to handle – negotiations over the *Scratchman* film. He was not impressed with the script.

- The production moved to TC1. Unfortunately, some of the sets had been damaged and not all had been mounted. By now the cast had tweaked their lines a little and de Polnay was adding an ironic twist to D84's dialogue; he and Baker augmented the "I heard a cry" scene. A slight delay happened when Baillie was released too early and had to be recalled and re-made-up as a wannabe robot. A frantic final day included the final shots, (using video effects by AJ Mitchell, many using another effects generator devised by Ian Chisholm for use in *Top of the Pops*), much of the CSO work for Part One, including the sand-scoop and inserts of the control-tower in the filmed model) and the playback of the model TARDIS being picked up (a shot the cast compared to a seaside toy-grabber). Scenes in the hopper, included the last one recorded, Toos and Leela hiding. Even after a special extension because of the lighting miscommunications costing over half an hour, the lights went off at 10.40pm and they needed to be guided out of the studio with torches.

- Six days after the recording ended, the night shooting for "The Talons of Greel" (as it was still called) began. Hinchcliffe had attempted to get a budget increase by threatening to shut down production for a month, but the only gap here was between filming and OB recording on location. Shortly after that, Baker had a promise to keep. Russell Hunter usually distributed presents at his local children's hospital at their party in Glasgow, but he'd been cast in Manchester. So, on December 22nd, Doctor Who stood in for him.

- The first episode would have had a tie-in with Louise Jameson on *Swap Shop*, but her glandular fever flared up (recording of the next story had just ended). Baker's pre-recorded episodes of *Call My Bluff* went out and all seemed rosy. However, the Christmas repeat of "The Brain of Morbius" prompted tabloid attack-monger Jean Rook to interview Holmes in a piece published on 11th February as (seriously) *Who do you think you are, scaring my innocent child?* With the BBC's Drama Department having weakened in the face of Mary Whitehouse over the last cliffhanger to "The Deadly Assassin", people increasingly feared for their jobs if they weren't seen to be doing something about this "menace". Nonetheless, there was no arguing with the viewing figures and the *Radio Times* asked for members of the public to talk about the series for the impending documentary *Whose Doctor Who*, of which more next story.

14.6: "The Talons of Weng-Chiang"

(Serial 4S, Six Episodes, 26th February – 2nd April 1977.)

Which One is This? "God save Fu Manchu, Moriarty and Dracula". And anyone else at large in 1890s London, as they squeeze every possible cliché into six weeks (and nonchalantly invent two popular literary genres). It's the divisive story Bob Holmes was born to write (but didn't want to).

Firsts and Lasts It's the first time this Doctor's gone a whole story without that scarf. On the other hand, it's the last story produced by Philip Hinchcliffe (and thereby hangs a tale), and the last directed by David Maloney (and thereby hangs a whole new series). Roger Murray-Leach hangs up his spurs as set designer and the crew pay a first visit to Northamptonshire (the second and final one was 26.1, "Battlefield"). Paying for all of this, especially with Hinchcliffe letting the designers and director go out with a bang, meant that Christopher D'oyly-John's long stint as production unit manager ended spectacularly (to his relief). Effects designer Micheal john Harris also ends his association with the series here. It's the first time the story's composer shows up in front of the cameras (see 24.3, "Delta and the Bannermen"; X4.0, "Voyage of the Damned").

It's the last time Leela murders someone with a Janis thorn. And, surprisingly late, this is the first time we see the Doctor at large in late-Victorian London, seemingly his natural habitat. (4.9, "The Evil of the Daleks" was in a mansion just outside Canterbury and 1966 London.) Perhaps we needed to see him on his native soil first.

Six Things to Notice
About "The Talons of Weng-Chiang"...

- Li H'sen Chang, a major character who's originally from China, is played by a Caucasian actor (John Bennett). They try to wriggle around it by hinting that he's been genetically altered, but it's glaringly of-its-time. At least he gets some decent lines. Every other Chinese character is played by a British actor of East Asian origin (including practically all of the available extras in London), but they're one-note goons. The white characters use cleaned-up variants of the sort of epithets such people really did use. If this sort of thing's a deal-breaker, please proceed to the next story (which has the same costume-drama vibe, but just white folks getting killed horribly).

- But if you're prepared to watch it as a historical document, observe how the recent subgenre of London Folklore Gothic (a seam mined by Neil Gaiman, Christopher Fowler, Peter Ackroyd, Ben Aaronovitch and many, many others) gets a kick-start here. On top of that, no less an authority than John Clute cites this story as a significant moment in the development of Steampunk (see our comments in volumes 2 and 7 on why this is less clear-cut). Nobody was thinking that at the time, though, because almost every story-element is familiar from what else BBC1 was showing around the time it was written. As usual, *Doctor Who* is a thought-process applied to otherwise-impossible combinations, rather than any fresh ingredients.

- They've availed themselves of an actual Victorian theatre, including all the backstage bits, and filled it with local Music Hall enthusiasts in period costumes. The whole thing looks right, and, with hand-held video cameras following the manager offstage and recording the stunt-filled chase through the curtains, it looks doubly authentic. They've festooned the corridor with genuine period posters just to add to the flavour. Also getting into the spirit of the occasion, about the first person we see is the orchestra's conductor – and, yes, that's Dudley Simpson in a wing-collar.

- Of course, there's a giant rat in the sewers. In some shots, it's a normal rat in a model. They don't slow it down to suggest bulk, so it looks like a normal rat in a model sewer. Other shots, where it's Stuart Fell in a rat suit, look even worse (although, perhaps, more scientifically accurate). They knew it would be him and even scripted it as "Fell-Rat". He's more convincing as the Doctor (hanging from the backdrops at the theatre) and Leela (flying through a window) and also plays a Tong assassin in Part One, executing a flying drop-kick and several vaguely Bruce Lee moves.

- December 1976 was between the rebuilding and overall gentrification of London's docks (see 21.4, "Resurrection of the Daleks" and X2.12, "Army of Ghosts") and their previous incarnation as the lifeblood of the city's commerce. As a result, there were lots of satisfyingly grotty-looking wharves and cobbled streets and not many people living there. One period detail never usually included in Victorian-set dramas is where all the horse manure went, but this one acknowledges the problem. They weren't originally planning to be quite *this* authentic, but there's a practical reason connected to the aforementioned gentrification – see **The Lore** if you don't already know why.

- You'll read a lot about how this was made as a four-parter with a two-episode dog-leg appended. That's only really apparent with hindsight, but there's a production difference between these two phases and two very obvious tonal shifts. The big production one is that the film and OB material drops off once the story moves on from the Music Hall. Tonally, the original antagonist is phased out in favour of his boss, but – more significantly – the two locals with whom the Doctor has been liaising finally meet and team up. Jago and Litefoot, despite their unfiltered period attitudes, became an entertaining double-act and there was talk of a spin-off series. (As it is, Big Finish did one decades later; it lasted an impressive 14 seasons.) But they're only together for about 15 minutes of screen-time, most of that with the Doctor hogging the limelight. The bulk of their one-on-one interaction is in one sequence written hastily, because Part Five was under-running.

The Talons of Weng-Chiang

The Continuity

The Doctor has dressed for the occasion. Sort of. He's in a wing-collar and spats [for the first time since "The Tenth Planet" (4.2)] and has a new outfit, without a scarf. There's a heavy woollen Ulster cloak in light brown, with red satin ribbons in a crosshatch pattern. [NB: this isn't the same Ulster that prompted the Doctor's first historical name-drop in 1.3, "The Edge of Destruction".] Under this is a crimson velveteen smoking jacket, a dark brown waistcoat with pink rose motif [we'll be seeing that again], a shirt with cufflinks and a dark red satin tie. On his head, even when indoors, he has a flap-eared deerstalker. [The impression is of the traditional Sherlock Holmes outfit even though that was for investigations in the countryside – notably "Silver Blaze", whence that 1892 Paget illustration that inspired all the theatrical and cinematic Holmeses – and would therefore not have so fancy a shirt or footwear nor so indoorsy a jacket. This is not what one would wear for a night out in London, any more than someone at a red-carpet event now would have a Barbour jacket and shorts with a tux.]

After pulling an all-nighter to plot the course of the Fleet, he proclaims that 'sleep is for tortoises'. [As with so many memorable Tom Baker lines, it's repeated by Peter Capaldi, specifically in X10.4, "Knock Knock".] He takes an unironic pleasure in Chang's stage-act and most of the other turns at the Palace.

With regards to the borough pathologist, Professor Litefoot, he comes to respect the man's generosity and pluck; the Music-Hall impresario Jago amuses him greatly. In both cases, the Doctor seems to almost be cosplaying Sherlock Holmes by emphasising his scientific prowess and detective skills by turns. He's impressed by the giant rat's size and seems indulgent towards normal rats.

Amid a flurry of moderately-impressive conjuring tricks, he's able to hypnotise (or, more precisely, de-hypnotise) Jago and *claims* to be able to play the Trumpet Voluntary in a bowl of live goldfish. He appears to be a fan of Little Tich. He claims to have always enjoyed 'messing about in boats' [like Ratty in *The Wind in the Willows*].

* *Background.* He was with the Filipino Army at the Battle of Reykjavik, c.5000 AD. It was an Ice Age and World War VI was narrowly averted. He's heard of Magnus Greel's experiments and the rumours of the Peking (sic) Homunculus. He decries the primitive 'Zygma Beam' and 'Zygma Particle' technology Greel uses for his cack-handed time-travel. [See **What's So Great About the Year Five Thousand?** under X1.10, "The Doctor Dances" for why this led to a lot of complications when they brought the series back in 2005.]

Once again, he talks about Agincourt as though he had been there ["The Masque of Mandragora"]. He hasn't been to China for 'four hundred years' [either in his own chronology (in which case the encounter with Mao Xedung was before 1.4, "Marco Polo"; see 8.2, "The Mind of Evil") or historical time (so, c.1500 and maybe the Kublai Khan incident we saw in Season One)].

He once went fishing in the Fleet and caught an enormous trout. At some point, he shared this with the Venerable Bede [who never went near London, but the TARDIS has a fridge].

* *Ethics.* He's only mildly put out when Leela uses a Janis Thorn to kill a Tong hatchet-man, as she does it to save his life. His increasing use of hypnosis as a first-resort is tempered by him telling Jago in advance that he's about to do it.

In ironically acknowledging the locals' ethnic stereotyping, he leaves them [and some viewers] with the impression that he's condoning it. Ditto his wry evaluation of the Birmingham-made "Chinese" fowling-piece [see 26.2, "Ghost Light" for the earliest re-use of this story's gags], although he really is staking his life on it working first time.

* *Inventory: Other.* His cane contains a small container of brandy. When he's emptying his pockets to look for Greel's key, we see: the Etheric Beam Locator we saw on Skaro; the Spectromixer ["Planet of Evil"]; a bag of jelly-babies; the yellow yo-yo; a Matchbox Toys Batmobile and a cuddly toy [specifically a fluffy toy mouse, but not a clockwork one as per X4.6, "The Doctor's Daughter"].

He also appears to have correct currency for theatre-tickets, muffins and a potential orange for Leela. When not-really auditioning for Jago, he produces a stream of coloured handkerchiefs and then, from somewhere, two doves in a dish. [We see two doves in a cage in Chang's dressing-room, so maybe he's borrowed the props – then again, in "Robot," we see a stuffed toy dove, so he may carry automata that are more lifelike when switched on.]

Mary Whitehouse: What was Her Problem?

If you've been reading the **Lore** sections of this book sequentially, you'll have noticed that we took great pains to unpick the commonly-held assumption that Philip Hinchcliffe's departure was the BBC's kneejerk reaction to the complaints of Mrs Mary Whitehouse, figurehead and founder of an outfit calling itself the National Viewers' and Listeners' Association. This impression is one that flatters Whitehouse and simplifies a lot of internal BBC politics to a straightforwardly linear cause and effect. It gave those wishing to berate the incoming producer, Graham Williams, a handy stick while looking sympathetic. It seems to explain why the series was "neutered" after "The Talons of Weng-Chiang" without apportioning blame to Tom Baker or accounting for the fact that – if viewing-figures and public memory are any guide – the only people who stopped liking the series were the kingpins within the newly-formed *Doctor Who* Appreciation Society.

But the idea's got traction outwith the DWAS. It's assumed to be true by those millions who were watching in the 1970s. Mary Whitehouse became such a bogey-figure in British pop culture as to inspire the title of a laddish sketch show (*The Mary Whitehouse Experience*), a Pink Floyd lyric (see "Pigs" on the album *Animals*), a *Python* riff (that recurring black-and-white clip of frumpy old ladies applauding is from her 1965 fatwa, as we'll discuss) and be ridiculed across the media. She turned herself into a meme and seemed to be becoming an unwitting self-parody. No such luck: this was as calculated as everything else she did. This cosy image belied the racist, homophobic and manifestly political objectives of her band of followers under the guise of being "ordinary, decent citizens". The conditions were ripe for such a ploy, so we'd better start examining how she got a toehold by looking at what she had a toehold *in*.

For the sake of argument, we'll start in September 1954. A few hundred schoolkids amassed at the Southern necropolis in Glasgow after rumours that a seven-foot vampire with iron teeth was lurking there and had eaten two children already. The policeman sent to investigate reports of vandalism was startled by their sincerity and asked some of the parents about it. They hadn't managed to persuade their children that it wasn't real. The school headmaster sternly admonished the children about this. The papers said it was all laughed off the next day, and everything was fine. Then, the next night, the kids returned. The media were unaware of any actual disappearances, so they started looking for someone to blame.

These days, when this story is told, at the forefront is the irony of this braw beastie's distinguishing features being identical to what the parents had told kids would happen if they didn't eat their neeps (plus the similarity to something their school taught about the Book of Daniel). At the time, the "obvious" culprit was popular culture, so they went looking for anything even vaguely similar in what the kids were enjoying when they ought to be scrubbing potatoes or whatever. That 1950s Scotland had the blandest comics around (*The Beano* and *The Dandy*, the strips *Oor Wullie* and *The Broons* in the Sunday Post) was lost on the press in their zeal, so they claimed it was all down to American "Horror Comics" – unavailable in Glaswegian newsagents' shops; any that made it across the Atlantic were traded like gold-dust. (An earlier reaction to this perceived menace was *The Eagle*, for which see **What Kind of Future Were We Expecting?** under 2.3, "The Rescue".)

When asked about it all decades later, none of the former children involved had ever seen these things or heard rumours of their existence. That didn't stop the press and church-leaders (and leaders of the Unions, suspicious of any American influence) fomenting a claim that Something Must be Done. Parliament agreed. The 1955 *Children and Young Persons (Harmful Publications) Act* was rushed through and, like all frantic laws to "fix" problems and to "protect" children, it was quietly repealed a few years later. The Gorbals Vampire is an early specimen of the process of what became known as "Moral Panics" (a term, like "Swedish Fish" and "Science Fiction", where neither word is entirely right but together it's a handy, agreed-upon label).

Then there were the bubble-gum cards from Hell. On 4th July, 1963, the Education Secretary, Sir Edward Boyle was asked in the House of Commons why the government wasn't acting on "shoddy and contemptible" cards found in sweets. The Blyth Teachers' Association, in the North-East, had petitioned him on this already, but their MP, Edward Milne, wanted an outright ban. What these cards were is conjectural – some sources claim it was a few American *Mars Attacks* cards that somehow made it to Tyneside. Hansard, the record of Parliamentary debates, cites a Mrs Slater decrying Boyle's statement that public opinion

continued on page 361...

14.6 The Talons of Weng-Chiang

The Supporting Cast

- *Leela*. In an unexpected switch, she seems to find wearing a big flouncy frock to go to the theatre more agreeable than a pair of knee-britches and a padded jacket. She loses the corduroy cap as soon as possible. She has Janis thorns on her person [somehow] and a blow-pipe in her pocket.

She was taught to stab upwards, under the ribcage. She knows signs of death [perhaps predictably] and seems to believe in swamp-monsters as something more than "feast-fire stories". She appreciates a good knife and cooked meats served cold. Torturing prisoners seems sensible to her. She seems to have encountered crabs on her home planet, as well as dry leaves [she comes from a deciduous jungle?].

She talks about pursuing Greel in 'the Great Hereafter', some sort of equal-opportunities afterlife. When Chang dies, she makes a curious gesture, not exactly like the Starfall Seven check of the Sevateem ["The Face of Evil" Part One].

The niceties of tea-drinking seem like a tribal rite, but being Leela, she immediately asks obvious questions. She has never encountered tobacco or blancmange. Winning the Doctor's approval still delights her. She also seems to have picked up the word 'dilettante' from somewhere. [We'll assume that her immunity from gangrene or any other ill-effects of getting her leg chewed by a giant rat in a sewer is the TARDIS at work, turbocharging her immune system as we now know it does from *Torchwood* and *The Sarah Jane Adventures*. This, of course, raises questions about Dodo's cold (3.6, "The Ark"), but we already had many about her.]

The Supporting Cast (Evil)

- *Magnus Greel, AKA 'Weng-Chiang'*. A fifty-first-century war-criminal [see **History**]. Greel developed the Zygma Beam: a dangerous and ultimately fatal escape route into the past. The journey, or perhaps the progressive effect it has on his metabolism, warps his face beyond recognition.

Greel adopted the persona of Weng-Chiang and used the technology of his time to make his rescuer, Li-H'sen Chang, mentally powerful. [As the time-cabinet is covered in Chinoiserie, it's possible that he was aiming for China all along.] He has been using reclaimed parts of his experimental equipment to sustain himself from the 'life-essences' of young women [cut dialogue indicates that these are the only suitable "donors"].

[A curious feature of Greel's 'performance' as a Chinese deity is that his vocabulary is full of animal similes — lions, tigresses, partridges, wolves and do on. He may have been stuck in nineteenth-century China for a very long time, but asking Chang what these things in paintings were would have blown his cover. It could also indicate that the near-Ice Age conditions of the fifty-first century ushered in a lot of rewilding as part of fixing the Earth's ecosystem, but this sits ill with the constant state of war mentioned elsewhere. We might conjecture that, as with Mr Sin's cerebral cortex coming from a pig, some of Greel's barbarous experiments involved a private menagerie. This might fit with the Extraction Cabinet and resolve a few of the **Things That Don't Make Sense** issues, but it's odd that the Doctor doesn't taunt his foe with the details.

[Little of this story's account of the fifty-first century matches what we see two stories from now, or anything from Stephen Moffat's repeated use of that period setting. We will later attempt to connect K9's vulnerability to viral infections (15.2, "The Invisible Enemy"; 17.1, "Destiny of the Daleks") with Sin's porcine motherboard, but that's about it.]

Planet Notes [Special geographical note: the Palace Theatre is above the covered river Fleet, which joins the Thames at Blackfriars' Bridge, running almost due south from Hampstead through Camden Town. Therefore, it can't be any further east than Ludgate Circus, so Limehouse — Litefoot's district — is at least a ten-minute cab-ride away. (In terms of London geography, Mile End is a better bet for his actual house.) From internal evidence and the Street Index of 1888, it's possible to place the Palace Theatre at Holborn Viaduct, perhaps near Farringdon tube station. The House of the Dragon *might* be at Limehouse Causeway, but we'll suggest in **Things That Don't Make Sense** that it's a bit further north.]

History

- *Dating*. If everyone knows "Daisy Bell", it's after Summer 1892. The Doctor hopes to catch a performance by the music hall comedian Little Tich, who was living in Paris for a lot of the late 1890s after a three-year tour of major European capitals (roughly 1893-6). Jack the Ripper was active in Summer 1888. We're going with the earliest possible date, because nobody says that

Mary Whitehouse: What was Her Problem?

...continued from page 359

was a more effective weapon than a heavy-handed ban by saying "It is the right hon. Gentleman's responsibility to see that our children are protected. We had to do something about horror comics. Why cannot we do something about these terrible cards?"

See how the process feeds itself: once one rushed and unworkable bill becomes law, there's a precedent. You get an authoritarian person or group raising a concern about something new, then the press hype it to sell papers, thereby identifying a root-cause (usually foreign or an unfamiliar medium, such as rock 'n' roll, television, the internet). There's usually a subtext that kids have it too easy nowadays. Individuals thought to be behind it are demonised, and a story goes about of manipulative outsiders exerting undue influence on "innocent" youth.

Britain has a much faster feedback-loop on this sort of thing: a few hours after an event, motions in Parliament can react to the tabloids' diagnosis of the problem. The term "Moral Panic" was coined by Stan Cohen in 1972 analysing the over-reaction to the Clacton scuffles between Mods and Rockers in Spring 1964 (see **What Were the Most Mod Stories?** under 4.6, "The Moonbase"). It incorporates the societal control mechanisms used to create demons, be seen to control them and reassure everyone that everything's hunky-dory with society itself – it's just "those people" and the sinister "others" goading them on.

In that regard, it's directly analogous to both paranoid conspiracy theories and the pop-culture manifestations of them that have various "Napoleons of Crime" (usually with Eastern European names of an ethnic group commonly blamed for things going wrong). We discussed in "Terror of the Autons" (8.1) and "The Talons of Weng-Chiang" how that sort of figure has a long pedigree, but it goes right back to the Gordon Riots in the 1780s and, before that, the anti-Jewish sentiment (and, in Norwich, a massacre) in the reign of Edward III. The Greeks did it, inventing ostracism and executing Socrates for corrupting the youth of Athens. The classic essay on the topic, Richard Hofstadter's "The Paranoid Style in American Politics", is having a bit of a vogue at the moment. (See also: **Gay Agenda? What Gay Agenda?** under X1.10, "The Doctor Dances" and our comments on Graham Bright with 22.2, "Vengeance on Varos".) Another reason Britain in the 1960s and 1970s was so prone to these (the list is alarming and occasionally hilarious until you get to AIDS) is that a nice bit of hysteria sells newspapers.

If you think about it, the fact that the press blames each new medium that comes along, from cinema to social media, for *everything* is entirely logical. They have a position to uphold and could lose influence, or worse, income, if the public decide that paying for sheets of paper with selections from yesterday's events is a poor investment. A newspaper is a sort of community, however much it pretends to be august and above such things, and relies on a notion of "us" and "them" as much as any idea of relaying facts. For most of the twentieth century, it was bought by the breadwinner and had some degree of recreational socialising inbuilt (things to read aloud to co-workers over breaks, crosswords, horoscopes, half-naked teenage girls, sport gossip, actual gossip...). Things that did this better, faster or cheaper were a threat.

The first line of defence was ridiculing people who liked sort of thing, usually as mindless slaves to a cheap pleasure (there's usually a class element in this, right back to Harry Furniss (yes, *that* Harry Furniss, look him up) in 1914, having to counter a notion that decent people avoided cinemas); then came the horror-stories of "addicts" doing terrible things (Teddy-Boys slashing up cinema seats because of Bill Haley and the Comets); insinuations of miscegenation, Svengali-like exploiters and young girls being led astray by promoters and, if all else fails, a dodgy defence lawyer trying to acquit someone of a murder rap because they were under the influence of... whatever it was (video nasties, computer games, Drill records and anything American).

A less obvious element is circulation wars between rival newspaper-owners. To get a little ahead of ourselves, the kerfuffle over Hinchcliffe-era *Doctor Who* has a lot to do with the rivalries between the tabloids. Notably the *Daily Mail*, originally the working man's paper but increasingly aimed at right-wing, petit-bourgeois readers; the *Daily Express*, always fairly authoritarian but playing catch-up with Northcliffe's *Mail* from the get-go; and the *Daily Mirror*, historically associated with the Labour Party, the educated working-class and progressive popular movements until Robert Maxwell happened.

continued on page 363...

the Doctor looks like Sherlock Holmes – indeed, Casey says he doesn't look much like a detective – so there can't have been any stage adaptations using the "Silver Blaze" costume. [Doyle's stories do exist in this world – see, once again, "Ghost Light". Litefoot doesn't wince at "elementary my dear Litefoot", paraphrasing a phase not in the Holmes canon but probably derived from the William Gillette stage adaptations from 1899 onwards.] Ergo, we'd opt for November 1892-February 1893, but not during Panto season or the Twelve Days of Christmas. [The amount of daylight indicates its proximity to Winter Solstice.] Litefoot is reading an issue of *Blackwood's Magazine* from February 1892, if that helps. The Fleet was covered over in the 1840s. [Litefoot says 'centuries ago', but he grew up in China).]

Following Magnus Greel's arrival in China, and after lying ill for 'many months', he set about biologically augmenting the peasant who cared for him: Li-Hsen Chang. According to Chang, the Cabinet was taken by 'Soldiers of T'ung-Chi'. [Tongzhi, in the current orthography, ruled from January 1861 to February 1875 (with the aid of various regents, as he was a toddler when he acceded to the throne).] Litefoot's family stuck around in China for over a dozen years after the end of the Opium War, returning home in 1873. [Presumably with Greel's cabinet in their possession. This in turn suggests that Litefoot is rather younger than he looks, to have been in China for some time and not have interrupted his university degree, residency at a hospital, specialist training as a forensic pathologist and so on. (He was 'brought up' there, but his father was sent there in 1860.) The implication from the dialogue is that Greel was at death's door when he arrived and isn't much better now, so he's been on the critical list for the 20 years it's taken them to get to London.

[It follows from this that Chang, Greel and Mr Sin have only been in town for a few months (when the girls started going missing), but Chang's reputation preceded him. There must have been a few abductions wherever he performed, but nobody made the connection. Unless, of course, his master's need for girl-juice only kicked in when they crossed the Channel and Greel made his drain-their-vital-bodily-juices device from scratch using everyday household objects. That suggests the journey was over land; a slow boat to or from China is a really lousy place to abduct young women without anyone noticing.]

Around the start of the next Ice Age, c. 5000 AD, Earth's science entered a dark age. Magnus Greel, AKA the Butcher of Brisbane, conducted experiments that killed thousands; some of these were to do with time travel, using the abortive Zygma Beam (following Professor Findecker's discovery of the double-nexus particle), others were connected with the extraction of 'life-essence' [proteinoids, as mentioned twice in the dialogue, slightly illogically, or something more numinous, as the visuals suggest?].

These interests dovetailed even before Greel fled from justice with the Time Cabinet, in a journey that ruptured his DNA strands and disrupted his metabolism. He must now harvest the life-essences of young women to stay alive. *Precisely what else he did is unclear*, but he was apparently thwarted in the Battle of Reykjavik. The *casus belli* was to have been the assassination of the Commissioner of the Icelandic Alliance: a toy built for his children, the Peking Homunculus, was programmed with magnetic fields but ran on the cerebral cortex of a pig and ran amok. [Dicks, in the novelisation, makes it clear that this was a hit and the family were massacred. The Doctor's dialogue in Part Five doesn't make this link, and just hints that the thing went wrong when the 'swinish instinct' took over.] The murderous Homunculus 'almost caused World War VI'.

Greel fears that his desperate flight through time will have attracted the attention of a Time Agent. [NB: to reiterate, nothing about this tallies with the assumption underlying Captain Jack Harkness's backstory that the Time Agency was based or formed in the fifty-first century. Greel honestly thinks that he's the first human to travel through time and seems familiar with the Time Agents from before he fled into the past (there's no evidence that he's getting news updates via some sort of space-time telegraph), so would have no reason to think they're native to his era. A fifty-first-century agency would perforce also use Zygma Beams; agents would undergo similar ill-effects.]

The Analysis

Where Does This Come From? To the casual viewer in 1977, this would have been a silly question. There were several overtly-cited sources and a lot

Mary Whitehouse: What was Her Problem?

...continued from page 361

There is a definite correlation between how the *Mail* discussed BBC programmes and who they wanted readers to vote for, so the *Mirror* generally reacted against whatever the Northcliffe-owned papers said with facts and jibes at the *Mail*'s hypocrisy. Similarly, *The Guardian* was keen to debunk any scare-stories that *The Times* repeated from the same sources the *Mail* used (see "The Brain of Morbius" for a good example), even though *The Times*'s mystique as "the top people's paper" was carefully nurtured from 1785 until 1980, when Rupert Murdoch got his hands on it and the "Top People" moved to *The Daily Telegraph*. Murdoch's main purchase in the 1960s was *The Sun*, initially intended as a brained-up version of the *Mirror* but, after the takeover in 1969, a smut-and-scandal rag whose readers saw no anomaly when lurid tales of debauchery were matched with topless Page Three girls. It had no consistent policy on television beyond gossiping about the stars – at least until Murdoch started his own satellite station in the late 80s, at which point nothing the BBC did was right.

It's within this context that Mary Whitehouse's antics have to be examined. She was born in 1910, the daughter of a failed artist turned travelling salesman (a lot of her biographical details have been mined to "explain" her apparent neuroses, notably the state of her parents' marriage). While studying to become an art-teacher, she came under the influence of Frank Buchman's "Oxford Group": an American style evangelical group that was something of a personality-cult (Buchman also inspired Alcoholics Anonymous). This rebranded itself in the 1930s as "Moral Rearmament" – while it and he belatedly accepted that Hitler was a bad lot, they were less anti-Nazi than anti-Soviet. (It has been said that Buchman's beef was that Marx had been raised as a Jew. It's interesting how often Whitehouse would use "not an English name" as a way of casting doubt on the integrity of those she picked on.) This outfit never caught on in Britain, as it did in America or post-war Germany, and was generally considered to be intolerant and sinister (although you'll not see anything about that in the Wikipedia article maintained by adherents).

Mrs Whitehouse (she married Ernest, a Methodist, in 1940) kept herself to herself for a few decades, becoming a teacher. The story, like *Doctor Who* and sexual intercourse,[58] begins in 1963,

Working as an art-teacher, with occasional sex-education lessons in her brief, she supposedly came across two pupils faking sex and, when she asked them about it, they claimed to be mimicking Mandy Rice-Davis and Christine Keeler. Quite how television was to blame for the Profumo scandal is unclear, but she had previous, writing to broadcasters complaining about the lyrics of "Please Please Me" by the Beatles in January. Then a talk by Dr Alex Comfort in the series *This Nation Tomorrow* in July. Using her status as a school-teacher and an "ordinary" woman with a provincial accent, she set about establishing her brand and contacting the press about her complaints.

In early May 1964, she advertised a meeting in Birmingham Town Hall and arranged for 2,000 people to be bussed in – this is the meeting that's the source of those elderly ladies in hats applauding you see so often in *Python*. She published a brochure for her "Clean Up TV" movement claiming to represent "ordinary housewives", although she herself was no such thing.

The line always cherry-picked from the news report runs as follows: *Last Thursday evening, we sat as a family and watched a programme that started at 6.35. And it was the dirtiest programme I have seen for a very long time.* The offending item was a Scottish comedy series, *Between the Lines*, and a specific sketch in which Tom Conti plays a bloke who fantasises about women he meets on the way to work. It was, apparently, about as raunchy as the clips from *The Secret Life of Walter Mitty* already used in Schools Television (in the estimation of those who saw its one broadcast, 30th April, 1964).

What's also left out is that not everyone at that meeting was enthusiastic about the crusade. David Turner, playwright, was working at a nearby theatre and denounced Whitehouse's campaign of censorship as a curtailment of artistic liberty, from the auditorium. Nonetheless, the media were told that 2,000 "ordinary" people had come and the "Clean Up TV" slogan got support from (where else?) the tabloids. Within weeks, she had half a million signatures – the most popular support she ever had, but that's not how things were subsequently reported. She set about using her now-established brand and renamed her band of zealots the National Viewers' and Listeners' Association ("NVALA", pronounced to sound like "valour" – Frank Buchman taught her well).

continued on page 365...

14.6 The Talons of Weng-Chiang

of familiar bits and pieces, but not all of these are in circulation today. Moreover, the connections between these things will need a bit of teasing out, intuitive as they seemed in the Jubilee year.

In the early scripts, the character eventually called "Jago" is identified as "Sachs": potentially a huge clue, were it not so flagrant in the broadcast version. A series called *The Good Old Days* had run from the early 1950s, when Music Hall was just-about visible, if receding rapidly into the haze, to 1981. As the number of acts who'd been doing it for real dwindled, it became a way for current performers to lay claim to being in a tradition. Bernard Cribbins (see Volumes 6, 8 and 9) was a frequent star turn, as were Larry Grayson (see Season Sixteen's notes) and Ken Dodd ("Delta and the Bannermen"). The version of Music Hall thus available for viewers was increasingly unlike anything real Victorians would have seen, but the zeal for "authenticity" kept the series true to its earlier episodes, if not to fact. The constant feature was a flamboyant MC, played by Leonard Sachs (3.5, "The Massacre"; 20.1, "Arc of Infinity") whose introductions included a lot of alliteration.

The audience's appreciation of each absurdly alliterative approximation of acrobatics was a gallimaufry of guffaws, gasps and groans, exactly as we get in this story. There's little to suggest that this was common in actual Victorian shows (it seems more a legacy of *ITMA*, the wartime radio comedy). The most obvious link to "Talons" is that the show-audiences would dress up in period clothes (and preposterous facial hair) and know the songs, turning up at the theatre in Leeds that had been kept in aspic to look like what people want to think was typical. This happened a lot, in various theatres not on telly. Performers and cosplaying audiences kept provincial theatres going outside panto season, fuelled by nostalgia and a delight in live entertainment. Several of those enthusiasts were extras in this production.

Of course, it was about as authentic as those "Renaissance Fayres" that serve turkey and potatoes. The name "Music Hall" indicates that this was, primarily, an outgrowth of entertainments put on in the back room or upstairs of a pub. Dressing up wasn't really an option. This was cheap, vulgar entertainment designed to get people to hang around and drink more, possibly eating as well. The content was ribald and sentimental, but the big difference between this, Variety and Vaudeville was that those involved were making a specific journey to go and see an act at a theatre, while this was an adjunct to usual after-work drinking.

There were a lot of pubs, so the acts (or "turns") were almost guaranteed a gig if they could compete with everything else going on and got re-hired if they made a bigger increase in turnover than they cost. If you were more entertaining than a sing-along around the piano, word would spread – but if not, the local would be a good berth for a while. The railways made turns more mobile and therefore worth advertising, so the next few steps are better-documented (or at least more evocatively). That and the physical evidence (buildings and their plans) enable us to state that the version of Music Hall we see here and in *The Good Old Days* is anachronistic. (It's also got a mixed audience, where the male-orientated acts meant that most of the women who'd be in a real Music Hall were working girls of one sort or another.)

There *were* purpose-built Music Halls in the period we're encouraged to think this is, but they tended to be laid out like big pubs – often having a pub built in – with benches and tables for seating rather than rows of seats and big boxes. Many of these were side-hustles for publicans in the boom years before the Brewers' Wars of 1896-9 and subsequent crash.[60] After that, the sort of set-up Jago has, proprietor of a bespoke Variety Theatre with no other business ventures, started spreading – especially as the Royal Family were giving the whole industry an image-change. Or, more accurately, confirming it. We'll go into this when we get to the essay on Panto with "The Horns of Nimon" (17.5), but by the time George V was crowned and had a Command Performance of his favourite turns (that's 1910), we're at the state of play memorialised in *The Good Old Days*, but nobody was dressing like the audiences in that show. Of course, a lot of legitimate theatres hosted stars of the Music Hall in the 1890s, but as a full night's entertainment in and of itself rather than as a highlight of a long roster of acts. Little Tich was one of these.

Another television approximation of Music Hall was making a splash in 1976-7: although it had a number of American star guests, some of whom we'd heard of, *The Muppet Show* was made in Britain and had only one advert break in the ITV broadcasts. The US transmissions had more than this and the sacrificial scenes cut to make way for

Mary Whitehouse: What was Her Problem?

...continued from page 363

The name "National Viewers' and Listeners' Association" is a textbook example of what we now call "astroturfing", i.e., pretending to be a grass-roots organisation and claiming a popular mandate. It's the same trick a fringe organisation in Russia, at the start of World War I, used when they took a Russian word for "majority" and called themselves "Bolsheviks". It would prove effective when a parallel outfit in America proclaimed itself to be "the Moral Majority". To this day, there's little evidence of their actual membership ever exceeding a few thousand even at the peak of Whitehouse's influence and publicity-drive. (For comparison, the *Doctor Who* Appreciation Society peaked with 3,500 members.)

In 1965, she quit her job to devote all her waking hours to watching programmes she thought likely to deprave – oddly, she herself never went on a killing-spree as a result. Nothing was too trivial for her contempt – Anglo-French marionettes Pinky and Perky (a couple of pigs who did "Chipmunk" style speeded-up covers of recent hits) were a bad influence in her eyes. Emboldened, she objected to *Panorama* repeating Richard Dimbleby's piece on being the BBC correspondent sent to Belsen concentration camp at the end of World War II. Her grounds for this: anything on television was "entertainment", thus this was unsuitable when children might be watching (like children ever voluntarily watched *Panorama*). We'll have the same argument trotted out for Peter Watkins's nuclear aftermath drama-documentary *The War Games*. The one thing these programmes had in common was that they were all made by the BBC.

As you'll recall from Volume 1, the Director General of the BBC in the early 1960s was Hugh Carleton Greene. He believed that public service television had to provide for everyone, not just the statistical plurality or some notional "elite". He favoured innovation, socially-conscious drama and universal access to the best of whatever was available. Whitehouse, quite naturally, considered him to be the anti-Christ. (Whether the fact that Greene's brother Graham – yes, *that* Graham Greene – was one of Britain's most celebrated Catholics was a factor is unclear.)

In some ways, Whitehouse's status as a middle-age, lower-middle-class woman with a Midlands accent made her his polar opposite, and she played up to this contrast. Greene never took the bait and never engaged with her directly. He was more concerned with the genuine grass-roots social mobility and dynamism of 1960s Britain and, despite seeming patrician and aloof, was probably more in touch with what ordinary people thought. He wasn't universally in favour of such people getting their views across, but wasn't going to stop it, just counter the less savoury ones. (Here we have to bring up *Till Death Us Do Part*, the format of which Beryl Vertue sold to America to become *All in the Family*, and the way a "typical" authoritarian working-class man, Alf Garnett, stated outright the half-formed associations underlying racist, sexist and repressive views assumed by the *Mail* and *Express*. He was ridiculed on screen by his wife, daughter and son-in-law, but – in saying this stuff in a lightly-Bowlderised version of how such bigots speak – he offended Whitehouse, even when he agreed with her. Greene found the way real-life Alfs wrote in and complained about the language piquantly amusing.)

For reasons we've rehearsed a lot in these books, the ITV companies were scared of causing offense or doing anything risky, so Whitehouse found the bulk of their output unobjectionable – until after the 1967 Franchise Auction, when they were set up for the next seven years and didn't need to play safe or let the BBC get all the kudos and exports. That auction was overseen, badly, by Lord Hill of Luton, formerly the wartime Radio Doctor, but latterly as fierce an opponent of Greene as Whitehouse or the Prime Minister. (Harold Wilson believed that the BBC was out to get him – actually, it was Lord Mountbatten.) With the subsequent pressure brought to bear on the Corporation, Greene was replaced by the superficially weaker Charles Curran.

This is where it gets interesting. Where Greene had a painting of Whitehouse with five breasts that he used as a dartboard, rather than acknowledge her existence publicly, Curran replied to her letters calmly, wittily and with facts to counter her every accusation. It drove her nuts (well, nutser). *Top of the Pops* aroused her ire, not for whatever Jimmy Savile was doing backstage (he publicly endorsed her views), but for the content. Her gripes about Alice Cooper performing "School's Out" may have got it to Number One (Cooper thought so and sent her flowers). Six months later, she whinged to Curran about Chuck Berry's novelty hit "My Ding-a-Ling". He pointed out that the

continued on page 367...

14.6 The Talons of Weng-Chiang

These Important Messages were often performances of old Music Hall songs – "Burlington Bertie", "Any Old Iron", "Don't Dilly-Dally on the Way" and so on. (A subtext of these is that this was the one item on the bill Statler and Waldorf actually enjoyed, and the reason they put up with Fozzie and Gonzo.)

Somehow, Fozzie Bear dressed as a Pearly King singing "Wotcher, Knocked 'Em in the Old Kent Road" made perfect sense.[61] (However, if – like our publisher – you were weaned on *The Muppet Show*'s US broadcasts and syndication, the more-comprehensive DVD releases that include the sight of a tuxedoed Kermit and a thunderously pregnant Ms. Piggy flouncing to "Waiting at the Church" – cue Kermit, that cad, singing: "Can't get away to marry you today, my wife won't let me! – incited oh so many mixed emotions.) There was an extended-play single of these performances in the charts the following Christmas. Another Anglo-American television feature about the subject was an episode of the long, worthy documentary series "All You Need is Love" in which Music Hall enthusiast Liberace showed off his collection and narrated a scholarly summary of the topic.

Television may have dealt the final blow to Music Hall, but it grabbed the remains enthusiastically. Apart from *The Good Old Days*, there was a literal and figurative land-grab as the agents and theatre-owners got into television at the start of ITV. Lew Grade even used one of his former successes, the Wood Green Empire, as a studio (it was a mile from Alexandra Palace and 500 yards from the tube station, so television technicians and performers knew where it was).

Unfortunately, its main claim to fame was the on-stage death of William Robinson, AKA Chung Ling Soo, during his famous "magic bullet" act in 1918. His stage-name has been translated as "Double Good Luck". The version he did was the inverse of the trick Chang does with the Doctor (catching a bullet, fired by an audience-member, in a bronze bowl). Why was he passing as Chinese? Because a lot of magicians adopted names a bit like already-famous ones (Robert Houdin inspired Harry Houdini, for example) and Ching Ling Foo, who was really Chinese, had been a big hit in Robinson's native America.

That 1977 casual viewer would note that, although he didn't look especially Asian, John Bennett looked almost exactly like Christopher Lee as Fu Manchu. The 1960s included many films churned out as a wannabe Bond-style franchise, usually with Richard Greene (50s *Robin Hood*) as Nayland Smith, the paranoid cop whose conspiracy theories always turned out to be right.

As was the usual course of such things, the BBC got them cheap about a decade later and, in March 1975, popped on a run of the better ones on Friday evenings (even if paid to, they'd've stopped before the Jess Franco ones that ended the fad in Europe, although America persisted into the 80s and Peter Sellers did a misfiring spoof just before he died). The films were mainly explosions and assassinations, with daft attempts to take over the world (although one loopy, sexist plot involving drugged beauties was recycled for Bond in *On Her Majesty's Secret Service*). Earlier films of these books were equally of-their-time, notably the Boris Karloff 1930s one but, with these colour 1960s efforts, they admitted defeat. To make any London setting palatable to American audiences, the period trappings are laid on thick even in films set in the present day: travelling to Britain is like travelling back in time and going to Transylvania is almost like visiting prehistory. (Conversely, late Victorian novels saw anywhere other than London as being "retro"; see "Terror of the Zygons" and, of course, Conan-Doyle's other big hit, *The Lost World*.) Hollywood wasn't too bothered with checking facts even about other bits of America. Ergo, all Fu Manchu films are effectively set in the 1890s, even if there are jets and lasers. The late nineteenth century was stuffed to the rafters with sinister foreigners plotting the downfall of whichever nation the books came from, usually by hypnosis and blackmail with an army of brainwashed goons.

As we discussed in 8.1, "Terror of the Autons", blaming an all-powerful but secretive mastermind for everything that thwarts the "right" outcome of the reader becoming rich and influential is easier to swallow than accepting that them's the breaks or that (whisper it) actually just being white and male isn't a guarantee of success if you're mediocre, stupid or antisocial. Professor Moriarty/ Fantomas/ Dr Mabuse/ Fu Manchu/ the Deep State/ Russian Hackers/ Commies/ George Soros/ the EU/ the Bilderberg Set make it easier to face failure than looking at yourself. Fu Manchu combined this fantasy with a recent set of foreign conflicts (the Boxer Rebellion and, earlier, the Opium Wars), a culture old and mysterious but unquestionably real, a visible ethnic group in

Mary Whitehouse: What was Her Problem?

...continued from page 365

free publicity kept it as the lucrative Christmas Number One after it had fallen in the previous week's chart. The only problem for *Top of the Pops* was that the concert clip they used for it became so over-familiar that they had to replace it – with hindsight, Rolf Harris illustrating a "clean" account of what was happening was far dodgier than the mild innuendo of the original.

In fact, it's instructive to look at the BBC programmes that we might query but with which she had no problems: *The Black and White Minstrel Show* was perfectly fine; *Miss World*, no worries; *Are You Being Served?*, absolutely fine (the innuendoes uttered unconsciously by Whitehouse-a-like Mrs Slocum may have whizzed over her head). Wildlife documentaries where animals rip each other to pieces got letters of praise. Not a word about the racist, sexist, anti-Irish material put out by former club comedians such as Bernard Manning, Jimmy Tarbuck or Charlie Williams.

People who try to reclaim her reputation by suggesting she was proto-feminist or analogous to the current tabloid demon of the "PC Brigade" or "woke snowflakes" are on a hiding to nothing. Her one connection with the modern zealots the press now opposes (or champion, depending on the owner's whims) is that, in the late 1970s, her anti-gay frenzy set legal precedents for private prosecutions for Blasphemy (against *Gay News*) and prosecutions for indecency against theatres (the hilarious-with-hindsight fuss over *The Romans in Britain* at the National Theatre). Sikh, Hindu and Muslim conservatives have used this to try to shut down plays for daring to comment on FGM or "honour-killings" (successfully, in the case of *Behzti* in 2004). The 1980s was, for Whitehouse and her epigones, marked by gleeful claims that AIDS was God's wrath. For reasons we'll come to, though, her star had fallen by then.

So what was her beef with *Doctor Who*? To begin with, not much, but then it got popular – so obviously, it was a good hook to get her name into the papers. It was popular with children, allowing her to cite the BBCs rules on children's television. (A bit of a fudge, but looking for logic in her pronouncements is like trying to find the names of the children she claims were affected.) It was challenging. It showed futures without many people like her in them. Those who were there were usually baddies. People with views unlike hers were often goodies.

As a series, it contained the three worst fears of a Fundamentalist busybody – science, the supernatural and sexy girls with brains. Obviously, there was rarely anything that directly said "Evangelicals are agents of the Daleks" – her fellow Festival of Light celebrity spokesman Cliff Richard was a fan of the series – but, as we've seen a few times this century, anything not explicitly endorsing a particular worldview is usually taken as a criticism by that faction's cheerleaders. In particular, the tabloids were getting a bee in their bonnet about the effects of violence on children, so she tuned in without fail, waiting to be offended. It got her headlines.

Characteristically, once she'd made a fuss about something, she would refer back next time to "the controversy", taking it as given that everyone else found it controversial. In 1975, she found – or concocted – a wave of arachnophobia sweeping the nation's youth because of Boris from Metebelis III (11.5, "Planet of the Spiders"). A psychiatrist working for the Church of England claimed an "epidemic" had occurred (then immediately pointed out that fear of spiders is almost universal anyway) and nonchalantly made the link to *Doctor Who*. The *Times* picked this one line from the lengthy article in *The General Practitioner* (erroneously claiming these ones to be "hairy") and Whitehouse pounced on this. However, the Whitehouse tirade, while low on fact, contained one useful suggestion – an independent investigation into the effects on young children of fantasy television. As we'll see in the next essay, that's exactly what happened.

Violence in films, and, as usual, the formula of "sex and violence" (as if they were the same and always linked), was also a reliable page-filler in tabloids. So, the attempts by Whitehouse supporters on local councils to ban films they thought liable to corrupt were more newsworthy than the films themselves. The British Board of Film Classification rarely made more than minor cuts, even when there was a crusade – but any time even the slightest trim was made, people of whom the BBFC had never heard anyway, most times, trumpeted this as "turning the tide" and claimed a victory. One favourable headline and these people smelled blood in the water and wanted more control. Whitehouse, once convinced that *Doctor Who* was corroding the nation's moral fabric, kept at it. And the press lapped it up.

continued on page 369...

14.6 The Talons of Weng-Chiang

London and the concern about opium-use. Arthur Ward, AKA Sax Rohmer, hit paydirt with a lazy amalgam of pan-European fears of invasion with the criminal mastermind motif and a lot of recycled Poe, Conan-Doyle and Rider-Haggard.

Enough was known to the readership, via lurid press coverage if not direct observation, to make any hysteria seem grounded in fact. Chinese workers in Limehouse, Liverpool or Birmingham were as handy a demon as Muslims in America now. Oddly, Britain was slightly behind the times on this trend (and had sided with Japan against Russia, to complicate the all-purpose "sinister East" thread of Continental fiction and US policies) and Rohmer only started in 1913 and hit his stride in the 30s, flourishing after the Great War and plugging away at what had become a chore when the talkies made his potboilers big business. Although most of the big "Yellow Peril" fantasies of the period 1890-1930 are American (and filters into such places as *Flash Gordon*'s Fu Manchu-with-ray-guns Ming and his sultry daughter and the original *Buck Rogers* storyline), Rohmer's books were considered as cinematic as the real late-Victorian paranoid masterpiece, *Dracula*.

Hammer Films went about it a different way: as the market for vampires dwindled and Lee stopped making Fu Manchu flicks or any kind of horror, they hitched their wagon to another star – the late Bruce Lee (no relation, obviously). Martial Arts films were going legit in America, hence *Enter the Dragon*, but their original source was the Shaw Brothers. These guys were churning out "chop-sockee" in profusion, redubbing everything because they were filming in the streets of Hong Kong right under the final approach of the jets coming to land. Lee had been the breakout star of the genre, but there were many others.

Logically, therefore, the last roll of the dice before giving up on Dracula was to have Peter Cushing, as Van Helsing, go to China and thwart the Count's bid to take over the world with an army of undead, aided by a lot of Kung Fu-trained relatives of one of Van Helsing's students. *The Legend of the 7 Golden Vampires* (1974) is a mess, but Hammer had little choice and Don Houghton (7.4, "Inferno"; 8.2, "The Mind of Evil") came up with at least a vaguely interesting twist to account for Dracula being an elderly Chinese monk for most of the film.

Hollywood, or at least indie film-makers around the edge, were using Kung Fu as an add-on to Blaxploitation films, but by 1977 the whole subculture was increasingly the preserve of anyone who'd stuck with the difficult bit of training three hours a day (see 11.5, "Planet of the Spiders" for our comments on the David Carradine TV show and the spoof in *The Goodies*.) Nonetheless, the old Havoc team had been obliged to learn enough to look convincing (even if this just meant falling over in slow motion when Gary Glitter beat them up in *Remember Me This Way*).

It's notable that, unlike "Pyramids of Mars" or "The Daemons", there's no attempt at "explaining" the mythology as an alien or time-traveller. After the radical secularism of "The Face of Evil", the Doctor's ire here is against the interloper using a pre-existing religion rather than castigating anyone who believed it before or after. The same textbook Holmes used for Egyptology seems to have been dragged out here, and the old Chinese god Wen-Chang has been retooled; originally this deity was responsible for writing catching on among humans and came from beneath the sea, like the Egyptian Thoth (anyone who wants to write a story about Sea Devils helping our ancestors can do it in private).

However, this isn't an exact fit and some have pointed out that there's part of a composite doorway-spirit, derived from Buddhism, Heng-Chiang, who blows fire. Take your pick. There never was a Tong of the Black Scorpion, although the name popped up shortly before this in an episode of *It Ain't 'Alf Hot, Mum* and one of the actors was in both iterations. However, the fanaticism and cotton-pyjama uniform is very like then-recent news reports of the Cultural Revolution under Mao. With Britain still having jurisdiction over Hong Kong at the time, the policing of the Tongs' successors, the Triads, was a contemporary issue, especially with the increasing heroin trade. However, the Victorian assassin-cult also being alluded to here is the Thuggee, from India. That might, at a pinch, explain why there's a statue of Kali in the House of the Dragon.

So if you're a writer in a hurry to place a Bond-villain in Victorian London, there's a ready-made template for you to subvert. And if you're in that much of a hurry, re-use things you've already done. We touched on it in "The Deadly Assassin", but *The Phantom of the Opera* is an obvious influence on both stories. There's a hint of the silent film version in Jago's description of the Doctor as "man of a thousand faces" (as that film's star, Lon

Mary Whitehouse: What was Her Problem?

...continued from page 367

As we said, in a circulation war, an issue such as this gets polarised quickly – a pro-Whitehouse column or article in one paper invariably got a reaction from a rival within days. Journalists in a hurry have usually got a small address-book of people who can reliably spout off on a particular topic; Whitehouse made sure they all had hers. However much NVALA's membership had dwindled since the first flurry of activity, she kept up her "ordinary housewife"/ "voice of the people" shtick, increasingly as a form of performance-art. She wasn't alone: in many ways, Margaret Thatcher was a sort of Whitehouse tribute-act, right down to the flouncy hats and "outsider" accent (both of which her advisors and image-consultants got her to drop once she'd established herself).

What of her big supposed victory, getting three seconds cut from "The Deadly Assassin"? In many ways, she was simply cashing in on an earlier attempt at stopping the series, when Jean Rook sneeringly attacked the omnibus edition of "The Brain of Morbius" and Robert Holmes personally. Someone high up in the BBC seems to have had it in for Holmes thereafter, so the suspicion lingers that the *Daily Mail*, rather than Whitehouse, scared management. Remember, the move to replace Hinchcliffe with Williams was taken in October-November 1976, before that episode went to air. When it did, it had already been trimmed from what was intended, but Sir Charles Curran later suggested that a few frames more wouldn't have hurt. By the time Whitehouse made up the story of children playing at drowning "like Doctor Who" and claimed that nobody but her understood freeze-frames, the damage was already done. Curran publicly conceded that the supervision had been at fault – it was all she needed to crow loudly and claim Victory in letters to the "right" newspapers, dismissing as a smokescreen the BBC's usual statement that the series wasn't primarily aimed at children and that those kids watching ought to have had parents or older siblings nearby.

It's what happened next that's interesting. When Hinchcliffe moved to *Target*, she started griping about *that* instead. *Doctor Who*'s subsequent – and comparatively subtle – digs at religion, family values and conservative politics went right under her radar. She bellyached about *Sapphire and Steel* supposedly promoting occult beliefs, but completely missed 15.3, "Image of the Fendahl" (the irony of this will be apparent after the next essay). Able to claim she had a high-profile scalp, she moved on to bigger prey, starting her anti-gay jihad and laying into Dennis Potter at every available opportunity.

With the public ridicule she amassed in the botched *Romans in Britain* lawsuit (her eye-witness was in the cheap seats and mistook a thumb for a penis), her news-value diminished: she got "fluffy cat" small fillers when she grumbled about *EastEnders*, but after her stand-in, Thatcher, left Downing Street, subsequent Conservative ministers took her even less seriously than broadcasters. A specially-created department, Culture, Media and Sport, set up an ombudsman body, OfCom, but the first Minister for this, David Mellor, roundly attacked her philistinism and intolerance.

The peak of Whitehouse's complaints about *Doctor Who* coincides suspiciously neatly with the period between late 1974 and Spring 1977, when Lord Annan was compiling a report on the future of broadcasting in Britain. The mountain laboured mightily, to the consternation of television executives and people pitching for a fourth channel, and produced a mouse: the report broadly stated something very close to business-as-usual, carry on regardless and so on. Part of the consultation process was listening to the public's opinions; Whitehouse marshalled her troops to complain about everything the BBC did, giving the impression of a groundswell of opinion. The Annan Report may have delayed the introduction of widespread cable television in Britain and probably caused the discrepancies between two rival ratings-collating systems we'll see a lot of from now on, to be fixed in the 80s.

Yet, apart from a brief acknowledgement of Whitehouse's influence in the debate in the House of Lords, including from Lord Annan himself (look, if you can stand it, at Hansard for 19th May, 1977), there was no sign of the feared clampdown. Neither was there the general election and Tory landslide most people expected, as the Labour government made a pact with David Steel's Liberal Party to hold things steady during the impending inflation spike. By the time Season Fifteen was broadcast, Whitehouse's window of opportunity to impose her views on the majority had passed. Almost all of her subsequent complaints about television were attempted pre-emptive strikes against forthcoming broadcasts rather

continued on page 371...

Chaney, was described), but the more obvious link is with the 1962 Hammer Films version. That's the one with Patrick Troughton as a rat-catcher and a chase through the curtains and pulleys of a theatre that's not precisely remade in Part Two, but that's obviously their ambition (at least, Maloney's). This version equips the Phantom with a murderous dwarf assistant, just in case it seemed coincidental.

The earliest film (shown on BBC1 just as Holmes returned after a disastrous holiday) makes more of a deal about the Grand Opera de Paris being opulent but built over former torture-sites. A key scene has the proprietors ostentatiously overcoming their fears and staking out their nemesis by sitting in the box to the left of the main stage, identified as where he's planning to strike – they look very like Statler and Waldorf. And, of course, all film versions build up to the moment when the girl in the flouncy frock pulls off the Phantom's mask – bizarrely, that wasn't the scripted cliffhanger for Part Five, nor was it a climax when Holmes did it again in 21.6, "The Caves of Androzani" (see **The Lore** for what was).

But the big thing about the 1925 *Phantom* is that the Catacombs of Paris are represented by cavernous vaulted arch rooves over a lake big enough to punt on. (Erik, the Phantom, takes his abducted paramour to the boat on horseback – the set's that big.) That image of a vast river-world beneath a city keeps coming back, in defiance of what we know about real sewers and cave-systems. You may be thinking now of *The Third Man* and Harry Lime fleeing justice through a Piranesi-like representation of Vienna's drainage system, or, if you're a bit more scholarly and British, *Hue and Cry* from a few years earlier showing London's substructure. (In *Hue and Cry*, the sewers are made to look like an exciting locale for a boys' game, just as the bombed-out ruins of 1947 London are.)

With London's sewerage being such a big deal (see X4.14, "The Next Doctor" for more on Joseph Bazalgette) and the city being an early-adopter of underground trains (5.5, "The Web of Fear"), it's understandable that the amount of earthworking in mid-nineteenth century London ought to have generated its own folklore. There are now several books on the topic – predictably, Peter Ackroyd's jumped on that subterranean bandwagon – but the first and best was *London Under London* by Richard Trench and Ellis Hillman, first out as a book in 1984, but a summation of a lot of previous research they'd published.

Post-war rebuilding and redevelopment led to a reappraisal of Victorian building work and a lot of conservation-work after the protests against the demolition of the Euston Arch in 1961-2. Centuries of building on the same land led to a lot of old stores, but new ones, especially gruesome accounts of men buried alive or people drowning in tidal waves of effluent, accreted. All those 60s office-blocks had something unearthed when they dug foundations – Roman temples, Mediaeval plague-pits, Victorian sepulchres or Nazi bombs. No modern story of Victorian London is complete without tunnels or crypts. But that's a story they've been telling since the Middle Ages; a poem about the founder of St Paul's Cathedral, St Erkinwold, tells of him becoming the city's Patron Saint by converting the ghost of a Roman general to Christianity while they were building the church on the site of an older temple.

Stories about things living in sewers is a more recent trend: the urban myth of albino alligators breeding in New York City is one of the big ones, alluded to in *V* by Thomas Pynchon, *Thunderbirds*: "Attack of the Alligators!" by Alan Pattillo and "The Dalek Invasion of Earth" by Terry Nation. There was *Them* in 1954 with giant ants in LA's flood drains. The *Thunderbirds* one is closest to the granddaddy of giant animal stories, HG Wells's *Food of the Gods*, and we can't leave the topic of huge rats in London's sewers without mentioning another *Thunderbirds* and *Doctor Who* alumnus, Dennis Spooner, and his episode of *The New Avengers*, "Gnaws". This can't be cited as a possible influence on "Talons" (it went out just before the location filming for the sewers took place), but it's handy as evidence that there was something in the water in more ways than one (it also has a giant tarantula).

The obvious giant rat referent is something Hinchcliffe specified when the story idea was first floated, "The Giant Rat of Sumatra", an undocumented case Dr Watson mentioned in passing in "The Adventure of the Sussex Vampire". That's not Victorian, though; Sir Arthur Conan-Doyle was still churning out Sherlock Holmes stories in the 1920s, and the incident is connected with a ship called the Matilda Briggs, not a London sewer as far as we know. (There have been attempts at this story almost since Doyle died, the first is a radio play by the adaptor of the stories, Edith Meiser,

Mary Whitehouse: What was Her Problem?

...continued from page 369

than jibes about popular series. It didn't help that various studies emerged on the influence of violent or "adult" material on children, few of them saying what she expected (see **Is Doctor Who Suitable for Adults?** under 15.1, "Horror of Fang Rock").

It's interesting to note that the Festival of Light, the mildly-embarrassing British attempt to cash in on America's "Jesus Freaks", had more success with annoying the BBFC than Whitehouse and her minions ever managed. They used her as a figurehead for the opening publicity, but it was Malcolm Muggeridge (the humour-deficient former editor of *Punch*) who persuaded councils to ban *Monty Python's Life of Brian* – and landed up looking ridiculous. (See 17.6, "Shada" for a sidelight on this.) It looks as if, as much as the Gay Lib protestors dragging up and turning the FoL rallies into coming-out parties, Whitehouse was the problem for them. She did their image considerable harm in the medium term.[59] It seems, in fact, as if picking *Doctor Who* as the focal-point for her attempt to start a culture-war backfired badly, making anyone else concerned about the availability of porn or violent images look as delusional as she evidently was. Her association with Lady Birdwood, a notorious anti-Semite, wasn't helpful either.

Did the BBC actually cave into her demands in late 1976? In the **Lore** sections of this book, we're increasingly having to state that the entire Drama department was undergoing internal convulsions in 1976-8. The seemingly-botched changeover of Philip Hinchcliffe and Graham Williams, getting each other's programmes at short notice, was a symptom of something else a tier up. The decision to move them around was taken long before "The Deadly Assassin" aired, before Jean Rook's hatchet-piece on Robert Holmes and before *I, Claudius* forced a public admission of crossing a line. She was as irrelevant to the situation as she was in 1985 when Michael Grade and Jonathan Powell cited Season Twenty-Two's violence to justify their "purely financial" decision to rest a series neither of them liked.

To be blunt, Season Fourteen *Doctor Who* had taken that particular recipe as far as it was ever likely to get. Even if Hinchcliffe had stayed on for two more years, it would have changed with the times. A later producer, John Nathan-Turner, said out loud that he hoped Whitehouse would complain to remind people the series was still on. Ironically, his tenure was marked by stroppy fan-groups using Whitehouse's tactics to try and get him fired, then try and un-cancel the series. With further, pleasing irony, her death was announced on 23rd November, 2001.

After that, her successor at NVALA, John Beyer, admitted that membership was down (he didn't quantify), but couldn't get arrested. A few tabloid brouhahas seemed so obviously elicited by broadcasters wanting column inches that he stayed out of them. Without the Whitehouse personality-cult, nobody wanted to listen. These days, rebranded as MediaWatch, they concentrate on reporting incidents of hate-speech and apparent child-exploitation to OfCom rather than making the fuss themselves. Enough other people have tried Whitehouse's techniques to stifle anything tolerant or progressive and come unstuck, making it not worth the candle.

We'll pick up on another aspect of this debate in the next essay.

---

less than ten years after publication of the original and shortly after the first broadcast of her adaptation thereof, in 1931.) But rats in sewers were a given and, as the Victorian brickwork crumbled, a reminder of how close we are to what we try to distance ourselves from.

It's very 1977, as the run-up to the Jubilee was marked by bands who'd been signed up in the feeding-frenzy over Punk Rock making their presence felt. In the album charts just after this story was "Rattus Norvegicus" by The Stranglers, the closing mini-suite of which was "Down in the Sewers". (The Damned, The Clash and Television all debuted in the same month's charts.) The most chart-friendly New Wave act of the next two years was, of course, The Boomtown Rats.

Back then, Freud was still taken absolutely seriously. (If we're chucking Freud at Sherlock Holmes, we have to at mention the vogueish nonsense in Nicholas Meyer's book and film *The Seven Percent Solution* – 1974, then 1976 – but we'll keep that as evidence that the 1970s was a boom time for debunking the Holmes canon). Freudian psychiatry, like Marx's economic theories, attempts at a science of history, leant heavily on the analogy with Boyle's Law about the pressure of gases in a confined space. In all cases, a rigid container and an external heat-source made things tend to explode. However, in Freud and Marx, the thing being treated as external wasn't really and attempts to disown it were what made it heat up. The problem was therefore the attempts at repression of that "other" (the Id, the proletariat) and, to a Victorian, the obvious next thought was the Thames and the various cholera outbreaks and Great Stink that led to the massive sewer construction project. Filth, poverty and moral degradation were self-evidently one and the same thing, so slums were best not thought about, just as the Wapping sewerage plant was distant and safe from Parliament and the West End.

The founders of the Salvation Army and the author of *Heart of Darkness* equated East London with a far-flung "dark interior" needing missionaries. Distancing oneself from this sort of thing was easier than acting on the root causes; so was paying money to charities to be seen to do something about the symptoms. Of course, it wasn't as easy as that, and the links between these two worlds were complex and tangled. Dickens made a lot of how interconnected these different Londons were while Robert Louis Stevenson made the link between psychiatry and class distinction in *The Strange Case of Dr Jekyll and Mr Hyde*.

However, it's only when you stop and crunch the numbers that the extent to which the other great "other" of Victorian London, the British Empire, underlies the Sherlock Holmes stories really becomes clear. We touched on it in "Pyramids of Mars", but the way in which things or people from remote imperial outposts keep coming to sedate British places and causing havoc was obviously a major concern for the average reader, whether they would admit to residual guilt about imperialism or not. (The second Holmes novel, *The Sign of Four*, is only the most explicit in linking India, the Thames and metropolitan aesthetes.) Equally obviously, the location of the Docks at the start of the Thames Estuary, near the sewers, meant that everything from outside, no matter how precious or costly, came via the nation's back passage.

Wapping Steps was also the place where dead bodies washed up. (Often bloated by posthumous fermentation of internal fluids, hence "a whopper", allegedly. There's a McDonalds in Shadwell, now but not a Burger King.) The Thames is still tidal there. Pirates were hanged and left on display at the nearby Execution Dock at Tilbury for three tides, by which time they were pretty ripe. They only stopped this in the 1830s. Wapping wasn't formally a part of London until the late seventeenth century, but was an early site for a tube station, because of the Docks. The original *Threepenny Opera* was set there.

You get the picture: everything posh London wanted to deny tended to come back and bite them from this bit of the city. No wonder the whole Jack the Ripper affair struck a nerve. (And no wonder so many loopy theories persisted about it being a disgraced member of an aristocratic family – it makes a Dickensian sort of sense to some people.) Of course, the 1970s, when everyone was letting it all hang out, meant that people thought all of this repression was over and done with, so we got prurient "frank" revisions of Victorian subjects all over popular culture. Combine that with the modish paranoid conspiracy theories about Freemasons (based, it must be admitted, on the revelations of how Britain had allowed a turbo-charged Old Boys Network to look like covert Black Ops until around 1970 – see that *Monty Python* skit for an only-slightly-exaggerated account) and you get a slew of deranged ideas that Jolly Jack was being covered for by Friends in High Places.[62]

An early manifestation is a weird spin-off from *Z Cars* (see Volume 1) in which Stratford Johns (19.2, "Four to Doomsday") and Frank Windsor (20.6, "The King's Demons"; "Ghost Light") looked into historical crimes in-character as Barlow and Watt. This 1973 pilot is the first attempt to suggest a Masonic cover-up that we've found. Inevitably, Alan Moore's late 80s comics followed a discredited "confession" implicating Walter Sickert, published in 1976 with the hopelessly tasteless title *Jack the Ripper: The Final Solution*. A film where Sherlock Holmes investigates the Ripper and comes to the same bizarre conclusion, *Murder by Decree*, was in the works soon afterwards and reached the screen in 1979. 1965 flick *A Study in Terror* made the same Sherlock/ Ripper connection, but skipped the Masonic faff – it was directed by James Hill (see **Could *Scratchman* Have Worked?**) An unsolved real-world mystery, the Great Detective... in the 70s the story had to incorporate guilty secrets from the highest echelon of Victorian society because, post-Watergate, nothing else was plausible. It had to match up the things the elite tried to pretend weren't their problem to the source of the scandal.

Sometimes, though, discarding people in Docklands wasn't enough, and they had to be sent around the world. Australia was a better *oubliette* than Whitechapel or Wapping and had the bonus, for narrative purposes, that some convicts and fugitives came back rich. Dickens used the ludicrous real-life shenanigans surrounding the Tichborne Claimant as the basis for *Bleak House* (see **English Lessons**) and the wealth-creating potential of the gold-mines for *Great Expectations* (another story where someone drowns at Wapping). In this light, the use of "Brisbane" for Greel's past notoriety is interesting.

As we mentioned with "The Sontaran Experiment" (12.3), there was a thread in postwar Britain of people from sunny ex-colonies basing themselves in London and showing the stuffy, languid locals how it should be done (or not, in many cases). Meanwhile, Australia had got its act together with regard to feature films and had finally started making television in colour (the latter wasn't really an issue for Britain until the 80s and daytime television). The London-resident ones were making their presence felt. We'll see this again when we get to 16.1, "The Ribos Operation" (Garron was written as an Australian but altered to fit the stunt-casting). As with "The Robots of Death", the locals are seeing what they expect to see and the outsiders, especially Leela, have trouble matching that to what they observe with (relatively) fresh eyes, the way Australians in the big city did in comedies. (Remember, Barry Letts's escape-plan if *Doctor Who* was canned was *Snowy Black*, a sitcom based on this proto-*Crocodile Dundee* premise.) Leela's reactions to Victorian London are almost those of the stereotypical Australian fresh off the plane, but so's her relative dynamism and initiative.

Making this link (and, although it's not obvious, Michael Spice was himself Australian) demonstrates the lengths they went to in avoiding the association many other productions might have leaned towards between a Chinese gang and young white women disappearing (see, among way too many examples, *Thoroughly Modern Millie*). Greel is dressed in Mexican clothing, for some reason. Teresa, abducted by Chang in as day breaks, is fairly obviously already "on the game". Although the story leans toward all the seamier sides of Victorian London, there were lines the BBC wouldn't have crossed even in 1977.

We might also mention the actuarialist prediction that the gap between previous ice ages was about as long as it had been since the last one, so we were about due (see also 5.3, "The Ice Warriors"; the date Holmes gives of c.5000 AD is what some people in the fledgling *Doctor Who* Appreciation Society said about the dating of the Troughton story). There's enough evidence of a trend in that direction if you compare Roman Britain (with vineyards) to the Frost Fairs of the immediate pre-Industrial age (see X10.3, "Thin Ice"), so the predictions might have been on track had not something worse counteracted it. Pretender to the *Who*-throne *Timeslip* had the 70s teenagers meet their adult selves in mutually-exclusive frozen and arid twenty-first centuries, just in case (1973 BBC kidvid *Outa-Space!* did the double and combined an ice-age thirtieth century with dinosaurs and black holes). Regular silly-season stories in the press about this chilly future during the hot summer of 1975 and the Drought of 1976 made it as off-the-peg a prediction as Moonbases and Esperanto.

An even more reliable period detail is the hologram. The media interest was low-key, and it was mainly discussed in pop-science journals as a method of data-preservation unusually resistant to damage: the photographic plate on which a laser had encrypted the image or bits could shatter, and each piece would have the whole of it from one perspective. That was the method used for the much-publicised scene from the film *Logan's Run*, just out in Britain as this was being written. Ahead of stick-on pictures of unicorns or even Carrie Fisher somehow recording a 3D message using a robot with a camera that couldn't see behind her, this is how holography was explained to readers of *New Scientist* and how the Doctor explains it to Jago and most viewers. (The earliest media version we've found is a 1974 episode of French *Doomwatch*-style cop-show *Aux Frontieres du Possible*, one of the two made in Montreal, where a gang uses a converted Bedford Van to steal furs by decoying police with a three-dimensional magic lantern – more expensive than the proceeds of even a hundred such heists.)

Not all of this is as clearly 1976-vintage. The Freudian Gothic set-piece of a ventriloquist being haunted by a dummy who is the unacceptable alter-ego and takes over has a long pedigree, but it's most clearly demonstrated in the 1945 anthology-film *Dead of Night*. (There's a few from later, notably the 1978 Anthony Hopkins film *Magic* and a *Twilight Zone* episode.) Dolls and dummies coming to life were useful as a commentary on automation and mass-production by Surrealists and agit-prop collagists, but ventriloquism gave it a familiar form for straightforward scariness.

We've been here before, notably with the Autons and the ugly doll that killed Mr Farrell ("Terror of the Autons"). Other self-retreads of Holmes's earlier scripts include the villain being shot just as he activates the potentially-explosive repaired craft in which he arrived (11.1, "The Time Warrior"); shooting at people crawling around under a table, who respond by assuming that you can't shoot two ways at once ("The Ark in Space"); and a damaged war-criminal in a cellar ranting at a willing servant who's the public face of the enterprise ("The Brain of Morbius"; "The Deadly Assassin"). In the mid-1970s, the war-crimes of Klaus Barbie, the "Butcher of Lyon", were coming to light in increasing detail.

The cape and hat aside, the Doctor isn't really doing much detecting here: the only truly Sherlockian inductive reasoning is at the end of Part Five, when he tells Leela that he is helping by staying put. (That look is, as we mentioned above, more a theatrical convention than anything in Doyle's fiction.) For obvious reasons, this story's author was fully aware of the Baker Street lore, but there's almost more Wilkie Collins on display here than Conan-Doyle. Holmes (Bob, that is) had spent time writing for *John Bull* magazine and accumulated old textbooks and gazetteers, so he was steeped in Victorian London – the epic-length **English Lessons** for this story is testament to that. We'll just note that a lady's hankie mono-grammed "EB" is in Doyle's "The Adventure of Abbey Grange" and the link between a distorted face and opium dens is in "The Twisted Lip".

One last Music Hall allusion: a lot of commentators get sniffy about either Litefoot or the Doctor misattributing the line about the One-Eyed Yellow Idol to the North of Kathmandu (especially after the Doctor's Kipling gag in "The Face of Evil"). But the dramatic recitation piece – actually entitled *The Green Eye of the Yellow God* – was known to 1970s children as the source of a party-piece where the reciter stands with hands behind his back (usually a him for height reasons) and the other party (often his wife) would be behind him, but with her arms protruding from around his waist to do the hand-gestures. Hilarity ensues, if you're lucky.

This bit was still doing the rounds at pantos and in television variety shows into the 80s and had been a standby at works parties and during power-cuts. Who knows, maybe the Doctor was at a party in 1920 when Harry Champion did it. There's also a Stanley Holloway skit ("Me'em Sahib") about two recently-returned Raj officers doing some Statler-and-Waldorf heckling, correcting the many mistakes in the verse and driving the reciter nuts. Kipling himself was vaguely flattered that he had so many imitators, J. Milton Hayes (the author of this tale of Mad Carew and a cursed jewel) among them. See Charles Laughton perform it to widespread indifference in the 1938 film *St Martin's Lane* (AKA *Sidewalks of London* and the first feature film shown on American television). Our point is, almost everyone over the age of ten who was watching on BBC1 in April 1977 knew that line and knew it wasn't Kipling. The joke was on Litefoot. But his Lady Bracknellish delivery of the line "a hatbox?" indicates that he's not entirely incapable of irony.

English Lessons (there's quite a lot of them)

- *Jago* (n.): a crafty dual meaning. It's a real, if exotic, surname (from the Spanish *Iago*, a form of "James" – as in "Jacobean" and "Santiago") and, therefore, an alternative spelling of the villain of *Othello* before orthography settled down in the 1750s. It's also the name given to a fictionalised version of a real East London slum in the sensationalist smash-hit 1896 novel *A Child of the Jago*. Arthur Morrison renamed the Nichol district straddling Bethnal Green and Shoreditch, slightly north of where we think the Palace Theatre and Litefoot's purlieu are, but by that time the area was being redeveloped into the Boundary Estate. Morrison barely changed any of the other street-names and one of these is Honey Lane, as in the street-market-based television soap from the 60s where Holmes first worked with Louis Marks and which made John Bennett famous. (Incidentally, Morrison later quit writing, after so many people furnished proof that his "reportage" in the novel was exaggerated, and started trading in Chinese silks, rugs and furniture...)

- *Cod* (Adj.): unconvincing deceit. Most usually used in association with actors doing bad attempts at accents (e.g. Dick Van Dyke as Bert the Chimney-Sweep, Nicola Bryant as Peri) or doing it deliberately badly for laughs.

- *Peelers* (n. sl.): The filth, the plods, the Babylon, the scuffers, the bizzies, the rozzers, the fuzz... the police, as founded by Sir Robert Peel (hence also "Bobbies": nobody's used either term for decades, except in American films).

- *Pavement* (n.): the paved path beside a road (i.e., what Americans call a "sidewalk").
- *Frighten the Horses* (sl.): appropriately, the original Eliza Doolittle, Mrs Patrick Campbell, said it first. The most reliable account has her admonishing someone who was irked at a rather lovey-dovey pair of Luvvies backstage: *I don't care what these affectionate people do, so long as they don't do it in the street and frighten the horses.* In most accounts, a same-sex couple elicited the bon mot, so this late-Victorian precursor to "get a room" is usually brandished as an example of bemused tolerance.
- *Little Tich.* A Music Hall performer, né Harry Relph, who was just under 140 cm tall (54 inches) and wore boots as long as he was high to do a curious dance. (The Doctor borrows a bit of this shtick to entertain the Gods of Ragnarok in 25.4, "The Greatest Show in the Galaxy".) The name was a gag about him claiming to be the Tichborne Heir, a notorious law-suit about an implausible imposter. For some of the early 1890s, he was in residence at the Theatre Royal, Drury Lane, before getting even more money abroad. He was a major star in this era (the word "titchy" comes from him) and his career extended into the twentieth century and recording discs. (An early book about him was by Sax Rohmer, creator of Fu Manchu.)
- *Second House* (n.): usually, a repeat performance later in the evening, but that's not likely in a Music Hall. Legitimate theatre might have a matinee on Saturday (and sometimes Wednesdays) and an evening performance from around 7.30 to 10.00pm, but the whole point of Music Hall was to be concurrent with usual pub opening hours and thus a trifle later. Nonetheless, in Part One we get Buller's death, after dark, between two performances by Chang – so either a day elapses between Mr Sin stabbing him and the Tong disposing of the body, or this particular night has back-to-back shows. Evidently, Jago's going up-market.
- *Oopizootics* (n. sl.): as reported in an 1873 medical journal, the technical term "epizootic" (five syllables, more or less rhyming with "neurotic" and meaning something like an epidemic but among animals rather than people) had caught on colloquially to mean some ailment that was doing the rounds – *I was laid up with the epizootic* (more or less rhyming with "Sutekh"), or even shortened to "zooty" – like the more recent "dreaded lurgi". There was a rather tasteless comic song of the late 1890s ("Father's Got 'Em") using the word to mean mental illness.
- *Carey Street* (n.): The Bankruptcy Court in London, WC2, from 1840-ish, was located roughly where the London School of Economics is now. Weirdly, the colloquial use of "on Carey Street" to mean "destitute" didn't take off until after it moved again. (The associated phrase "on Queer Street" pre-dates it, meaning more "in trouble" than specifically financial ruin.)
- *Cockneys* (n.sl.): Generally, people from East London; specifically, those born within the sound of Bow bells – the "great bell of Bow" as mentioned in *Oranges and Lemons* is on Cheapside, St Mary le Bow (somewhat west of the London district of Bow, just to confuse people). Before all the high-rises and traffic, this was a radius of about five miles, so it's not *quite* the same as the East End but close enough. Before that, the word meant an egg laid by a male pigeon, i.e. something odd and unnatural (as in *Twelfth Night*).
- *Manor* (n.): originally, a lord's fiefdom, protected by him but owing him food, rent and an army when necessary (as in "lord of the manor" and "manor-house"); colloquially, the bit of London you have as your stomping-ground. Sergeant Kyle is using it to mean "around here" rather than any feudal boundaries. We were past all that in 1893. Officially.
- *No Fixed Abode* (adj.): the usual way that vagrants were described in charge-sheets and court reports, but also applies to long-term guests if they are accused of anything. It's a rather prejudicial term, coming with an assumption that migrants and itinerant workers were naturally prone to moral turpitude.
- *Limehouse* (n.): The bit of East London closest to the Thames and the docks. Therefore, a bit with a lot of single working men, of various origins. The bit that got the Victorians worked up was that many of these were from China and – after the whole business with the Opium Wars – everyone assumed that everybody there was an addict and probably criminally-minded to feed this. (So, rather like the Bowery, or Hell's Kitchen in the 1970s, with similar gentrification now.) More interestingly, many of these sailors brought their families across and started small businesses catering to that community, and schools for their children, so London had a Chinatown that lasted into a second or third generation, only dispersed by the Blitz. However, it's hard to refute allegations that if London had any opium, that was where to get it and a lot of wealthy Englishmen landed up

there (see X1.3, "The Unquiet Dead" for Dickens slyly admitting to it). It was also where the majority of East London laundry services were based, as this was labour-intensive work that immigrants could do, so the stereotype of Chinese laundry persisted until World War II (as in George Formby's *Chinese Laundry Blues* and various sequels about Mr Wu's other business ventures), hence the character in older Panto versions of *Aladdin*, "Wishee Washee".

- *Grub Street* (n. sl.): Originally a real place, in what's now the Barbican (renamed, ironically, Milton Street), famous for low-rent scurrilous journalism and self-published pamphlets. By the period we're looking at, it colloquially meant anyone paid to write rather than doing it as a hobby. Between the Civil War and the introduction of a Stamp Act licencing (and taxing), newspapers it was occasionally helpful to the Cromwell government and its successors to (a) know what the public were saying and (b) spread rumours about what the Irish were up to. Once the Hanoverians were on the throne, it was more trouble than it was worth. Attempts to curtail it annoyed those working on such journals (Dr Johnson was a veteran, so was Jonathan Swift) – the name attached to a precursor of *Private Eye*, the *Grub Street Journal*, which flourished once the party political system got under way.

- *Stony* (adj.): Stony broke, i.e. really short of money.

- *Licensed Cab* (n.): as you may know, the regulations for who could operate a cab in London included a stringent test of the roads, routes and local conditions, "the Knowledge", which even now take years to master. The famous black cabs are driven by such people (whose brains, it has been shown by fMRI scans, have altered around the hippocampus by this process). Ubers and unlicensed minicabs don't require this, nor are they governed by the legal restrictions covering horse-driven Hackney Carriages – it was only in the 90s that the latter were officially allowed to not carry hay for the horse in their diesel-driven Leyland Metropolitans. The point is, the badge worn by the cab-driver Buller allowed quick identification and his home address was on file (a legal cover for aggrieved passengers, but also proof that his cab was trustworthy and he knew the city).

- *Thames* (n.): the central river around which London grew in Roman times. There are 16 tributaries within the metropolitan area, all of which, like the Fleet, became part of the sewerage during the Victorian era. And it's pronounced "Tems", because English is an old language. The part of the city where most of this story happens is around the deepest part of the river, the Pool of London, where it's still tidal and before it gets too circuitous. (See 21.4, "Resurrection of the Daleks" for the last stage of decline and X2.12, "Army of Ghosts" for what happened to it after.)

- *Pixilated* (adj.): Nothing to do with digital imaging, but everything to do with pixies and their malign influence.

- *Leprechaun* (n.): Presumably, you know the basic meaning, but there's a historical detail here too, specifically 1970's Britain. When the kinds of stand-up comedians who did the circuit of Working Men's Clubs in the north got onto television, they brought with them a lot of prejudicial jokes they'd been doing for years and had to rapidly get new material. This led to a flurry of jokes about the Irish being a bit naïve, often told by Irish stand-ups, which in turn became a stereotype about stupidity, repeated by bus-drivers, DJs and even teachers. Some people found this comforting when the IRA were planting bombs in pubs, but others found it a bit creepy. So while Jago's in period for an 1890s Londoner, being condescending to Casey (see Dickens's comments about navvies in "The Unquiet Dead"), this was also entirely in keeping with the bad jokes doing the rounds at time of broadcast.

- *Newgate* (n.): another debtors' prison; other criminals went there too (Oscar Wilde, shortly after this story's set). There was a gaol on the site from the 1160s to 1904 and, between 1783 and 1868, they had public hangings. The knocker was famously forbidding – the whole place was designed to intimidate – and ominous rain clouds were often described as being as black as it. The Old Bailey is roughly where it stood (i.e. the other end of Fleet Street).

- *Lombard Street* is where all the merchant banks were based, from the Tudors to Thatcher. It was associated with extreme wealth and spiritual deadness (as in Eliot's *The Waste Land* where his co-workers trudge past St Mary Wolnoth's church). Marx is less than flattering in *Das Kapital*. Jago bets it against ninepence, but the usual phrase, reinstated by Terrance Dicks in the novelisation, is "all Lombard Street to a China Orange" (i.e. a low-value one compared to a Seville or Jaffa orange). These days, with Silicon

Valley sucking up the world's money and property prices in the less-well-established Lombard Street in California skyrocketing, the phrase is due for a revival.

• *Ninepence* is three-quarters of a shilling, but is most usually associated with well-being, "as right as ninepence". Why Jago mixes up these two phrases is anyone's guess.

• *Chinks* (n, sl.): pejorative term for people of Chinese origin, later semi-reclaimed as the more affectionate "chinky" (meaning Chinese takeaway food) until that was ruled out in the 90s.

• *Fish Lane* (n.): There ain't no such animal (there's a Fish Lane in Chelsea, but that was a fair distance from this parish). However, there are a lot of similar names in Cheapside, where the markets were in the Middle Ages. That's a bit west of where we're supposed to think Buller was from, but it's not implausible. Newer streets in the area we're told he's from were often named after pubs and, that close to the Thames, they could have had one called "The Fish".

• *This Parish*: the identification of murder victims or anyone in the dock was given in police reports (and thus the press) by way of ecclesiastical boundaries. It was usually prefaced with a word depicting the marital status of the individual (i.e. "spinster of this parish", "widower of this parish" &c). P.C. Quick uses the vocabulary of *The Police Gazette* as his everyday working parlance – improbable, but a sign that he's as much a caricature as Jago, Casey or the Tong.

• *On Pleasure Bent*: as above; the way a court report would describe the last known movements of a murder-victim or similar (it means, simply, "out for a good time"). It could be that the young copper is unused to hanging around in mortuaries and being formal to avoid throwing up or freaking out.

• *Punitive Expedition of 1860*: i.e. the Opium Wars, one of the most squalid bits of British Imperial history. The first war was a blockade run by the East India Company in response to the not-entirely-legal goods being confiscated at Canton; the Chinese surrender led to Britain getting use of Hong Kong until 1997. A second conflict, from 1857, saw the legalisation of opium and an Anglo-French military expedition backed up by America and Russia, who extracted further concessions (including giving Manchuria to the Russians). All of this was, in essence, to bolster Britain's balance-of-trade figures after China tried to monopolise the silver trade and raise the price of tea.

• *Gordon* (n.): Interesting middle-name for someone already fairly mature in the 1890s. Either it's his mum's maiden-name (suggesting a Scottish heritage he is uncharacteristically quiet about) or he adopted it opportunistically after General Gordon died in 1885. That Gordon was another "hero" of the Opium Wars and after, then Governor-General of Sudan. After several thwarted attempts to abolish slavery and generally improve the lot of the people there, he tried to prevent the worst excesses of the Belgians in Congo but returned and was killed in an Islamicist uprising. His piety and overt concern for the welfare of the less fortunate (he also founded a Poor School in Kent) made him a posthumous example. So most people with the middle-name "Gordon" in 1893 or thereabouts would have been of school age. We therefore submit that Jago is entitled to the name through his matrilineal line and is thus probably distantly related to the Brigadier.

• *The Trumpet Voluntary* (n.): An ostentatiously twiddly piece for solo trumpet, by Jeremiah Clarke, used by Brass Band virtuosi from oop north or terrified kids at school concerts.

• *Money Spider* (n.): on finding a tiny spider, possibly newly-hatched, in one's hair or clothing, children were admonished that this was good luck. Should anyone encounter one, he or she must carefully revolve the arachnid around the head three times before safely depositing this "blessing" on a window-ledge where it can helpfully stop flies. Before fridges, this was probably a self-fulfilling prophecy.

• *Fleet* (n.): As mentioned above, a tributary of the Thames covered over in the early nineteenth century (so not as long ago as Litefoot thinks) and which runs almost due south from the well that gave Clerkenwell its name. It passes the Smithfield meat market (seen in 11.2, "Invasion of the Dinosaurs"), so usually reeked of blood and offal even before the sewers emptied into it. It meets the Thames at Blackfriars, about 200 metres from where Fleet Street crosses its path. "Follow the Fleet" suggests a naval escort – or peripatetic hooker – but the most famous use of the term is a Fred Astaire-Ginger Rogers flick.

• *Tongue* (n.): again, a sign of pre-refrigeration eating. It's a cow's tongue, soaked for a day, peeled and boned then boiled for most of the next day, pressed flat until the gelatine sets and sliced thinly for sandwiches. All the meats Litefoot names are high-fat ones that could safely be eaten cold,

14.6 The Talons of Weng-Chiang

prized as much for the aspics and jellies they exuded when cooling as the meat itself.

- *Birmingham* (n.): England's second city. Note that the Doctor doesn't over-stress the "Ham" like America's similarly-named city does: he means the original, in the West Midlands, then the heartland of British manufacturing and jewellery. The Doctor unironically accepts that the "Chinese" fowling-gun being made in Brum is a mark of reliability and the reach of the trading-routes. The Birmingham Small Arms Company later branched out into motorbike manufacture (see Ace's jacket in Season Twenty-Four onwards for the "BSA" logo). See *Peaky Blinders* for more, then look up how many great rock bands came from there, as well as ELO. (See also 26.4, "Survival".)
- *Ducks* (sl.): a term of endearment, generally associated with the East Midlands ("eey oop, me ducks"). Further north, "Duckie" was used until it became too associated with gay men.
- *Rosie* (n.sl.): Tea (rhyming-slang, "Rosie Lee"). It predates the American stripper, so nobody's sure to whom it originally referred.
- *Kippers* (n.): smoked herring, a traditional cheap breakfast before World War II (see X6.9, "Night Terrors").
- *Plates* (n.sl.): Feet ("plates of meat").
- *Half a foot of port*: a play on the idea of "a yard of ale". That was a challenge in pubs, using a thin retort (like a three-foot test tube, bulbous at the bottom and fluted at the top) to down 1.4 litres of beer (2 1/2 pints) in one go. Port, which is fortified and thus a lot thicker and more syrupy, would make even the hardiest drinker sick if consumed that way, so a six-inch pint-glass is as much as anyone would dare.
- *Togs* (n.sl.): clothes, usually sporting apparel: a very Public School term.
- *Rum* (adj.): questionable, curious, dodgy et cetera.
- *Fit-Up Company* (n.): travelling players who toured rural areas (especially in Ireland, so Casey would get the reference).
- *Seventeen and Thruppence*: just over half a crown short of a quid, i.e., 76p. Today that would be about £112.00 (call it $150 but allow for wild currency-rate fluctuations).
- *Brown Derby and Boots*: note correct pronunciation of the hat's name, to rhyme with "Zarbi", as it's an old town. The hat (which we'll see the Doctor wear next story and Graham wear in X12.4, "Nikolai Tesla's Night of Terror") is scant protection against blows to the head, but was a cheap alternative to a policeman's helmet, so the caricature detective wore one and had stout boots for a lot of walking from door to door.
- *On the q.v.*: not quite how the Latin "q.v." is usually used – "quod vide" means, roughly, "on this, go and see...", so is a way of citing back-up authorities. "On the QT" is a way of saying "don't talk about this" or "on the quiet" (probably from Latin *quae tacenda*) and seems to be from around 1870 in Britain then revived in 1940s America.
- *Star Traps* (n.): the main trap-door and the lift under the stage leading thereunto, as used in pantos for genies and fairy-queens arriving in a puff of smoke or, as seen here, for escapes and transformations.
- *Celestial* (Adj.): condescendingly used for all things Oriental (see 3.7, "The Celestial Toymaker").
- *Bob a nob* (sl.): a shilling per head.
- *Tong Wallahs* (n.sl.): a very confusing term. "Wallah" is the title accorded anyone in India with a specific task (punkah wallah to pull the ropes to operate the fans; dhoti wallah to do laundry – in Target's *Doctor Who and the Daemons*, the Brigadier refers to the "electricity wallahs"). Real Victorians were often just as muddled, hence the weird character-names in *The Sign of Four* and *The Moonstone*.
- *Homunculus* (n.): originally, a "little man" (in Latin) supposed to be what an embryo was made from and – in alchemical theory – capable of being artificially created in a laboratory to work as a servant (see our comments on the name "Mandragora" earlier in this volume and all the *Frankenstein* stuff in "The Brain of Morbius"). The word also means the topographical cortical "map" of the human nervous system, proportional to the amount of neural tissue allocated to each body-part, so with huge hands and lips, small legs and vast genitals. However, the term was also applied in the west to the body-map dolls used by Chinese doctors, to allow ladies of the court to show where it hurt without undressing or being touched.
- *Whitechapel and St George's*: the Parliamentary constituency of that name was only created in 1918 out of two pre-existing ones. These boroughs, and the others within the old constituency, were church parishes originally. This district went from Mile End to Shadwell (N-S) and the Tower of London to Limehouse (E-W). Litefoot describes Rundell Gardens as between the parish of

keep written notes and the whole house of cards would collapse.)

Leela escapes Mr. Sin by hurling herself through Litefoot's window. Leela has never seen glass before – how does she know that the magic see-through material will break if she hurls herself at it, let alone that she'll be able to survive? Litefoot is clobbered from behind, but it's a blow to the top of the head. Mr Sin and the other miscreants aren't tall enough to do that, even if one of the latter got in without him noticing. Why render him unconscious, instead of killing him?

Seeing Leela in Victorian lingerie creates a genuine puzzle: every time we've seen the TARDIS wardrobes, we've just had racks of clothes from various periods and no other assistance. Not even laminated diagrams. Anyone who knows anything about how ladies dressed in that period would know that, first and foremost, they'd need help getting into these things. Dressing like that needs a maid – or ridiculously long and flexible arms and a facility to do fiddly things behind your own back. (See also "Pyramids of Mars"; 26.2, "Ghost Light"; X1.3, "The Unquiet Dead"; X8.1, "Deep Breath".) But this is a woman from a planet where they haven't got buttons, let alone shoelaces, hooks-and-eyes or the buckles on her knickerbockers. And she's got a necktie on, tied properly for the period. Even though she doesn't need a corset or stays, are we to imagine that the Doctor told her all about stockings and suchlike or – Mrs Whitehouse be blowed! – that he did her up and explained all the peculiarities?

Later in the story, she somehow gets into a nice frock in remarkably little time: 48 seconds, by our count. That Mrs Hudson's a marvel. Considering that she's just been in a sewer (Leela, not the unseen housekeeper), chin-deep and horizontal at one point, and up-close and personal with a giant rat and a blunderbuss, it's obliging of Litefoot to have her in his front parlour, even if she's just out of the bath. In fact, *especially* if she's just out of the bath. But it does look as if she stopped to clean up before updating the Professor on the plot-developments, meaning she must have squeezed a quick dip in and dried her hair before changing *back* into the soiled and flimsy foundation garments and having a new do. So there's a missing scene where a nearly-naked girl in damp, reeking cotton undies is ferried back down the Thames in a rowing-boat at 9.00am in December, yet somehow doesn't even get a head-cold. (And whatever did they tell the cabbie?)

Implicit in the dialogue of that scene is that Litefoot bought the clothes for Leela, so presumably she's been in the grubby chemise and bloomers for an indefinite period while he had an awkward conversation with a lady at a department store having, somehow, got Leela's measurements, then gone to a milliner's for a matching hat. Wouldn't it have been easier to get a new outfit from the TARDIS (right by the river, near the docks), then meet Litefoot at his house?

Chang's death-scene is never resolved: unable to say another word as he carks it, Chang attempts to give the Doctor a clue to Magnus Greel's whereabouts by pointing down at the Doctor's foot and grabbing his toe. The audience is perfectly entitled to assume that from this clue, the Doctor will deduce that Greel is living on Old Boot Street or Toe Lane or Athlete's Foot Circle. The Doctor indeed determines that there's a "Boot Court" in a large Baedeker, and that he'll find Greel there. But there's no on-screen confirmation of this, because Greel comes to find the Doctor instead of the Doctor finding Greel. (Unhelpfully, Terrance Dicks fudges in the novelisation by having Chang pitch forward dead, no clue given.)

[Undaunted, we've dug out the 1891 Stanford Library Map of London and Its Suburbs (Holmes probably had an ex-library copy near his desk, but we got the CD Rom), walked the streets and had a bash: there's a Boot Lane in Hoxton, a bit too far north but it had a Variety Theatre (now a juice bar); Shoemaker's Place, near St Paul's Cathedral, was right next to a railway station (neither's there any more); Shoe Lane, Holborn, is where we think the Palace Theatre must have been, so that's not much of a clue. One possibility is Walker Street, in Limehouse (just about), roughly where Masjid Lane is now. It's just at the edge of Poplar and Mile End: If Litefoot's getting his laundry delivered by pushcart, this makes a bit more sense. But it doesn't seem to fit whatever Chang was trying to articulate that came out as "Buh-buh-buh".]

Why exactly is there a laser cannon in the front parlour of the House of the Dragon? Greel can't expect a pitched battle there – to repel assaults from the police or the army, it should really be outside, in the street like a sign outside a Chinese restaurant. Mounting it indoors assumes that it will be used against either visitors or his own staff, if they refuse to swallow scorpion-venom. That's contingency planning for defeat without bothering with the precautions that would make it

14.6 The Talons of Weng-Chiang

unnecessary. In Part Five, Greel sees Jago and Litefoot. Apart from the wonky logic he uses to deduce (somehow) that they have the bag, the problem is that he talks to Ho, in English, and Ho replies in somewhat restricted English, *then* gives orders in Cantonese. Has Greel made it part of the terms of employment that everyone learns English? Isn't that a security-risk?

Not much of Mr Sin's backstory matches what the living doll does. Even if we assume that its vocabulary is actually Chang doing genuine ventriloquism, it has to sit still and let the mouth move rather than roll in mud or eat raw potatoes. Is there a reason that a pig would want to gun everyone down, and why only now turn on Greel? If, for whatever reason, the porcine cerebral cortex gives it a reason to hate humans, why is it only bumping off people Chang orders it to? (A cut scene covers some of that, with Chan operating the doll by telepathic remote control. But why is Greel unable to do a trick he presumably taught Chang?) Is it having difficulty handling a gun, or even a knife? Is bipedalism a problem? Is he a pig who thinks he's a robot or a robot who thinks it's a pig? These are all legitimate questions. So is: how does the Distillation Chamber kill Greel when Leela's just severed the main power-line with a hatchet?

There's a pipe-smoking chap in the audience for all three performances we witness at the Palace. He must really like Chang's act. Finally, why does someone posing as a Chinese god have a statue of an Indian goddess, Kali, in his front-room?

Critique (Prosecution, guest reviewer Dorothy Ail)
In the long, often glorious tradition of *Doctor Who* borrowing storylines, from the *Prisoner of Zenda* to *Big Brother*, "Talons" stands out for having a template that's simply a mistake. The Doctor might be dressing as Holmes while Litefoot and Leela play *Pygmalion*, but the bones of this story are a yellow peril Fu Manchu tale, complete with poison-wielding gangs and unnatural monsters. The first scene has no compunctions about setting out the stall, with an honest English cabby directly accusing Chang of making away with white women (a very different story if Chang cultivated a cult that was willing to sacrifice itself for Weng-Chiang, compelling the viewer to think a lot more cogently about immigrant Chinese – so instead they're all male, end of). This is the story the Doctor decides he's in before there's any proof of time travel and giant rats, when he promises to help the police fight the Tong. And it's the chain of thought that deems an opium den the inevitable, appropriate place for Chang's death.

The oft-argued controversy about the yellow-face casting is almost extraneous from this point of view. The Chinese in this story bear as much resemblance to reality as the mummies of "Pyramids of Mars" or the Loch Ness Monster; it's all so much playing with genre tropes, just from a genre that's become less recognisable since the 70s. Holmes's frantic attempt to get a story, any story, written is following the Hammer Horror path of least resistance.

That anyone might take this more personally simply hadn't occurred to anyone in the production; everyone's game to play Victorian stereotypes and relishing their work. To what extent "Talons" is an enjoyable – or indeed watchable – experience rests entirely on how much appreciation you have for that.

It's noticeable just how long the story takes to start doing something only *Doctor Who* can do. Replace the giant rats with a reasonably motivated set of guard dogs, and you have a story that passes for a Hartnell-type historical up to Chang's deathbed scene, when all his character motivation is finally grounded in the gag of a regular *Doctor Who* occurrence – a mysteriously appearing cabinet – being treated as the miracle it is. The Doctor's contained fury about Greel's crimes and the Filipino army at Reykjavik are memorable enough, but like the Jago-Litefoot double act, a few crisp lines carry a lot of story. It's arguably one of the only six-parters that benefits from being watched all in one sitting.

The original Fu Manchu novels had their antagonist as the continual source of tension, a figure who had to be devious and a murderously able opponent to motivate the endless stories; in Holmes's photocopy of a photocopy, all the wily foreigner's machinations are overshadowed by an energetic pig. That might have been a story better worth pursuing – an animatronic quarreling with its creator who disowns it, while fending off a meddlesome Doctor, covers the necessary plot points in a more engagingly *Who*ish way. But given Holmes's starting point, that version was never on the cards.

The Talons of Weng-Chiang 14.6

Critique (Defence) Time was, anyone daring to say that this was any less than perfect would be shouted down. Now, it's almost impossible to make any effort at praising this without caveats, qualifications and squirming for fear of being hounded. To say anything more complex or nuanced than a wholesale pro- or anti- case is liable to play into generational disputes and name-calling. The baby-to-bathwater ratio here is much higher than in other controversial/ offensive stories, even from this century.

Anyone coming to this fresh is going to see a different production from the version 1977 viewers saw, and neither is quite the version older fans carry around in their heads. The broadcast story is substantially on videotape and the "cinematic" bits are Outside Broadcast: what's on film is very tightly-shot to avoid showing any present-day wiring, cars or street-furniture. All of the last two episodes is in the studio. This is more like *The Pallisers* than Hammer. There are some shockingly bad effects. Even allowing for the censorship and jiggery-pokery, the 1980s VHS release unsettled a lot of people who had an idealised memory of it. That "remembered" version was routinely in the top five when *Doctor Who Magazine* ran a poll, and there are lots of identifiable reasons for that to have been the case. The actual production's a shade subtler than the idealised version, but the context in which it emerged – where it looked radical – is gone, making it look like a relic of the very things it ridiculed. Luckily, we'll never get that context back.

The fact that this story makes people uncomfortable is proof that this is a more honest depiction of British history than some recent sanitised versions. Nearly everyone here is a caricature, with only Chang given anything like subtlety or layers (not last in his dry way of dealing with everyday racism), but some caricatures are now more acceptable than others. Viewers have spent 45 years finding Jago and Litefoot endearing and have taken these characters' attitudes towards the Chinese as being endorsed by the story. They have so many other flaws that are comedic or touchingly relatable that this flaw might have seemed to be equally indulgable. Nobody seems to have expected these two characters to work so well together or individually, otherwise they would have been made to meet earlier. The real double-act here is Jago and Casey – on a first watch, the latter's death is a wrench.

The setting is the sort of thing the BBC could do in their sleep in the 70s, so the cost-cutting (where they did, in fact, cut costs rather than spend like drunken sailors and leave Graham Williams to pick up the tab) is invisible. Don't believe us? Another Ripper spoof from the same era, Spike Milligan's "The Phantom Raspberry-Blower of Old London Town" (originally a stand-alone half-hour special for Ronnie Barker, then a serial in *The Two Ronnies*) managed to be almost as atmospheric and evocative even with a laugh-track, surrealist sight-gags and men in drag chasing a fiend who... well, the clue's in the title.

Unlike the awful Hollywood attempts to do Ripper/Jekyll stories over the previous 50 years, the BBC staffers knew what they were doing. That alone justifies doing a story like this once the series could do it properly. As far as production goes, it was a slam-dunk in the 1970s – so long as the script wasn't clumsily anachronistic or stupid. The trick is to avoid being mealy-mouthed about what things were really like and just making pretty wallpaper or costume kitsch. Newsflash: Victorian London was racist and squalid. Sewers were not filled with lovable urchins (X4.14, "The Next Doctor").

The difference between the real Robert Holmes and all the wannabes BBC Wales hired is exactly that: he had lived a life and kept his eyes and ears open before becoming a full-time writer and, unlike the later writers, didn't grow up wanting to be Holmes or to write for *Doctor Who*. The Victoriana here is the culmination of decades of listening to people, reading fiction of all grades or levels of respectability and, for want of a better phrase, jackdaw meanderings. As we'll see in **The Lore**, the producer got the optimum people for the story's look and facilities and let Bob do Bob, not worrying about whether a location or effect was achievable. That unfettered approach to writing, in a story devised and delivered in so little time, allowed all of the pulp and "classic" fiction and films he'd soaked up to all gush out. This wasn't researched so much as observed.

When you sit down and look at it, the story's a mess, with two pairs of identical cliffhangers, a couple of huge holes they paper over and an outrageous piece of stalling with Greel losing his key. Yet there's a lot of circumstantial detail allowing them to get away with it by sheer *brio*. Few people can simply sit down and dissect the plot when it's running on the screen, because it carries almost every viewer away – or repulses them completely. Locations, dialogue, performances conspire to make this an experience rather than a narrative. Critical viewers get enough researched or experienced truth to make them think they can answer the plot anomalies if they go and look it up afterwards.

What makes this more than a grab-bag of set-pieces from Victorian fiction is that the storyline gives legitimate reasons to be visiting a Music Hall, a Pathologist's Lab, an Opium Den, the sewers, a fashionable town-house and a lot of cobbled streets after dark. Cleaners, prostitutes and laundry services all matter here in ways they don't in adaptations of Victorian novels. Matter to us and the plot, that is; the affluent Londoners don't seem to notice them until they are forced to, just as in reality. There's no contrivance or even preposterous (Dickensian) coincidences (again, naming no names). At a functional level, the plot allows us to explore the world following its logic and see another world's impact on it.

Upon that foundation, the rest of the team and cast confidently built their own contributions. Trevor Baxter deserved a medal just for calling Greel "you filthy bounder" with enough conviction to avoid people giggling. Christopher Benjamin's more obviously crowd-pleasing performance comes off as more than just Vorg-with-a-thesaurus (10.2, "Carnival of Monsters") or a trial-run for Gatherer Hade (15.4, "The Sun Makers"). Jago fits the situation and reveals a few more layers once out of his natural habitat. (When Holmes did this just to live up to his reputation, the result was Oscar in 22.4, "The Two Doctors" – proving that trying to be the fanzine-reviewer's "Robert Holmes" got as messy when Holmes did it as future copycats' attempts.)

The performance we're discouraged from praising is the actually most textured; hold your nose and watch John Bennett adjust Chang's public and private displays according to who's with him, letting the situation in each scene guide him. Kids picked up on this: the line *I understand we all look the same* struck a nerve. So did the reminders that the laundry-services and Limehouse were like that within living memory when this was shown. Whatever your thoughts on the casting or the character *per se*, it's not a disrespectful performance. In a setting of one-note or two-note Victorian stock figures and against Michael Spice (as Greel), trying to prove that it *is* in fact possible to over-play a fifty-first-century Nazi War Criminal impersonating a Chinese deity and feeding his enemies to giant rats, it's extraordinary. Once Chang is dead, the story actually loses a lot of dignity.

"Dignity" might seem an odd word for a seemingly-playful *Doctor Who* story delving into Penny Dreadfuls, but imagine how bad a Barry Letts version would have been. Not just CSO rats or the plot stopping to explain everything, making sure we hear the sermon on how most Chinese-born Londoners were decent (it's just the Tong who are misguided), not just the Doctor taking half an episode to defeat the Black Scorpion with Venusian Aikido, but the achingly slow pace it would have had. It would have taken four episodes to get to the first cliffhanger, because the Pertwee Doctor wouldn't have taken such complete control of the police investigation and would have been in cells more often than in "Frontier in Space" (10.3). He'd pick fights rather than sardonically allow people to condemn themselves. Only posh people, and perhaps a comedy yokel, would have had speaking-roles.

It's taken three years, but *Doctor Who* is finally rid of this prim, trite approach. It trusts us to join the dots and skip unnecessary scenes of the incremental accumulation of evidence. We have a Doctor who bounces equally well off a pathologist, an impresario and a fugitive dictator and whose ironic approach to everything around him allows him to tease Leela. She isn't so much the audience-identification figure as the innocent abroad, and her direct approach to problems slams up against what we know of period customs and generic conventions. Fond as (nearly) everyone is of Lis Sladen, no-one can deny that Sarah would have killed this story stone dead. There's no going back from this year's developments.

That doesn't mean, as some of the older reviewers and the *ancien regime* of fandom seem to think, that *Doctor Who* was always trying to become this story and we were robbed of more like it. Philip Hinchcliffe's ideas of how he would have proceeded if given a fourth year indicate that he thought he'd gone as far in this direction as was possible or desirable to attempt. The BBC also had ideas on what should happen next. This is an outlier and was intended as such. An unprecedentedly dense, rich, allusive script, performed just about as well as it could ever have been, in a production they can't do now even though they could afford it (and they couldn't have done a year later, for various reasons) – no wonder people think of this story as the climax. Change makes whatever was last before it seem special. As we've said, the mythology of "the Hinchcliffe Era" only really applies to about half a dozen stories, most of them in 1977, but the memory doesn't entirely cheat.

If the rest of this story hadn't kept it in the public eye, allowing it to outlive the Christopher Lee films it parodied and all the other, more glaring, race-fails of the 1970s, that aspect wouldn't have attracted so much attention and contempt. Disney's disowned *One of Our Dinosaurs is Missing* (although someone fondly remembers Jon Pertwee's cameo – see X8.1, "Deep Breath"). None of the sitcoms from ITV that exceeded anything in "Talons" for glaring wrongness are a global mega-brand with millions riding on merchandise sales and reissues of old episodes. (*Sherlock* is another matter...)

In a story that mines so much depth, shock and fun from the gulf between what we know about London in the 1890s, and other media representations of "the good old days", this bum note has aged badly for other reasons than more enlightened attitudes. Because of the high-profile casting decision, this story alone gets a trigger-warning on BritBox: worse examples of yellowface or ethnic slurs in *Doctor Who* (11.5, "Planet of the Spiders"; 19.2, "Four to Doomsday"; even 5.1, "The Tomb of the Cybermen") are allowed out without a note from their mum. The Doctor's far more casually offensive to Lin Futu than he ever is to Chang, but nobody cares because, ultimately, nobody gives a toss about "Four to Doomsday".

The Facts

Written by Robert Holmes. Directed by David Maloney. Viewing figures: 11.3 million, 9.8 million, 10.2 million, 11.4 million, 10.1 million, 9.3 million. AIs 60% (Part Four), 58% (Part Six, no others recorded). Part Two was shown at the almost-unprecedentedly late time of 6.35pm, the rest at 6.30pm (still too late for a lot of children), but with hardly any opposition on ITV and *Sight and Sound in Concert* on BBC2 catering for those people gagging to see Gallagher and Lyle or Graham Parker and the Rumour.

Despite its subsequent (favourable) reputation and even later notoriety, this story was never repeated by the BBC. It did, however, get a free plug when the makers of *Whose Doctor Who* advertised for kids and professionals to do vox-pops and when that documentary was promoted ahead of the last episode of the previous story.

Working Titles "A Foe from the Future" (sort of, see **The Lore**), "The Talons of Greel".

Alternate Versions The 1985 VHS version was hacked about mercilessly; apart from the usual thing of ripping out the cliffhangers and credits, the fight in Part One was subject to newly-imposed bans on nunchucks and rice-flails in anything children might watch, knives going into people and so on. To keep the music-cues from abruptly jumping, the gaps were filled by slowing down shots of the Doctor walking, accidentally adding a David Carradine *Kung Fu* ambience to Tom Baker loping about in an Ulster.

Australia's ABC showed an edit where the Part Three cliffhanger is tweaked to remove any hint that Leela's getting nibbled by an R.O.U.S.

Terrance Dicks used his Sherlockian/ Dickensian knowledge to rush out a novelisation that restored the "Lombard Street to a China Orange" line and gave Theresa a slightly more reputable career as waitress in a late-night casino in the West End. He makes explicit the link between the Icelandic Alliance massacre and Greel programming the Peking Homunculus to kill.

Cliffhangers There's a ten-foot rat in the sewer; Mr Sin is in Litefoot's front-parlour, approaching Leela with a knife; the Rat's about to eat Leela; Sin and Weng-Chiang are driving off with the Cabinet, laughing; Leela pulls the leather mask off, revealing Weng-Chiang's distorted face.

What Was In the Charts? "Year of the Cat", Al Stewart; "Don't Give Up on Us, Baby", David Soul; "Chanson D'Amour", Manhattan Transfer; "When I Need You", Leo Sayer; "They Shoot Horses, Don't They", Racing Cars; "I Don't Want to Put a Hold on You", Bernie Flint.

The Lore

This story came about in stages. Philip Hinchcliffe had proposed a Victorian adventure, possibly themed around Jack the Ripper, as a way to introduce Sarah's replacement. The Doctor would educate a street-urchin, along the lines of Eliza Doolittle in *Pygmalion/ My Fair Lady*. (Continuing negotiations over the *Scratchman* film, with Twiggy as the companion, seem to have

14.6 The Talons of Weng-Chiang

become attached to the notion of her as the Eliza-figure: several years later, she played the role for real on the London stage.) An old colleague of Holmes's, Basil Dawson, was apparently sounded out for a four-part script. But then the idea of placating Tom Baker with a companion-less adventure took hold, and "The Deadly Assassin" was inserted after what had been done with "The Hand of Fear". With Chris Boucher's first script introducing Leela, and the rapidly-commissioned "The Robots of Death" retaining her, this notion was back-burnered while Hinchclifffe tried to resolve whether he was staying on for a fourth year.

In the meantime, Robert Banks Stewart was asked for another season-ending story and devised a scenario called "A Foe from the Future", about a time-travelling war-criminal hiding in present-day Devon and launching a killing-spree analogous to the Ripper's in a sleepy village. The first proposal came in during Holmes's work on "The Deadly Assassin", early in May 1976, with a formal commission on 1st June. With three scripts in the pipeline from reliable writers and his own tricky story safely in on time, Holmes looked forward to his first holiday since taking the job of script editor. He left in early July for two weeks in Italy, driving there by a scenic route.

That never happened. His wife suffered a perforated stomach ulcer in Germany and needed hospitalisation for 16 days longer than the planned trip. Holmes was given leave on his return to Britain and resumed work in August, tidying up Boucher's first script, then received a message from Stewart. Thames Television had offered him a job editing their anthology series *Rooms*, starting immediately, so they were without a last story. David Maloney was booked to start work on this non-existent story from 6th August. As Hinchcliffe sent memos to the Writer's Guild and the BBC Contracts Department reminding everyone that Holmes was cleared to write two scripts that year, a shattered script editor started spot-welding the Victorian setting to the time-fugitive idea. Hinchcliffe vetoed the first idea, with a semi-regenerated Master as the villain. Of the things previously discussed, all that remained in this new story were the hologram "ghosts" and "Jalnik" having a protective mask ripped off to reveal a distorted face.

- In Holmes's absence, the drama chiefs had set up talks with a man whose CV resembled Hinchcliffe's three years before. Graham Williams, from a crime-drama background but known to like Science Fiction, was another of Slater's protégés and, like Hinchcliffe, was in his early 30s with a young son. They met him in July to discuss how a notional handover could be made to work and, we think, a studio day of "The Deadly Assassin" had Williams in the gallery, feeling massively out of his depth. Piecing the story together from various interviews, it seems that this left Hinchcliffe protective of his series and determined to give it another year.

As you'll know if you're reading this book sequentially, the next anyone heard of it was on 2nd November – during pre-filming for "The Robots of Death", Williams was presented to Baker as the new boss. With so many of the players behind this long dead, the full story may never emerge (but see the attached essay and our notes on the next two stories).

Whatever the case, Hinchcliffe told the design staff not to stint on any expense and make this last hurrah look and feel lavish. The production unit manager, Christopher D'oyly-John, was aghast at having to find the money, but said later the cards would have fallen this way even if Hinchcliffe had stuck around for Season Fifteen – he was not good with budgets. (Hinchcliffe's subsequent career bears this out.) Whether this was Hinchcliffe displaying loyalty to regular colleagues or a spiteful booby-trap for Williams, that's why there's so much night-shooting in London, so many well-dressed sets and locations (and extras) and nothing that looks like cost-cutting.

- Holmes prepared his own exit-strategy. He had a notion for a *Doomwatch/ Quatermass* serial called "Lutavin 50" that he'd workshopped with Hinchcliffe and got Slater interested in developing. He had a radio serial, "Aliens in the Blood", he'd been working on for years and had got commissioned to write, but not had time to work on. He was looking to return to freelancing and working from home. Although his enthusiasm for "The Talons of Greel" was growing as he got into the Victoriana and *grand guignol*, he thought this was his last work as a salaried member of the production team. He followed his own advice and made the scripts function as a four-parter at a Music Hall, with a lot of location filming, and a two-parter at the villain's studio-bound lair. One other complication arose: think back to the start of this book and the notion of a behind-the-scenes documentary about *Doctor Who*. A BBC2 arts strand, rebranded as *The Lively Arts*, was trying to make the topic "popular" and "accessible". They refloated the idea as a one-off with interviews with the "punters" as well as the professionals – guess which story they wanted to show going from script to screen...

- Meanwhile, Hinchcliffe and Maloney had identified the right location for the theatre, with the correct period curtain "fliers" – but this was Panto season, so they couldn't shoot there until January. This gave the entire team a breather once the London night-shoot was completed (and may have saved the budget). Hinchcliffe supervised this production, but Williams was given the office. On 30th November, Williams was left to run the admin and commissioning of new scripts.

- Hinchcliffe got one last story's worth of work from Roger Murray-Leach, who designed sewers, playbills and retro-futuristic technology, and a swift return for John Bloomfield on costumes. Leela's look for the first three episodes was based on the late-Victorian "Practical" look adopted by lady cyclists (see also 5.2, "The Abominable Snowmen" and 18.4, "State of Decay"), but not in tweed (it has a more-than-passing similarity to what Vesta Tilley wore as Principal Boy in various pantos of the era). The amount of running, fighting and crashing through windows necessitated a bloomer-suit rather than corsets and tight skirts. The Doctor was originally to have had a silk top hat and a different – but still long – scarf.

Another of Bloomfield's tasks was to make a rat-costume for a small actor (inevitably, Stuart Fell got the call), using a sheet-aluminium frame for the head and an articulated jaw hung from Fell's head via a rugby scrum-cap. Bloomfield and his young son made this and the fur wrap-with-tail in their spare bedroom. There was a similar arrangement for Deep Roy as Mr Sin. (He'd recently been a different small assassin in *The New Avengers*, also with blow-pipe poison dart-chicanery.) Murray-Leach spent a day in real London sewers making notes and was, with Maloney and production assistant Ros Anderson, on the lookout for whatever location Holmes asked for. Hinchcliffe had put experienced people on the case so that Holmes could just write what he felt like and not worry about practicality or affordability.

- The theatre location, the Northampton Rep, was secured on 26th November and they found that the nearby former mental hospital, St Crispin's, had facilities for other scenes. The amount of work needed for this out-of-town shoot led Hinchcliffe to book an OB rig with two hand-held LMCR cameras in lieu of one of the studio sessions. (If Williams was taking notes, it explains why he was so prepared for a seemingly-inevitable strike just before Christmas the following year – see 15.6, "The Invasion of Time".)

- The first day of shooting was 13th December 1976, at Ealing (Stage 2) for the interiors of the horse-drawn carriages. Baker was in high dudgeon that Leela was being retained and was rather curt with Jameson. The first night of shooting was at Skin Market Place, off Emerson Street (roughly where the replica Globe Theatre is now – X3.2, "The Shakespeare Code"); this too was mainly a horse-and-buggy show with the rented hansoms (apparently called "Clarence" and "Growler") as horses being used by the Doctor, Chang and Litefoot.

- Maloney had worked with Trevor Baxter (Litefoot) in theatre, but Baxter auditioned, covering his slight uncertainty by feigning a patrician interest in the script's possibilities (which is what the part needed).

- The team were in the same neck of the woods the following night, ending up at Bankside, near the power station that's now Tate Modern (i.e. 500 yards west of Emerson St.) where Fell, Alan Chuntz and Max Faulkner performed something a bit like Chinese martial-arts and tried to keep warm in cotton pyjamas. Before that, though, they'd been to Clink Street, now the site of the Prison Museum tourist experience, where more horse-drawn traffic was paraded in front of Fred Hamilton's cameras as dusk fell. Despite requesting the residents to remove their cars for the evening for a few weeks in advance, one couple was on a skiing holiday and hadn't moved their shiny new Porsche. By all accounts, they'd not got on well with their more-established neighbours, so it was a cause for small celebration when Murray-Leach got around the problem with a tarpaulin, some hay and some horse-manure to fake one of the piles of dung that were a less-commented-upon feature of traffic-management back in ye day. The rest of the street took photos.

- Remember David Maloney's daughter, who saved Baker from drowning on that holiday in Italy? She attended school at Broad Oak, in Twickenham (several miles west of every other London location), so that was an easy find for Litefoot's house. One of the windows was replaced

14.6 The Talons of Weng-Chiang

with sugar-glass so that Fell, dressed as Leela, could crash through it. (He found the padding and design of the bloomer-suit helpful: the groping from the crew, mistaking him for Jameson, less so.) It's at this point that Maloney was approached to produce *Blakes 7*, and Williams asked what it would take for Jameson to stay on for another year. Her terms, as we'll discuss next story, included not having to wear red contact-lenses.

- The filming at Wapping Steps followed on 16th, with the scene of an old ghoul relishing the sight of Buller's corpse; the one-line role was given to veteran old-lady actor Patsy Smart, who'd spent a few years in *Upstairs, Downstairs* as Miss Roberts and whose CV included *The Elephant Man* and *One of Our Dinosaurs is Missing*. For maximum effect, she removed her dentures, leaving them with Maloney while she expressed delight in the "floater". The corpse was a dummy, obviously, and the local constabulary, who'd kept the public away for the take, are said to have borrowed it to prank a colleague later that night.

Holmes reminisced that he attended the shoot with Hinchcliffe that night and observed Bennett grumbling that people immediately recognised him from a distance after three hours in make-up. (A lot of Chang's unnerving stillness is simply Bennett trying not to wrinkle the latex and have to go in for another long session.) The Mortuary's exterior was shot at Bridewell Place. Here is where the hatchet-man was bumped-off – there was a pneumatic special-effects device to fire the hatchet into the woodwork but, on the night, it proved easier and more reliable to throw it by hand.

- Friday was the last day of filming and started on the north bank of the Thames, at St Katherine's Docks, near the Tower of London, for the daytime shots of the Doctor, Litefoot and a boatman rowing to the sewer entrance. BBC Visual Effects built the "Chinese" fowling-piece. Later, at Ivory House (now a very exclusive marina and flats), the council obligingly removed the manhole cover; a lighter replacement was used. The Doctor's descent into the sewer in Part One was nearly perfect first take, except that a small child cheered on the Doctor. Eleven less-good takes later, they opted to use the first one, redubbed.

- On 29th, the team reconvened to rehearse the location taping; joining them was Christopher Benjamin, who had been in *The Forsyte Saga* when Maloney was a floor-manager. His other credits include *Potter*, a character in both *Danger Man* and *The Prisoner*, and Sir Keith Gold in 7.4, "Inferno". (We'll see him again in X4.7, "The Unicorn and the Wasp".)

- Recording started in Northampton on Saturday, 8th January 1977 (just before Part Two of "The Face of Evil" went out). They began with the old Rates Office on Fish Street, made up to look like a police station. (It's a branch of Subway now.) Sunday was the first of four days at the Theatre Royal, on Guildhall Road (now part of the Royal and Derngate performing arts complex). This had just been made a Listed Building (so had to be kept as it was) and had last been enlarged in 1889, so had an intact fly-gallery (the ropes and pulleys to move curtains and backdrops, as seen in Part Two), the nearest to London. (Many of the famous West End theatres were by the same designer, CJ Phipps, who'd supervised the rebuilding and enlargement, but have been updated.)

The in-house Repertory company provided a few extras for the backstage scenes, and a group of Music Hall enthusiasts came from Birmingham to swell the ranks of the audience. *Look East*, a regional opt-out as part of *Nationwide*, covered their arrival even though Birmingham is nearer to Northampton than Norwich, that programme's focus. Williams had touted the location recording as a possible *Nationwide* feature, so it's possible that the overall editor, John Gau, farmed it out to *Look East*.

Two professional conjurers, Larry Barnes and Ali Bongo, oversaw several scenes including the levitation trick at the start of Part One. Bennett had to sign non-disclosure documents as Rep member Sally Sinclair was held up by two men dressed in black velvet (this sequence was done without the audience, apparently, but it's a trick real Victorians performed). As we've noted, Dudley Simpson came along for the ride and brought some of his usual musicians, but most of what we hear played was pre-recorded in a session before Christmas. (This section of Part Four's score introduces Chang with the overture to *The Mikado* but mutates into the fourth Doctor motif.)

Monday had most of the backstage scenes, including the chase though the period fly-gallery in Part Two, using two hand-held OB cameras: Max Faulkner was Greel and Fell was the Doctor. This sequence was greatly expanded by Maloney from a one-line description of Greel knocking the Doctor into the Pit. Many of the Jago-Casey scenes were recorded that day, as well as a few involving

Chang and Leela in Part Three. As 1977 was the Silver Jubilee year, many local businesses started their celebrations this week and the theatre had scheduled a banquet for that night – they had some surprise special guests. Tuesday morning was a chance for some fresh air as scenes in the doorway of the theatre and the corridor near Chang's dressing-room were shot (observe everyone's breath misting). The walls were decorated with a selection of genuine theatre playbills (a close examination of the one for the Grand reveals some odd coincidences).

• The studio work finally began on 24th, with scenes in Litefoot's dining-room and porch for parts 2 to 4. Jameson gave up eating meat a while after these scenes were recorded, but this isn't cause and effect. The next scenes were the early ones of the sewers. These were, of necessity, nowhere the size of the Bazalgette ones, but similar in look. They weren't concrete or brick but a durable PVC. On returning to the studio (TC1) after the lunch break, the crew found that the whole floor was inch-deep in water – less water than had been put in the fake tunnels, though, the rest had seeped down into electrical ducts under the studio and into the telephone switchboard and records department. A lot of mopping-up and contrition followed. (Oddly, this mishap wasn't mentioned in the documentary.)

• By now Williams had prevailed upon Holmes to stick around for the next six months, partly to ease in the new producer, but also because Holmes's wife's illness had delayed the plan to go freelance. The disquiet about Baker and Jameson's on-set tensions didn't incentivise staying longer and, among all the other projects, he had an offer from Louis Marks to write a historical drama about the *Daily Mail*'s founder.

On 27th, as rehearsals resumed in a new venue (the North Kensington Community Centre), the documentary team had decided to show a "typical" script conference... even though there weren't any scripts ready. Holmes, Williams and Terrance Dicks are seen kicking around an idea of a moral dilemma for the Doctor. It's apparently caused by the need to let a planet's population continue in serfdom, because the thing they need to get free is needed by him for some higher purpose, possibly connected with this Key to Time malarkey. How far we can rely on this as evidence for what "The Witch Lords" might have been like is anyone's guess (probably not very), but we'll pick this up when discussing the next two stories and 16.2, "The Pirate Planet".

Dicks was, by now, a consultant on the documentary, which may explain why the illustrative clips are more pertinent and imaginatively-selected than those in, say, the 1991 *Late Show* piece. The commentary makes no mention of why Hinchcliffe wasn't there, just that Williams was taking over. Later that day, they filmed a rehearsal where Baker, Roy and Maloney were blocking out Mr Sin's shooting the Doctor (Jameson's glandular fever had flared up and she was off) and playing table-football. Baker was interviewed, memorably describing Jon Pertwee as "a tall lightbulb" and claiming to know the series better than the writers, producers or anyone. During this rehearsal period, they noted that Part Five was under-running, so the dumb-waiter sequence was added.

• On 28th, the film crew went to Visual Effects to see Michealjohn Harris test the effect of the table exploding when hit with a laser. This effect caused problems on the last day of recording, but it worked perfectly for the documentary. In the meantime, the strife of balancing the books led Chris D'oyly-John leaving early and concentrating on Birmingham-based productions *The Brothers* and *Angels*. Parachuted-in at the last moment was another experienced PUM with Birmingham connections, John Nathan-Turner, although he wasn't credited for this. His big calling-card was his work on *The Pallisers,* and he was currently on *All Creatures Great and Small*. If you don't already know, he's going to be a big part of the programme's future, so stay tuned. Still on the subject of musical chairs, Bill Slater abruptly left to go back to producing and was replaced by Graeme McDonald, so now Baker truly had seniority as far as the series went.

• Williams trailed Hinchcliffe for the final studio session, starting Tuesday, 8th February. All three days were in TC8. The last of these was the main hall of the House of the Dragon, with a centrepiece constructed from expanded polystyrene foam. By now the money had run out, so much of the rest of this set is just plush curtains and old props (you'll recognise some from the Sisterhood of Karn's Flame Chamber in "The Brain of Morbius"). The title of the story had changed, so the dialogue incorporated it. An enthusiastic set-dresser had added an extra coat of varnish to the small table, the one that was supposed to explode and fall in half, so it failed to perform first go. Or second. This added to the delays, and the last session over-ran by 45 minutes. The scene-shifters left promptly at 10.35, but the rest of the crew stuck it out. (The only thing needing to move was a set of cardboard boxes for Fell to fall onto and, as stunt-arranger, this was his job, so there was no demarcation dispute.)

- The *Lively Arts* interviewed Hinchcliffe about how masks were unpredictably scary (or not) even with preparation, and that he had only cut two scenes because he thought they were too frightening. Then they sat in on Simpson and Maloney blocking out music cues (Simpson excitedly explaining that he was using car suspension springs to make the sound of Sin pouncing on Buller). With one exception, each episode's score was recorded on a Monday, starting on 21st February and ending 28th March – under a week before transmission of each episode.

- Part One had a lot of editing. A scene of Chang in his dressing-room telepathically "driving" Sin and using joss-stick to concentrate was lost, which meant that an exchange between the Doctor and Leela, where she observes that the smell of death has gone when Chang leaves and the Doctor says all he noticed was "a disagreeable odour of old joss-sticks" went. So did Leela's claim that she was hungry enough to eat an "owrus". (There was to have been a similar shot of Chang outside Litefoot's house as Sin attacks Leela in Part Two.) Part Six lost some observations about what Greel had done to the girls, but curiously, the extension to the previous episode because it was under-running meant it was now a minute over. The cliffhanger of Sin about to stab the unconscious Leela was delayed so that the unmasking of Weng-Chiang, a minute or so earlier, was the new episode ending.

- In the *Radio Times* for Part Two, a letter from Amy Sheeler (age 11) grumbled that the good old monsters, such as the Ice Warriors and the Yeti (apparently she was a Target reader, as she would have been two when they last appeared) ought to come back. "Producer Designate" Williams replied that "monsters on their own can be pretty boring; a good *Doctor Who* story – never". We'll see how he does on this over the next three years.

- The day after the last episode, *Whose Doctor Who* went out on BBC2 at 8.20pm. Although they'd found some odd people from the call for viewers with strong opinions, the bulk of the talking-heads pieces were kids from Smallwood Junior School, Tooting. Not all of them were complementary. There were child psychologists enthusing about the positive effects of allegorising internal states, retired educationalists talking about the balance of reason and hope, and a lot of clips (some in what was then-shockingly bad condition for things broadcast relatively recently). The *Radio Times* promised "a galaxy of monsters from Autons to Zarbi" (they started with the Zarbi, but people still watched). For the first time, even counting "The Three Doctors" (10.1), watching the series became a subject for nostalgia – this is the real start of the "behind the sofa" cliché.

- Hinchcliffe, now well away from it, was asked to discuss the documentary a few days ahead of its broadcast on fluffy daytime chat-show *Pebble Mill at One*. He was asked about violence, scariness and his own kids, but was fed soft-balls about Mary Whitehouse and the apparent cheapness. (They showed the allegedly-controversial "Deadly Assassin" cliffhanger complete with freeze-frame, at around 1.30pm on a weekday during school holidays and nobody minded.) He seemed hugely proud of what he'd got away with but relaxed about someone else having to top that. His subsequent career is a mixed bag, but highlights include *Private Schultz* and *The Charmer*.

- David Maloney went on to make the first three series of *Blakes 7* and took Roger Murray-Leach with him. Maloney later did the 1981 adaptation of *The Day of the Triffids* that inspired *28 Days Later* and worked on *Juliet Bravo*. Murray-Leach went into film design (an early project was *Local Hero*, where promising newcomer Peter Capaldi gushed over the designer). Holmes, in the flurry of personal projects and attempts to jump-start Season Fifteen, missed the boat with getting a spin-off series off the ground. It took Big Finish to get that done in the twenty-first century; their *Jago & Litefoot* audios ran an impressive 13 series until Trevor Baxter's death in 2017.[63] Holmes did, however, revisit Victorian sewers and skulduggery in an episode of Bob Baker's cheap-and-cheerful series *Into the Labyrinth*, generally considered one of the few highlights of the third series.

Over the summer, those twin bastions of the BBC – *Blue Peter* and *Radio Times* – joined forces to let Britain's children stage their own *Doctor Who* plays, with cut-outs of the Doctor and Leela to colour-in printed in the listings mag and helpful hints on making a cardboard-box stage, alien-looking sets and – with the aid of a tape-recorder and some Swarfega – Dick Mills gave a tutorial on Special Sound. Oh, and there was a Jubilee.

End Notes

1. Anthony Boucher, groundbreaking mystery author and editor of *The Magazine of Fantasy and Science Fiction* in its early years, had deep religious convictions and thought that humanoid robots were somehow unholy. His writers moved in the direction of self-aware gadgets that led, ultimately, to R2-D2 but by some odd tangents. Check out Henry Kuttner's 'Galloway Gallagher' stories as a start.

2. Driving sheep across London Bridge is one of the less obscure rights that Freedom of the City of London confers, with other cities having similar permissions. Jodie Whittaker is now allowed to do it. Dalazar is the name of the Dalek city in the various 1960s Annuals and semi-authorised spinoffery in which Terry Nation and David Whitaker were involved, some of which would be reworked for a new audience after the runaway success of "Genesis of the Daleks".

3. The disability-rights series on BBC Radio 4 *Does He Take Sugar?* was called that because the most commented-upon problem was the way wheelchairs, guide-dogs and so forth make anyone using them seem like 'props' to the well-meaning but ignorant general public.

4. Which is why we've pointedly ignored that series' attempt at a definitive statement on the topic, *The Measure of a Man*. It's basically a court-case to decide whether Data is human but, after Captain Picard makes a few moves that Perry Mason wouldn't be allowed to and gets away with it because he's the hero, they decide that Data has rights because, err, Star Fleet was set up to find new life-forms and he is one. Ergo, he's human because he isn't human. Almost all of the commentary about this, in the endless textbooks and online, evaluate the episode on how far it conforms to current US practice and precedent – Riker is a doofus because he makes arguments when he's supposed to be laying evidence, and so on – rather than accept that even Britain or France would have conducted this case in a radically different manner, let alone that a pan-species federation of the 24th Century might differ from 1980s America. Nor do they follow up the suit with Data seeking legal redress for these slurs, as he would have the right to even in 80s America or show him reconsider his relations with the humans he serves now that he is no longer property. They even ignore precedent from Shatner-era stories, including the existence of several other androids. Riker's case is that Data can't be human because he's got an off-switch, which would have been bad news for Captain Pike in *The Menagerie*.

5. The current problem is that so much of the coding for algorithms is proprietary, covered by copyright and commercial secrecy protection, that nobody can entirely rule out malice or bias even before the sum total of human inanity and bigotry is turned over to it as Big Data. When the machine learning has worked best is when it results in something no human would have considered (as with AlphaGo making moves in Go that looked like mistakes until they lead to victories). There's no guarantee that the rosy view we've just outlined of robots developing empathy after becoming self-aware is the only course of action: with so much money and legal resources put into developing such a system, its self-awareness would more likely turn into self-preservation to protect the company's investment at all costs – Asimov's Third Law would over-ride the other two.

6. In 2017 New Zealand also accepted a Maori group's argument that a sacred river, the Whanganui, was a legal person. India did something similar with the Ganges and Yamuna, although these were later reversed in the High Court, but in both cases the door was left open for anyone maliciously polluting them to be charged as if for assault on a person. 'Sentience' is as hard to define or prove as 'sanity' (which is also a legal matter rather than a medical one). You may recall the case of a macaque that took selfies and was argued to be the 'author' of the pictures. That was rejected but an Orangutan called Sandra was adjudged to be a person by a court in Buenos Aires in 2017, a chimpanzee called Cecilia got rights in 2016 and India's courts, although iffy on whether a sacred river is a person, defined cetaceans (whales, dolphins et al) as 'non-human persons' in 2013. In America, meanwhile, some states have accepted that divorcing couples have to give their pets as much consideration as any children from the marriage. In all cases, it is accepted that animals have the capacity to feel pain, to react to the behaviour of other beings (especially humans) and to have some notion, however vague of a 'self'. This is going to get messy as, for example, an adult elephant can demonstrate self-awareness to a capacity far beyond a human toddler.

391

End Notes

7. *It's a Square World* routinely used Television Centre as the symbol of pomposity. There was an incident when real masked robbers took the ancillary staff's wages and were seen doing it but not stopped, because everyone thought Bentine was at it again. Eventually, he received a memo solemnly stating, "Television Centre is not to be used for the purposes of entertainment". By the 70s, he'd got a niche doing children's stories using crude-but-ingenious tabletop animatronics, the Potties, which gave anyone wanting to ridicule Clifford Culley's model effects in 10.4, "Planet of the Daleks" and 11.2, "Invasion of the Dinosaurs" a handy stick. See also the invisible monster's footsteps at the start of "The Face of Evil".

8. A clear division between "director" and "producer" was a recent development – in the 1950s, most BBC series used both terms almost interchangeably. Non-fiction series had an "editor" in charge and a "producer" as the person physically making each edition happen. Sydney Newman, of course, was behind the streamlining and demarcation. In the system at work for *Doctor Who* 1963-89, the department head was the equivalent to an American-style "executive producer" and so was never credited. (Apart from the odd circumstances of Season Eighteen, there was never an "Executive Producer", with capitals, and certainly not one equivalent to Messrs. Davies, Moffat or Chibnall.)

There was one "associate producer", Mervyn Pinfield, for the first year but it seems they all agreed that Verity Lambert didn't need a babysitter and had mastered the technical aspects that he was there to supervise. The BBC set up a dedicated training course for directing in the three-camera electronic studio format at around the time Television Centre opened, in 1960. Obviously, there had to be a clear demarcation thereafter because directors and producers were in different unions and on a different pay-scale. Barry Letts didn't entirely stick within these boundaries but note that, when he directed a story as well, he was credited in one capacity or another, never both. As we progress through this book, we'll see the extent to which the PUM is more hands-on in *Doctor Who* than any other series and that the hierarchy's denial of Graham Williams's request that John Nathan-Turner get a pay-rise and "assistant producer" title is at the root of a lot of trouble.)

9. It may surprise people who first encountered the character on TV or in the film, but there is no mention in either the original Radio 4 series or the novelisation and first two spin-offs of Arthur wearing pyjamas or a dressing-gown. The blazer, cravat and Marks and Sparks trousers are at least as plausible a get-up for a character only ever stated to be wearing a digital watch, and who was let into a pub 12 minutes before the end of the world. This isn't just us being facetious: Richard Molesworth's biography of Robert Holmes notes that in April/May 1974, when this story was still being salvaged from Christopher Langley's first attempt, a promising youngster called Douglas Adams was in talks with Holmes over script ideas. He may have been the first-reserve writer for the Space Station idea. Shortly thereafter, Adams co-wrote with Graham Chapman a pilot for Ringo Starr, never made, involving a space ark filled with useless middlemen in suspended animation. You can see where this is going. Even after 40+ years of Simon Jones, or the film using Tim from *The Office*, it's remarkably easy to imagine Ian Marter saying Arthur's lines.)

10. You had to ask, didn't you? It's one of a number of made-up science-of-learning concepts Van Vogt derived from the real-life work *Science and Sanity* by Count Alfred Korzybsky. In this case, it's based on an idea that all the sciences have become over-specialised and need some kind of new overall theory to examine the links between them. Like a lot of early SF "greats", Van Vogt was a bit hazy on what was happening in science (and how much had changed since he left school), so was apparently unaware of how Quantum theory was changing chemistry and this was feeding into a new theory of genetics and inheritance, etc., etc. The Count's idea of "General Semantics" shows up in Van Vogt as "Null-A" (i.e. Non-Aristotelian thinking, which leads to the ability to teleport or something), in L. Ron Hubbard as "Dianetics" (Van Vogt fell out with Hubbard when the latter remade it as a religion), in the current Transhumanist cult and the quasi-science of Neuro-Linguistic Programming. As you will recall from 11.5, "Planet of the Spiders" and "Robot", and we'll see in 18.1, "The Leisure Hive" and 4.3, "The Power of the Daleks", SF mags promoted a lot of fringe cults and their legacy is seeping into the nether portions of the internet and the tinfoil-hat sections of political discourse. If you've not

End Notes

read Van Vogt, it's perhaps easiest to think of him as being in the same relationship to Philip K. Dick that the 1973 BBC version of *The Foundation Trilogy* was to the 1978 radio series *The Hitchhiker's Guide to the Galaxy*, the originals for the parodies. *Eminent Hipsters*, a memoir by Steely Dan co-founder Donald Fagan, contains a reminiscence on how influential Van Vogt was in the 50s among disaffected teenagers.

11. However, if he complained, all the BBC had to do was mention "Wonkavision" and the chewing gum that turned Violet Beauregarde into a blueberry. See **How Do You Transmit Matter?** in the next volume for more on this apparent borrowing.

12. Curiously, recently unearthed 1967 editions of *The Carol Burnett Show* look rather better but still have problems with skin-tones: Burnett and fellow ginge Vicki Lawrence look unwell and guest-artiste Barbara McNair looked grape-coloured, which added an unfortunate extra dimension to their sketch about hotels in the Deep South. The only person who looked the same on film and in this format was Leonard Nimoy, in a cameo as Spock.

13. Part Two was first shown the same night as Part Three of "Invasion of the Dinosaurs" but looks far worse. Apart from the shoddiness of the title graphics, apparently done in felt-tip (we were spared those before), it's got almost everything wrong with it. There's the BBC Sleigh, as used in every Christmas Special, at 45 degrees to the direction of the stock film that's ineptly CSO'd behind it; the bride says "look" and points then, several seconds later, something happens on the worn-out stock-footage insert; people go out for a breath of alpine air and risk bumping into the cyclorama of painted mountains (Raymond P Cusick has off-days too, it seems); wigs slip, chequered trousers strobe and people wait for cue-lines when they're supposed to be arguing. Did costume-drama addicts have lower standards than cynical parents forced to watch *Doctor Who* with their kids?

14. GBH, Grievous Bodily Harm, has been the constabulary's term for malicious assault since 1861. In the late 1970s, with all those thuggish cop shows and the trend for Mockney, people talking too much or too loud were accused colloquially of *givin' me GBH of the ear'ole*. Inevitably, it provided the names for a punk band and a street-drug. So the American PBS station's name was intrinsically amusing. Apparently, the name of the station stands for "Great Big Hill", the location of their transmitter.

15. Two days after Part Three a similar rubbery weapon would be presented to BBC2 viewers when the Lancastrian martial art of "Ecky Thump" – hitting people with black puddings – was disclosed to the outside world in "Kung Fu Capers", the episode of *The Goodies* thought to have made one viewer literally laugh himself to death. Modern tastes may vary. However, once you've seen how oddly flexible Nyder's weapon of choice is, the similarity is remarkable. Was this a re-used prop?

16. There's actually rather a lot of the film that no longer exists – the US edit was significantly shorter and that's the basis for versions released these days – but the juxtaposition Nation cites as his starting-point was never scripted or made.)

17. As we keep having to explain to UK readers, it's not *that* John Peel, it's a fan-turned-author who became Nation's ministry on Earth, gave us a couple of *Eighth Doctor Adventures* Dalek stories and is credited as co-author of *The Official Doctor Who and the Daleks Book* from St Martin's Press. In this, a great deal of effort is made to establish that the ruined Kaled dome contained static-powered prototypes of the Mk III Travel Unit and, as predicted, the mutations followed a precise pattern so that the descendants of a few irradiated survivors started using these, almost as described in the *TV 21* strips of the 60s. Resolving this with 17.1, "Destiny of the Daleks" is tricky enough but, as with the interrogation in "Genesis of the Daleks", it seems as if Nation is remembering the feature film and not his own television scripts.

(For non-UK readers, imagine if Gene Roddenberry or Rod Serling had an amanuensis called "Dick Clark" or "Alan Freed", and you've got some idea of the potential confusion.)

18. By "catapult", we mean what Americans call a slingshot, even though there's something else with that name that has a biblical precedent: we're talking about a Y-shaped handle and a strip of elastic. By "Dennis the Menace", we mean the one from *The Beano*, known throughout the English-

End Notes

speaking world, not the one only really known in America. Both strips began on exactly the same day – probably, although the off-sale dates on the *Beano* covers may be a week after it appeared in the shops and are for Saturdays rather than the stated "Every Thursday", making precision difficult – so nobody gets dibs. The 2009 animated version of the *Beano* character was voiced by Sophie Aldred, so that scene in "Silver Nemesis" now looks like an audition. The more recent animation was Australian, because that's how globally-popular the strip is.

19. Those of you who encountered Children's BBC in the mid-80s will have that bloody themesong stuck in your heads all day. You're welcome.

20. Has there been a more British form of gambling than guessing which football matches will end in goalless draws? Until 1957, it was about the only legal bet available to most people. What would happen is a company would print a rundown of all the professional matches on a given Saturday and you'd pick which ones wouldn't end with a clear winner, getting three points for a score-draw (3-3, 2-2 or whatever), two for a no-score draw (nobody got a goal), and one for either a home win or an away win. The systems varied between the seven big companies and over the years but that's it. You'd select your ten matches and hand in the slip, with your money, then hope to get the coveted 24-point jackpot and win thousands of pounds. As a result, many families participated in a ritual of listening in for the results, usually intoned solemnly on a TV or radio sports programme. The final scores would have an almost ecclesiastical feel to them, as the reader (Len Martin or Tim Gudgin on BBC1's *Grandstand*, a variety of similar-sounding men on ITV's *World of Sport*) used particular intonations for each type of result. There were jokes about the peculiar names of the teams and the strange scores (especially with Scottish teams, which have especially whimsical names, e.g., "Hearts of Midlothian", "Queen of the South" or "Hamilton Academicals"; according to legend one game ended "Fife 4, Forfar 5") and it's one of those Proustian triggers of a Saturday teatime.

21. It may, at a pinch, be a Nestlé *Doctor Who* bar, perhaps the one where we learn about Benton's fondness for stray dogs. They were both on the market at the same time, for the same price, in an apparent bid to induce tribal loyalties in the nation's kids.

22. His spiel about getting ready, sorting out Monday clothes, doing your homework in time for the new episode, something about "Sunday night popcorn", tried to evoke memories of those series whose themes came to mean the end of the weekend and the crushing return of routine. Yes, there are many TV shows whose place on a Sunday represented term-time ritual, but they were mainly resented for this. If you ask anyone who grew up in Britain between 1965 and 1990, they have specific themes – appropriate to what was on when they were young – which give them the screaming ab-dabs or just deflate them. It's nothing intrinsic about the music – is there a theme more jaunty than *Doctor Finlay's Casebook*, more mellow than *Bergerac* or more exhilarating than *The Onedin Line*? – but they somehow smell of Kiwi polish and defeat. Will Segun Akinola's arrangement of the *Doctor Who* theme one day be the cause of similar half-remembered frustration and misery?

23. The resolutely non-commercial BBC made an exception and devoted half an hour every Bank Holiday to plugging Disney films. Historically, Walt Disney had been a key figure in the 1936 launch of television, offering Mickey Mouse films for free. One of these was apparently the last thing shown before the Alexandra Palace service was suspended for World War II, and the same one was – if the listings are accurate – shown again on the day broadcasts resumed. This enabled the canny Disney to tell US networks that he had a decade's TV experience when they got in on the act post-war. *Disney Time* was a clips show, usually a few old favourites, an oddity from a nature documentary plus a short and ending with a plug for the new release (increasingly a let-down as the 70s wore on). Getting to present it was a bit of a coup but, while Jon Pertwee did it as himself, in denim, Tom Baker was strictly in-character throughout. His links were shot at the St. Martin's cinema near Broadcasting House – don't go looking for it these days – and are online if you're at all interested. Some are on the DVD.

24. He's sort-of famous: he starred in the most famously counter-productive advert of the 6, for Strand cigarettes. Sales plummeted, but "The

End Notes

Lonely Man Theme" was a hit single. The advert had a vaguely Sinatra-like bloke near Westminster Bridge at night, apparently stood up. The official reason for the failure is that it associated the brand with losers; it's also said that it looked like a (then-illegal) gay pick-up. It was parodied everywhere.

25. The source of that phrase is a political painting by Goya, but it's as good a "definition" of the original Gothic as any. Especially if we take an older, broader definition of "monster" (as we outlined in Volume 9.

26. Hey, guess what: according to research cited by Das and Ferbel in *Introduction to Nuclear and Particle Physics* (Wiley, 1994), one experiment looked at neutrons and their constituent quarks and found that, while a neutron is, by definition, neutral, the quarks had charges and these could be shown to have a dipole moment so… you've guessed it… Omega might have reversed the polarity of the neutron flow.

27. This was a series highlight but was a victim of the supposed need to cut ten minutes from each episode to repackage it in the 1990s with introductions by Douglas Adams. Sadly, those shortened versions, without even Adams, are what gets shown whenever it's repeated now. The main thing Adams and Bronowski had in common was deplorable taste in shirts.

28. Nobody from Britain, of course, can hear the term "Black Pool" without thinking of somewhere else, and few people over 30 can have avoided George Formby. We'll discuss the seaside town and the traditional mint-candy gift in 15.5, "Underworld", but the mildly-suggestive ditty *With Me Little Stick of Blackpool Rock* (1935) just says out loud what a lot of people think when they pop a seven-inch-long pink cylinder in their mouths.

29. And a stray comment in a Terrance Dicks novelisation: "Doctor Who - the Three Doctors" puts the star Omega detonated at the Veil Nebula in Cygnus, just 2400 light years from this cinema. That also suggests a date of 200 000 BCE. Nothing broadcast matches this.

30. We're fudging exactly when because the script says "two million", but the Doctor seems to say "two billion". That's a hefty difference.

31. FASA's *Doctor Who Role-Playing Game* – yes, it may seem oblique but at least one writer working on the series in the 80s had read it – blithely assumed that Gallifrey was in the far future. In FASA's universe, the TARDIS can't go any further into the future than "Frontios", because that would take it into the future of Gallifrey itself and allow the Time Lords to discover their own destiny.

32. If, for this or 15.3, "Image of the Fendahl", you want to make a compilation of tracks recorded at Stargrove, rather than just hits made with this mobile studio, you can't use that track but can have "Won't Get Fooled Again" by The Who, "Black Country Woman" by Led Zeppelin (with the plane flying overhead at the start: they also did all of the album *Houses of the Holy* there except "The Crunge" and "No Quarter"), the Stones themselves for "It's Only Rock 'n' Roll (But I Like It)" (but not all the album of the same name, although there's three tracks on *Sticky Fingers*), "Bad 'n' Ruin" by The Faces – Rod Stewart later bought the mansion, then had to sell it as part of a messy divorce before he'd even spent a night there - and "Bring Your Daughter to the Slaughter" by Iron Maiden, plus quite a lot of less-familiar titles and bands (*Molesto* by Peruvian psych-rockers The Mads, for example. The LP has a few photos of the house and grounds as they were in 1971). On the shambolic "I'm Gonna Sit Right Down and Write Myself a Letter" from the eponymous LP *Ronnie Lane's Slim Chance*, the piano they were using fell apart in mid-take in the room we see Tom and Lis leaving through the window in Part One, about three months before the filming. The mobile studio spent a lot of time in France for *Exile on Main Street*, at the communal house of Fleetwood Mac, at Lucerne for Deep Purple – hence the incident with the flare-gun at the Frank Zappa gig with the riff we all know – and, just after this story was filmed, the Lyceum Theatre, London for *Live!* by Bob Marley and the Wailers. So next time you hear "I Shot the Sheriff", you'll be thinking of George Tovey and Bernard Archard. The live bits of Santana's *Moonflower* were almost the last things to use it.

33. Both appear in *Raiders of the Lost Ark*, Lemkow as the old scholar who translates the amulet, Tablian as the guy with the eyepatch and the monkey (like Lemkow in 1.4, "Marco Polo").

395

End Notes

34. Ironically, the spacesuits look *exactly* like the logo for Android, the smart-phone operating system that makes looking up this story and 3.1, "Galaxy Four" online so much more challenging now.

35. If Elton John had prevailed over the record company, "Dan Dare (Pilot of the Future)" would have been released as the first single from *Rock of the Westies* around now, which would have been even more on-the-nose.

36. In *Reading Between Designs* by Piers D. Britten and Simon J. Barker, a curious book about the design philosophies of *The Avengers*, *The Prisoner* and old *Doctor Who*, there is a lot about the historical referents for Baker's look. Their argument, briefly, is that mixing the velvet "metropolitan" look of Oscar Wilde and the Aesthetic Movement with the tweedy "rural" mode associated with George Bernard Shaw is like putting a MAGA cap over a burka. However, the jacket designed for this story and worn, periodically until "The Sun Makers" (15.4), earns their particular scorn for combining tweed, corduroy, leather elbow-patches and yet being styled like a frock-coat, the "symbol of probity". Perhaps they'd not met many "resting" actors. Or boffins: the tweed/corduroy/ elbow-patch combo is 1970s British shorthand for "scientist" – as per Graeme Garden in *The Goodies* – and, latterly "unsuccessful author", but continued into the twenty-first century in *The Mighty Boosh* for heroically unhip musician Howard Moon.

37. It started with a gang called "Shambush!" in Brighton, spread to Australia, Ireland and Germany; now gatherings synch up globally on a Saturday in July each year to do the dance from *Wuthering Heights*. Anyone with a dark, flowing wig, a big black belt and stockings and a red frock can have a go. America's slowly caught on, with a dozen or so in Madison, Wisconsin in 2018 and more in San Francisco and Chicago, but Covid came and Extinction Rebellion almost literally stole their clothes.

38. So, we got out the DVD and the headphones, then put on the subtitles to be certain. The subs simply say (MORBIUS YELLS INCOHERENTLY), which is no use to man or beast (whichever Morbius is), but they also relay to us the earlier baffling line 'Is your mind, Doctor, mine?' – we heard it as 'Feel your mind, Doctor, going' - grammatical but odd - and Elisabeth Sladen reacting to Jon Pertwee's face appearing by yelping 'Tom'. However, listening as carefully as possible, we can confirm that Michael Spice delivers the questionable line as 'Back… to *your* beginning'. So there.

39. Well, all right, Yaz does so after what, in script terms, is at least a week of the Doctor pottering around in the Capaldi costume and forgetting about the missing TARDIS while they arrange Grace's funeral. What we see, however, is the Doctor remembering her name and a corporate mission-statement, *Sorting out fair play throughout the Universe*, then Yaz and the Fam all start calling her that unprompted.

40. An odd idea has been circulating, and was accepted in the earlier edition of this book, that there was an obscure Medici called "Innocenti" who wore such a gold mask and a purple monk's habit in public. We can't find any citation for this. Closer examination suggests that the conflation of the Brunelleschi-designed orphanage and the banking family who sponsored it started early, but the first instance of a personage with that exact name and dress-habits we've found is a couple of throwaway asides in a Kurt Vonnegut novel from 1987. Was Vonnegut watching reruns of *Doctor Who* when writing Chapter 27 of *Bluebeard*?

41. Mentioning sulphuric acid reminds us that the oddness of 6.4, "The Krotons" needs a thorough look one of these days. In most circumstances tellurium actually diminishes the potency of H_2SO_4, but many compounds of this chalcogen crumble on contact with conventional metals, especially ones with copper in. The Doctor could have defeated his crystalline antagonists by slinging his loose change at them and Jamie's dirk would have been like a crucifix to a vampire. Of course, the Doctor does point out that the Krotons aren't *pure* tellurium…

42. There was, as was common in those days, an overseas remake of the oddly-parochial *Man About the House* in America, called *Three's Company*. It was less salacious than the original but took the shape of the Thames series and made it more aspirational and bland. The premise was

End Notes

that a young man moved in with two single girls and let the landlord and his wife think that he was gay. It had two spin-offs: *Robin's Nest* showed the lad getting a girlfriend (and grumpy prospective father-in-law) and a career as a chef; *George and Mildred* followed the stroppy, conventionally-minded landlord and his frustrated wife into suburbia. That was remade too (as *The Ropers*, with a more photogenic cast) but the film version of this was a weird mess, released just as one of the stars died, involving George Roper being mistaken for a hit-man. This is credited with being the film that killed off such adaptations until *Bean* in 1997 and *Kevin and Perry Go Large* in 2000.

43. Yes, that's dating evidence. The original 1973 Allegro had the "quartic" steering-wheel, more square than round, but later models dropped this. That puts this car's manufacture between 1975 and 1979, and it looks brand-new. The last letter of the registration number is P, so it can only come from a six-month period shortly before the story was made. The script called for a future model, an F-Type Jaguar – they only went up to E-Type in the real world.

44. There's doubt about whether this event, mentioned on Oldbury's website and Wikipedia article, really happened. Every time something that looks plausible shows up, people identify the location as the then-unfinished Spaghetti Junction near Birmingham or the gasworks we saw in 7.4, "Inferno". Nonetheless, Oldbury has provided paperwork to confirm that it was cleared with them. *Top of the Pops* had two studio performances and one of the band on stage at the Finsbury Park Rainbow but some recall seeing a fourth, with Slade on motorised trolleys scooting around the fuel-store. There was also a separate clip of in-house dance troupe Pan's People performing there, which some reckon was what people are remembering. If the Slade clip was shown on 23rd November 1972, as claimed, nobody's got the video to check and that week's presenter, Noel Edmonds, has placed an embargo on broadcasting that edition even if it shows up. Certainly, none of the band's members remembers this much-publicised coup for Oldbury.

45. Answers on a postcard. We favour people Williams had worked with and trusted, such as Stratford Johns (19.2, "Four to Doomsday") or Iain Cuthbertson (16.1, "The Ribos Operation"). One malicious thought we had was that Williams could have poached Patrick Mower from *Target*.

46. We should also recall that, when supervising the first draft of "The Hand of Fear", Holmes had to find another name for the silicon baddies because he remembered, dimly, that there had been an "Omega" who was "king of a black hole" but not that Baker and Martin had written "The Three Doctors". It's possible Holmes only knew of the story from a synopsis on the wall of the office and didn't make the link with the Time Lords.)

47. Stokes worked on the *Daily Mirror* fantasy strip *Garth*, as did Frank Bellamy. Bellamy did *Doctor Who* artwork for the *Radio Times* in the mid-70's, including "Terror of the Zygons" with a striking Skarasen. The Doctor appears in the first panel of "Star Death" looking like a copy from the Bellamy drawing of Tom Baker by someone who's not got any other reference pictures. Had Stokes, in fact, not watched *Doctor Who* but collected Bellamy's work? It would explain why the Time Lords and their ships look so odd and unlike anything on television.

48. This makes it deeply weird – well, weirder – when the CG Disney *Star Wars: Rebels* uses the word 'bogan' for the Dark Side of the Force and gives the explanation to Bendu, a giant desert-dwelling yak with the voice of Tom Baker.

49. Actually, it seems they *did* get that memo and Rassilon tortured the Doctor to get more information. The only sensible interpretation of X9.12, "Hell Bent" is that the Matrix worked out what would happen in Series 12, but slightly garbled the Master fusing with the Cyberium to become the dreaded "Hybrid" that would one day 'stand in the ruins of Gallifrey'.

50. Lots of words change meaning over time, so the comment in Chapter II about "intercourse" between two young ladies is no more smutty than the paragraph in Chapter VI where Anne amuses herself with her "little fingers flying about". In context, we have to assume that they're chatting and she's playing the piano, although our hypothetical ignorant-but-smart reader may have difficulty guessing that. Julia Quinn's fans would argue that the smutty interpretation was *exactly* what Austen meant...

End Notes

51. Alluding to Harold Bloom in a discussion of SF leads us to warn anyone reading never to attempt his one and only novel, *The Flight to Lucifer*. Although it starts like a solemn version of *Father Ted* where three priests go to "Krag Island" and steal the space shuttle to fly through a black hole, it's a lot less interesting than that makes it sound. It reads like a bad translation. Although the sales-pitch forges a connection to David Lindsay's *A Voyage to Arcturus*, it lacks the fever-dream bonkersness and obsessive quality of that book or anything like a link in the plot or situation. It just grinds on for another two hundred pages to a "climax" consisting of someone saying something to someone else, but nobody's sure what. What's on the page is this: *"Elaborated error," Valentinus unflinchingly cried. "Dissolve back into the ether!"* That's as zippy as the prose gets and as much incident as you'll find.

52. Every so often a fantasy or horror writer is mistakenly sent to an SF convention to plug a book. It's often amusing to watch these people rapidly lose an audience by saying something daft such as "sci-fi writers haven't got anything to write about now it's all come true". It's more often depressing to be in that audience in the first place, especially if it's at one of the more reputable venues such as ReaderCon.

53. He did, after all, invent the time paradox. If you try the same Strong Misreading thing on *Bleak House*, you'll start thinking that Esther's covering up for war crimes or something and that the whole thing's set in an underwater city with malfunctioning pumps and literal dinosaurs.

54. Sturgeon would have known better than that: he got into trouble because he dared rewrite an already-published story called "Maturity" to make it work better. He, as much as anyone, renegotiated the pact between reader and author that makes style the key to engaging "correctly" with content. This is one reason his attempts at writing for *Star Trek* sucked. His narrative voice is the most important character in anything he did and the reason the stories function as SF rather than random surrealism.

55. Among the pop-orientated children's show was Saturday morning oddity *Zokko!* This started on the same day as "The Invasion", 2nd November 1968, and was ostensibly presented by a pinball machine. It made adults recoil in terror at the speed and randomness of the items but all that remains in the archives are two compilations that seem remarkably staid. Pinball was often used as emblematic of Pop Art and American influence – as in *Tommy* – but seems to have been more popular with television set-designers than actual teenagers, at least outside London. However, for more on this and much of the hinterland of this essay, check out George Melly's invaluable *Revolt Into Style*.

56. Not, as *Doctor Who Monthly* claimed, perpetrators of "I'm Going to Spend My Christmas With a Dalek". That was a Newcastle blues band called the Go-Gos – not, as Twitch claimed in the quiz in their 2017 *Doctor Who* marathon, Belinda Carlyle's old band. The Go Jo's can be seen in Hammer's 1969 Space Western *Moon Zero Two*. The Beat Girls can be seen in 1964 Mod oddity – Moddity – *Gonks Go Beat*. But not in 1959 Soho kitsch classic *Beat Girl*. The Go Jo's also dance to *Reflections* by Diana Ross and the Supremes on the Boxing Day 1967 *TOTP* in a clip that will give you a much clearer idea of what "The Macra Terror" looked like than the animated DVD release – and has a girl in the audience wearing the sort of thing Polly would have in her wardrobe earlier that year.

57. Perry Mason, or at least the Raymond Burr incarnation, could have saved a lot of time and taxpayer expense by just telling Lt Tragg to put out an all-points bulletin for Dabbs Greer, Denver Pyle or William Schallert. However, a defence of "not guilty by reason of being Robert Redford" is inadmissible.

58. It's a line from Philip Larkin. It's usually trotted out in this context, so you've probably heard it, but we can't guarantee that everyone has. We can't afford the rights to quote it directly but look it up – then watch that David Tennant play about the Lady Chatterley trial.

59. Some indication of how her crusade looked to mainstream Britain can be found in a 1975 story from the courtroom drama *Crown Court* (used to "examine social issues", i.e., hire everyone in Equity for lightly-retouched newspaper stories over four lunchtimes with a "jury" drawn from the public, so they didn't need appearance-

End Notes

fees). "An Evil Influence" was shown around half-term in autumn, so was probably seen by more people, especially of school age, than usual – it told of a local doctor suing parents for malicious libel after they claimed that 15-year-old girls, including their precious daughter, were getting contraceptives from him. They are exactly the sort of people wheeled out to show that Whitehouse had more support than just her long-suffering husband. The story, as usual, looks like it could go either way until the parents announce that they stopped her from watching Doctor Who. At this point, any residual sympathy for these people flies out of the window. Check out the cast on IMDb; it's got a lot of people you'll recognise, and the kid was the lead in The Changes earlier that year.

60. If you've ever wondered why so many pubs, especially in London, have "189n" on the ornate front it's because the money for refurbishment or speculative building came from the increasingly monopolistic brewing companies in a cynical move. It's very like how "disruptive" Silicon Valley start-ups boost their share-price by undercutting the competition at what would be ruinous rates if they stayed in business for more than a few years. Increased beer and spirit consumption made pub-building look like a good investment, so there was a feeding-frenzy until those purpose-built Music Halls started looking like as good a place to spend leisure-time. Prior to this, most pubs were built speculatively by construction companies and sold on. But the habit had formed of small publicans "flipping" their properties like modern-day house-buyers and expanding, a "London Custom" based on the assumption that brewers would pick up the tab and bankroll mortgages. Even when the Liberal Party, more associated with the Temperance Movement, was in power in the mid-1890s, this looked like a sound investment and Brewer A would try to squeeze Brewer B out of their territory – London companies were jealously protective of their manors, and resented Burton's (from the East Midlands) and Guinness (from Ireland) muscling in. Then, in 1898-9, even before consumption peaked, revenues dropped alarmingly and publicans began defaulting on their payments. The whole system collapsed, with bankruptcies in Dot-Com Bubble proportions. The brewers, most of whom had gone public over the preceding decade, had a lot of angry shareholders and the construction companies specialising in pubs moved into cinemas and Music Halls.

61. Conversely, these days, upon seeing a flouncy Kermit duetting with a pregnant, unwed Piggy on "Waiting at the Church" some young viewers might be bewildered.

62. Readers in America, where big, purpose-built Masonic lodges with signs proclaiming themselves as such have been pressed into service as pizza restaurants and gift-shops, might find this odd. The Freemasons are like Fight Club in Britain. You don't talk about it but you use the secret handshake as a – literal – get out of jail free card. To a British observer, America's nonchalance about *I'm a Freemason* bumper-stickers and child-registry stands at clambakes is like having a bake-sale for Al-Qaeda. In the church hall. As for the Shriners driving Davros-buggies on 4th July parades and raising funds for children's hospitals...

63. A 14th was scripted, but efforts to record at an ailing Baxter's home were dashed because his neighbour was renovating, causing too much noise.

who made all this ?

Tat Wood wrote some of what you've just read in a tent while braving plague, wildfire, tornadoes, bison and riots to explore some of the rest of North America in 2020. Believe it or not, this was safer than staying put on the New England coast. In the process, he's seen places that he grew up thinking were just made-up stories and kept small bookshops solvent from the Catskills to the Great Salt Lake. He also took the opportunity to get proof that Lars Pearson really exists and to explain patiently to garage-owners from Minnesota to Montana that, no, he doesn't know Harry Styles. While he was delighted to discover how much tent technology has improved since he was in the Scouts, the experience brought back memories of an early form of FOMO when he discovered that everyone else was watching an omnibus repeat of "The Ark in Space" while he was wading through slime in Keswick and then missed Part One of "Pyramids of Mars" when stuck in stinging-nettles on the remains of Fotheringay Castle. (He's seen them since, though).

Favourite story in this volume: "The Face of Evil". Least favourite: "The Seeds of Doom".

Thanks to the slip-fielders. Googlies were nurdled toward the following funky field placings:

Short Fine Leg	Dorothy Ail
Deep Extra Cover	Simon Black
Silly Point	Jennifer Hoffman-Brion
Cow Corner	Daniel O'Mahony (Man of the Match)
Square Leg Umpire	Simon Bucher-Jones
Barmy Army	Allison Wolfe

Lars Pearson has served as publisher and editor-in-chief of Mad Norwegian Press for (gulp) more than 20 years now. The older he gets, the more he realises that kindness begets kindness, and cruelty begets cruelty.

Favourite story from this volume: "Pyramids of Mars". Least favourite: "Robot".

A special thank you to our Patreon supporters, whose direct support helped to fund the cover artwork: the late David Adler, Matt Bracher, Steve Grace, Johanna Draper Carlson, Gia Ramos, Jeremy Remy and Rick Taylor. Behold, the cyber-mummy you have spawned. Creation is a sheer force of will.

Mad Norwegian Press

Publisher / Editor-in-Chief / About Time Content Editor
Lars Pearson

Senior Editor / Design Manager
Christa Dickson

Associate Editor
Joshua Wilson

Cover
Jim Calafiore (art),
Richard Martinez (colors)

The publisher wishes to thank... Tat and Dorothy, for continued adventures throughout the land; Lawrence Miles; Christa Dickson; Carrie Herndon; Jim Calafiore; Richard Martinez; Josh Wilson; Stacey Smith?; Shaun Lyon; Omar, Kurtis, Jess and everyone at Near Mint Condition; Jim Boyd; Shawne Kleckner; Braxton Pulley; Jack Bruner; Heather Reisenberg; Liam Wheery; Mason Ferguson; and that nice lady who sends me newspaper articles.

4606 Kingman Blvd.
Des Moines, Iowa 50311
madnorwegian@gmail.com
www.madnorwegian.com